# Sport Psychology in Practice

THE UNIVERSITY OF
WINCHESTER

Mark B. Andersen, PhD

Victoria University, Melbourne, Australia

Editor

HUMAN
KINETICS

**Library of Congress Cataloging-in-Publication Data**

Sport psychology in practice / [edited by] Mark B. Andersen.
  p. ; cm.
 Includes bibliographical references and index.
 ISBN 0-7360-3711-X (soft cover)
 1. Sports--Psychological aspects. I. Andersen, Mark B., 1951-
 GV704.S64 2005
 796.01--dc22

                2005010554

ISBN: 0-7360-3711-X

The Web addresses cited in this text were current as of May 26, 2005, unless otherwise noted.

**Acquisitions Editor:** Myles Schrag; **Developmental Editor:** Amanda S. Ewing; **Assistant Editor:** Bethany J. Bentley; **Copyeditor:** Patricia MacDonald; **Proofreader:** Sarah Wiseman; **Indexer:** Gerry Lynn Messner; **Permission Manager:** Dalene Reeder; **Graphic Designer:** Nancy Rasmus; **Graphic Artist:** Kathleen Boudreau-Fuoss; **Cover Designer:** Keith Blomberg; **Photographer (cover):** Sarah Ritz; **Art Manager:** Kelly Hendren; **Illustrator:** Kelly Hendren; **Printer:** Sheridan Books

Printed in the United States of America  10 9 8 7 6 5 4 3 2 1

**Human Kinetics**
Web site: www.HumanKinetics.com

*United States:* Human Kinetics
P.O. Box 5076, Champaign, IL 61825-5076
800-747-4457
e-mail: humank@hkusa.com

*Canada:* Human Kinetics
475 Devonshire Road Unit 100
Windsor, ON N8Y 2L5
800-465-7301 (in Canada only)
e-mail: orders@hkcanada.com

*Europe:* Human Kinetics
107 Bradford Road, Stanningley
Leeds LS28 6AT, United Kingdom
+44 (0) 113 255 5665
e-mail: hk@hkeurope.com

*Australia:* Human Kinetics
57A Price Avenue
Lower Mitcham, South Australia 5062
08 8277 1555
e-mail: liaw@hkaustralia.com

*New Zealand:* Human Kinetics
Division of Sports Distributors NZ Ltd.
P.O. Box 300 226 Albany
North Shore City, Auckland
0064 9 448 1207
e-mail: info@humankinetics.co.nz

For Izora Alice Andersen
and Bille Stanford Andersen

I chose my parents well.

# Contents

Preface     ix

Acknowledgments     xiii

## Part I    Teamwork: Doing Sport Psychology With Groups

### 1    The Selling or the Telling of Sport Psychology: Presenting Services to Coaches     3

*Harriet D. Speed, PhD, Mark B. Andersen, PhD, and Jeff Simons, PhD*

The Shopping List Model 5 • Telling and Sharing Stories 5 • Parallel Processes 7 • Models of Sport Psychology 7 • Counseling 8 • The Variety of Presentations 10 • Training in Presentation Skills 12 • Respecting and Involving Coaches 13 • Being a Role Model for Coaches 14 • Resistant Coaches 15 • Conclusion 16

### 2    Integrating Mind and Body: Presenting Mental Skills to Young Teams     17

*Clay P. Sherman, PhD, and Artur Poczwardowski, PhD*

Integrated Instruction 18 • Integrated Perspective 19 • Developmental Issues 19 • Consulting in Youth Sport 21 • Goal Setting and Daily Practice Objectives 23 • Working on Awareness and Arousal Control With Young Teams 32 • Conclusion 43

### 3    But Coach Doesn't Understand: Dealing With Team Communication Quagmires     45

*Kevin L. Burke, PhD*

Communication Theory and Research 46 • Coach Just Doesn't Understand: A Team's Story 48 • Bull in the Ring 55 • Reinforcing the Coach 56 • Conclusion 58

4  "I have a friend who . . .": Group Work on Weight
   and Body Image                                              61
   *Mark B. Andersen, PhD, and Kirsten Peterson, PhD*

   Issues for Group Presenters 63 • Tag-Team Presentations 64 • Presentation
   Outline 65 • The Group Begins Work 67 • Conclusion 74


Part II  Not Exactly on the Map: Surveying Old
         and New Territories

   5  The Skin Game: Extra Points for Looking Good               77
      *Mark B. Andersen, PhD, and Helen J. Fawkner, PhD*

      Body Image Disturbance 77 • The Male Ideal and the Prevalence
      of Body Dissatisfaction 78 • Eating Disorders in Men 79 • At-Risk
      Populations 80 • Reasons for Elevated Eating Disturbance and Body Image
      Disturbance 81 • The Gravity of Weight: Erik's Story 83 • Conclusion 92

   6  Returning to Self: The Anxieties of Coming Back
      After Injury                                               93
      *Britton W. Brewer, PhD, and Albert J. Petitpas, PhD*

      Psychological Responses to Sport Injury 93 • Psychological Intervention 95 •
      Working With Injured Athletes 96 • Identity and Ambivalence: Chris'
      Story 98 • Summarizing Chris 107 • Conclusion 108

   7  On Stage: Mental Skills Training for Dancers              109
      *Stephanie Hanrahan, PhD*

      Why Do You Dance? Tracy's Story 110 • Injuries 112 • Performance
      Anxiety 113 • When Others Are Nervous 115 • Self-Talk 116 •
      Self-Reflection (Dealing With Mistakes) 117 • Concentration and
      Attention 119 • Imagery 121 • Self-Confidence 123 • Conclusion 127

      Commentary on Chapter 7                                   129
      *Kate F. Hays, PhD, CPsych*

      "Comptrasting" Sport and Dance 129 • Mental Skills 131 • The
      Dance Milieu 132 • Consultant's Knowledge and Skills 133 • Dancers'
      Expectations About Performance Consulting 134 • Conclusion 134

   8  Facilitating Change: Alcohol and Violence
      Among Athletes                                            135
      *Robert D. Stainback, PhD, and Robert E. Taylor, PhD*

      Alcohol Use, Risk Taking, and Violence 136 • Changing Problem
      Drinking 137 • Facilitating Change in Problem Drinkers 139 • Alcohol
      Treatment 139 • Intercepting Anger: Josh's Story 141• Professional
      Issues 155 • Conclusion 158

   9  Over One's Head: Referral Processes                       159
      *Mark B. Andersen, PhD, and Judy L. Van Raalte, PhD*

      Doubt About What? 159 • Referral for What? 161 • Who Can Do
      What? Questions of Training 163 • Performance and Personal
      Issues 163 • Thor Descending: Lucien's Story 164 • Referral
      Networks 167 • The Referral Process 168 • Conclusion 169

10    Touching Taboos: Sex and the Sport Psychologist        171
      *Mark B. Andersen, PhD*
      Roots of Attraction 171 • Why Don't We Talk About "It"? 174 •
      Other Barriers to Exploration 178 • Star Crossed: The Story of Jake
      and Joanna 179 • Conclusion 191

      Commentary on Chapter 10                               193
      *William B. Strean, PhD, and Herbert S. Strean, DSW*
      Sex, Countertransference, and the Sport Psychologist 193 • Exploring
      Concepts 194 • Countertransference in Action 195 • Countertransference:
      Beyond the Erotic 197 • Conclusion 198

## Part III    Expanding Repertoires and Understanding Self: Diversity in Service Delivery

11    Raising the Bar: Developing an Understanding
      of Athletes From Racially, Culturally, and Ethnically
      Diverse Backgrounds                                    201
      *William D. Parham, PhD, ABPP*
      Psychology's Legacy With Respect to Culturally, Ethnically, and
      Racially Diverse People 202 • The Tre-Nine Approach 208 •
      Conclusion 214

      Commentary on Chapter 11                               217
      *Heather Gridley, MA*

12    Able Athletes With Disabilities: Issues and
      Group Work                                             223
      *Stephanie Hanrahan, PhD*
      What Is a Disability? 223 • Types of Disabilities and Accompanying
      Issues 224 • Introductory Group Session 229 • So What? 245 •
      Conclusion 247

13    Straight Guys Working With Gay Guys: Homophobia
      and Sport Psychology Service Delivery                  249
      *Matthew P. Martens, PhD, and Michael Mobley, PhD*
      Gay Male Athletes in Sport 250 • What Kind of Issues Might
      Emerge? 252 • Coming Out, Backing Off, and Coming Back: The
      Story of Matt and Bryan 256 • Reaction to the Case Example 261 •
      Conclusion 263

14    The Elephant in the Locker Room: Opening the Dialogue
      About Sexual Orientation on Women's Sport Teams        265
      *Heather Barber, PhD, and Vikki Krane, PhD*
      Social Identity Perspective 267 • My Teammates Are So Negative:
      Jasmine's Story 269 • I Know I'm the Only One: Susan's Story 274 •
      But It's My Personal Life: Ellen's Story 278 • Implications of the Cases 283 •
      Educating Ourselves 284 • Conclusion 284

**15    Coming Full Circle: From Practice to Research        287**

*Mark B. Andersen, PhD*

Evidence-Based Practice 287 • Confessing Prejudices on Research
and the Field 289 • Historical Roots 290 • The Research
Relationship 291 • Examples of the Researcher's Own Stuff Making
Things Messy 292 • Missing the Point 295 • One Model for the
Qualitative Researcher 296 • How Research and Practice Can Go Pear-
Shaped 296 • Conclusion 298

Afterword by Robert C. Eklund, PhD                          299
References                                                  305
Index                                                       326
About the Editor                                            332
About the Contributors                                      333

# Preface

Another applied sport psychology book? That question is the same one I asked in the preface of *Doing Sport Psychology* (Andersen, 2000) five years ago. I argued there (and here) that what we need are applied sport psychology texts that examine the processes of applied sport psychology service delivery. The style of the previous book was to present models of service and theories of behavior change and then show how those models and theories are reflected in actual practice. Almost every chapter contained extensive conversations between practitioners and performers. Coupled with the dialogues were in-depth commentary and analyses of what was going on in the practitioner–client working relationships. The book was designed to illustrate the *how* of doing sport psychology.

When we finished *Doing Sport Psychology,* my editor, the redoubtable Linda Bump, and I looked at each other and said, "Well, that was fun. Let's do it again," but it would be five years before this companion volume appeared (about the long delay . . . don't ask). The first book covered a wide range of topics, but it was far from exhaustive. We believed there were several obvious gaps. For example, one of the most common services of sport psychologists is delivering group presentations to teams on a variety of topics (e.g., goal setting, relaxation, concentration). Except for the chapter where a coach talked to his team about mental preparation, and a segment where three retired athletes met with a sport psychologist, no attention was given to what a sport psychologist does when standing up in front of a team.

Another missing service is working with diverse clients. Nowhere in *Doing Sport Psychology* do any of the chapters address the issues of working with athletes of color, gay and lesbian performers, or disabled participants. Attention is also needed in other areas (alcohol abuse and violence, referral processes, erotic transference and countertransference, and coach–athlete communication problems). We also decided that some extremely complex areas (eating disorders, injury, and identity) in the first book needed to be revisited in order to paint a broader picture of these convoluted issues.

## Organization of the Book

This book follows the same format as *Doing Sport Psychology,* with one additional feature. In three of the chapters (7, 10, and 11), a "guest star" provides a commentary. A commentary on each of the chapters would have been unwieldy, so I chose these specific contributions because their contents represent areas that are controversial or outside the usual realms of sport psychology service issues. This feature's addition stems from Murphy's (2000) observations in the afterword of the first book, where he noted that as he read the chapters, he often came up with alternative case formulations and different interpretations and analyses of what was occurring between the athlete and the sport psychologist. The processes Murphy went through as he read the book are exactly what I hoped *Doing Sport Psychology* would do for most readers: provoke debate, discussion, and controversy. The three guest critics bring some of that lively debate to the book and, I hope, spark even more argument and discussion.

*Sport Psychology in Practice* is divided into three parts. In Part I, the authors address the processes of presenting sport psychology to groups. In our psychology training program at Victoria University, we ask gradual students (no, that's not a typo; they call themselves that because they *gradually* get their degrees) to give group presentations to fellow students who role-play teams of athletes and coaches. In the early stages, even after seeing demonstrations of effective group presentations, the students often begin in lecture mode (telling athletes about the topic, e.g., relaxation) instead of getting athletes to tell their stories, following the athletes, and using those stories to illustrate points about, say, the importance of playing loose. Effective group presentations are not easy for a neophyte to accomplish. They involve thinking quickly on one's feet, sussing out (Aussie term for determining what is actually going on) group dynamics, and having the sport psychology canon down pat.

In chapter 1, Jeff Simons, Harriet Speed, and I discuss one of the most important group presentations a sport psychologist is likely to give: talking to a group of coaches for the first time. Sport psychologists, if they want to work, need to sell themselves, and we illustrate some good, and some not so good, ways of convincing coaches that the services we offer are worth paying for. Clay Sherman and Artur Poczwardowski, in chapter 2, illustrate another difficult audience to approach—young athletes. This chapter covers working with a group of children and teaching them relaxation. Telling stories and playing games are prominent features in working with a group whose collective attention span is somewhat less than that of adult athletes. In chapter 3, Kevin Burke presents a case of communication dysfunction between coaches and teams, what I believe is probably the most common presenting problem in sport psychology service delivery. Such dysfunction can lead to athlete anxiety, depressed mood, and withdrawal from sport. Kevin shows how he helps a team develop favorable ways of getting what they need from the coach. Finally, to end this section, Kirsten Peterson and I discuss presenting the sensitive topic of eating disorders to a mixed men's and women's team of divers. We discuss the use of media presentations, such as the National Collegiate Athletics Association's videotapes on eating disorders and nutrition (NCAA, 1989). This chapter also shows a "tag-team" approach and how a male psychologist and a female psychologist can work together with a mixed team. One of the main objectives of such a presentation is to demonstrate how safe and nonjudgmental sport psychologists can be, as well as how they can help. One of the markers of a successful presentation is when an athlete, afterward, self-refers for treatment.

In Part II, the authors take on sensitive issues in both topics of concern to athletes and the ethics of professional practice. Two of the chapters cover topics presented in the first book (eating disorders, injury) but take alternative approaches with these markedly different cases. This section is the logical extension of the clinical and counseling section of *Doing Sport Psychology*, with cases that require great sensitivity to deal with athletes (and sport psychologists) in fragile conditions and precarious situations.

In chapter 5, Helen Fawkner and I document a self-referral that results from an eating disorder presentation similar to the one illustrated in chapter 4. A male diver comes to see me, at first for performance enhancement, but as the relationship evolves, weight, eating, and the issue of having a "female" problem emerge. Britt Brewer and Al Petitpas, in chapter 6, present the case of an injured athlete getting ready to return to competition. The anxieties around the possibility of reinjury, of not competing up to past form, of no longer being an athlete, and of a loss of identity are almost paralyzing. The authors show how to help the athlete move from paralysis to action. In chapter 7, Stephanie Hanrahan presents some cases from her work within the highly charged atmosphere of dance. In all chapters, knowing the language of the sport is central to good service delivery. This chapter also demonstrates how knowledge of the art and being able to "talk the talk" serve important functions in the working alliance. Accompanying this chapter is commentary by Kate Hays, who wrote the performing arts chapter in *Doing Sport Psychology*.

Rob Stainback and Robert Taylor, in chapter 8, show the development of a relationship with an athlete referred for mandatory counseling after a violent, drunken bar brawl. The authors trace how the athlete moved from resentment, to cautious interest, to a strong working alliance, and finally to a referral for more intensive treatment.

Judy Van Raalte and I tackle, in chapter 9, the delicate ethical matter of referring athletes when their issues are beyond your ken. How do you tell athletes that their problems are such that another expert needs to be called in? Also, how do you do a brutally honest self-assessment of what you can and cannot treat? Supervision (my favorite topic) enters as a support system for the referring sport psychologist. In the final chapter of this section, the taboo specter of sex and the psychologist rears its head. The topics of transference and countertransference were major themes in *Doing Sport Psychology*. Here, I take those topics and open up the closet of erotic attraction between sport psychologists and athletes. Supervision of a young male sport psychologist, whose erotic interest in a female athlete is obviously returned, is the story for this chapter. My colleague and adversary Billy Strean and his dad, Herbert Strean—the dynamic duo—offer a fascinating critique of the supervisor's work and the sport psychologist's case. They take my basic psychodynamic formulations to a deeper level, and I learned a lot from their observations. Billy's dad is no longer with us, and I am so happy to be able to present one of his last works in print.

In Part III, the authors tackle issues related to working with diverse athletes. This section is *not* about what athletes of color are like, or what gay and lesbian athletes expect, or what disabled athletes need from sport psychologists. Articles in those veins necessarily contain generalizations that in many cases just do not apply (see Andersen, 1993; Lee & Rotella, 1991). These chapters tell the stories of diverse athletes and, most important, the processes the sport psychologist goes through in working with them. Through these chapters you will read about the challenges diverse athletes face, but also of central importance are the development and evolution of the sport psychologists as they work with these athletes, uncovering and understanding their own prejudices and how those prejudgments get in the way of good service.

In chapter 11, William Parham thought (and I agreed) that an introduction to diversity in sport psychology would serve well here and set this section in a broader context of understanding differences through a sociocultural lens. In a true sense, all sport psychology encounters are multicultural. Sport psychologists and athletes bring their unique ontogenetic histories and their worldviews to the working relationship. The magnitude of overlap of those histories and viewpoints will always vary, and in some cases, those from different groups may actually have more overlap with each other than those from the same group. To use a statistical analogy, differences within groups will always be much larger than differences between groups. Parham's chapter is the odd one out in that there is no dialogue, but it serves as a broad introduction to the commentary and three chapters that follow. Heather Gridley, a community psychologist and an expert on aboriginal issues in Australia, offers some observations on this chapter.

In chapter 12, Stephanie Hanrahan discusses group presentations with disabled athletes. She relates in intimate detail the processes she goes through as she works with this challenging and appreciative group. Matthew Martens and Michael Mobley, in chapter 13, examine subtle and not-so-subtle aspects of internalized homophobia within sport psychologists, along with helping gay male athletes cope with the very real threat of being "outed" and the potential repercussions (e.g., getting dropped from the team, being violently attacked). For chapter 14, Vikki Krane and Heather Barber explore similar territory when working with lesbian athletes. They also discuss the sometimes troublesome lesbian–straight splits that develop on some women's teams and how interventions from the sport psychologist can make for healthier team environments.

In chapter 15, I bring the book back to the very beginning and turn the tables, taking the practice of sport psychology back to what it has to tell us about doing research in the field. Finally, Bob Eklund, a truly wise member of the clan, reflects in the afterword on what the authors have done.

Second and third children are supposed to be easier. Not true (in this case). Editing and writing is something of a love–hate experience in which pleasure (e.g., finishing a chapter) and pain (e.g., spending 30 minutes agonizing over a sentence), approach and avoidance often get pathologically mixed. Whew! Glad this third child has been put to bed.

I would like to thank all the authors for their great efforts and for putting up with my inordinate delays and possibly obsessive–compulsive tendencies. Again, I learned heaps from them.

# Acknowledgments

Books are creative and collaborative efforts, and the best metaphor I can come up with for that cooperation and joint venture is *family*. In the case of this third child, it is a global, extended, funny, diligent, hardworking, loving, and quirky family with sons, daughters, nieces, nephews, grandparents, mums, dads, aunties, weird uncles, brothers, and some wonderfully evil stepsisters.

I will have to start by thanking Linda Bump. I have known and laughed with Linda for many years, and she is the one who pushed me to have another go at publishing with Human Kinetics. Next in line is Amy Clocksin, who stood by me with loving care and attention as the book started, stalled, started again, floundered, and finally made it into a home stretch. Her therapeutic encouragement and empathy helped combat my doubts, fears, mental disorders, and to be honest, indolence. Myles Schrag took over from Amy, and she really knew the best person to take up that baton. The phone calls with Myles were often hilarious, and just when I thought we were going to start picking out curtains together, the bastard abandons me and inflicts me on Amanda Ewing. Amanda is, in a word, fabulous.

My head of school, Terry Roberts, gets a big thank-you for giving me time to get this puppy finished. I have a bucket load of adult children, some of whom were the first critical audience for this book. My students Lisa, Pippa, Trevor, Dr. Li, Emma, Jillian, Andrew, Becky, Sean, Cadeyrn, Little Joey, David, Michelle, and Gavin all helped, with their feedback, to make this a better piece of work. Speaking of evil stepsisters, Dr. Harriet Speed is a constant source of jocularity and constructive feedback, and thanks to her, and all the other authors in this book, I think we have come up with something sport and exercise psychologists will find useful and informative for practice. And finally, thanks to Jeffrey—and he knows why.

# Teamwork

*Doing Sport Psychology
With Groups*

# The Selling or the Telling of Sport Psychology

## *Presenting Services to Coaches*

Harriet D. Speed, PhD, Mark B. Andersen, PhD, and Jeff Simons, PhD

A sport psychologist gets a phone call asking if she would be willing to talk to a bunch of developmental squad coaches about how sport psychology can be beneficial for their teams. Now what? That is a good question, one that has been answered in some excellent and some suboptimal ways. How do we talk to coaches about doing sport psychology in ways that increase the chances they will be interested in our efforts, invite us to work with their teams, and pay us for our services?

Gaining acceptance of sport psychology among coaches and athletes has been a long struggle and will, no doubt, continue to be so (Gardner, 1995; Ravizza, 1988; Simons & Andersen, 1995). One of the problems facing legitimate, hardworking, and sincere sport psychologists is that the field has a glamour halo about it that also attracts charlatans, self-appointed gurus, and crackpots. When I (Mark) was a full-time practicing psychologist working at Arizona State University, I was seeing up to 35 athletes a week and using other resources (e.g., graduate students) to help handle the load. About once every two months or so, someone would call the intercollegiate athletic department and offer his or her services for helping athletes with their mental games. Some of these people even claimed to be sport psychologists, even though the word *psychologist* is protected in the United States.

I once received a call from a guy claiming to be a transpersonal psychologist (whatever that is); he told me he had a lot to offer the athletes. I was thinking, *Oh, no, another one!* but I was curious as to what this particular transpersonal guy had to say. So I said, "Please tell me what you have in mind." He then told me he could help adjust the "auras" of the athletes. Well, I am not a new-age sort of person, and I don't know much about auras except that they are some sort of glowing energy field around people, with different colors, and that some "attuned" people can perceive them. I asked the guy, "Why might the athletes need their auras adjusted?"

He responded, "It's about all the jet travel they do to get to competitions."

"Interesting," I said, trying to keep the patronizing tone out of my voice. "Tell me more."

He went on, "You see, when they take off in jets, the *g*-forces shove the auras behind them, and they are not integrated anymore. I can help fix that." Sounded like an acceleration-induced "aurotomy."

I said, "OK, but when they land, wouldn't their auras bounce back to where they should be?"

He paused, as if considering something he had not thought of before, then responded, "No, it doesn't work that way; the takeoffs are too severe." I politely thanked him and said we probably couldn't use his services.

It is a scary tale on a variety of levels. What would a coach or athlete think of someone who claimed to be a psychologist and then talked in this manner? Such a description of sport psychology service would provide a ton of reinforcement for the prejudice that psychologists are fruitcakes. It is also scary because the person was so convinced of his own worldview, and of his messianic ability to heal, that he could not even see how such claims would be viewed by the sporting community. Being a sport psychologist is a constant battle, and people who claim to be sport psychologists and then present such ideas to coaches make the job for the rest of us that much more difficult. The aura approach is an extreme example, but all it takes is one bad experience with a sport psychologist to turn a coach against the whole field. And coaches talk to other coaches, and they talk to their athletes.

Throughout their careers, sport psychologists will encounter hostile, indifferent, and enthusiastic coaches. The latter species are relatively easy to work with; it is the former two who present challenges to the sport psychologist in the hard, the soft, or the medium-firm sell.

The authors of this chapter are three practitioners who have, collectively, worked with athletes and coaches for more than 50 years. We have determined over the decades what seems to work, and not work, when discussing sport psychology service with coaches. Coaching is a relatively conservative profession, with traditions handed down from one generation of coaches to the next. Coaches have a wealth of knowledge, and when we talk to them, we try to use that knowledge to help us get our points about sport psychology across in meaningful ways.

The dialogues and commentary in this chapter resulted from the three of us sitting down and discussing our experiences of introducing sport psychology to coaches and of working with coaches in general. We recorded our conversations, transcribed them, and then edited them into major themes.

For a beginning sport psychologist, a first meeting with coaches to "sell" sport psychology service can be a daunting and threatening experience. We hope our dialogue will help both neophyte and more seasoned sport psychologists feel a bit more comfortable and confident when talking to a group of coaches. The "what sport psychology can do for your team" talk to coaches is probably one of the most difficult presentations a sport psychologist will make.

The problems with talking to coaches usually start at the very beginning when sport psychologists try to sell themselves and the services they offer. Sport psychologists often start with a usually suboptimal focus (i.e., themselves). Why this approach is taken is unknown, but it probably stems from professional insecurities and learned patterns of communication that put the psychologist before the client.

# The Shopping List Model

Mark: What beginning sport psychologists often do is say, "Here, these are the services I have to offer. I can do goal setting, relaxation, imagery, self-talk," and then describe how these interventions can be beneficial to teams. It's the "here I am, here are my skills, here's what I can do" approach instead of getting coaches to tell stories about how they see their teams, the strengths and weaknesses and so forth. So we end up trying to sell Harriet or sell Jeff or sell Mark.

Jeff: We're talking about a shopping list, or a menu, and the assumption is that people are coming to the sport psychology restaurant, and they're going to get an appetizer, a main course, and a desert. The assumption is that coaches just need to see the selection and then pick and choose, and we'll deliver those things to the table. I don't think this approach really connects with coaches because, first of all, you're just cataloging things such as imagery, goal setting, relaxation, and maybe counseling as well. Coaches don't know what to do with menus. It's a bewildering array that may seem overwhelming. What you have to realize is that coaches in most cases are not really looking for another person to manage. And in many ways, you need to be an answer to a problem or question that they have rather than an extra burden, someone they have to manage or figure out how to use or how to work into their systems. So part of it is trying to figure out how you answer coaches' questions or help them deal with problems or issues, rather than presenting a whole bunch of stuff that seems to add on to what they already need to do.

Harriet: And menus or shopping lists really don't reveal anything about how you do your work. Experienced coaches know something about many of the tools of the trade such as goal setting and imagery. What they don't know is how you're going to work with the athletes and coaches themselves in these areas. And, for me, that information probably comes more through getting to know me as a person, experiencing my personal qualities and idiosyncrasies, than anything else.

There are a couple of ways to start. In apparent contradiction to what we have just said, it's okay to begin with the sport psychologist, but not with a shopping list. Rather, ask the coach some questions and tell the coach some things about how you work, some real-life stories that coaches can relate to their own experiences.

> Get a feel for where coaches are in their conceptions of sport psychology service.

# Telling and Sharing Stories

Harriet: Tell some good stories. I think that is the crux of getting the information across. Coaches want to listen to stories. They don't want to listen to a sport psychology lecture, they want to listen to stories of things that are of interest to them.

Jeff: If I can back up a second before we get to the storytelling. If I think it is going to be a tough sell, and I don't have a lot of background on the coaches, I'll just say, "When I say the term *sport psychology,* what does it mean to you? What do you imagine?" and have them tell me. You can also ask, "What things are mental in what you do?" Ask them about what they do in the mental game. "What's psychological in coaching?" or "What's in the psychology of coaching?" You're asking questions, and they're providing you with not only the answers but also much more, about themselves and their attitudes. The information they provide can further the discussion and give you some clues as to which of your stories will most likely be heard.

Harriet: Sometimes, though, taking the approach of asking, "What do you know about sport psychology and about sport psychologists?" may not be so helpful. When you get a hostile response from one or more coaches—for example, "It's all right for some people, but it's a load of crap if you ask me," or "You're a bag of raving lunatics"—you can get caught defending the profession and being dragged away from the focus you wanted. I find that approaching it from the perspective of having the coach talk about his or her own experiences and perceptions of sport psychology, that is, what he or she relates to rather than what you as a sport psychologist do, usually results in a more constructive discussion. For example, "What have you observed to be some of the important mental aspects of athlete performance, or the important team dynamics?" Or alternatively, the important mental aspects of coaching because that strikes them right where they live, and often they can get into things such as communication. I think, having gone the route of "What is sport psychology to you?" that often coaches can be opinionated, and you can waste a lot of time.

> Have stories ready to tell coaches; show them you're not a cookie-cutter psychologist.

Mark: I think one of the things to try to avoid is giving coaches a quiz. But I also use that question, "When I say *psychology,* what pops into your head?" After they tell me, I usually reply in a way that's self-deprecating, in a way that makes fun of myself, in a way that says, "I'm not a raving lunatic, and I know all the myths and funny stories of people lying on couches and meditating on navels." Injecting a bit of humor may help both the coach and me relax.

Jeff: I agree that you don't want to make it a quiz, but you can include lots of good examples of normal psychological aspects of sport such as decision making, dealing with training, dealing with injuries, dealing with teamwork, dealing with miscommunication. You need a whole bag of good and quick examples to pepper in there. They may be able to see a lot of things that they readily recognize. And so instead of its seeming like an open-ended quiz, you're feeding it, and they carry it on. Some examples: "Do you ever wonder whether somebody is going to make it back from an injury?" and "Do you wonder how they will rejoin the team?" "Do you recall some times when people were very good at decision making and other times when they were very poor at decision making?" "How do people deal with stress differently when the pressure's on, or during a pressure play?" So if you have some examples ready, then you're actually starting to talk their work, and they then start talking about coaching and not psychology.

Harriet: I think sport psychologists often talk to groups of coaches about sport psychology within a very general context and about sport psychologists in the context of . . . all sport psychologists. I tend to make it a lot more personal, a lot more specific. I try to look at a specific example, and I talk about me as a specific sport psychologist and the ways in which I would deal with specific situations, not just generalize across situations and the profession. I would probably go back to giving some examples, such as "OK, you said that you've tried sport psychologists. What's one particular thing that you thought a sport psychologist may have been useful for? What's that specific situation? OK, well, let's look at it," and I present it within a personal framework rather than relate it to the whole field and the whole profession. Because it's really about you and the way you work with the coaches and athletes, not about general practices and principles or sport psychology as a profession. I think also doing that, the coach telling the tale and the sport psychologist using the story, affords the opportunity to convey to the coaches aspects of yourself—your attitudes, your knowledge, how you work, and also something about your own personal qualities.

Jeff: Let's say you are a communication specialist, and you want to let the coach know something about how you operate. You may have an informative but short talk prepared about the way you see communication issues among coaches and athletes. If a coach says communication is an issue [and in our experience, it is one of the most common issues], that can be a really good introduction because it gives you a chance to tell about yourself, about the way that concepts of communication actually flow into sport. It gets people thinking. It's interesting. And they can begin to make the links between their problems and your service.

# Parallel Processes

In supervision of sport psychologists, there is often a parallel process in the supervisory sessions that mirrors, in part, what is happening with the psychologist and the athlete. For example, a psychologist may be helping an athlete with irrational thoughts by using principles such as cognitive restructuring. In supervision, the supervisor may use similar principles to help the psychologist address his own unreasonable beliefs about needing to be a perfect practitioner. The process, when talking to coaches, often closely parallels what happens when we first meet athletes and try to understand their stories (see Andersen, 2000, for an example of an intake interview).

Mark: When I'm talking to coaches, I'm trying to call on a lot of the skills I use when I'm doing an athlete intake interview. It's not like, "Well, what brings you here today?" In the intake interview, what you're trying to do is get a complete story about what this athlete's world is like. With coaches the goal is to get the story about what that coach's world is like. It involves the same sorts of principles. There's a data-gathering phase; there's rapport building. There's the retelling of the story; there's genuine interest and care. It's sort of an almost Socratic process, in that with your help and caring, your sport midwifery, they'll tell you what their psychological needs are. I think it's an extremely difficult thing to do well.

Harriet: I agree, and having heard you make that analogy reminds me of the actual time and effort I often devote toward building rapport with coaches, which is sometimes substantial. Although my primary agenda and outcome goals may be about data gathering, the main mechanism through which I achieve that is the same as in a counseling session with an athlete, when trying to understand the athlete's world, by building a personal relationship with that person.

# Models of Sport Psychology

In keeping with parallel processes, behind our interactions with coaches, just as with our encounters with athletes, models inside our heads guide what we do and how we talk. Models help us know where we are, how we interpret stories, and how to proceed. The most common model in sport psychology is the cognitive–behavioral one. So we often listen for stories about the contingencies of reinforcement and punishments along with the thinking patterns, both positive and negative, behind those stories. But the overarching model is a psychoeducational–developmental model that employs cognitive–behavioral principles.

Harriet: I think also that sport psychology is often presented or considered within a sports medicine framework. The medical model in particular, as it has developed historically, can be perceived by people as being a relatively static model, one that is "Band-Aid" oriented or otherwise cure oriented. It is prescriptive in a way that says (a) here is the problem, (b) here is the prescribed way of dealing with it, and (c) everyone deals with it this way. I think that tossing that medical model and relating sport psychology to the way that coaching *is* can be helpful. In psychology, and in coaching, there are many different ways to solve problems or deal with particular issues. You've often got many different parts of your background and experiences to draw on, and coaches also teach a lot through their own experiences, as we do. We don't just practice sport psychology from a prescriptive textbook. We practice through our own experiences. When talking to a group of coaches, I would probably relate things directly to their work and profession and look at the commonalities between coaching and what I do as a sport psychologist and the way that I approach my work, not necessarily the actual content, but the way that I approach problems and explore options.

Jeff: What Harriet is talking about is more of a developmental model. There is also the excellence model and the high-performance model, but I think sometimes those use too much jargon [e.g., zone of optimal functioning] and are a bit of a hype. In talking about the excellence model, we're talking about supernormal performance and all that. That's sometimes a bit overblown. And maybe the coaches can't relate because it all sounds as if somehow we're special, the "zone doctors," and we're way above everyone else. But if you contrast the medical model we've described here with its curative "take this for that problem" doctrine and instead talk about a developmental model—which is more about learning, developing, educating, becoming, moving, and having an idea of where you're trying to go—coaches often really relate to that because they are teachers, and many see themselves in that light.

Mark: The medical model sets up a doctor–patient dichotomy, whereas a developmental model lends itself more to collaboration. A rough analogy is the distinction between talent identification and talent development. In talent identification the experts come in, like doctors, and "diagnose" who will be good athletes. In talent development, a team works together to nurture the athlete.

Jeff: In developmental models you assess, you observe, you try things out, you listen, and it's a process that coaches can appreciate because they are teachers. Those coaches who aren't teachers can have a hard time understanding this approach. Some coaches just coach in their own ways and don't reflect, and it's going to be a long haul working with them. I think the big thing is to get coaches on side. They are the really big movers on teams. They are the people you are probably going to do the most effective immediate work with, anyway. And then in time you can gain some trust and some credibility, and then you can work with some of the people who are a little harder to win over, such as administrators and parents. If a coach is on side, then more than half the battle is won.

Mark: In working with coaches, I've tried to identify myself as being a teacher, as being an educator, as being a type of coach. I try to say from the beginning that we have some common ground. I may have some special areas of expertise that may be useful in sport, but I still identify myself as an educator, teacher, coach. And so when you're tapping into that developmental model, you're tapping into the coach's world. You're not coming from the doctor's world or the super special world. You're not using the hype of snake oil or the sporting equivalent of Buzz Lightyear's "to infinity and beyond." You are saying, "I have common cause with you, and I hope that 'I' can become 'we' in time."

Connect with coaches by emphasizing that you are both teachers.

# Counseling

Sport psychology service is often viewed, at least initially, as primarily performance enhancement. Coaches and athletes usually do not have many problems with accepting that domain of service. The more threatening area of service involves counseling and clinical issues that can arise in sport.

Mark: What I'd be interested in when you're talking to coaches is whether you actually make inquiries about working with their athletes on clinical and counseling issues. For example, some coaches may have said, "I've got a couple of kids here; they're having some nightmares [or they're stressed puppies, or they're really anxious], and I'd like them to talk to somebody one-on-one. What can you do for me and these kids?" How do you approach the whole issue of what to say to coaches about counseling issues? What do you say to them about confidentiality and those sorts of things? For example, here's a story. I had been working with a team, doing some psychoeducational group presentations but no one-on-one services. I was called to a meeting with two coaches, a head coach and an assistant, and they talked about counseling services for an athlete. We started discussing her, and I said, "When she and I move into this relationship, then certain rules start to apply, and one of those rules is that everything that goes on between her and me when we're talking to each other is sacrosanct." And then I explained why it's sacrosanct—because I have to develop trust with that athlete, and the athlete needs to have confidence in me and know that, except in rare cases, anything she says won't get back to anyone else. Because if she has a suspicion that I might talk to the coach, then important material may not come up, and that will limit the therapeutic process. I explained to the coaches that confidentiality is a cornerstone of treatment but that I would also encourage her to talk with them about what's going on, but if she doesn't want to then they should not try to force her to do that. It's laying down those sorts of ground rules but explaining what the therapeutic process is about, explaining why confidentiality and privilege are so important. It's a really delicate thing to talk about and to get across.

> It is important with coaches to lay the ground rules of confidentiality in counseling relationships.

Harriet: I think that explaining *why* the relationship is going to change is equally important as describing *how* the relationship will change.

Jeff: Harriet makes a good point about the "why." Most coaches do pretty well if you say, "If we get into this counseling thing, there will be a different relationship. We are no longer talking about your athlete's performance, we're talking about a person on her own. She is no longer only your athlete. She is no longer just a team athlete." So the relationship is really different. It's kind of as if somebody has a personal medical problem, or somebody in her family has a medical condition. That's not the coach's or the team's business unless they need to be informed for some change in training or something like that. Most coaches can cope pretty well as long as you say, "When I'm talking with this athlete, realize that I'm not just talking to her as your athlete. I'm talking to her about her probably very personal world, so it kind of changes our orientation." A second thing that helps sport psychologists deal with the issue of counseling, particularly critical issues, is having multiple support people around the team. For example, when an athlete has an eating disorder, you can often call a huddle of other people who will help manage athlete care. So you form a management team. Maybe the head coach stays somewhat privy, but you have the medical doctor, the nutritionist, and yourself, and that's the group that's going to help. Then everything's not on you, and coaches can see that it's a special case, and that's what we've done, for example, with gymnastics.

Harriet: I had a really interesting experience where a coach asked me to talk to an athlete because the athlete was appearing unfocused during training, sort of vague in the head, and the coach was really getting fed up with her. Her behavior toward the athlete was actually rather confrontational on the court. I agreed to check things out with the athlete, which I did, but what happened in the course of that weekend was that the coach came back to me several times about the athlete's behavior, and that enabled me to actually talk to the coach about how she was coping with this athlete. And so the counseling had a collateral branch that provided an opportunity to work with the coach. That was a positive learning experience for that coach about confidentiality issues, the whys and wherefores of the counseling process. What came up was a whole lot of stuff going on in the coach's life, and we explored directly how her stress was manifesting itself in her coaching and in dealing with others. Aside from helping her personally, it helped her develop an awareness of what goes on in counseling sessions with me.

Jeff: For more serious cases, I see myself as being a liaison person for athletes and coaches and other professionals. If the athlete has a clinical problem, I will help him find resources to deal with the problem. So when I explain that this relationship is changing and that I'll probably pass it on, most coaches actually deal with that pretty well. You don't have to go too much in depth about all these things. It's hard for a lot of people to understand; it's really hard to describe to the layperson who hasn't gone through professional counseling or hasn't had to deal with these things. Coaches talk among themselves about athletes' personal issues all the time, just loosely, and it's very hard for them to understand things such as confidentiality in the same way. So you just say, "The relationship has changed, and it's really nobody's business but that person's, and this is the way I'll have to handle it." I find at least it works with most cases. For me and in my practice, I would probably not carry on a long-term counseling relationship with an athlete. The main reason is I don't want to get caught in a lot of relationships that are outside the team environment, and I would rather the athlete call somebody from the outside even though I would be happy to collaborate. These are my own choices in practice. And that does go along with what Harriet's talking about in terms of not taking all of sport psychology as a single entity. Some of us focus on performance; others do more counseling.

## The Variety of Presentations

How we first interact with coaches, introducing ourselves, happens in a variety of ways. It may be an informal discussion over the phone. It may be a request to present formally to a group. It may be an invitation to come down to practice and observe and chitchat. We need to be prepared for navigating those different avenues of entry into service.

Jeff: I think a big thing for me is that I don't like coming in and doing those introductory talks. I really don't. I much prefer sit-down discussions with individuals, and the main thing you're trying to get across is that "I can sit, I can listen, I'm not going to suddenly jump in and ruin your job or hurt your position." And I also have really gotten away from the classic "teach them all about sport psychology so they'll know when to use you" mode. It's more like "I'm here to try to understand what you're doing." Usually if you tell people, "I study in this area," they'll take you at face value. If you're studying it you must know something about it. So you don't have to prove its worth right off the bat, and in fact you probably *can't* prove it right off the bat. You say, "This is my area of specialty—understanding how people perform, listening to what they do, how they are able to deal with stress, deal with training, deal with all the difficulties that are involved and the challenges that are within sport. That's what I specialize in, and that's also something you do. If I can be a resource for you, I will." And then let them start talking about what they need.

Harriet: I find I sometimes get caught when they come back to me and say, "But what do you do?" It sometimes seems simpler for them; they will often just want a list of things I do. I can't change their need for information, but I can answer their question in a way that is far more interesting to them as listeners and that will provide them with a better understanding of what I am about, personally and professionally, than giving them a lecture on sport psychology. I take a very interactive approach, such as, "Well, let's throw a few ideas around. What are some issues that have come up recently?" I might ask, "What are some of the issues that sport psychologists you've worked with before have tackled?" if that's relevant. It's really about being responsive to them rather than directing a discussion or presentation at them. Every group will be different and will need to be addressed differently. I think that as a communicator you've got to be able to read your group and respond to their needs in any situation. And if you don't interact with them, and have them interact with you, the session will break down. I also like to use group sessions as a means of getting the athletes and coaches to know me better. I want them to know me not as a lecturer but as someone who relates to and is interested in their situations, who listens and hears what they have to say. It's important for me to show them that I can be serious, and have a sense of humor, and be sensitive, and be confronting, all of those qualities that make me a normal person in their eyes, not ones that make me look like a special or important sport psychologist.

Mark:    I think there's a lot to be said for actually trying to avoid those sorts of group presentations because they put you in the most difficult situation to communicate.

Harriet:   But we're often hired to give exactly that kind of talk to a group of coaches, and we don't have the option of talking informally with them, for example, over lunch. I think what we're doing today is covering a whole lot of different ways in which you can interact with coaches. And that's a good point in itself. We need to have a range of different presentation styles and tailor each interaction or presentation to the specific needs of a group or the situation in which we work. We need to be able to talk to coaches about what we do under formal and informal circumstances, in group sessions or one-on-one, over lunch or in an educational workshop. I've had the opportunity to cover pretty much all those situations, and although each one may have been structured differently, the general principles I go by remain the same. Encourage the coaches to tell their stories, follow their leads, give them some idea of who I am—my personal qualities—tell a few stories of my own, and have a few laughs along the way.

> Have a range of presentation styles so you can present in any situation—one-on-one session, informal meeting, or formal group presentation.

Jeff:    You come in to do a talk, or you're paid to do a talk, and the coaches are in a sense "trialing" you. Then I would suggest you pick a narrow area and say, "I'm going to share with you a principle, a technique, an idea"—a something, something you really feel good about, and you have stories to tell, and you can really do a tight and entertaining talk in the time you have. Find a very specific area, something you feel really comfortable with, give a whiz-bang presentation on this one little topic, and make it really clear that this is just one single thing you thought they might be interested in. "This is not all of sport psychology, but you've asked me to come and talk, and I was thinking that this would be a good topic. Obviously, with a team of this size, this kind of issue is really important." You give a tidbit—don't give them everything. What you do is keep it really concise, and you keep it to the one singular topic. OK. On the other side, if I'm not in the position where I have to give that kind of talk, I'm a lot more vague. If they say, "What do you do?" I say, "I listen. . . . I listen, try to understand, and see where I can help. So I'm going to spend a couple of weeks here" or "I'm going to spend this day" or whatever the time is. "I'm going to be chatting with people, finding out what's going on . . . and then we'll all together figure out something that can contribute." So I make it very vague and then go about the process of determining details and gathering information by actually talking to people. I always find things to talk about, and if you're listening really well then you find meanings there, and you find things that are going on. But you're not making that up.

Mark:     In another type of presentation, I'm a big fan of the lunch consultation. That is to say, the coach is interested in some sport psychology, and my approach is "You know what, we can do this over a meal. Why don't we go to lunch and you tell me a whole lot about your team, and then I'll tell you a bunch of stuff about what I do, and we'll see how we might be able to work together. How about we do that?" Move it down to the everyday, nothing special. Let's go out and tell some stories about how things are going, and then maybe we can figure out how we might be able to incorporate me into part of the team. Something like that.

# Training in Presentation Skills

Our discussions so far highlight a key principle of presenting sport psychology to coaches: Be flexible. How we introduce sport psychology to coaches depends on several interacting factors, including our own preferences for particular presentation styles; our knowledge of, or our perceptions of, the expectations of coaches; the situational opportunities afforded to us by coaches; and the desired outcomes of presentations. How we manage these interacting factors determines, to a large extent, our success in achieving those wished-for outcomes. Unfortunately, and for the variety of reasons already discussed, sport psychologists are often not very good at recognizing, acknowledging, and managing those factors. Training in presentation skills is an important part of the education of sport psychologists, and like athletic performance, it requires practice to refine and retain those skills.

Harriet:   Now that I am watching sport psychology students at my university giving talks to class groups and to coaches or athlete groups, it seems that they're very keen to try to cover everything. And being very impersonal about it, being very academic about it. If I think back to when I first started out, that's probably the way I was, too. Presentations were about my agenda, what I felt comfortable with and what felt safe to me. But that's pretty normal when you're just out of grad school. What we really need to do is provide students with a much broader training ground so they have confidence in working within a wide range of settings and learn how to tailor a presentation to the particular situation. I guess that's basically what we're doing now at Victoria University, but I also think it could be introduced more rigorously into the training courses.

Jeff:      I think that's part of where this begins. I think we need to document how we actually do this, how we go about that process. One of my big early mistakes was my own "classic" introduction for sport psychology. I would try to cover all the different things that might be psychological in sport and get everybody *aware*. I was on a mission! Then I would follow up and say, "Here are all the reasons why people don't think sport psychology is good," and try to pick them off. "OK, so what about your belief that psychological skills are preset and unchangeable?" and then I would argue against that. I was trying to set up these straw men and knock them down, and I thought that would somehow prove sport psychology works. So I was doing a version of this teach-everything approach, but it was trying to convince people by argument that sport psychology would be worthwhile. But people aren't interested in debates. And also, they are not really interested in your introducing why it is they might think they don't want you. You know, it's a very strange thing. It's a good academic exercise that I was taught, but it's not a good applied presentation. And so we need to be careful about those academic types of talks that try to describe everything or hit on all things or create these arguments and debates and things like that because most people don't want to hear arguments and debates, they just want to hear about stuff. You know, "Give us some interesting ideas, talk about some interesting stuff."

Mark: In the training realm, what we do at Victoria University is tons and tons of group role-plays where a student is the presenting sport psychologist and the rest of the class role-plays coaches, athletes, or parents. That process really gives students a live-action feel for how and why academic lectures don't work. We teach them how to engage their audience, to get some stories from them that help illustrate their points. Those group role-plays are actually a whole lot of fun. You should see our graduate students regress to 14-year-old female gymnasts in a New York minute. We have had several students come back to us years later and say, "Thank you for forcing us to do those terrible group presentations. They helped heaps."

> Lecturing to coaches is suboptimal; instead, provide interesting stories to those you are presenting to.

## Respecting and Involving Coaches

When we talk to coaches, we are talking to people who have expertise in the skills, techniques, and training methods of a particular sport. We are also talking to people who, in many cases, have an intimate working knowledge of the psychological demands that particular sport places on the athlete or team. Coaches may not use the same terminology as sport psychologists do, or necessarily interpret things in the same way, but to assume they do not know much about sport psychology is at best naive and often a gross error of judgment that can undermine the rapport-building process. Yet this assumption often happens, particularly when a sport psychologist holds the perception of having "special knowledge." When the sport psychologist and coach combine their expertise and their working knowledge of each other's specialist areas, and when they share their stories and their experiences, the level of understanding by both parties, and the building of rapport, is likely to be substantially enhanced.

Jeff: It's more a matter of your understanding where the coaches are, not their understanding where you are. If I'm talking to a group of coaches, I usually assume that they're fairly uninterested in sport psychology and that I've got to find some way of captivating them or bringing them in or softening down the resistance. And that comes through discussion and their offering information to me—their participating. The point here is to have coaches as involved as possible in the process, and I guess what you're trying to cut down is the "us and them" kind of barriers. I really try to move away from being so different from them. I try to show a lot of respect and understanding for where they might be, even if I don't know a lot of what is going on with them. What I try to do is probe or find out what the coaches think are the issues, what they think would be helpful, what they find is interesting, what preconceived ideas they may have. I think that if you are going to work with them, you need to show a great deal of respect for their profession and also be very careful about implying you know more about psychology in their sport than they do. I'm always very careful, as careful as I can be, to show a great deal of deference to people who actually work with the athletes day in and day out, and I try to cut down that artificial gap—the expert professional psychologist versus the lowly coach.

Mark: I often say right out front, "You guys are the experts, and I need you to help me out because you know the sport much more than I will ever know it," and maybe that sounds like ass-kissing, but it's really important ass-kissing. The other thing is that it's true. You go in with the attitude that you are the expert and you have something to give and then not recognize the coach's expertise, or not tell the coach that you recognize that expertise, then I think you are starting to get on a slippery slope there.

Jeff: Acting as though coaches have never done anything about goal setting and don't know anything about imagery, about stress or communication or any of the things that constitute competence, and assuming they don't know anything about those topics is very naive. And most coaches have read articles; they do training. Many of them have degrees, or have gone through coaching courses, and so they are familiar with these ideas. To assume that this is just a whole new area that we're feeding to them is one of the stumbling blocks as well.

# Being a Role Model for Coaches

Coaches and sport psychologists both work with athletes and teams on issues relating to performance enhancement. Coaching and sport psychology also share several key features in their service delivery (e.g., effective communication, feedback). In addition, coaches may use in their coaching practice many of the same techniques or tools as those used by sport psychologists. Most coaches, for example, incorporate some form of goal setting in their preseason and early season preparation of athletes. Some coaches are skilled in their use of those tools; some are not. Unlike sport psychologists, coaches have few, if any, opportunities for instruction or training in these matters, with knowledge and practice usually passed generationally from one coach to another. The intensive training that sport psychologists receive puts them in an excellent position to help coaches by modeling systematic applications of psychological principles in sport.

Harriet: Often coaches have been using some of the tools we come in with for a long time before we arrive. I had an instance early on when I was away on a pre-season camp, and I'd talked to the coaching staff about doing a goal-setting session. I was quickly informed that the head coach runs the goal setting. Upon talking to the head coach it became clear that goal setting was something that was her domain, and she had the belief that it was her role to do. Her focus was purely on performance outcome goals (i.e., wins and losses), so what I did was discuss with her how this could be extended to include other areas of focus, both for the team and for individual athletes. What I found was that by doing a goal-setting session alongside a session run by the coach, but on different aspects of performance and using a different style of presentation, aside from extending the use of tools already familiar to the coaches, I also became a model for the coaches in the way that they presented sessions and talked to the athletes. It is really important to be aware of what coaches already use in terms of the tools or skills we bring, what we might label sport psychology stuff. But it's equally important to be aware of how we might assist the coach in using those tools and also to present a good role model for others to learn from.

Jeff: It's very different if you say, "I have a system for goal setting. Would you like to hear about that?" as opposed to "I'm going to tell you all about goal setting." I often say, "There's a system I like, and there are some basic principles I use. There are lots of different ways to do it, but this is one I find really effective." Essentially I am asking permission: "Do you want to hear about that?" Now even coaches who are very experienced will say, "Yeah, go ahead and show me the way you do it," and then they feel they have permission to ask questions—to challenge and say, "Oh, I do it a different way," and then we have a discussion about it. Instead of representing that I'm going to tell them everything about sport psychology or any specific topic, I say, "This is something I thought would be useful," or "This is something I have seen people use very well." So it's always an "example of" rather than the definitive. And that is part of the difficulty of when we try to sell ourselves; we try to say, "We have special knowledge," and we then go on to either tell the coaches all about it or assume that everything we say is everything there might be. And that's just not the case.

# Resistant Coaches

Mark:   Can we just switch it here for a bit? I'd like to hear some stories on when you're talking to coaches and there's a particularly hostile one in the group. "I know all about sport psychology, and I'm sorry, you know, I don't buy it. Convince me." Do you have any stories about how you've handled that? For example, in a group setting—maybe we're only talking two or three here, like a head coach and a couple of assistant coaches. And you've got the one who is really resistant.

Jeff:   Sometimes you're in a situation when you are down to crunch time and something has to be produced right away. I have had a situation where we were coming up against a trials period, and suddenly here is this coach saying, "All this preparation stuff and all this psychology stuff is worthless. We always talk about it and nothing ever happens and . . . blah blah blah." And my challenge is, "So we're going to do nothing? So how powerful is the path of nothing? Don't mind which way you go, but what is it you're suggesting? What is it you suggest we do?" And he says, "Well we should just go the normal way." *The normal way?* "Well, can you explain to us what the normal way is? And how that is the best form of becoming successful?" "Well, I don't know. . . . We just do it." And it begins to become evident to the people sitting around him that "You're not talking about a plan here." All he is talking about is "I'm really bothered" or "I'm really nervous," and it shows up. The point here is to ask, "What is it that you perceive needs to be done? Is it nothing?" and try to get the person to describe what he or she actually thinks. In the case of someone who says, "Well, this stuff never works. We've had these people before," respond with, "Well, what was the experience? What did you actually do or didn't do that didn't work? Because I'm interested. And if it didn't work, well, I'm not going to suggest something that failed. I don't want to go with that, so tell me about that past experience."

Mark:   I think one of the things I do in a group presentation with a resistant coach, and thank goodness there aren't very many of them, is immediately agree with the person who says, "We've tried it, and it's crap." I say, "You know, I'm sure what you're saying is true. And there are so many ways to be a poor sport psychologist, just as there are so many ways to be a poor coach. There are so many errors you can make and so many things you can do in coaching, and you've seen plenty of bad coaching in your day; you've seen bad coaching technique. Same thing in sport psychology. All sport psychologists aren't the same. There are some that are more competent than others. And you know the sport psychologist who comes in and says, 'I want to give you relaxation, and it's going to help your team'? Man, I'd run the other way, too. Because that's maybe not what your team needs. And besides, each individual on your team probably needs something different. So the fact you've had bad experience with sport psychology in the past doesn't surprise me at all." You completely agree with the person, and that disarms and says you're not like the others. You're not here to prescribe, just as we started out this conversation. I find that agreeing with a hostile coach and taking that hostile coach's story and interpreting it in a way that says "You are right. This probably has been worthless in the past" is a way to move him or her past hostility and on to interest—and maybe even fascination.

Harriet: There's Mark's favorite word. And on that note, I think we ought to stop here.

# Conclusion

We have covered a lot of territory here, and we hope that our conversation has been helpful for sport psychologists faced with the daunting task of presenting themselves, and the field, to coaches. In a final note, we think the content of this chapter is useful, but equally, we believe the process of this chapter has a lot to say. The act of taking time, sitting down with colleagues, arguing, telling stories, and trying to figure out what it is we do when we do sport psychology has been central for all three of us and our professional development. We strongly encourage both neophytes and seasoned practitioners to engage in such processes. Such bull sessions have helped us become better psychologists and serve as a form of continuing education and professional development.

## CHAPTER 2

# Integrating Mind and Body

## Presenting Mental Skills to Young Teams

Clay P. Sherman, PhD, and Artur Poczwardowski, PhD

For much of the past century, community sport enthusiasts and educators, as well as parents and average citizens, have lauded the psychological benefits of sport involvement for youth participants (Coakley, 1998; Sage, 1990). Characteristics such as positive self-perceptions, self-confidence, social consciousness, self-motivation, and the ability to cope with stress are some examples of the benefits. What is clear today is that these benefits, as well as many others, do not automatically result from involvement in sport (European Federation of Sport Psychology, 1996). Both positive and negative attitudes and behaviors are learned in the sport environment.

Bredemeier and Shields (1995), after a thorough review of character development in the sport literature, aptly conclude that "whatever advantages or liabilities are associated with sport involvement, they do not come from sport per se but from the particular blend of social interactions and physical activities that [constitute] the totality of the sport experience" (p. 184). Although not explicitly stated in this quote, psychological development is associated with social interactions and physical activities and may lead to positive and negative outcomes. Furthermore, Weiss (1995) indicates that if positive social and psychological characteristics are to result from sport participation, they must be "purposefully planned, structured, and taught, as well as positively reinforced" (p. 40). Thus, to a large degree the psychological and social benefits from sport involvement are derived from the social and psychological milieu that makes up a specific sport experience.

Although some applied research and practice have targeted the sport medium to help children and youths develop positive social and psychological skills (Danish, 1996; Danish & Nellen, 1997; Orlick & McCaffrey, 1991; Zhang, Ma, Orlick, & Zitzelsberger, 1992), sport psychology practice, applied research, or both have traditionally focused on collegiate, Olympic, elite, and professional athletes (Brewer & Shillinglaw, 1992; Burton, 1989; Davis, 1991; Lloyd & Trudel, 1999; Page, Sime, & Nordell, 1999; Turatto, Benso, & Umilta, 1999). This work with high-level athletes has furthered the sport psychology literature and enhanced the performances of numerous athletes through educational, counseling, and clinical practice. Practice at only these levels, however, is limited in its preventative and long-term focus (Sinclair & Sinclair, 1994). An alternative approach addresses the holistic, developmental, and educational needs of youth sport participants and prepares them for a life full of performance situations.

Many professionals advocate holistic, developmental, or educational mental skills instruction with youth populations (Danish, Petitpas, & Hale, 1995; Vealey, 1988; Weiss, 1995). There have, however, been few examples of the actual work between sport psychology consultants and youths in sport environments. This chapter addresses this limitation. First, we describe support for integrated approaches suitable for teaching youths physical and mental skills. We offer integrated instruction as the central theoretical construct that drives our practice. Second, we discuss some of the developmental concerns of working with young athletes. Third, we present examples of integrated instruction in action as the relationship develops between a sport psychologist and participants of various age-group teams. Finally, we draw some implications related to structuring mental skill development in the youth sport environment.

# Integrated Instruction

One purpose of this chapter is to discuss and demonstrate the practice of integrated instruction. The importance of purposefully integrating sociology, psychology, and social psychology concepts into physical education and youth sport experiences is well supported (Hellison, 1996; NASPE, 2004; Vanden Auweele, Bakker, Biddle, Durand, & Seiler, 1999; Weiss, 1995). Recently, integrated instruction was discussed in both the physical education and sport psychology literatures as an approach that can systematically develop learning, performing, and coping strategies in young people (Mohnsen, 2003; Pangrazi & Darst, 1997; Placek, 1996; Sherman, 1999; Sinclair & Sinclair, 1994; Vanden Auweele et al., 1999; Weiss, 1991, 1995). Placek (1996) defines integrative instruction in physical education as " a curriculum in which subject matter from other subjects is included in PE classes . . . or [in which] social or thinking skills are consciously selected and specifically taught" (p. 290). Instructional approaches that embrace crossdisciplinary integration as well as emphasize social and psychological learning domains are becoming the gold standard in physical education (Mohnsen, 2003; NASPE, 2004; Rink, 1998).

Others have provided comprehensive discussions and examples of how to integrate psychological principles into sport and physical education. For example, Vanden Auweele and colleagues (1999), working cooperatively with FEPSAC, the European Federation of Sport Psychology, edited a book specifically for physical educators. *Psychology for Physical Educators* describes theory and practice specifically related to the why and the how of including psychological principles in daily physical education. Also, Sherman (1999, 2000, 2001) provides specific examples of curricula and lesson plans to facilitate the integration of psychological principles into physical education and youth sport. Through the purposeful incorporation of psychological principles, teachers, coaches, and sport psychologists can help youths achieve affective, social, and cognitive gains in physical education and youth sport in addition to the more traditionally sought psychomotor and organic gains.

The United States National Education Goals (National Education Goals Panel, 1999) and the current literature on education reform reverberate, at the core, with a similar integrative message. The K-12 curriculum must emphasize *how* to learn as opposed to *what* to learn and must help students assume responsibility for their own learning. It is not a stretch to suggest traditional sport psychology methods and skills fit nicely into this approach (see Anderson, 1997; Lidor, 2000; Sinclair & Sinclair, 1994; Singer, 1988). Additionally, the K-12 curriculum must focus on the integration of important principles across the curriculum (i.e., instruction must integrate content areas in an interdisciplinary fashion). Clearly, concepts from psychology, including the development of positive self-perceptions and intrapersonal skills (e.g., coping skills), and concepts from sociology, including the development of interpersonal skills (e.g., group decision making and effective communication), are both important parts of the physical education curriculum.

## Integrated Perspective

Weiss (1995) uses the term *integrated perspective* as a vantage point for understanding and explaining children's participation and behavior in sport. (We use the terms *children* and *youths* interchangeably to cover the ages from early childhood to early adolescence.) This perspective is essential for understanding children's learning, performance, and participation in sport. Her model includes the important interactive influences of physical, biological, social, and psychological factors in sport participation and performance. Without this integrated sport science approach, it is difficult to understand (and efficiently assist) children in sport or to determine their participation and performance patterns and their general health and well-being (Weiss, 1991).

Intrapersonally, integrated instruction can include mental skills training from a preventative and developmentally appropriate perspective. That is, children can learn skills at critical periods in their lives that can lead to successful coping behaviors later in life. For example, as a result of actively involving children in the process of learning new skills and learning how to perform (e.g., self-motivation, cue identification and focus, arousal regulation, self-evaluation), children learn about learning (Bloom, 1981). In addition, children may ultimately assume greater responsibility for their own learning as a result of an autonomous environment that promotes effective learning and enhances intrinsic motivation and self-esteem (Deci & Ryan, 1985). Furthermore, an integrated instructional approach capitalizes on an ecologically valid environment (i.e., sport or physical education environments) for developing mental and physical skills simultaneously. Specifically, when mental and physical skills are taught in an integrated manner, learning can be more efficient, more meaningful, and as a result, more effective. Sinclair and Sinclair (1994) outline the rationale for, and underlying philosophy behind, integrating physical and mental skills instruction:

> We recognize (a) that effective mental management skills are crucial to proficient performance, (b) that mental management skills are an inseparable part of the learning process, and (c) that the practice experience, by design, presents and permits the management of a learning environment which purposefully integrates the physical, mental, and emotional aspects of talent. (p. 15)

## Developmental Issues

As youngsters move from childhood to adolescence, they continue to mature not only physically but also cognitively, socially, and emotionally. Although growth in each of these areas contributes to normal human development, children's cognitive development seems the most relevant to their progress in acquiring and applying psychological skills and, ultimately, benefiting from an integrated instructional approach. According to Piaget and Inhelder (1969), the cognitive development of children between the ages of 7 and 11 is characterized by the ability to perform concrete operations. Children at this stage are increasingly able to think logically and systematically about concrete objects, events, and experiences. In addition, they "gradually attain the ability to mentally modify, organize, or even reverse their thought processes" (Payne & Isaacs, 1999, p. 34). It isn't until the formal operational stage (11 to 12 years and beyond), however, that children begin to deal with complex abstractions and reason about hypothetical situations.

Current generations of children may progress through developmental stages faster than specified by Piaget (Wood & Wood, 1999). Orlick (1992; Orlick & McCaffrey, 1991) has written extensively about the capabilities of children as young as 5 years of age to learn and apply mental skills to improve life performance (i.e., everyday living). In addition, some research supports the use of psychological skills for performance enhancement among boys and girls between 7 and 12 years old (Weiss, 1991; Wrisberg & Anshel, 1989; Zhang et al., 1992).

Attentional processes improve significantly beginning at about 7 to 8 years of age (Haywood & Getchell, 2005). Although selective attention matures by around 12 years, beginning at about age 7, children are better equipped to attend to multiple aspects of a problem and to determine the best solutions. At this age, most children also develop the capacity to mentally organize or modify their thought processes. With practice, the development of cognitive schema significantly reduces the time needed for information processing (Bee, 1995). Similarly, memory capacity improves with age. Children as young as 5 can learn memory control processes such as rehearsal, labeling, and grouping (Bee, 1995). Finally, children can learn to monitor their own performances and recognize the strategies or solutions used in a particular situation. For example, children as young as 4 to 5 years develop the ability of knowing about remembering or knowing about knowing (executive processes or metacognition, respectively) (Bee, 1995).

In summary, what is most important from a practitioner's perspective is that each of the previously discussed mental functions improves with repeated exposure to problem-solving situations (i.e., practice and performance). This improvement is due to increases in the activity-specific expertise or knowledge base (Bee, 1995; French & Thomas, 1987; Haywood & Getchell, 2005; Vealey, 1994). Practice improves declarative knowledge (i.e., facts and information), procedural knowledge (e.g., how to perform sport or mental skills), and strategic knowledge (e.g., how to arrange mental skills into a precompetitive routine). Once instructors and children work through the initial stages in learning new skills (lots of support, encouragement, and skilled instruction is necessary), children will experience more success with the skills and likely experience more satisfaction. As feelings of perceived competence increase, motivation to continue involvement in the activity also increases (Weiss & Chaumeton, 1992).

We have focused most of our work on young athletes who are more than 10 years old. There is, however, no magic number with age. Some 10-year-olds are able to contribute to discussions and complete instructional tasks designed to help them apply mental skills to real and hypothetical situations, while some 15-year-olds struggle considerably doing the same. As discussed previously, there is evidence that children much younger than 10 can benefit from mental or coping skills instruction. Our philosophy rests on the understanding that it is useful to expose children early in life to skills important for healthy and functional living. Children who are introduced to psychological skills at an early age—and provided with the opportunity to practice those skills—are more likely to successfully utilize those skills later in life (Orlick & McCaffrey, 1991). We may be long gone by the time some of the youths we work with successfully apply mental skills learned under our tutelage.

# Consulting in Youth Sport

Researchers and practitioners in sport psychology understand the interdisciplinary potential of applying psychology concepts across learning and performance domains, whether it be test taking, the performing arts (e.g., music, drama), interpersonal skills, exercise pursuits, or the study and practice of any profession (Orlick, 1992; see also the first issue of the *Journal of Excellence*, Orlick, 1998). The sport environment presents continual opportunities to learn mental skills in relation to learning and performing physical skills. Although several resources describe what mental skills and concepts to include when integrating mental and physical skills (Anderson, 1997; Mercier & Hutchinson, 1998; Sherman, 1999; Vanden Auweele et al., 1999), how those skills are included, and the process of integrated instruction, is much less clear. In this section we provide examples of integrated instruction in the youth sport domain.

The examples (excerpts of dialogue) are based on integrated instruction conducted by us in coaching and consulting roles with young swimmers and water polo players (11 to 14 years old) as well as speedskaters (11 to 15 years old). Instead of focusing on a single team or sport, we chose to draw from different experiences to illustrate integrated instruction. Although we discuss a progression of how mental skill development may occur in the youth sport environment, the reality is that many potential differences exist in any given coaching or consulting situation, and more than a general framework is impossible. For example, the type and quality of a consultant's relationship with a sports team will factor into how quickly an integrated curriculum can be implemented. Head coaches are in the best position to begin integrating mental skills into practice. Hired consultants, assistants, and volunteer coaches can expect at least some resistance from athletes, other coaches, or both. Also, cognitive developmental differences between boys and girls are influenced by parent, teacher, and peer sex stereotyping as well as biological differences (Kohlberg & Ullian, 1974). As a result, developmental readiness to accept or understand psychological concepts will vary. From our experiences working with children, we have found that, generally, 10- to 12-year-old girls are often able to listen to, learn, and implement concepts related to goal setting, relaxation, and attentional focus quicker, with fewer reminders, and more effectively than 10- to 12-year-old boys. In addition, the level (e.g., recreational or seasonal, year-round club program, junior development team) and the type of sport (e.g., team or individual; predominantly closed or open skill), as well as language and socioeconomic issues, influence the speed and effectiveness of implementing an integrated instructional approach. Last, the cultural homogeneity of many sporting environments places additional demands on group leaders such as coaches (Corey, 1995).

Coaches who provide integrated instruction (e.g., physical and mental skills instruction) need to be aware of dual-role relationships. Dual-role relationships include functioning as a coach and a sport psychologist for athletes and can be, potentially, problematic from ethical and practical standpoints (Brewer, 2000). Although most coaches providing psychoeducational instruction (e.g., use of goal setting, arousal regulation, attention training) are not functioning as psychologists and are not bound by the ethical principles and codes of psychologists (e.g., APA ethical principles and code of conduct, 1992), coaches need to work within their competencies. When a coach teaches mental skills, some athletes may feel that the coach has opened the door to talk about more personal states and conflict. Opening the door is great, but having other doors to walk through is even better. When athletes present issues to coaches that are of a clinical nature—eating disorders; substance abuse; or issues related to sexuality, identity, or relationships—coaches need to refer these athletes to qualified professionals. See Andersen (2001) regarding referring athletes in or out for counseling or clinical issues. Furthermore, coaches providing psychoeducational instruction as part of a holistic training package should adequately prepare themselves for this additional facet of their coaching repertoire (e.g., through graduate coursework or degrees, workshops, supervised experiences, or preferably a combination of all three).

## Spending Time in the Environment With Young Athletes

Both research studies and anecdotal reports indicate that a consultant's immersion (Poczwardowski, 2001) into the sport setting is critical to the effectiveness of the intervention (Botterill, 1990; Bull, 1995; Neff, 1990; Partington & Orlick, 1991; Simons & Andersen, 1995; Thompson & Ravizza, 1998). One major advantage of teaching mental and physical skills simultaneously in an integrated fashion is that the coach or consultant (the less cumbersome term *consultant* will be used from this point on), because of the relationship, spends a lot of time with the athletes, getting to know them, building trust and rapport, and developing positive relationships. In addition, the consultant is in a good position to observe athletes over an extended period of time (e.g., during practices and simulated competition-like or game-type experiences). In this respect, the consultant is able to gather firsthand information and get a feel for which athletes seem to have adequately developed learning and coping mechanisms and which athletes seem less well adjusted (e.g., those that appear distracted and have trouble focusing, those that express anger or frustration impulsively, those that have trouble self-motivating). During this initial immersion in the environment, the consultant can begin to form generalizations related to understanding and appreciating individual and team strengths and limitations.

## Introducing Mental Skills to Young Athletes

From an educational standpoint, athletes can be equipped with tools to self-motivate and establish immediate, short-term, and long-term purposes for their training or practice. This work can begin at the first practice using the progression outlined in the next section. Athletes can also learn to identify and attend to the relevant learning and performing cues related to any specific skill. This work can also begin immediately as daily objectives and process goals, often stated using words, phrases, or images (e.g., cues) meant to direct an athlete's attention and ultimately lead to performance improvements. To illustrate, in one of our examples we discuss the development of a daily practice objective for increasing freestyle stroke efficiency. In this example, age-group swimmers are talked through a guided discovery episode that encourages them to develop several cue words or phrases to help them improve stroke efficiency. Through the use of one or more of those words or phrases, each swimmer can focus on a concrete idea while working on that day's objective of increasing freestyle stroke efficiency.

Excessive nervousness, tension, fear of failure, and other anxieties can inhibit an athlete's ability to attend to or focus on relevant learning and performance cues (Sherman & Poczwardowski, 2000). Consultants can help athletes develop cognitive strategies to reframe unrealistic or maladaptive thought patterns as well as strategies (e.g., relaxation) to reduce physical tension and cognitive anxiety. For example, later in this chapter we guide speedskaters through a number of different competition-specific scenarios that may elicit negative emotional states. The focus of this group work is on developing and practicing preventative and compensatory strategies to diminish these negative affective responses.

The remainder of this chapter presents dialogue between the consultant and athletes designed to (a) help athletes develop self-motivational strategies and direct their attention purposefully by learning to identify and focus on relevant learning and performance cues and (b) assist athletes in both awareness and moderation of arousal levels. Facilitative self-talk, imagery, and performance routines are other important mental skills (referred to by some as methods; see Vealey, 1988) that could be included in an integrated curriculum depending on the length of the season, type of sport, and amount of time available to spend with individual athletes.

# Goal Setting and Daily Practice Objectives

Goal setting is a method for increasing volition (Vealey, 1988). It is also a skill that needs repetition and practice. A recent strategy to help children and adolescents understand the goal-setting process and increase their ability to set effective goals for themselves is to develop the concept of goal setting in a three-step learning progression (Sherman, 1999). We use this progression to ease athletes into the process of goal-setting behavior. In the first step, we introduce goal setting to athletes by stating objectives at the beginning of practice. We like to think of this as a bottom-up approach. Instead of focusing on long-term or dream goals from the beginning, we first provide athletes with the experience of grappling with daily objectives. In short, based on the focus of the practice, the coaching staff (and later each athlete) determines daily practice objectives (i.e., what athletes should strive to accomplish by the end of practice). After several weeks of accomplishing daily practice objectives, athletes will get used to having a concrete objective guiding their daily practice behaviors.

This first example is an approximation of one of many similar sessions with an age-group swim team. I (Clay) was the head coach of this particular team, and I occasionally go back as an assistant and resident sport psychologist. My tours of duty usually last between one and four weeks. I have a good relationship with the coaching staff, the swim team board, and the swimmers (many I coached as younger swimmers). This relationship is a good example of integrating mental and physical skills: My primary responsibility is to introduce and facilitate the development of psychological skills, although I am also on the pool deck assisting the coaching staff in providing physical skills instruction. When I am in town, I attend the regular daily and weekly coaches' meetings, and normally I am asked to provide specific instruction at specific times of the year. I generally have 10 to 15 minutes after the dryland warm-up to set up the practice objectives and cover any other psychology-related topics (these topics, incidentally, are almost always woven into that day's practice as well as future practices). The coaching staff is a regularly contributing part of this process (in terms of support, perspective, and reinforcement).

## First Step

The first step of the goal-setting progression might look something like this example as I discuss increasing stroke efficiency as the daily objective with mostly 11- to 14-year-old swimmers.

Clay Sherman
(CS):    As Denny [the head coach] said, today we will work on increasing the efficiency of our freestyle strokes. What are some ways we can do this?

Brian:    Use swim fins. [I rely heavily on humor to maintain a light and fun atmosphere when I consult. This tactic is often contagious.]

CS:    Good, Brian! But how about another way, perhaps within the rules. [Period of silence.] Hmmm. Let's go back to the swim fins. Why would using fins potentially increase our efficiency?

Kim:    We could go faster.

CS:    Yes, Kim! What else? [Pause.] What about energy expended? [Pause.] Think about the difference between swimming 1,500 meters versus 50 meters?

Paul:    Sprinters are lazy. [Mixed outbursts.]

CS: Actually, sprinters just have to be fast. Most good sprinters are efficient as well. But distance swimmers must be efficient to be successful. So what is efficiency? [Period of silence.]

Kim: Swimming hard without bonking. [This term, in some countries, has sexual connotations, but it is common usage for North American swimmers to connote giving too much and not having anything left to finish the race.]

CS: Interesting, Kim. I guess it is not clear to me what you mean by bonking.

Kim: I don't know, [pause] not running out of energy.

CS: OK. [Smiling, nodding approval.] So, if you don't want to bonk, or run out of energy, and you have to swim a predetermined distance, you need to be? [Pause for athlete response.]

Kim: Efficient?

CS: Yes. So, according to Kim, efficiency is being fast or swimming long without expending much energy. What are some things we can do to increase our efficiency? [After a few seconds of silence, I look at Josh and smile while making an S-shaped movement with my hand across my body to encourage a response.]

Josh: [Showing the pull pattern.] Using an S-shaped pull.

CS: Yes, Josh! What does that allow? What are the benefits of an S-shaped pull?

In about a two-minute period I have engaged four different athletes. As apparent from this example, not all comments are serious or accurate. I use strategies such as ignoring, silence, clarification, and acknowledgment to encourage or discourage athletes in various ways. Sometimes minor misbehaviors or irrelevant comments are ignored if drawing attention to them would accomplish little and perhaps reinforce poor or off-task behavior. Silence sends the message that I am not always responsible for continuing the discussion. I will often wait five seconds or more for "the team" to move the discussion along. For some athletes, contributing to a discussion is easy and natural; for others, it is a risk. I try to encourage all athletes to take part in discussions (e.g., through nods and smiles). I acknowledge athletes for their contributions with nonverbal behaviors and verbal comments. I try to get as many athletes involved in discussions as possible by moving around the instructional area, making eye contact with athletes, providing hints, nonverbally and verbally encouraging athletes to respond, and so on. In Josh's case, we had just talked about the underwater stroke pattern for freestyle yesterday. A nonverbal reminder allows Josh to participate in the discussion. The dialogue continues until several strategies for achieving the goal (increasing efficiency) are identified. In this particular example, athletes (with some guidance from me) identify

- searching for still water (to keep pressure on the hands),
- keeping the head low in the water, and
- using long strokes that emphasize body roll.

These are written on the whiteboard for all to see. The cues—pressure on the hand, head low, and body roll—are underlined for emphasis and for possible use as cue words while in the pool.

The purpose of displaying the strategies (or cues) where they can be seen is to remind swimmers before and during the upcoming set. Perhaps more important, however, athletes who make a contribution get to see their suggestions publicly displayed. In addition, I try to help athletes develop an educational perspective of the training and coaching process by involving them in the process. My ultimate goal is for athletes to develop a sense of responsibility for their personal development and move toward self-reliance.

The previous dialogue also illustrates a guided discovery style of teaching (Mosston & Ashworth, 1991). Although it would be less time consuming to simply tell athletes about efficiency (direct instruction), I value the process of discovery and the internal thought processing that each athlete experiences as various questions emerge.

> CS: OK, as I said, today we will focus on increasing freestyle stroke efficiency. Last week we counted the average number of strokes per pool length each of you needed to complete an all-out 100 meters. Today, by the end of practice, I am sure each of you will be able to decrease the number of strokes needed to complete an all-out 100 by one-half to two strokes per length—that is, two to eight fewer strokes for the 100 [25-meter pool].

At this first step in the goal-setting progression, I will determine daily objectives as well as a method to measure attainment of each objective (allowing some athlete choice—see dialogue to follow). My thinking here is, I want to model the process of effective goal setting by structuring the process into daily practices (i.e., integrated instruction). This first step may last several practices to several weeks or more depending on how well athletes seem to be grasping the process. For example, some athletes, particularly those that are younger, are less skilled, or have trouble focusing, initially need constant reminders to focus on important cues. Athlete focus is easy to estimate either in advance or retrospectively simply by asking athletes (see Sinclair & Sinclair, 1994). The dialogue that follows takes place during a warm-up set (eight by 50 meters or 75 meters depending on the lane and skill level, with a 20- to 30-second rest interval). The team has been instructed to think about one or more of the cues (listed on the whiteboard) before and during each repetition.

Marisa is 12 years old and a first-year swimmer. She is often the slowest in her lane because of inefficient technique. She will likely decrease the number of strokes to complete the 100 meters by more than eight strokes, potentially a big confidence builder. I also happen to know from past experience that Marisa has trouble paying attention and is easily distracted. It is important to me that she, and several others like her, experiences success in this practice.

> CS: Marisa, before you take off, what do you plan to think about to increase your efficiency?
>
> Marisa: What? [A stalling response.]
>
> [I pause here, smiling, and look at her, knowing that she heard me.]
>
> Marisa: Uhhh, [clearing the water out of her goggles and looking toward the whiteboard] I am going to keep my head low and reach or, uhh, roll my body.
>
> CS: Excellent! Before each 50 meters, if you need to, take a look at the board to remind yourself of one of the three cues to think about.

**Avoid answering for your athletes. Pause, and give them time to come up with the answers on their own.**

With novice swimmers, I try to keep it simple by instructing them to focus on one cue at a time. I move over a couple of lanes to talk with Bryce, who just finished a 75. Bryce is a strong kid with mediocre technique. He wastes a lot of energy. The objective for this practice suits him well. Bryce, while fun loving, is also pretty squirrelly.

> CS: Bryce, you look tired! What were you focusing on to help you stay efficient?
>
> [In this case, I move in front of the whiteboard to block Bryce's view. I want to know what he was thinking about, not if he can find the cues on the board.]
>
> Bryce: [Pausing and stretching to see the board.] Those cue things.
>
> CS: Hmmm. Any one in particular? [Smiling and keeping it light.]
>
> Bryce: Uh, not really.

CS: [More serious now.] Bryce, I think you will improve your times if you are able to increase your stroke efficiency. What do you think?

Bryce: I'd have to agree. [Smiling.]

CS: Good. How do you think you can increase your stroke efficiency? [I move out of his line of sight to the board.]

Bryce: [Smiling and reading.] Head low, pressure, and rotate.

CS: How do you feel about thinking of one of those cues during each of the next four 75s? [I know he has four remaining because coaches know these things.]

Bryce: I can do that.

CS: Good. I'll check with you again to see how it's going.

Bryce: Cool!

A variation of this dialogue is repeated several times as I move from lane to lane to provide feedback based on the use of the efficiency cues. I am not always able to interact with each swimmer every set, but I make a concerted effort to know which swimmers will benefit most from the psychological principles stressed in each set, and I make a point to get to these swimmers.

After participating in the first step of the progression for several sessions (i.e., practices), athletes have firsthand experience with

- aiming for specific daily task-related objectives,
- utilizing the cognitive process often involved in striving to achieve daily objectives (e.g., directing attention toward task-relevant cues),
- individualizing objectives, and
- using feedback mechanisms to evaluate the effectiveness of particular objectives.

During this first step, athletes can begin to assume some responsibility for the process. For example, a range is provided so athletes play a role in individualizing each objective. During the main set for this practice session, athletes are given a target time (based on previous times recorded) for each all-out 100-meter swim. They then determine a stroke target within the range I have suggested. Athletes work in pairs; one athlete counts strokes and keeps track of time while the other athlete swims. They rotate until the set is complete. I quickly circulate among the group swimming first to find out the number of strokes each athlete is trying to reduce his or her total stroke count to. Some swimmers respond quickly, some less so.

CS: Jon, what is your number?

Jon: I don't know. [A bit apathetic.]

CS: [Enthusiastically.] Jon, I know you can get your stroke total down and increase your efficiency. What do you think would be a good number to shoot for?

Jon: How about one stroke per length?

CS: OK, good! Four is your number.

Jon: Four for the 100?

CS: That's right. How do you plan to do it? What are you going to think about during this 100?

Jon: [Looking toward the board.] Pressure on my hand [ad-libbing] all the way through the finish.

CS: Sounds great! I'll check back to see how you did.

Jon: OK.

# Second Step

In the second step of the goal-setting progression, I try to take athletes a bit further in becoming self-reliant and fully applying the goal-setting process. Sometimes I will decide the daily objective (as in the first step) but encourage each athlete to think about how he or she plans to achieve the objective. For example, I may ask the swimmers to think about ways to increase their turn proficiency (e.g., speed in transitioning to the opposite direction and power generated leaving the wall). I instruct athletes to come up with two strategies they can use in the pool today to help them improve their turns (they get to pick which turn—fly, back, free, breast). Although the strategies they come up with are normally adapted or adopted from feedback statements provided by the coaching staff, athletes often feel as if they developed the strategies for their specific needs. I write their turn strategies down and use them as a basis for dialogue with each athlete during the remainder of practice (I typically work with 12 to 15 swimmers at a time, so this task is doable).

The athletes also decide how to evaluate whether or not they have improved their proficiency. At this point in the progression, we have repeatedly discussed the need for some type of evaluation mechanism to determine if they are improving.

CS: [To the entire group.] I would like us to figure out how we will know if the strategies you use help you improve your times. Any ideas? [Period of silence.]

Brian: We could have some type of competition. A relay race! [Cheers from the group.]

CS: [Speaking softly until the group is quiet.] Hmmm, I like the excitement generated from your idea. Any other ideas?

Kim: How about like the start practice we had before? You know, when we do our best starts off the blocks and you judge us like divers, from 1 to 10.

CS: Go on.

Kim: I don't know. [Pause.] Well, you could watch our turns and hold up 1 to 10 fingers to tell us how good our turns were.

CS: That sounds interesting. I'm not sure if I like all that pressure on me, though. How about if each of you practices your turns and gets judged and also serves as a judge for others?

Group: Yeaaaaah!

CS: OK, here's the deal. I have designed a set to help you practice your turn strategies. Before you complete that set, I will assign you to one of several small groups. Each of you will perform four regular turns, without thinking about your new strategies. Just do your turn as you normally do. Each of us watching will rate each turn by holding up 1 to 10 fingers. For each turn, figure out the average score from the judges. That is, determine the total score by adding all the scores and then dividing by the number of judges. I can help you with this. I will write down the averages for each of you. Then, you will all swim my special set designed to give you lots of turn practice, and not much rest I might add. During this set you will consistently focus on your new turn strategies every time you approach the wall. Finally, we will return to the turn judging. Also, after each of you has completed four turns, share your strategies with your group. Any questions?

Jennifer: I'm lost.

CS: [Smiling.] I know, I am lost a bit, too. Fortunately, Denny is writing this all down and will keep us on track. [More serious.] We will help remind you what to do and when.

Josh: How will we know how to rate other people?

CS: Excellent question, Josh. I was hoping someone would bring that up. What do you think?

Kim:    How about the speed of the turn? We could use stopwatches.

CS:    Excellent, Kim. Anything else?

Magnus:    How about the streamline off the wall?

CS:    Great, Magnus. Any others? [Pause.] OK, I will write the scoring criteria on the board. Three points possible for the speed of the turn—that is, how quickly you can change directions. Three points possible for the streamline off the wall, and a new one I just thought of, three points possible for the power of your turn as you push off the wall. So [writing on the board], you have to be quick, streamlined, and powerful or travel really far off the wall. The last point is only given if the turn looks perfect in every way.

I try to provide a model or demonstration whenever possible, so I ask two of my more resilient swimmers to perform four turns for everyone to see. I then evaluate them based on the criteria we just developed.

This small-group evaluation is a hoot; the team has a lot of fun with it. It provides an appropriate challenge for the swimmers to practice their turns under more meaningful circumstances (i.e., they know they will be evaluated by their peers). This allows the swimmers to maintain some motivation after an hour or so of physically and mentally demanding practice. This evaluation device is obviously subjective, but it is fun and reinforces the need for an evaluation feature in the goal-setting process. Also, each athlete shares his or her strategies, and feelings of similarity, uniqueness, and collaboration, along with their results. The small-group focus fosters these positive outcomes. Furthermore, swimmers are not spotlighted in front of a large group but instead are able to practice using new strategies in a relatively safe environment.

A second way I move athletes from dependence on me to more self-reliant goal-setting behavior is to discuss their uniqueness. Often, each of them will be working on specific skills or skill elements. I guide each athlete toward the understanding that goals are best determined individually (with assistance from other coaches and me).

This next example is with a club water polo team I (Clay) am currently working with. The head coach, a previous student of mine, asked me to help out, and I agreed to work with the team two days per week. The team has recently started training again after a layoff. They have been training daily for three weeks. Most athletes are 11 to 15 years old (most older athletes have begun training with their high school teams). The typical format with this team is to do about 15 minutes of dryland work, with coaches participating, and then chat for a couple of minutes before getting in the water. During this brief chat period, I provide some direction related to mental skills. We have just finished the dryland work.

CS:    During the last couple of weeks, Bud [head coach] and I have provided daily practice objectives for you to work toward. We'd like you to begin to get comfortable with determining your own practice objectives or daily goals. So, as you warm up in the water today, I'd like you to think about an element of your game that needs work. Anyone care to share an element of your game that you'd like to focus on?

*[Pause to give them some time to think.]*

Melissa:    I need to get fit.

CS:    [Smiling.] Your extended vacation has caught up with you? OK, Melissa, so you'd like to work on conditioning. Others?

John:    Swimming with the ball.

CS:    Good, John. Others?

Amanda:    Getting the cramps to go away in my calf.

Alan:    Making good passes.

Ian:    Getting a stronger eggbeater kick.

CS: Excellent suggestions! Once you have selected an element of your game that you'd like to work on, I'd like you to think about what you can do today to improve in that area. Alan, you want to work on making good passes. What makes a pass good? [I have selected Alan to keep his attention and that of those near him. I move toward them as I continue with the line of questioning.]

Alan: Well, it can't be taken away, and it is easy to catch and play quickly.

CS: OK, so Alan might choose to focus today on a couple of things to increase the chances that a pass he throws is not taken away and is easy to catch or play quickly. What words or thoughts might help Alan?

Dawn: Well, the person getting the pass needs to be open.

CS: Yes! What else?

Dawn: The pass needs to hit me right in the hand, up high, but not too high.

CS: Good! Anything else? [Silence for about 10 seconds.] OK, based on your suggestions, Alan may quickly consider these two points before every pass: (1) Is my teammate open? and (2) Where do I need to put the ball so he can play it quickly? Then, Alan can pass the ball confidently to that spot.

Although Alan has good throwing mechanics, he tends to make bad decisions when passing (e.g., throws the ball to a teammate who is closely covered). I know about Alan's poor passing decisions based on observations over the last two weeks and discussions with the head coach. Thus, I have chosen to direct Alan to use cues related to making good decisions as opposed to throwing mechanics.

CS: So, to keep it simple, Alan may choose to think, *Open? Where? Confident pass!* to remind himself of the important cues to focus on before each pass. So Alan's goal for today could be to remember to use this sequence before each pass. How will we know if Alan is successful?

Mark: If he doesn't make any bad passes.

CS: OK, yes, eventually. For today, however, we might be more interested in whether Alan remembers to think about the cues before each pass. Later, we might be interested in Alan's percentage of good passes during scrimmages. Alan, I know this is a new thing for you—what do you think?

> In group situations, try to keep the discussion on track. If athletes wander, gently bring them back to the topics at hand.

Alan: [Smirking and playing the studious athlete role.] I can remember to think about the cues: open, where, confident pass.

CS: Good, my man. In what percentage of your passes today do you think you can practice these cues?

Alan: All of them.

CS: Really? Remember, that means when we are warming up, in drills, and in scrimmage.

Alan: OK, I can do it.

CS: Great! How about I check with you during practice to see how you're doing?

Alan: That's good.

I choose to provide an example for the team of what I expect at this step. During the warm-up and initial drill portion of practice, I will ask each athlete individually for a skill he or she would like to work on this session. Of course I write these down so I can follow up with the athlete later during practice. I help each athlete determine how to address his or her concerns or how to operationalize his or her goals.

CS: Melissa. What are you focusing on today?

Melissa: Getting in shape.

| | |
|---|---|
| CS: | OK, how do you plan to work on that today? |
| Melissa: | Well, last week you talked about downtime. You know, when we get to practice early or when we wait in line for RBs [rear backs] or some other drill. |
| CS: | Yes. |
| Melissa: | Well, I could keep moving some way, or after each RB I could swim hard to the other end of the pool and get back in line. |
| CS: | Good. I like that. So when there is downtime waiting for your turn, you will get some sprint work in and keep your heart rate elevated? |
| Melissa: | Yeah. |
| CS: | How many sprints do you think you can get in during drills? |
| Melissa: | I don't know. Maybe 10. |
| CS: | Good. Let's start with 10 today as a goal and see how that goes. |
| Melissa: | OK. |

## Third Step

Eventually athletes will be exposed to the third step, which includes more in-depth understanding and practice setting short- and long-term goals. Although possible short- and long-term goals of some athletes were discussed during the first two steps of the progression, the focus was on achieving and then selecting and achieving daily objectives. By the time athletes get to the third step, most have a good feel for the important components of daily practice objectives: individual, specific, measurable, and challenging. Now, these components can be transferred to short- and long-range goal-setting practices.

When I share relevant past or present stories from my life with athletes, they are usually interested and appreciative. Sometimes I will self-disclose to build rapport or to give athletes a glimpse into my life. In this particular instance, I self-disclose to draw a parallel between goals I have used and the goal-setting process. In the following dialogue, I share one of my experiences related to goal setting with the water polo team. Then, I ask athletes for experiences they may have had with goal setting. Finally, I help athletes put all the pieces together in understanding the goal-setting process by writing big, small, and daily goals (I will use the terms *big* and *small* as synonyms for *long-term* and *short-term)*. The following discussion and exercises are best conducted in a setting with few distractions and accommodations for paper-and-pencil work (e.g., classroom, gym bleachers).

| | |
|---|---|
| CS: | To earn my doctorate, I had to take a big exam covering three years of coursework. In preparing for the exam, I knew it would last 3 days, eight hours per day. There was so much information that I knew I would need to study really hard. My big goal was to pass the exam. I knew 60 days in advance when the exam would take place, so I had 60 days to really cram for the exam. I determined, with my adviser, 45 topics that I knew would probably be on the exam. In 60 days I needed to prepare for 45 topics. That's about 6 topics per week. I decided that I would spend two hours every morning, from 5:00 to 7:00 a.m., and complete 1 of the 45 topics. I would do this Monday through Saturday for two months. Any ideas why I shared this story with you? |
| Melissa: | So we don't feel bad about 5:00 a.m. workouts? |
| CS: | Well, that is an additional benefit of my story. What is my story really about? |
| John: | Goal setting. |
| CS: | Yes. What about goal setting? |
| John: | Well, you had a big goal to pass your test. |
| CS: | Yes! What else? |

| Amanda: | You also had a plan for how you were going to study for the tests. |
|---|---|
| CS: | Absolutely! This is a sharp group. Amanda and John were right on. I had a big goal and a plan for how I intended to meet the big goal. We could call this plan my short-term and daily goals. From a short-term perspective, I needed to study six topics each week. From a daily perspective, I needed to study for two hours every morning. Any of you have examples of goals you have set for yourself? |
| Melissa: | [After a period of silence and some nonverbal encouragement from me.] You worked with me on a plan for increasing my fitness. |
| CS: | That's right, Melissa. Would you mind sharing? |
| Melissa: | Well, I guess my big goal was to get in better shape or increase my fitness. [Pause.] |
| CS: | Good. What was your plan to do this? |
| Melissa: | Well, to put in about an extra 5,000 meters every week. You suggested I could get to practice 10 to 15 minutes early for a long warm-up in the rec-swim lane after I told you it seemed to take me a long time to warm up, and I came up with doing extra sprints during drills when there is downtime. |
| CS: | Yes. So your short-term goal was to complete an accumulation of 5K extra every week, and your daily plan was to get to practice early for an extended warm-up and take advantage of downtime in the pool with some short sprint work. |
| Melissa: | That's right. You also suggested that I have some way to tell if I am getting in better shape. Should I talk about that? |
| CS: | Please do. |
| Melissa: | OK, well, I know when I am in shape, I can feel it, so I have that to go with. But you said we should have some other way to tell as well. When I feel in shape, I can do 20 100s on the 1:30 [i.e., repeat 20 100-meter swims, starting a new 100 meters every 90 seconds]. Right now I can barely do 5. That's when you said you would do that set with me every two weeks. |
| CS: | Ah, yes. So Melissa has a long-term, or big, goal; a short-term, or small, goal; a daily plan to help her achieve her goals; and a way to tell if she is making progress. [I summarize these four steps on the whiteboard for the athletes to see now and refer to during the exercise to follow.] |

> Share personal stories, when relevant, to engage your athletes and help make your point.

At this point I could ask for examples from other athletes. Melissa's example, however, is clear enough that the risk of muddling up a good model outweighs the benefit of getting other athletes to share. Furthermore, the next task is designed to allow athletes to share their long-term goals with at least one other person and work through the goal-setting process together.

| CS: | Each of you has a worksheet in front of you. Notice the worksheet has a place for you to list a long-term goal, up to three short-term goals, and several daily goals. Recently we asked you to think about something you'd like to accomplish by the end of this season. As we said before, it should be something you are pretty sure you can accomplish if you work very hard. For our purposes now, use that as your long-term goal. Write that in the space provided using a pencil. [Passing out pencils and providing two or three minutes for them to complete this.] Now, I will pair you up with one other person. Please listen carefully, and quickly find a spot to work with your partner. |
|---|---|

I often allow athletes to select a partner (or partners) when we work in pairs or small groups to increase the chance that each athlete will pair up with someone they feel fairly comfortable with. In this case, however, I assign an older athlete to work with a younger athlete, hoping the older athlete will perhaps understand the process a little better and provide leadership or guidance.

CS:     I'd like you to share your long-term goal with your partner now. Together I'd like you to come up with first a couple of short-term goals and then a few daily practice objectives to help each of you meet your long-term goal. Jot these down in the spaces provided.

I provide enough time for them to give this task some careful thought. I watch them, circulate among them, and help them stay on task by facilitating the collaborative process. My plan is to help provide some direction without giving answers.

Megan and Steve are using this time as a social hour. I can tell by their blank sheets and boisterous conversation that they are a bit off task.

> When working in group situations, help athletes stay focused by asking questions directed to each athlete.

CS:     Steve, what is Megan's long-term goal?

Steve:   To be the starting junior varsity goalie at Canyon next year.

CS:     Excellent. What are her short-term goals?

Steve:   I don't know. We haven't gotten that far yet.

CS:     Why don't you ask her?

Steve:   [Smiling.] Megan, what are some of your short-term goals?

Megan:   Well, I know I need to increase my leg strength and stamina. . . .

And they're off. In this case, Megan and Steve just needed a little jump start. Others will need some extra explanation and perhaps some modeling of the process. As indicated, I provide feedback as the partners help each other develop short-term and daily goals and some method of accountability. I try to empower, not undermine, each athlete in helping a teammate. Eventually, each athlete will have long-term, short-term, and daily objectives written down on paper. The athletes will also have a means of knowing whether they met their goals. Additionally, at least one other person (other than the coaching staff) will know about their goals and will help hold them accountable. In future sessions, I will discuss dealing with adversities that may get in the way of goals that we set for ourselves and the need to be flexible and adjust goals. This process will be ongoing throughout the season. From a responsibility or accountability standpoint, athletes at any given time should be able to tell the coach exactly what they are working on to meet their long-term goals. The head coach throughout the year constantly reinforces this expectation.

# Working on Awareness and Arousal Control With Young Teams

The previous section demonstrates how the sport psychologist can help athletes learn and practice self-motivational strategies, as well as direct their attention purposefully, while they learn and practice physical skills. Similarly, application of an integrated instructional approach provides the opportunity to help athletes not only increase their awareness of psychological arousal states but also modify these states when necessary. The next series of dialogues is based on Artur's work with a speedskating team. We illustrate how work on awareness and adjustment of arousal levels can be initiated in a group setting. In addition, because team building was one of the items on the coaches' agenda for the sport psychology intervention, we continue to devote attention to the dynamics of team interrelations that relate to integrating psychological skills into sport practice and performance.

The head and assistant coach of a team of 12 young skaters (boys and girls ages 9 to 15) and 2 more-advanced male athletes (ages 18 and 23) invite me (Artur) to develop and deliver a mental training program. The two coaches (both strong believers in psychological preparation) request that the sport psychology service delivery take place in their regular practice and performance settings. The settings include outdoor venues (parks and running trails), weight training facilities, and the speedskating rink. On "mental training days," the coaches allow for 10- to 15-minute time segments at the beginning of the practice for team instruction, and later I am free to move around and work with athletes on an individual basis. Similar to Clay's relationships with the coaches described earlier, both speedskating coaches contribute significantly to the process of mental skill building through their ongoing presence, support, reinforcement, and sharing of personal examples and experiences.

Developing awareness of a specific psychological state precedes any work on developing and using skills that attempt to control this specific psychological state (Ravizza, 2001). For example, before learning to control activation levels, athletes must develop awareness of bodily and mental energy levels (Sherman & Poczwardowski, 2000). As Weinberg and Gould (2003) note, self-awareness training for arousal control involves self-monitoring and making the connection between one's psychological state and the level of performance. In the pursuit of these objectives, I use the following steps:

- Brainstorm with athletes the importance of awareness and arousal regulation skills.
- Make use of guided group discussions and individual conversations.
- Help athletes learn the skills.
- Assign homework, practice, and competition assignments.
- Follow up and use reminders.

The first dialogue is representative of our group guided discovery discussions on a number of mental training topics. During the previous practice session, the head coach announced the team would work on awareness of psychological states. The location for the following dialogue is a weight training gym. This dialogue takes place immediately before their warm-up.

| | |
|---|---|
| Artur Poczwardowski (AP): | Good to see you guys in such great shape! [Pause; hellos from the athletes.] I imagine that some of you may expect an hour meditation session after coach Ron [the head coach] told you about our topic for today. [Smiling and laughing.] We will sit in a lotus position facing east and think about the universe, right? [Smiling, closing eyes, and attempting to "levitate."] Well, that's some other time. Today, we'll try to understand what self-awareness can be regarded as. Let me give you a brief example. Being aware means paying attention to what is happening inside and around us. For example, I can see you sitting on the floor and mats. I am aware of my attempts to project my voice strongly enough so all of you can hear me. I can feel the pressure on my feet that comes from the weight of my body. Now, I am interested in some of your thoughts. Would anybody like to share some of the things that you are aware of right now? [Extended period of silence.] |

It's been almost three weeks since our last mental training session ("How can mental skills enhance performance?"). It seems necessary to introduce an icebreaker to help move the group into the "performing" mode that we had reached three weeks ago (or working stage, Corey, 1995). Clearly, an initial joke about meditation and brief examples were not enough. Such "resistance" after a break (or going back to a transition stage, Corey, 1995) is natural. My next strategy is to devote attention to the group communication process and to pick up the dialogue from the last discussion. This regression to topics that were already covered may be enough to get the discussion going if initial levels of trust and comfort were established at the beginning of the relationship with the team (and if high comfort and trust exist among teammates and coaches regardless of your presence).

> Sometimes, with sessions after hard training, the participants in group discussions can be quiet. Icebreakers and recaps of previous sessions are good ways to help athletes become engaged.

AP: Let me go back to our last session for a minute. Some of you can still remember when we talked about how useful mental practice can be. As I recall, we agreed mental training can help with concentration, help us relax, and also help us get more out of a practice session. [Looking around, nodding, and establishing eye contact with a number of skaters.]

Kirk: Yes, I remember. We also said that mental training needs to be done every day.

AP: Exactly, Kirk! [Smiling.] Wasn't it Caroline who told us she was thinking, even before the practice, about how she wanted to improve her position on turns?

Caroline: Yeah. It was me! [Smiling.] I have been doing it for the past three weeks since your last meeting with us.

Both Kirk and Caroline are the group leaders (for the entire team and the group of girls, respectively). I established good rapport with them last session (first, they were the most mature athletes on the team, and second, it is easier to initiate or change group processes with their help). Not surprisingly, they help move the group into a more productive direction (as demonstrated in the following dialogue).

AP: For the next couple of weeks I will be around more often. I hope we can get a lot done! So let's get back to this "awareness stuff." For example, when you skate, what are some of the things you are paying attention to during your practice? Your personal examples and stories can make our discussions more real for us.

Caroline: It's just like my thinking about the turns. I know exactly what I want to do during the practice. I know where my head, shoulders, and knees need to be. To know it, I need to think about it.

AP: Great observation, Caroline! So how does it help you?

Caroline: I think I can concentrate better because of that. Ron and Tracy [the other coach] always say that once you're concentrating, the muscles will give more energy out.

AP: OK, good! Anybody else?

Brad: Isn't it about feeling the muscles in your legs, like when Ron ran us up and down the hill yesterday?

Ron: Guess what, guys, if you keep complaining, you can expect more of the hill runs after today's practice! [Everybody laughs—they know he is kidding. I appreciate the coach's support in loosening up the atmosphere. He's been around, and he knows the group needs his input to encourage their involvement and sharing.]

AP: Right on, Brad! How about the rest of you? [Establishing eye contact with a few of the younger athletes.]

Cristal: Well, it may not be the same for everybody, but for me I felt the butterflies in my stomach way too much before our last regionals.

AP: Cristal, thanks! [Smiling and nodding.] We need to be aware of what's going on with us during both practice and competitions, even if it is an unpleasant feeling. We will talk about, learn, and practice ways of reducing or minimizing these butterflies and other problems of a troubling nature. I appreciate the examples you have provided so far. At this point, I'd like to share with you another example of being aware. A few judo competitors—you know they still are my favorite examples [smiling]—shared with me their lack of competitive drive before some of their matches. They were aware of no "bounce" in their legs, they yawned a lot, and they didn't care much about doing well. Instead, they wanted the competition to be over as soon as possible. In working with them, I wanted to tap into their environment to help them develop feelings of energy and fighting spirit. After several sharing sessions with the judo athletes similar to our discussion now, one athlete shared that the judo mats underneath his feet reminded him about the energy that has been absorbed and stored in these mats. I asked him for more details. Well, as you know when they practice, they throw each other on these mats. Their throws are fast and powerful. This one athlete believed he could plug into this absorbed and stored energy and use it to psych himself up. What helped him most was feeling the texture of the mats on his feet during the prematch warm-up. I would love to hear more about your own personal stories that speak to our topic of self-awareness.

Our guided discovery dialogue evolves into a focused discussion on awareness of arousal levels before and during races. At the same time, through the judo example provided, I attempt to illustrate a natural link between the awareness and arousal regulation skills, as well as to further stimulate group sharing through encouraging them to take on a teaching role concerning their sport.

Kirk: I used to feel the pressure to perform well. I kept thinking about the other people who count on me. Too often I thought I needed to do well for the rest of the team to perform well. It was like not being able to stop these thoughts, so I could not have a good warm-up and had trouble listening to Ron giving me last-minute cues and reminders. Now, I know when it's coming, and I can easily stop these thoughts in my head. [Pause.] Yeah, that's it.

AP: Thanks, Kirk. I appreciate your sharing your thoughts with us. We all learn better because of it.

I recognize and reward the risk that Kirk took in his sharing. I know he still struggles with high levels of cognitive anxiety before major races; the past tense he uses in his narrative is to let the others on the team know that he is in charge of his mental game and can effectively influence them as one of their leaders.

AP: Well, let me summarize what I heard from you. Awareness is knowing what is going on in our bodies and inside our heads. Awareness is also knowing what's going on around us and how it affects us, how it makes us feel and do things. It is paying very close attention to your experience. Awareness is the first step to control. What I mean here is that once you're aware of what or how you feel, and how it makes your practice or race better or worse, you can begin to develop skills that help you regulate or adjust your energy levels. Just as Kirk, after becoming aware of his negative thinking, learned how to stop it.

We find that youngsters respond better if the planned instruction is divided into a few smaller segments. For most segments, we make an effort to provide opportunities for athletes to share and for leaders to make summarizing statements (e.g., "Let me summarize what I heard from you," "I am curious about your comments," "I'd like to add . . .").

> With younger athletes, plan shorter instructional segments.

AP: Now, the task for today's practice, both before and during your lifts, is to be aware of yourself—for example, your muscles, your breathing, and the environment. I will circulate around the gym and chat with you and make myself available for your questions. One exercise I want to complete with you is related to how much energy you feel at any given time. I'd like to use a scale, or number system. We will use the numbers from 1 to 10 to help you estimate your energy levels. You can think of a *1* on this scale as being totally asleep. A *2* on this scale would be total relaxation. A *3* may be how you feel when you wake from a good night's sleep: calm, relaxed, wanting to do nothing but just enjoy the sense of being rested. At the other end of the scale, *10* would be when you feel so much energy in your body and there are so many thoughts racing through your head that it is difficult to think or do anything that makes sense. You may be really angry, afraid, or nervous. [Pause.] Believe me, some people get that angry or that nervous occasionally. If you watched Jim Carrey in *Mask* you know what 9.5 is on our scale. [A few skaters laugh; pause.] Let's think of your normal activities as 4 and 5. Sound OK? [A few nods and affirmative verbal reactions.] Today, I'd like you to focus on how much energy you feel from 1 to 10.

Cristal: So for me, when I am at school in class it can be 5, and when I am back home I can feel 4, or 3 when I watch TV and relax, right?

AP: That sounds good, Cristal! I want you to know, however, that the numbers on the scale may work differently for every person here. For example, for a student who has trouble learning, school could be a 9, very stressful, and home a 2. So although Cristal gave us a nice illustration of how she experiences different situations and levels of activation during her day, these numbers may be different for you or for someone else. This is precisely the point: self-awareness, or being aware of your own experience. [Pause.] Other comments? [Pause.] No? OK, if questions arise later, you know I'll be cruising around.

At this point, the athletes proceed with their warm-up and their strength training under Tracy's leadership. Tracy closely supervises a couple of the youngest skaters who use their own body weight as resistance (no weights). It is now time for me to work with them individually. My goal is to help these athletes get some practice focusing on self-awareness and how much energy they feel. Later we will use their developing awareness skills to determine their arousal regulation needs.

AP: Hi, Jim! Do you still remember our energy scale? [Jim nods.] Good. On this scale from 1 to 10, how much energy do you feel in your body at this moment?

Jim: Somewhere between 6 and 7.

AP: Tell me more about it.

Jim: You know, I feel I have more energy than at school, and I am kind of pumped up for my lifts to go up more since I have improved so much recently.

AP: OK. So school would be somewhere between 4 and 5? [Jim nods.] I like your insights. OK, go through your set now. And do focus on the experience, all right? When you're done, I'll ask you the same questions. Ready? [Pause while Jim finishes his set of bench presses.] Can you talk now? [Jim nods.] OK, on the scale from 1 to 10, how much energy did you feel in your body during the lift?

Jim: Probably a 7. No, maybe 8 because it was a tough lift, and I was really trying hard.

AP: Good! Try to continue paying attention to your energy level during your lifts today. Try to remember when you rate yourself high and when you rate yourself low and what you are doing during those times.

I want to model a reflective and thorough approach to this self-examining activity. With the reinforcement that I provide (i.e., praise, interest, encouragement) and the detail-oriented questions, I hope to send to Jim a message indicating the importance of being aware of one's experience as well as illustrate the need of working on awareness in a serious and focused manner.

I structure a similar interaction with each skater. The examples, language, and humor change based on individual differences, such as skill level, age, and personality. The focus, however, remains on "experiencing" the skill (e.g., movement, bodily sensation, thoughts and emotions, images) rather than "performing" it, or getting it done (Ravizza,

2001). These interactions are structured to help athletes focus on their own experiences and develop self-monitoring skills that later will become the goal for their homework (or away-from-practice applications). Toward the end of the first week of the two-week awareness and arousal regulation training, the skaters will be encouraged, reminded, and invited to share their experiences in figuring out the connection between their arousal levels and their performances (during practice and competition).

During their stretching routine, the head coach invites me for another brief interaction with the team. This "free to move" part of their workout is also a good opportunity for me to observe patterns in the interactions among the skaters.

AP: Guys, you're becoming experts at observing yourselves during practice. Nice! So what are some examples of things you're aware of during your lifting? [I direct my eyes to a group of four skaters who sit together and laugh occasionally while going through the stretches; three of them did not participate verbally during the previous guided discovery activity. Given their outgoing mood at the moment, it seems a good time to invite them to the team exchange and sharing.]

Kirk: My breathing and the burning feeling in the muscles. [I nod encouragingly.]

Jim: The air traveling through my nose, and the bar in my hands.

AP: Good. Kristin?

Kristin: The form of the lift and counting in my mind. [I nod, pause, and establish eye contact with Todd, the fourth kid in their pack.]

Todd: Nothing. [Laughs.]

AP: Yes, quite a variety, huh? Guys, you know your stuff! [Reinforcing their contribution to the team learning; acknowledging a joking "nothing" with a shade of a smile—Todd plays the role of the showbiz guy and, most likely, has just performed one of his tricks for the team.]

The idea for this brief sharing activity is for the athletes to hear from themselves examples of what enters the field of their awareness. Thus, mere listing of these experiences satisfies the activity objective. The comment from one athlete (Todd) could easily be interpreted seriously (i.e., experiencing "nothing"). Feeling "nothing" may be indicative of flow, or "being in the zone." Thus, this situation presents a teaching moment. The team may benefit if I proceed as follows:

AP: "Nothing"—that's an interesting one, Todd. I heard you laugh, but I sense that you had something important to say. [Pausing and looking toward Todd.]

Todd: Well, kinda. I certainly did not feel this way today. I am still dead tired after our hill runs [looking at Ron and smiling; everybody laughs], but I felt this way a few times during practice and also during a couple of races. The thing is that it felt great, and these were the best practices I have had in a long time, and I improved my personal bests during the races.

AP: An awesome account. Thank you, Todd! Indeed, some athletes report feeling nothing, or more often thinking nothing, when they are "in the zone" or when they are "on automatic pilot." Athletes who have reported being in the zone say that everything works without thinking about it. The mind is so clear that this experience may be described very accurately by the word *nothingness*. Anybody else felt something like that? [A couple of skaters share their experiences of having a flow sensation in practice and competition. Ron offers his insights into how being in the zone helps mobilize all muscle energy and builds on training efforts, ultimately leading to a powerful race.]

AP: Nice job, guys! And thank you, Ron, for your examples. Again, different things work differently for different people. We can learn a lot by just paying attention to our bodies. [Pause.] Let this be our homework for the next couple of days:

Pay attention. Pay attention to what you feel, what you think, and what you do. [Pause.] Pay attention and learn! [Reaching for a notebook and getting out blue sheets of paper.] Here are some reminders for you to collect as you leave. You remember the scale, from 1 to 10? You'll have five scales on the form for five different activities. My intention is to give you lots of practice developing your sense of awareness. Ron and Tracy will remind you what to do.

> Acknowledge the contributions athletes make through interacting with you. Praise their insights and offer reinforcement; this approach encourages others to participate.

I was particularly pleased with the responses coming from the junior and less-experienced athletes on the team. While working with groups (as well as in individual consulting), it is critical to assume a nonjudgmental perspective, offer reinforcement for comments that are on task, and acknowledge the risk that the participants take while sharing their own experiences. These techniques develop trust and acceptance, caring, freedom to try, commitment to behavior change, and self-disclosure, to name a few characteristics of a well-functioning group (Corey, 1995), and are the building blocks of a consultant–client alliance (Andersen, 2000). The more trust between the group facilitator and the group members, the sooner members focus on group tasks and goals. From an educational standpoint, providing early reinforcement often results in further learning through increased interaction, motivation, and self-involvement.

The next vignette illustrates the interaction with the team when I introduce ideas and experiences to set a foundation for later sessions on arousal regulation. Mental skills instruction is again integrated into their typical activities performed in their natural practice setting. Three days before a competition (home meet), we brainstorm ideas on how to deal with negative feelings and thoughts before and during their races. The emphasis at this point is on paying close attention and learning from the observations made about one's reactions and attempts to cope before and during the competition.

AP: Let's get back to our last lesson where we focused on paying attention and learning. We will try it on Saturday and Sunday. Your races will be a lot of fun, no doubt! Now, do you think that you may also experience some negative feelings or thoughts before them? [Pause, allowing time for their reflection and response.]

Kristin: My dad will be watching. I always want to do well when he comes to races and stuff, and I get nervous.

AP: Great point, Kristin! I know a number of athletes who want to please their parents, coaches, and teammates. That's natural and fairly common. Anybody else who feels this way before their races? [A few skaters raise their hands.]

AP: Go ahead, Kirk.

Kirk: I had similar experiences with my dad. He used to come to many practices to watch me. He'd have a talk with me before every competition, telling me I gotta focus and race hard, don't give away an inch to other kids. Then it was really hard for me to race, remembering what my dad would say.

AP: I wonder whether you could share with us what you decided to do about that.

Kirk: I don't think I'll tell you how my dad found out that this was bothering me. But we had a great conversation about his not coming to my practices and races for a while, and it helped a lot. Now, even if he comes it is different. I mean, I feel different about it.

AP: Less pressure?

Kirk: Yeah, exactly. Plus, he wants me to have fun most of all. That works for me. . . .

AP: Great story, Kirk! When I listened to Kirk and Kristin, I started to think about how some of you may be trying too hard sometimes.

I am fairly directive in my consulting approach with groups and teams; I am also willing, however, to be redirected if my hypotheses are inaccurate. Although I believe this directive approach works very well for me, I realize it is not for everyone.

AP: Kristin, did you find that wanting to do well so much can in fact make you lose your concentration on what needs to be done, thus leading to worse performance?

Kristin: Oh, yeah, that happened to me! And Tracy said that, too, many times when she talked to us about her racing in national and international meets.

Nicole: And for me, there will be so many girls who are older, you know? I may not feel like racing against them. Kind of, why even bother? I am not that strong.

AP: So, Nicole, you may find yourself not having enough energy and motivation to warm up properly and to try your best against these older girls. Is that how you feel?

Nicole: I think so. You know, they seem too strong for me.

AP: Good example, Nicole. We'll see what we can do about that in a few minutes. Jim had his hand up.

Jim: I may be too cold and rush through the warm-up.

AP: Yes, this seems like a serious concern, too, Jim. We'll come up with some ideas how to handle situations such as these you guys have just mentioned. Any other thoughts on how you guys might feel this weekend before and during your races?

I want to involve as many athletes as I can at this point. I hope the athletes discover that, regardless of their individual experience, most have issues and concerns relating to their races. Also, the variety of meaningful examples from the athletes provides an opportunity to deal with authentic negative states.

AP: Very good! I like the richness and details in your observations! [Pause, allowing the time for the praise to be absorbed by the younger athletes.] Now, what are your thoughts on what to do to feel good about yourself and about the upcoming races? [Long pause.] What I am looking for here are your experiences. But also you may choose to share solutions that you haven't tried yet but you have heard about and somehow they make sense to you. [Another pause.] For example, Jim might pair up with somebody for the race warm-up to make sure he will go through his routine without rushing and skipping any moves and stretches. [Jim is nodding.] Also, on Saturday morning while still in bed he could visualize his warm-up as if he were doing it on ice. OK, Jim? [He nods again.] So what do you guys think?

Jim: This visualization session in bed sounds cool!

AP: Let me know how that goes, Jim. We could work together to make an audiotape if that would help. Caroline, you wanted to add something?

Caroline: Yeah! What I do when there is too much pressure is play my favorite CDs after my warm-up and between my races, you know? It relaxes me just fine.

[I nod approvingly.]

Todd: I always tell myself that it's gonna be my best race.

AP: Sounds as if Caroline and Todd have tried a few things to stay calm and relaxed under pressure. Any other thoughts? [Pause.] Another thought I have is to think about the race as just another practice. I have heard many Olympic athletes speak about this technique. You've completed your races in practice so many times! And Ron and Tracy tell me that most of you improved your best times from last year. Where did those improvements take place?

Brad: In our practice trials three weeks ago.

> AP: Is that so? So how about seeing Saturday and Sunday's races as another practice time? There will be skaters from other clubs and a group of parents watching. That's great! They will be there, but for you, think about your races as just another practice, another opportunity to improve your personal best.

At this point, I think it is a good time to proceed with an experiential illustration of one of the skills we talked about (i.e., I told them about a skill or technique, now allow them to experience it). I lead the group through a brief guided imagery session in which they pick their most recent practice when they felt good about their performance and themselves. After reliving some of those feelings and thoughts, we process their experiences, and I make a transition back to our awareness training.

> AP: Again, the goal for these races is for you to pay attention to what you're experiencing. Some of you may decide to try a skill that we have just brainstormed here. However, the goal stays the same. Yes, go ahead and try the skill, but most of all make efforts to notice what your thoughts and feelings are before and during the race, what your energy level is on the scale from 1 to 10, and how well you perform. The coaches will hand out the same sheets that you used for your homework. You will be provided some time, immediately after the competition, to fill these out and process your races a bit. Then, we will talk about this next week. At the meet, pay attention, learn, and have fun! I will be there on Sunday.

During the practice, I approach the athletes on an individual basis and follow up with further exploration, clarification, and brainstorming regarding their experiences with arousal regulation strategies. I offer my support and encouragement, and I re-emphasize using process orientation in their mental preparation during the upcoming competition. My presence on Sunday serves as a reminder of their awareness training. The next week, the coaches summarize their performances, offer feedback, and ask questions about the mental training. They also announce that I am coming back to conduct relaxation training the following week.

I start the relaxation session with questions about skaters' experiences during the competition. They offer a variety of insights and comments concerning their awareness and attempts to control their activation levels (e.g., reducing the feeling of butterflies in the stomach by remembering these races were really only another practice opportunity, visualizing going through the planned warm-up routine). While reinforcing their "paying attention and learning," I make the transition into presenting techniques that athletes use to reach deep relaxation states, specifically autogenic training. Before getting into the technique itself, I preview for them the entire learning and application process. We believe it is important to situate a psychological skill in a larger perspective to help athletes make connections between what they are doing at the moment and the ultimate goal of integrating their mental skills into their sport behavior.

> AP: Just as I said, we'll start slowly. I'll lead you through the autogenic training today and a few more times this week and the next. You'll learn the relaxation progression, and we will encourage you to practice it at home for a few weeks. I have made audiotapes to help you practice and learn this technique. Now, let's get the mats from the pile over there. Lie down and make yourself comfortable.

I proceed with autogenic relaxation training as described in our chapter in *Doing Sport Psychology* (Sherman & Poczwardowski, 2000). The introduction to the skill, the script used, and major components of the learning experience (e.g., processing, building on strengths and elements that work well) remain the same. A few modifications are made to account for group instruction and the age of the participants. For example,

- more time for sharing (or processing) is planned;
- mutual care for each athlete's reactions, experiences, and insights is nurtured and reinforced;
- the instructional language considers the participants' frame of reference;
- fewer repetitions of the suggestions are performed to better keep the young skaters' attention; and
- more concrete examples are provided.

I start the first relaxation session with a short dialogue aimed at refreshing skaters' recollections of what *2* on the activation scale means.

> AP:  I hope that today most of you will be able to experience 2 or 3 on our 1 to 10 activation scale. Well, most likely you'll find yourself today even more calm and at peace than after waking up from a good night's sleep. [Pause.] We will accomplish this relaxation through a special kind of relaxation training. It's called autogenics. It's like learning how to tell your mind and body to relax. Autogenics means that this relaxation state comes from within you. It is you who will teach your mind and body to calm down through a set of suggestions. What it also means is that after some practice with my help, your tapes, and the coaches, you will not need anybody or anything to relax. Amazing, isn't it? You are doing this relaxation yourself! [Pause.] Initially, I will be telling you what you might be experiencing, but at the end it is you who produces these feelings. OK! So what's your task today? I want you to repeat these suggestions in your head and passively respond to them. By passively, I mean just be there, listen, repeat, and wait for your body to respond. Sound OK? [Smiling, reading the team reaction, and waiting for their nonverbal signals of being ready to proceed.]

Because young athletes seem to rely more on adult guidance, we use a short preview of what is coming with respect to the intended instruction. While the athletes are getting comfortable on their mats, I use this time to influence their expectations of the upcoming relaxation experience.

> AP:  I know a number of Olympians who have used autogenic training. They say there is no better way to relax really deeply. But it does take practice, just like improving your skating technique. [Pause.] We'll begin with focusing on your breathing. Then, I'll describe for you increasing feelings of heaviness and warmth in your body. You'll repeat the words to yourself—just think them or say them to yourself. I will start with the instructions for your arms. [Pause, raising my right and left arms.] We'll repeat the same suggestions for your legs. [Pause, lifting my right, then left, leg.] Next, I'll allow a couple of minutes for you to really experience this relaxation state. Once we are finished, we'll talk about what you've experienced. Any questions at this point?
>
> Todd:  How are we going to remember what to do?
>
> AP:  Good question! [I sense that this preview might have gone for a bit too long.] I'll lead you through each step. Just listen and let your body follow my instructions. Later, you will have an audiotape to help you remember when you practice on your own, and eventually you will remember how to do it on your own. For now, just repeat the suggestions of heaviness and warmth in your head. Just repeat without forcing anything. Again, that's what I mean by passive. Repeat and kind of be there to see what happens next. Let's begin. I want you to find the most comfortable position you can. Good! Now turn your head to the left, now to the right, and relax the muscles in your neck. Nice! Now shrug your shoulders a few times and relax the muscles in your arms. Now, the same with your feet: left and right, tense and relax your muscles as

we have practiced previously. Yes! Close your eyes. [Pause, slowing the speaking rate and lowering the tone of voice.] I'll switch from saying *you* to saying *I*. It'll be easier for you to repeat. Good. . . . My eyes are closed. I pay attention to my breathing: inhale, exhale, inhale, exhale, in, out, in, out. . . . Good. With every breath I take, I am becoming more and more aware of my body. [Pause.] This is my head [pause], my shoulders [pause], my arms [pause], my hands [pause], my torso [pause], my hips [pause], my legs [pause], my feet. [Pause.] Good. . . . Breathe in, breathe out, in, out, in, out. Nice and easy. . . .

The first session takes about 15 minutes. We proceed with group processing of how it went. After responding to a few comments related to some of the athletes' experiences, I conduct the final part of the relaxation training—generating some ideas for how the relaxation skill can be used.

AP:    Now, most of you have experienced deep relaxation, so let's talk about some potential uses of this skill for your skating. I will make the first deposit in our idea bank. You might use relaxation to clear your mind after a hard day at school so you can focus better for your practice.

Kirk:    I have never before been so calm and relaxed. I think that for me it would be a great way to go to sleep at night before my races.

AP:    Excellent!

Cristal:    What about resting after practice? I still have a lot of homework to do.

AP:    Good point! It can help you to rest and regain your freshness, and scientists have also found that your muscles will recover faster. There may be a bit less muscle soreness, and you'll be able to work harder next day during your workout. Your coaches will like that. Bonus, huh? Nice comment, Cristal!

Todd:    This floating experience that I reached reminded me about those feelings of nothing and this flow thing that we talked about the other day. That was cool!

AP:    Right on, Todd! Sounds as if you had a peaceful, floating experience. Anybody else?

Jessica:    I don't know whether it fits or not, but after doing our awareness training, you know, I could focus on myself so easily during our relaxation training tonight. Like there were no other things, just me.

AP:    I am glad you're bringing this up, Jessica. Indeed, with relaxation practice, athletes gain more knowledge about their bodies and reactions. Good point, indeed. So far we've heard about being able to be more aware of yourself, about using this technique before you go to sleep—especially on nights before races—and about helping muscles recover after hard workouts. [Pause.]

Ron:    This all sounds good. When can we expect to see some results?

AP:    To enjoy these and other benefits that we mentioned, you need to practice relaxation. I'll be back on Wednesday. After a few times, you'll practice relaxation on your own. I will give tapes to those who are interested. We will work on your trigger words so you will be able to use these skills whenever you choose. It is coming along. As I said, developing psychological skills such as awareness and relaxation takes the same commitment to practice and improvement as developing physical skills. [Turning to Ron.] You know about that.

This last dialogue with the coach reflects our philosophy that it is important to start slowly and gradually integrate the mental fabric into sport behavior. In the delivery of psychological skills training, we use the following cycle:

- Introduction of the topic
- Brainstorming of ideas and drawing on athletes' and coaches' experiences

- Mental skill acquisition
- Mental skill refinement
- Progression of mental skills from practice settings to competition (from less to more important), allowing for fine-tuning
- Integration into one's sport behavior

# Conclusion

We find our work with young athletes rewarding and challenging. For the most part, children are enthusiastic and willing to try new experiences, especially if a fun element is structured into the learning. Although much lip service is given to the importance of teaching mental or life skills through the medium of sport, our observation is that life skills instruction is rarely purposefully and intelligently integrated into the total sport experience. Children will not learn discipline, self-control, or how to focus in sport without leaders who not only model those qualities but also structure them into practice activities. In this chapter we provide several examples of integrating mental skills with practice of physical skills. Our philosophy is that mental skills are best learned in a context that is important and meaningful to young athletes. For many, that context is a sport or physical activity setting.

# But Coach Doesn't Understand

## Dealing With Team Communication Quagmires

Kevin L. Burke, PhD

In the world of sport, clear and precise communication can be the deciding factor for learning new skills, eliciting high team satisfaction, and determining the outcome of contests. Building an effective communication system may be one of the more important aspects of strengthening any team (Hardy, Burke, & Crace, 2004). Good communication is a central skill that sport psychologists (as well as coaches, athletes, referees, umpires, and sports managers [Burke, in press; Haselwood et al., in press; Lambrecht, 1987]) must have. Numerous authors have written about communicology, linguistics, body language, proxemics, encoding, decoding, sending, receiving, and other related communication topics (Anshel, 2002; Beebe, Beebe, & Redmond, 1996; Burke, 1997; Carron & Hausenblas, 1998; Haney, 1979; Infante, Rancer, & Womack, 1997; Knapp, 1978; Martens, 2004; McGough, 1974; Mehrabian, 1968; Sullivan, 1993; Weinberg & Gould, 2003; Yukelson, 1997, 2001).

In the business world, past investigations have shown that good interpersonal relations are a key predictor of profitability and bottom-line advantages (Hanson, 1986; Ouchi, 1981; Peters, 1988). Whetten and Cameron (1991) state that supportive communication is a proven competitive advantage for managers and organizations. Von Gunten, Ferris, and Emanuel (2000) structured a seven-step approach for the communication of important information in the medical profession. Regardless of the venue—interpersonal relations, business, medicine, or sport—effective communication increases the healthiness of the working environment and helps people understand their roles in groups (teams).

Most colleges and universities offer courses and majors in communication. Communication problems, however, are prevalent in all areas of life. One reason for communication difficulties is that many people feel that others, rather than themselves, are ineffective communicators. Investigating more than 8,000 employees in universities, governmental agencies, hospitals, businesses, and the military, Haney (1979) found that most believed they were communicating better than, or as well as, everyone else. These findings indicate that suboptimal communication may remain prevalent because most people perceive poor communication as someone else's problem.

Communication is a core issue in many aspects of sport, such as skill improvement and attainment, motivation, concentration, self-confidence, task and social cohesion, leadership, goal setting, expectations, and overall satisfaction (Burke, 1997; Carron & Hausenblas, 1998; Lambrecht, 1987). Although technology (e.g., e-mail) has improved the efficiency and speed of some types of communication, comparable progress has not been achieved in the interpersonal aspects of communication. Whetten and Cameron (1991) state that "ineffective communication may lead individuals to dislike each other, be offended by each other, lose confidence in each other, refuse to listen to each other and disagree with each other as well as cause a host of other interpersonal problems" (p. 233). Therefore, effective communication is necessary among teammates, coaches, and players.

# Communication Theory and Research

Although the area of communication appears relatively lacking in theoretical foundations (Watkins, 1991), some interpersonal and group communication theories may be relevant to sport situations. One interpersonal theory applied at the beginning of relationships is known as the uncertainty reduction (UR) theory (Berger, 1986). The foundation of this theory is that during initial interactions between two people, both seek to reduce uncertainty about each other. The seven interrelated factors in dyadic exchange (information-seeking behavior, intimacy, liking, nonverbal expressiveness, reciprocity, similarity, and verbal communication) are included within UR theory (Infante, Rancer, & Womack, 1997). Again, UR theory is designed for the early stages of relationship development, so its application to sport circumstances would be limited to initial (but still important) interactions.

A more intriguing interpersonal theory is the predicted outcome value (POV) theory (Sunnafrank, 1986). POV theory involves anticipated costs and rewards in relationships. Sunnafrank postulates that relationships are advanced by the anticipation of more positive than negative denouements. In other words, the rewards and costs a person expects in a relationship will influence the choice to avoid, constrain, or pursue further involvement with another person. If players expect to benefit personally and athletically from their coaches, they will be more likely to initiate interactions with coaches that will further develop their relationships. If athletes expect negative outcomes from their coaches, they will communicate in ways that impede relationship progression.

Cahn's (1984) theory of perceived understanding suggests that development of interpersonal relationships is affected by perceived feelings of being understood or misunderstood. For example, if players perceive their coach understands or empathizes with them, the athletes will develop feelings of emotional intimacy, which will lead to more interactions with the coach. If athletes feel misunderstood by the coach, they will most likely curtail communication. Both POV theory and the theory of perceived understanding have roots in behaviorism and, more specifically, operant conditioning.

The previous theories were developed with one-on-one communication issues at the core, but models of group communication processes also exist. Three group communication theories or models are the symbolic convergence theory (Bormann, 1986), the interaction system model (Fisher & Hawes, 1971), and the multiple sequence model (Poole, 1983). Symbolic convergence (SC) theory emphasizes choices and personal translation; it postulates that the stories and anecdotes told by members of a group disclose group norms and rules. In a sport setting, for example, the anecdotes basketball players share with teammates—about each other or their opponents—augment team norms and develop a team identity. Team members learn more about members of the group and what the group represents through these symbolic converging behaviors (storytelling). SC theory places significance on the meaning stories have for a team or group because these stories help the members form a rhetorical vision (Bormann, 1986). This rhetorical vision is the view of the team identity among group members and in relation to persons outside the group. The strength of the SC theory is its potential to explain group processes such as the development of norms, rules, and cohesiveness (Infante, Rancer, & Womack, 1997).

The interaction system (IS) model emphasizes interactions among group members rather than individual actions (Fisher & Hawes, 1971) to explain group behavior. The IS model focuses on group members' behavior patterns, their responses, and the interaction of message patterns (Infante, Rancer, & Womack, 1997). In other words, the IS model claims that to understand team behavior, one must analyze the interactions among team members instead of just the behaviors of members within a team. According to Fisher and Hawes, verbal statements may be categorized as to the function performed in the group (e.g., clarification, substantiation, interpretation, decision making). Applied to a sports team, the IS model could be used to attempt to identify how a team interacts (message patterns among teammates) and the processes transpiring in making team decisions.

Another communication model for group decision making is the multiple sequence (MS) model (Poole, 1983). Poole identified three group-communication tracks—labeled task, relational, and topical—that develop at the same time yet at various rates. The task track describes the processes a team uses to accomplish a task, such as analyzing situations, accumulating information, and choosing solutions. The relational track refers to how well or poorly a team works together. The content (issues and arguments) of the interactions are represented by the topical track. The task and relational tracks focus on processes, whereas the topical track emphasizes content. One aspect of the MS model that may have the most relevance for sports teams is the influence of group history. Expectations of the future depend on what happened in the team's past (Poole, 1983). According to Poole, three aspects of group history affect decision making:

- Group involvement (e.g., low or high level of involvement of team members)
- Beliefs of leadership (e.g., coach or team captains)
- Procedural norms relating to group roles and rules

For example, a basketball team with good social cohesion (i.e., players enjoy interacting and cooperating with each other) and confidence in the coach's decisions, and whose members clearly understand their duties and roles within the team situation, is able to more effectively confront team issues than a team who lacks any of these aforementioned variables.

In addition to these previously discussed theories and models, Byrne's (1971) reinforcement theory proposes that principles of reinforcement explain most interpersonal attraction occurrences. Simply explained, we like and are attracted to people who reward us, and we dislike and are repelled by people who punish us. Byrne also predicts that persons with similar attitudes find the relationship rewarding and, hence, will like each other.

Research related to improving communication of sports teams has been scant within the field of sport psychology (Hanrahan & Gallois, 1993). Sullivan (1993) found that after an intervention of seven interpersonal communication skill activities, athletes in the interactive sports of basketball, water polo, and volleyball reported being better aware of their communication abilities. One 12-week investigation on enhancing interpersonal relationships in team sports (Di Berardinis, Barwind, Flaningam, & Jenkins, 1983) noted improvement in skills, and those gains were positive predictors of athletic performance. Other related studies investigating team cohesion have found, in interactive team sports, that success and performance are dependent on effective communication (Bird, 1977; Martens & Peterson, 1971; Nixon, 1976). Studies investigating coach–athlete relations (Carron & Bennett, 1977; Haselwood et al., in press; Smith, Smoll, & Curtis, 1979) and coaching sports (Williams & Widmeyer, 1991) suggest that communication may be integral to success or performance in sport.

In the field of sport psychology, the teaching of communication skills, instead of research in this central area (Delia, 1987), has usually been emphasized. Several book chapters or journal articles in sport psychology discuss the significant elements of communication (Anshel, 2002; Burke, 1997; Carron & Hausenblas, 1998; Hardy, Burke & Crace, 2004; Weinberg & Gould, 2003; Yukelson, 1997, 2001). These authors also describe principles, guidelines, commandments, or techniques to improve communication in sport. Nevertheless, it is rare to observe or read transcriptlike descriptions about communication enhancement techniques sport psychologists employ. The goal in this chapter is to share my experiences of working with a university women's volleyball team coached by a male head coach and a female assistant coach. I am not suggesting in any way that the techniques I use are the only way to go. Most of my interventions involve group discussions with the team (either the entire team or a subunit) and one-on-one meetings with the head coach or assistant. Except for team goal-setting or imagery sessions, the head coach and assistant are never present while I meet with the team. This arrangement allows the volleyball players the freedom to speak their minds openly.

I try to illustrate how some of the theories and models of communication just discussed get translated into how I help athletes and coaches work with each other. I operate from the cognitive–behavioral perspective, with influences from the family systems approach, in dealing with team and coach communication issues. The family systems approach (Corey, 2001) suggests that people are involved in living systems. Therefore, it is necessary to assess interactions within the dynamic system to better understand the person. As applied to sports teams, this perspective necessitates that to understand athletes, the entire team's interactions must be assessed. Also, actions by one component of the team (e.g., player, manager) affect the entire team. In examining the team's communication patterns, I attempt to discover what is maintaining (the contingencies of reinforcement and punishment) the current maladaptive communication patterns. My goal is to intervene to alter these contingencies toward healthier communication pathways. My belief is that self-statements and operant conditioning principles play an influential role in changing the communication patterns within a team.

## Coach Just Doesn't Understand: A Team's Story

In my initial meeting with the head coach, Norman, he expressed his belief in sport psychology. Although his volleyball team at this university has yet to have a winning season during his two-year tenure, Norman is positive about the potential of this group of athletes. He believes techniques and mental skills such as visualization, goal setting, confidence, motivation, and concentration are important; therefore, he wanted a professional to come in and help with those issues. Norman gives me free reign to do anything I believe will benefit the team, and he seems sincere in his belief of the value of sport psychology service. Although he had reason to be concerned, his bringing me in last year was not a desperate attempt to save his job. The intercollegiate athletics administration probably requires several unsuccessful seasons before it would consider dismissing the volleyball coach. Norman feels little external pressure to become a conference contender. Nevertheless, it is definitely Norman's goal to contend for the conference championship.

My initial meeting with the volleyball team (12 players) this season involves individual meetings at a team practice, held on the volleyball court in full view of everyone. While practice is taking place, Norman sends the players over one by one to sit down and meet with me on the sideline for a 5- to 10-minute session. These brief one-on-one contacts allow me to introduce myself to the new players and to check up on what the veterans did over the summer and what they are looking forward to for the upcoming season. I also give the newcomers a brief rundown of what services I might offer them.

Many of my group meetings with the team deal with psychological skills such as goal setting, mental imagery, concentration, and confidence. Near the end of one of the psychological skills training meetings near the middle of the season, I sense the players might need to vent or let off some steam. In terms of wins and losses, the team is not doing well. I think that being able to express their frustrations openly will serve some benefit—a catharsis, so to speak. Here is how the meeting goes:

Kevin Burke (KB):  So, ladies, how are things going? [The team looks a little surprised by the inquiry.] We've spent several sessions working on psychological skills. I have an idea that your season is not going as you expected, and I'm just interested in how you feel about the team, coach, university, or anything else you would like to discuss.

LaToya:  Can we talk about Coach?

KB:  Sure you can. Remember, anything we discuss in here is totally confidential. I will not tell the coach anything you say unless you want me to. So what about your coach?

Nadia:  We want him to be more involved.

At this point, I think being "more involved" means more emotion at the matches. Off the court and away from practice and competition, Norman is a congenial person who has a good sense of humor and interacts very well with the athletes at social functions. At the matches, however, he rarely applauds his team, and his facial expressions almost never change. Also, 90% of the comments he makes to his players either involve technique correction or are negative rather than encouraging. He is definitely not a cheerleading coach. Many times he shows no external reaction to either good or bad play by his players. I would not classify him as a "Dr. Jekyll and Mr. Hyde" off and on the court, but he does act differently toward his players during practice and games, as compared with other times off the court.

KB:  Explain what you mean by more involved.

LaToya:  Well, at practice, he just stands back and lets Brenda [the assistant coach] run things. Every now and then he steps in to tell us when we do something wrong. Most of the time he is just there with a sheet of paper in his hand.

KB:  So you would like to see him more personally involved during your workouts?

Nadia:  Yeah. We don't know what he is thinking at all!

KB:  So you want Norman to open up a little bit.

Tammy:  No! A lot! [Team laughs.]

Bronwyn:  Also, we want more encouragement at the matches.

KB:  Tell me specifically what you mean. Give me some examples.

Lynn:  Look at the coaches for the other volleyball teams. They stand up and cheer, shout for their teams. We think that's cool. We don't feel as if our own head coach is supporting us as he should. If we make a mistake, *then* Coach will have something to say, or he may just ignore us. We'd almost rather that he yell at us than ignore us. We would just like to see him cheer for us every now and again.

KB: Norman does have a very stoic demeanor on the court. He is very analytical and a keen observer. That is just his style. What would you like him do in particular?

Aileen: We want him to say more positive stuff to us. Stand up and clap when we make a good play. Even when we get a good kill or spike, he just sits there looking at his clipboard.

KB: OK, I get it. Would you like me to share with him what we talked about today?

Pam: Do you think it will do any good?

KB: I can't promise you anything, Pam. But I think Norman would want to know your concerns and will respond.

Pam: Tell him, please.

Chandra: Also, could you tell him one other thing?

KB: Sure, what?

Chandra: Tell him we are tired of eating at Wendy's [hamburger chain; team laughs]. After every match he takes us to Wendy's. We want to go somewhere different.

KB: Do you seriously want me to tell him that?

Francesca: Yeah. Tell him we would like to choose where we can eat sometimes.

KB: OK, I will tell him about Wendy's and your other comments. Please remember, just because I share your comments with him, don't expect an immediate change. Just as you have developed a style as a player, Norman has his style as a coach.

> As a sport psychologist, there are times you may be called on to tell coaches about criticisms and complaints that athletes have.

After this rather interesting encounter, I decide to go immediately to Norman to express the team's concerns. Although it is usually best for players to deal directly with the coaches, I believe there are times it may be fruitful for the sport psychologist to serve as the "messenger," or mediator. Because of the way Norman chooses to interact with his players, the team does not feel comfortable speaking with him about these kinds of issues.

Although most of the players and coaches have spent several months together (and in some players' cases, a couple of years together) uncertainty reduction theory (Berger, 1986) may be applied here. The players want to reduce their uncertain feelings toward the coaches so they can better know what to expect from them—especially from Norman. They want more information-seeking behavior and, particularly, more verbal communication from Norman. Byrne's (1971) reinforcement theory may also explain why the team–coach relationship has not been more deeply established. The players receive more punishment and nonreinforcement than positive reinforcement from Norman. Therefore, according to Byrne's theory, the players will not seek to interact much with Norman.

As I became better acquainted with Norman, I saw a different side of him. He is easy to talk with and can be humorous. Since I have begun working with his players, I have had numerous conversations with Norman. We play softball on the same team and go to lunch now and then. I consider him a colleague of mine. Norman is not standoffish by any measure and is willing to listen. I know he considers me an asset to his team because of the conversations we have had about his players, the way he lets me work with them, and his inclusion of me in his decisions and recruiting processes. Although our relationship probably makes it a little easier for me to work with him and his team, I still find it a little uncomfortable when I have to share team criticisms with him. I use self-talk to tell myself three facts before I speak with him. First, if I were the head coach (I have been the head coach of three NCAA Division I tennis teams [two women's and one men's]), I would want to know what my team is thinking. Second, the upcoming conversation is for the good of the team. Third, I owe it to the players to share their concerns with Norman.

As I share the players' comments with Norman, I carefully rephrase them to convey what the players stated in as positive a manner as possible. Norman is a conscientious coach and gets a notepad and pen to record what we discuss. Here is a portion of our conversation:

KB: Norman, at the end of our team meeting, I asked the players if they wanted to discuss how their season is going, which included the team, you, the university, and so on. Anything they wanted to talk about was fair game.

Norman: OK.

KB: Let me first say that whether or not you agree with what they said, I suggest it is important that you take this information into consideration. True or not, these are their perceptions.

Norman: I understand. Don't worry, Kevin. I can handle it. [Smiles.]

KB: They asked me to share a few suggestions with you.

Norman: Let's hear them.

KB: In a nutshell, your team wants more interaction with you.

Norman: Oh, really? That's nice—I think. In what way?

At this point I explain that the team wants more involvement by him at practice, more consistent discipline, more enthusiasm at the matches, and generally more positive reinforcement. Norman expresses some concern at these suggestions.

Norman: That's just the way I am. I know I am not a big cheerleader on the sideline.

KB: I understand. You are what I call "calm, cool, and collected." However, I think it is neat that your players want more interaction with you. They seem to want to know you better than they do. I think that is a great compliment!

Norman: I guess so. So they don't think I reinforce them enough, huh?

KB: That seems to be their perception. They indicated that most of the time you seem to respond mainly to tell them what they have done wrong.

Norman: That one sort of surprises me. I really feel that I reinforce them a lot.

KB: It may be that you do. However, this is what they are perceiving. And as you know, what they perceive is probably more important than reality. Let me share with you a similar experience that I had coaching men's and women's tennis teams.

I could tell that his team's perception of not being reinforced enough bothers him. To take the focus from him temporarily, I share with Norman a similar experience I had while coaching tennis. (I thought it would be easier for Norman to accept this criticism if he knew I had experienced a similar situation.) I had called a team meeting because of rainy and cold weather one afternoon. I met with both the men's and women's teams simultaneously and asked each player to give both positive and negative comments about me or about how I had been running the team. I was shocked to hear several of the players state that I did not give them enough positive reinforcement. At first I wanted to deny their perceptions because I had just graduated with a PhD in sport psychology—surely I knew the value of proper reinforcement! After some self-evaluation, I came to three conclusions:

• The players probably just remembered more of the negative criticisms I had given them.

- I really needed to offer more positive reinforcement.
- The second conclusion was more likely than the first one.

> Just as telling personal stories about yourself (self-disclosure) can be beneficial when working with athletes, it can also be useful when talking to coaches.

Norman seems to appreciate this story and says he will really work on his cheerleading, especially at the matches. He seems less interested in providing encouragement at practices. I decide not to question him on practice behavior; if he really begins to reinforce more at the matches, he will notice the positive results and then probably begin to incorporate it more in practices as well. I also explain to Norman how to use the sandwich approach (Smith & Smoll, 1996) to help the players see his corrective interactions with them as more positive. With the three-step sandwich approach, Norman would begin instructing each player by calling her by name and beginning with a positive statement (e.g., "Kirsten, nice hustle on the dig"). Using her name makes the interaction more personal. Starting with a positive statement catches the player's attention because she is probably expecting a negative criticism, especially if Norman's comments are occurring after a mistake. Next, he would give her future-oriented feedback such as, "The next time you see the opponent about to spike the ball, get as low to the floor as you can." By focusing Kirsten on what she should do the next time a spiked ball is coming toward her, Norman can help her be ready for the next attempt and keep her from thinking about the recent error. He would then end the interaction on a positive note by giving Kirsten a compliment (e.g., "I really appreciate the way you go all out at every practice"). Ending with a compliment toward Kirsten will help her to remember what he said and to see their interaction as positive. These types of positive interactions are what the players want from Norman.

| | |
|---|---|
| Norman: | Can you give me more specifics about what they meant by more consistent discipline? |
| KB: | Sure. An example they gave was on some days when they don't hustle after the balls at practice they have to run, while on other days you seem to ignore it. |
| Norman: | They are right about that. I just don't want to punish them every time they do something wrong. |
| KB: | I don't think they see that side of it. |
| Norman: | I guess not. I will take care of that beginning today. |
| KB: | Along with consistent discipline, the team would probably really benefit from positive reinforcement when they do hustle or otherwise show good effort. |
| Norman: | I will try to work on that. It is hard to break habits. |
| KB: | I know. I don't think they expect an overnight change. That would seem fake to them. I think they will appreciate your efforts. |

Finally, I end our meeting by mentioning the team's saturation of fast food at Wendy's after the matches. We both chuckle at this comment, and Norman says he will definitely begin giving the players a choice of where they would like to eat. Although this concession seems like a small action, I believe it makes an excellent first step toward bettering his relationship with the volleyball team. Once Norman gives the players the option of where to eat, they will see this change as evidence that he will listen to them and allow them some influence over their team. Norman's change also makes me even more credible in the players' eyes.

Cahn's (1984) theory of perceived understanding seems to explain the lack of close relationships between the volleyball players and Norman. Because the players do not perceive themselves as being understood, they do not try to develop a closer relationship with him.

After what Norman and I believed was a fruitful team meeting, we decide it might be a good idea to hold team meetings devoted to getting this type of feedback for him. Norman may not be comfortable enough with his team to ask for information himself. Nevertheless, I believe that if he or the assistant coach had been present at the last meeting, the team would not have openly expressed themselves. Therefore, after approximately three weeks (which included several away matches), I meet with the team again to discuss whatever topics they bring up. No psychological skills training is performed during this meeting.

KB:     The purpose of this meeting is to discuss anything that you want to. Again, unless you ask me to share this with your coaches, the contents of this meeting will remain confidential. Ladies, what is on your minds?

[The players remain silent.]

KB:     How are things since our last meeting?

Jenn:     We got to eat somewhere besides Wendy's! [The team cheers enthusiastically.]

KB:     [Laughing.] I am glad to hear that. See, Norman does care about what you want.

Kirsten:     Yeah, that's cool.

KB:     So let's talk about your interactions with Norman. How have things been since we last met?

[Several of the players look at each other before anyone responds.]

Aileen:     It's a little better. Practices are about the same. He did clap for us more and tell us "good job" more than he usually does at the matches.

KB:     That's good. Do you think it helped you?

Tammy:     Yes, but he only did it for the first couple of games, then he was back to "Normal Norman."

KB:     I see. Remember you are asking him to make a big change—something he is not used to doing. It takes time to make a big change like that. Please be patient with him.

The rest of this session we discuss how much they enjoyed the brief occurrences of Norman's reinforcing attitude. I tell the team to be patient with their coach and remind them that he does care for them and is doing what he thinks is best for the team.

Before meeting with the team for another session, I give considerable thought to how their situation might be handled. I meet with Norman to discuss how things seem to be progressing since the meeting when I informed him the team wants more reinforcement from him. Norman believes he responded to their suggestions but also realizes he did not keep it up for very long. I ask Norman how he would rate his relationship with his team on a scale of 1 to 10, with *10* representing a great relationship. Norman rates his overall team relationship at about a 6. I ask him why he feels this way.

Norman:     I really think that our losing seasons have a lot to do with it. If we were conference contenders, much of this probably wouldn't matter.

KB:     You may have a point there. So you believe that the losing seasons have helped to make issues bigger than they really are, or have blown things out of proportion?

Norman:     Yeah. If we were winning, I think most of this stuff would be swept under the rug or seen as minor details.

KB:     You gave the team relationship rating a 6. What do you think, besides winning, would help this?

Norman:     I am really not sure. I will keep trying to be more enthusiastic at matches [I could sense uneasiness here], but that will take some time. I have never been that type of coach.

| KB: | I am sure your team would appreciate and respond to that. |
| Norman: | You know what bothers me sometimes about my players? |
| KB: | What? |
| Norman: | Many times they will just walk by my office, make quick eye contact, and move on. Only a few of them will smile, say hello, or even bother stopping in for a chat. |

An important piece of the puzzle clicks into place. I know the players' side of the story, but until now had not heard more details from Norman's view. I believe Norman's response indicates that he is keeping a distance from the players because of the distance they keep from him. It seems the team and their head coach are in a cycle of "he's distant, so we are distant; they are distant, so I am distant." Obviously to make communication progress, this cycle needs to be broken.

POV and Byrne's reinforcement theories seem to provide a manageable model for dealing with the communication quagmire between Norman and the team. Neither the coach nor the players anticipate more positive than negative experiences from each other and have not pursued further involvement. Neither party is providing each other enough rewards to seek more interaction with each other.

Another piece of the puzzle is the assistant coach, Brenda. What is her role in this situation? Brenda is only a couple of years older than the players, just a year or two removed from competing in what most would see as a higher level of collegiate volleyball. She often participates (as a player) in practices and always leads the warm-up before the matches. Norman and Brenda plan the practices together, and Norman welcomes her input in all areas of the team. He lets Brenda "run the show" at practice while he stands back to analyze and make strategic comments when necessary. Norman has always let his assistant coach operate in this manner because he believes it is good coaching training for her. In my opinion, it is also self-serving for Norman in that it allows him to "hang back," which fits the persona he usually shows to the team.

Fortunately, Brenda does much more good than harm, but issues still arise. Although the team is fond of Brenda, eventually the players complain to me about her constant yelling and "naggravating" (nagging and aggravating) comments. They are definitely tired of hearing her say, "When I played at . . .". Brenda often tells the players how she and her teammates met challenges, motivated themselves, worked harder, never gave up, and so forth. The team informs me at one of our sessions that they like having Brenda around and know she means well, but they have grown tired of her tactics and "just wish she would lay off a little bit" (as Byrne's theory would have predicted). As instructed by the team, I meet with Norman to share the players' comments. He thinks Brenda will accept this type of feedback better if it comes from him. Norman meets with her and relates the team's feedback. Brenda's feelings are hurt somewhat, but she says she will take it as a chance to try to improve as a coach. From my later conversations with her, however, I predict she will probably mostly blame the "lower level" of team she is working with.

**As suggested in the family systems approach, all participants' influences (including assistant coaches, managers) should be considered among the team dynamics.**

Brenda once came to me to complain about Norman. She was frustrated and having a difficult time with Norman's practice and match demeanor. She believes he is not as consistent a disciplinarian as he should be. Although Brenda enjoys running the practices, she senses that Norman should be more involved.

When I first started working with the team, I assumed that Brenda had a better relationship with the players than Norman did. It is not unusual for an assistant coach to have a better personal relationship with the players, but Brenda's association with the team really does not help or hinder Norman's relationship with the athletes. It would be interesting to see how Norman's relationship with the players would develop if he did not use an assistant coach. I know he depends on his assistant for various on- and off-court coaching duties. Unfortunately, Brenda has intimated to me that her two-year coaching experience, which she had eagerly anticipated in the beginning, might keep her from ever seeking another coaching position.

# Bull in the Ring

Summarizing the overall situation at this point, I believe the team wants more enthusiasm, positive reinforcement, consistent discipline, and more involvement from their head coach; they also want him to open up more. The players do not see their practice and match environments as "playful," nor do they view them as military exercises. They see their team environment, or climate, as somewhere in between. The coach simply wants the volleyball players to be more friendly toward him outside and during practice. I believe both sides want one similar factor from each other—more positive personal interaction. Neither side, however, is sure how to go about it.

Before dealing with this essential communication problem again, Norman asks me to meet with the team. He thinks some destructive cliques are developing, along with some hard feelings among the players. He asks if I will meet with the team captains (three players—two seniors and one junior) to try to deal with this problem. The captains report two players in particular who seem not to care anymore. These two players are telling the team they are not going to play again next year and will possibly quit before this season is over. Their practice and match behavior has become lackadaisical. They are also having a negative effect on some of the younger athletes' attitudes. The team seems to be dividing into camps based on those who care and those who do not. After listening to the captains' concerns, I ask them what they think should be done. After much discussion, we determine we should hold a team meeting to discuss the situation and get it out in the open.

At this team meeting, neither Norman nor Brenda is present. I begin by stating that the purpose of this meeting is to deal with a "players-only circumstance"—in other words, this situation does not involve the coaches. I tell them I am aware that a lack of team unity and communication is hurting their performances and enjoyment of playing intercollegiate volleyball. I begin to wonder how much their perceived relationship with Norman may have influenced this circumstance. Also, their lack of winning matches is certainly a factor. I ask the team to brainstorm with me on why a lack of team togetherness has occurred and what can be done about it. Although this session gets emotional for some of the players, some are quiet and aloof. Some progress is made and some issues are brought forth, yet I believe it is necessary to hear from everyone in this session. Therefore, I decide to employ what I call a "bull in the ring" (BITR) session. I like using this intervention because everyone gets involved, and when handled properly, it can be quite an eye-opening self-awareness session. I usually use BITR only when most of the team or group has been together for at least one year or season. BITR is held in two parts. First I ask the players to sit in a circle. I place a chair in the center of the circle. For the first part of the session, I place an item that represents the team on the center chair. The item could be a media guide, a team T-shirt, or simply a card with the team's name or mascot on it. For this session, I use the team's media guide. I give them the following rules:

- Speak freely, honestly, and forthrightly.
- Don't explain your brief statements (discussion may occur later).
- Do not openly react to the statements.
- Keep an open mind.

Going clockwise around the circle, I ask each player to make a constructive negative statement about the team while looking at the media guide on the center chair. Players are not allowed to make statements about any individual but must make relevant statements about the team. For each "round," it is usually a good idea to grant the first person to speak a 30-second pause to give enough time for a thoughtful response. After hearing all the negative statements, each player is required to make a positive statement about the team, following the same guidelines. Once this round is finished, each player is allowed to make one comment or ask a question, of any teammate, concerning the positive or negative comments made. During this session, the volleyball players make negative statements about not playing together as a team, not supporting each other, low attendance at the home matches, a possible rift between some of the veteran (junior, senior) and newer (freshman, sophomore, transfer) players, not hanging out together outside of volleyball, and lack of caring pervading the team environment. Some of the positive statements include having fun playing college volleyball, getting to know their teammates, and staying in good physical shape. Some brief discussion concerning these statements seems to begin an "out in the open" attitude where the team feels more comfortable talking about these topics.

The second part of BITR follows the same format, but each player is required to sit in the center chair. This means that each player (the bull) will hear one positive and one negative statement about herself from each of her teammates. I give each player the opportunity to select whether they hear the positive or negative statements first. Players must look the bull (teammate) directly in the eyes while making all comments and may pass only once if they are not ready to respond. Each time a new round begins, the person who began the previous round of comments takes her place in the center chair; the next player in the circle begins the new round.

Obviously this activity can be a sensitive encounter for all. My role (ringleader) is to enforce the rules, keep the team on task, and help the process flow. After all the players fulfill their turn in the center chair, I give each player a chance to ask any one of her teammates *one* question. Most ask a question regarding a negative statement. These questions bring about brief discussions and interactions between teammates who apparently did not interact all that often. In some cases, depending on whether the climate is facilitative, after the second part of this exercise, any players who volunteer may make one comment, or ask one question of any other teammate, as long as the comment or question does *not* relate to the statements made during BITR. After the conclusion of any BITR session, the ringleader may wish to have the group discuss the process just experienced. The group may discuss the interactions both with and without the leader present. Also, group members should have the option to discuss the session individually with the ringleader in a separate session.

A BITR session can be an excellent method for reducing uncertainty among teammates. Through this session, players learn what everyone else is thinking about the team, as well as how they are perceived by their teammates. BITR therefore promotes self-awareness because players see themselves through others' eyes. Another purpose, applicable to this team in particular, is to clear the air about issues that are hurting their team chemistry and to promote better communication. Many times this type of session will promote a bonding experience for the players, as happens with this team. The three goals of BITR are to (1) improve cohesion, (2) open and improve communication, and (3) clear the air of any issues that may be hurting the team.

# Reinforcing the Coach

Although this bonding session seems to benefit the team, there is still the lingering issue of more personal interactions between the coach and players. Sometimes more personal interaction can be promoted through a team get-together at the coach's home or an outing such as bowling, miniature golf, or even playing another sport together, such as basketball. Although Norman has done some of these things, they help only temporarily. The players seem to be expecting Norman to improve the personal interaction circumstances. Also, Norman seems to be expecting the team to take some first steps in becoming more personable with him. It appears the best possible solution is to work at this situation from both ends. Keeping in mind the tenets from POV and reinforcement theories, I first meet with Norman.

KB: How are you getting along with handing out more positive reinforcement, using the sandwich approach, and being more personable with your athletes?

Norman: Well, I'm trying. I like the sandwich thing. It's just going to take me some time to remember to do it that way. During a match I have so many things going through my mind, it just makes it difficult to do.

KB: I know. We all know that change does take time and effort. We know you are willing, and that's important. Would you prefer further assistance with making the transition by having someone videotape you at matches or observe and record your actions at games or practices?

Norman: No, I don't want that. I hope it won't come to that. I don't want to feel under the microscope just yet. I would just appreciate your honest opinions for now.

KB: I can assure you that I will give you that.

Norman: I want you to be aware of something.

KB: OK.

Norman: I think a big reason I have sort of kept a distance between my players and me is the male–female thing.

KB: You mean a male coach with female athletes?

Norman: Yes. I have always wanted to keep clear boundaries so the players, or anyone for that matter, don't get any wrong ideas that could jeopardize my job. That's one reason I have always had a female assistant.

KB: Do you think your well-meaning attempt to mark clear boundaries has maybe gotten in the way of your just being yourself around your athletes?

Norman: I know it has. Without a doubt.

KB: I certainly understand that. But I know they would enjoy getting to see more of the "real Norman." For example, I think you have a great sense of humor. I don't see you showing that side with your athletes.

Norman: There are times I show my humorous side to them that you don't see. I show it to some of the players, especially if I'm meeting one-on-one with them. But I probably could employ it more at practices and matches.

My goal for this session with Norman is to try to get him to be himself more with his athletes. Again, I am around Norman a lot and know the players do not get to see a side of him that I think they would enjoy. Another variable of the player–coach relationship the players are not aware of is Norman's preference to maintain a certain distance from his players. His apprehension toward intimacy with his players because of potential innuendos of sexual impropriety is a hindering factor in the relationship development between him and his team. Predicted outcome value theory (Sunnafrank, 1986) may explain Norman's choice to constrain a deeper level of involvement with his players. Norman anticipates an enormous "cost" (i.e., negative rumors, being fired) if he attempts closer relationships with his team. By keeping his distance, he keeps his reputation and job.

> Determining the perceived costs and benefits of the coaches and athletes of a communication system may lead to a more thorough understanding of the present team interactions.

The purpose of the next session with the volleyball players is to make them aware that they can help Norman make the transition they are looking for.

| | |
|---|---|
| KB: | How are things going with Norman? |
| Francesca: | Well, he is a little better. |
| KB: | That's good. Again, I ask that you be patient. |
| Kelly: | It just seems that he is more responsive after we have these team meetings, then within the next match or two he is pretty much back to his old self. |
| KB: | Is there anything you could do to help him become more enthusiastic at games and give you more positive reinforcement? |
| Kelly: | Maybe if we could string together a couple of wins, that would pep him up. |
| KB: | Yes, that would probably help a lot of things. [Pause.] I think there are some things you can do as a team to help Norman be more like the coach you want him to be. Are you willing to try? |
| LaToya: | What do we have to do? |
| KB: | You know how much you want positive reinforcement from him, right? |
| Jenn: | Yeah. |
| KB: | I think you need to give Norman some of that same positive reinforcement. |
| Kelly: | How can we do that? |
| KB: | Well, every time he says something to you that you think is positive, either smile or say, "Thanks, Coach," or do both. For example, after a match when he gave some good comments, tell him, "Hey, Coach, thanks for all of the encouragement during the game—it really helped." You see, by telling him how much you appreciate his encouragement, you are reinforcing his reinforcement. In other words, he needs to know how much you appreciate his reinforcing you. Do you think you could do that? |
| LaToya: | We can try. |
| KB: | Think about it. We are trying to get you to bring out the behaviors from your coach that you desire. I think you can help him make the change more quickly by reinforcing his positive behaviors. You might also kid around more with Norman. He has a good sense of humor. If you show him your sense of humor, it might help to loosen you both up. [Pause.] I also have another suggestion for you. |
| Tammy: | What? |
| KB: | Take some time to get to know your head coach a little better. I think both of you—team and coach—would benefit from getting to know each other better. Stop by his office every now and then, even if it is just for a minute. That is a small gesture on your part that could mean a lot for all of you. |

# Conclusion

With these sessions I have attempted to get both parties to take partial responsibility for a situation they both want to improve. Using the family systems approach (Corey, 2001), I attempted to change components (i.e., players and coach) of the team in order to cause a change in the entire team's communication patterns and system. Norman was asked to interact more positively. As UR, Byrne's reinforcement, and POV theories would suggest, reinforcement from each other would bring about further involvement and lead to less uncertainty toward each other, leading to improved relations among the entire team. I would not characterize the team situation as a bad one but as one that is common in sport. Although Norman and the volleyball team do not fare much better in the win–loss columns, I notice a more optimistic outlook. It is unrealistic to expect a "dramastic" (dramatic and drastic) improvement overnight. Nevertheless, I see a slight progression in the development of their relationships. Both seem to be trying to make adaptations to bring about positive changes for the team. Also, Norman begins actively participating in the practices rather than hanging back. Norman's decision to take a more engaged role in practice has an immediate positive influence on the team. The players receive more interaction from him, and they feel Norman is more immersed in the team. These practice actions allow the players and coaches more encounters, which allow them to get to know each other better. Another influential factor is that past "problem" players either leave or are removed from the team. Their departures also help the team environment by removing their negative influences.

My approach to this communication situation is to serve mainly as a mediator. I do not meet with both coaches and players at the same time to deal with their communication problems. Considering the coaches' and players' lines of communication, that approach might be counterproductive in that both sides might be less likely to express themselves openly. As long as both parties show patience and continue to make sincere effort and progression, their team environment may become more conducive to open and honest dialogue. For the immediate future, it would probably be helpful to continue to monitor this situation, especially the coaches' and players' perceptions of their relationships and team climate. As their communication improves, I hope the coaches and athletes will be willing and able to deal with their internal conflicts without my presence.

## CHAPTER 4

# "I have a friend who . . ."

## *Group Work on Weight and Body Image*

Mark B. Andersen, PhD, and Kirsten Peterson, PhD

We start off by saying this chapter describes a real "nuts and bolts" approach to working with groups on body image and eating disorders. We do not do a massive, or even medium-size, review of the literature on eating disorders and body image. That has been done over and over again, and the reader can consult Petrie and Sherman (2000) and the following chapter (a focus on males) for references. We want to show our real-life approach to working with athletes on these sensitive topics.

The success of a group presentation with athletes lies, in part, in the ability of the presenters to move beyond merely delivering information to engaging the audience to participate in the exchange as much as possible. Depending on the specific personalities involved in a group of athletes, the attempt at engagement can be a challenge for presenters. With potentially sensitive topics such as body image and eating disorders, the hurdles are even more formidable. Add to the mix a co-ed group, and the dynamics become more complicated still.

Before the presentation even begins, it is always a good idea to know, in advance, why a team has asked us to talk about these issues. Our approach would be somewhat different if we were being called in to deal with an identified problem for some athletes on the team rather than simply provide an educational forum for these issues. Sometimes coaches are uncomfortable dealing with an athlete with an eating disorder or body image problem and hope that our group presentation will take care of the matter. It is not a well-thought-out plan, in our opinion, to use a group session as a way to target someone with a body image problem or eating disorder. Although we would not necessarily change our presentation given what's going on in the group, knowing the team culture around eating, as well as whether any athletes have active problems, can help us guide the discussion. I (Kirsten) have been in a situation where, as the presenter, I became "infected" by the coach's anxiety about how to handle the situation of some athletes on his team having eating problems. His fearful approach to the situation caused me to feel as if I were walking on eggshells throughout the entire presentation.

In buying into the coach's anxiety-driven perception of his team's problems, I never allowed myself to test those assumptions or try to see the team in a different way. I ended up protecting the team from any meaningful discussion about what might or might not have been troubling them, and no doubt my fear of their issues influenced the athletes' confidence in my abilities as a professional. Certainly, my presentation did not inspire any athlete to seek additional help from me! My professional blunder speaks to the issue of *approach* and the models the presenters publicly display on how to talk about such sensitive topics.

> Know why you've been asked to present to a group. Are you simply providing information, or are you addressing an identified problem?

Following the edict of "do no harm," our primary goal is to provide an atmosphere for discussion that allows group members, first and foremost, to feel safe and unthreatened by what gets talked about and by how discussion is handled. We typically do this by setting a stage for healthy communication, which includes some ground rules. Such rules might include agreeing to speak to each other respectfully, to address each other directly if appropriate, and to keep whatever gets said during the session in the room. We encourage athletes to develop their own set of ground rules as well. In addition to such rules of engagement, we also pay attention to the interactions between group members once discussion ensues. Monitoring this process well requires us as presenters to hone our skills of observation, both of verbal and nonverbal exchanges within the group. If we notice, for example, that one or a few group members are speaking as if they speak for the group, we might intervene, thank them for their contributions, and suggest that there are others who have some different stories to tell. Doing so can validate the experiences of other athletes who might indeed hold different opinions or have different experiences.

Once we have addressed safety issues, we do a few things to mitigate the tendency for groups to be passive, or worse, inattentive or disruptive. One way to deal with situations such as these is to confront them, using the athletes' expertise to our advantage. At the beginning of presentations, it can be useful to engage athletes by pointing out their obvious experience in sport, that they are often more "expert" in the topics to be discussed than we are or they would not have come this far athletically. We follow this introduction by encouraging the athletes to speak up and share their knowledge with their teammates, saying it will be more fun for them to hear from each other than to listen to us talk. How seating is arranged for the group is also important. Instead of a classroom style that allows some athletes to distance themselves physically from the presenters or from teammates, having the group seat themselves in a circle can keep everyone on relatively equal footing and lessen the formality of the setting. On the other hand, if our goal of the moment is not necessarily to bring out discussion, or if we know that the topic of body image and eating disorders is a potentially scary one for some of the athletes, we might allow the classroom style of seating to give athletes the choice of how "close" to the action they would like to be.

Because eating disorders and body image are often perceived as particularly sensitive topics for many athletes, simply asking (or worse, telling) them to feel comfortable talking about these issues may not be enough. We might confront the "elephant in the room" further by suggesting to the group that talking about eating disorders and body image is difficult, and it would not be a surprise that no one wants to talk about them. It can be useful to throw a question to the audience, asking them why body image can be a difficult topic to talk about. We tend to avoid asking questions of specific individuals so as not to put a particular athlete or subgroup of athletes on the defensive. If answers are not forthcoming from the group, one of us may do some self-disclosure (described in more detail in the next section).

In the case of a co-ed diving team, the dynamics can be more complicated because of the different ways that men and women perceive their bodies, think about eating, deal with stress, and communicate about sensitive topics and their feelings surrounding them. The literature and our experience, in general, suggest that issues about weight, eating, and body image are more prevalent for female athletes than for male athletes—though in body-conscious sports such as diving, such generalities probably need to be discarded. But even in diving, we may expect that women have more knowledge of these areas because much greater attention is paid to women in the popular press, but we can't assume that this generalization is true. Sometimes it can be helpful to ask groups what they already know about eating disorders and body image as a way to test some of these assumptions.

It can be useful for presenters to anticipate some gender differences in how athletes perceive and react to emotional issues. In our experience, female athletes tend to be more vocal about their body image, along with the emotions that come with those perceptions, because they also tend to be more comfortable talking about their feelings. Male athletes, for whom discussions of body image or eating disorders are often even more taboo, may find themselves choosing not to respond or denying that any problems exist. If the team culture is such that denial is prevalent (e.g., men outnumber women on the team), those athletes, typically women, who speak up may feel pathologized if they think, or worse, admit, otherwise. This scenario is another example of a safety issue that must be dealt with quickly, or the group may cease discussion altogether. Of course, these differences are not always gender based, and presenters should be ready for them but not closed to the possibility that some men may be more verbal or some women more closed off from their emotions or ability to discuss these issues.

> When giving presentations about weight and body image, be prepared for the different ways men and women react to these topics.

## Issues for Group Presenters

Gaining an understanding of the group's ability to process issues of body image and eating disorders is important, but so is knowing about ourselves as presenters in terms of our own "baggage" of body image or eating disorders. This topic can be a difficult one for both athletes and presenters alike, but it is particularly difficult if an individual on either end is coping at the moment with his or her own issues of body image or eating disorders. For example, if I as a presenter have had trouble with eating or if I dislike my body, I may be less prone to feeling comfortable helping others discuss these issues. I may transfer my own negative feelings onto those I am trying to reach and even prevent potentially fruitful discussion to keep others from feeling my discomfort. Alternatively, I may assume that my experience is the same as others' experiences, without really listening to what the group is saying, and end up trying to validate feelings of group members that are not really there.

Effective presenters share some basic characteristics, including the ability to maintain a balance between being friendly and being professional. It is less a science than an art to take a body of knowledge and turn it into compelling presentation material without going overboard into stand-up comedy, sensational storytelling, or boring lectures. There is also a balance between encouraging active audience participation and communicating the important concepts. Presenting to athlete groups is different from teaching a class in that you usually have only one shot at developing a positive atmosphere with the audience. So, good presenters look for ways to engage the audience early, through getting them involved in the process and by using relevant and well-organized material. Athletes tend to respond better to presenters who have had experience talking with other groups of athletes, or even better, other athletes in their sport. It should not come as a surprise that a presenter who can easily speak the athletes' language would invite more trust and credibility. A central key to a good presentation is getting athletes to tell stories you can use to illustrate exactly those educational points you want to cover. When you incorporate the athletes' stories into the discussion, you do several things. First, you get the points across in ways that have immediacy and personal relevance. Athletes begin to feel that their stories are valued and useful. You also set up an atmosphere of friendly dialogue, and you start to establish a sense of "we are in this together."

In our case scenario dealing with body image and eating disorders, another important characteristic of a presenter is approachability. It is our hope that in addition to providing information about body image and eating disorders, we motivate athletes with problems to seek out personalized assistance. Given that hope, our manner or presentation style cannot seem intimidating or overly clinical; if it is, we may lose the chance to make a connection with someone who might be contemplating getting some help. Again, sharing with the group our experience working with other athletes in this area can inspire trust and increase the chance that an athlete will seek us out.

Some presenters find it helpful to use personal disclosure as a tool for destigmatizing the concept of having a problem with body image or an eating disorder. For example, Mark may say, "When I was a swimmer, I hated my body. I was too skinny. I needed more muscle, and when I saw some of the other guys, I just despaired of ever getting to that ideal body for my sport. It was a real bummer, and I called myself the 'poster boy' for anorexia." Or Kirsten may say, "When I was competing, I would get on the scale and see I had gained some weight and think, *Oh, crap, Hindenburg City! Now I really need to work extra hard.*" Such disclosures model being comfortable talking about dissatisfaction and send a message that we all have at times experienced some dissatisfaction. It lets the athletes know that the presenters are also human; we can talk about these topics candidly and with some humor.

Informing athletes of your own struggles could lessen other people's feelings of being alone with their problems and could strengthen their bond with you as the presenter. On the other hand, an audience might be uncomfortable with such self-disclosure if it seems that the presenter is still conflicted and struggling with the problems. In general, using this tactic requires a great deal of self-awareness of the presenter to not subtly take the focus off the audience with such self-disclosures. We have seen presenters on pathogenic eating literally manifesting their struggles through telling graphic stories of their experiences in ways that resemble the psychological equivalent of purging. And we have watched audiences slowly withdraw from a presenter, collectively thinking, *Whoa! Boy, does she have some problems.* When we talk in a matter-of-fact manner, with self-compassion and a touch of humor, about our own struggles with how we look and how we have eaten, we model that it really is OK to talk about these things. That modeling may help athletes feel more comfortable about doing some of their own self-disclosure.

## Tag-Team Presentations

For a host of reasons, when addressing groups of athletes, it can be helpful to have copresenters. Although many of us as sport psychology consultants by necessity work on our own, there are several advantages to working as part of a presentation team. First, it takes the pressure off one presenter to be "on" all the time. Presenting and interacting with a group of athletes are hard work, and alternating or sharing the stage can provide some relief. Second, as the saying goes, "two heads are better than one." With two presenters, one person can present while the other observes, gauging audience reactions or catching useful topics for future discussion that might otherwise be missed. So, expanding on the example from the previous section, my copresenter might become aware that my own experience with body image is influencing how I am facilitating the group discussion. He might intervene with some observations from a different perspective that could help offset my unintended effects on the group.

Another positive effect of copresenting is the ability to teach through doing. Copresenters who model compassionate ways of interacting with each other can help a group do likewise. When a team discusses body image and eating disorders, for example, there might be some peer pressure to not discuss the topic, and group members obey this unspoken rule because they fear conflict. Presenters who come with different opinions and who work through those differences in front of the group can be effective in helping the group recognize that within-group differences can actually be handled productively. Modeling these interactions in front of the group can show the athletes how we as copresenters work through the process and not just the product of conflict management.

When addressing the topic of body image and eating disorders to a co-ed group, in addition to the general usefulness of a team approach, it is also helpful if the presentation team consists of both genders. Having a co-ed team of presenters can serve as a model for both males and females in the group. If, for example, the presenters notice that the women in the group are being shut down verbally, the female presenter can model more assertive behaviors, or at least observe and comment on why women may be more silent. Alternatively (or in addition), the male presenter can model behaviors inviting participation from the women and can act as a model for the male athletes to engage women in the process. In the case of body image and eating disorders, having both male and female presenters talk about the issues may lessen assumptions that this topic is for women only.

> When part of a copresenting team, try to have both a male and a female presenter. This approach provides an opportunity for modeling behavior.

## Presentation Outline

To begin our session, our initial goals are to simply ease, as best we can, anxieties about this topic and get the team engaged in some thinking about the issues. To start, we set up the room before the athletes arrive, with a circle formation of chairs so all athletes are on equal footing with each other and us, the presenters. Once the athletes arrive, we each introduce ourselves and briefly outline the goals of the presentation. To help the group feel more comfortable with the topic, it can be helpful, initially, to get the group to feel more at ease talking with each other. It's a mistake to assume that just because a group of athletes is on a team, they know each other particularly well, or they interact better than any other group. In our experience, teams often come to listen to a presentation right after either a practice, a sports medicine session, or a meal. In any event, the athletes are, at best, likely to feel tired or sore and perhaps are still processing some inter-team conflict from an earlier practice session. Although it would go well beyond the scope and time frame of our presentation to deal with those issues, taking some time to help the athletes make the transition to the topic at hand can prove beneficial.

There are many ways to help a group feel more comfortable with each other. A possible first step would be to have each member introduce herself and answer a few simple questions about her sport involvement. One fun exercise is "the agony and the ecstasy" game, where each athlete identifies one thing he really loves and one thing he really hates about his sport. To get the ball rolling, one of the presenters will usually go first. For example, Mark may say, "What I really liked was joking with the guys in my lane during practice. We had a blast. What I really hated was having to do the 200 free in competition. I never hurt so much, and the coach kept making me do it." This exercise models that it is just fine to have mixed feelings about a sport, a point that is truly important when thinking about body image and eating.

We also use more active team-building exercises as alternative or additional icebreakers. These types of activities get the group physically moving—an attention-getting change of pace all on its own and something athletes tend to respond to. We often instill a within-team competitive element, such as the idea that the team members need to continually improve their performance in the exercise. Not surprisingly, adding this competitive element to an exercise is usually highly salient and a great motivator for athletes. One exercise is "the lineup." We ask the athletes to line themselves up as fast as possible from tallest to shortest. This tactic gets them up and moving. We time each stage of the exercise to add an element of competition. The next lineup may be month of birth. This stage gets them talking a bit. The third lineup may be distance from where they came from originally—more talking and some joking about being geographically impaired. The next stage gets closer to the issue of how they look, and we might have them line up by who they think has the best diving suits. In conducting such an exercise, its utility is limited to an in-the-moment experience if we don't make the effort to connect its lessons to those we are heading toward in our presentation.

> Open the session with activities that get the athletes up and moving.

We might begin our preliminary discussion of body image and eating disorders by having the athletes talk about what, if any, pressures they experienced as a result of this fun but admittedly competitive exercise. The next question would be for them to tell us what relevance this exercise and the ensuing discussion has for them as they compete in the sport of diving. With any luck, someone will mention the pressure of maintaining appearance or of how she looks in a bathing suit, which of course can serve as a great segue to the topic at hand. Even if no one mentions appearance or eating as a specific pressure, just conducting the exercise and getting the team talking about perceived pressures can take you a long way toward easing them more comfortably into a discussion of body image and eating disorders.

As presenters, we then need to take the initiative to offer up body image or eating as other possible issues the team feels pressure about and use that lead to start a focus on those issues for the presentation. One method we often use is showing a videotape of athletes discussing the issues of weight and body image. We have found the NCAA tapes (NCAA, 1989) on eating and weight to be quite useful, but many sport psychologists may not have access to them. If they are not available, it is relatively easy to find a graduate student or another athlete who would be willing to talk in front of the camera about struggling with these issues. Seeing an athlete on tape forthrightly discussing the problems in her or his sport can help put the focus "out there" and make the topic a bit less threatening.

After showing the tape, we ask athletes to form groups and discuss what they have just seen. We give some example discussion topics to help the process along. We may say, "When talking about the tape, you might want to consider some of the following: (a) [start out with a 'safe' topic] How believable was the athlete? (b) Do you yourself or people you know have similar difficulties? [again, playing safe with the 'I have a friend who . . .' approach] (c) How do you think the sport makes things difficult for athletes? [more safety with vague 'things'] and (d) How do you think we [coaches, teammates, psychologists] might be able to help athletes struggling with weight and how they look?" It sure sounds as if we are treading very lightly here, and that is intentional. We need to open a door, and when the issue on the other side of that door is threatening, we need to help people believe it is all right to open it just a crack.

To help athletes feel more comfortable as they react to the questions, we suggest dividing them into small groups of usually no more than three or four. If for some reason (e.g., the team culture) we believe that male and female athletes are uncomfortable relating to each other, breaking the team into same-sex small groups can enhance athlete comfort. Doing this can, for example, allow the women on the team to process the emotional issues they feel prohibited from dealing with when the men are present. Time permitting, and if there is some utility in it, we bring the small groups back together to share their insights with the team as a whole. We are more likely to take this route if the athletes are interacting well together in their small groups and generating thoughtful answers to the questions, so that the group as a whole would benefit from the shared knowledge. Otherwise, it can be just as worthwhile to allow the processing to end with the small groups.

If we bring the small groups back together, we begin to discuss what they have shared. Facilitating an effective group discussion of issues after the videotape presentation can be very helpful in moving the information from the abstract to the personal level for each athlete, as well as helping team members begin to interact with each other about this often difficult issue. We, as presenters, need to be clear between ourselves as to our goals for this type of interaction. We must take care to differentiate between group processing of the information presented and group therapy revolving around eating disorders, though the lines can get blurred rather quickly. There is surely an art to the balance necessary to encourage a discussion that also feels relatively safe for all involved.

And that gets us to the title of this chapter, "I have a friend who. . . ." Over and over again we have found that athletes are willing to tell body image and eating stories about acquaintances, friends, other athletes they have heard of, and so forth. We suspect, however, that many of the stories they tell are about themselves. Just as a gay athlete who is tightly in the closet may tell a story about "a guy I know," so may a closeted athlete with eating problems tell a story about "a friend I know back home." We take those stories and use them, respecting the athlete's privacy and sensitivity, but we never challenge whom the story is about. Months later, when working one-on-one with athletes who were part of the group presentation, we have had the experience of athletes telling us, in a confessional tone, that the story really was about them. They were just too afraid and embarrassed to come out of the closet in front of their peers.

## The Group Begins Work

One of the factors we have not discussed is the role of the coach in this group interaction. The two of us are of the same mind regarding the role of the coach. We want the coach involved, and we certainly want the coach to know and approve of the group session. Ideally, in most cases, we would like the coach to be present at the start of the session, say a few words emphasizing the importance of the topic, . . . and then leave with parting words of "OK, team, you guys listen up and have a good discussion. The stuff you talk about in here is between you and the shrinks. I don't need to know what you are saying in here, but if you want to, I'll be around to talk with any of you after the session or any other time in the season." As nonthreatening as coaches may be, their presence still may act as an inhibitor. In our dream fantasy, we are working with a team whose coach is willing to be at the presentation and tell stories of how she struggled with bulimia and saw herself as fat. How wonderful would that be? It hasn't happened yet, but we can dream.

In the real world, coaches can be threatened by the topic and feel forced to let us present because such sessions may have been mandated by the administration, bowing to pressures from the university or the student health center or the national governing body. We do our best to make sure the anxious coach knows we are not on a witch-hunt or trying to uncover pathogenic coaching practices but rather are acting in an educational role to help any athletes who may be struggling.

Here we start with our talk to some divers, males and females, at an NCAA Division I university. It could also be a developmental squad visiting the Olympic Training Center.

The general processes are the same. The session starts out with the supportive coach, whom we have asked to say a few words before he leaves.

Coach: OK, gang. I'm going to take off now. You listen to these two. They have good stuff to say. And what you talk about is between you and them, but I'll be glad to talk to you later, too, if you want. I think this stuff is important, and it will help you be better divers. [Coach begins to leave.]

Kirsten Peterson (KP): Thanks, Coach, we'll see you in about 45 minutes or so. I think introductions are in order. I'm Kirsten, and I have worked a lot with Olympic athletes, divers among them, and this guy here is Mark; he has been doing work with divers for many years. We are both in the field of sport psychology, and we actually love our jobs. We enjoy helping athletes get better at the mental aspects of their sports and also get better in other areas of their lives such as school, careers, and relationships with family, friends, and other loved ones.

Mark Andersen (MA): We want to start with getting to know you a bit better. How about we go around the room and each of you can tell us a little about where you're from and something about the agony and the ecstasy of diving for you. By that I mean what in diving really, really makes you happy and excited and what in diving is a major pain in the butt. I'll go first. . . . I was a swimmer in California. I just loved working out with my teammates every day. It was a great bunch of guys, but man, doing the 200 free in competition I just dreaded every time. It was my worst nightmare. So who is next?

KP: For me, I was generally the same as Mark, and my sports were softball, basketball, and field hockey.

Allison: I am from Oak Park, Illinois. I just hate my inward dives, especially learning a new one. I think I'm going to kill myself. [Silence.]

KP: And what do you really like?

Allison: Oh, I don't know, probably the postmeet parties! [Laughs.]

KP: Now there's an honest athlete! I remember plenty of those parties, and I think I understand a bit about those frightening inwards. I don't dive, but just watching inwards sometimes scares the heck out of me.

This agony and ecstasy exercise is not used just to get the athletes talking. What Kirsten is doing in responding to the athlete is telling her that her brief story was heard, that we are listening, and that we do have some understanding of the scariness of the sport. In these sorts of exercises, a sport psychologist should not just go around the room, let each athlete say something, and then say, "Thank you for sharing." Every story needs to be recognized, commented on, and verbally appreciated. We want to send the message that we are here; we are listening, and we care. The athletes in this group session tell their stories around the room, but it is Phillip, the last to talk, who gives us the best bridge to the topics at hand.

> Recognize what each athlete says. It shows you are listening and you value what he or she has to contribute.

Phillip: I really love the rip of a perfect dive, but what drives me nuts is getting on the lard-o-meter every couple of weeks.

MA: I think I know what you mean about that rip. I just love the sound of it. Perfect. [Pause.] Seems as if those weigh-ins are a major pain. What do you hate about them?

Phillip: It's just a bummer, especially if you've been trying to drop some pounds.

KP: And it's a reminder that you aren't where you want to be?

Phillip: Exactly!

MA: Phillip brings up a point that gets to what we want to talk about today. And that is the constant issue of how you look and feel out there on the board or the platform.

KP: This sport puts a lot of pressure on you to look good out there. We know that with all other things being equal, looking good in the suit is probably going to help you in the scoring department. I know in my sports I was always conscious of my weight, even hypercritical, because I thought if I put on some pounds then I wouldn't move as well on the field or on the court.

MA: While in my sport, swimming, with all those other muscled aqua-monsters, I was always conscious that I was too skinny and would put on my Speedo and jump in the pool as fast as I could. Thank God I didn't have to stand around on the pool deck as you all do.

KP: What we would like to focus on today is how you all are feeling about the pressures of maintaining a certain weight and look, some of the problems you may have had trying to get that look, and what you have been doing with nutrition and weight training for your sport.

MA: We know this topic is not one many of us are comfortable with, and before we go much further, we would like to establish that we are all equals here, and that we respect each other, and that anything we talk about stays in this room. I hope we can agree on that. [We pause and look around the room, catching each athlete's eyes for nods of confirmation.]

Kirsten and I take Phillip's comments and use them to do a couple of things. We acknowledge that the pressures to look good are rampant in this "judgment" (and judgmental) sport. We also do some minor self-disclosure about our own struggles with weight. We hope our comfort with the topic will transfer over to at least some of the athletes. We have not used the "ED" words (eating disorders) yet, and that omission is purposeful. We want to stay away from diagnosis-like language and labeling. The topic is threatening enough without us sounding as if we are looking for pathology. We have also set some ground rules of mutual respect and group confidentiality.

We know we can probably come back to Phillip if we need to in order to get the ball rolling, but what we would like to do is get some more stories about weight and looks from some of the other divers. To draw them out, we phrase our next question in a way that gives them an out about talking directly of their own experience. In this part of the dialogue, Kirsten uses the phrase "in the past" intentionally to help some divers be comfortable telling a story about someone else a bit distant.

KP: I know several of you have been in diving for a long time and have probably had some worries about your own looks out there on the board. You've also probably seen teammates in the past who were having trouble in the weight department and doing some maybe unhealthy stuff with eating and exercise. Anyone have some stories, either about yourself or someone you know?

Julie: I knew this chick back home. She looked fantastic. And when we would go out for a team meal, she would eat like a horse. We asked her, "How do you do that?" 'cause we were jealous and all eating salads, and she would say, "I have a fast metabolism, so I don't worry about it." We found out later that she had been puking her guts out every day, and she ended up in the hospital with some rips in her throat.

KP: That's a perfect story, and it gets at a lot of the problems in diving about weight control. Here you have a diver who looks great but who is really worried about getting fat, so she starts taking some drastic measures to keep that good look. She is also probably ashamed about what she is doing, so she puts on a good face and is compelled to tell an untrue story so people don't suspect what is going on, and she can stay in the bulimia closet.

MA: Thanks, Julie. It's a sad story, too, because she probably felt all alone and didn't know any other way to keep her weight steady but to do things that landed her in the hospital with serious damage. And that is the big problem in trying to get that perfect look for diving. Most of us don't know a lot about how to eat really well, and some divers then resort to starving or bingeing and throwing up. The weird thing is that you can have a lot of success with that sort of stuff, initially, and that is reinforcing, so you keep doing it. You all have young bodies, and they can take a lot of abuse, but sooner or later it catches up, and the damage is done.

Michelle: [Raising her hand hesitantly.] I have a question.

KP: Yes, Michelle, what is it?

Michelle: I am not a snarfer and barfer, but I really hate those weigh-ins, and I don't eat the whole day before we have to get on the lard-o-meter. Is that gonna hurt me?

Kirsten and I look at each other, and we both want to run over and give Michelle a big hug. Her question contains so much about looking good, weight, pressures in the sport, public embarrassment, and the anxieties about poor eating practices. Her shy hesitance and her initial statement about not being bulimic may be just discomfort and an accurate description of what she does not do. There is also a common phenomenon in confessional tales, however. People who are involved in some perceived major transgressions will often confess to a lesser sin in order to deflect scrutiny and have a minor *mea culpa* that lets them off the *big* hook. To give a distressing example of this phenomenon, in Australia an ad campaign ran on television about violence against women. A 30-something male comes on the screen and says, "I may shove her around a little, but I am not a wife-beater." The screen goes dark, and the following words appear: "Yes, you are." We don't offer such a challenge back to Michelle because what she says may be perfectly true, and we don't want to introduce any unnecessary element of threat. We both, however, mentally note the story for future reference.

KP: Not eating for a day, generally, will not really hurt you, especially if the weigh-ins are only every two weeks or so. It would become a problem for your health if you had lard-o-meter days a couple of times a week. Because you're divers, there is, however, a problem with going without food for a day and getting out there on the platform or boards.

MA: When you don't have a lot of fuel on the days you aren't eating much, you may be increasing the risks in your sport. When blood sugar is low from not eating, or you're dehydrated, then you don't have a lot of resources to call on when diving.

KP: A couple of things happen—you don't have good concentration or focus, and we know that can be dangerous on the boards. You'll also get fatigued faster, so toward the end of practice you're more likely to botch your dives, and the risk of hurting yourself goes up. So if you are going to not eat or drink on the weigh-in day, make sure right after the weighing, and throughout practice, that you start taking in plenty of water and eat some fruit. We've seen how you guys can down bananas. You've always got a box of them around. [Bananas are often the fruit "on deck" for many diving teams we have worked with.] They're good; they can help with blood sugar, and they have good minerals to keep the body functioning well.

Michelle: OK, thanks. . . . Hey, Jerry, toss me a banana.

The quality of the communication here needs some examination. We are not taking a pathogenic weight control story and saying, "This is wrong." We first acknowledge that the practice of fasting, in usual circumstances, probably does not pose a threat to health. We never say, "Don't do it," but we do tell a story that brings eating back to performance and risk, told in a rational and nonjudgmental way. We also tell them that if they are going to starve for a day before the weigh-in, then there are ways to compensate for the risk. This tactic communicates that we know and appreciate the pressures of diving and that we are primarily concerned with their health, safety, and well-being.

We don't want to overwhelm the divers with lots of information or try to delve really deeply into their anxieties. Small steps toward talking about body image, weight, eating problems, and the pressures of the sport may help athletes approach these topics, and in that way we may avoid overstimulating defensive reactions. Michelle and Phillip have given us a topic we can focus on, the weigh-ins, and that will be plenty for now. We (Kirsten and Mark) look at each other, and in presentational simpatico, and sotto voce, say almost simultaneously to each other, "Weigh-ins." We now have a focus for the rest of the group session.

> Take the slow approach and tread gently. Try to find some relatively safe ground.

KP: Michelle and Phillip have talked about the pain of the weigh-ins. We would bet that there are others here who hate them, too. We know it must be frustrating to get on the lard-o-meter and see that you haven't lost any weight or that you have gone up. Is there anything positive about getting on the scales?

Tommy: I don't mind it. Coach usually says something nice, such as "Looking good," so it doesn't bother me.

Jerry: Yeah, but look at you, Mr. Buff-o-Rama! [Group laughs.] You have no worries.

MA: Don't some of you just want to shoot Tommy?

Several divers: You bet!

KP: Some of us, like Tommy, seem to have won the genetics sweepstakes, and keeping that good body look for diving is not a problem. For others, we are fighting the genes Mom and Dad gave us. It does sound as if the coach can be encouraging, though, when the weigh-ins happen.

Allison: Oh, Coach is nice enough and doesn't get mad or anything, but he sometimes looks disappointed, which kind of makes you feel bad.

MA: When you get on the scales, and it's not all right, it may feel that you've failed the coach in some way.

Allison: He's a good guy, not like this other jerk of a coach I heard about who had these weekly weigh-ins, and the diver who gained the most weight had to wear a little pig on a chain around her neck for the whole week.

KP: To be honest, that really makes me angry. Must have been terrible for the diver who got pig-of-the-week. Sounds as if the weigh-ins are not a lot of fun for many of you. Is there anything you would like to change about them?

Phillip: Not have them!

MA: Have you spoken to the coach about that?

Phillip: No way!

KP: You know, after this session, the coach is going to ask us how everything went. As we already said, everything we talk about in here stays in here unless you want it to go outside these walls. What we will say to the coach is something like, "Went well. . . . We had some nice discussions about trying to keep that good diving body and how to eat healthy." No more than that. Is there something else you want us to say to the coach?

Tommy: Could you ask him to stop the weigh-ins, or cut them down, or maybe do them privately?

Tommy's suggestion surprises us. He seems to be the one on the team who has no problem with weight. We know him as a bit of a peacock, but now he is showing a side of himself that is empathetic and insightful into the anxieties of the other members. We spent a fair amount of time observing the team in practice and competition before we started working with them. We noticed, especially during competitions, that Tommy is always encouraging and caring of other divers, so maybe the empathy is not so surprising. We suspect, even though he appears to have no problem with weight, that he may have struggled in the past. It is good to see that the one person with apparently the least concern is also the one who makes the most concrete suggestions on what to do. Tommy may feel a bit guilty about not having to worry about weight, at least in the eyes of the other divers. He may actually have to work really hard at looking the way he does, and maybe the peacock in him won't let his sensitive side tell a personal story of battling weight. But his sensitive side wins out in a solid suggestion to help all the other athletes with a painful part of their diving. In helping the team, he may also be helping himself. How perfect is that? Everyone may win. We don't know what is going on inside Tommy, and these speculations may be off the mark, but we are fascinated by, and appreciative of, what Tommy has just done.

MA: What do the rest of you think about Tommy's suggestion?

Marylin: But what would you say to the coach?

MA: Kirsten and I get along really well with the coach, and I am sure we could convey your worries about weigh-ins in a way he would appreciate. We could talk about how you all really like him but how some of the team feel intimidated or worry about disappointing him, and then we could talk about how after a weigh-in maybe some divers can't get focused on practice and how that might make practice less productive. I think if we bring it all back to getting the most out of diving practice, he will see the connections.

Allison: He's never going to give up weigh-ins.

KP: You're probably right, Allison, but maybe we can make the argument that weigh-ins could be done once a month in private. I know he has a scale in his office. We could suggest that maybe he has a monthly meeting, outside of practice, with each of you individually where you talk about how the diving is going for you, and how other things such as school are going, too, and then you have a weigh-in and discuss it, and that it is all just between you and him.

Allison: You think that'll work?

MA: We'll give it a shot. What do you all say?

The divers all agree for us to talk to the coach. We usually encourage athletes to speak directly to coaches about their problems in the sport, but because weight is such a complex team and personal issue, we are more than happy to act as intermediaries. In an ideal world, our intervention with the coach would lead to the complete abandonment of weigh-ins. We are not idealists. Weigh-ins are entrenched in many diving teams; getting rid of them altogether may be setting the bar too high. If we can help move the coach to a more personal and humane approach to weight, then we have made progress, and then maybe in the future we can make more progress. And if we are successful in this small change at this time, then we feel we have helped make the sport a better place to be for both the athletes and the coach.

> If the situation calls for it, be an intermediary between the athletes and the coach.

What have we accomplished in our session with the divers? The main outcome may appear small, but the implications for the team climate and the personal health and well-being of the athletes may be quite large. We come away with a mutually agreed upon plan to change a feature of diving that has implications for diver self-esteem, coach–athlete relationships, communication, health, and happiness—no small feat. We do not address eating disorders among team members directly but get to the point with the "I have a friend . . ." story. And that is good enough for now. We think the previous conversation shows how two psychologists can work together in tackling these sensitive issues in ways that communicate respect, humor, and care. The results of this session may reach further than the changing of a counterproductive coaching practice. As illustrated in the next chapter, some divers may now feel a bit more comfortable about individually approaching us with their eating and body image concerns. Now, how do we talk to Jim, the coach? We meet him after practice once all the athletes have left for the day.

Jim: So how did that go?

KP: Really good. We discussed weight and how one looks out there, and the athletes told some good stories.

Jim: Anything I should know? I don't want to push you, though.

MA: The divers did want us to talk to you about one thing, and we got their permission to tell you about it.

Jim: OK, shoot!

KP: It seems that some of the divers get rather anxious when they have those weigh-ins every two weeks.

Jim: [Defensively.] Oh, but I don't yell at them or anything if they weigh too much.

MA: [Placating.] Not at all. Several athletes said you were really nice about weight. It was just that they didn't like getting on the scales in front of everyone; they sometimes felt embarrassed and worried that they were disappointing you.

Jim: OK, but I gotta keep tabs on them.

KP: We know, and we came up with some suggestions that could still let you keep tabs, but in another way.

Jim: Well, what do you suggest? [Still somewhat defensive.]

MA: We and the athletes came up with a change that they felt they would like, and that change would be to meet with you one on one outside practice time once a month, go over how things are going for them in diving and school and such, have a weigh-in, and then discuss with you how to proceed, maybe with the help of the nutritionist over in sports medicine.

Jim: Well, I guess I could do that.

KP: Some athletes told stories about being anxious and distracted during practice in the days before and the day of the weigh-in, so we thought that if we could lower that anxiety then they could focus better on practice and get more out of their diving.

Jim: OK, I see your point.

MA: And we would be happy to sit down with you, the nutritionist, and the athlete all together if you think that would help keep the diver healthy and on track.

Jim: OK, I'll have a talk with them tomorrow. Could at least one of you be there?

KP: Sure can, and thanks, Coach. It really is great working with you.

Along with group presentations to coaches, a team session on weight, body image, and eating is probably one of the more difficult tasks that a sport psychologist may be asked to do. Like the topic of sexuality in sport, these issues are fraught with anxiety and embarrassment and are often closeted. Sport climates and coaching practices are usually conservative and resistant to change. Coaches often use coaching models they experienced as athletes and create climates similar to the ones they witnessed. Changes to those models can be perceived as threatening, and you can see from the previous examples of talking to both the athletes and the coach that we trod very lightly. Moving in on a team with a messianic zeal to right the wrongs of a pathogenic sport milieu may get one excised permanently from the environment. When a sport psychologist begins to point a finger at a coach, it may happen that a coach begins to point back and say, "You are done here now!"

I (Mark) recall working with a women's gymnastics team years ago. I had taken great pains to approach the issues of weight and body image slowly and nonthreateningly. This process had continued off and on over the course of a year. I was then asked to take on an intern from student mental health who wanted to work with gymnasts. She started sitting in on our weekly group meetings and seemed to be eager to be involved with the young women. But she was on a mission, and I suspected it had to do, in part, with some of her own history in an "appearance" sport. She started to talk to the women in a strongly assertive manner about the tyrannies of weight and appearance in gymnastics. I asked her to tone it down. She did for a while, but as a supervisor I failed to be sufficiently assertive myself. She grew to despise the gymnastics coach, and although he was problematic, at least he was on the same page with me.

After the intern had an unpleasant encounter with the coach, I was called into his office. He said, "Mark, I don't know about this girl from student health. I don't like what she's doing. If she stays around, I am going to have to think about your continuing to work with my girls." I said, "Coach, I agree. She is out of here. We probably shouldn't have let her start. Sorry. It won't happen again." I excised her myself. That may sound brutal, but it was necessary because a year's worth of work helping the women talk about the issues important to them was under serious threat. The intern and I did discuss in detail the whole experience, and I hope she came to understand that working with athletes and coaches on eating, weight, and body image is a process of slow and gentle seduction, handled with kid gloves and not a true believer's truncheon.

# Conclusion

We hope this chapter has been useful to those of you who will be embarking on the journey of addressing weight, eating, and body image in sport. We have never encountered a team in which these issues, at some point sooner or later, do not make an appearance; they are ubiquitous and a great deal more common in men's sports than many believe. The athletes who participated in this dialogue did get to have their one-on-ones with the coach, and the threat of public weigh-ins disappeared. The group presentation helped initiate a change in the climate, and it was even more fun than usual to be out on deck with the team.

# Not Exactly on the Map

*Surveying Old
and New Territories*

PART

II

## CHAPTER 5

# The Skin Game
## *Extra Points for Looking Good*

Mark B. Andersen, PhD, and Helen J. Fawkner, PhD

Until recently, interest in body image focused on the study of women's dissatisfaction with their bodies, driven by the reported relationship between body dissatisfaction and eating disorders (Cash & Brown, 1987; Keeton, Cash, & Brown, 1990). Since the mid-1980s, there has been increased interest in men's body image, in both the popular media and academic research, and increased recognition that a similar relationship may exist for men. A growing body of literature describes body dissatisfaction and associated body image disorders among men. In this chapter, we trace that literature and provide a case example of these issues with a male diver.

## Body Image Disturbance

Cash (1996, 2002) conceptualizes the development of body image disturbance within a cognitive–social learning framework. There are myriad issues associated with body image disturbance, but they can be separated into two major categories: historical (causal) and current (maintaining) factors.

At least five types of causal factors determine body image attitudes:

- Cultural and interpersonal influences (e.g., societal norms, vicariously acquired attitudes about appearance)
- Developmental factors (e.g., timing of puberty)
- Physical attributes (e.g., changes in weight or other aspects of appearance)
- Personality attributes (e.g., extent to which an individual is appearance focused)
- Body shape image attitudes (i.e., schemas, ideals, self-perceptions)

Body experience is driven by everyday events (e.g., body exposure, social comparison, social scrutiny, eating, exercising). These events activate schema-driven processing of information about, and self-appraisal of, one's appearance (Cash, 1996). Self-appraisals draw on existing attitudes of body image and discrepancies between self-perceived and idealized physical traits, resulting in implicit and explicit cognitions about one's body. These cognitions produce body image affect (and vice versa), which motivates a range of adjustment strategies and behaviors designed to reduce the emotional consequences of a negative body appraisal. Such wide-ranging adjustment strategies can be relatively positive behaviors (e.g., seeking social reassurance) that may reduce dysphoric experiences. It is possible, however, that the adjustment strategies can be potentially harmful (e.g., unhealthy changes in exercise and diet) and likely to result in further maintenance of body image disturbance.

Body image disturbance can also be conceptualized as a continuum (Cash, 1996; Thompson, Heinberg, Altabe, & Tantleff Dunn, 1999). For some men the level of dissatisfaction is slight, but for others it may be more extreme. At the extreme end of the continuum, body image disturbance has been associated with a range of negative psychological and physical health outcomes. Body image disturbances are the central defining feature of several psychological disorders: eating disorders, body dysmorphia, some forms of somatic delusional disorders, and koro syndrome. Also, body dissatisfaction has been associated with poor self-esteem, depression, social anxiety, inhibition, and sexual dysfunction (Cash & Grant, 1995). This link to psychopathology is stronger in individuals who are more psychologically invested in their appearance (Cash & Syzmanski, 1995). Furthermore, body dissatisfaction is thought to underlie a variety of health risk behaviors such as sexual risk taking (McMurray, Bell, & Shircore, 1995; McMurray & Gazis, 1995), excessive or damaging exercise (Yates, 1991), and steroid abuse (Blouin & Goldfield, 1995; Brower, 1992; Buckley et al., 1988).

# The Male Ideal and the Prevalence of Body Dissatisfaction

Ample evidence suggests that both men and women perceive the male ideal as mesomorphic—an average, well-proportioned build with good muscular development and definition of the shoulders, chest, and arms, along with a slim waist and hips (Fawkner & McMurray, 2002; Grogan, Williams, & Conner, 1996; Ogden, 1992). This shape is preferred to both the ectomorphic (thin) and endomorphic (fat) physique and is expressed regardless of age. Boys as young as five years have shown this preference (Lerner & Korn, 1972), as have adolescent and young adult males (Diabiase & Hjelle, 1968; Jacobi & Cash, 1994; Lindner, Ryckman, Gold, & Stone, 1995; Mishkind, Rodin, Silberstein, & Striegel-Moore, 1986; Salusso-Deonier, Markee, & Pedersen, 1993; Tucker, 1982, 1984). Although some males idealize the hypermesomorphic physique typified by professional bodybuilders (Deno, 1953; Tucker, 1984), this extreme is perceived by many people to be unnatural and even repulsive (St. Martin & Garvey, 1996).

Mishkind and colleagues (1986) hypothesize three major sociocultural changes that might be responsible for a growing body consciousness and concern among men. First, as a result of the declining number of purely masculine domains, increased muscularity is one of the few ways available for men to express their masculinity. Second, preventable diseases (e.g., cardiovascular disease) are now among the leading causes of death (Sarafino, 1998), resulting in increased importance being placed on the self-management of one's health. Being healthy has erroneously become equated with looking healthy, and looking healthy has become associated with a lean but mesomorphic physique for men.

Finally, cultural attitudes toward the male body have changed. Men's bodies have become increasingly visible in popular culture (Mort, 1988), and men are now being targeted in advertising for products such as diet soft drinks and cosmetics that previously were considered to be feminine products and unappealing to men (Mishkind et al., 1986). These changes challenge traditional masculine icons and encourage men to become more aware of how they look (Mort, 1988).

Analysis of both written content and graphic images reveals that men are subtly pressured to conform to the mesomorphic ideal. For example, Andersen and Di Domenico (1992) examined 10 of the most popular magazines for young adults. They report that men were exposed to more than three times as many advertisements and articles advocating changing their body shape as they were to articles advocating dieting and weight loss. Pope, Phillips, and Olivardia (2000) report that the proportion of magazine images in which men are undressed or naked has risen from 3% in the 1950s to 35% of images in the 1990s. Additionally, the idealized images presented to boys (e.g., action toys such as G.I. Joe and Star Wars characters) and idealized images of men (e.g., Playgirl centerfolds) have become increasingly muscular (Pope, Olivardia, Gruber, & Borowiecki, 1999; Pope et al., 2000).

A number of cultural trends suggest that these societal changes have increased body consciousness among men. For example, substantial increases have been noted in the incidence of cosmetic surgery (Catalano, 1996; Marinos, 1997), the sale of men's grooming products (Mishkind et al., 1986), and the number of men who attend exercise facilities and diet clinics (Davis, Dionne, & Lazarus, 1996). Empirical evidence also suggests that men are increasingly experiencing body concern and consciousness.

Many college-age men experience discrepancies between their perceived size and shape and their ideal size and shape (Abell & Richards, 1996; Drewnowski & Yee, 1987; Mishkind et al., 1986; Raudenbush & Zellner, 1997; Silberstein, Mishkind, Striegel-Moore, Timko, & Rodin, 1989; Silberstein, Striegel-Moore, Timko, & Rodin, 1988). As many as 95% of studies report such a discrepancy (Mishkind et al., 1986); approximately equal numbers desire a larger body size as those who desire a smaller body size (Abell & Richards, 1996; Drewnowski & Yee, 1987; Raudenbush & Zellner, 1997; Silberstein et al., 1989; Silberstein et al., 1988). Despite methodological shortcomings with this approach to assessing body dissatisfaction (see Gardner, Friedman, & Jackson, 1998), these discrepancies provide some evidence of body dissatisfaction among men and have been interpreted as a desire for a more mesomorphic body (Drewnowski & Yee, 1987). This species of body dysmorphia has been called, in non-DSM-IV terms, "bigorexia" or the even more colorful "megarexia."

Further evidence of increasing body concern among men comes from a series of national studies conducted in the United States (Berscheid, Walster, & Bohrnstedt, 1973; Cash, Winstead, & Janda, 1986; Garner & Kearney-Cooke, 1997). In 1972, 15% of men reported experiencing overall appearance dissatisfaction, but these figures had nearly tripled by 1997 to 43% of male respondents. Increasingly, men have reported the greatest dissatisfaction with their abdomens, weight, muscle tone, and chests, confirming the notion that the mesomorphic physique is the ideal to which men aspire. Garner and Kearney-Cooke (1997) conclude that body dissatisfaction is soaring among men, and it would appear that the gender gap in body dissatisfaction is narrowing. On the basis of a meta-analysis, however, Feingold and Mazzella (1998) argue that such a conclusion is premature. Nevertheless, evidence suggests that a large proportion of men experience body dissatisfaction.

# Eating Disorders in Men

Estimates of the prevalence of eating disorders among men in the general population vary greatly, but bulimia and binge eating appear to be more common among men than anorexia (Olivardia, Pope, Mangweth, & Hudson, 1995). Among men, the incidence may be as low as 0.02% per year for anorexia (Lucas, Beard, O'Fallon, & Kurland, 1991), between 1 and 5% for bulimia (Drewnowski, Hopkins, & Kessler, 1988; Schotte & Stunkard, 1987; Striegel-Moore, Silberstein, Frensch, & Rodin, 1989), and at least 1% for binge eating (Hoek & van Hoeken, 2003). Studies examining eating disorders indicate that men constitute from 5 to 10% of people with anorexia (Oyebode, Boodhoo, & Schapira, 1988) and 0.4 to 20% of people with bulimia (Carlat & Camargo, 1991; Drewnowski et al., 1988; Halmi, Falk, & Swartz, 1981; Pope, Hudson, Yurgelun-Todd, & Hudson, 1984; Schotte & Stunkard, 1987; Striegel-Moore et al., 1989; Striegel-Moore, Silberstein, & Rodin, 1986), and the rate of eating disorders may be increasing among men (Braun, Sunday, Huang, & Halmi, 1999). Braun and colleagues compared the 51 males and 693 females admitted to an inpatient eating disorders service between 1984 and 1997. Although male patients made up only 6.8% of the total admissions, the proportion of male patients increased significantly across this time. Given that eating disorders are popularly considered "female" problems, there is probably significant underreporting of the incidence and prevalence of these clinical syndromes in males.

The clinical picture for men with eating disorders is similar to that for women, and examinations of other psychopathology associated with eating disorders (e.g., Axis I and II disorders) have revealed more similarities than differences between men and women (Braun et al., 1999; Olivardia et al., 1995). Nevertheless, some gender differences have been reported (Herzog, Bradburn, & Newman, 1990). Men have a higher age of onset (Braun et al., 1999; Carlat, Camargo, & Herzog, 1997), are less likely to seek therapeutic intervention (Olivardia et al., 1995), and are less likely to have good treatment outcomes (Oyebode et al., 1988). Oyebode and colleagues report that only 20% of males, compared with 50% of females, had good outcomes following treatment. The majority of men (70%) had what could be considered poor outcomes, compared with only 30% of women. Additionally, there appear to be some gender differences with respect to preferred methods of weight control. Some evidence suggests that women are more likely to use purging, diet pills, and laxatives (Braun et al., 1999; Johnson, Powers, & Dick, 1999), and men are more likely to use saunas and steam baths (Johnson et al., 1999) and exercise to control their weight (Davis & Cowles, 1991; Drewnowski & Yee, 1987).

# At-Risk Populations

Two groups of men, gay men and athletes, are thought to be at greater risk of body dissatisfaction and eating disorders. Siever (1994) hypothesizes that gay men might be more vulnerable to body image disturbance and eating disorders as a result of a heightened emphasis on appearance and physical attractiveness in the gay culture. Research has shown that gay men experience both greater body investment (Finch, 1991; Siever, 1994; Silberstein et al., 1989) and body dissatisfaction as compared with heterosexual men (Berscheid et al., 1973; Finch, 1991; Garner & Kearney-Cooke, 1997; Siever, 1994; Silberstein et al., 1989). Examinations of eating attitudes and behaviors in nonclinical samples generally reveal that gay men, as compared with heterosexual men, have significantly higher levels of eating disturbance (French, Story, Remafedi, Resnick, & Blum, 1996; Gettelman & Thompson, 1993; Herzog, Newman, & Warshaw, 1991; Siever, 1994; Silberstein et al., 1989; Williamson & Hartley, 1998; Yager, Kurtzman, Landsverk, & Wiesmeier, 1988). Only a few studies did not support this trend (Brand, Rothblum, & Solomon, 1992; Mangweth et al., 1997; Olivardia et al., 1995). Studies of clinical populations confirm that eating disorders are more prevalent among gay men (Carlat et al., 1997; Carlat & Camargo, 1991; Herzog et al., 1990; Herzog, Norman, Gordon, & Pepose, 1984; Kearney-Cooke & Steichen-Asch, 1990; Schneider & Agras, 1987). The percentage of men who are gay has been estimated between 4 and 10% (Singer & Deschamps, 1994); as many as 33% of men with anorexia (Dally, 1969) and as many as 50% of men with bulimia were found to be gay (Herzog et al., 1984).

Associated with the underreporting mentioned earlier, Herzog and colleagues (1984) warn that it is possible that heterosexual men may be underrepresented not because of an absence of the disorders but because of a greater reluctance to present for treatment. Their study of men with eating disorders revealed that 67% of gay men presenting for treatment were self-referred as compared with 29% of heterosexual men.

The relationships between exercise, sport participation, and body image disturbance are complex and still not fully understood. Regular physical exercise has been associated with a number of physiological and psychological benefits (Davis, 1997; Davis & Cowles, 1991), and it seems plausible that exercise participation might result in a positive body image and reduce the risk of eating disorders. There is some support for this hypothesis from both cross-sectional (Anderson, Zager, Hetzler, NahikianNelms, & Syler, 1996; Davis & Cowles, 1991; Huddy & Cash, 1997; Huddy, Johnson, Stone, Proulx, & Pierce, 1997; Huddy, Nieman, & Johnson, 1993) and longitudinal research (Salusso-Deonier & Schwarzkopf, 1991; Tucker, 1982, 1983). It has even been suggested that athletes might be protected from developing eating disorders (Fulkerson, Keel, Leon, & Door, 1999; Wilkins, Boland, & Albinson, 1991).

Nevertheless, Yates (1991) suggests that exercise might be a maladaptive behavior—an analogue of anorexia, a strategy in the pursuit of the ideal body (Rosen, 1990; Yates, 1991). Exercise may even provide an environment that fosters an unhealthy preoccupation with weight and appearance, thus increasing the likelihood of body dissatisfaction and eating disorders (Davis, Fox, Cowles, Hastings, & Schwass, 1990; Katz, 1986).

Research has revealed support for this hypothesis. Several studies have shown exercisers and athletes to be significantly less satisfied with their bodies than nonexercisers and nonathletes (Armstrong, Lange, & Mishra, 1992; Kiernan, Rodin, Brownell, Wilmore, & Crandall, 1992; McDonald & Thompson, 1992). Further, there are reports of significantly greater eating disturbance among athletes such as runners, rowers, weightlifters, and body-builders as compared with nonathletes (Andersen, Barlett, Morgan, & Brownell, 1995; Franco, Tamburrino, Carroll, & Bernal, 1988; Pasman & Thompson, 1988; Stoutjesdyk & Jevne, 1992; Thiel, Gottfried, & Hesse, 1993). Male athletes have been reported as being at greater risk of developing an eating disorder than the general male population, and some athletes are at greater risk than others (Stoutjesdyk & Jevne, 1992). Stoutjesdyk and Jevne compared eating attitudes and behaviors among high-performance athletes representing three different types of sports: sports emphasizing leanness (gymnastics and diving), sports with weight restrictions (lightweight rowing and judo), and sports with no weight restrictions and low emphasis on leanness (volleyball and heavyweight rowing). For the male athletes, although there were no differences in levels of eating disturbance as a function of sport type, the small percentage of men displaying clinical levels of disturbance competed in weight-restricted sports and were engaged in their sports at a national or international level.

# Reasons for Elevated Eating Disturbance and Body Image Disturbance

There are at least six reasons why exercisers and athletes might experience greater body dissatisfaction and elevated levels of eating disturbance. First, although body dissatisfaction might motivate exercise behavior, it may not change the anatomical features that are the source of the dissatisfaction (Davis, Durnin, Gurevich, LeMaire, & Dionne, 1994). Although many men exercise for the purpose of weight control (Davis & Cowles, 1991; Drewnowski & Yee, 1987), exercise alone is not an effective way to lose weight (Durnin

& Passmore, 1967) and may not result in a more positive body image, possibly leaving an individual frustrated and vulnerable to eating disturbances.

Some athletic and exercise activities are more likely than others to promote body satisfaction (Davis, 1997). For example, weight training can quickly result in increased muscle mass, thus moving the individual closer to the mesomorphic ideal (Tucker, 1982, 1983) and possibly explaining why athletes engaging in these weight-based training activities might experience greater satisfaction. Not all athletic and exercise activities will have this effect, and not all sports demand or produce mesomorphic physiques. For example, McKay Parks and Read (1997) examined body image concerns, attitudes toward weight and eating, and reasons for exercise in adolescent football players and cross country runners. Cross-country runners were more dissatisfied with their size and shape, but they were less dissatisfied with their weight. These differences might be attributable to cross country running's requiring and producing a lean physique. The masculine ideal, however, is mesomorphic, and thus, the runners may experience conflicts, resulting in body dissatisfaction (McKay Parks & Read, 1997).

Investing time and effort in one's body via exercise participation may lead to increased expectations about one's body shape, weight, and level of fitness (Davis, 1997; Katz, 1986; Loosemoore, Mable, Galgan, Balance, & Moriarty, 1989). Even though an individual may achieve objective improvements in body composition and fitness levels, increased expectations might result in dissatisfaction. Armstrong and colleagues (1992) note a complex relationship between fitness satisfaction, body weight perception, and exercise frequency. Exercisers who were more satisfied with their weight were more satisfied with their fitness than those who were dissatisfied with their weight. As exercise frequency increased, so did fitness satisfaction, but the difference in fitness satisfaction between those who were satisfied with their weight and those who were not became more pronounced. Exercise moderates the negative effects of body weight perception on fitness satisfaction for moderate-level exercisers, but as exercise frequency increases, the protective effect is eroded (Armstrong et al., 1992). People who exercise five to seven times per week hold more critical standards than those who exercise a more moderate amount.

Davis (1997) suggests that social comparison between oneself and others in the exercise or sport environment may result in negative self-comparison and, thus, increased dissatisfaction. The likelihood of dissatisfaction might be heightened in sports where comparisons not only are made internally but also form part of the competition process (e.g., diving, gymnastics). In these types of sports, success is determined not only by technical prowess but also by grace and physical appeal (Davis, 1997). Attractive people have been shown to be advantaged in numerous social situations (Dion, Berscheid, & Walster, 1972), and there is evidence of appearance-related bias in sports such as gymnastics (Ryan, 1995). Ryan notes that in 1972 the winning women's gymnastics team had an average height of 5 feet 3 inches and an average weight of 106 pounds; by 1992 the average height was 4 feet 9 inches, with an average weight of 83 pounds. An examination of the reported heights and weights of male Australian divers suggests a similar trend—those with higher national and international rankings show a trend toward more mesomorphic physiques and lower body mass indices (Fawkner, 2005). The perception that thinness is rewarded could contribute to development of both body image disturbance and elevated eating disturbance in athletes participating in judgment sports such as diving and gymnastics.

Davis and colleagues (1990) suggest that exercise, through biochemical or social reinforcement, may play a central role for some people in the development of obsessive preoccupations with appearance and excessive concerns with weight and dieting. Although these processes would explain why some participants (irrespective of the type of exercise undertaken) experience greater body dissatisfaction than do nonexercisers, a word of caution is warranted. It must be remembered that the former underlying motivations of individuals who participate in sport and exercise need to be considered. McDonald and

Thompson (1992) examined body image, eating disturbance, and motivations for exercise. They report that men who exercised for appearance, as opposed to health, mood, or enjoyment, had elevated scores on the measures of eating disturbance and body dissatisfaction, and the more men exercised specifically for fitness, the lower the level of eating disturbance.

Finally, the role of individual and psychosocial factors needs consideration. For example, Beren, Hayden, Wifley, and Grillo (1996) report that individual and psychosocial factors moderated vulnerability to eating pathology in gay men. Men with a greater affiliation to the gay community experienced a greater degree of body dissatisfaction than those with lower affiliation. Similar affiliation and identity processes may occur in sport. It is possible that athletes with a greater sense of self-identification as athletes may be more at risk for eating disorders and body dissatisfaction, particularly if they participate in sports in which thinness is seen as desirable. Factors of this nature need to be considered both empirically and clinically if we want to better understand the complex relationship between exercise and sport participation and vulnerability to body dissatisfaction and eating disorders.

## The Gravity of Weight: Erik's Story

Armed with this background, we now move to the case of Erik, a collegiate diver. Erik comes to see me (Mark) two days after an eating disorder group presentation similar to the one described in chapter 4. It is my usual day to go out to the diving well and observe practice, talk to the coach, and catch up with the athletes. I often have an additional role of "videoman," and I videotape the practice dives of the team members. The divers are appreciative of my amateur video efforts because no one else has the time to provide such a service, and they really love seeing themselves on tape. I hold on to the tapes for about a week so the athletes I am working with individually can watch themselves, and we use the information on the tapes for further sport psychology work.

My role as videographer is a boon for divers hesitant to approach me individually. Watching videotapes is a safe way to start interacting with a sport psychologist. The focus is on the video monitor and the dives, and watching the tapes gets the athlete in my office, where we begin talking about dives; then, as comfort grows, we may begin to talk about other issues the athlete is dealing with.

Erik knows me from the team meetings and my pool deck activities but is not a one-on-one client. About 15 minutes before practice, he leans into my open doorway and says:

Erik:     Hey, gotta minute?

Mark Anderson
(MA):     Sure, what's up?

Erik:     Today at practice, when you're taping, could you maybe get a bunch of me? I'm working on two new dives, and I need all the help I can get.

MA:     No problem. Some days I just shoot whoever is on the board or platform, and some days I focus on one or two divers—as I did with Julie last week. We can make this an Erik day.

Erik:     Great, that would be cool. . . . And I got this new suit—kind of like to see how it looks when I am diving.

MA:     OK, I'll be out on deck by the time you get through with dryland. Shall we make a time to take a look at the tapes?

Erik:     Yeah, maybe we should do that before practice tomorrow.

MA:     OK, it's a plan. See you at the pool.

Erik:     Cool, Doc.

Several things have occurred in this brief interchange. Erik has made the first move of coming to talk to me, a move that does not push his comfort level too far. I also know that Erik is a bit of a loner who does not actively seek out others, so I take his making the move as a small success for my efforts with the team. In his statement about "needing all the help I can get" lies a marker of the potential developing relationship—the question "Can you help me?" My response to his implicit question contains the statement "We can make this an Erik day." The wording is intentional. I use *we* to emphasize that we are working together and *Erik day* to underline that it is a special time for both of us to focus on him. That simple communication about working together and my being there on deck especially for him may have let him feel more comfortable and willing to add his second concern to the mix—his worries about his new suit and how he looks. That concern tweaks my body appearance radar, especially because the request for video services

> Athletes often "talk around" issues of weight and eating; listen carefully for subtle hints of conflicts.

comes close on the heels of our eating disorder presentation. I do not explore the suit issue but take a mental note that when we look at the tape together, if he does not comment on the suit, then I will probably ask, "Well, so how do you think the suit looks?" Divers constantly make social, physical, and fashion comparisons with other divers, and as the title of this chapter says, one does get extra points for looking good. To help Erik along in his request for help, I make the move (using the first person plural) to suggest we set aside a time to watch the tapes. I take it as a good sign when Erik mirrors my use of *we* by saying, "We should do that . . . tomorrow," and when he takes his leave with the familiar and affectionate "Cool, Doc."

At the diving well, I tape most of Erik's dives and make sure I get every attempt he makes at the two new dives he is trying to master. He has some flubs, but he also has some rather clean attempts.

The following day, Erik shows up in my office about 40 minutes before he is due at practice. I have video editing equipment in my office that allows athletes to watch themselves in real time, slow motion, or frame by frame. The athletes I videotape really enjoy sitting at the console and operating the equipment. Erik is no exception; he thinks seeing himself in action and stopping and running dives forward and backward is informative and entertaining.

> Erik: This video stuff is so cool. Thanks!
>
> MA: My pleasure. It's loads of fun, isn't it?
>
> Erik: I really like the single frame stuff.
>
> MA: Yeah, it can help with analyzing what's going right and what's going wrong with the dives.
>
> Erik: [Pointing to the monitor.] You can see on this flub where I started to go wrong all the way back at the hurdle.
>
> MA: It will be good to go over this tape with Neil [his coach] soon and do some analysis. I'll copy it and have it for you after practice.

Erik is quite engaged in the process of examining and discussing his dives. Having been a swimmer, I spent a lot of time around pools and swimmers and divers and know quite a bit about the sports. I can see on the tape where many of his technical difficulties are occurring. I could ask Erik, "What do you need to do differently?" or something like that but would also keep steering him back to discussing the technical aspects of his dives with his coach. Sport psychologists working with athletes in sports where they have a lot of technical knowledge can easily, and unintentionally, suggest things that stray over into the coaching realm. Early in my career as a psychologist, when working with swimmers and divers, I had to make a concerted effort to bite my tongue when it was obvious to me what the technical problem was. I have gotten better at deflecting technical talk back to consultation with the coach, but there are still plenty of times when I really want to say, "Just try doing it this way. . . ."

> Erik:   Great, thanks. I'll talk to the coach about it. [Pause.] So what do you think about the suit?

Often when viewing videotapes, I will ask athletes questions about thoughts, feelings, and behaviors (the holy triumvirate) before, during, and after the event to get at where some psychological interventions may be helpful (e.g., changing thinking, reframing emotions, modifying behavioral routines). Erik and I have not yet gone down that performance enhancement path when he poses the question about his suit. Asking me about fashion is like inquiring of a tropical beast what he thinks of snow. That Erik brings up how he looks so early in our second meeting suggests that it is a topic of high importance and that he is ready, at least, to start talking about it. Also, his asking my opinion suggests he values what I think (another good sign of the forming working alliance), or it may be a type of test: "Does this guy see the flaws I see in my body?" I am not sure what is behind his request for my personal opinion, so I answer as honestly as a fashion-impaired guy can and then turn the question back to him.

When discussing performance with athletes, it's easy to find yourself coaching. Make a mental note to keep your session about psychology.

> MA:     It's quite striking, very colorful. Looks good. What do you think?
> Erik:   Maybe draws too much attention, especially to my fat ass, you think?

I have worked with many divers, and they are one of the bluntest groups when it comes to talking about their bodies. My turning the question back to him resulted in a comment about how the suit was unflattering, then he turned the question back to me again ("you think?"). Awkward for me, to say the least, and he is not going to let me off the hook. He has asked my opinion twice already, so I know he is invested in talking to me about something that has to do with how he looks. As I always tell my students, if clients bring something up that you do not adequately address, not to worry—they will bring it up again and again until you do. In Erik's last statement and question we have moved from the suit to his body, one part of which he is not pleased with. This move stirs in me concerns about his body dissatisfaction and possible body dysmorphia.

So how does one respond to such a statement and question? To me, most elite divers have amazing bodies, and it is hard for me to see flaws. For divers, however, even small imperfections may be exaggerated and perceived as fatal disproportions. I do not want to respond with "I don't notice a fat ass; you seem well proportioned" because that contradicts his perceptions. I also do not want to agree with his assessment of the suit and its effect on his shape because that will only reinforce his negative perceptions. Directly answering his question seems like a no-win situation, so I take a reflective–interpretive tact.

> MA:     You don't sound too happy about how you look in that suit.
> Erik:   You know diving—gotta look perfect. [He pauses for a while.] Wish I could afford a butt tuck so my shoulders would fit my hips.
> MA:     Feeling a bit unbalanced proportion-wise?
> Erik:   A bit? . . . A lot! . . . Hey, Doc, I gotta get some stuff done before practice. Thanks for the tape. I'll pick up the copy later. Gotta go.
> MA:     OK, see you later.

Talking with a psychologist often resembles a dance of approach and avoidance on the client's part. In some cases, psychologists also join in that dance, approaching and avoiding areas clients bring up because of their own discomfort with the topics. My arguments about the better way to address Erik's concerns may sound, on the surface, like sound psychological care, and I am sure my reflection had some benefit. Well, maybe not—he ran away. But his dramatic exit tells me a lot about how much valence this body concern has. My reflection–deflection of Erik's question also has possible roots in my own struggles with body dissatisfaction. I was never happy with how I looked as a swimmer, especially in a Speedo, and so Erik's concerns strike very close to home. I tell my students to try to use their own struggles to help them understand and empathize with clients. I also have to keep telling myself the same thing.

So far with Erik, I have some ideas about what is troubling him. On the body side, he feels unbalanced. His hips are too big for his shoulders, so he may be trying to both increase his shoulder size (through resistance training) and decrease his hip circumference (through restricting food intake or bulimic behavior). These tactics, especially if occurring simultaneously, are doomed to failure.

Erik is worried about his body shape and wants to talk about it, but when I make observations that go deeper than my opinion on how he looks and that touch on his dissatisfaction, he suddenly has to be somewhere and disappears. I let him leave and do not pursue. I feel we have made a start; I also feel he is in that ambivalent state of *I want to* versus *I don't want to.* Later when he picks up the tape, I ask him if he would like to talk more about his diving and maybe work on the mental aspects of getting those two new dives down. He says he would like to, and we arrange another meeting. In the approach and avoidance dance, Erik has moved to the avoidance side. Asking him if he would like to discuss his body shape more would probably push him further into avoidance. So I offer him an alternative (performance enhancement) that is much safer and will move him back to approaching and talking to me.

I suggest we work on performance issues to help him continue to build trust in our relationship. As Erik gets more comfortable with me, he may start to readdress those body issues that are probably more central to his life and his sport than learning new dives. Classic sport psychology service delivery (e.g., relaxation, imagery, goal setting) offers a comfortable way for athletes to build up trust and ease into talking about what is really bothering them. This tactic works with Erik. We spend the next four sessions doing performance enhancement work on his new dives, using a lot of relaxation and imagery. On our fifth session, Erik comes into my office very flat.

> If you sense an athlete wants to talk about several issues, establishing trust in one area is a good bridge to these other topics.

| | |
|---|---|
| Erik: | Hey, Doc. |
| MA: | Come on in, Erik. How's the week going? |
| Erik: | OK. |
| MA: | Well, I gotta say you don't look OK. . . . You're looking kind of down. |
| Erik: | Just having a bad week. |
| MA: | So tell me how the week went bad. |
| Erik: | Well, it started with the goddamn weigh-in on Tuesday. [Pause.] |
| MA: | What went on? |
| Erik: | [Silent for a while.] I have been trying so hard to trim up, and I got on the scales, and I was three pounds heavier than the last weigh-in, and the coach said, "Better watch that." . . . I would love three pounds if it was upper-body muscle, but I am sure it was three pounds of fat. |
| MA: | You sound both bummed out and really pissed off, too. |
| Erik: | I probably am; it's just that I've tried everything to lose some fat and get stronger, but it just isn't working. |
| MA: | I can see on your face that you are really frustrated. You said you tried everything; what all does that include? |
| Erik: | Shit! I have been on about five different diets, and I have been doing lots of weights for upper-body stuff. . . . |
| MA: | Have you tried anything else? |

Erik: [Long silence.] You won't tell anyone?

MA: Erik, our relationship is special; nothing goes outside this room unless you want it to.

Erik: OK. . . . I got this problem. . . . I sometimes just start eating junk, and I can't stop, and pretty soon almost a half gallon of ice cream is gone, and then I feel like shit and say, "Well, that's going straight to your ass," and then I go and puke my guts out. . . . [Erik has been looking away from me the whole time he tells the bulimic story, but when he finishes he makes eye contact with me.] Pretty gross, huh?

MA: Well, not so sure about gross, but it sounds like quite a roller coaster. Eating a lot of ice cream, which tastes and feels good, then eating too much and feeling like shit, and worrying about weight, and then throwing up, which *is* kind of gross, but I bet it actually feels good to get it all out, but then you feel bad and grossed out about the whole thing. Sure sounds like a whole lot of ups and downs.

Erik: Exactly! Like after the weigh-in, I was so bummed out I went home and massacred a tub of mint ice cream and a box of chocolate cookies.

MA: The barfing must have been rather colorful.

Erik starts laughing at my joke, and the laughter turns into some silent tears. I could see a wave of sadness, confusion, shame, and possibly relief move across his face.

> Using humor in a session can be a good tension breaker. Make sure, however, it is used judiciously.

Erik: Sorry, Doc, I just never told anyone about it.

MA: No apologies necessary, Erik—actually I feel privileged that you were willing to tell me about your worries and struggles with weight and eating. That took a lot of guts, so to speak. [Erik smiles.] I can see you're concerned about all this, and I will be more than happy to work on this stuff with you. What I would like to know is now that you have come out of the bulimic closet, what is going on for you at the moment?

Erik: I am so embarrassed . . . but I am a bit relieved. I know I have to do something about it all.

MA: And you don't have to do it all on your own.

Erik: Thanks, Doc, but I have tried to stop, and I just can't do it. I am fine for a few days, and then, boom! I am back at it again, and yesterday there was some blood in my puke, and that scared the crap out of me . . . so to speak. [Mirroring my joke.]

MA: OK, Erik, that worries me too, and one of the first things is to get you a full medical once-over. We won't send you to the team physician. We'll have you go to a doctor I know in student health, Dr. Yoshi; she's wonderful. No one but you and me and the doctor will know what you're there for. But before we do that, I think it would help if I got the whole story. I know we talked briefly about how you looked in your suit a few weeks ago, and I bet your concerns with weight and how you look and your sport go back a ways. So can you take yourself back to when you first noticed you weren't happy with your body and you started some eating behaviors that led to where you are now?

Erik: I can tell you exactly when it started. In high school, I was a star—made second at state championships, but when I got here, it was as if I turned into a pig.

MA: Good, Erik, there's a start. We will get to the pig years soon enough, but first I would like to hear about your high school diving. Tell me some stories from that time.

Much has occurred here for both Erik and me. Erik is worried about what others might think ("You won't tell anyone?") and what I think (that what he does is gross). Bulimic behavior carries with it a great deal of shame and self-loathing along with a profound sense of being out of control. Erik has confided in me, and I try to retell his story for him so he understands that I have heard it and am sympathetic. My retelling serves another purpose in that I do not sound shocked or disgusted, but I acknowledge that parts of what he does do seem gross—not that I am repelled by the behavior but that I understand how "gross" he feels.

Now why do I make the joke about colorful vomit? Those words probably serve a couple of purposes, at least one to help Erik and one to serve my own needs. With that joke, I want Erik to see that I am not repelled and that I can see some humor in his situation. It is a type of normalizing comment, taking his behavior and treating it in a matter-of-fact way with a touch of humor. This use of humor can communicate that everything is not horrible and awful but interesting and even possessing of something humorous about human frailty. That Erik can laugh at my joke is a good sign. Humor is also often used when things start to get too painful for the parties involved. It is a type of defense against the powerful emotions that come with such a topic. My joke probably serves my needs to steer away, at least for a moment, from what Erik's story brings up in me. I am actually physically hurting when Erik tells his story; I know I am having a strong personal reaction tied to my own anxieties about my body and my appearance. The joke is designed, unconsciously, as a momentary relief for both of us. Reinforced by the relief the joke gives us both, I make another small joke about it "taking a lot of guts" to tell the story. I do get back on track and let Erik know that his story is one I value highly and feel honored to have heard.

Erik wants to do something, but he feels powerless. Even when I tell him he does not have to do it all alone, he is still resistant and brings up how he has tried and failed. The blood in his vomit calls for immediate attention, and I jump in and get directive. With closeted medical and psychological conditions, many athletes at North American universities are loath to see their sports medicine team members. Although confidentiality should be the rule in such institutions, I have seen the rule breached as much as observed. Athletes are often fearful that information will get back to the coach or other teammates. That fear is not totally unjustified. I try to allay Erik's fear by letting him know that I take his medical symptom very seriously and that we will go about taking care of it in a way that protects him.

Erik has "dropped the bomb," and he can trace the bomb back to a specific change in his life. I could ask him to start talking about how, and in what ways, his concerns about his body and his eating behaviors began to go off the rails. I will get to that story eventually, but for now I ask Erik to go back to a halcyon time when he was king of the board. Again, the path I choose probably helps me as much as Erik in that I want to see some smiles on this kid's face (major countertransferential big-brother protective response) about his past successes. I also think that going back to the good old days might reveal some material that will be useful in grappling with his current concerns.

Going back to happier times can result in stories that can be used as models for current problems (confidence, success, joy of functioning). It can also stimulate comparisons with current functioning. I have seen many athletes relate past glories with big smiles on their faces and then lapse into deep sadness and grief over the comparison with how they are now. That roller coaster has much to tell us about how the sense of self has taken a beating: "I was a prince; now I am crap." The change from royalty to the position of just another diver, and the loss it entails, can move athletes to take radical measures to try to recapture that sense of competence and worthiness. "I am not what I used to be. In this new world I am so much less, all the way down to an animal [and a porcine one at that]. I must do everything to get rid of my piggishness and climb back up into the blessed realm, otherwise I truly am crap." Erik's use of the word *pig* is perfect, for that is how he feels about his body and appearance, the "skin" he is in, and his attempts, in all sorts of maladaptive ways, to shed that skin.

Erik begins his stories about past glories with enthusiasm, and they are wonderful to hear, but the roller coaster hits the peak of its trajectory, and he plummets back down, not only into body image concerns but also questions of masculinity.

Erik:    And now I just hate going to practice; I'm fat, and I got this girlie problem, and . . . [He slumps in the chair and looks defeated. I remain silent for a considerable time.] What am I gonna do, Doc?

MA:    Erik, I'm not really sure what you are going to do, but we can work together and figure out what might be helpful for your diving, your fat, and your "girlie" problem. What do you say?

Erik:    OK, but what are we going to do?

MA:    I don't know. Maybe we should pick something and start talking. So where do you want to begin? With diving, or your body, or the bulimia–girlie stuff?

Erik:    Let's start with the dives. This last one I am working on is such a bitch.

MA:    There's a start; we will take things one at a time. Why don't we move over to the video, and you can talk me through what's going on in the tapes of this new dive.

Erik is dancing again, and I need to let him dance. He makes some rather large approach moves in exploring his problems and puts some sensitive material out on the table (girlie concerns). He again asks for help ("What am I gonna do?"), and I tell him I do not know exactly what we are going to do, but we are in this endeavor together. When offered the choice of what to explore first, he retreats from the probably more emotionally taxing issues of feeling fat and having what he considers a female problem to the safer realm of performance. All along, Erik has been coming close to painful issues (and to me) and then backing off, then coming back. It is a dance of trust and a dance of self-exploration. I let him dance, and given our brief history, I am fairly sure he will come back to his other concerns in time. For Erik, just admitting his abhorrence of his weight and his bulimia is a huge step. He views these problems as awful and disgusting but still is not quite ready to go into them in more depth, precisely because of the import they have for his view of himself and what a catastrophe of shame and worthlessness his life is. His models for interpreting his problems are not helping.

What I am trying to do as he approaches his demons is to be a model of showing interest, having concern, taking things matter of factly, having a sense of humor, being encouraging, and above all, being the caring other who has complete positive regard for Erik no matter what. The most important element that needs to be missing from this model I am trying to communicate is being judgmental. I am hoping by modeling a judgment-free interest in his struggles that eventually Erik will start to internalize that model and begin to free himself of the harsh condemnations of his behaviors and the hypercritical perceptions of his body. That internalization process has a great deal going against it. Erik's environment is full of punishments and contingencies of reinforcements that help maintain his pathological worldview. So how does the internalization work? It works through the quality of the developing working alliance. As our relationship grows it becomes a model for how to communicate, how to problem-solve, how to share, and how to "be" with each other, relatively free of judgment but full of fascination and interest. A well-built alliance can counteract the multitude of pathological contingencies in Erik's environment.

> Model being judgment free.

I am convinced that the first line of treatment for athletes with eating and body image concerns is the working alliance between the psychologist and the athlete. The literature on eating disorders and athletes strongly emphasizes adopting a team approach (Petrie & Sherman, 2000; Thompson & Sherman, 1993), often involving a nutritionist, a physician, a psychologist, and even the coach and family. I do not want to knock such an approach, and bringing in others for athlete care is sometimes immediately necessary (as with Erik's bleeding). The team approach, however, sometimes has more of a feel of managing the disorder than caring for the person. Bringing so many others into the athlete's world, and making the athlete go over the problems again and again with each practitioner or significant other, can be overwhelming and counterproductive.

Of the many athletes I have worked with who had eating concerns, the majority started out wanting to talk only to me. Even gentle suggestions of a visit to a nutritionist would often be met with fierce resistance. I have found that in many cases it would take several months before the athlete would be ready to venture outside my office for other help. I think we need to give the athlete the breathing room to explore with us their concerns without the pressure to go and do it all over again. As they become comfortable with us and begin to internalize a model of how to look at their problems, then they become more willing to expand treatment. The team approach to athletes with eating disorders may be the gold standard in current thought, but such an approach probably works best once a really solid working relationship is established with the psychologist.

Returning to Erik's case, he does come back to his other problems in time. Regarding his concerns about having a "female problem," he starts approaching it, as so many of us do, with a story about a third party, a male cheerleader. In the U.S. collegiate system, student cheerleaders are usually part of the intercollegiate athletics department, sharing locker rooms and sports medicine facilities with the other athletes.

| Erik: | I ran into Ronnie, the cheerleader, today. |
|---|---|
| MA: | Oh, how is he doing? |
| Erik: | Probably not too well. . . . [He does not continue.] |
| MA: | Is he having some difficulties? |
| Erik: | Maybe. I met him coming out of that bathroom down the hall, the one that no one ever uses, and he looked like crap, and when I went to the toilet I could smell the vomit. God, I'd never puke here at school. |
| MA: | Sounds as if Ronnie either has the flu or maybe has some things in common with you. |
| Erik: | I don't think I have much in common with him. |

More dancing. Erik brings up Ronnie because that story encapsulates some of his concerns (e.g., bulimia, having a female problem, masculinity issues). Cheerleaders in the U.S. intercollegiate sport system are the low men and women on the totem pole. They are often considered by other athletes and staff as not really athletes. They are also derided, with the women stereotyped as "blonde bimbos" and the men as "cheer queers." Erik has seen Ronnie in a situation that suggests Ronnie is struggling just as Erik is. He recognizes himself in Ronnie but is repelled by that recognition (his denial that they have anything in common). As for masculinity issues, diving is already a suspect sport that has as its recently most famous icon a gay man. Having a female problem, having something in common with a "cheer queer" like Ronnie, and being a diver all adds up, in Erik's mind, to people thinking he is gay. I do not want to move directly to Erik's anxieties about what others think of his sexuality. He may leave the dance. So I first do some normalizing about the number of males with eating disorders.

| MA: | I wouldn't be surprised if some people on the cheer squad have eating problems. They do have something in common with diving in that they need to look good out there. I used to be surprised by how many male athletes had eating problems . . . not anymore. I was trained that it was primarily a female problem. Well, whoever came up with those statistics did not work for intercollegiate athletics. I see guys in all sorts of sports, and especially the weight class ones, struggling just like you, and I bet there are a lot more out there |
|---|---|

who are in the closet because they think it's a female problem, and they are embarrassed.

Erik: I certainly haven't told anyone else besides you and Dr. Yoshi.

MA: Sometimes the closet is a good place to stay. There can be a lot of worries about what others—such as your teammates and coaches—will think.

Erik: Oh, yeah, if they knew it would be, "Yup, girl problem. It figures; we thought he was a fag."

MA: It can be hurtful when people don't know us and jump to conclusions about who we are.

Erik: And I have enough problems getting a date without people thinking I'm gay.

Erik is a straight guy in a sport where his sexuality is more likely to be questioned than in some other more traditional male athletic endeavors. Erik is also homophobic. Most of us are homophobic, straight and gay people alike; it is a question of parts per million. Erik has a substantial amount of "parts." Erik's homophobia is not in any way a malevolent kind. It has more to do with fears of being labeled and what others (coach, teammates, family) may think. These worries are another burden on top of his anxieties about how others will view him if his eating disorder becomes known.

I am not working with Erik to explore and treat his homophobia or even "cure" his eating disorder. My job is to help a young man who is painfully out of control gain some sense of balance. The treatment of an athlete with an eating disorder is well outlined in a case study presented by Petrie and Sherman (2000), and I will not go into such details here. But over the course of several months, Erik and I work on his behavior; his thinking; and his emotions surrounding food, his body, his diving, and his relationships with others. For his bulimia, we do some log keeping to discover the emotional and situational triggers for his bingeing and purging, but one intervention that seems to help is to schedule a time (well after his medical condition is under control) for him to binge and purge. We start with once a week, on Wednesdays right after the TV show *Seinfeld*. As odd as that sounds, encouraging the client to binge and purge, it is a different way of going about it. Having a schedule gives Erik, at first, a small sense of control, and that sense of control slowly grows to the point of occasionally starting the binge and then saying no. *Seinfeld* becomes a kind of running, but informative, joke with us. I might ask, "How was the *Seinfeld* episode this week?" Erik will sometimes say, "Didn't even have to watch *Seinfeld* this week."

Erik and I work together for more than a year. He doesn't turn into an NCAA champion and is never more than the "second" diver on the squad. His weight does fluctuate, but less and less over the year. His bulimic behavior never goes down to zero, and he stays in the bulimic closet. About five months after we start working together, he sees a nutritionist, but not the one associated with the athletics department. As Erik and I progress through our relationship, we move more and more away from diving and into other realms. We spend a lot of time on his awkwardness with women, his dreams about his future, and the nuts and bolts of studying and getting through his university degree.

Working with Erik pulls up a great deal of countertransferential material for me, and I believe my own struggles help me help Erik. I tell my students that despite my time in psychotherapy, I have never gotten over any of my neuroses; they are still with me. They crop up again and again, as they do with Erik, except now they do not tend to overwhelm; they are not the huge monsters they once were but have evolved into (usually) manageable gremlins. Erik is not cured of his behavior and his anxieties, and there are no wonderful stories about athletic glory and podium visits. I know, however, that he is happier, a state not usually purchasable with some gold currency that hangs around the neck.

> Identify the underlying problem for the athlete. Is it a control issue? Self-doubt? Once you've identified the core problem, other issues will tend to emerge and work themselves out.

Two years after I lose track of Erik, I receive a letter from him. He is working in marketing and has met a woman and fallen in love. He writes that he is so excited and has been telling her all about his diving, his problems, and our work together and that things are going really well for him. Letters such as this remind me why I am in this profession and can keep me going for months.

# Conclusion

In the hypermasculine world of sport, many mental and behavioral disorders are kept firmly in the closet. There are, however, some exceptions. Some forms of narcissism and antisocial behavior may actually find havens for their expression. Eating disorders, especially among men, are not socially acceptable in the sporting arena and thus are kept locked behind those closet doors. These disorders are associated with shame, anxiety, and perceptions of unmanliness. For males (and females) struggling with issues of weight, appearance, eating behaviors, and others' perceptions of their sexuality, the sport atmosphere is hostile. These problems are signs of weakness, and the inimical sport environment often leads people to struggle alone and in silence. The office of the sport psychologist may be the only safe place where athletes can approach these issues and tell, often for the first time, their stories.

Most sports are associated with one or more of the following: weight, appearance, strength, muscularity, and proper nutrition. The majority of sport psychologists have personal experiences with the world of sport, performance demands, and competition. If we, as sport psychologists, take a brutal and honest inventory of our histories, most of us will find traces of these body issues in our own sporting endeavors and recognize the struggles of our athletes as something personally familiar. The athlete with an eating disorder is truly the "other" in sport. But the "other" is also us. That recognition will help us help athletes open those scary closet doors, just as our encounters with these athletes will also help us explore our own closets around eating, weight, appearance, and ultimately, who we are.

# Returning to Self
## *The Anxieties of Coming Back After Injury*

Britton W. Brewer, PhD, and Albert J. Petitpas, PhD

njuries associated with sport participation are ubiquitous, both across sports and around the world (Caine, Caine, & Lindner, 1996). Many sport injuries are minor, requiring minimal treatment and having little effect on sport involvement. Other injuries, however, such as bone fractures and ligament tears, can involve protracted periods of rehabilitation and difficult transitions back into sporting activity. In some cases, severe injury may preclude a return to sport participation.

Depending on their nature and severity, sport injuries may pose considerable physical challenges. Recovering from physical trauma, regaining lost physical functions, and resuming sport-specific physical training are among the tasks that athletes with injuries face. In addition, as researchers and practitioners have suggested in a sizable body of literature (e.g., Bramwell, Masuda, Wagner, & Holmes, 1975; Brewer, 2001; Heil, 1993; Little, 1969; Pargman, 1999; Williams & Andersen, 1998), psychological factors may play an important role in the sport injury process. From a biopsychosocial perspective (Brewer, Andersen, & Van Raalte, 2002), psychological factors are thought to influence not only the occurrence of sport injuries (Williams & Andersen, 1998) but also the processes involved in healing sport injuries and eventual rehabilitation outcomes (see figure 6.1).

## Psychological Responses to Sport Injury

Psychological variables assume added significance in the rehabilitation proces injured athletes experience dysphoria that hampers their ability to perform in oth of their lives. An estimated 5 to 24% of athletes experience clinically meaningfu

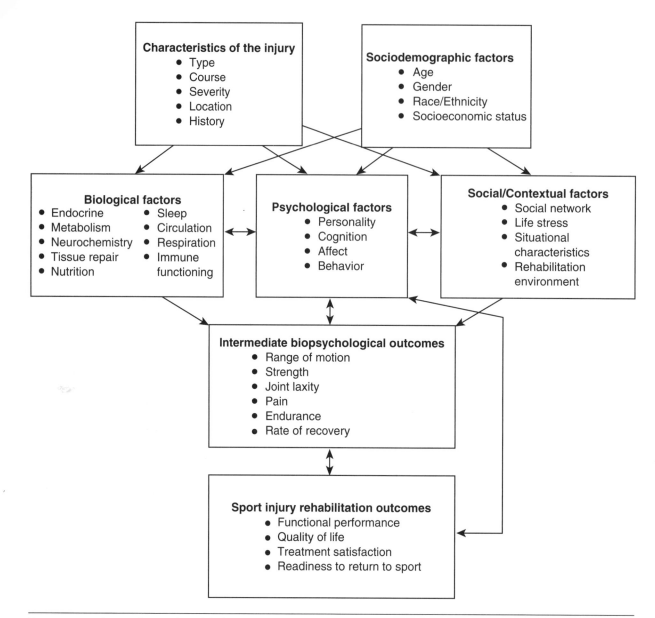

**Figure 6.1** A biopsychosocial model of sport injury rehabilitation.

Reprinted from B.W. Brewer, M.B. Andersen, and J.L. Van Raalte, 2002, Psychological aspects of sport injury rehabilitation: Toward a biopsychosocial approach. In *Medical aspects of sport and exercise*, edited by D.I. Mostofsky and L. Zaichkowsky (Morgantown, WV: Fitness Information Technology).

of psychological distress after an injury (Brewer, Linder, & Phelps, 1995; Brewer, Petitpas, Van Raalte, Sklar, & Ditmar, 1995; Brewer & Petrie, 1995; Leddy, Lambert, & Ogles, 1994). Further, there is evidence that athletes with injuries experience elevations in negative emotions relative to their preinjury emotional states (Leddy et al., 1994; Smith et al., 1993) and in comparison with athletes without injuries (Brewer & Petrie, 1995; Chan & Grossman, 1988; Johnson, 1997, 1998; Leddy et al., 1994; Pearson & Jones, 1992; Petrie, Brewer, & Buntrock, 1997; Smith et al., 1993).

Contemporary models of psychological response to sport injury (Brewer, 1994; Johnston & Carroll, 1998; Wiese-Bjornstal, Smith, Shaffer, & Morrey, 1998) suggest that a variety of factors may contribute to emotional reactions to sport injury. Briefly, these factors may be categorized as personal characteristics, situational characteristics, cognitive responses, and behavioral responses. Personal characteristics are relatively stable attributes, such as age (Brewer, Linder, & Phelps, 1995; Meyers, Sterling, Calvo, Marley, & Duhon, 1991; Smith, Scott, O'Fallon, & Young, 1990), athletic identity (Brewer, 1993), competitive trait anxiety (Petrie et al., 1997), hardiness (Grove, Stewart, & Gordon, 1990), investment in playing a professional sport (Kleiber & Brock, 1992), level of sport involvement (Meyers et al., 1991), and pessimistic explanatory style (Grove et al., 1990).

Situational characteristics include sport-related factors (e.g., time of the season when injury occurs), injury-related factors (which correspond to "characteristics of the injury" and "intermediate biopsychological outcomes" in the biopsychosocial model depicted in figure 6.1), and aspects of the social and physical environments that may vary over time (i.e., "social and contextual factors" in the biopsychosocial model). Among the situational characteristics that have been associated with postinjury emotional functioning in research studies are current injury status (Alzate, Ramirez, & Lazaro, 1998; Brewer, Linder, & Phelps, 1995; Quinn, 1996), injury severity (Alzate et al., 1998; Pargman & Lunt, 1989; Smith et al., 1990; Smith et al., 1993; Uemukai, 1993), impairment of daily activities (Crossman & Jamieson, 1985), level of sport participation (Crossman, Gluck, & Jamieson, 1995), life stress (Brewer, 1993; Petrie et al., 1997; Quinn, 1996), recovery progress (McDonald & Hardy, 1990; Quinn, 1996; Smith, Young, & Scott, 1988), social support for rehabilitation (Brewer, Linder, & Phelps, 1995), and social support satisfaction (Petrie et al., 1997; Quinn, 1996).

Current perspectives on psychological responses to sport injury (e.g., Brewer, 1994; Johnston & Carroll, 1998; Wiese-Bjornstal et al., 1998) ascribe a key role to cognition in influencing emotional and behavioral reactions to sport injury. Injury- and rehabilitation-related thoughts and interpretations have been deemed especially important in mediating psychological adjustment to sport injury. Cognitive factors that have been associated with emotional responses to injury include appraisals of injury coping ability (Daly, Brewer, Van Raalte, Petitpas, & Sklar, 1995), attributions of injury cause (Brewer, 1999b; Tedder & Biddle, 1998), and confidence in recovering fully (Quinn, 1996).

Behavioral responses constitute the most observable, and some would say, most important, psychological component of the sport injury rehabilitation process. Aside from a growing body of work on adherence to sport injury rehabilitation programs (Brewer, 1999a), however, researchers have conducted little formal study of how athletes actually behave after injury. Nevertheless, on the basis of their clinical experience, Petitpas and Danish (1995) identify a number of "warning signs of a poor adjustment" to injury, including becoming dependent on the sports medicine practitioner, boasting about sport or nonsport accomplishments, denying the impact or importance of the injury, displaying guilt and other negative emotions (e.g., anger, anxiety, depression), and withdrawing from social interactions.

# Psychological Intervention

Only rarely do sports medicine clinics have a sport psychologist on site as a member of the treatment team (Cerny, Patton, Whieldon, & Roehrig, 1992; Larson, Starkey, & Zaichkowsky, 1996). Consequently, it is necessary for sports medicine practitioners to make referrals for injured athletes to receive treatment of a psychological nature. Despite the prevalence of emotional and behavioral concerns among injured athletes, referral of these athletes for psychological assistance is far from commonplace among sports medicine practitioners. Sports medicine physicians are likely to have referred at least one of their patients to a psychologist (Brewer, Van Raalte, & Linder, 1991), but the practitioners who typically have the most day-to-day contact with athletes during the rehabilitation process (e.g., athletic trainers) are much less likely to have done so (Larson et al., 1996).

The reluctance of sports medicine practitioners to refer athletes with injuries for psychological assistance is noteworthy in light of the receptiveness of athletes to treatments such as counseling, goal setting, and imagery during injury rehabilitation (Brewer, Jeffers, Petitpas, & Van Raalte, 1994) and the growing body of evidence supporting the use of psychological interventions in the prevention and treatment of sport injuries (Cupal, 1998). Although sports medicine practitioners have acknowledged the importance of psychological factors in the rehabilitation process (Francis, Andersen, & Maley, 2000; Gordon, Milios, & Grove, 1991; Larson et al., 1996; Wiese, Weiss, & Yukelson, 1991), they are unlikely to make more referrals to sport psychologists and other mental health practitioners until they overcome the challenges of identifying the athletes for whom referral is most appropriate (Brewer et al., 1995) and become more comfortable with referral practices (Brewer, Petitpas, & Van Raalte, 1999).

# Working With Injured Athletes

Many challenges confront sport psychologists in working with injured athletes. As shown in figure 6.1, multiple factors can influence psychological responses to sport injury, and these responses, in turn, can affect biological functioning, the social environment, and ultimately, rehabilitation outcomes. From a practical standpoint, it can be difficult for sport psychologists not only to delineate the presenting concerns of injured athletes but also to identify the possible sources and potential consequences of the concerns. Consequently, it is vital for sport psychologists to gain a solid understanding of athletes with injuries and their perceptions of the injury situation before intervening. Petitpas and Danish (1995) present a framework for psychological intervention with athletes who are injured. The framework consists of four interdependent and potentially overlapping phases:

- Rapport building
- Education
- Skill development
- Practice and evaluation

## Rapport-Building Phase

The main task of the rapport-building phase is listening carefully and nonjudgmentally to athletes while they describe their injuries, the personal meanings they ascribe to the injuries, and any associated issues. Such an approach can enable sport psychologists to simultaneously build rapport with their clients and gain valuable information about likely treatment focuses. Petitpas and Danish (1995) advise sport psychologists to make every effort to help injured athletes feel understood and accepted in initial contacts.

The main task of the rapport-building phase is listening carefully and nonjudgmentally to athletes while they describe their injuries, the personal meanings they ascribe to the injuries, and any associated issues.

As athletes with injuries discuss their situations with sport psychologists, themes pertaining to emotional disturbance, identity loss, separation and loneliness, anxiety, and loss of confidence may emerge (Petitpas & Danish, 1995). Although more severe injuries are generally associated with more extreme emotional responses (Alzate et al., 1998; Pargman & Lunt, 1989; Smith et al., 1990; Smith et al., 1993; Uemukai, 1993), that is not always the case. A relatively minor injury, if interpreted in such a way that the athlete perceives a major threat to her self-worth, can elicit a strong negative emotional response. Conversely, athletes who have sustained serious injuries may experience little emotional disturbance depending on their sport career goals, the time of the season in which the injuries occur, and other factors (Brewer, 1994; Johnston

& Carroll, 1998; Wiese-Bjornstal et al., 1998). Only by exploring athletes' injury-related cognitions can sport psychologists understand the basis for the presence or absence of emotional distress in injured athletes.

For many athletes, sport participation is a central source of self-worth and self-definition (Brewer, Van Raalte, & Linder, 1993). Injuries, particularly when they are long lasting or career ending, can threaten the self-identity of athletes. The temporary or permanent loss of identity resulting from injury can contribute to the emotional difficulties encountered by some athletes (Brewer, 1993; Sparkes, 1998). Although sport psychologists may be tempted to encourage athletes going through an injury-induced transition away from competitive sport to develop new identities and focuses not involving sport, such a tack may be met with considerable resistance by athletes if introduced too early in treatment. Even when confronted with objective evidence contraindicating continued sport involvement, athletes may be reluctant to shed their athletic identities. Accordingly, it is generally best for sport psychologists to assess the extent of identity loss during the rapport-building phase without initiating a treatment based on this assessment.

Because athletes are often isolated from their customary sport environments while they are receiving treatment for their injuries, it is not surprising that injured athletes sometimes report feelings of separation and loneliness while undergoing rehabilitation. Further, the uncertainties associated with receiving medical treatment (e.g., prognosis, potential surgery) and the lack of opportunities to practice important sport skills can lead these athletes to feel anxious and insecure about their current status and future prospects. Exploration of these sorts of injury-related concerns can help sport psychologists identify possible targets for intervention with injured athletes.

As a positive emotional bond develops between sport psychologists and athletes with injuries, sport psychologists can instill a sense of control in and boost the confidence of the athletes by enlisting them as collaborators in the process of identifying treatment goals and planning and implementing treatment strategies (Petitpas & Danish, 1995). Adopting such a collaborative approach enables sport psychologists to solidify the rapport they have built with athletes who are injured and contributes to the development of a working alliance (Brewer, Van Raalte, & Petitpas, 1999) in which the sport psychologists and athletes reach an agreement as to the focus and direction of treatment.

## Education Phase

For sport psychologists to work effectively with athletes who are injured, it is essential that the athletes have accurate information regarding their injuries (Petitpas & Danish, 1995). Although sport psychologists are not typically the ones to impart medical information to athletes (at least initially), they may inquire as to athletes' understanding of their diagnoses, medical treatments, and prognoses. It is vital for sport psychologists to get "on the same page" with athletes in terms of their injury and treatment status to facilitate the setting of appropriate goals for psychological intervention. During the education phase, sport psychologists may need to translate the judgments and prescriptions of medical practitioners into terms the athletes fully understand.

> Make sure both you and the athlete understand the athlete's injuries.

## Skill Development Phase

After identifying treatment goals through collaborative inquiry, sport psychologists and injured athletes can choose from a wide array of interventions to address the athletes' specific concerns (for an extensive list of interventions, see Petitpas & Danish, 1995). In selecting an appropriate intervention, it is important to consider the extant coping strategies of athletes with injuries. Before introducing new techniques, sport psychologists should assess the self-help skills (e.g., goal setting, relaxation techniques, imagery) that athletes already possess and can enlist to enhance their injury rehabilitation (Petitpas & Danish, 1995).

Whether the focus of treatment is on developing new coping skills or transferring existing skills to the rehabilitation domain, formulating a plan for implementing skills and evaluating progress can improve the effectiveness of psychological interventions. It is important to allow sufficient time for injured athletes to acquire proficiency in the desired coping skills and to specify concretely how the skills can be applied toward achievement of treatment goals. The potency of psychological intervention can be enhanced further by identifying barriers to accomplishment of treatment aims and devising ways around roadblocks to goal attainment (Petitpas & Danish, 1995).

## Practice and Evaluation Phase

During the practice and evaluation phase, athletes apply the skills they acquired in the skill development phase to their rehabilitation. Sport psychologists monitor athletes' progress toward achievement of their treatment goals, provide support and feedback, and if necessary, recommend additional skill acquisition. Because rehabilitation often does not progress as anticipated, Petitpas and Danish (1995) recommend that sport psychologists help these athletes develop an action plan in the event that they experience setbacks in the recovery process. Preparing for termination of the counseling relationship is a final task of the practice and evaluation phase. Sport psychologists can facilitate successful termination by reviewing and reinforcing the skills the athletes learned during treatment, affirming their belief in the meaningfulness of the counseling relationship, and discussing ways in which treatment outcomes may generalize to other areas of the athletes' lives (Petitpas & Danish, 1995).

# Identity and Ambivalence: Chris' Story

For injured athletes who seek out psychological assistance of their own accord or who follow through on recommendations to do so, interaction with a sport psychologist can be a productive experience. The case that serves as the centerpiece for this chapter is a vivid example of the issues faced by athletes during injury rehabilitation, the influence of psychological factors on adjustment to injury, and the ways in which consultation with a sport psychologist might be of benefit to injured athletes. In the case of Chris, consistent with both theory (Brewer et al., 1993; Pearson & Petitpas, 1990) and research (Brewer, 1993; Sparkes, 1998), self-identity assumes a primary role in affecting how she feels and acts during her rehabilitation and attempts to return to sport participation.

Chris is an internationally ranked downhill skier who has experienced repeated knee injuries. The cumulative effects of the multiple physical traumas threaten her dream of becoming an Olympic champion. After her latest surgery, her team physician stated that he did not believe she could recover sufficiently to compete at a World Cup competitive level. Chris downplayed this prognosis and came to the United States to seek further medical assistance at a sports medicine clinic specializing in skiing-related injury rehabilitation. After several weeks of rehabilitation, Chris' athletic trainer is becoming increasingly concerned about her emotional outbursts and failure to stay within the limits of the exercise prescriptions.

Although the athletic trainer fears that Chris would be resistant to the idea of speaking to a counselor, he decides to discuss options with the clinic's sport psychology consultant (Albert Petitpas). They consider several strategies to facilitate a referral, finally deciding that Chris might be receptive to speaking with someone about the mental aspects of high-level competition rather than her inability to cope with her physical limitations. During the next rehabilitation session, the athletic trainer waits for Chris to say something related to the psychological aspects of sport in order to introduce the idea of using her downtime to further strengthen her mental skills. Although Chris expresses some hesitation initially, she agrees to meet with the sport psychologist in hopes of improving her ability to stay focused during qualifying runs. The following exchange takes place during the initial consultation.

Albert Petitpas (AP): Hi, Chris. Dave [the athletic trainer] has told me a little about your situation.

Chris: Well [pause], I'm stuck in rehab for a while, and Dave suggested that I work on some of my mental skills while I'm waiting to ski again.

AP: How long till you ski again?

Chris: Probably another month or so.

Although it is extremely unlikely that Chris will ever ski again at a high level of competition, it would be premature to confront her at this point. Instead, the goal is to build rapport and to establish a collaborative working relationship.

AP: Help me understand what you mean by mental skills.

Chris: You know, staying focused and sharp.

AP: I know what that means for me, but I want to be certain that I understand it from your perspective.

Chris: It's being ready to burst from the gate, seeing the flags, being in total control.

AP: How do you know when you are focused and sharp?

Chris: [Pause.] I don't know, it just happens. I'm not thinking about anything else. I'm just ready to go.

AP: That's really helpful. So one thing is there are no distractions. You are there mentally in the moment, ready to do the things you have practiced and perfected.

Chris: Well, I wouldn't say perfected because we are always trying to get better.

AP: OK, then, practiced.

Chris: Sure, I know I can do it, and I can't wait to get out of the gate.

AP: It also sounds as if you are confident, and your energy level is up.

C: Yeah, it's a rush—everything flows, and I'm in total control.

AP: You keep coming back to feeling in control.

Chris: Well, yeah, I just know what to do.

AP: I can imagine that's a great feeling.

Chris: It is, it's a rush. I wish I could be like that all the time.

AP: How often are you in this focused state?

Chris: I don't know, it comes and goes, but I always have my best races when I'm there.

AP: So during rehab, you want to spend some time working on your mental skills so you can be in that focused state more often.

Chris: Yeah, especially during qualifying runs. Sometimes I just start thinking of everything that can go wrong instead of focusing on what I need to do.

AP: How do you try to get back in focus?

Chris: Sometimes I just try to focus harder, but that doesn't work very often. It's almost as if the harder I try the worse it gets.

AP: OK, so trying to force things doesn't work. What else have you tried?

> Repeating words the athlete uses shows you are paying attention.

Chris:  You know, paying attention to my breathing or doing those deep breathe things.

AP:  Such as?

Chris:  Trying to get the air into my stomach. You know, the stuff they teach you at the centers.

AP:  It doesn't sound as if you bought into that stuff.

Chris:  I don't know. If I'm thinking about my breathing, I'm not focused on the count.

AP:  OK, I see. If you are thinking about internal stuff such as your breathing, then you are not as focused on getting ready to burst from the gate.

Chris:  You've got it.

AP:  Has anything worked?

Chris:  Not really.

AP:  It is interesting that you have more trouble getting focused in the qualifying runs than in the actual competitions.

Chris:  Probably because I have less to lose.

AP:  What do you mean?

Chris:  You know, I'm expected to make the finals. It would suck big time if I wasn't even good enough to just qualify. At my level, I'd never forgive myself. [Laughing.]

AP:  It sounds as if skiing is a big part of your life.

Chris:  You've got it.

During this last exchange, Chris has provided an entry point (see Giges & Petitpas, 2000) to explore the strength and exclusivity of her athletic identity, but I believe it is still too early in the counseling interaction—a solid working alliance has not yet been established. On the other hand, even though Chris' comment about not being able to forgive herself was said with a laugh, it still must be taken seriously and evaluated as a possible indicator of potential for self-harm. I choose to avoid confronting the comment directly at this point, but I remain vigilant for other signs of depression. When faced with decisions such as this, I have found it helpful to ask myself whether I am choosing to avoid confronting the client at this point because I am uncomfortable with the confrontation or because I believe it is in the best interest of the client.

AP:  It also sounds as if you put a lot of pressure on yourself.

Chris:  Well, pressure comes with the territory. If I wasn't at this level, it would not matter as much.

AP:  I know some athletes who feed on pressure and others who just learn to cope with it. You sound like a coper.

Chris:  I guess so. Sometimes it's easy, but there are some races when I can really feel it.

AP:  Where do you feel it first?

Chris:  I don't know where I feel it first, but sometimes my hands are shaking, and my mind is all over the place.

AP:  It sounds like what you were talking about before.

Chris:  Yeah, it's the same crap over and over again.

AP:  So you've been battling this for a while?

Chris:  Yeah, but not all the time.

AP:  OK, but if I understood you, it's likely to happen most often when you put a lot of pressure on yourself, like during qualifying.

Chris:  [Pause.] I guess so.

Although Chris' response suggests some agreement with my previous statement, her tone, facial expressions, and body language indicate she is not ready to acknowledge that she may be putting a lot of pressure on herself. I am also fearful that I am setting myself up in the "expert role" by interpreting her behaviors. As a result, I attempt to create a more collaborative relationship by self-disclosing my fear that I am controlling the counseling exchange and stating my intentions to try to understand her situation from her perspective.

AP: I feel as if I'm putting words in your mouth, but I'm trying to understand what you are going through.

Chris: I know, but sometimes I don't know what I'm feeling. How can you?

AP: Well, if you feel comfortable working with me, maybe we can figure it out together.

Chris: OK, if you think it will help.

AP: You would never have made it this far if you did not have good mental skills. Let's see if we can figure out what is getting in the way.

Chris: Sounds like a plan.

AP: What is your schedule like on the days you are here for rehab? Can you come in before or stay for a while after?

Chris: I'm here every day now, but my rehab sessions are on Monday, Wednesday, and Friday.

AP: How about Fridays about this time, and then you have plenty of time to get ready for rehab?

Chris: Ok, I'll see you at 10:00 on Friday.

AP: See you then, and we'll see if we can get a handle on what is going on inside your head.

I believe that this brief contact illustrates how fragile the working alliance can be when working with athletes who are faced with the threat of a career-ending injury. Although I attempt to build some initial rapport with Chris, I am also careful to avoid challenging her beliefs about returning to competitive skiing. Nonetheless, based on one of her early statements, it appears that I have less than a month to develop a working alliance. Therefore, even though I do not want to push Chris too fast at this stage in the relationship, I also feel some pressure to address the possibility that her skiing career might be over. Fortunately, Chris gives me an opening to discuss her current situation, and I decide to invite her to speak about her potential career-ending injury using an indirect strategy.

AP: Hi, Chris, how is it going?

Chris: About the same.

AP: What do you mean? Rehab? Life in general?

Chris: You know. Rehab can be so boring. It's the same old shit. . . . Excuse the French.

AP: Yeah, especially for you. From the look of your knees, this is not the first time you've gone through this.

> You should invite, but you cannot force, clients to self-disclose.

Chris then takes me through a long description of her multiple injuries. Although she provides more information than necessary, I decide to just listen patiently and to use this exchange as an opportunity to shift some of our focus to her current situation.

AP: You've been through a lot. Just to be able to put up with all that shows how much you love skiing.

Chris: It's all I've ever done.

In efforts to build rapport with Chris, I try to let her know that I appreciate the importance of skiing in her life. By identifying some of the experiences that I believe she is likely to have through skiing, I attempt to validate their importance and, by so doing, foster some understanding of the strength of her athletic identity.

> AP: I can only imagine what it is like to be at that level of excellence, competing for World Cup points, traveling the world, meeting new people, skiing the best mountains.
>
> Chris: It's the best.

Chris is looking up and seems to be thinking about some of her skiing experiences. I decide to remain silent and allow her the space to focus on these memories. After a brief time, she looks directly at me, and I take this shift in attention as a cue to continue.

> AP: It looked as if you were enjoying something.
>
> Chris: Pardon me?
>
> AP: It looked as if you were thinking about something, and your face just seemed to relax.
>
> Chris: Oh, yeah, I was right there, and it was wonderful.
>
> AP: I could tell. Your whole body seemed to just release.
>
> Chris: What do you mean?
>
> AP: You seemed to just let yourself go. It's the first time I've seen you relaxed or peaceful. You were so into the memory.
>
> Chris: I guess I was. There is nothing better in the world than coming down a run and feeling the wind and the snow, the speed and the rush.
>
> AP: I think that is the best thing about being an athlete. You have experiences where everything is perfect, and you are perfect, and nothing else can ever match that feeling. Although I'm not a skier, I can remember having similar experiences with my sport. There is nothing like it.
>
> Chris: What sport?
>
> AP: Basketball, but even though that was years ago, I still can be driving in my car today, and a memory of a particular shot or move will come to my mind and bring a smile to my face. That's one great thing about sports that some people will never experience.

Although this type of self-disclosure, by discounting the uniqueness of an athlete's experience, can interfere with efforts to build rapport, I think there is enough trust and understanding built at this point in the relationship that Chris will believe I am identifying with her feelings at the moment. Nonetheless, there is always some danger in disclosing personal sport experiences in efforts to "prove" yourself to an athlete client. In the previous exchange, I believe that my self-disclosures came out of the flow of the interaction. Rapport is typically built at a mutually regulated pace between the athlete and sport psychologist. Attempting to force rapport by listing your sport involvement early on in the helping relationship can impede the development of trust.

> Self-disclosure in order to prove yourself serves the needs of the psychologist rather than the needs of the athlete.

> Chris: I don't know if it's that zone thing, but it's a great feeling.
>
> AP: Maybe so. When is the last time you had that feeling?
>
> Chris: Probably last March, a couple of days before this last crash.
>
> AP: Are you ever able to recapture that moment?
>
> Chris: Not since I've started rehab, that's for sure.
>
> AP: You seem really down again.
>
> Chris: When will this crap be over? I just want to get back on the slopes.
>
> AP: What would you do if you could never ski again at that level?
>
> Chris: I don't know. I don't even want to think about it.

I do not want to say anything at this point, so I lean forward in my chair and allow the silence to continue. Chris is looking down at the floor and seems to be getting upset. After 20 or 30 seconds, I continue the dialogue.

|       |                                                                                                                                          |
| ----- | ---------------------------------------------------------------------------------------------------------------------------------------- |
| AP:   | That thought seems to be pretty scary.                                                                                                   |
| Chris: | I don't want to talk about it.                                                                                                          |
| AP:   | OK, let's move on, but maybe we could talk about a contingency plan for later on when you are ready to retire.                            |
| Chris: | What do you mean, contingency plan?                                                                                                      |
| AP:   | Oh, it's just something that I've done with athletes who want to use their off-season time to plan for their next career.                |
| Chris: | I'm not ready to quit.                                                                                                                   |
| AP:   | I can tell. [Brief pause.] It's something that these athletes did to help them down the road. Just like our using your downtime to practice some mental skills for when you are back competing. Let's get back to that. |

Chris is becoming upset, and I sense that I may have introduced the idea of planning for retirement prematurely. I decide to back off and spend the rest of the session talking about her precompetition rituals. I ask her to use imagery to recall her feelings and thoughts as she is getting ready for a specific event. Although Chris appears to be relieved that we changed the topic, she does not have a lot of energy for the imagery exercise, and she seems to be somewhat emotionally detached throughout the remainder of the session. I interpret her reactions as signs that she is "shutting down" in an effort to ward off the anxiety resulting from my "threats" to her athletic identity. The session ends on time, and Chris leaves to get ready for her rehabilitation appointment.

Later that day, I wonder how Chris has reacted to our session, so I speak with her athletic trainer. Dave says she really pushed herself, and he had to tell her repeatedly to slow down or stop. Dave's comments reinforce my beliefs that Chris is feeling threatened, and her overdoing rehabilitation is a further indication of her fear and anxiety. Although I am not scheduled to see Chris until the following Friday, I make a point to come into the clinic on Monday to see how she is doing during her rehab.

|        |                                                                                                                          |
| ------ | ------------------------------------------------------------------------------------------------------------------------ |
| AP:    | So this is what you do during rehab.                                                                                     |
| Chris: | Yeah, this and a bunch of other exercises, mostly Cybex stuff.                                                           |
| AP:    | How is it going?                                                                                                         |
| Chris: | Ok.                                                                                                                      |
| AP:    | You don't seem to be saying that with a lot of enthusiasm.                                                               |
| Chris: | I just can't seem to get over the hump. No matter what I do, my range of motion stays the same. Then if I try to push it, Dave butts in and tells me to ease off. What's his problem, anyhow? |
| AP:    | Maybe he is afraid you will push too hard and not allow your body to heal properly.                                      |
| Chris: | What, are you taking his side, too?                                                                                      |
| AP:    | Who else is on his side?                                                                                                 |
| Chris: | Everyone.                                                                                                                |
| AP:    | Everyone?                                                                                                                |
| Chris: | What's the matter? Can't you listen, either?                                                                             |
| AP:    | Can we talk about this after your workout?                                                                               |
| Chris: | No. I'm sick of you and everyone else getting on my case.                                                                |
| AP:    | Ok. [Pause.] I'll check on you later in the week.                                                                        |

I pause for a moment to see if Chris would change her tone and reconsider my offer for a meeting, but she ignores me and continues her exercises. As I walk away, I wonder if she is displacing her frustration and anger onto me as part of her denial and defensive system. I notice that Dave is working his way around to Chris' exercise station, so I go to my office. I sit down in my chair, worried that I have overstepped the boundaries of our professional relationship by initiating contact before our scheduled meeting. I also wonder if Chris will come for her appointment on Friday. I see Chris on Wednesday and say a quick hello, but I do not stop to try to strike up a conversation. When I arrive at my office on Friday, there is a note from Chris stating that she had a conflict and would see me next week.

> Initiating contact with an athlete outside of a scheduled appointment is best done after a solid working alliance has been formed.

As part of my work, I meet with a colleague periodically to discuss cases and to gain feedback and suggestions. After describing the situation to my peer supervisor and sharing my fears and concerns, I feel some reassurance that I have not destroyed the working alliance. We both believe that Chris' behavior over the past week and her note to me about rescheduling the appointment are indications of her fear and ambivalence. Nonetheless, she continued to initiate some contact, so it appears to us that at least a part of Chris wants to continue to meet with me. I do not see her again until the next Friday.

AP: Hi, Chris.

Chris: Hi. [Looking away.]

AP: How are you doing?

Chris: I don't know.

AP: I was thinking back to last week, asking myself what I could have said to show you that I was trying to be on your side.

Chris: Probably nothing.

AP: Maybe so, but you seemed to be sitting on so much emotion . . . anger . . . sadness. I just did not know what to say. I'm trying to be helpful, but I'm not sure what you really want. Maybe you don't even know yourself.

Chris: I'm not angry with you, but nobody believes me.

AP: About?

Chris: About getting better. They just keep telling me I'll never ski again. Shit! I've heard that for the last five years, but every time I made it back. Now they are telling me it's over. Well, it's not—I'll show all of them.

AP: I'm not a medical person, so I don't know how bad your knees are, but I *am* concerned about how hard you are pushing yourself, both mentally and physically. I've always believed that you need to allow yourself to heal and get stronger. You can't push it or force it to happen. I'm just afraid that if you keep pushing beyond your physical limits and keep bottling up your feelings, you are not going to have enough energy to get better.

Chris: What do you mean?

AP: What I'm trying to say is I don't know if you will ever ski again at a highly competitive level, but I'm afraid you are using up so much emotional energy that you are not giving yourself any chance of making it back.

Chris: That's crazy. You have to push yourself, or you'll never get to the top.

AP: Oh, I agree, but there is a big difference between working smart and grinding. Even after a daily workout, your body needs to recover both physically and emotionally. You need to recharge the batteries. But emotional recovery takes a lot longer than physical recovery. I'm just afraid you are not putting enough into your emotional recovery, and as a result you're not psychologically ready to get the most out of your physical workouts.

Chris: I don't know.

> AP: Maybe you are different, but many of the athletes that I've worked with talk about peaking at the right time or planning their workouts so they are physically and mentally on top of their game for the major competitions.

> Chris: I understand that, but what does that have to do with my rehab?

> AP: It's the same thing. If you are having trouble controlling your emotions during a competition or rehab, you are not getting the most out of your efforts. [Pause.] The other day when I talked to you during your workout, you seemed to be grinding, and it didn't take much to set you off. At least that is what it felt like to me.

> Chris: I said I wasn't angry with you, but it's hard sometimes.

> AP: I can only imagine what you are going through. [Pause. Chris is looking down at the floor.] Maybe it's because you are in this alone. [Pause.] Maybe just having someone to talk with will help you, no matter what happens with the rehab. [Pause.] Maybe that is how I can help.

> Chris: Being down here [in the United States], I really don't know anyone.

> AP: Well, maybe I can help out for a while.

Although I find myself doing most of the work in this session, I believe it is important to try to re-establish our working relationship as quickly as possible. Chris has apparently established her own personal recovery date (Petitpas & Danish, 1995), the date when she believes she will resume competition, and it is only three weeks away. I am not sure how she will react if she does not reach her personal goals, and I want to make sure I have established myself as one of her support people. During the remainder of the session, I continue to reinforce my availability and eagerness to be part of her support team, and I also receive her permission to speak with Dave in order to get a better handle on the physical part of the rehab process.

> Often, you may be one of only a few support personnel an athlete has. Take care to foster that supportive relationship.

When I meet with Dave, I learn that Chris has had a "bad week." She had several emotional outbursts, and she left the gym in the middle of one of her workouts. Dave even questions whether the counseling is doing any good. Although I feel myself getting a little defensive, I choose to ignore Dave's comment and keep my focus on Chris' situation. I continue my discussion with Dave and learn that Chris is planning to return home in a month. She is also well behind her own estimates of where she should be in her rehab. As I leave the meeting with Dave, I wonder if Chris has used me to get a status report so she would not have to hear it directly. My next contact with Chris occurs on Monday when she comes to my office.

> Chris: Hi. . . . I got here early, and I was just curious what Dave had to say.

> AP: Well, he said you were doing well by most standards, but far behind by your own.

> Chris: Yeah, that sounds like him.

> AP: How would you rate your progress?

> Chris: Shitty! [Pause.] What do you expect when no one really helps you?

> AP: I don't know what happens between you and other people. I sense that there are people who are trying, me included. [She does not respond.] I know that skiing is your life, and now there is a possibility that you will never compete again. [She appears to be on the verge of tears but does not respond immediately.]

> Chris: [After about 20 seconds.] Fuck you!

*[I say nothing, but move my chair closer to hers. After a few moments of silence, she begins to cry and leaves the office.]*

After Chris leaves, I sit in my chair wondering if I should go out and look for her, but I decide to stay put. I think about Chris' comment and Dave's earlier statement questioning whether the counseling is doing any good. I begin to replay the significant events involved in my work with Chris. Did I push too fast? Did I fail to reach out to her? Was I insensitive to her feelings? Did I let her down? With no clear answers to any of these questions, I begin to second-guess and wonder about my own competencies.

Later that day, I learn that Chris left the clinic immediately after our interaction, and she failed to show up for her rehab session. I know that I may have opened an emotional floodgate, so I call her apartment. She is not there; I leave a message on her answering machine, stating that I will be in the office the next day if she wants to talk. Otherwise, I will see her on Friday. I also leave my pager number to make certain she has a way of contacting me should the need arise.

> When needed, contact your athletes to let them know you are available at any time.

When I arrive at the office, there is a message from Chris on my answering machine received at three in the morning: "Sorry I was such an asshole. I'll see you Friday, if not before." Although I continue to be very concerned about Chris in her present emotional state, her message offers some relief. Later that day, I peek into the gym area to see if Chris is there. We make eye contact, so I go over to her workout station. She says she is really tired and does not want to talk right now. I ask if she is OK, and she reassures me that she is fine, but she is tired from being up most of the night. She then says, "Don't worry, I'll see you Friday." I see Chris again on Thursday to say hello, and the following exchange takes place on Friday during a regularly scheduled meeting.

AP: Hi, Chris.

Chris: Hi. [Silence.]

AP: It seems as if you had a rough week.

Chris: Yeah. [Silence.]

AP: I can only imagine what you have going on inside. [Chris remains silent.] I worked with another athlete who was in your situation, and he described it as an emotional roller coaster.

Chris: What happened to him?

AP: He was in a different sport, and he tried rehab, but he never made it back all the way. He said he got a courtesy tryout for the national team, but he didn't make it.

Chris: What did he do then?

AP: He went back to school and finished his accounting degree. He then tried to start a small printing business, but his heart was never in it. Now, he is running a gym and working with young kids. He says it doesn't give him the high that he got from competing in front of thousands of people, but he is still connected to a sport he loves, and he enjoys the little things that happen with the kids every day.

Chris: Does he still miss it?

AP: Do you mean the big-time competition?

Chris: Yeah.

AP: I'm sure he does, but at least he has something that most people will never know. He knows what it is like to work hard and achieve spectacular things. It is like when you described the rush you got from competing in World Cup competitions. [Pause.] Do you realize how few people will ever know that feeling?

Chris: It still must hurt him.

AP: Sure it does. Even years later, he still has some regrets, and he gets a little down every once in a while. On the other hand, the last time I spoke with him, he was joking about how smart he was to take early retirement. [Pause.]

> It looks as if he is making the transition from one part of his life to another. Maybe he will find something else that will give him as much enjoyment as his sport. Maybe he won't. At least he has learned to cope with his emotions much better, and he is open to whatever will happen.

Chris: What's his name?

AP: I can't tell you because of confidentiality, but it sounds as if you two have at least a few things in common.

Chris: Yeah, but I'm not ready to give up yet.

AP: I'd be very surprised if you were. [Pause.] I think, at some level, he knew he wasn't going to make it back to the national team, but he owed it to himself to give it his best effort, and he probably would have felt worse if he hadn't at least tried.

Chris: I'm going to prove everyone wrong.

AP: I hope you do, but in any event, I'll do whatever I can to support you.

Chris: Do you really think I can do it?

AP: It sounds as if the odds are against you, but I'll do what I can to help you manage your emotions so you'll be able to give it your best shot.

Chris: That is all I want.

It is not until this point in the helping relationship that I believe a working alliance is established with Chris. During the remainder of this session and the next two meetings, I work with her to develop her ability to manage her emotions by using the stress management strategies I described previously in *Doing Sport Psychology* (Petitpas, 2000). Skiing has become a central part of her identity, and the last injury threatens her sense of self. As a result, I do not challenge her behavior as denial of the reality of the situation but instead focus on developing a supportive working alliance. During this process, I use several indirect strategies to allow us to discuss the possibility of her never skiing again without causing her to become overly defensive. In particular, the information about contingency plans and the story about the other injured athlete provide her with information without forcing her to confront the overwhelming medical evidence against her full recovery. Although I fabricate some of the information about the other athlete, I use his story to educate Chris about what might happen to her, thereby normalizing some of the strong emotions and confusion she is experiencing. In the end, I believe that my support and some of the stress management skills she learns enable her to work through this forced transition reasonably well.

Chris is not able to gain sufficient stability in her injured knee to ski at a competitive level. She returns to her home, and I continue to have telephone contact with her on a weekly basis for about 6 months. I still receive e-mails from her periodically some 18 months later. Chris has had some emotional ups and downs over the months, and she sometimes talks about giving competitive skiing another try. Nonetheless, she is much more realistic about her situation, and she has begun to invest a lot of energy into her graduate program (exercise science), a new relationship, and her part-time job as a ski instructor. Although the consulting relationship did not facilitate the outcome that Chris desired, I believe I was able to become a part of her support system at a time when she was feeling confused and abandoned.

# Summarizing Chris

Chris' case highlights important aspects in the process of psychological adjustment to sport injury, the influence of self-identity on athlete behavior, and the provision of psychological services to athletes with injuries. Chris clearly demonstrated some of the difficulties that athletes can encounter in adjusting cognitively, emotionally, and behaviorally to injury. She experienced noticeable psychological distress that, consistent with models of response to sport injury (Brewer et al., in press; Wiese-Bjornstal et al., 1998), was influenced by personal, situational (or injury-related), and social and contextual factors. In particular, Chris' emotions and behaviors seemed to be affected greatly by her pattern of self-identification with the athlete role, her medical status, and her interactions with the sport psychologist and members of the sports medicine team.

Chris' situation vividly illustrates some of the beneficial and detrimental effects of identifying strongly with the athlete role (Brewer et al., 1993). Although Chris' strong and seemingly exclusive self-identification as an athlete undoubtedly contributed to her tenacious approach to rehabilitation and her ability to persevere despite challenging physical and psychological circumstances, it appeared to exacerbate her negative emotions (Brewer, 1993) and leave her unwilling (at least at first) to consider options outside of sport (Pearson & Petitpas, 1990).

Providing psychological services to injured athletes requires a clear understanding of the meaning that athletes place on their injuries. As exemplified in Chris' case, athletes who have a strong and exclusive identification with their sport personas can become defensive when faced with any threats to their continued participation in sport. Much of the case example illustrates the difficulties that can arise when a sport psychologist attempts to build a working alliance with an athlete in a situation similar to that of Chris. Building enough rapport to help an athlete withstand the anxiety associated with the threat of a forced termination from sport can be a difficult and challenging task. Sport psychologists working with athletes who have experienced career-ending injuries are likely to find themselves walking a fine line between supporting these athletes' attempts at gaining a full physical recovery and helping them come to terms with the reality of their situations. Sport psychologists often need to develop fluid, modifiable treatment goals and learn to function in collaboration with, yet autonomously from, sports medicine personnel. The intense emotional reactions that can surface require careful management, and the support of a peer supervisor or colleague can be of enormous help to the sport psychologist.

# Conclusion

Although the literature contains numerous suggested treatment strategies for working with injured athletes (e.g., Petitpas & Danish, 1995), little has been written about the process of establishing a collaborative working alliance with an athlete facing a career-ending injury. This chapter provides one illustration of some of the challenges practitioners must deal with when working with people who face a genuine threat to their strong and exclusive identification with sport roles. Careful consideration of the processes inherent in attempting to establish rapport with athletes facing forced career termination will enable sport psychology consultants to operate more comfortably through the ups and downs that may occur as the counseling relationship evolves.

# On Stage
## *Mental Skills Training for Dancers*

Stephanie Hanrahan, PhD

In sport psychology, mental skills help athletes enhance their performance as well as their enjoyment of participation. The same concepts and principles can be applied to many areas of performance. Although the majority of my applied work has been with athletes, I also work with dancers, singers, actors, and business people (I am currently working with a group of accountants). Anyone who is interested in performing can benefit from developing skills of self-reflection, anxiety control, concentration and attention, and self-confidence.

When I first began working with dancers, a few factors caught my attention as being somewhat different from working with athletes. Generally speaking, their concept of personal space is less obvious. Greeting each other with hugs and kisses, although commonplace among dancers, would be fairly rare for most sports teams. Touching seems to be part of the communication system for some dancers. At first it was rather disconcerting to have the hand of someone I did not really know on my arm when speaking. Whether due to my increased involvement as a psychologist with performing artists or my own personal participation in Latin dance, I no longer find the touching to be strange or uncomfortable. My expectations regarding personal space, however, do vary depending on the performance area of my clients.

> Personal space may be less traditionally defined when working with dancers.

Another notable difference with dancers is their incredible physical flexibility and their tendency to stretch. Particularly when conducting a session after a class or a rehearsal, it is fairly status quo to see dancers stretching during that time. I will never forget the time I was speaking to a dancer who, very casually, while talking, placed his foot behind his head.

Athletes in team sports sometimes need to adapt to different-size playing fields (e.g., baseball, Australian rules football), but most sports have regulations regarding the competitive arena. Although many athletes must contend with environmental changes, few have to adapt to different performance spaces to the same degree as dancers on tour do. Gymnasts with a choreographed routine always perform in the same-size space. The same is not true for many dancers. The size, surface, and in rare cases, slant of the stage as well as the presence, absence, or location of wings and curtains are constantly fluctuating. The audience may be far away or extremely close, on the same level as the dancers or above or below stage level. Variations in lighting and sound can influence the feel of the piece as well as create situations where it is difficult to hear the music or see marks on the stage. Although these changes can be quite off-putting to novices, requiring cognitive and behavioral adjustments, experienced dancers tend to take them in stride as evidenced by the following quote from a series of interviews I did with dancers:

> On some tours we never know where we are going to dance . . . or how big it would be. It could be half the size of this room or across stage could be like four times as big as this room. You take your body and the space and just do what you can. You're given a routine and you have to put it in different spaces. You just have to do it automatically. After . . . the first few times you . . . think, "Oh, yes, this is going to be OK, this will be cool." You have to do it a few times as soon as you get there . . . [to] get [your] mind used to it. (This quote has not been published elsewhere, but a summary of the interviews can be found in Hanrahan, 1996.)

One area in which I see no differences between athletes and dancers is in their competitiveness. I naively assumed that because most dancers do not regularly take part in competitions (the exception being ballroom dancers), they would not be competitive. I was definitely wrong. Although structured competitions are not the normal forum for dancers, they are almost continually competing for roles. Before obtaining employment, they are competing for jobs. In some instances, their fear of being replaced by an understudy forces them to dance when medically they would be advised to rest. I say "would be" because some dancers do not even take the steps of having their various ailments medically evaluated.

The previous observations give people familiar with sporting environments a glimpse into the dancing milieu as a brief introduction to this chapter. The structure of the rest of this chapter is somewhat different from that of the other chapters in this book. Rather than take the readers through a single session or a series of sessions from start to finish, I instead provide a series of snapshots from sessions with a dancer. The dancer in this chapter (let's call her Tracy) is an amalgamation of about 12 dancers. I have selected topics that a large percentage of dancers with whom I have worked found to be important. My aim is to familiarize readers with some of the issues in the performance area of dance while at the same time providing some insight into the way I practice.

# Why Do You Dance? Tracy's Story

Asking people why they do what they do is a useful method of getting them talking. The responses often provide insights into their connections with the activity—whether, generally speaking, they are content, frustrated, or bored. Through the exploration of why people participate, I have had clients who were despondent in day-to-day participation remind themselves that they have freely chosen to participate and enjoy the activity most of the time. As a result of this reflection, they recommit to the activity. Conversely, I have had clients who realize they are participating only out of habit or because someone else expects them to. Many of these clients end up making the decision to quit or to switch to a different activity. Even when there are no earth-shattering revelations, discussions of the "why" provide useful insights and often easily lead into other topics. Although some of the athletes I have worked with are sometimes slow in providing an answer, and some are unable to answer the question with something other than "Because I do," I have yet to work with a dancer who is unable to come up with an immediate positive response. Enthusiastic responses can be revisited in later sessions when the person's love of dance is temporarily overshadowed by specific issues.

| | |
|---|---|
| Stephanie Hanrahan (SH): | Why do you dance, Tracy? |
| Tracy: | Just dancing. The exploration of movement, of myself. That's probably why I enjoy it the most, the exploration in movement. Finding out more about my own body. I think that's why I like contemporary best. One of the main qualities of contemporary dance is that you get to move around a lot in an unrestricted manner, and I find that exhilarating. I just like jumping and traveling across the floor as much as I can. I also like the performance side of it. |
| SH: | When you say the performance side, what do you mean? |
| Tracy: | I suppose it is quite a thrill to get up in front of people and do something and have them enjoy it. If they really enjoy it, you know it, from the applause, from the reaction. There's also a down side as well. If you're trying to express something and they don't react to it. |
| SH: | So you take a chance with it, with your performance? |
| Tracy: | Oh, yes. It's a big chance, a big risk you take. I enjoy it. |
| SH: | When the risk pays off, what does it feel like? |
| Tracy: | Well, that's actually really weird. My best performance I don't remember at all. I remember beginning it, I remember a blur, and I remember getting up off the floor afterward, because I finished on the floor. I can't remember any of the performance. |
| SH: | Why do you know it was your best performance? |
| Tracy: | I think because it touched so many people. They had never seen me dance before, and afterward I was just shaking, I was shaking like this. [She shakes.] I mean, uncontrollably, and it really freaked me out afterward. I stood up and I thought, *Holy shit, what did I just do? What am I doing here?* That's all I remember. Well, no, not exactly. I don't remember *how* I did it; I just know that I did it. |
| SH: | Did you get the shakiness from muscle fatigue or from emotion? |

It probably would be better to just ask what the shakiness is from rather than provide my ideas of what it might be. In this case I am lucky—my narrow interpretation of the shakiness does not confine the dancer to the same interpretations.

| | |
|---|---|
| Tracy: | I don't think it was muscle fatigue. No, I definitely don't think it was muscle fatigue. It may have been emotion and more possibly adrenalin. Because I don't rely on that feeling, but I always know it's there, especially when I'm nervous. Afterward I was given a lot of respect. I think that is why it was my best performance. |
| SH: | Because of what happened after the performance? |
| Tracy: | Yes. But that's the only time I've completely forgotten an entire section of five or six minutes, where I just can't remember anything, anything at all. I remember starting, and I remember getting hassled. A couple of guys in the third row started yelling out something, and I remember a girl in front of them turning around and telling them to shut up. Then everything went blurry, and I don't remember the rest of it. |
| SH: | You were on automatic pilot. |

Tracy: Yes, everything just clicked without my really trying. Sometimes performances feel really good, and you feel as if you've just woken up after a really good sleep, and you just want to go on and do it, and then you realize that you have already done it. You've already done the performance. Because most of the time after a performance you're so concentrated on the one thing that it sort of wears out your mind and body at the same time, so you walk off and think, *I'll have to do it again tomorrow night.* But sometimes it just works and you don't feel so stuffed, and that's when performing is really, really nice.

SH: Do you ever try to recreate that feeling?

Tracy: Yes. You know, you do try to recreate it, but the feeling of it, I think. Well, for myself, if I lose it afterward, I try to recall it—like actors when they're doing method-type stuff. They recall different events in their lives. In this I try to recreate it as a feeling.

From this brief dialogue, I begin to form a picture of this person in my mind. Since I have a strong research background in motivation, I automatically think in terms of particular motivational theories. I believe that Tracy has a high level of task orientation but also shows signs of ego orientation (Duda & Hall, 2001). The dancer also appears to be close to the intrinsic motivation end of the self-determination continuum (Ryan & Deci, 2000). She wants to perform well in front of others but also enjoys the exploration of movement. Individuals who give responses related only to ego orientation and extrinsic motivation set off alarm bells in my head. They tend to endure great difficulty when they either experience low levels of perceived competence or fail to receive the recognition from others that they think they deserve.

I ask Tracy if she ever tries to recreate the feeling of a great performance to learn if this feeling can be used in the future during periods of low confidence or high performance anxiety. In a way I guess I am already starting to explore the possible cognitive–behavioral intervention techniques that may be useful for this person.

This dialogue also builds rapport. Because I am genuinely interested in why people participate in their chosen activities, I do not have to put any effort into exploring this area. My sincere desire to understand is usually appreciated by clients. In addition, most people like to talk about good experiences. Sharing previous positive experiences can help lay a foundation for the future exploration of potentially less comfortable topics.

# Injuries

Lack of motivation is rarely an issue for dancers. As one dancer said, "People who haven't got the motivation shouldn't be in the profession." Instead of being concerned about having the motivation to get to class, rehearsal, or performance, dancers often need to learn when to take a break. *Recovery* is a term that has gained acceptance in most sports but still tends to be a foreign concept in the world of dance. The good news is that dancers generally feel that their injuries have no effect on their long-term progress, and many dancers with previous injuries indicate they are now more careful when dancing. They try to use better technique, stretch more, and modify exercise to avoid injury (Macchi & Crossman, 1996).

Tracy: When I sustain an injury, it takes me a bit longer to get over it because once I've got an injury, I don't worry about it, I just keep going, keep pushing myself. A lot of people do that. They get an injury and they think it will go away, so they just keep dancing. If it's not a major injury, I'll just keep going. If I have, like, a sore knee, I don't really worry about it. I'll go and see the physio. Like the other day I had a sore knee because I've been doing a new strengthening program for the last two months. My knee was getting a bit sore, but I kept doing weights, and I kept dancing. I'm not the injured type. Some people tend to exaggerate and complain, like, "Oh, no, I've got a sore knee, I've got a sore knee." And I'm just, "Yeahhh, so?" I don't think about it. I go for it. Pretending to be sick is useless.

SH: What if you have a serious injury and really can't dance?

Tracy: If you can dance on it you will. But if it is completely impossible, what can you do? To some degree it's great. You can just sit down and watch and maybe learn something that way. You can get out and have a rest and do nothing. But after a week of it, it gets really difficult because you really want to get up there and dance. Once you get used to doing it five, six, sometimes seven days a week, and then you have to sit down for a week and do nothing, you basically have to control yourself not to get up there and ruin yourself again or do yourself more damage. Because you just get into so much of a routine, and if its something you're doing well, it's something you want to get up and do. It's frustrating. Also, the longer you're out, the greater the chance that someone else is going to take your position, take your role. When you're not dancing you're getting worse, and everyone else is getting better. Then again, look after your body. It's your living.

SH: What about when you are sick?

Tracy: I tend to push myself too much sometimes. If I'm sick I do keep dancing. The only way it really stops me sometimes is if I'm just about half dead. Everyone who dances is motivated. You don't put your body through that unless you're motivated.

Hamilton (1997) states that many dance teachers encourage their students to keep working in the face of discomfort and pain, and one out of four dancers reported being expected to keep working even with a serious injury. Hamilton also indicates that pain is often associated with progress in the performing arts, especially in overachievers. This ethic advocating personal sacrifice, risk taking, and performing with pain may require a philosophical intervention directed at countering the influences of the prevailing sociocultural climate (Shaffer & Wiese-Bjornstal, 1999). Working in a multidisciplinary environment such as a performing arts medicine center makes it easier to establish a structure where dancers are encouraged to report injuries early and recognize the importance of short-term recovery for long-term gain. Performing arts medicine centers, similar in intent to sports medicine centers, currently exist in more than 20 major international cities (Hamilton, 1997). Emphasizing the sense of personal accomplishment when dancers attain small achievements in terms of healing, range of motion, or strength gain can be helpful in any environment. Goals related to being healthy and injury free should be a regularly included domain in any goal-setting program with dancers.

> As a sport psychologist working with dancers, you'll come across, as in sport, the attitude that pain, personal sacrifice, and risk taking are good and expected.

## Performance Anxiety

Performing in front of others is a basic facet of being a dancer. Whether the first recital of a novice or the thousandth performance of a professional, all dancers have at some time experienced performance anxiety. Just as performing in front of scouts or judges can be anxiety provoking in the sporting world, auditions can be nerve racking for dancers. Unlike some sports where objective measures of speed, strength, and skill are readily available, there are no objective measures in dance. Whether assessing an audition or reviewing a performance, the process of evaluation is entirely subjective. One frustration for many dancers is the inability to know what is expected or desired by the people doing the evaluating. Dancers often take rejection personally because audition personnel rarely give feedback (Hamilton, 1997).

When first working with dancers, I thought that *stage fright* would be the term comparable to *competitive anxiety* in sport. Once again, I was wrong. Stage fright is most commonly defined as anxiety about performing in front of an audience, but for dancers, stage fright refers to a state of being completely frozen and unable to move. Regardless of the terminology, performance anxiety is a common experience for dancers. Just as in most sporting situations, however, nerves can sometimes play a useful role. A complete absence of nerves can result in a flat performance.

Tracy: I get really frightened. I have on full makeup, put on false eyelashes, and do my hair. Everything is perfect, and then it is so exciting that you are nervous. It's weird; I actually find all that nervousness really comfortable

SH: So you know it's right, and then . . . ?

Tracy: Yes. Once you get in there it's fine, but it's the waiting, and you think, *Have I prepared myself for this?* and then, *Right, I've prepared myself for this.* Your heart races just before you dance. It's bad when you get to the point where you can't control your nerves anymore, they just take you over too much. They take you over that anxiety level where it's helpful. There is a point—it's not that hard to reach and control, once you get used to it—where the nerves give you that boost of adrenalin. Once you get out there, and then you just know you're there and you can't do shit about it, you just go for it. That adrenalin is still going and it keeps coming. But it's hard to control all the time.

SH: What happens when you don't control it?

Tracy: The performance sucks. I worry that everything I'm doing is wrong, which makes my performance even worse. But it doesn't happen that often.

SH: When does it tend to happen?

Tracy: I don't know. It happened once when I was really worried about making a good impression.

SH: So who is in the audience affects how nervous you get before a performance.

Tracy: Yes, you could dance a piece of repertoire for five nights. Sixth night comes, a choreographer or someone special, a director of a company, is in the audience. Then you start to think, *What if my three turns don't come off? What if my leg isn't as high as it usually is?* What if this? Or what if that? You start to worry because that person is in the audience. Well, you wouldn't have worried about that the other five nights. That's definitely true—who is in the audience. I constantly make mistakes when people I know are out in the audience. I don't usually get nervous, but the other day . . . well, I wasn't nervous, I just tried too hard. A lot of the time if someone is in the audience or, like, the videotape is on and I know someone important is going to watch, I'll try too hard. Because I try too hard, I tense up a little bit, then I make a mistake from trying too hard to look good.

SH: When you are trying too hard, are you overanalyzing what you are doing? Can you describe it?

Tracy: I think it's just that I probably rush, like I'm trying so hard that I rush it, and I suppose I would rush into what comes next. And I'd rush into the next step, and then I'd do the step wrong because I just rushed into it, and I hadn't done the full step, and I've made a boo boo of it. Trying too hard, I tend to rush it and not do my best. When that happens I probably look too tense, also.

SH: How do you think you could deal with that?

Tracy: With special people in the audience, I don't focus on the step. I focus on the fact that they're in the audience. What I guess I should be doing is focusing on myself and just doing the performance.

SH: How can you do that?

> Tracy: Go through a meditation process before getting on stage. Basically just breathing and focusing. Just concentrating on things. Even just saying your own name over and over again, or focusing on a spot on the wall and trying to see through the wall.
>
> SH: When you say breathing, what type of breathing?
>
> Tracy: Deep breathing. Trying to get a grounding effect, trying to think of being planted to the ground. I'm not going to go out there and dance in the air.

Many dancers or athletes who have had no previous mental skills training have developed effective techniques for controlling anxiety, focusing attention, or enhancing confidence. Early in my career, I made the mistake of thinking I had to teach them everything from scratch. In many instances, sessions with me serve as a reminder to clients of the skills they already have. My role often involves fine-tuning those techniques or helping the client use the techniques in a systematic manner. In the previous scenario, I go on to explore the breathing technique or techniques that Tracy has used in the past—does she have one method she always uses, or does she do a bit of this and a bit of that? I also try to determine when the techniques have been used effectively; when they have been used ineffectively; and when they haven't been used but, in retrospect, could have been. From this exploration of her use of breathing, we develop a plan for her to implement systematically.

> Often, athletes and dancers have already developed their own relaxation practices; you may just need to fine-tune what they've created.

## When Others Are Nervous

Most dance performances involve dancers working or performing with others. Just as in team sports, where the mood or attitude of one athlete can infiltrate a team, dancers can be affected by the people around them.

> SH: How does it affect you if a partner or someone else in a group piece is nervous?
>
> Tracy: It annoys me greatly because it affects me if I'm dancing in a group. I had to do that once. This girl, when she gets really nervous, she dances fast. She does everything a count ahead. And because she was in front, we just had to follow her. That just goes against everything I do because she shouldn't have been put there in the first place. If you can't cope with it, then you shouldn't do it. Because that means the four of us who are behind her cope with that as well, as well as with our performance problems, concentrating on that. And I mean, everyone knows it's because we had this choreographer who hadn't been here before and hadn't worked with us. And like, she's fine in class and everything, she's really good, so that's why she's put in front. As soon as we're on stage she speeds up. All they could say is, "Keep with her," even if we were with the music. The four of us were with the music, and she was out on her own. "Keep with her, she's in front." How annoying. I used to get a bit uptight about that.
>
> SH: What about when you're partnering with someone?

I don't pursue the specific situation of the dancer who danced too fast because we discussed that particular incident before as part of a bigger issue. There had been a lot of interpersonal conflict with that particular dancer, and she is no longer in the country. Generally speaking, Tracy gets along with most people, so I feel it's best to move on after she has her little vent.

> Tracy: It's hard when the guy you're dancing with is just a very negative person. He's very worried about himself, and you obviously haven't got much trust in him.

I had a partner that I didn't trust at all. Then I talked it over with someone, and the reason why things weren't working out was because I had no trust in him. He probably felt that. So the next day I walked in, had all the trust in the world, just let myself go. It worked! Obviously, he found it easier. He sensed I was thinking, *I know you're going to catch me.* So you've got to be strong for yourself so your partner is strong.

[SH remaining silent.]

Tracy: Thanks. Thanks for making me think of that. I need to remember that.

I love it when that happens. All I did was ask a question. The client answers the question and in the process of doing so provides herself with some useful advice. I have had a number of sessions where I felt I haven't done anything. I just listened and asked a few questions. Clients have come to their own realizations that in some instances have had a minor effect on how they approach a particular activity but in others have had a major impact on their attitude toward life. Sometimes I need to remind myself how important the skill of listening is. When I first began consulting, I felt obligated to provide the client with knowledge or solutions, almost forgetting the role of the microskills I had learned in my counseling class (Egan, 1982). The impact of a safe environment brought about through trust and rapport should never be underestimated.

> Let athletes and dancers create their own advice. Sometimes all you have to do is ask a question and listen.

## Self-Talk

Self-talk, or the monologue that runs in our heads, can affect performance positively or negatively. Positive, or constructive, self-talk may aid performance through its impact on self-confidence, anxiety control, effort, mood modification, or attention control (Hardy, Jones, & Gould, 1996). Although there is no agreement as to why self-talk affects performance, there is a general consensus that it does.

Tracy: Last week I had a class, it was a classical class, and I'd probably say it was my best ever because it was the first time I knew I'd done a perfect double pirouette. So it was like, *"Wow, I got it. Great!"* Everything flew after that, and then the next day for some reason I was back to my usual stuff. After that really good class, I'm thinking, *"OK, I can do this,"* and then I start thinking too much about doing it and stuff up.

SH: Did you think much about how you can do it, not just that you can?

Tracy: No, I thought just that knowing I had done it before would make me be able to do it again. But then again, when I couldn't do it, I started thinking a lot about the "how." I think about all of the feedback and comments that teachers have ever made to me. I think, *"Feel the plumb line through the body,"* *"Spot,"* *"Lock ankle,"* *"Brace knee,"* *"Brace hip joint,"* *"Strong control over abdominal muscles,"* *"Don't let the lower back round out,"* *"Firm hold of turnout,"* *"Get full extent of turnout,"* *"Whip arms."* I start thinking so much that I don't do anything right.

SH: So thinking too much about the "how" results in a poor pirouette.

Tracy: Yeah. When I did it right, I wasn't thinking about so many things.

SH: What did you do to do it right?

Tracy: I held my position throughout. I had everything firm and braced.

SH: Do you think it would be useful to focus just on that, holding position or being firm and braced, rather than try to think about every single technical aspect at the same time?

Tracy: It would make it a lot easier.

> SH: Which phrase works better for you, gives you the best sense of what it feels like to do it correctly: "hold position" or "firm and braced"?
>
> Tracy: How about just "brace"?
>
> SH: Does that get the feeling of a good double pirouette across to you?
>
> Tracy: Yeah, I think so. Either that or "hold position."
>
> SH: Well, you can try both "brace" and "hold position" and see which works best for you.
>
> Tracy: I think I like "brace" better—it's shorter.

This is the first time she provides a specific example of when she thought she had done something perfectly. I ask a lot of questions because I believe it is an opportunity to develop a strategy she can use when things are not going perfectly. I use questions as a form of "query theory," encouraging improvement in skill techniques through self-awareness (Hadfield, 1994). Guided questions encourage her to determine what cognitions might be useful.

Some sessions I hold in my office, and other sessions I hold at the client's place of training or performing. It is useful if the client can immediately physically try the skill while using the chosen cue word. If we are in my office (carpeted floor) or the dancer needs to be warmed up and stretched before doing the skill, I work with the client to create a plan as to when and where the cue word could be trialed. Procedures are also put into place concerning the evaluation of the cue word's usefulness. Sometimes my presence at training or class situations serves as a reminder to the client to practice certain techniques. Immediately discussing the process of different techniques or the efficacy of their implementation is often more fruitful than waiting until the next session in the office.

# Self-Reflection (Dealing With Mistakes)

In dance, training diaries or training logs are rarely used. Incorporating regular self-reflection by using a dance diary, however, can be useful (Taylor & Taylor, 1995). Diaries can help dancers monitor their use of various techniques, along with their effectiveness. Self-reflection (best if written) allows dancers to recognize improvement and good performances as well as target specific tasks for future work. The writing process can help the dancer develop a positive approach to dealing with mistakes. Some dancers have a tendency to blow up minor errors into catastrophes. Self-reflection can keep the molehills from becoming mountains.

> Tracy: Like, if you come off stage and you know that you've made a huge mistake and you think, *Shit*, and you're really upset about it. Nearly every time someone will say to you, "It doesn't matter, it doesn't matter." They don't know what you're doing. They don't know anything about the dance. All they see is that dance, they saw it right then and there. They didn't see it before. I usually ask for some sort of reassurance that it wasn't that bad from someone who knows. I usually go to the choreographer and say, "How noticeable was that?"
>
> SH: Do you do anything to try to keep the mistake from happening again?
>
> Tracy: Usually directly after the performance, I come off the stage and think, *Oh, shit,* and go through it. If I'm with a partner I say, "Come here." I never leave it until the next day. I don't know why. I correct it by memory and by using a mirror.
>
> SH: Rehearsing the correct way of doing whatever it was keeps the mistake from happening again.
>
> Tracy: Usually, but mistakes are still going to happen. You get told that all the time in last-minute rehearsals and that sort of thing. Little things go wrong. They

just say ignore that, "Keep going, keep going." Especially if all of a sudden you just go blank. That's a bit of a scary thing to happen. The hardest and yet the easiest way to get out of it is to just keep moving.

SH: So you're doing something, and you don't remember what it is that you're doing. . . .

Tracy: And then you listen. If there is music you listen to it, and while you keep moving you think about what is coming up. Like a place where you can step into what you remember of the rest of the dance.

SH: Do you ever feel as if you have paused forever and in fact it was like half a second?

Tracy: Yes, that's right. But I think because the adrenalin is rushing so fast you think really, really fast during a performance. There is the most ridiculous detail, and when something does go wrong your adrenalin gets hit even harder, and so you're thinking three times as fast as you would normally. And so that's why . . . yes, that seems a long time.

*[SH remaining silent.]*

When I first started applied practice, I was uncomfortable with pauses in dialogue. I now recognize the usefulness of allowing time for clients to gather their thoughts or approach the topic from a different viewpoint. At times my eagerness to break a silence has disrupted a client's chance to determine introspectively the course of the conversation.

> Silence is often useful. Let pauses in the conversation be a time for clients to think about what's being said.

Tracy: Sometimes mistakes really frustrate me. I get really angry with myself, but I try not to let it affect what's going on. You can't let it show. Like during a performance if you make a mistake, you think about it for that instant, then try to block it off and keep going.

SH: You deal with it later.

Tracy: Yeah. After the performance, no matter how wonderfully you danced. After that one little mistake, you just go back to that mistake and think, *Mistake, mistake.* It doesn't matter how great the rest of the performance was. You just think about that little mistake. The audience, they wouldn't even know. But you know. You sit there and punish yourself afterward. Stupid mistake.

SH: Do you ever sit down after a performance and think to yourself about the good stuff?

Tracy: No, you only remember the mistakes, unless it was like that performance I couldn't remember.

SH: You know how you are already completing the evaluation sheets after every class, rehearsal, or performance, noting what mental techniques you used and how effective they were? Well, I think it would be useful to add two open-ended questions to those sheets. I don't want to overload you, though. Do you think you'd have another two minutes to regularly address a couple of questions?

Tracy: Yeah, I've got the time. Especially since we've already talked about deleting the recording of my activation level, since I seem to really have that under control.

SH: Well, the two questions, more really filling in the blanks, are (1) One thing I did really well today was . . . and (2) What can I do better next time? The basic idea is that no matter what happened in the studio or on stage, you would have done something right. You probably did a lot of things right. The idea is to pick the highlight of the day. The second half, what can I do better next time, is to get you thinking about what you can do differently that will result in a better performance instead of continually playing in your mind a mistake or getting sucked into focusing on the negative. OK, so the performance wasn't perfect. Instead of getting down about it, start looking to the future and looking for the positive. What can you do next time to make it even better?

Tracy: Yeah, that probably would be more productive. It's funny—when someone else I'm dancing with makes a mistake I often help him look at it positively, but I never do that for myself. That is, of course, assuming he hasn't dropped me or anything.

SH: So other people can learn from their mistakes but you can't.

Tracy: No, I can, but I don't. If I make a mistake, I just think how stupid I was to have done that.

SH: People who make mistakes are stupid?

Tracy: No. Everybody makes mistakes. I guess you're stupid if you don't do something about it and keep making the same mistake over and over.

*[SH remaining silent.]*

Tracy: And you're saying that if I think about what I can do differently next time instead of just getting down on myself, then I'm doing something about it. I'm not being stupid. I guess I've always been tougher on myself than on other people.

# Concentration and Attention

To perform effectively, people need to pay attention to task-relevant cues and ignore task-irrelevant cues (Moore & Stevenson, 1994). What dancers attend to is somewhat dependent on the style of dance (Hanrahan, 1996). In abstract classical ballet, for example, where the emphasis is on shapes in space, the focus is on technique (e.g., body lines) and timing. In a narrative modern dance intended to evoke emotion, however, the focus is also on the feeling of the movement or the mood being expressed. Although it is essential to concentrate on the task at hand, dancers also must be careful not to attend to every single detail as a separate entity, which may result in the loss of movement fluidity. Consciously attending to every step of execution can lead to overanalysis and a decrement in performance because it can get in the way of automaticity, a quality associated with highly skilled performance (Singer, Lidor, & Cauraugh, 1993). Nevertheless, the opposite extreme (e.g., thinking about what to have for dinner after class or the show) will not allow for top performance.

Tracy: Like if exercises bore me shitless, I just tune out. I usually think about stupid little things that don't really matter to me, like having to go into town or having to buy a new pair of socks. Nothing of major importance.

SH: Do you think you would get more out of classes if you weren't thinking about these other things?

Tracy: Yes, but they just wander in. They come in there when you might be practicing something 100 times, and you just sort of think, *Oh, what are we going to have for dinner? What can I cook?*

SH: What effect can that have?

Tracy: You get all *Come on!* because you usually stop concentrating, and you hear someone say, "Plié, tendu," and then you hear "Now, one, two," and you think, *Oh, God!* That happens a lot to me. I have to learn to be in class in my mind as well.

SH: You feel you should concentrate more during class?

Tracy: Yes, but it depends on the class. See, it's different again in every class I do. In classical, I should think a lot about technique. Also, because I know that I'm never going to be performing in it, that changes the way I dance. So I'm not doing all these flowery things and trying to make it look good, which is bad because it's not what the teacher wants. So you get the ignore treatment. So I work on my technique and do that as best I can. For example, if I'm doing pliés in second, I'll think of using my adductor muscles when I am recovering from the plié. I'll think about actually using a specific muscle, and I feel it tighten when I think about it. When my arms are in second, I have to consciously think about the curve in my arm. On the other hand, when I'm in contemporary, then it's totally different. I work on technique and images. I develop images. If it's something like going down, what it would feel like if you were falling, say. I think of the falling image and apply that, and that really helps.

SH:    You apply imagery to what it should feel like when you dance.

Tracy:    Even what it would look like, what it would feel like. Actually use the falling sensation and really make it fall.

Here it would be easy to get onto the topic of imagery, but I want to get a better understanding of Tracy's focus and thought process while dancing (rehearsals and performance), not just in classes. Sometimes I find it useful to jot down the topic being considered at a particular point in time, to help me stay on topic. It can be useful to note other topics or issues that arise during the discussion to refer to at a later date. If every potential tangent is explored at once, the session can feel as if it has no direction, leaving both parties frustrated or confused.

SH:    What do you think about or focus on during rehearsal?

Tracy:    It depends on whether I know I can pick it up easily. It depends what repertoire, if it's like contemporary or classical. I just concentrate on the step. But years ago when I was a student, I didn't. I wasn't concentrating on the steps. I did rehearsals like a class and didn't worry about it until a week before we went on. I sort of, like, went through the motions, so I didn't have to work. That was my attitude years ago. Professionally, though, you can't get away with that—you have to pick up the steps.

SH:    When you say that you are working on picking up the steps, do you think about it as a list where this follows that follows this, or is it in reference to the music, or is it what it feels like?

Tracy:    It should go, what is this step? What is that step? On two, three in a row. But for me, it's *OK, what's this step and how do I work that step? How do I do that step really well? The next step, how do I do this step really well?* It should be, what's this step? What's that step? What's the next step? And then go back and make it look good. Whereas I go, *What's this step? Make it look good. What's the next step? Make it look good.*

SH:    And you think that makes it harder for you to pick up the steps.

Tracy:    Yes, just thinking about it now, yes.

SH:    So you're thinking so much about how to make it look good that you're not learning the steps.

Tracy:    Yes. Then I'll miss a step. I might do one step really well but then completely miss one. I don't keep it consistent. That would get in the way a fair bit.

SH:    What about during performances, once you have learned the steps?

Tracy:    If it's a classical performance, I think about the technique because it is so refined, and I'm not quite definite on it. I'm not so sure of it. It's different when it comes to something contemporary or jazz or something.

SH:    So then you think about . . . ?

Tracy:    I think about how much energy I can give to them and get back. Play about a bit more with something easy, something like contemporary jazz. That sort of stuff I have fun with. Classical can be nerve racking.

SH:    Because that's not your preference or just because—

Tracy:    [Interrupting.] Because you know that when you're performing, there's going to be somebody out there who knows exactly what you're supposed to be doing and whether or not you're doing it. Basically you fail. You fail as a technician.

SH: That sounds really black and white—success or failure.

Tracy: Well, in classical ballet there is the correct way of doing things, the correct look, the correct line. Anything else is wrong. In more contemporary pieces there is more room for individual expression. Unless it is a well-known piece, no one is going to know exactly what it should look like because they haven't seen it before. In classical ballet, you can be compared with all the great dancers who ever danced that role. Even if your technique is as good, if you don't have the right body, it will look wrong. You fail.

SH: So anyone doing a classical piece that doesn't do it exactly the same way as some previous prima ballerina is a failure.

Tracy: In a way, yes. That probably sounds really harsh. I guess you're not really a failure, but you aren't really good either. I guess I'm more biased against classical ballet than I realized. I don't know if it's sour grapes, knowing that I'll never be a great classical dancer, or just that I really love contemporary.

# Imagery

Imagery is commonly used in dance, but rarely systematically (Hanrahan, 1996). In a controlled study of dancers, imagery resulted in a significant improvement in technique (Hanrahan, 1995), suggesting that systematic use of imagery would be beneficial for dancers. Imagery has been shown to enhance performance of both ballistic movement (e.g., battement) and sustained position (e.g., arabesque) (Hanrahan, Tetreau, & Sarrazin, 1995). Imagery can have many purposes for dancers. In addition to enhancing technique, imagery can be used for learning choreography, building confidence, and calming nerves (Hanrahan, 1996).

SH: Do you ever image yourself dancing?

Tracy: In classes sometimes. If it's an exercise that you have worked on for a while, you can sort of slip into it and start thinking, *Wow, I wonder what this looks like on the stage?* Even sometimes at home, I'll be sitting and thinking about what happened in class, and I'll stand in front of this big mirror we've got and practice doing it and think that this is what they see—the image.

SH: Do you ever image your performance before you go on stage, or in the wings?

Tracy: That's one thing that helped me to relax, actually. Because, I don't know, I can't say I didn't know what to do before I went on, but usually I found after the first night, before I went on, I'd stand out back and think, *Right.* I could actually picture myself, and then the crowd, and I'd just go through the routine in my head.

SH: So you'd see it as if you were watching it on video?

Tracy: Yes, I used to see it as if I were watching from the back.

SH: As if you were standing behind yourself.

Tracy: Yes, I'm standing behind myself, and I could see myself do all these things.

Although I have never come across this imagery viewpoint when working with athletes, many dancers have told me they see themselves from behind when they use imagery. Dancers have also reported using internal imagery, but with no feeling. They see the visual feedback they would normally experience while dancing, but with no sense of kinesthetic awareness during the images (Hanrahan, 1996). Classical, rather than contemporary, dancers use this internal visual perspective. My guess as to why is that classical dancers may define success by how something looks, whereas contemporary dancers may tend to incorporate the feel of the movement when initially learning it. A step in classical ballet is deemed to be correct when it looks right. A step in contemporary dance may be seen as correct when it feels right.

SH: Do you ever do it from the inside? You're inside your body and you feel yourself doing it.

Tracy: No. When I was doing it, no. Usually when I was thinking about it, I was always watching myself from behind. Probably so I could see the steps I was doing.

SH: Do you think trying to feel it instead of just see it would be useful?

Tracy: Yeah, I guess. Well, yes, I suppose it would—particularly for when I get a mental block. I get a lot of mental blocks in class, and I think, *I can't do that.* Then I try not to get those mental blocks for things such as pirouettes on the left side. I'm a lot worse than on the right side, and I know that I can do them just as well because I have done them once. But now I continually have a mental block. Like pirouettes on the left side, *My God, I can't do this.* And I try not to say that, but I think it.

SH: And it only gets worse because you're thinking, *"Well, I know I shouldn't be thinking it, and I'm thinking it."*

Tracy: Yes.

SH: But you've tried.

Tracy: I have tried to think positively and visualize what I'm going to do on the left side before I actually do it.

SH: Well, when is the last time you did a good pirouette on the left side?

Tracy: It was this year at the end of class when everyone had left and I was just standing at the mirror practicing it. I went around and had a good finish.

SH: Can you recreate that moment?

Tracy: I'm trying to.

SH: Not as a pirouette, actually doing it. But can you, like, push replay in your mind?

Tracy: I haven't tried that.

SH: And try to replay what it felt like then?

Tracy: No, I haven't done that—I should try that.

SH: Let's try it now. Are you comfortable in your chair, or would you prefer to lie on the floor?

Tracy: I'm comfortable here.

SH: Close your eyes. Recreate that day after class when everyone had left. See where you are in the room. You've just finished class, so you are probably warm and a bit sweaty. Your muscles feel warm and relaxed. No one is watching. It is just you in the room. You prepare in fourth position to do a pirouette to the left. Left foot back. Left arm in front, right arm to the side. Your weight is evenly balanced on both legs in a demi plié. You feel balanced and in control. When you are ready, you pull up onto the ball of your right foot as your shoulders and arms pull you around to the left. You spot yourself in the mirror, hold the position, and finish cleanly in a perfect fifth position. Feel yourself relax. In your own time, once again prepare in fourth, and feel yourself execute a clean pirouette to the left. [Pause.] When you have finished, open your eyes.

*[Tracy opens eyes after several seconds.]*

SH: Could you feel yourself doing the pirouette?

Tracy: Yeah, that sense of being balanced and in control really worked. I pulled up and, bam, hit it perfectly. I actually want to do a pirouette now.

SH: Well, unfortunately between the carpet and your not being warmed up, that can't happen. But you should be able to replay that feeling, replay that pirouette in your head, anytime you want.

Tracy: Yeah, instead of just trying to think positively, telling myself, *You can do it*, when half the time I don't believe myself anyway. I can instead close my eyes and feel myself doing it the way it should be done. I'm actually feeling it, so I know I can do it, because I know what it feels like. I've done it already.

# Self-Confidence

A wavering level of self-confidence is probably one of the most commonly found psychological performance issues in dance. A lack of self-confidence can lead to good dancers quitting. Failure to believe in one's ability can result in poor performance, failed auditions, and eventually unemployment. Many dancers believe they cannot control their level of confidence (Hanrahan, 1996). It is something they want, but they sometimes think that either you have it or you don't—and too bad if you don't.

Tracy: A lot of emphasis is placed on aesthetics in the dance world these days, particularly for classical. If you're big or bigger, especially for women, I mean that sounds horrible, but if you're bigger you've got to be twice as good as a person who looks stunning. In classical, how well you do is based as much on what you are born with as what you've actually developed. It's such a stupid system. We get really fed up with it. A lot of girls do.

SH: Ballet requires a specific look.

Tracy: Classical ballet does, but in contemporary you've got more leeway with the figure, in what's acceptable and what's not. Whereas classical, it's just so strict, you know, skinny, tall, long legs. This is for classical. If you don't look like that, then you don't even bother with it. You've got no career in this, and often we're discouraged against going on with it. That's another reason why I have that thing about classical—I get no encouragement in that area because, even though I've got a high standard, it's like they can see, she's not going to make it in that area because of her body.

SH: She's never going to be a classical ballerina.

Tracy: No, she's not going to be in ballet, so I've never been put into a classical piece that's gone to performance. I'm always in the contemporary ones. It doesn't worry me because I prefer contemporary anyway. If it was someone else, though, who really loved doing classical and was not put in them because of that. . . . It's just not fair.

SH: So is your opinion of yourself as a dancer determined by comparing yourself with others?

Tracy: There are so many other confident dancers, I get worried that I'm not as good as they are. When I watch other people I think how good they are, and then I start to think of how bad I am. It's not too good watching. To be a professional dancer you need to be confident. After years and years of training it should just be *Bang, have a look at me*, but it's not, it's *Oh, God*.

SH: So your level of self-confidence is not as high as it should be.

Tracy: No. Well, not always. For example, in class if I do something well, I sort of feel proud of myself. But if I do something poorly, I can feel that my self-esteem is lower. I creep to the back of the class and do it there. I'm a person who gets very easily intimidated, and then I start putting myself down.

| SH: | As a dancer? |
|---|---|
| Tracy: | Yes. Other dancers don't even have to do anything. Usually it's me looking at them and thinking, *I wish I could look like them,* or something. And then I think that's why I believe in ability and not just build. Because I look at them and think, *Well, I might not look that good, but I'm a better dancer, and I know that.* And so that's the way I can boost myself up again. It's not stable. I am on a high one minute, thinking, *I'm getting so strong here, this is great.* Next day you walk in and you come home and think to yourself, *Oh, God, I am hopeless, what the hell am I doing in this place?* Really that extreme. High and low, high and low. There's just no middle ground. Sometimes you can just get really down about it. |
| SH: | What do you do in that case—when you're feeling down about it? |
| Tracy: | You have to believe in yourself. That's the only thing I can do. I just believe in myself. I think to myself, *Look. Fine, I don't care what you do. You do what you want to do. You can dance that way, and look how you do. This is what I've got. This is what I can work with.* So I work to my own potential. And if I'm any good, then something will come of it, and that's what I believe in. I just believe that I can make it, and then I will, hopefully. |
| SH: | Are you able to believe in yourself whenever you want to or need to? |
| Tracy: | No. It's probably when I most need to that I can't. |
| SH: | Have you ever systematically tried to work at building your confidence? |

> Be careful not to ask too many yes or no questions because they can stifle the conversation.

With other clients, asking two yes or no questions in a row could bring the conversation to a grinding halt. As has most likely been evident from the dialogue presented, though, this dancer is naturally talkative and independently continues after answering with a yes or no.

| Tracy: | No. I figure it's something you pretty much have or you don't. I never thought of it as a technique or a skill, something you can work on. |
|---|---|
| SH: | Do you have your dance diary with you, where you have been recording your daily highlights and your "what I can do better next times"? |
| Tracy: | [Fumbles in bag, pulls out diary.] Yeah. |
| SH: | I'd like you to randomly open it to any completed page, and then just read to yourself the next four daily highlights. |

*[Tracy reads diary.]*

| SH: | How does reading that make you feel? |
|---|---|
| Tracy: | Good. Yeah, I remember doing that. |

*[SH remaining silent.]*

| Tracy: | I see. . . . If I regularly read these positives that I write, I can give myself a boost in confidence. Writing them has made me less negative about myself after class or a performance, but I tend to go over the "remember for next time" stuff rather than what I did well. |
|---|---|
| SH: | You don't even have to read them regularly, just when, as you put it, you need a boost in confidence. There are a lot of other techniques that can help people develop and maintain confidence. Would you like me to pick one and have you try it, or would you rather I describe a few possibilities and then you pick the one you like the best? |

I call this my "menu approach." I provide a menu of methods for developing a particular skill. For group presentations the menu is fairly lengthy, but in individual sessions I try to limit it to three or four possibilities. Mentioning multiple techniques not only increases the knowledge base of the participants but also, in my opinion, increases their sense of control and motivation because they are the ones selecting the techniques. I also think the menu approach is appropriate because I believe there are very few techniques that are effective for everyone.

Tracy:    Yeah, give me a few. Who knows, I might want to use more than one.

SH:    OK. Let's look at the possibilities of video highlights, positive affirmations, imagery, and attributions. Video highlights is probably the easiest to explain. Basically you begin to create a personal highlights videotape. You probably have a collection of videos from previous performances, and maybe even some from rehearsals or classes.

*[Tracy nods.]*

SH:    Well, instead of watching them through from start to finish, you just pick the best bits. You record onto your highlights tape the sections where you can see or feel that you were doing something really well.

Tracy:    Yeah, I love a video I have of a performance we did a few years ago. I only had a really small solo—like two minutes—but I nailed it.

SH:    Do you think combining that solo with other good bits of past performances or classes would give you a tape that would remind you of your ability and improve your confidence?

Tracy:    Yeah, I like that idea. And I have a friend who has an editing machine—it would be really easy to do. Plus it would be fun going back through all my old videos. If nothing else, I'll have a good laugh.

It is fortunate that Tracy has access to video editing equipment. Before offering this option, I always make sure the company, club, or team has access to video editing or that I can access the equipment for them through the university where I work.

SH:    Well, before starting to edit your videos, do you want to hear about some of the other possibilities?

Tracy:    Yes, but I think I'll definitely be doing the video thing.

SH:    OK. Well, something close to video is imagery. We've previously talked about imagery and how you can push replay in your head and re-experience a good performance. Before, we talked about using imagery in reference to a specific skill—I think it was pirouettes. But you can also use imagery to see yourself performing an entire piece the way you want to.

Tracy:    I think I like the video thing better, but then again, I can't always have a VCR backstage when I might want to watch the video. I think I might start with the video thing and then eventually add in a bit of imagery.

SH:    Are you happy to leave it at that, or do you still want to hear about a couple of other possibilities?

Tracy:    No. I love this. Keep going. It would be so cool to have lots of things I can do to be confident when I want to.

SH:    We've talked about self-talk in terms of technical cue words, but there are other types of self-talk. One of these is positive affirmations. Affirmations are basically positive self-statements. They are statements about your strong points. The affirmations should always begin with *I* and be stated in the positive—what you do rather than what you don't do. So for example, instead of saying, "I don't choke when the pressure is on," you should say, "I maintain my cool under pressure," or something like that. Can you think of a positive affirmation for yourself related to dance?

Tracy:    I'll try. [Pause.]

This time it's the client who is pausing. Once again, 10 or 15 years ago I would have jumped into the pause after about three or four seconds because I would have been uncomfortable. Silences are not to be avoided. Often they are evidence of productive thinking time.

Tracy: Err . . . How about, "I have good extension?"

SH: Yes. Excellent. But this time say it as a statement rather than as a question.

Tracy: I have good extension. [Said in a regular speaking voice as if part of a conversation.]

SH: Good. Now this time say it as if you really mean it—that there is no doubt in your mind that you have good extension.

Tracy: [More forcefully.] I have good extension!

SH: Perfect. Now as far as confidence building goes, it can be useful to create a list of about 10 affirmations. You can then record those affirmations onto a tape in such a way that when you play it back you don't just laugh and think, *Yeah right, as if,* but instead really believe the statements when you hear them. You can listen to the tape before auditions or backstage before a performance. Of course you want to keep track of the tape to make sure it doesn't end up on any public address systems. In addition to recording, you can just read the statements out loud to yourself. Some people like doing this in front of a mirror. You can also write the affirmations on index cards and then leave the cards in places where you will run across them throughout the day—on your bathroom mirror, in your desk drawer, in the cupboard with your cereal bowl, or in your car. Just seeing the cards reminds you on a regular basis of your abilities as a dancer.

Tracy: I like the idea of making a tape, but I don't like the card thing. I mean, I don't live alone, and I wouldn't want other people coming across my cards. They'd think I had the biggest ego in the hemisphere.

SH: That's fine. Often just making the list is a productive exercise. Also, recording the affirmations onto a tape usually takes a few tries until it sounds the way you want it to. That process in itself is useful.

Tracy: OK. . . . What else?

SH: Attributions. This last technique is a bit more complicated, not quite as straightforward as the others, but can be easily incorporated into your dance diary. Basically, attributions are the reasons we give for what happens to us. So, for example, if you had a really good performance, what might you attribute that good performance to? What do you think might have caused that good performance?

Tracy: I was really familiar with the choreography.

SH: OK. Good. What else?

Tracy: The choreography suited me.

SH: Yes. Anything that's not related to choreography?

Tracy: I kept focused throughout the performance.

SH: OK. Good. Now, what about the flip side? What attributions might you make for a less than wonderful performance?

Tracy: I rushed. I forgot the steps. I was too nervous.

SH: Right. So in terms of confidence, the idea is to try to make attributions that help you rather than hurt you. You were tending to do that anyway. For example, you want to attribute good performances to internal and stable reasons. If you performed well it was because of what you did, something inside you. Also, whatever that cause was can be there again at the next performance and the next. So instead of attributing good performances to luck or the fact that you only looked good because everyone else was so bad, you take personal credit for your successes.

Tracy:   That makes sense. What about for failures? I don't think I want to be blaming other people for my failures.

SH:   You're right. You want to try to attribute failures to unstable causes—factors that can change. For example, you might attribute a less than wonderful performance to a lack of effort, to inexperience, or to poor concentration—focusing on who is in the audience instead of what you are actually doing on stage.

Tracy:   So if I make a mistake, it's not because I suck but because I got distracted or didn't prepare well enough.

SH:   Exactly. You want to be sure, however, that you believe these attributions, that you're not saying one thing but really thinking something else.

Tracy:   Yeah. I can believe it. I mean, for any one performance there may be a lot of factors that contribute to my performance. You want me to focus on the factors I can control.

SH:   I couldn't have said it better myself.

# Conclusion

I am fortunate to have had an extensive background in dance before I became a sport psychology practitioner. Dance performance may not have a lot in common with discus throwing, but the overlap with the aesthetic sports, such as figure skating, rhythmic gymnastics, and synchronized swimming, is extensive. For those not familiar with the world of performing arts, Hamilton's (1997) text is a great place to start. As I mention in chapter 12, homework is essential. One of the wonderful things about working with dancers is that it exposes sport psychologists to a whole new world where they can learn to apply their skills in new and different ways.

Dancers are athletes with many of the same issues found within competitive sport. They may have a slightly different definition of personal space, but they are competitive and strive to enhance their skills and the consistency of their performances. Unlike many sports, however, there are few objective criteria for "good" performance. Dancers can become frustrated by the combination of not knowing what is expected and receiving little direct feedback during auditions. Overall, the same mental skills used in sport are beneficial for dancers, although working to develop self-confidence generally may be a higher priority for dancers. Being a sport psychologist is a career-long learning process, and the lessons acquired in this aesthetically oriented environment will serve the practitioner in many future encounters with athletes and other performing artists.

# Commentary on Chapter 7

Kate F. Hays, PhD, CPsych

**W**hat's a chapter on dance doing in a book on sport psychology? Although atypical, it reflects recent interest in the broad area of performance; Andersen's *Doing Sport Psychology* includes a chapter on music performance anxiety (Hays, 2000). Since then, an entire issue of the *Journal of Applied Sport Psychology* has been devoted to the generic perspective of performance excellence (Gould, 2002). In the chapter under consideration, Stephanie Hanrahan looks at the application of mental skills to dancers, whether in relation to ballet or contemporary, students or professionals. In doing so, she adds to a small performance literature concerning dance both as it pertains to talent, skill acquisition, and expert performance (e.g., Starkes, Helsen, & Jack, 2001) and other performance issues (e.g., Hamilton, 1997; Hays & Brown, 2004; Taylor & Taylor, 1995).

Hanrahan articulates issues confronted by dancers as well as ways in which a consultant can address these concerns. Consultants more accustomed to working with athletes will see both similarities to and differences from their usual practice. In commenting on her chapter, I examine these similarities and differences, share relevant information about the dance milieu, reflect on the knowledge and skills a consultant brings to dance consulting, and describe dancers' expectations concerning performance consulting. In doing so, I draw on a number of sources, in particular Hanrahan's work, research conducted on expert performers (Hays & Brown, 2004), and my own observations in working with dancers.

## "Comptrasting" Sport and Dance

In what ways are sports and dance training, practice, and performance similar, and in what ways different? "Comptrasting" (my neologism) these two large fields involves comparing and contrasting, examining areas of overlap in the curves and exploring regions of uniqueness.

Often, we think of dance as being aligned with other performing arts, such as music or acting. Yet one of the primary features of dance is the central role of the body in motion. Unlike many other performing arts, dance shares with gymnastics, figure skating, and various martial arts the full use of the active body and a need for memory of large-muscle movement sequences. As with various types of both performing arts and sports, the sequences occur (usually, though not always) in relation to audio accompaniment. The engagement of the performer's rhythmic sense is important both to practice and performance. Further, music can serve as an aid to complete learning.

Hanrahan points to differences between athletes and dancers in need for personal space, physical flexibility, tendency to stretch, and capacity to adapt one's performance to the available performance space. These reflections seem apt and relevant.

We do not tend to think of dancers as being either competitive or involved in a competitive activity, and yet, as Hanrahan describes, competition is a regular aspect of everyday functioning for dancers. In class, dancers compete for the teacher's attention; within a dance company, they experience differences in status (e.g., principal dancer versus member of the corps de ballet) and regularly compete for roles from one performance piece to another. If they dance independently, they need to deal with auditions, whether for parts in an upcoming production or to become part of a company.

Although Hanrahan does not mention gender, it is a central feature of dance life. As with certain artistic sports, such as figure skating, whether in schools or dance companies, the vast majority of dancers are female. There is an overabundance of highly talented and skilled females competing for too few spaces; the few men who are involved become lionized and may be less disciplined and less focused than their female counterparts (Hays & Brown, 2004; Wootten, 2001).

One of Hanrahan's clients speaks of the connection with the audience, finding it thrilling to dance in such a way that the audience enjoys the performance. The issue of audience in some ways differentiates sport from the performing arts. Sports competitions include spectators, and sports attendance reaps lucrative financial rewards. Sports sponsorship and commercials at times may be seen to be driving forces, yet in terms of the sport itself, it would be possible to hold many sports competitions without the presence of spectators. Not so the performing arts—one central purpose is presentation to an audience.

Hanrahan also speaks of the interesting interplay between motivation, recovery, and injury. Because of the rigorous training demand in ballet, those with flagging motivation may be weeded out, in a Darwinian process, earlier rather than later. We think of dance as an ethereal activity, but there is probably good reason why Degas painted both dancers and racehorses. In both instances, intense musculature built up over time allows for extraordinary stamina. The physical stresses on dancers' bodies are comparable to those placed on athletes engaged in contact sports (Hamilton & Hamilton, 1994). "The show must go on" is accompanied by an expectation that one will perform, no matter what. Similar to sports subcultures, the dance community subscribes to, and reinforces, beliefs and values supporting pain tolerance that may well increase the risk of injury, particularly through overuse (Mainwaring, Krasnow, & Kerr, 2001). Dancers who are injured and cannot perform often feel an intense amount of guilt and responsibility (Hays & Brown, 2004).

The subjectivity of dance judgment, which Hanrahan addresses, is not dissimilar to artistic sports. It differs in part because of the long history of dance, especially ballet, with its very specific focus on line and form. As Hanrahan notes, one of the most challenging aspects of this subjectivity is the frequent lack of feedback. Particularly with intrinsically motivated, perfectionistic dancers, it becomes nearly impossible to create a mental or emotional space devoid of self-blame and self-criticism.

Hanrahan comments that for dancers, stage fright appears to mean "being completely frozen and unable to move." I would suggest that this deviation from the traditional definition reflects that performance anxiety is considered the norm for performing artists (Hays, 2002). Performers are expected to experience "nerves"—the issue is one of management rather than occurrence. Thus, if performance anxiety is anticipated, one needs a different term to designate "really bad performance anxiety." *Stage fright* serves that purpose.

# Mental Skills

Hanrahan describes a number of mental skills that she uses with dancers. Among these are self-talk, concentration and attention, and imagery. Passing mention is made of diaphragmatic breathing. The value of a preperformance plan is emphasized. Because mental skills are the "canon" of applied sport psychology (Andersen, 2000), it is worth discussing the ways in which mental skills are taught and practiced among dancers as compared with athletes.

In the dialogue Hanrahan uses to illustrate concentration and attention, the dancer roams around the topic, touching on issues such as distraction, concentrating in class as compared with rehearsing for a performance, teacher attention, kinesthetic awareness, sequencing of learning and fine-tuning, technique versus energy, striving to replicate a preset ideal, rigid thinking patterns, and classical compared with contemporary dance. This dialogue is marvelously energetic for us to read. And it offers the dancer the opportunity to explore these different important areas while paying attention to how she goes about paying attention.

Hanrahan notes the very interesting imagery position of seeing oneself from behind. This imaginal perspective not only includes kinesthetic awareness but also replicates the dancer's experience of looking toward other dancers, whether viewing another dancer's body while in line at the barre or as a member of the corps de ballet. It is neither the perspective of the audience nor the self-observing of the self in the mirror that surrounds the dance studio. Although this positional perspective is not something I have encountered before, it now makes me wonder if I have asked the right questions! Hanrahan speculates that this positional perspective occurs among ballet dancers because they are so focused on how things look as compared with how movements feel. It may also reflect how ballet dancers in some ways learn to disconnect from their own bodies. This detachment can become seriously problematic if or when they disconnect from bodily sensations of hunger or from attention to injury or illness.

Hanrahan encourages one of her dancers, in dialogue, to begin mapping out a preperformance plan for herself. I have found that this critically important mental skill is one that is not taught to performers. Those who even demarcate and consider the management of preperformance tension tend to roam haphazardly among methods. Ultimately, often by trial and error, a method may be selected. One ballet dancer describes the following: "I always did a barre [practice routine] before performance, half an hour or forty minutes of repetitive physical activity in a predictable sequence" (Hays & Brown, 2004, p. 121). A contemporary dancer comments: "I had one or two little rituals that I would always do: I'd go onto the stage before the curtain went up and do a deep plié [knee bend] on the stage. That was my one little talisman thing. I always had to do that. And in my makeup case, I always had one of those tiny little bottles of Metaxa brandy, and I always had a sip of Metaxa before—just one sip. I didn't want to have the whole bottle—I mean we're talking about one of those little mini bottles. Those two little actions, one sip of brandy and one deep plié on the stage before the curtain went up" (Hays & Brown, 2004, p. 120). When I conduct workshops, I have found that dance students appreciate the opportunity to focus on the development of individual preperformance plans.

Hanrahan only briefly touches on breathing. Her dancer describes deep breathing in order to "get a grounding effect," to feel as if she is "planted to the ground." I have noticed that most dancers, whether ballet or contemporary, become markedly uncomfortable even contemplating expanding their abdomens and ruining aesthetic lines, yet this is a key element to diaphragmatic breathing as we teach it to athletes. Some athletes, such as gymnasts or skaters, are also disinclined to breathe in this way, for the same reason. Instead, they may become intrigued if offered the opportunity to learn to create the same diaphragmatic effect through expansion of the sides or the back. In this way, instead of fighting "having to stick their bellies out," they can learn the myriad pockets the body contains for complete breathing.

It is often useful to find out what breathing methods students have learned and build on them, whether via correction, reinforcement, or instruction. Getting them to demonstrate how they go about "breathing deeply" can be informative; for many, thoracic expansion is a sign that they are adding to performance nervousness. Some students may have studied yoga, or the increasingly popular Pilates, and learned effective methods of diaphragmatic breathing. They may know that it is good for them in a vague, generic way but may not fully understand the anxiolytic effects that proper breathing will allow.

Hanrahan's dancer notes, "My best performance I don't remember at all." Although one of the common aspects of PST workshops involves training for peak performance, I too have found that this element of flow, the loss of self-consciousness, is one that dancers more than other performers have mentioned. One dancer, for example, describes in detail the moments just before he went on stage, "and that's the last thing I remember from the performance. But I know that it was a very good performance" (Hays & Brown, 2004, p. 195).

# The Dance Milieu

Although Hanrahan does not speak directly about the milieu of the dance student and dancer, some aspects are critically important for the consultant interested in working with dancers. Among these are location, types of dance, the impact of others, corrections, taking classes, finances, the weight of the history of dance, and health habits.

The milieu of the ballet dancer is quite different from that of the contemporary dancer. The prototypical ballet dancer begins training as a young child; may need to board at a dance school by her early teens; and is likely at some points to experience old school, autocratic teachers who have no patience with the positive perspective of many North American educators. For this student, "anatomy is destiny"; she will or won't be a ballet dancer in part depending on whether her body type will sustain a prepubescent form. Unless she has a naturally thin body, she will need to function in semi-starvation much of the time to sustain low body weight. Even if she completes high school, she is unlikely to attend college or university but rather will seek work within a dance company at the earliest possible age. A contemporary dancer may come to this form of dance with previous ballet training, or she may have chosen contemporary dance directly. In the latter case, she may have begun dancing in adolescence. There is likely to be more institutional flexibility about her body type. Her years of most serious dance study may occur in a postsecondary program.

Both types of dancers will be serious performers, devoting as much of their waking time to their art as possible. Once she has completed dance school, the dancer will continue taking dance classes on a regular basis throughout her career. Finances are likely to be tight, and she may well need to maintain a day job. Often, this work will not be especially remunerative because she will not have advanced skills, having devoted so much of her time and energies to her dance life.

In class, a dancer is surrounded by mirrors that offer the opportunity for self-judgments, which are often negative. If she is fortunate, her teacher will notice her and comment—tellingly, this form of attention is called "correction." She will be told what she is doing wrong. She may or may not be instructed as to how, specifically, she can rectify the error(s). Renowned ballerina Karen Kain writes:

> In the perfectionist world of dance, teaching traditionally emphasizes "corrections." [My teacher] singled me out, giving me a dozen corrections every class, while everybody else got two or three. Nobody thought for a minute that these

frequent corrections meant I was making more mistakes than anyone else; in the elite world of dance, only those who have promise are given these attentions. (1994, pp. 15, 11)

Hanrahan suggests an important antidote to this mental state of self-criticism. She encourages the dancer to reflect in her journal, on a regular basis, both what she did well and what she could do to improve performance the next time. In this reflective process, she learns a number of skills. She can assess her own performance from a learning perspective. Observing herself with an evaluative eye instead of a judgmental one, she can move out of the relentlessly self-critical space; she can attend to striving for excellence rather than perfection. This method can easily be used by other types of performers as well. Shortly after reading Hanrahan's chapter, I suggested to a swimmer, who was already keeping a journal, that she try asking herself these two questions for the next two weeks. She was immediately enthusiastic.

Dance schools and dance companies are predominantly female, although qualitative research suggests that the academy and the studio are both perceived by the participants as not being "girl friendly" (Wootten, 2001). In this same research, girls are more commonly identified as perfectionists, whereas boys are viewed as physically competitive.

Particularly in classical ballet, developing dancers experience the burden (as well as the joy) of tradition. "You can be compared with all the great dancers who ever danced that role," one of Hanrahan's dancers comments. The combination of a few hundred years of history, a visually transmitted culture, and a closed and militaristic system engenders particular pressures for the developing artist.

Two very troubling aspects of the dance milieu are health habits and self-care. Especially striking is the frequency and prevalence of eating disorders, or at the very least, disordered eating. Because the social system is predominantly female, because there is such emphasis on how one looks, because of the historical tradition about shape and line, because a ballet dancer needs to maintain her weight at 85% of normal levels, it is nearly inevitable that weight preoccupation and disordered eating, if not eating disorders, will run rampant (Hamilton, 1997). Not unassociated with this is the heavy use of nicotine, in part as a weight control mechanism, in part because of the artist culture and glamour associated with smoking. Other risky health habits, such as the use of alcohol to "self-medicate," especially during injury recovery (Hamilton & Hamilton, 1991), are also of concern.

## Consultant's Knowledge and Skills

In her chapter, Hanrahan is wonderfully forthcoming about her own style and method. Of particular interest are her judicious use of the pause, interested inquiry, solution-focused methods, and sharing of options (a "menu" approach), along with her own extensive knowledge of classical ballet.

"The right word may be effective," commented Mark Twain, "but no word was ever as effective as a rightly timed pause." Hanrahan has figured out the accuracy of this maxim and puts her knowledge into practice. She acknowledges this as a learning process. Sometimes less is more; we do not need to let our clients know everything we know—at least not all at once!—and in fact we can offer them the opportunity to use their own resources for self-understanding. "You always want to be one step behind the client," Donald Meichenbaum once said at a conference I attended, and it is this supportive, inquiring, option-offering method that most allows such a stance

It helps, too, that Hanrahan is so knowledgeable about dance. Her detailed imagery script gives the dancer the specificity she needs to image the pirouette. In the process, the dancer shifts from "mental blocks" and self-doubt to a sense of excitement and eager anticipation.

# Dancers' Expectations
# About Performance Consulting

In this chapter, Hanrahan does not speak of the ways in which dancers have made contact with her, but it is an area that bears some exploration. Consulting in the performing arts is a newly developing field. It is emerging as a result of two current trends. Some forward-thinking dance programs are aware of performance enhancement training in sport and are intrigued about applications to their own domain. Performance medicine, itself connected with sports medicine, is the other route to development of this field. The former perhaps has more of an educational and skill development bent, whereas the latter aims to restore previous functioning and tends more toward rehabilitation, focusing on injury or, occasionally, injury prevention.

My own experience is that performing artists, including dancers, are comfortable with the idea of psychotherapy but not necessarily familiar with performance enhancement (Hays, 2002). This can have a number of consequences. These performers may initially be more positively inclined toward the helping professions than are athletes. They may also, however, misinterpret the available resources. Thus, performing artists may assume that any services offered either are or should be long term, rehabilitative, in depth, and designed for psychological or emotional exploration—and for all these reasons, that this process will be fairly costly. Typically, neither arts institutions nor individual performers have much discretionary financing available. The interested practitioner may need to provide a fair amount of education in order for dancers or program directors to appreciate the relevant array of potential services.

If there is little money to spare, group presentations offer the best value. Useful areas of focus include preperformance planning or counteracting perfectionism while striving for excellence. In general, people are often looking for methods to increase self-confidence, decrease self-criticism, maintain focus, and cope with the uncertainties associated with life in the arts.

# Conclusion

Mental skills training for dancers is an exciting emerging area, one that offers new opportunities and markets to sport psychologists. Hanrahan's chapter is on point: A number of the mental skills that have been developed and researched with athletes can, with appropriate training and adaptation, be of considerable benefit to dancers as well.

## CHAPTER 8

# Facilitating Change
## *Alcohol and Violence Among Athletes*

Robert D. Stainback, PhD, and Robert E. Taylor, PhD

Hardly a day goes by without mention in the media of an athlete experiencing alcohol- or drug-related problems. In addition, it is often the case that violent behaviors, ranging from barroom altercations to homicide, are associated with alcohol use and abuse. If athletes are experiencing alcohol-related difficulties, it is a fair assumption that their health and well-being and certainly their athletic performances have deteriorated, or will deteriorate, as a result. Therefore, coaches and other professionals interested in the welfare of athletes (e.g., sport psychologists, athletic trainers, sport physicians, counselors) would be well advised to familiarize themselves with the incidence and prevalence of alcohol use and abuse and violence among the athletes they serve. This knowledge is the first step toward developing a strategy for preventing these problems from occurring and reacting constructively when they do occur.

Our primary goal in writing this chapter is to familiarize the reader with a clinical approach to intervening with and facilitating change in an athlete (in this case a college football player) who presents with problems related to his alcohol use and violence. In keeping with this goal, the case study in this chapter is the focal point from which we hope to pass along our primary message to the reader, which is an effective method for helping an athlete with alcohol problems. Our principal lessons are incorporated into the commentary in the dialogue between the sport psychologist and the athlete. Additional matters of clinical importance are covered in the section Professional Issues following the case study. Before embarking on the case study, however, we present background information on alcohol use among college students generally (and college athletes specifically) and on issues concerning risk taking and alcohol-related violence in these populations. We also provide information on how and why individuals change problem drinking, on how helping professionals can facilitate this process, and on components frequently found in specialized alcohol treatment programs.

# Alcohol Use, Risk Taking, and Violence

Recent epidemiological data indicate that per capita alcohol consumption in the United States reached a 35-year low in 1995 and showed an 11% decrease from 1990 to 1997 (Nephew, Williams, Stinson, Nguyen, & Dufour, 1999). Despite this decrease, alcohol clearly remains the drug of choice in the United States relative to nicotine and illicit drugs, as indicated by data from the National Household Survey on Drug Abuse (Substance Abuse and Mental Health Services Administration, 1999). This survey, with a nationally representative sample of the noninstitutionalized civilian population of the United States aged 12 years and older, found that 81% of the target population reported lifetime use of alcohol, 64% indicated use in the past year, and 52% reported use in the past month. Reported use of other drugs in this survey pales when compared with these figures.

Given these results, it is not surprising that alcohol use among college students is widespread even though purchasing it is illegal for most of this population. Recent national survey results (Johnston, O'Malley, & Bachman, 1998) indicate that 87% of college students reported lifetime alcohol use. Most alarming are the apparently frequent occasions of heavy drinking (sometimes referred to as binge drinking), measured by the reported incidence of five or more drinks in a row in the two-week period before the survey. Thirty-eight percent of the college students reported binge drinking, which represents a recent low but is still considerably higher than the 31% of high school seniors reporting binge drinking. When compared with their noncollege age peers and high school students, who have been showing a net decrease in binge drinking since 1980, college students' binge drinking has been maintained at a relatively consistent high rate. There also were significant gender differences in alcohol use among college students. College men reported significantly higher rates of daily drinking (7.8% versus 2.1%) and binge drinking (51% versus 31%) than did college women.

In a resurvey of college students' alcohol use, Wechsler, Dowdall, Maenner, Gledhill-Hoyt, and Lee (1998) found that binge drinking (defined in this study as five drinks in a row for men and four drinks in a row for women during the two weeks before the survey) changed little from 1993 to 1997 and remained at a troublesome level. The 1997 results indicate that 43% of students were binge drinkers, 19% were abstainers, and 21% were frequent binge drinkers (students reporting bingeing three or more times in a two-week period). Among student drinkers, increases were noted from 1993 to 1997 in frequency of drinking, drunkenness, drinking to get drunk, and alcohol-related problems. Binge drinkers in both 1993 and 1997 showed increased risk of alcohol-related problems when compared with nonbinge drinkers. These problems included some with serious consequences, such as driving after drinking, damaging property, and suffering personal injuries. Also, nonbinge drinkers at colleges with high binge drinking rates experienced increased risk for secondhand effects of binge drinking (e.g., had been insulted or humiliated, had to take care of a drunken student). In 1997, fraternities and sororities continued to be the focus of heavy drinking, with two thirds of fraternity and sorority members reporting binge drinking. For those living in Greek houses, 80% of students reported binge drinking, and 50% indicated frequent bingeing.

What do all these alcohol-related statistics about college students mean for college student-athletes? Unfortunately, participation in college athletics does not appear to provide immunity to heavy alcohol consumption and other risk-taking behaviors. There is evidence that athletes may actually engage in high-risk behaviors with greater frequency than their nonathlete peers (Nattiv, Puffer, & Green, 1997). Athletes took greater risks than their peers by demonstrating

- a lower likelihood of always wearing seat belts,
- a greater likelihood of riding as a passenger with a driver under the influence of alcohol or drugs,
- greater quantity and frequency of alcoholic beverage use,
- greater frequency of smokeless tobacco and anabolic steroid use,
- lower contraceptive use, and
- more involvement in physical fighting.

Male athletes were more prone to risk taking than were female athletes, and those in contact sports showed more risk-taking behavior than those in noncontact sports. Finally, athletes with one high-risk behavior tended to report multiple risk-taking behaviors.

A recent review of the effects of alcohol on behavior and safety (United States Department of Health and Human Services [USDHHS], 1997) indicates that alcohol consumption is a risk factor for a variety of threats to health and safety. These include traffic accidents, drowning, occupational injuries, and violence (either as perpetrator or victim). Although research suggests that the relationship between alcohol consumption and violence is complex, with biological, psychological, interpersonal, and contextual influences (Chermack & Giancola, 1997), both experimental and correlational work indicate that individuals consuming alcohol have an increased probability of subsequent violent behavior (Lipsey, Wilson, Cohen, & Derzon, 1997). In young males, the relationship is particularly strong. For example, Pernanen (as cited in USDHHS, 1997) found that young adults (aged 20-29) were at greater risk for alcohol-related violence than persons of other ages, and young men were at the greatest risk for this type of violence. Collegiate male athletes certainly fit into this high-risk age group.

# Changing Problem Drinking

Before discussing problem drinking, we define terms commonly found in the alcohol literature and delineate how they are used in this chapter. *Alcohol abuse* and *alcohol dependence* (commonly referred to as alcoholism) are the diagnostic names in the American Psychiatric Association's *Diagnostic and Statistical Manual of Mental Disorders* (APA, 1994). In both of these disorders, significant impairments or distress are directly related to alcohol use. Alcohol dependence is demonstrated by more significant impairment than is found in alcohol abuse and may include physiological dependence on alcohol.

*Problem drinking* and *problem drinker*, terms commonly found in the behavioral psychology literature, are conceptually related to the DSM-IV nomenclature. These terms, however, refer to any drinking pattern that results in problems for the drinker regardless of whether DSM-IV diagnostic criteria are met. *Alcohol use* or *social drinking* suggests alcohol consumption that is not associated with recurring physical, psychological, or social problems.

In the United States, most people have experience with alcohol during adolescence, and for many this life stage is a time of repeated experimentation with alcohol. The majority of adults (85-90%) drink moderately or not at all, and drinking poses no significant threats to health or social functioning. For a subset of drinkers, however, alcohol use progresses into problem drinking, which may also include alcohol abuse and dependence. Given the potential serious health-related consequences of alcohol dependence, helping professionals should have knowledge of how people abusing alcohol recover and what role the professional may play in facilitating this process.

Although it was once believed that people with alcoholism needed to progress to severe consequences in order to make changes in their drinking, more recent research, fortunately, indicates that people abusing alcohol can and do make changes in their drinking earlier in the addictive process. For example, a popular transtheoretical model of change (DiClemente & Prochaska, 1998; Prochaska, DiClemente, & Norcross, 1992) suggests that changes in addictive behaviors occur in stages, which may take place within or independent from treatment. Stainback (1997) summarizes these stages—precontemplation, contemplation, preparation, action, and maintenance—as follows:

> Precontemplation is the stage in which there is no intention to change behavior in the immediate future. Most individuals are unaware or underaware of their problems at this stage and therefore are resistant to recognizing or modifying a problem. As described by G.K. Chesterton, "It isn't that they can't see the solution. It is that they can't see the problem." (cited in Prochaska et al., 1992, p. 1103)
>
> Contemplation is characterized by the individual's being aware that there is a problem and thinking seriously about changing but not being ready to commit to action. An important activity during the contemplation stage is the individual's considering the advantages and disadvantages of the problem and the potential solutions to the problem.
>
> Preparation is typified by the individual's intending to make changes, and perhaps beginning to move in that direction, but not yet reaching the point of sufficient action to terminate the problem. In the case of problem drinking, the individual may have made changes in drinking (e.g., reduced frequency and amount) but has not been able to reach criterion for effective action, such as abstinence from alcohol abuse.
>
> Action is the stage in which an individual takes direct action to overcome a problem. During this stage, the individual makes substantial overt efforts to change a problem behavior. For the problem drinker, this action may take the form of treatment, attendance at self-help groups such as Alcoholics Anonymous, or individual efforts to discontinue or moderate drinking.
>
> Maintenance is determined by the individual's efforts to prevent relapse and solidify behavior changes that have been made in the action stage. (pp. 129-130)

An important tenet of this change model is that progression through the stages is nonlinear and is characterized by relapsing and recycling to previous stages. Also, at each stage, individuals must engage in specific processes that enable them to negotiate and progress through that stage. For example, consciousness raising (learning more about the problem and how one is reacting to it) is a process people typically use during the contemplation stage. It is important to remember that people can engage in these processes and move through the change stages while in therapy or through self-change.

The stage model of change has important implications for a helping professional seeking to facilitate the process (Prochaska, DiClemente, & Norcross, 1992). The model emphasizes the following:

- Assess the person's readiness for change, and focus interventions on the processes the person must use to negotiate each change stage successfully.

- The greatest efficiency in change depends on use of the correct process for the current stage. A mismatching of processes and stages results in change becoming more difficult. For example, if interventions focus on specific actions needed to change an addictive behavior (action stage) before the individual reaches awareness of the problem and its potential solutions (tasks involved in the contemplation stage), then the interventions and stage are mismatched, which will likely lead to client resistance and a less than satisfactory treatment outcome.

- The majority of people will cycle through stages many times before successful long-term maintenance of nonaddictive behavior occurs. The helping professional expecting a linear progression through the stages will invariably be disappointed and may invite the same disappointment in the client.

# Facilitating Change in Problem Drinkers

A number of research findings have significant bearing on facilitating positive changes in problem drinkers (see review in Stainback, 1997). The majority of alcoholics do not seek treatment and do not typically discuss their drinking with helping professionals until late in the course of their drinking problem, after significant social and physical impairments have occurred. Also, many people who abuse alcohol recover without treatment. Many of these individuals apparently furthered their self-recovery by using a cognitive evaluation or appraisal of the pros and cons of their drinking. These findings suggest that helping professionals may serve a valuable purpose, with respect to problem drinkers, by stimulating natural recovery capabilities, which may include a cognitive evaluation of drinking (a process that may actually already be under way when the client is initially seen).

Motivational interviewing (Miller & Rollnick, 1991), a brief intervention used by clinicians to encourage this cognitive evaluation by their clients, has shown significant positive direct effects on drinking as well as on help seeking among problem drinkers. This positive effect on drinking and help seeking may be related to the intervention's influence on motivation for change. Once this motivational impact occurs, persons may change their drinking with or without formal treatment. Miller and Rollnick indicate five basic principles of this approach to guide the therapist:

- Express empathy.
- Develop and amplify in the client's mind a discrepancy between present behavior and important goals.
- Avoid argumentation.
- Roll with resistance by offering new information and perspectives for the client to consider.
- Support self-efficacy by reinforcing the client's personal responsibility for change and by suggesting a variety of alternatives for action.

Although this approach has its beginnings in the addiction literature, motivational interviewing has reached far beyond these boundaries to influence strategies for changing health behavior generally. For example, similar approaches are used by practitioners to help patients change various health behaviors such as overeating and physical inactivity, as well as to help patients adjust to chronic conditions such as heart disease and diabetes by making life changes. In their recent book *Health Behavior Change: A Guide for Practitioners*, Rollnick, Mason, and Butler (1999) provide an excellent description of the theoretical foundation for this approach, as well as specific descriptions of the tasks involved in facilitating health behavior change. Their book is an excellent resource for practitioners wanting to incorporate these strategies in their practice, and aspects of motivational interviewing are incorporated throughout the case example.

# Alcohol Treatment

In the previous section, we discuss approaches to facilitating change in problem drinkers. Alcohol treatment specialists may use these methods, but perhaps the most valuable places for their application are general care settings. These settings include primary care physicians' offices; university counseling centers (including the work performed by sport psychologists with college athletes); and social service agencies where helping professionals see clients with alcohol-related problems, although their drinking may not meet the diagnostic criteria for alcohol abuse or dependence. In this section, we briefly explore care provided by helping professionals with specialized training or experience with addictions.

The Institute of Medicine (1990), in its book *Broadening the Base of Treatment for Alcohol Problems,* offers the following definition of alcohol treatment:

> Treatment refers to the broad range of services, including identification, brief intervention, assessment, diagnosis, counseling, medical services, psychiatric services, psychological services, social services, and follow-up, for persons with alcohol problems. The overall goal of treatment is to reduce or eliminate the use of alcohol as a contributing factor to physical, psychological, and social dysfunction and to arrest, retard, or reverse the progress of any associated problems. (p. 46)

This definition is inclusive of a variety of services that form a continuum of care to meet the needs of people with alcohol-related problems, including minimal, moderate, or severe cases.

Professional help for problem drinkers comes in various forms and intensities. Professionals representing a variety of backgrounds—including psychology, medicine, social work, counseling, nursing, and vocational rehabilitation—may be involved in treatment. Professional assistance can be separated into two types:

- Pharmacological treatment, including drugs for withdrawal management and for use in long-term rehabilitation
- Psychological treatment, including behavioral and psychodynamic approaches

Comprehensive treatment programs typically include both of these types of care. In addition to professional services, patients also may be referred to self-help groups (e.g., Alcoholics Anonymous, Adult Children of Alcoholics, Rational Recovery).

Depending on the severity of the alcohol problem, treatment settings and intensities vary and may include services delivered in residential, inpatient, intermediate (e.g., a halfway house), and outpatient facilities. Inpatient and residential facilities provide 24-hour care or support. Intermediate care facilities provide care or support, or both, in a partial (less than 24 hour) treatment or recovery setting. Outpatient facilities provide nonresidential treatment services on a scheduled and nonscheduled basis. The choice of treatment setting depends on various factors, including the severity of the alcohol abuse and related problems, the person's ability to attend activities in a particular treatment setting, the availability and consistency of environmental support for treatment goals, and the client's motivation to alter drinking patterns and to obtain necessary help in doing so.

Although treatment models vary, most include basic stages (or phases) of care, including acute intervention, rehabilitation, and maintenance (Institute of Medicine, 1990). Acute intervention services might include medically supervised detoxification and crisis intervention counseling. Also included in this stage are screening activities to identify individuals with alcohol problems and to facilitate referral for treatment.

During the rehabilitation stage, the client is assisted with reducing or discontinuing alcohol consumption and improving physical, psychological, and social functioning. This stage includes a comprehensive evaluation of the client's current functioning and the development of a comprehensive treatment plan (conjointly devised by the therapist and client) to address issues that have either contributed to or resulted from the drinking problem. This evaluation leads to therapeutic activities focused on altering the drinking and related problems. Rehabilitation activities may occur in any of the treatment settings mentioned previously.

In the maintenance stage, the focus of treatment attention is on maintaining gains made during rehabilitation. Also known as aftercare or relapse prevention, many treatment professionals regard the successful completion of this stage's activities as essential for long-term sobriety. The maintenance stage may include treatment delivery in a domiciliary setting for individuals unable to return to independent living in the community.

As Miller (1989) describes, effective alcohol treatment is the result of a negotiation process between the therapist and client. After a comprehensive assessment of the client's alcohol-related problems by the therapist, negotiations proceed through four levels, including determination of treatment goals, levels of intervention, types of intervention, and maintenance arrangements. Finally, a follow-up assessment is completed to evaluate the effectiveness of the entire intervention process.

# Intercepting Anger: Josh's Story

The following case outlines an effective intervention approach for an athlete demonstrating problems with alcohol and violence. We want to emphasize that this approach is by no means the only one, but it is one grounded in the ideas about change presented earlier in the chapter, as well as in our clinical experience with athletes and problem drinkers. The case represents an amalgamation of clients we have seen and is presented in a brief format for didactic purposes. In the section after the case study, we discuss professional issues related to the case and seek to connect these issues with the material reviewed in the introduction. This approach is in keeping with our belief that effective clinical work is enlightened by a knowledge base of the presenting clinical issues, in this instance problem drinking among college student-athletes.

Josh is a 21-year-old college football wide receiver referred to me (Robert Stainback) after a recent arrest for participating in a barroom fight. At the time of the referral, the coach indicates that Josh has a history of behavioral problems while on the team, including breaking curfews, arguing with teammates, and fighting. Most of these problems are apparently associated with Josh's consumption of alcohol. Josh has also experienced problems with his grades and has been on academic probation in the past. Other referral information indicates that Josh has a family history of polysubstance abuse and violence. Apparently, his father has successfully completed an alcohol treatment program and is currently abstinent, and he has siblings who also have experienced problems with substance abuse and violence. Presently, Josh is suspended from the football team indefinitely, and the coach is requiring him to meet with me before he will consider reinstating Josh's eligibility to play. The following initial session with Josh occurs the day after the coach's referral.

The initial goals of the clinical interviewer are to establish a working relationship and set the stage for change. This process is under way before the actual meeting and is influenced by preceding events. I have information that may create suppositions and raise questions; Josh has undoubtedly been told something about me that will give rise to assumptions on his part. Background information has positive and negative aspects. It can set the stage for deeper understanding, or it can foster inaccurate preconceptions. Some professionals prefer to form their own first impressions without the clutter of data from various sources. Others may want to gather as much as possible from all parties involved in the referral. My preferred stance is to regard all information as potentially useful while remaining skeptical about its factual accuracy.

Knowing that Josh has been raised in an addictive environment, I suspect he is unlikely to perceive anyone in a position of authority as emotionally or behaviorally consistent and is apt to cast me in that mold. I wonder about the extent to which his background fosters angry, distrustful assumptions and how I might penetrate that armor. I will need to decide how much of my foreknowledge I can share with Josh and when to do so. How was I described to him? Might he present a physical threat? Has he done any drinking to fortify himself for the interview? Who are the nurturing people in his life, and how can I ally myself with them? What other stresses are lurking in the background? How does Josh view his role in this interview? He does not have a strong academic background and is unlikely to view this process as a welcome opportunity to learn anything useful. We think of such considerations as the setting for the story about to unfold.

Robert Stainback (RS): Hello, Josh. I am Rob. Please come in and have a seat and make yourself comfortable. I understand that your coach has asked you to come here today. Can you tell me what that's all about?

Josh: [After a perfunctory handshake, an angry stare, and a slouch into the chair.] I can tell you this, I'm not happy to be here, and I don't have to tell you anything I don't want to. The coach has really gone too far this time. I can't believe that he has probably shelved me for the rest of the year for some stupid little fight where nobody really got hurt too bad. And now I have to come see you instead of being out on the practice field. I am really angry about it, and I don't understand it. [Josh's volume has continually risen, and his face is reddening. The intensity of emotion is unmistakable.]

Josh's distress is palpable. As I try to quiet my own anxiety over this dramatic start to our session, I take note of the manner of his handshake, initial eye contact, tone of voice, and bearing. I do note with a bit of surprise that he has kept the appointment and is punctual.

> In certain situations, using first names at introductions can be disarming and may ease some of the athlete's anxieties.

In the initial address, first names can be strategically disarming as a means of not casting oneself as an authority figure. I do not approach everyone routinely in the same manner, however. For some, more formality would be preferable. I could also ask Josh what he prefers to be called in this setting. It is often good to offer a choice of seating options ("Where would you like to sit?"), thereby allowing the athlete to exercise control over his psychological comfort zone. Such options may be especially important if the psychologist and athlete are not of the same gender. Meetings in less formal settings, such as bleachers or a training room, deserve similar considerations. The athlete's sense of territory must be respected.

Efforts to put the athlete more at ease include tone of voice, attire, personal physical comfort, and a positive welcome ("I'm glad you came here today"). I try for an individual style that is facilitative for the athlete and me. My initial query serves as a marker for several things. We are going to get down to business without a lot of social small talk and will begin the therapeutic discourse for which I am responsible. I will outline the agenda and ask Josh to participate in developing it with me. I also take note of my internal processes. Where are my muscles tense? What is going on in the pit of my stomach? Am I giving full attention? What am I communicating in my posture? How do my pre-encounter predictions about Josh jibe with the actual experience? I also try to remain ready for surprises, and Josh does surprise me a bit. He discloses strong feeling, and I consider his frankness a gift.

I now have several options. One is to clarify "not happy." Does it reflect anger in response to anxiety? Is he upset with me, his coach, or the world of authority in general? What might reduce Josh's anxiety? I do not want to fall into the trap of placating his anger, which will denigrate his feelings. If we are to work together, it will be necessary for him to become more at ease in my presence. Later in our work (assuming we get there), I might want to raise his anxiety about some things, such as the trouble he makes for himself. In this moment, my intent is to become an anxiety-reducing and positively reinforcing presence. It is not always easy to do so. When confronted with strong negative affect and judgment, my perception of self-worth and expertise are threatened, and I am tempted to begin operations that will restore my good opinion of myself. My yielding to this temptation is the first step on the path to disordered communication (see chapter 3 in this volume).

Josh has quickly introduced the coercive factor (i.e., the coach is requiring that he come to see me), which raises an immediate barrier between us. I wonder what aspect of his self is at risk here. How can his negative expectations be empathically acknowledged without endorsing them? I have been given the opportunity to acknowledge the importance of his feelings and reinforce his expression of them. I might choose to build a bridge to other situations that have engendered similar feelings. Does Josh feel this way often? Do the feelings have anything to do with getting into fights, especially when his judgment is impaired by alcohol? The coach is being held responsible for Josh's feelings. I must take steps not to incur the same fate. Further, I do not want to be put in the middle of Josh's disagreement with his coach. Such a "squeeze play" will ensure continuation of their conflict and embroil me in it as well. It is a scenario familiar to anyone attempting to intervene in domestic disputes. Without taking on the role of intermediary, I want to help Josh become more skilled at managing the relationship with his coach.

Josh is not a prisoner—he does not "have" to see me, and I hope to make that clear to him in a manner he will not interpret as rejection. Josh hasn't taken to heart his own actions leading to this interview. In his mind, his personal behavior is not connected to consequences, and some other person or event must have determined his fate. Owning up to personal responsibility for the consequences of his actions can become part of our therapeutic agenda, but our current relationship does not allow such an intervention now. There is also an element of minimizing damage. How bad is "too bad"? Is Josh amnesic for some actions when drinking? Josh not only is seeing himself as being punished unfairly but also is accusing me of being part of it. Though I have not really had an opportunity to do anything with or to him, I need to monitor my own anger and defensiveness while resisting any impulse to behave in a punitive way, which would only confirm Josh's expectations. I cannot allow myself to react rather than process. Fortunately, Josh does admit to some confusion, which allows me a means of becoming useful.

> RS: I can see that you are upset about your situation, Josh. But I am having a hard time understanding everything that has happened. Can you please back up and tell me in more detail the circumstances that led to your coming here today?
>
> Josh: As if you don't already know everything about it. I'm sure the coach has bent your ear plenty about me. [The intensity in Josh's voice remains high, and his eyes are still glaring at me as if to say, "I know your game, and I want no part of it."]
>
> RS: Actually, Josh, your coach explained that you were having some problems he felt I might help you with. I would like to get the specifics from you.

Josh has been provocative. I choose to model, without verbal elaboration, a nonconfrontational response to this provocation by seeking more information. The negative feelings are acknowledged, but it is not my intent to be Josh's buddy or win his favor by endorsing those feelings. I certainly do need his help, however, if we are to proceed, and I will not deny that I have already heard some things about him. What we both need is his version of the story, not someone else's. I am still trying to learn the relevant facts from his perspective and appreciate the origins of Josh's feelings while remaining grounded in the present. Were I doing long-term intensive psychotherapy, I would expect to be digging far and deep. Such is not my purpose, and I hope to have more opportunities to gather relevant background information while staying mindful that Josh is in need of immediate relief.

> With defensive, angry athletes, model nonconfrontational responses to provocation.

The session is only a few minutes old and I have already entered Josh's domain of persons or things to be defied. His categorization of me need not be rational. It could be all blue-eyed people, anyone who asks him to do something, or even anyone sincerely interested in his well-being. His defiance could simply be his characteristic mode of responding to the world at large. I do not take his resistance personally, and I wish to avoid an interpersonal power struggle. Josh's prime mode of opposition consists first of attempting to shift the focus of the interview from him to me. It is not a planned strategic counterplay on Josh's part. He is simply being himself. I could choose to focus on what is happening between us right now, or I might silently await developments. I also think about what I am communicating through posture and countenance. Holding the arms across the chest and shifting to a belligerent tone like Josh's is not a great way to go.

I like to think of myself as catching a hard-thrown ball. Josh has every right to know my role with respect to his coach. Although not wholly agreeing with Josh, I will avoid argument and long explanations, which are apt to be a way of distancing myself in the relationship. Contention would also divert us from the primary theme of the interview, which I reiterate for Josh. I cannot expect to be clearly heard or understood on the first intervention. Josh and I both know he does not have to comply, and it is wise to bear that in mind. He could just snarl and walk out. I hope that at some level, not even clearly conscious, Josh recognizes that his welfare, or more specifically his athletic career, is at stake in just how well our discussion proceeds. I reinforce the idea that he is the important person here and that I value what he has to say.

> Josh: So now I get to tell you all about myself, and then you can go back and tell the coach all about me. [This statement has a sarcastic ring to it, which may be Josh's way of controlling his obvious frustration and anger.] I think he already knows enough, and what's my business is my business and none of yours or his.
>
> RS: Perhaps we should back up here for a second, Josh. You are obviously very angry about your situation, and I can't say that I blame you. [I am trying to let Josh know that I empathize with his plight.] It sounds as if football is very important to you, and not being able to play is extremely frustrating. I would like to hear more about it; I think it is important, however, for me to lay a few ground rules about our discussion. First, I am not here to punish you for anything. I am here to try to help you and to hopefully speed your return to the team. From my brief discussion with your coach, it appears that he is interested in the same outcome, that is, your coming back to the football team in good standing and in a position to contribute to the team's success. Second, my talks with you are strictly confidential. What is said between us stays here. I will talk with other people only if you give me written consent to do so. I would really like to help you, Josh, but I need your cooperation in letting me know what is going on.

Josh views his coach's referral to me as an act of betrayal rather than a matter of genuine concern. He sounds likely to view me as similarly untrustworthy. He clearly resents the coercive element and does not see it as a reflection of how valuable he may be to the team. I am guessing that Josh is not very good at taking orders, at least outside the realm of football, and I had better not offer any symbolic medicine that he is required to take. He does demonstrate the ability to cooperate when there is a concrete personal benefit, or he would not be psychologically able to pursue an athletic career at all. The coach cannot be indifferent about how well this referral progresses, and he probably does have an investment in how well Josh performs for the good of his own career, for Josh, and for the team. The coach's input is helpful to me, and judging from Josh's sensitivity, anger, and vehement response to his referral and the related circumstances, his drinking is likely to be a significant issue in our work together. It is too early in the process, however, for me to conclude anything about his drinking. For now, I simply note Josh's emotional reactions to our discussion and continue to focus on building our alliance.

I know that "telling" is a high crime among siblings and in the lower school grades. So it is, too, for the mental health professional, possibly leading to license revocation or painful experiences in civil court, but there is no absolute way to prove that I am an upstanding, trustworthy, ethical, and sincere person. All relationships involve risk of one sort or another, but that knowledge is a function of emotional maturation. It is easier to think in idealized and categorical clear-cut propositions. Almost any interpersonal undertaking requires some degree of trust. Trust is a component of the coach–athlete dyad, and it is a positive sign that Josh probably has been able to respond to coaching in order to advance his career in sport this far. Why am I not communicating these ideas to Josh? Well, we are not in a lecture hall, and I remain more interested in trying to empathize with his situation in order to build a working alliance. By backing up, I can acknowledge that we are not moving in a mutually meaningful fashion. Josh is entitled to feel whatever he feels. In attempting to clarify and label present emotions, I make another offer of alliance without straying far from the basic purpose of the interview. I do not openly address whether or not Josh and I can work together. I do recognize that I am the primary party responsible for building our relationship and that I can be defeated in the effort to do so.

I doubt that disavowing punitive intent assures that I will be believed. My subsequent actions will convey the real message. Although I tell Josh I want to help, perhaps I should explain more specifically with appropriate examples. I need to take care that the examples do not sound as if I am violating past confidences. Josh raises the issue of whom I am working for, and it is vital to clarify this point in my own thinking. Josh is helping me, albeit reluctantly, with this process, and there may be a way to thank him for it. At the moment I want him to know that he, and no one else, is the client despite the coercive aspects of our encounter. Our meeting, however, is not coercive for me. I can decline to see him or refer him elsewhere. Confidentiality is vital, but it is also conditional. I cannot maintain silence in the absence of knowing what may be disclosed. What if some of the altercations involved criminal assaults, rape, or other offenses, and Josh threatens more of the same? Should I want to seek consultation concerning Josh, he will be informed and his permission requested. If the coach or other school official calls, I am not obligated to say whether this interview took place. I do not go into the details of these issues for the moment because the more that is said, the more likely that Josh will seize on some aspect of it to present further resistance. I make a mental note to elaborate on confidentiality for Josh if we terminate here or come to an agreement to continue. I try to encourage him to help us arrive at some problems to work on together, and I imply by my direct request that he is capable of doing so.

> Josh: What's going on is that I have been thrown off the football team indefinitely, and I am not sure how I will get to play again. [The tone in Josh's voice suggests that he is fearful of not being able to play again and at the same time thoroughly perplexed about how he might regain playing privileges.] I think the coach doesn't understand me. I don't get what the big deal is with a few drinks with the guys and a few scuffles here and there.
>
> RS: Tell me more about the drinks and the scuffles, Josh.
>
> Josh: A few nights ago, me and some of the other guys on the team went to one of the local hangouts and had a few beers. Some loudmouth got up in my face, so I decked him. That started a kind of free-for-all for a while before the cops showed up, and I got arrested. Then the coach tells me I am suspended from the team until I can get some help. I have no idea what he means by help. I feel just fine.

Josh still is not grasping the connection between alcohol use, violence, returning to the playing field, and his presence at this interview. I know this symptom of his immaturity—separating actions from consequences—is a psychological defense that is not thought out or even consciously known. He is genuinely confused, but it will not be useful or palatable for him if I attempt to lead him out of it. It is more important that he make some discoveries for himself. My job is to help him get on the right path.

Josh again tries to draw me into his differences with the coach. Were I to be seduced into playing "you and me against the coach," I would become the next target. More important, he is marginally cooperative in volunteering a specific drinking incident instead of categorical generalizations, and his brief story is something we can work on right now. That Josh cooperates by recounting the precipitating incident suggests a slight appreciation of what I am trying to do.

I think about how to provide positive reinforcement to Josh and to help him find a way to gain some control of his situation. He is unaware that he is out of step with regard to policies applying to all athletes on his team and is trying to portray himself as singled out for persecution. Josh presently lacks sufficient perspective to assess the total context of his actions. I want to keep him talking without commanding or leading him. Through my tone of voice and facial expression, I try to convey my interest and concern. I doubt he really feels "fine" in the psychological sense, but I do believe he experiences temporary euphoria when he cuts loose aggressively with his anger. No doubt he will hold me accountable for any negative aspects of this interview. I am tempted to explain "help" and all that I could do, but now is hardly the moment. To do so would only be a way of reassuring myself and quelling my personal anxiety and of no real use to Josh.

> **Keep your clients talking without commanding or leading.**

RS: It sounds as if the coach is concerned about you, Josh. What do you think he is worried about?

Josh: I'm not sure. I just wish I could play football.

RS: In the interest of reaching that goal, Josh, I think it is a good idea for us to take a look at what might be preventing you from playing football. Would you be willing to do this with me?

Josh: What do you mean, what is preventing me from playing football? [Josh shows exasperation with my comment.] It's the coach and his ideas and rules that are preventing me from playing. But since I have to be here, I don't see any reason not to talk about it. I got nothin' better to do.

I am going to frame the problems for Josh and put the issues in a context where active problem solving might take place. I will phrase Josh's difficulties within a parameter that we can manage for the duration of this conversation. Josh is a bit of a magical thinker. He would like wishes to come true, especially without any effort on his part. I have good reason to believe that the coach has told Josh exactly what he is concerned about and that Josh genuinely did not comprehend the message. I ally myself with Josh's confusion, clarify what I intend to do, and formulate a possible common goal. Josh likes to pretend that his situation is not really serious, but I will not make an issue of that point. I consider ways to praise Josh for what he has disclosed thus far about his quandary. He gives me a grudging acquiescence with the proviso that he does not want to be held responsible for the consequences of his actions. I take his statement as a first indicator of trust in small measure, though cast in a no-choice vein ("But since I have to be here . . ."). I will not be drawn into trying to make Josh and the coach a happy couple. All problems have a history, and it is time to elicit more about Josh's past.

RS: It sounds to me as though the coach has concerns about your drinking and the behavior that results from drinking, such as arguing and getting into fights. Can you tell me about other times when these behaviors have caused problems for you?

Josh: Sure, I guess. I have been drinking since I was 13 or so and fightin' for at least that long. [The tone in Josh's voice is matter of fact, suggesting he does not place great importance on these behaviors.]

> R: Who else besides your coach has expressed concern over your drinking and fighting?
>
> J: Oh, my mom has talked to me about it and said that I needed to change. My dad never seemed too concerned about it. I have gotten in trouble with a few other coaches who warned me that they would suspend me from the team for fighting, but no one ever has until this coach.

I am not judging or blaming, but the link between actions and consequences must be drawn if we are to move toward Josh's responsibilities for his circumstances. His behavior while drinking seems serious—he is not talking about late-adolescent carousing. The troubles may go beyond what I can directly address in my present relationship with him. I probably do not have to ask if anyone else has been worried. I believe I already know. I am leading Josh toward hearing himself admit it. My query is also an indirect way of letting Josh know I am familiar with these waters. He appears more comfortable talking about the fighting, and the drinking has been conveniently omitted.

> RS: Anyone else?
>
> Josh: Well, my girlfriend said she wouldn't stay with me if I continued to get into fights. I have been with her for a while, and I would hate to lose her, but I don't really understand why she is so concerned. I don't fight around her.

Many people like Josh are incredibly fearless when emotionally aroused and act with total disregard for the potential danger to themselves or others. They may be seen as laudably brave in physical fighting or intensely competitive in sport. When the pattern moves into the context of intimate relationships and social interaction, their partners often become anxious about potential consequences and are unwilling to remain with someone whose behaviors could endanger relationships via legal sanctions or actual loss of life. There is clearly more to know about how violent Josh has been. This area can be a difficult one to explore because it has direct implications for just how safe I might be in his presence. Therapists are not required to be heroes, and I know that assaults by clients are grossly underreported. I will not get swept up in Josh's denial of potential harm to himself and others. Josh has once again avoided the alcohol issue and focused on the fighting, but at some level he knows alcohol is a genuine problem. I presume he wants to lead me away from the real cause of the fighting. It is time to reinsert that piece of the puzzle.

> RS: Tell me about the circumstances that usually lead to your fighting.
>
> Josh: Well, I usually get into fights when I've had a few drinks and I'm out with the guys for a good time. It always seems to happen that someone pisses me off, and the next thing I know I take a swing at him.
>
> RS: What role does alcohol play in all this?
>
> Josh: I guess drinkin' and fightin' kind of go together. As a matter of fact, I can't remember the last time I was in a fight without having had a few drinks. It seems to loosen me up, and I guess it gives my temper a quick fuse.

I wonder what constitutes a "good time" and also note that Josh holds others blameful for his negative feelings. He does not separate the feeling from the action. So it is with toddlers. Josh is functioning at a level where the feeling also justifies the action. The referral information suggests that he probably shares this attitude with others in his family. The regressive effects of alcohol further enhance his developmentally regressive thinking. He is almost dissociated from his own body, as if his fist just flies out on its own and does the damage. I attempt to connect the links in Josh's account. It seems to me that alcohol use functions as a sanction for certain behaviors in Josh's way of thinking. I will not be intimidated away from the alcohol abuse exploration. I stay with the presenting problem without delving into the interpersonal patterns or intrapsychic conflicts underlying them at this time.

RS: So you think you are quick to anger when you are drinking?

Josh: That's right. For the most part I'm a pretty easygoing guy, and I don't let things bother me too much. When I drink, things seem to upset me much quicker than when I don't drink.

RS: How long has that been the case?

Josh: For as long as I can remember; I guess I don't think too straight after I have had a few drinks, and people can get on my nerves in a hurry.

I reflect and reinforce Josh's increasing participation. Nothing in this interview suggests to me that Josh is as easygoing as he might like to believe. Although he is still trying to dissimulate and minimize, I am encouraged by his effort to actually reflect on his behavior, which gives me an opening for continuing this process. I explore his history for other indications of alcohol abuse. I could make other choices such as asking what things usually bother Josh, what happened immediately before the last incident, or who else Josh has been around becomes violent when drinking. The likelihood that Josh had a physically abusive childhood is sounding more probable. Although Josh certainly is not thinking of symptoms, I note his impaired judgment and the opportunity the alcohol use provides for Josh to unload his anger on others. I am sure he is angry long before the first drink, but he has not learned much about other ways to manage negative feelings. I make a mental check to put anger management on our agenda in subsequent interviews.

RS: Besides your temper getting short, are there other things that happen differently while you are drinking?

Josh: Yeah, I guess. I sometimes can't remember things that happened to me the morning after a night out on the town. Sometimes I find myself back in my room and not remembering how I got there.

RS: What do you think about that?

Josh: It scares the hell out of me. It's really a strange feeling to be in a familiar place but not have a clue how you got there. Sometimes my friends tell me I did funny things the night before, and I have no memory of it.

RS: For example?

Josh: Oh, I might tell jokes or say something stupid to somebody, who may get upset about it, but I can't remember it the next day when my friends tell me about it.

As I explore symptoms, I remain ready to mention possibilities that Josh may overlook. I find his disclosure about blackouts (memory loss associated with heavy drinking) an unusual admission for a first interview. I believe that Josh is at least a little in touch with a frightening aspect of problem drinking, which creates the opportunity for me to advise that he could, indeed, use a very specific form of help (e.g., programmatic outpatient substance abuse treatment), though I do not intend to blurt it out at this moment. My focus stays on Josh, and I know there has to be more to his story. Comedic drunks can be entertaining, but they do not get arrested.

RS: Anything else about your behavior when you are drinking that concerns you, Josh?

Josh: I don't know. [Pause.] There are times I have thought about cutting back on my drinking or quitting altogether, but I don't want to miss out on fun with my friends. I mean, most people my age in college drink on a regular basis. I don't see where I am any different from most people out there. So why should I change something if I like it?

RS: It is certainly true that a lot of people your age are drinkers. It sounds as if you are having a difficult time reconciling the fact that a lot of your friends drink and that you would like to join them, but for some reason alcohol is associated with some unfortunate circumstances for you, for instance, your short temper, your fighting, and your not remembering things after a night out on the town.

Josh has just told me that there are aspects of drinking he really does not like, that he has been worried to the point of thinking about initiating changing on his own, but that alcohol use seems like an essential component of socialization. I infer that he is not particularly at ease in social situations off the athletic field (a familiar place for Josh where there are many convenient rules about how to behave) and that underneath the bravado he is adrift and unsure of himself. I suspect that "easygoing" is more of a passive going along with the group than an expression of his temperament. I could bring up consequences of the fighting, such as arrest, suspension from the team, girlfriend problems, and today's interview, but it would not be wise to lay the whole case out right now. I will wait until the summary and recommendations phase of the interview process. We are still struggling to develop a style of working together.

> Josh: [With a thus far uncharacteristic reflective look on his face.] You know, Doc, I really don't want to give up something that is fun to do with my friends, but I also want to play football. I think my chances to play at the next level are pretty good, and I don't want anything to mess that up.
>
> RS: What are some things that you think might mess that up? [I am looking for a way for Josh to discover the discrepancy between his present drinking behavior and its consequences and his achievement of goals that are important to him.]
>
> Josh: Well, if I continue to drink like I am and continue to get in trouble like I am, I may be messing up my potential future in football. I think I would have a hard time if I short-circuited my prospects in football by continually getting into trouble for rules violations having to do with my drinking and fighting. [We are moving in the right direction.]
>
> RS: That sounds like something that concerns you a lot.
>
> Josh: You are damn right it does. [Stated emphatically and seriously.] I really want to play at the professional level, and I think I am capable of doing it. And these days just signing a contract at the pro level can put a lot of money in my pocket.

Josh is displaying a serious and reflective aspect of himself, which I am rather surprised to uncover, while providing me with a "hook," a means of enlisting him in further discussions. His use of *Doc* suggests that I am becoming a real person to him rather than just another symbol of authority to be resented. His anxiety level is going down, so we are on the right path. He may not yet realize that the "anything" standing in his way is himself, but he is moving toward such insight. He has given me the chance to enlist him in the problem-solving process and is on the edge of taking responsibility for his actions and changing them.

The mutuality of our exchange also is heartening by establishing the likelihood that Josh came to this interview sober and able to think coherently. I am really impressed by the shift from laying all the problems on the coach to the admission from Josh that the circumstances are at least part of his own making. It is all too easy to blame the alcohol and disown one's part in using it. Josh is hinting at just how important a sports career is for his future and his sense of personal identity. Football may be much more than just a means of earning a living. Now I can build on the motivational aspects of his interests and place myself on his "team." He is showing me indications of positive self-regard that can be used when the process moves to the matter of taking action. He is articulating a concrete goal in the distant future. Such a goal, however, is usually not sufficient motivational incentive for impulsive persons. We need something closer to home.

RS: That is true indeed. We have spent a lot of time talking about the circumstances that brought you here, Josh. I would really like to know what's so appealing to you about playing football.

Josh: [Josh's eyes light up, and his enthusiasm spills out without restraint.] It's the coolest sport ever. I love the contact, and I like the challenge of beating the defensive back trying to cover me. At my best, I don't think anybody can cover me. I like the idea of being able to show my stuff every week on the field. It's really a high for me!

RS: It's wonderful that you have found something you really enjoy and that you are very good at. Are there any negative aspects to playing football for you?

Josh: I don't like all of the rules, and I don't like practice too much. I particularly don't like coming in for curfew every night during the season. But if it gets me to the next level of competition, I am willing to do it.

RS: What are some things that you think could make you a better player?

I am looking for psychological and emotional incentives and building bridges to material Josh has yet to explore. Josh is providing me with a metaphor that can be employed as an instrument for change. Can Josh beat alcohol abuse? Can he do it better than anyone else? How might alcohol deaden the performance-induced pleasures? Josh does not know it, but the dialogue is now on two levels. Interchange *drinking* with *football* and the intervention possibilities are widened. Josh's academic performance leads me to believe that he has difficulty engaging in behaviors that involve postponement of gratification, even when they may be in his long-range self-interest. That remains as a fundamental challenge for us. The interview is flowing well, and I resist the temptation to offer remedies prematurely. The art of proper timing does not come naturally.

> **Timing of interventions is learned and is critical to success.**

Josh: I think I am real good, but I know I have some areas where I could improve. I could definitely be a better blocker, and I would like to be able to concentrate better before catching a ball in the middle. As much as I like contact, I don't like the idea of a defensive back taking a free shot at me while I am trying to catch a pass.

RS: Sounds as if there are some mental aspects of the game that you feel you could do better.

Josh: Yeah, I guess in many respects it's a mental game. Do you think you could help me with any of that stuff?

RS: That's one of the main reasons I am here, Josh. Yes, I think there are some things we can do to help you become a better player mentally, and I would be glad to talk with you about that later. Right now, I would like to recap our session today. When you first came in here today, you were understandably upset and angry about your circumstances. You told me you enjoy going out and having a few drinks with the guys, and you would like to continue to do that. It seems, however, that your coach is concerned about your behavior when you drink, in particular your fighting. Apparently, he is so much concerned that he has chosen to suspend you from the team as a result of your recent drinking and fighting episode. You also told me that other people have expressed concern about your behavior while drinking, such as your mother and your girlfriend. You believe that your skills in football are at a level that will make you competitive to play professionally, and you would not like anything to get in the way of that goal, particularly things you have direct control over. Apparently, you think your drinking and fighting may potentially short-circuit your prospects in football, and you would like to prevent that from occurring. Last, you shared with me that you enjoy the physical contact aspects of football and the challenge of beating the defensive back covering you. You've acknowledged that football is to a large extent a mental game and that you feel you could improve that aspect of your game. Does this accurately summarize what we have been over today, Josh?

Now we are on cognitive–psychological ground, and Josh has picked up on the "mental" aspects with little help from me while wondering if I can really be useful. I embed the idea that Josh is the one who has to control his drinking while using his fear of being controlled by others as a positive motivational agent. Josh entered this interview defiantly, transferring blame to authority and coping by an attempt at bullying. He has a history of breaking rules, which actually leads to further tightening of controls, and he has been forced into the interview. I can use his fear and his wish to be in command by linking them with his ability to control himself and make the decisions, which will put him back on the playing field. I do not argue with him about what he should do. I am no longer an obstacle to be attacked or avoided but can be viewed as a potential collaborator facilitating Josh's objectives. The process is put in the context of Josh's own avowals rather than something imposed from without. By rolling with his resistance in this manner, our reason for being together is being transformed.

Josh:   Yeah, I guess that gets it in a nutshell. I want to play football, and anything that keeps me from it, I want to do something about. Can you help me get back on the field?

RS:     I am not sure of the specifics of how the decision will be reached about your return to the field, Josh. I suspect that the timing of your return to football depends on you, your coach, and health professionals who are responsible for your care, such as the team physician. What I would like to do is help you take a closer look at the events that have led you to be suspended from the team and discuss ways in which you can change the associated behaviors. My suggestion is that we set another appointment time to begin taking a closer look at things and exploring our options. Are you game for that?

Josh:   Sure, I guess so. Do you have any idea how long this is going to take?

RS:     At the moment I don't. We should know some more as we explore your background a little more in depth and come to some conclusions about a direction to take.

Before a remedy can be prescribed, I ask Josh to consider matters not yet discussed. His family background has set him up for substance abuse as a primary coping tendency, tremendous anger, impulsive and violent tendencies, and unstable current relationships. Patience is not one of Josh's great strengths. I will have to move on quickly and formulate a concrete initial therapeutic task for him. I begin by making it easy for him to return.

Josh:   Are you gonna talk to my coach?

RS:     As I explained before, our sessions are confidential unless you would like for me to disclose information to another person. If we feel that including your coach in some aspects of our work together would be beneficial, then we can discuss it at that time. Otherwise, I would like to proceed without him for the time being.

Josh:   Sounds fine to me, Doc. What time do you want to meet again?

RS:     I would like to meet with you again tomorrow at 2:00 p.m. Also, Josh, I would like for you to refrain from drinking during the next week or so while we are meeting and deciding what direction we are moving in with respect to our work together. Would you agree to do that?

Josh:   [Josh gives me an incredulous look and pauses for a second, seemingly mulling over his answer.] I guess I can do that, but I don't really want to.

RS:     Thanks, Josh. I understand that you don't want to, and I appreciate your willingness to make that change for now. I will see you tomorrow at 2:00.

Josh is asking, not assuming, as he did at the beginning of the interview, if I will betray his confidence. Until now, he has not said anything that would lead me to break confidentiality. The trust implied in his question deserves my full respect. At the onset of the next interview, I am obliged to spell out the exact limits of confidentiality in the context of our relationship; obtain his consent to them; and establish the administrative aspects of my responsibilities such as availability by phone, encounters in other contexts, and scheduling protocol. I am already thinking that I may need to help him enlist in an alcohol treatment program while he and I continue on the specifics of how he can get back on the playing field and perform even more effectively there. Somewhere down the road we might even explore his fears of intimacy and social anxieties.

I ask Josh to refrain from drinking partly to decrease the risk of further problems but also to see whether he is able to comply. My intent in doing this is to see whether he continues to drink and have related problems despite his current predicament. Continuing alcohol-related problems in the face of significant negative repercussions would suggest to me that Josh might require more immediate and intensive assistance (e.g., inpatient or residential care) than I might plan otherwise.

In the next two sessions, occurring within a one-week period, I spend time gathering a general history on Josh, paying particular attention to alcohol use and its effects on important life areas, such as school, work, relationships, and perhaps most important to Josh, his athletic performance. He made it clear in our first session that football is an exceptionally important part of his life, and he is willing to entertain changing his drinking behavior if he thinks it might deter him from excelling on the field. This fear of not excelling is an important potential motivation for Josh to take steps necessary to change self-defeating alcohol use patterns. Fortunately during these sessions, Josh reports that he has not had anything to drink and has not been involved in any fighting since we started our work together.

I also decide that input from significant people in Josh's life would be valuable at this point, both for information gathering on my part and for Josh to hear directly from these people their thoughts regarding his drinking. I speak with Josh about calling his parents and girlfriend in separate conference phone calls to solicit their input. After some hesitation, he agrees to the calls, and I obtain essential confidentiality releases to include these parties in a phone call. Based on what Josh has already shared with me, I am fairly certain that each of them will be supportive of his taking the necessary steps to make changes in his drinking. I ask Josh to call each of them and arrange for a mutually convenient time for the conference call. My focus in these calls is largely on Josh's behavior when he is drinking and when he is not drinking and on concerns for his general welfare as it relates to his alcohol use. Ideally, I would bring these parties in session with Josh so that he may hear what they have to say in person, but in this case, I judge that time is critical, and the information I could gain from these important people in Josh's life by phone is valuable to my work with him and to the success of a possible referral for alcohol treatment.

> When necessary, and if the athlete agrees, involve other people in your sessions, such as parents and significant others.

As it turns out, their information is helpful, solidifying my impression that Josh's problematic alcohol use dates to his high school years and that the trend appears to be worsening (e.g., increasing frequency of heavy alcohol use, more fights, deteriorating relationships). His mother tells me that Josh had repeated difficulties in high school concerning fighting and drinking, and she is not surprised that he is having difficulty at the university. She adds that she is saddened by the fact that so many in their family have problems with alcohol, but she knows that help is available if Josh would take the important step of accepting his problem and realizing that he needs assistance.

After three sessions with Josh, I believe I have sufficient information supporting the existence of an alcohol problem and the need for a referral for specialized alcohol treatment. My task now is to use this information in such a way as to help Josh come to the same conclusion. At this juncture in our work together, I judge him to be in the contemplation stage of change (see the section Changing Problem Drinking on pages 137 and 138 for explanations on stages of change). In the last two sessions, he has indicated that he has not fully realized the damage his drinking causes family members and friends. He has also reiterated his desire to change whatever behavior is necessary to give himself the best chance to be successful in football. In the fourth session, I decide it is time to discuss the possibility of Josh's enrollment in an outpatient alcohol treatment program.

RS: Hi, Josh. How have you been since our last session?

Josh: Fair, I guess, but I sure miss being on the football field.

RS: I know it has been difficult for you to be away from what you love to do. How have you been spending your time since you haven't been able to practice and play with the team?

Josh: Well, I have been doing a lot of thinking about what we have been talking about and my drinking and all.

RS: And what exactly have you been thinking?

Josh: I guess I have been kind of mad about everything. I was really tempted to go out and have a few beers with my friends last night, but I knew that would do nothing but lead to more problems. So I went for a long walk to clear my head and think about things.

RS: What did you think about?

Josh: I thought about what a screwup I have been lately. It seems I can't keep from messing up. Every time things are going well for me, I do something to mess it up.

RS: How so?

Josh: Well, I guess mostly when I drink I mess things up. I mean, since I have stayed away from the alcohol for the last week, I have stayed out of trouble, but I also don't seem to be able to have fun with my friends, either. I hate to think that I will have to give up having fun along with drinking.

RS: Sounds pretty frustrating for you, Josh.

Josh: Yeah, it sure is. There has got to be a way for me to be able to have a normal life with my friends and all and still be able to drink occasionally. I mean, I am 21 years old! [Josh raises his arms in exasperation and lets them flop back onto his thighs.] I can't back out of my social life just because of a problem I may have with alcohol.

RS: I agree, Josh. Your problems with alcohol should not preclude your having a social life. I sense that you are really struggling with the issue of living a life you can enjoy while also dealing with the problems that drinking has posed for you. Would you like some suggestions on where to go with that issue?

Josh: Please, Doc, suggest away!

RS: Well, Josh, based on what you shared with me over the last week and on discussions we had with your parents and girlfriend, I believe your drinking and the effects it has on your behavior pose a significant roadblock to your potential happiness and to your effectiveness in life. You told me about problems related to your alcohol use that date back to your teenage years when you first started to drink. These include problems in school, with your friends and family, and with the law. Apparently, when you drink, you have significant changes in your behavior such that you are prone to fighting with the slightest provocation. This aspect of your drinking has caused you problems for a long time, and is the reason you are now suspended from the team and here seeing me. You also told me about memory lapses that occur when you drink that have scared you. Also, we have yet to explore the possible negative effects of alcohol on your athletic performance. Your drinking may very well negatively affect your ability to remember plays, sustain concentration, maintain self-discipline, and work cooperatively with your teammates and coaches. All this information taken together, Josh, indicates to me that you are paying a very high price for your drinking and have been for a long time. To alleviate these problems and to decrease the price you are paying, I believe you need to make some changes to your drinking. In other words, I don't think you can lead an enjoyable life, pursue your goals, and at the same time continue to drink in the fashion you have been drinking. I also believe that the best way for you to make changes in your drinking is to get help from someone who specializes in helping people who have difficulties with alcohol.

Josh: So you think I need to go see an alcohol shrink?

RS: I think you need to see a specialist at the outpatient alcohol treatment program, which is located a couple of miles from campus. His name is Alan Grant.

Josh: What is he going to do for me that I can't get from you?

RS: Josh, Mr. Grant is a specialist who focuses his practice on helping people who have problems related to their alcohol use. I would refer you to him so that you can get the appropriate help for the difficulties you are having with alcohol. I would continue to help you with the mental aspects of becoming a better football player.

Josh: I don't know about this. How am I going to get back to playing football if I am going to see this guy at the alcohol treatment program all the time?

RS: I am not sure what your schedule for seeing him would be. That would be arranged with him. With respect to returning to play football, I believe that going to see Mr. Grant could be a step in that direction. If I call to make an appointment with him, would you be willing to go?

Josh: I am not crazy about the idea, but I realize I have got to do something to change the direction I am going in now. If I agree to go, will you promise to continue to work with me on getting back to football?

RS: What I promise to do is work with you on becoming a better mentally prepared player. I believe that your improvement on the mental aspects of the game will make you a more effective player, generally. With your permission, I also would like to stay informed about your progress in working with Mr. Grant. When the time comes, I would like to be involved in the decision about when you will return to practice and games.

Josh: I guess that sounds like a fair deal to me.

RS: Good, Josh. I will call to set up an appointment for you with Mr. Grant, and then we can set up a time for you to come back and see me.

Josh: Let's do it.

Josh is agreeing almost too readily and will need a lot of follow-up support on my part. Referrals of this nature frequently do not "take" on the first try. My making the appointment for Josh with Mr. Grant during our session should increase the probability of a successful referral. I have a solid working relationship with Mr. Grant, and I am prepared to give knowledgeable answers to Josh's questions. I expect that Josh will occasionally "slip" to former drinking habits, and his self-esteem and determination to alter his drinking pattern will likely fluctuate. I am willing to help enlist others as Josh builds a support network to facilitate change. I can continue to link athletic performance enhancement with the benefits of avoiding alcohol abuse, which I expect will serve as motivation for Josh to continue with his positive change process.

> Successful referral is supported by understanding the dynamics of motivation for change.

# Professional Issues

Josh's case presents numerous professional issues for consideration. For didactic purposes, we pose these issues in the form of questions that we feel the sport psychologist would benefit from exploring, perhaps with a consultant or supervisor, depending on the professional situation.

**Is Josh's drinking atypical among his peers?**    Based on the initial sessions with Josh, I believe I have enough information to answer yes. Additional corroborating information in the context of his treatment at the alcohol treatment program would be helpful. Presently, there is sufficient evidence that his drinking is causing serious interpersonal problems for him and that it is a factor in his violence and his suspension from the football team. As we learned earlier, heavy drinking is not an uncommon activity for college students, and college male athletes certainly are not immune to heavy drinking and related consequences. Josh's behavior while drinking (anger outbursts, violence, episodes of memory loss), however, indicates that even if his consumption of alcohol is not unusual in the context of his peers' use, his response to alcohol is. This history, along with his positive family history for substance abuse and violence, suggests that Josh's drinking will continue to cause problems for him unless he takes purposeful actions to change.

**Does Josh's drinking pose a threat to his and others' health and safety?**    Of course Josh's drinking and its effects on his behavior pose threats to his and others' health and safety. Often, however, it is the question with the obvious answer that fails to be addressed by the clinician. In Josh's case, the clinician must be mindful of his potential for harming himself and others and of the duty of all helping professionals to protect members of society, generally. Every time Josh "goes out with the guys to have fun" and the fun includes drinking (which seems highly likely given his reported history), he poses a potential threat to himself and others. The issue for the helping professional is what to do about it. Because we have no magic wands to change his behavior, and he has committed no offenses that warrant his incarceration or commitment (at least in our current awareness), we must work with what we have—him and his attitudes and motivations for changing his behavior. Fortunately, Josh gave some indications in the first session that he has, at times, been concerned about his drinking and has actually considered cutting down. For now, this motivation for change, small though it may be, is what we have to work with.

**What level of awareness does Josh have regarding the seriousness of his drinking?**    A different and perhaps more useful way to phrase this question is What change stage is Josh in presently? At the beginning of the first session, I would have placed Josh squarely in the precontemplation stage. His statements suggested that he considers his "drinkin' and fightin'" as part of his life; he does not think either is a problem and does not voice any desire or need to change. Later in the interview and in subsequent sessions, however, Josh indicates an awareness of some of the negative aspects of his drinking (blackouts, potential loss of his girlfriend, threat to his football career) and reports that he has even considered altering his drinking. These self-reports suggest that he has moved into the contemplation stage, at least for periods of time. Josh's reports of awareness of negative consequences of drinking are a positive thread for me to recognize and nurture in hopes that he will continue along this path of contemplation and later move into the preparation and action stages.

**Is the case example reflective of motivational interviewing strategies?**    An examination of the case dialogue indicates that the five basic principles of motivational interviewing suggested by Miller and Rollnick (1991) are being applied:

- Express empathy: I take every opportunity to express empathy for Josh and his predicament, being careful not to become enmeshed in the disagreement he is having with his coach. Maintaining my objectivity about his situation is critical so that I will be in a favorable position to suggest and explore behavioral alternatives with him as he progresses through the change stages. Genuine empathy is a special kind of deep interest in another, communicated through good listening and learning the client's verbal and nonverbal language. It is not a feigned concern or restricted to only one aspect of the client's personality. When skillfully expressed, empathy encourages the client to feel safe in letting down the persona presented in casual relationships.

- Develop and amplify in the client's mind a discrepancy between present behavior and important goals: As it happens, Josh really helps me out with this motivational principle when he reflected on how important football is to him and how he does not want to jeopardize a possible future professional career. He started developing the discrepancy on his own; it is my task to help him proceed further by exploring various ways his drinking and violence might, if unchanged, block him from his ultimate goal—playing professional football. As we continue to explore various facets of his drinking and violence, I am confident there will be numerous opportunities for me to amplify this theme. The odds for Josh to play professional football are not known as yet. Furthermore, even if it is a long shot for him to play professionally, now is not the time to challenge or dismiss his ambitions, particularly if they may fuel his motivation to change his present counterproductive behavior.

- Avoid argumentation: This principle is put to the test from the outset of the session with Josh. He obviously came to the interview with anger and frustration about his situation, part of which was directed at me. He also voiced distrust of my intentions and questioned the confidentiality of our interview. It was important that I not respond emotionally to his confrontational style but rather allow him to vent and then return the interchange to the issues that led to his coming to see me in the first place—his drinking and violence.

- Roll with resistance by offering new information and perspectives for the client to consider: The best example of this principle is my reflecting and embellishing on the idea he presented that he wants to do whatever it takes to do away with potential roadblocks that might interrupt his path to playing football. I suggest to him that he ultimately needs to control his drinking, which will enhance the likelihood that he will control his own fate with respect to football. Because Josh is resistant to external control of his behavior, the opportunity to control his future in football is self-rewarding.

- Support self-efficacy by reinforcing the client's personal responsibility for change and by suggesting a variety of alternatives for action: The drinking–football metaphor mentioned in the dialogue commentary is one way for me to support Josh's self-efficacy regarding his ability to change his drinking. By using a metaphor that ties directly into football, I suggest that the skills that have made Josh great as a football player can also make him great as a behavior changer—in this case the behavior to change is problem drinking. With respect to alternatives for action, I recommend Josh to an alcohol treatment program and suggest that he continue to see me for sport psychology interventions. Because I am familiar with the program I referred Josh to, I know he will receive a variety of treatment options there. I also will monitor his progress in the program and introduce additional alternatives as I see fit.

Motivational enhancement therapies, such as those described here, have been found to be more effective than 12-step facilitation (based on the disease model of alcoholism and on Alcoholics Anonymous principles) and cognitive–behavioral therapies in treating alcoholic patients with high anger levels (Matching Alcoholism Treatments, 1998). These results suggest that our use of motivational enhancement strategies is particularly appropriate given Josh's problems with anger control.

**Is referral for alcohol treatment warranted in Josh's case?** Given recent research results (Dinh-Zarr, Diguiseppi, Heitman, & Roberts, 1999) indicating that treatment for problem drinking is effective in preventing alcohol-related injuries, Josh's possible entry into alcohol treatment takes on added significance. I suggest this possibility in the commentary: "The troubles may go beyond what I can directly address in my present relationship with him." Reaching a reasoned conclusion to this question requires consideration of many variables with respect to Josh. Some of the factors that need evaluation include the severity of his alcohol-related problems, the risk that Josh poses to himself and others, the presence of other psychological problems, and the validation of his self-reports through history taking with Josh and with significant others (e.g., family members, friends, teammates). If some form of alcohol treatment is indicated, choices of level and type of interventions must be negotiated with Josh. It is best to try the least intensive intervention (outpatient rather than inpatient treatment, as I have done in this case) that is likely to meet Josh's needs and goals first. If these interventions are unsuccessful, more intensive care may be considered.

As sport psychologists, we must be mindful of how athletes' participation in sport may interact with their participation in treatment. For example, the acute intervention stage, when an alcohol problem is first recognized, may be delayed in athletes because of their superior physical conditioning and youth relative to the general population, which may bestow on them temporary resistance to the physical effects of heavy drinking. Conversely, because successful sport performance demands advanced physical skills, the acute intervention stage may actually be hastened for the athlete relative to the average person. During the rehabilitation stage, a significant amount of the athlete's time must be focused on attainment of treatment goals. Therefore, depending on whether the athlete is in a competitive season, this stage of treatment may significantly disrupt any sport-related activities. During the maintenance stage, the athlete may face a difficult readjustment to training and competitive routines, depending on how long treatment required him or her to be away from sport.

Another issue bearing on whether and when a referral for alcohol treatment is made in Josh's case is my level of training, experience, and comfort in dealing with the clinical issues that he presents. In addition, I must consider my role with respect to the referral source, the football coach. If I am an independent clinical practitioner with alcohol treatment skills, I might feel very comfortable working with Josh on an outpatient basis until clinical progress, or lack thereof, dictates otherwise. On the other hand, if I am a sport psychologist primarily involved in providing performance enhancement services to the athletic program where Josh participates, it is best for me to do an initial evaluation and refer Josh to specialized service providers.

**Can Josh transfer strengths from sport to his current problems?** This question relates to the issue of whether skills developed in sport positively transfer to the tasks involved in changing problem drinking. Individual differences notwithstanding, it is reasonable to assume that some sport-related skills will be useful in alcohol treatment. These may include goal setting, achievement motivation, accurate assessment of strengths and weaknesses, development of methods to capitalize on strengths and improve weaknesses, self-reward of incremental progress toward goals, time management, focusing attention on task-relevant issues, and accepting direction and guidance (coaching) to improve performance (Stainback, 1997). Whether or not Josh has developed these skills before treatment remains to be seen. In the event he has not, perhaps his treatment experience may help him acquire them, in which case the transfer of skills can work in reverse (i.e., flow from treatment to sport).

**What are important issues to consider if Josh enters alcohol treatment?** One important issue to consider is whether the time and energy demands of treatment will allow for Josh's continued participation in football, or perhaps more important, whether his participation in football is indicated given his recent problems. To a large extent, the time and energy demands will be determined by the intensity of treatment required for Josh. If Josh can successfully handle treatment in an outpatient setting, he may be able to handle his football responsibilities simultaneously. Whether or not Josh plays football is ideally a mutually agreed upon decision made by the coach, Josh, the sport psychologist, and other health professionals involved in his care.

Another important time for Josh in the course of his treatment will be the maintenance phase of care, which involves "trying out" his changed relationships with alcohol and with important people in his life (e.g., friends, family, coaches, teammates). This treatment phase is pivotal for Josh's ability to establish a new life that is not enmeshed with alcohol. He will face many challenges and will likely experience "slips" to his former behavior patterns. His successful completion of this treatment phase can be supported by his work with alcohol treatment and sport psychology professionals and by his reintegration into sport.

# Conclusion

Josh's case is complex, combining what appears to be a substance use disorder with tendencies toward violence when alcohol is consumed. Effective intervention with Josh requires patient and skillful interviewing, knowledge of alcohol abuse and violence, self-awareness of one's professional capabilities and limitations, sufficient knowledge of community resources for alcohol treatment to make an appropriate referral, and professional flexibility to work with Josh in conjunction with alcohol treatment professionals. Josh will tax professional skills, but we believe those sharpened skills, resulting from work with Josh, will be exercised repeatedly in the future with similar cases.

## CHAPTER 9

# Over One's Head

## *Referral Processes*

Mark B. Andersen, PhD, and Judy L. Van Raalte, PhD

We call ourselves sport psychologists, and so we open our doors to athletes who expect that we can help them with psychological issues. When an athlete reveals material that is particularly challenging, sport psychology conventional wisdom urges us to refer. If we send our athletes away to another practitioner, however, they can interpret the referral as rejection, even when the matter is handled with sensitivity. These referrals can backfire, leaving our clients feeling rejected over core issues (often evoking shame). Our athletes may take referral information, never follow up, and then cease all therapeutic processes. Always referring athletes to other practitioners whenever the situation becomes challenging is too simple a solution. Many other questions need to be answered before the complex process of referral is chosen.

"When in doubt, refer!" are the cautious watchwords that have been repeated to graduate students in applied sport psychology for many years (Andersen & Tod, in press; Van Raalte & Andersen, 2002). What an ethical ring these words have. After all, ethical guidelines clearly state that we should *not* practice out of our areas of competence (APA, 1992). Repeating this referral mantra aloud, some students have surely wondered, *If I always refer when I am in doubt, how do I gain expertise and expand my ability to help my athlete clients?* And that is an excellent point. Maybe we should instead be saying, "When thinking of referring, doubt!" Perhaps the way to figure out this quandary is to examine, more carefully, what exactly is meant by "when in doubt, refer."

## Doubt About What?

Doubt can come in a variety of flavors, including Cartesian radical doubt, theological doubt about the existence of a deity, or statistical doubt about the likelihood of some research results being accurate. The types of doubt that arise in sport psychology service delivery may center more on interpersonal and intrapersonal levels, such as doubt about one's competence to serve the client's needs. ("Do I understand the problem? Do I have the competence to help the person deal with the problem? I know what the first step is, but if that doesn't work I have no idea what else to do.") This doubt about one's ability to help an athlete may stem from a lack of knowledge and experience. ("I know nothing about coach–athlete sexual exploitation and have never worked with such a client, so how could I help in this highly sensitive area?") Doubt may also arise from the emotional reaction a client's problem brings up in us. ("When this athlete talks about sexual abuse by the coach, it brings up all these images and feelings about when my coach sexually abused me, and I become a complete mess; there's no way I can help.")

It is okay for sport psychology students to doubt their abilities, question whether what they are doing is helpful, and try to figure out where they fit in service delivery. Doubt is good; it keeps one honest and reflective. But doubt can also be paralyzing. If every time doubt creeps into service delivery, the practitioner hits the referral button, not much work is going to get done.

One would hope, through education and supervision, that sport psychologists would be able to make reasonably accurate assessments of what they are capable of handling and what is beyond their competencies and requires referral (see Van Raalte & Andersen, 2000). But there are sport psychologists who range from one extreme, thinking they know very little, to the other, thinking they know everything. The adjectival anchors for those extremes run from "very ineffective" to "downright dangerous." Solid, honest, and brutal assessment of one's skills will supply a foundation for decision making on whether to refer or not.

**When thinking of referring, doubt!**

We hope that sport psychologists' competencies constantly develop rather than remain static (Lesyk, 1998). One practices with the competencies one has acquired, and with supervision, one practices the skills one is learning. Constantly referring when athletes present with issues that would stretch one's repertoire keeps professional development at bay. I (Mark) recall clearly my first student-athlete client with an eating disorder. I was prepared to do a quick handoff of the athlete to people with expertise in the student health center. But the athlete was not really disposed to going to someone else ("I only want to talk to you"). (For stigma anxiety and resistance issues, see Linder, Brewer, Van Raalte, & DeLange, 1991; Linder, Pillow, & Reno, 1989; and Van Raalte, Brewer, Brewer, & Linder, 1992.) I began having serious anxiety over continuing to work with her. My supervisor (bless him) took me aside.

Supervisor: Don't panic! OK, now what is the problem?

Mark: The problem is I don't know what the hell to do.

Supervisor: Are you sure about that?

Mark: I have never dealt with eating disorders; I don't want to screw this up.

Supervisor: Hold on, and back up. Why don't you tell me what you know about eating disorders and athletes. [I do so.] See! You know quite a bit.

Mark: But that's just book stuff, not real life.

Supervisor: OK, but let's look at real life for a moment. How long have you been working with Alicia?

Mark: Been seeing her for almost three months. We meet almost every week.

Supervisor: And when did she drop the eating bomb?

Mark: Yesterday.

Supervisor: And so what does that tell you?

What I came to realize is that the athlete and I had done some good work together. We had established a strong working relationship; we liked each other; and she had, over time, developed enough trust in me to reveal a concern that was deeply personal and painful

(Giges, 1998; Petitpas, Danish, & Giges, 1999; Poczwardowski, Sherman, & Henschen, 1998; Simons & Andersen, 1995; Strean & Strean, 1998). Referring her may have met my needs and concerns about working with an athlete on a difficult problem, but referral was not an option for her or perhaps even in the best interest of this athlete. With my supervisor's help and support on eating disorder issues, I was able, ethically, to work with Alicia. With such guidance and support, I began to practice what I was learning: helping an athlete with an eating disorder. (For more on supervision, see Andersen, Van Raalte, and Harris [2000] and Van Raalte and Andersen [2000].)

Does this example mean that the new sport psychology mantra should be "When in doubt, do *not* refer?" Absolutely not. Knowing when to refer and when not to refer is a complex process. Referral was not necessary for Alicia. Another sport psychologist in this situation, without a supervisor with expertise in eating disorders to serve as a guide and a net, would need to comply with our ethical principles and refer the athlete.

So what should you do when an athlete drops a bomb with material that makes you, as a sport psychologist, uncomfortable (for a number of reasons)? We would suggest starting a thoughtful, self-reflective process with the aid of a knowledgeable supervisor. Carefully consider the available and best options for the particular client and situation given your skills, knowledge, relationship, and supervision.

> When an athlete drops a bomb, go through a personal, thoughtful, self-reflective process with the aid of a knowledgeable supervisor.

The next question in the referral process is "Referral for what?" We have focused on referral for psychological problems, but they are only one subset of issues that may be in need of referral.

## Referral for What?

For many sport psychologists, referrals are often the result of emerging psychological problems that practitioners believe are over their heads. A good portion of this chapter deals with exactly those scenarios. There are, however, many other referrals a sport psychologist may be called on to make. As sport psychologists, we will need to consider referrals for issues such as body composition, sport sciences, behavioral changes, and life choices. Of course, we will also need to consider referrals for athletes with mental health issues. A sport psychologist may also become impaired in some way (e.g., as a result of a mental disorder such as depression) and may need to refer an athlete to another sport psychologist. That issue is beyond the scope of this chapter, but more information on psychologist impairment can be found in Andersen, Van Raalte, and Brewer (2000).

We should, however, always keep in mind our motto, "When thinking of referring, doubt!" By taking this tack, we force ourselves to examine carefully whether or not referral is necessary. As an example, athletes may be trying to gain muscle. Their strength and conditioning coaches can help with the physical training part, but the eating and hydration aspects simply may be left up to the athletes (Swoap & Murphy, 1995). Proper nutrition for weight and muscle gain (and weight loss) is not straightforward. A perusal of muscle magazines reveals a bewildering array of different diets, nutritional supplements, and other regimens. Some of those diets may be solidly based in nutritional science; others may be fads, popular myths, or pseudoscience. Athletes on the path of losing or gaining weight may consult other athletes or the popular press—often unreliable sources—to get ideas about how to change. Or they may be instructed by the coach on what, and how much, to eat. We have heard dieting instructions from coaches that range from sound to ineffective to injurious. We recall one coach who told an athlete to eat huge amounts of protein; the athlete overcomplied (as athletes often do) and developed a serious state of ketosis. Having a sport nutritionist on board for referral should be a resource of every practitioner. You can prepare your coaches and athletes by talking up front about your nutritionist in your early meetings with the team. For more information about eating and nutrition for athletes, there is substantial literature available (e.g., Black, 1991; Burckes-Miller & Black, 1998; Martin & Hausenblas, 1998; NCAA, 1989; Petrie & Sherman, 2000; Putukian, 1994; Seime & Damer, 1991; Sours, 1980; Sundgot-Borgen, 1994; Swoap & Murphy, 1995; Thompson & Sherman, 1993).

In talking with coaches about our roles with their teams, we usually mention that if we come across issues outside our realms of expertise, then we have a referral network we use to address those athlete concerns. Because diet, weight, and body composition are such major issues in many sports, we make it a point to let the coach know about the sport nutritionists we consult. We say directly to coaches who do not have a nutritionist on board, "If you have any athletes who you think could benefit from gaining some muscle or losing some weight, then please send them our way, and we can connect them with a nutritionist who knows the demands of sport and training and who can help athletes start a diet that will be healthy and get long-term results." We also arrange for the coach to meet with the nutritionist. That small pre-emptive intervention may help the coach feel more confident in the sport psychologist as a resource for athlete development. Athletes with eating disorders are also candidates for referral to nutritionists, but their cases are more complicated and also fall under mental health concerns (see Petrie & Sherman, 2000).

Referrals for behavioral change and life choices may include time management, study skills, career exploration, and retirement (Baillie & Danish, 1992; Grove, Lavallee, Gordon, & Harvey, 1998; Lavallee & Andersen, 2000). These areas are often covered in many sport psychologists' training, but not in all. In high schools and universities, there are usually student services that can help athletes survive and thrive in academic environments as well as plan for future vocations (Etzel, Ferrante, & Pinkney, 1996). In terms of getting help in the physical aspects of training, many sport science departments have close connections with athletic teams. For athletes training on national teams, such as at the Australian Institute of Sport or the United States Olympic Training Center, sport scientists (e.g., biomechanists, exercise physiologists) are usually part of the support staff. A referral list of sport scientists would be beneficial for athletes training independently.

There is a range of mental health, career, family, spiritual, life choices, sport, and training issues that athletes may experience, and no exercise science or sport psychology practitioner can be expected to be able to handle all of them. Some mental health problems are extremely rare in sport, especially at the elite level, because the resources to train and compete are just not available to persons with these conditions. We tend not to see people with chronic schizophrenia in sport, and some Axis II diagnoses *(DSM-IV-TR*, American Psychiatric Association, 2001) are also uncommon (e.g., avoidant personality disorder). Nevertheless, athletes may experience a variety of psychological challenges, including substance abuse (Carr & Murphy, 1995), gambling problems, grief (Barney & Andersen, 2000), suicidal ideation (Cogan, 2000), existential concerns (Balague, 1999), family problems (Bobele & Conran, 1988; Hellstedt, 1995), sexuality issues (APA Committee on Lesbian and Gay Concerns, 1990; Andersen, Butki, & Heyman, 1997; Butki, Andersen, & Heyman, 1996; Cogan & Petrie, 2002; Griffin, 1992, 1998; Krane, 1995; Lenskyj, 1991), anger, unplanned pregnancy, steroid use (Gregg & Rejeski, 1990), religious belief conflicts (Barney & Andersen, 2000), injury (Brewer, 1994; Brewer, Petitpas, & Van Raalte, 1999; Brewer, Van Raalte, & Linder, 1991; Kolt, 2000; Petitpas & Danish, 1995), and many others. In terms of personality disorders, antisocial and narcissistic tendencies are prevalent in some sports (see Andersen, Denson, Brewer, & Van Raalte, 1994; Brewer & Petrie, 2002). Depression is the common cold of mental health and is seen relatively often in athletes and coaches, as are a variety of anxiety disorders. The case example in this chapter focuses on a mental health referral.

# Who Can Do What? Questions of Training

As we wrote this chapter, we thought that a chart or table might provide a clearer picture of what sport psychologists can and cannot handle, illustrating sport psychologists' training and backgrounds and where referrals would be necessary. The problem we encountered is the myriad ways in which sport psychology practitioners are trained and the idiosyncratic features of training backgrounds. For example, sport psychologists currently trained in Australia are psychologists first and sport psychologists second. Many practitioners in North America come from exercise science backgrounds. Current education in clinical or counseling psychology or exercise science often includes substantial cross-discipline training. It would be difficult, and possibly misleading, to describe models of training as deciding factors in when to refer. Again, we need to look at what we know and what we don't know. Knowledge and skills determine whether we refer or not. For example, plenty of practitioners from exercise science backgrounds have gained the knowledge, through professional development, to work with athletes with eating disorders. There are also counseling psychologists working in sport who do not have such skills. The knowledge, skills, and resources available to a particular practitioner, when making referral decisions, are more important than the department from which they graduated.

# Performance and Personal Issues

We have heard many sport psychologists say, "I work only with performance enhancement. If personal issues arise, I refer." We understand the basis for such a statement, usually from those trained in exercise science making sure they do not move into realms their training does not cover (e.g., counseling psychology, psychotherapy). But an examination of that statement reveals a fundamental flaw in conceptualizing performance enhancement service delivery. For many athletes, performance is central to their lives, often a defining feature of their being, intimately tied to feelings of self-worth, and sometimes inextricably enmeshed with family dynamics. Performance can be a source of joy, anguish, pride, terror, elation, and humiliation. So how is working on performance not a personal issue? For example, a "performance psychologist" works with an athlete for six months, and that athlete's performance improves to the point of her making it to the Olympics. The athlete's self-esteem has risen substantially; she is fulfilling a dream, and her communication with her coach and parents is greatly improved. Through maximizing her performance potential, she has become a happier person. Performance enhancement is a deeply personal issue. This argument is more than a decade old (Andersen, 1992; Rotella, 1992); the false dichotomy of performance enhancement versus personal issues is one we bring up again to emphasize that when we are helping athletes, we are helping people. The focus of the work may be improving a time in the steeplechase, but attached to that race is a whole world, some aspects of which may aid greatly, or harm seriously, the ability to perform in that race. No race or performance is an island; it is usually linked to vast continents, and we may need others (referral networks) to help navigate.

> The work you do with athletes doesn't affect just performance; it may affect many areas of their personal lives.

The important question is how does performance fit into the rest of the athlete's life? If the rest of the athlete's life is a mess, then the likelihood of performance enhancement techniques working well is probably low. Relaxation techniques to combat prerace anxiety are not likely to be effective if the anxiety stems from the anticipated withdrawal of Mom's affection and the dread of Dad's scorn and humiliation for failure. In this case, helping the athlete understand and cope with a dysfunctional family or referring to a practitioner who can help with these issues would be ideal (see Hellstedt, 1995).

In the situation of referring the athlete to a nutritionist, admitting you do not have the expertise to work in the area is an easy thing to do. Admitting you cannot handle the intimate intra- and interpersonal difficulties of the athlete who has grown to trust you is much more difficult. Professional impotence ("I can't help you") is painful to bear. The other painful process in a clinical or psychiatric referral is explaining to the athlete that he has a disorder that could benefit from the attention of a mental health practitioner. How do you soften the stigma, the resistance, and even the panic of a mental illness diagnosis? For example, how do you talk to an athlete who is having a depressive episode and meets the criteria for a diagnosis of major depression?

# Thor Descending: Lucien's Story

Lucien is a hammer thrower on scholarship at a major North American university. He is a gifted athlete and an Olympic hopeful, but also a rather "sad-sack" young man. After a few sessions, I (Mark) suspect that he struggles with dysthymia, which sets him at risk for depression. We work a lot on performance enhancement and communication with his coach. Like many people with dysthymia, he responds well to the attention of a caring parental figure. Over a period of about four weeks, I notice he has lost some weight, and he misses some appointments. He always calls to reschedule, however, explaining why he cannot make it. One day he misses an appointment, and I do not get a call. I am starting to worry, so I call him. I do not get an answer, so I leave a message. After not hearing from him for two more days, I go out to practice. The coach knows I am working with Lucien, so I ask if I could have a quick word. The coach informs me that Lucien is out with the flu. I call again that evening and get Lucien on the phone.

|  |  |
|---|---|
| Lucien: | Hello? |
| Mark Andersen (MA): | Hey, Lucien. |
| Lucien: | Oh, hi, Doc. Oh, shit, I missed an appointment. I'm so sorry. |
| MA: | Not to worry. I was just out at practice today, and Coach said you were down with the flu. And I wanted to call to see how you were. |
| *[Lucien: Long silence.]* | |
| MA: | Lucien? |
| Lucien: | Sorry, Doc, and sorry I never returned your call. |
| MA: | Lucien, don't worry about the call. I can hear something in your voice. Talk to me. |
| Lucien: | I don't know. . . . I lied . . . to Coach, of all people. . . . I don't have the flu . . . shit! |

With his missed appointment and no call, his repeated apologies, his silence and slow responses, I suspect he has fallen into a dark place. I use those terms to inquire about where he is.

|  |  |
|---|---|
| MA: | Yeah, it sounds like something bigger than the flu, as if you have fallen into a dark place that is sapping all your energy, and it's hard to see a way out. |
| Lucien: | [With a note of pained relief.] God, Doc, how did you know? |
| MA: | Lucien, believe me, I'm no mind reader. We have been working together for a good while. You always make it to appointments, and even when you have to cancel, you always give me a call. You're about the most polite and respectful athlete I know, so when you kind of disappeared I was thinking something was up. I noticed awhile ago that you had a bit of a melancholy streak, and now with the tone in your voice and what you have told me so far, it all makes me think that you have gone pretty deep down. |

Lucien: I don't know what is happening. I get out of bed, and then just end up on the couch. The thought of food makes me sick, and schoolwork has gone to hell.
. . .

MA: And if you open a textbook to read, you can't focus or remember what you read, and then you just give up and feel even shittier.

Lucien: That's it! What's happening? I'm scared, Doc.

At this point, I start to feel anxious and even physically ill. I am worried about potential suicide, and I am also having a profound empathic response. There is a history of depression in my family, and Lucien is bringing up all those memories in me. I use my experience with depression (e.g., calling it the dark place, relating the inability to focus and feeling even worse about not getting things done for school) to let him know I understand where he is. Using those empathic and historical responses helps Lucien make the big call for help. He is saying to me, "I am so afraid. I don't understand. Please help me understand what is happening."

MA: I know you are really afraid right now, and it feels as if you are paralyzed and sliding even deeper, but I want you to do something, OK?

Lucien: OK.

MA: I want you to get dressed and walk out the door and come to my office. Can you do that?

Lucien: I don't know, Doc. I'll try.

MA: I know you'll give it a great try. I have seen you pull out some fantastic throws after some really crappy ones. I know you can do it.

Lucien: OK, I am putting on my shoes.

MA: And you are going to walk out that door in a couple of minutes.

Lucien: I'll be there, Doc.

MA: I know you will. I am walking out the door, too. I will see you in a few minutes.

Lucien: OK, but I hate to pull you out at this time of night.

MA: Nice night for a walk. . . . Now get going!

Lucien: OK, see you soon.

> It is important to be as available as possible for your athletes; crises don't run on a workday schedule.

For someone experiencing depression, there is something therapeutic in pulling it together, walking out of the house, and going to see a psychologist. Just the act of moving toward working on what is going on is itself salubrious. I could have made the offer to go and see him, and I would have if this suggestion to come see me did not work. That he can make the move to come to my office is a good sign that he still has some resources available. I also notice that he kept using his name for me, "Doc." That repeated familiarity, that calling out for me by name, is another aspect of the call for help. *Doc* is an affectionate term, and his repeated use of it shows a need for connection with another person, one who may understand. Another good sign.

Lucien arrives at my office looking distressed. We go over what has been happening with him over the past weeks. I make a suicide risk assessment and am relieved that there is no plan, only vague ideas of "wanting it to be all over." Lucien fits many of the criteria for depression. He has no appetite, is not sleeping well, cannot focus on relatively simple tasks, does not enjoy activities he usually likes, feels worthless, keeps beating himself up about not getting things done, and is withdrawing from social connections. We explore the possibility of some precipitating event but cannot pin down anything specific. He does mention that when he was 14 something similar happened. His parents took him to all sorts of specialists, but "it just went away, after a while." I need to talk to him about his mental health and where we need to go from here.

Lucien:   What's happening? What am I gonna do?

MA:   Lucien, I am not going to sugarcoat what's going on. It looks as if you are having a serious bout of depression, and we need to take some action.

Lucien:   What does that mean? I know I'm a head case. . . . [Despondently.] I just want to lie down and not wake up.

MA:   We talked about those kinds of suicidal thoughts, of just wanting it to be all over.

Lucien:   I know, I know. I ain't going to do anything, Doc. I just wanna feel normal again.

MA:   I know you do, Lucien, and this depression you are going through may go away soon, just as it did when you were a teenager, but it may not. I don't know, but we can do something that may help this darkness lift.

Lucien is both depressed and anxious, and some of that anxiety may help fuel change. He wants to do something about his condition. Those who are depressed and who are in rather vegetative states do not have the resources to effect some change that people who are anxious and depressed do, such as Lucien. Lucien knows I am invested in him and that I care. My goal is to use that bond of trust we have to make the referral and suggest that he see a psychiatrist for an assessment. I believe Lucien could benefit from antidepressant medication such as those that work through serotonergic pathways (e.g., Zoloft, Cipramil). I cannot prescribe medication and really do not have the expertise to make a decision about which pharmacological agent to try.

Suggesting medication for an athlete is tricky. In Lucien's case, he is desperate and may grab on to the idea of medication as he would a life preserver. Antidepressants do not work for everyone, so the athlete may end up disappointed. Athletes are also wary of taking drugs that may be problematic when it comes to drug testing at competitions. Fortunately, antidepressants, and many anxiolytic agents, are not on the list of banned substances in sport. Having a copy of the list of banned substances (available from the World Anti-Doping Agency, www.wada-ama.org) for an athlete about to start pharmacological treatment may alleviate some anxiety about being on medication.

> Keep a list of banned substances in your office. Even though you may not be able to prescribe medications, it is important for you to know what is and isn't allowed.

MA:   Lucien, I am no expert in treating depression, so what I would like for you to do is go see a psychiatrist I know really well. She knows loads more than I do about depression, and she is a runner, too, so she understands athletes.

Lucien:   You've always helped me; why do I have to go see her?

MA:   You don't have to do anything you don't want to do. I don't want to push you. . . . Oh, hell, that's a lie. I *do* want to push you. I want you to see her because she can make a solid assessment of whether you could benefit from starting some antidepressant medication. I don't know if she will suggest some drugs or not, but I would like you to go and find out.

Lucien:   Drugs, Doc? I don't know. What about testing?

MA:   Not to worry. I have the latest list of banned substances, and so does the psychiatrist. Antidepressants are not on the list.

Lucien:   What about side effects?

MA:   The new drugs seem to have few side effects, but we are getting ahead of ourselves. Let's get you to Dr. Choi first, and then if she thinks some medication is a good idea, then you can get all the information you need from her. How does that sound?

Lucien:   OK, but what about you and me. Can I still see you?

MA:   Of course! We can still have our weekly appointments, just as we always have.

| Lucien: | Are you going to tell the coach? |
|---|---|
| MA: | Not unless you want me to. I think after you see Dr. Choi, maybe we can talk about what you might want to say to the coach. |
| Lucien: | He thinks I am a bit odd, anyway. This will probably flip him out. |
| MA: | You might be surprised. I know, for a fact, that someone close to him was depressed and was helped by medication. He has had at least secondhand experience with depression. |
| Lucien: | Really? Wow! |

Lucien accepts the referral, and I do not have to work too hard at selling it. He meets with Dr. Choi and begins taking Zoloft. Within a couple of weeks he notices changes, and within a month he has put on some weight. He does continue to have disturbed sleep for about two weeks, but he treats himself with a childhood remedy of a glass of milk half an hour before bed, and that seems to help. Lucien's referral was relatively straightforward because an ideal clinician (runner, knowledgeable about sports) was available. Lucien did not seem to feel rejected as a client when he was referred. He and I continue to see each other and begin to explore what happened to him at age 14. He never becomes a happy-go-lucky person, and he still has some melancholy and dysthymic features, but he is back in the sport he loves, functioning socially, and no longer paralyzed.

# Referral Networks

So how do you create a network of people you can use for referrals? As mentioned already, practitioners working in and around colleges and universities have potential referral systems that are easy to access—staff in university mental health centers and some academic departments are often available and interested in working with athletes. Practitioners in private practice or in more remote locations must work a little harder to create their own "invisible college" of resources. So how do you begin? For mental health consultants, you may want to start in the yellow pages of your local phone book. The American Psychological Association (APA) publishes a member directory by state. The Association for the Advancement of Applied Sport Psychology has a list of certified consultants on its Web site (www.aaasponline.org). Call local sports medicine clinics and talk to people in your community to find practitioners who work well with athletes. Finding names may be the easy part. The bigger challenge is cultivating relationships with these skilled referral sources so you can work effectively with your clients and the experts you refer them to.

Suggesting that you create and maintain a relationship with your referral sources may seem odd. After all, information shared between you and your athlete is generally confidential. Your individual relationships with the athlete are separate and private. Why bother getting to know these experts in other fields?

Actually, there are many benefits of knowing your referral sources well. First, in knowing your referral sources, you gain confidence that you are sending your athletes to competent people. As we already noted, athletes who are referred to untrustworthy or unskilled practitioners are unlikely to return to see the referral source or you. Second, knowing practitioners well allows you to tap them as consultants or pre-referral sources in challenging cases.

> Get to know your referral sources well. This network building enables you to make good decisions about whom an athlete should see.

What do we mean by pre-referral sources? I (Judy) once worked with a gymnastics team that raised money by putting on workshops for local kids. At one workshop, I observed a newer team member acting strangely. This gymnast was somewhat rude to some of the parents and rather critical of several young children with whom she was interacting. The gymnast was not quite rude enough for the parents or children to complain to the coach, but it struck me that her behavior was odd. The athlete was striking out, seemed emotionally shaky, and was teetering on the brink of acceptable behavior. After the workshop, I called my clinical referral source and had a pre-referral conversation. I discussed my observations and got feedback from an expert on the situation. We agreed that it was not time to intervene, but if the situation deteriorated further a referral might be in order. The athlete in question was not a one-on-one client of mine outside my team interactions. Because I was not going to be seeing the team for some time, I shared some of my concerns, my behavioral observations, and the pre-referral information that I had gathered with the team coach.

At my next meeting with the team, the coach took me aside. She told me the athlete had deteriorated quickly. A few days after the workshop, she had been found wandering around, in a neighboring town, barefoot, wearing pajamas, and disoriented. The coach said that the athlete had bipolar disorder and had discontinued her medication before the workshop, which seemed to have contributed to her problems. Although the athlete returned home, and a referral was not needed on campus, the coach was appreciative of the "heads up" provided by the pre-referral conversation. Indeed, the coach seemed to gain a greater appreciation for, and confidence in, applied sport psychology after this incident.

But what if the athlete had not left campus and a referral was needed? How does a sport psychologist make an effective referral? There is no one perfect way to refer an athlete, but there are some guidelines that can help make the referral process go more smoothly.

# The Referral Process

When it is clear that a referral is needed, a sport psychology practitioner can take a number of steps to facilitate this complex and sensitive process.

- **Prepare.** Referrals work best if the athlete is not taken by surprise when the referral is made. Preparation can begin at the first meeting with an athlete client. Inform the athlete that referral to other practitioners, such as nutritionists, sport scientists, academic advisers, and psychiatrists, is possible. To make sure this information is clearly conveyed to the athlete, it may be useful to develop a written handout about the consultation process that the athlete can take home (Strein & Hershenson, 1991).

- **Explain.** Be direct and clear in explaining to the athlete why the referral is being made (Bobele & Conran, 1988; Heil, 1993). Highlighting the sport performance benefits of following up with the referral may be helpful for athletes who are concerned about their sport outcomes. With a solid referral network in place, it will also be easy to explain how helpful you believe the referral source will be.

- **Educate.** Explain to the athlete what it will be like to work with the practitioner you are suggesting (Heil, 1993). Both athletes and nonathletes have expectations, prejudices, and concerns about counseling and mental health treatments that may be inaccurate (Miller & Moore, 1993). Be clear about the expertise and function of the practitioner (Bobele & Conran, 1988). It can be tempting to omit some of the details of the practitioner's expertise. Failure to reveal relevant information, however, violates trust and can make it difficult for the practitioner to work effectively with the athlete. It is also useful to describe the various forms of payment available (e.g., insurance, sliding scale, pro bono), but the practitioner should set the specific fee (Bobele & Conran, 1988).

- **Respect concerns.** Some athletes may be embarrassed to be referred to another practitioner, perhaps feeling they are "head cases." Providing support and enabling athletes to maintain dignity and save face is important (Brewer, Petitpas, & Van Raalte, 1999). Some athletes may be afraid that pursuing the referral may actually cause changes that will take away what made them great performers. Focusing on athletes' competition goals and their return to competition (if they want to return) is also important (Bobele & Conran, 1988).

- **Get consent to share information.** Information about the athlete can be shared with the referral source on a need-to-know basis if the athlete has given written consent (Strein & Hershenson, 1991). Some athletes like to have information shared so they do not have to start over with a new practitioner. All athletes should be informed about exactly what information needs to be provided to the referral source. Some coaches try to push the referral process by punishing athletes who do not comply, but placing these additional conditions on the referral process can make it impossible for the practitioner to work effectively with the athlete. If a coach or parents are involved, it may be useful to teach them about sport psychologists' responsibility to protect athlete confidentiality.

- **Consider stretching.** With appropriate supervision and guidance, it may be possible to work with an athlete on an issue that is just outside of your current level of competence or comfort. You may not need to refer right away. If you decide *not* to refer, reassess the situation on a regular basis to decide if referral becomes necessary. You do not need to wait for the perfect time to refer. There is no perfect time to refer.

- **Refer in.** Referral follow-through can be enhanced by "referring in," bringing the practitioner in to work together with the athlete and the sport psychologist (Andersen, 1992). Referring in can be convenient for athletes and may alleviate their fears that pursuing the referral will cause them to be abandoned by their sport psychologist. (For an example of an athlete resistant to talking to someone else and to the referral process, see Van Raalte & Andersen, 2002.) When referring in is not feasible, it is helpful to provide athletes with the information necessary to schedule an appointment with the practitioner. Some athletes prefer having the sport psychologist schedule the first appointment when the referral is made.

- **Follow up.** Assess the effectiveness of the referral to see if it was helpful. If the athlete decides not to follow through on the referral, discuss alternate strategies for dealing with the problem; you should not hesitate to reintroduce the idea of referral (Heil, 1993).

- **Parallel treatment.** Many athlete issues are best treated in parallel with a team approach (e.g., nutritionists, psychologists, and physicians for athletes with eating disorders). The team approach offers the positive aspect of comprehensive care, but it contains negative features such as high cost. In addition, bringing in three or four other experts on a case will often mean that the athlete has to go through the whole story again and again. Unless there is an emergency, we suggest that other practitioners are consulted and introduced relatively slowly to keep the athlete from being overwhelmed. Also, it is helpful to assure athletes that you will still be their sport psychologist during their treatment with another practitioner.

## Conclusion

And here is probably a good place to end this chapter, as we come full circle from the sport psychologist–athlete relationship, to referring to others, to coming back to the work. Much of what is contained in this chapter is not new. We have written specifically about referral processes in other works (see Andersen & Tod, in press; Van Raalte & Andersen, 2002), but we hope the story told here has added a bit more light to the complexities of sport psychology service delivery. In this chapter, we take a few new slants on referral and present a case example of how to go about helping an athlete see another professional. That example is only one small picture, but it demonstrates both specific (dysthymia moving into depression) and general (the process of referral) features of a service that all sport psychologists will face in their careers. We hope this chapter has been helpful for all of us who want to know our athletes' full stories and how we can provide, through ourselves and our referral networks, the best possible care.

# Touching Taboos
## *Sex and the Sport Psychologist*

Mark B. Andersen, PhD

The June 2004 issue of *Dialogue,* the newsletter of the Psychologists Registration Board of Victoria (Australia), features a report on a male sport psychologist engaging in sexually explicit telephone and Internet conversations with a 17-year-old female client. The young woman had recently attempted suicide; after her involvement with the psychologist, she was rehospitalized. This frightening report detailing a gross abuse of trust by a sport psychologist with an extremely vulnerable client illustrates that the phenomena of erotic transference and countertransference can result in dire, and even life-threatening, consequences. This case is the first I know of in which an identified sport psychologist sexually exploits a client. I fear it will not be the last. With that sobering tale of professional transgressions, let's begin by examining some foundations of the development of erotic attraction in sport psychology service delivery.

## Roots of Attraction

The terms *transference* and *countertransference* have their roots in psychodynamic theory. Freud used these terms to label the phenomena in which clients and therapists begin to respond (generally unconsciously) to each other in ways that reflect past responses to significant others in their lives. For example, a client may begin to act toward the therapist in ways that mirror his relationship with a parent. Therapists may also begin perceiving and reacting to clients in similar fashion. Past relationship patterns and the thoughts, feelings, and behaviors that accompany them are getting transferred to the current therapeutic encounter. These phenomena are not necessarily counterproductive. Some species of transference and countertransference actually fuel therapeutic change. Nor are these phenomena limited to psychotherapy. They appear in relationships between students and teachers, coaches and athletes, supervisors and supervisees, and sport psychologists and those in their care (Andersen, 2000).

There is no doubt that transference and countertransference can be damaging to relationships, and what is particularly worrisome is when these phenomena develop into erotic or romantic feelings. Discussion of the sexualization of professional relationships, although common in clinical and counseling psychology, rarely occurs in the field of sport psychology. I recall a presentation at the Association for the Advancement of Applied Sport Psychology (AAASP) where a panel of well-known sport psychologists discussed the joys and difficulties of mentoring students. A member of the audience asked the panel how they would handle issues of sexual and romantic attraction between graduate students and professors. One panel member seemed quite flustered by the question, saying, "I don't see why this would ever come up." Another member stated, "It's unethical; I just wouldn't let it happen." These responses seem somewhat naive and have a flavor of denial to them. One way of dealing with behaviors, thoughts, and feelings that cause anxiety (e.g., sexual attraction to students) is to deny that they occur or could possibly occur. Such denial flies in the face of reality because most people in sport psychology academia know at least one case of a student–mentor romantic liaison.

One member of the panel, however, said, "Thanks for bringing up something no one ever seems to want to talk about. We all know it happens, and the general response is to turn a blind eye." I think the blind eye approach about sums up the situation for student–professor romantic attraction. The story of psychiatrist–client and psychologist–client romantic or sexual involvement has been, and still is, a hotly debated topic in the ethics of service delivery (Avery & Gressard, 2000; Barnhouse, 1978; Bates & Brodsky, 1989; Bouhoutsos, 1984; Bouhoutsos, Holroyd, Lerman, Forer, & Greenberg, 1983; Brodsky, 1989; Dahlberg, 1970; Davidson, 1977; Kavoussi & Becker, 1987; Koocher & Keith-Spiegel, 1998; Pope, 1988, 1990a, 1990b; Pope & Bouhoutsos, 1986; Pope & Vasquez, 1998; Serban, 1981; Zicherman, 1984). Research has consistently shown that anywhere from 4 to 10% of male and 2 to 3% of female psychologists have had sexual relationships with clients (Ethics Committee of the American Psychological Association, 1988; Gartell, Herman, Olarte, Feldstein, & Localio, 1986; Herman, Gartell, Olarte, Feldstein, & Localio, 1987; Holroyd & Bouhoutsos, 1985; Pope, Sonne, & Holroyd, 1993; Pope, Tabachnick, & Keith-Spiegel, 1987).

Sexual impropriety is one of the most common formal complaints against psychologists (Vinson, 1987). In sport psychology, Petrie and Buntrock (1995) conducted a survey of AAASP members about sexual attraction and sexual behavior with athlete clients. Approximately 4% of the male participants had at one time become sexually involved with an athlete client. For females, the percentage was substantially less. Considering the prohibition on such behavior, it might be safe to conclude that the percentages reported here are underestimates of the actual prevalence of sexual or romantic intimacy between sport psychologists and athletes (cf. Holroyd & Bouhoutsos, 1985).

> Sexual intimacy between psychologists and clients is almost universally damaging (often to both parties).

The potential for harm resulting from psychologist–client sexual intimacy is great, and the literature reflects and documents the damage that can occur (Brown, 1988; Feldman-Summers & Jones, 1984; Pope, 1988, 1990a; Somer & Saadon, 1999; Sonne, 1989; Sonne, Meyer, Borys, & Marshall, 1985, Sonne & Pope, 1991). In a therapist–client relationship, there is always a power differential. The therapist is the expert authority, and clients are often in vulnerable states. Taking advantage of that vulnerability can lead to client feelings of betrayal, exploitation, and abuse. Depression and suicidal ideation are not uncommon results of therapist–client sexual involvement.

It is not surprising that most helping professions have explicit prohibitions against sexual intimacy with clients. The American Psychological Association (1992), in their ethical principles and code of conduct, states the following in sections 4.05, 4.06, and 4.07:

4.05. Psychologists do not engage in sexual intimacies with current patients or clients.

4.06. Psychologists do not accept as therapy patients and clients with whom they have engaged in sexual intimacies.

4.07 (a) Psychologists do not engage in sexual intimacies with a former therapy patient or client for at least two years after cessation or termination of professional services.

(b) Because sexual intimacies with a former therapy patient or client are so frequently harmful to the patient or client, and because such intimacies undermine public confidence in the psychology profession and thereby deter the public's use of needed services, psychologists do not engage in sexual intimacies with former therapy patients and clients even after a two-year interval except in the most unusual circumstances. The psychologist who engages in such activity after the two years following cessation or termination of treatment bears the burden of demonstrating that there has been no exploitation, in light of all relevant factors, including (1) the amount of time that has passed since therapy terminated, (2) the nature and duration of therapy, (3) the circumstances of termination, (4) the patient's or client's personal history, (5) the patient's or client's current mental state, (6) the likelihood of adverse impact on the patient or client and others, and (7) any statements or actions made by the therapist during the course of therapy suggesting or inviting the possibility of a post-termination sexual or romantic relationship with the patient or client.

The edicts from the APA seem explicit and hard-lined about the prohibition on sexual intimacies with clients. There has even been discussion to make the prohibition on sexual intimacies with former clients "forever" (see also Gabbard, 1989; Gabbard & Pope, 1989).

Sexual behavior with clients is so taboo, and the prohibitions are so strongly stated, that the result appears to have been (in the past) to discuss the topic no further than "It will not happen." Actually, the prohibition has such a final Talmudic quality (Thou shalt not sleep with clients) that just the mention of sex with clients raises suspicions that something is going on. This guilt by association, or suspicion about those who voice concerns, is probably another reason we rarely discuss the problem (Pope et al., 1993). Unfortunately, sexual liaisons between psychologists and clients do happen, and part of the reason they do is that we do not help graduate students develop the tools and personal resources to handle sexual feelings in service delivery (Hamilton & Spruill, 1999; Ladany, O'Brien, & Petersen, 1997; Pope, Keith-Spiegel, & Tabachnick, 1986; Pope, Levenson, & Schover, 1979; Pope, Schover, & Levenson, 1980).

I recently had a discussion with a graduate of one of the finest sport psychology programs in North America. She said, "When I was in training I had the unbelievable hots for one of the wrestlers I worked with. He was such a babe. I didn't do anything about it, but I also never mentioned it to my supervisor." That reluctance to talk about it with the people who should be most equipped to help students understand these phenomena speaks volumes about the closeted features of client erotic transference and psychologist countertransference. Why was the graduate student unable, or unwilling, to talk to her supervisor? Probably because the issue was never normalized and treated as another aspect of service in her training. Closets beget closets, and I hope this chapter throws open a few of those closet doors.

Sport psychologists may actually have solid reasons to be even more mindful of erotic transference and countertransference than their more traditionally practicing colleagues. Sport psychologists often operate in a generally looser atmosphere than other psychologists (Andersen, Van Raalte, & Brewer, 2001). They are at poolside, on the track, and in the locker room. They travel with teams and may end up sharing a lot of experiences with athletes (e.g., competition, practice, team dinners, airplane travel). Athletes are generally an attractive group and are often under a lot of pressure from people and organizations with agendas. The psychologist enters this familiar pressure-cooker world but has (or should have) no major agenda beyond the health and welfare of the athletes. Athletes may find in the sport psychologist a nonjudgmental and caring person whose only interest is their happiness. The sport psychologist may be seen as a human island of calm in the rather tempestuous sea of sport—and that, in itself, can be very attractive. So sport psychologists may have an even greater need for education and training in erotic feelings in service.

Research in the clinical psychology field reveals that those who received instruction in erotic transference and countertransference were more comfortable handling such situations than those who did not receive such training. Those with more resources were also less likely to cross that taboo and enter into a romantic relationship with a client (Hamilton & Spruill, 1999; Ladany et al. 1997).

# Why Don't We Talk About "It"?

Pope and colleagues (1993) identify some of the many reasons we avoid the topic:

- Guilt
- Anxiety about unresolved personal issues
- Fear of losing control
- Fear of being criticized
- Feeling unable to speak openly
- Confusion about boundaries and roles
- Confusion about what to do

> Issues of erotic transference and countertransference are not commonly covered in any meaningful depth in the training of sport psychologists.

When I was completing my master's degree, and later my doctoral program, I was involved in coursework, practica, and internships covering a variety of psychotherapy and counseling topics and work with diverse populations (college students, psychiatric patients on locked wards, incarcerated individuals). Not once was sexual attraction in therapy mentioned in all those years of education and training. I think my experience was not atypical.

My first serious discussion of erotic transference and countertransference occurred in my postdoctoral training; it came about because of a videotape and an aesthetic response to an exceptional athlete. Although this example involves a male therapist admiring the body of a male athlete, it does not have the erotic content of the major case study in this chapter, which is decidedly heterosexual. Erotic transference and countertransference between same-sex dyads, however, are probably common in sport and sport psychology (athletes fall for their same-sex coaches; locker rooms are often venues of disguised homoeroticism), albeit even more closeted phenomena than heterosexual attraction. In the case of gay and lesbian athletes and sport psychologists becoming erotically interested in each other, it would seem as if there would be a closet within a closet. In the case study of Jake and Joanna, it just as easily could have been Jake and John. Well, maybe not as easily, given the deep closet in which such attraction usually resides.

One of my first jobs as a full-time psychologist working for an NCAA Division I university (top university level of competition in the United States) involved a lot of time spent at the track, on the pool deck, at the archery range, and on the golf course. (I loved my job!) One of the services I provided was to videotape athletes during practice. I had rather sophisticated editing equipment in my office that the athletes and I could use to review practices and to make up best-shot tapes for them to use as part of mental rehearsal. The video service was often a way to begin working with athletes that led to more in-depth service as they got comfortable with me in the role of videographer (there are innumerable routes to service).

My supervisor, a psychiatrist who was the head of student mental health on the main part of campus, came over to my office in the intercollegiate athletics department to see how I had fixed up the place and to see the video equipment. I was showing him a tape I had made the previous day out on the track. When the decathlete I had been working with for a couple of months came on the screen, I heard this intake of breath from my supervisor, and he said, "Whoa . . . he is stunning!" I knew my supervisor very well, and I knew his response was that of a straight man to an aesthetic visual experience. The athlete *was* stunning; I was just surprised to hear the verbalization of such a response from my current model of professional behavior. My knowledge of service delivery was limited; back in my early postdoctoral career days, the gaps were substantial. I thought such responses to clients were to be acknowledged as errors and minor breaches of professionalism—and then neatly tucked away. One was supposed to see the person, not the body. I had developed a fairly deep transferential response to my supervisor and viewed him as the font of wisdom for all things therapeutic, but it was not a completely sycophantic transference. He encouraged me constantly to challenge him and to speak my mind. These behaviors on his part only endeared him even more to me. Here's my best reconstruction of a conversation that is now more than 15 years old.

| | |
|---|---|
| Mark: | Wow, Rick, that was quite a response. |
| My supervisor, Rick: | Excuse me? |
| Mark: | Your response to seeing Isaac on the screen, the "Whoa, he's stunning." |
| Rick: | Yeah, well, look at him . . . he *is* stunning. . . . You don't see that? |
| Mark: | Yeah, but . . . |
| Rick: | Hold that thought; I want to watch him do these hurdles. [I keep silent while we both watch Isaac go through his hurdles. He is poetry in motion.] OK, let's turn this thing off. [I do so.] Now, tell me. What surprised you about my responding to Isaac? |
| Mark: | [Starting to feel almost totally unsure of myself.] It just seemed like a kind of emotional response to one of my clients. |
| Rick: | Well, I have emotional responses to the stories you tell me about your clients all the time. Some of the stories make me sad; others make me angry. And you and I laugh a lot in supervision. So how is this emotional response different, or why is it bothering you? |
| Mark: | [I am actually beginning to feel a bit anxious.] Well, it seems like kind of an objectification of my client, as if he's a body and not a person. [I find it difficult to say those words to my supervisor.] |
| Rick: | Mark, right now he is a body to me, one in motion, who looks beautiful. I am not his psychologist; he is not in treatment with me. I had an aesthetic response to him, but I get the feeling you think that response was unprofessional. |
| Mark: | [I am a mess at this point. I have accused someone I deeply respect of behaving in a questionable manner.] No, no, it's just that . . . I . . . uh . . . |
| Rick: | Here, let me make this more difficult for you. How would you respond if I had said, "Wow, he's stunning. I bet he's gorgeous naked"? |
| Mark: | Well, I don't think you would say that in supervision to me. |
| Rick: | No, you are right there, but if you had shown me a beautiful female athlete, I might very well have thought that exact thing. So tell me, what was your first response to seeing Isaac? |

| | |
|---|---|
| Mark: | [Sheepishly.] I think I silently said to myself, *Wow.* |
| Rick: | Of course you did; he's an exceptional-looking athlete. I would have been highly suspicious if you said your first response was "I wonder what his performance issues are." You had a completely "human" response. And what did you think to yourself right after that? |
| Mark: | Probably something like *Put that away—get professional.* |
| Rick: | Did it work? |
| Mark: | Sort of, but I kind of felt bad about being so superficial. |
| Rick: | Boy, you're tough on yourself. Now, what would happen if an athlete walked into your office whose looks made you get instantly horny? |
| Mark: | I'd probably slam that door pretty hard. |
| Rick: | And how would you end up feeling? |
| Mark: | Rather unprofessional, still a bit horny, but . . . uh . . . [I am stumbling.] |
| Rick: | Go ahead; you can say it. |
| Mark: | OK, I guess I would feel ashamed that I was letting down all my mentors and my standards. |
| Rick: | Oh, Mark . . . boy, do we have some work to do on you and your standards. You want to start now? |
| Mark: | OK, I guess. [I really am not quite ready for what is about to transpire.] |
| Rick: | All right, let's go over in detail the most recent time an athlete walked into your office and you thought to yourself, *Whoa! What a babe!* before you slammed that door. |

That was how things got rolling in my first really in-depth discussion of erotic countertransference. About a year later, I attended day-long workshops on erotic transference and countertransference as part of my continuing education. From the dialogue, it is apparent that I was uncomfortable with the topic, but there is also much about my relationship with my supervisor, my wanting to please him, my not wanting to offend him, and how much I was emotionally and professionally tied to him. I think it is also apparent from his style why I had become so connected to him. He was "what you see is what you get," in touch with his own feelings and thoughts, avuncular but challenging, and instructive but not condescending. Such a supervisor made it relatively easy for me to discover finally that the flaws I perceived in him were really the projections of my own overactive professional superego and my naive understanding of my own emotional, aesthetic, and erotic responses to athletes.

A partial answer to the question of why we don't talk about erotic feelings in sport psychology is that they shock us when they occur. We don't really understand them; we suppress them, and we feel ashamed about them. All of these reasons only make the phenomenon of sex in sport psychology even more subterranean. My supervisor helped me let aesthetic and erotic feelings and thoughts about the athletes I worked with surface; he let me explore my unrealistic demands for an elusive and unreachable professionalism (indeed, an undesirable and inhuman kind of professionalism). Until sexual attraction between sport psychologists and athletes is a routine topic in graduate seminars, students (and professionals) will not have any models to refer to when such feelings surface (and they inevitably will) in service. Without models of how to discuss, approach, and handle erotic feelings, we are left with uncertainty, anxiety, and in the worst case, damaging action.

Another example of countertransference of a more intimate nature might illustrate how responses to clients can come from deeply felt past relationships and events in one's life. This emotional and regressive response to a swimmer I worked with, although undeniably sensual, does not have the overt sexual content contained in the major case study of this chapter, but it still shows the power of countertransference.

I met Jill several years ago after I moved to Australia. Right from the beginning, I was invested in the relationship, in no small part because swimming was my major sport (I was quite mediocre at it). Jill and I discussed, over the course of more than a year, communication problems with her coach, difficulties in her relationship with her boyfriend, the upcoming end of her swimming career, and her medical issues related to her swimming. I enjoyed my private sessions with her immensely and saw her often on the pool deck during practices and competitions. I found myself often thinking on Tuesdays, *Oh, how nice. Jill is coming to see me today.* Her transference to me seemed to have a positive good-father quality, and I believed my own feelings for her were tinged with the protective big-brother feelings I had often noticed in myself with many other athletes. Such a countertransferential response, if acknowledged and monitored, seemed to be a salubrious part of the developing working alliance between the two of us. In retrospect, my interpreting my countertransference in this positive light seems like grasping at a half-truth in order to avoid a more developmentally primitive response to Jill.

That response came to light in a dream I had about Jill during the time when I knew our relationship would be coming to an end (her career was ending, and she would be leaving the area). Jill was an attractive young woman with lots of curly long hair, and she often joked about her "big hair" problem. Her build was not typical of elite female swimmers in that she was quite buxom and more curvaceous than most (weight was a constant battle between Jill and her coach). She was actually a nurturing, almost motherly, person despite her age.

Although it is now many years later, I can still recall waking from the dream, startled and saying to myself, "What the hell was that about?" I put a lot of stock in dreams. They often seem to be signposts as to what is happening in our lives at the moment. I am no great dream analyst, but I like to look at dreams to see if they can shed any light on current relationships and functioning. In the dream we were in my office. I was in my chair, and she was on the couch (yes, I had a couch). I am sure I have forgotten much of the dream (repression in action), but I recall looking at her with a vague sense of longing. I don't remember what we had been talking about, but at one point she said, "Why don't you come over here?" With little hesitation, I moved to sit next to her on the couch. Then she said, "Just try to get comfortable; it will be all right, really it will." I then moved closer, wrapping my arms around her shoulders and laying my head between her breasts. I felt so safe and cared for. And then something extraordinary happened that is difficult to describe. I began to sort of melt, like a type of merging in which the boundaries between her and me were dissolving, and my last thoughts before waking were *This is right where I need to be.*

There are many ways to interpret a dream, and maybe I am offering only a superficial analysis. I hope the commentators on this chapter will suggest a possibly more in-depth account. Some context, however, is needed. The dream, and the beginning of the end of my relationship with Jill, were occurring at a time when the first anniversary of my mother's death was approaching. As I went through the day after the dream, I recalled another dream I had the night after my mother died. In the dream, I was in her hospital room, and there were tubes and monitors everywhere. She was trying to adjust her position in the hospital bed, and I asked, "Are you OK?" She responded, "I am just trying to get comfortable, but it will be all right." I interpreted that dream at the time as being about my struggling to become comfortable with her death, with her leaving me.

The parallels with my dream of Jill caught me up short (especially the features of becoming comfortable with a loss, of adjusting, of acceptance). The powerful feelings of wanting to merge with Jill now seemed like infantile desires to have union with the parent. Jill was also a mother figure that I would be losing soon, and to stave off that separation I dreamed of a melting and a dissolving with the love object (a kind of death, but also a kind of transformation). I had not understood the depth of my countertransference to Jill until that dream. Jill had become a replacement for a lost parent, one whom I had taken care of in more hospital rooms than I wish to remember. My care for Jill had been the care of a loving son. My merging with her in the dream had been the representation of a deeply regressed (and repressed) desire to be one with the parent, probably stimulated because Jill, like my other parent before her, would soon be leaving me.

> Transference and countertransference occur on a huge variety of levels, often reflecting past patterns and fantasies about significant others (e.g., parents, close friends, grandparents, siblings).

I guess the question is what does all this Freudian stuff have to do with the practice of sport psychology? I assume more than a few sport psychologists might say, "Not much." But I would have to say, "Just about everything." What I mean is that this story about Jill is a story of a relationship, and relationships are the central core of what we do and why what we do helps athletes. To understand relationships, we must understand both dancers in the dance and what they bring to their encounters with each other. I was bringing the death of a parent, a profound event by which many of us measure our lives. If I had not understood how I was relating to Jill, I might have engaged in some behaviors and had some responses that would not have been in her best interests (e.g., attempting to maintain contact way past termination, becoming angry with her for leaving) or mine (falling into a depressed funk when she left). Understanding my responses to Jill helped me get past them and say, "Whoa, that was all about me. Now, let me see if I can get back to Jill and figure out what will help her." I have seen too many sport psychologists working out their conscious and unconscious fantasies and desires through the athletes they serve (e.g., using the athlete to bring attention to themselves, identifying with athletes to bolster their self-esteem). In such cases, the phrase is actually "athletes they disserve."

Before I move to the more overtly erotic transference and countertransference of the case study, I think it will be helpful to examine a few more reasons why these topics of intense emotional, sensual, and sexual responses to and from clients have not received the attention they deserve.

## Other Barriers to Exploration

Nietzsche once wrote, well ahead of Freud, in an aphorism in *Beyond Good and Evil* (1886/1966) that "the degree and kind of a man's sexuality reach up into the ultimate pinnacle of his spirit" (p. 81). His dynamic insights provide clues, as do Freud's, for why we find our sexual responses to clients so shocking and disturbing and why we may wish to keep such responses closeted. Sexuality and sexual responses, as Nietzsche observed, stem from extremely central aspects of being; they let us know something about who we are and how we react to the world and people around us. Deeply personal responses to others are generally not for public consumption and are something we (usually) hold only for ourselves and intimate others. Social and cultural (including the culture of sport psychologists) prohibitions against public discussions of such personal responses influence our willingness to explore our own all-too-human reactions to clients and students.

To become a better therapist or counselor, one needs to "know oneself." If we can help our students and ourselves speak and write about erotic issues in service, then maybe the next generation of sport psychologists will be a little further down the road of self-understanding. As the example at the beginning of the chapter illustrates, some sport psychology supervisors are not really trained to handle erotic issues. The "thou shalt not" approach, like the instruction "don't strike out" to a batter in baseball, does not really offer a student any option other than suppression, hardly a healthy psychological response to a powerful reaction. On the panel of esteemed sport psychologists I described earlier, the depth of denial about erotic responses between supervisors and supervisees was encapsulated by one member's remark: "I don't understand why he is asking this question." If one cannot consider why the question is important, then the likelihood of getting to know oneself is limited.

Another possible reason we do not discuss sexual feelings in sport psychology service may be that just mentioning the topic raises suspicions. It is like the whistle-blower who then becomes the object of investigation ("If he's asking these questions, then what's going on with *him?*"). This irrational turning of a legitimate and important professional practice issue into suspicion illustrates exactly how profoundly uncomfortable many people are with the topic.

# Star Crossed:
# The Story of Jake and Joanna

I have disguised the protagonists and the sport for this sensitive case. Personally, I know most about Jake, so I will start with him. Jake is a master's student in counseling psychology. He is not what I would call a physically attractive young man. He has kind of an off-center face with an obviously broken nose and the traces of his history of being a wrestler in his ears. He is, however, a nice guy, with a goofy and often self-mocking sense of humor. I know Jake does not go out on dates much, and his self-esteem and comfort in the realm of interacting with young women are well below the median for college men his age. I met his parents once. They seemed to be loving, even doting, parents, and they were obviously concerned for their son's happiness. Jake's academic work is of generally high quality, although I think his main goal is human contact, that research and theory are quite secondary to making connections with athletes. I like Jake, and I see our relationship developing positively (he had a good model of relationships from his parents). Jake is in his first practicum class and has just started seeing his first athlete, Joanna, a member of the volleyball team.

Joanna is an exceptional athlete, especially in practice. She is on scholarship in her junior year. By any standards, Joanna is a knockout. She is intelligent, generous, tall, beautiful, and even though at times quite serious, rather funny. Her main hurdle in volleyball is translating stellar practice performances to competition settings. Flawless in her serving during practice, she often serves into the net during matches, and her competition performance is not up to practice standards in other areas as well. It is not that she is terrible in competition but rather that she has so much more ability than she shows. Joanna knows me because I work with the team. At the beginning of practicum, I introduced the team to some of the students and told them if they wanted some one-on-one attention, they could see a student. Joanna self-referred and actually asked specifically to see Jake. I am not sure why she chose Jake—maybe because of his goofy smile or his nonthreatening stature (he is five inches shorter than Joanna). I arranged for them to start a performance enhancement relationship. With the practicum unit just starting, the academic portion of the experience (group sessions with students for group supervision and discussion of theory and research in service delivery) had not arrived at the issues of transference and countertransference, much less erotic versions thereof (see Abramowitz, Abramowitz, Roback, Corney, & McKee, 1976; Guttman, 1984; Person, 1985). Besides group supervision, Jake sees me for weekly one-on-one sessions to discuss his work with Joanna.

Jake and Joanna quickly move to the heart of the performance matter and begin working on her competition anxiety and fear of evaluation by others. They use both a cognitive (thought stoppage, cognitive restructuring) and a somatic approach (breathing, centering) to counter the anxiety she experiences during competition. They are measurably successful within a few weeks. I count the botched serves in a match four weeks after they start working together, and the reduction is substantial. Joanna is really pleased, and after one of my biweekly sessions with the team, she comes up to me and says with a huge smile,

"Thanks for getting Jake to work with me. He's been super." I think little of the comment at the time, just basking in the reflected glory of one of my students doing a good job.

In supervision with Jake, I notice a change. He seems more confident and more animated. He is still in Stoltenberg's first stage (1981; being concrete, dependent, anxious) and needs lots of structure and guidance. Jake seems a bit intimidated by me (something that is often unavoidable in early stages of supervision), but that intimidation is something we discussed and are trying to get beyond. He was always enthusiastic, but now he is even more so, and coupled with the new confidence, he seems to be progressing more rapidly than most students. It looks as if he is maturing well and coming into his own. I have to admit, I attribute some of these apparent positive changes to the quality of supervision he is receiving (a narcissistic response). The changes were actually fueled by something a bit more romantic than that. On our fifth supervisory session, we start a new chapter.

> Mark: So how are things going this week with Joanna? [In a first practicum, each student has only one client.]
>
> Jake: Great. She has really gotten down the breathing and centering to use in the games, and even the coach has said nice stuff to me about how she is doing. Did you see her in the last game? She was awesome.

That last word—*awesome*—is one I particularly dislike, primarily because of its overuse in sport, but in this case it strikes a chord. I can see it in Jake's eyes as he is talking; my immediate thought is *Oh, no, this kid is in awe of his client*. There is also something more than awe in his eyes. I think I see pride, and I am getting feelings of, at least, a possible minor crush developing. Red flags are, if not starting to fly, just about to be hoisted.

As stated earlier, the admonition in erotic or romantic transference and countertransference to "just say no" is not helpful and can even be a destructive way to handle a sensitive development. I am not sure if Jake is even fully cognizant of his feelings. There is also the distinct possibility that I am misinterpreting an enthusiastic student's response to a fine performance by an athlete he is helping. On top of these vagaries, there is also the relationship between Jake and me. My initial response includes cheering for the underdog, hoping the outsider makes good and comes into the fold, wanting the nice homely guy to get the girl while the quarterback loses out: the Hollywood version of supervisor countertransference. So my responses to realizing that Jake might be developing a crush on his athlete are in rapid order: *"Oh, how nice," "Uh-oh, he's going to set himself up to get hurt,"* and *"Oh, shit!"* The first two responses are me going down a fantasy lane, and the third one is me bringing myself back to reality and professional practice. So just how can, or should, a supervisor address what may be the beginning of romantic interests between a student and an athlete?

> Mark: Sure sounds as if what you two are working on is actually helping Joanna.
>
> Jake: I think she looks more fired up and confident out there, and you know what? After the match the coach walked past me and patted my shoulder and said, "Nice work."
>
> Mark: You still have the grin on your face.

I think the questions "What are you thinking?" "What are you feeling?" and "How does that make you feel?" are all fine questions. An alternative to those questions for supervision (or service), where a good working relationship has been established, is to make a comment on current behavior that invites reflection on thinking and behavior (e.g., my comment on his grin). Even though Jake is a new supervisee, we laid ground rules that his responses, thoughts, feelings, and behaviors are going to be central topics of supervision. So he is already primed to respond to my behavioral observation.

Jake: I know; it was so great. It was as if I just won a race. You know how the coach has always been just lukewarm? Well, ever since that match she smiles at me more.

Mark: Mmm-hmm. [I pause; Jake is silent for a while.]

Jake: It's like I'm accepted now.

Mark: [I remain silent, but Jake doesn't go on.] Sort of a turning point? [A double meaning here—a turning point for Jake with the coach and with Joanna.]

Jake: Yeah, I feel I'm part of the team more. We had a big pizza feed afterward; it was great. Some of the players who have hardly said anything to me so far were talking to me. I guess I'm still grinning.

Mark: Feels good to be part of a team, and I bet it was nice to have all those women paying attention to you.

Jake: [Silent for a while, looking a bit sheepish.] Yeah, I guess it was.

Mark: Your face went from a grin to sheepish. What is that?

Jake: You make it sound as if I'm getting off on the attention.

Mark: Sorry if I sounded accusatory; I just thought you had a powerful response, and it's probably a good idea to look at it. There's nothing wrong with getting attention and positive feedback from your clients. Such responses from clients let us know we are probably doing something right.

Jake: I guess it was the "attention from women" that kind of got me.

Mark: OK.

Jake: Well, look at me, I'm a wrestling knucklehead geek. Women don't look at me, so yeah, it was nice to sit down for pizza surrounded by those great women. Was I doing something wrong here?

It seems as if I have triggered some defensiveness in Jake with my comments on attention from the team. His response has both a defensive and an open feel to it. He wants to justify his liking all the attention but knows at some level that those feelings are suspect. He also is responding, like many supervisees in the early stages of supervision, with a question that is concrete (Was I wrong? Was I right?). With beginning students, I find it is sometimes helpful to move into didactic mode because a discussion of that concreteness can help move them beyond seeing their responses and behaviors in monochromatic terms. Also, Jake is struggling, and I want to help him out.

> Issues of transference and countertransference, erotic or otherwise, are often uncomfortable for supervisees. They generate reactions such as denial, anxiety, and shame.

Mark: Jake, it's not a question of whether your liking the attention was right or wrong. How we think and feel about athletes we work with is not something we can slot into right and wrong. Right and wrong usually don't even make sense at the feeling and thinking level here. When you get to the action or behavior level, then those ethical questions come into play. How you think and how you feel are sources of information. They are data. They let you know something about you, something about your clients, and something about how your relationship with the athletes is developing. I get the feeling that you think I was passing judgment on you based on your feelings for the team. Far from it. I am just a data freak, and these data are really fascinating. Something's happened that has changed your position with the team, with the coach, and even with Joanna. Let's look at what that was about and how it happened. Your thoughts and feelings will help us here.

Jake: I don't know. It's just that I felt I had really made a breakthrough with the team.

Mark: And so you did, but what was that breakthrough for you?

Jake: I guess I felt accepted and a part of it all.

> Mark: Pretty good feeling, eh? As if you belonged and were a part of something bigger than yourself.
>
> Jake: Maybe that's it, and then maybe it was because I was getting some recognition.
>
> Mark: I still feel there is something about getting recognition that you think may be suspect. As if meeting your own needs is off base. Or did I give you the impression that you were feeling something a bit more ego-centric than client-centric?
>
> Jake: I think I just have some guilty feelings because it was all about me.
>
> Mark: Where do you think those feelings might come from?
>
> Jake: Well, you, probably.

Jake and I seem to be floundering here, but at least he feels comfortable enough with me to say, "Hey, you're making me feel guilty." That guilt has roots in the black-and-white thinking of neophyte practitioners (there's a right and a wrong way to proceed), and despite my previous comments that all this information is mainly interesting data, I haven't been able to help Jake beyond his sense of right and wrong. When learning something new, it often takes visiting and revisiting the same territory before concepts (and feelings) sink in. So I need to give it a second shot. Time to self-disclose.

> Mark: Jake, you've been doing a great job. The athletes and the coach are responding to you. They are listening and taking things you say to heart. They really appreciate what you are doing, and now you are more part of the team than ever before. In my books, all that is a fine accomplishment. But now I've spoiled your good feelings by asking you about them and giving you the impression that maybe you have done something mildly unprofessional. Sorry about that. It wasn't my intent. The sport psychologist is not just someone who delivers a service that others benefit from. He is someone who is in the profession because he, too, is getting something out of his athlete encounters. [I use third person here to help Jake get a little distance from himself.] What he gets out of his work with athletes is going to depend on his character. Let me tell you a story about you and me. When I am working with you, what I am trying to do is help you see, understand, and appreciate how what you do, and who you are, helps athletes change and get better at what *they* do. When your eyes light up over an interpretation of how you and your relationships with athletes act as positive forces in athletes' lives and how you personally are a large part of the change process, I get immense satisfaction. And when that lightbulb goes off, I often think to myself, *Cool, he got it; damn, I'm good!* Is that an ego thing? Sure it is, and that good feeling I get when you make progress is connected to my feelings of competence and my needs to help others. It's kind of a confirmation that what we are doing is working well. I think your experience is not so different.

I use the third person for some analytical distance and then move to the first person singular to tell a story. The intent of the story is to normalize his feelings of pride by letting him know his supervisor has similar responses, which brings us to the use of the first person plural, *we,* to suggest that all we are talking about is a shared and wonderful experience that is at the heart of what we do. The process Jake and I are going through is a question of questioning. Jake has all these rather "tingly" reactions as a result of what he has done and the responses he has received (not unlike getting a lot of positive attention from a coach for a new motor skill performed well for the first time). He feels good. I question those feelings. He becomes confused and doubts the validity of those feelings. We explore those doubts, question them, interpret them, tell stories related to them, and then (one hopes) Jake comes away with a deeper understanding of his feelings and better insight into himself as a person and a psychologist working with athletes. Rather than come "full circle" back to feeling good, I hope to lead Jake "full spiral" to feeling good again, with an understanding of those feelings at a deeper level. It's often a painful but rewarding process (much like physical training). It is sort of like moving from the superficial "I did that; it felt good" to the "I did and felt that way because . . . gee, that's really neat" understanding of self in relation to others.

> Jake: OK, so what I am feeling is not so bad. [He's getting it, but that beginning psychologist "good–bad" thinking is still hanging on.] It's part of the game.
>
> Mark: And it's a big part of what keeps us in the game. You had good feelings for a job well done. You also had good feelings from the attention of all those women. Now you have the tools to recognize where those feelings are coming from when they come up in the future. Pride and positive feedback about your service will help you be a more confident practitioner. I have already noticed an increase in your confidence over the past week. Recognizing those good guy–gal feelings will also help you keep them in check so you don't move into areas that are not in the best interests of your athletes.
>
> Jake: I think I need a date.
>
> Mark: You and me both.
>
> Jake: [Laughs out loud.]

> Moving supervisees from shame and anxiety to fascination with the sensitive topics of erotic transference and countertransference may take a long time to accomplish.

Now, that unprofessional response just slips out, and it is a self-disclosure that is not in the service of my supervisee but rather reflects my need to identify with Jake, his struggles, his frustrations with the romantic side of his life, and his fantasy of taking a break from all this heavy conversation and just going out and having some fun. I guess I need a bit of a break in the supervisory process, too. Supervision is extremely taxing, and my joke about a date helps me take a breather and have a laugh with Jake. In another respect, my narcissistic turning of the conversation back to me may be helpful in some small way. It could be interpreted by Jake as "Oh, wow, my supervisor is human, too." Supervisees often place their supervisors on unreasonable pedestals and don't consider that supervisors also have foibles, weaknesses, and all-too-human desires. Jake's laugh may have been one of relief, but my response was all about me. We all make mistakes; I just hope my response is not counterproductive.

In this session, we do not get around to addressing his potential crush on Joanna. I sort of leave it at the "recognizing those good guy–gal feelings" level. I do not think he is ready for the sort of intimate examination of a one-to-one countertransference that discussing Joanna would mean. He has made good, but difficult, progress with his feelings about the team, and I think he has done enough for the day. In retrospect, if we had discussed his crush, then he might have been better equipped for what happened next.

Two sessions later, Jake comes into my office, plops down as usual in the comfy chair, and looks at the floor. I don't take much notice of his somewhat uncharacteristic entrance and proceed as usual.

> Mark: So what's been happening this week?
>
> Jake: [Silent for a while, still looking at the floor.] She kissed me.

I cannot think of a better time for a supervisor to shut up than this one. Here's a prime, and extremely obvious, example of how first utterances in a session can signal the topic for the day (see Andersen, Van Raalte, & Harris, 2000). Jake has dropped a bomb, and he knows it. He also knows he will need to start talking about it. I let him gather himself together. After a while he looks up at me with an expression of "What's going on? Have I disappointed you?" and "You gotta help me out here." Now maybe some of those interpretations of the expression on his face are my projections, but I think I have come to know Jake well enough to have a reasonably good idea what is churning up inside him. He keeps silently looking at me, and I finally make a gesture with my face and both of my hands that signals (I hope) "It's going to be all right; tell me a story."

Jake:    Shit! Where do I start?

Mark:    How about what was going on before you got kissed? [Being mildly directive to help him out.]

Jake:    Well, it was after the competition last night. We had just had the postmatch talk by the coach in the team room, and then all the girls—'scuse me, women—headed for the showers. Joanna sort of held back and fiddled with her gym bag. Everyone had left. I walked over to her and said, "You were awesome tonight." It was one of her best matches ever. Then she said, "So were you," and she took my face between her hands and planted one right on the lips. Then she looked me in the eyes and then turned and disappeared into the showers. [Jake stops and just looks at me, as if asking, "What the hell is going on?"]

Mark:    [In the most gentle tone I could muster.] And then?

Jake:    I think I had a brain hemorrhage. I don't think I moved for several seconds. I was just too stunned. And then I just flew out of the gym and went home. I thought of calling you, but it was almost 11:00, and I remembered we had supervision this morning.

Mark:    So how are you doing the morning after?

Jake:    You wouldn't happen to have a morning-after pill, would you?

Occasionally, I just shock myself with my insensitivity and flippancy. Jake's situation does not call for a lame joke about the "morning after." The use of that term also implies there are much more serious client–practitioner issues (actual sexual intimacy) involved. My joke probably serves my need to lighten up what I know is going to be a heavy session that will tax both of us. Also contained in the morning-after comment is probably some of my irritation that he didn't call me the "night of" so we could start on the problem when it was fresh. My joke also allows Jake to distance himself with a joke about a morning-after pill. The symbolic content of that comment sends me on a dynamic spin. Jake wants a magic wand to take away all that occurred the previous night. Is Jake the one who feels impregnated by the event? Is there something growing in Jake that he wants to get rid of? Or are all these associations of mine the result of the overactive imagination of a dynamically oriented supervisor? I am going overboard with associations, but I do not make any of those interpretations for him. I back away from how he is feeling at the moment (more avoidance on my part?) and ask about what happened after he got home.

Mark:    So tell me about last night. What was going on with you once you got home?

Jake:    I couldn't sleep for several hours. I was just in a funk. I got into bed and tossed and turned for a few hours. I did nod off for a while, but I woke up real early and then went out for a run.

Mark:    Did that help?

Jake:    Not really.

Mark:    How about any dreams last night?

Jake:    Yeah, a few. One was about my sister and a formula-one car, but I don't recall much else about that one, and I did have one about being in high school.

Mark:    What was that one about?

Jake:    It's not real clear, but I think it was at a tournament. I know I had just lost by being pinned, and the coach said something about going over to the bench because he had to watch Phil wrestle. But I don't recall much more.

Mark:   So who is Phil?

Jake:   He was a guy in high school in a weight division above me.

I deflect Jake's attention to dreams for a couple of reasons. First, he is distressed and maybe some reflection on something else for a while may help him compose himself a bit more. There is plenty of emotional stuff left to come up in this session, and taking a step back to look at dreams may give him a problem to focus on for now. Second, dreams often tell us something about our inner states and the current turmoil we are in. Jake's dreams are almost too easy. The first one about his sister concerns an intimate female in his life going way too fast. That one is obvious. The next dream is probably about Jake and me. In that dream Jake has been pinned, and he has lost. Being pinned in wrestling is a physically intimate situation by any standards. It is also a type of failure. The coach (me) tells him to go over to the bench because he has to watch another wrestler. That scenario may have something to do with failing in my eyes and being dismissed. And that dismissal is connected with my turning my attention to someone else who is more worthy (a weight class "above"). I think the dream is about shame and the fear of losing me as his supervisor.

Mark:   Do either of those dreams seem to have any connection to what went on last evening with Joanna?

Jake:   I have been thinking about that because we sometimes talk about dreams. I remember being ashamed that I lost, and I feel kind of all mixed up about what happened and how I felt when she kissed me. [He's getting to the heart of the matter in the dream and in the kiss, and his statement is blending the two events.]

Mark:   So how did you feel when she kissed you?

Jake:   [Pause.] Shocked, I guess, but then, just for a quick second, I wanted us to start ripping clothes off, and then I just wanted to run.

Mark:   Sounds as if you felt a strong need to get away from a lot of things.

JA:     Man, I couldn't stick around 'til they got out of the locker room.

Mark:   Do you have some ideas about what you were running from?

Jake:   Well, Joanna for one. . . . [He was probably also running from his own erotic response, but we will get to that later.]

Mark:   [From his running, I move back to his returning to the problem.] What was it like for you walking up to my office today?

Jake:   I was sweating bullets . . . still am.

Mark:   So why the sweaty bullets?

Jake:   I guess I'm ashamed of how I reacted.

Mark:   [In my best collaborative empiricist mode.] So let's look at that dream and what went on in the gym and what's going on here. Being ashamed of losing and being dismissed to the bench may also be part of being ashamed of having a major sexual fantasy about an athlete, being ashamed of the kiss itself, and being ashamed of letting me down.

Jake:   I am such a mess.

Mark:   Sure you are, but messes are what you and I are so good at sorting out. Let's go back and look at what led up to that kiss.

Supervisees like Jake make what I do all worth it. The term I used—*collaborative empiricist*—conveys the atmosphere I try to nurture in both supervision and sport psychology practice. Jake and I are involved in an intimate, collaborative effort to understand the data of his experience, to understand his story, and to build and evolve a portrait of the developing psychologist who is Jake. He and I are on an adventure, and in almost every session Jake gets more and more of the picture of Jake, in his relationships with athletes, in his understanding of himself, and in his relationship to me.

It is interesting that Jake avoids reflecting on the dream with his sister. The incestuous quality of that dream may have been too threatening for consideration, but that avenue probably does not need attention at this time. Jake does, however, begin to see that his miasma of emotions concerning Joanna, himself, professionalism, and me is what needs to be sorted out. In the following discussion of what led up to the kiss, Jake speaks of some subtle events on Joanna's part that he did not mention previously in supervision (e.g., a touch on the arm, a quick sisterly hug after a game), some acts of his (e.g., giving her more attention than the other players during his attendance at practice and games), and some fantasies he was previously too embarrassed to talk about (e.g., Joanna in the showers). In examining the lead-up to the kiss, it appears that two people were slowly getting caught up in a minor whirlpool.

> Supervision, at its best, is a long-term, intimate journey for both the supervisor and the supervisee.

The kiss and Jake's overt sexual fantasy of getting naked with Joanna are the nearly predictable outcomes of a romantic dance that first came to the fore when Jake talked about Joanna being awesome. My failings as a supervisor at not addressing what I thought might be going on earlier only helped the dance along.

Shock, shame, and guilt. Jake's reactions are exactly the sort that keep erotic countertransference in the closet. Fortunately, Jake and I have a relationship that allows such feelings to be expressed and talked about. I give Jake the wonderful book *Sexual Feelings in Psychotherapy* by Pope and colleagues (1993) to take home and read. I often use bibliotherapy for my supervisees, and reading that book is usually a therapeutic act. It humanizes all the intense feelings that appear in the intimate encounters between psychologists and clients and offers ways to go about helping psychologists sort through clients' erotic reactions and helpers' own romantic responses.

Two related concerns need attention. The first is Jake himself and his jumble of emotions regarding what happened. The second is helping Jake figure out what he needs to do about talking with Joanna.

> Mark: So here we are. You got kissed, you got excited, and you got scared. How about we look at the excitement part first?
>
> Jake: You mean, like, the "let's get naked" part?
>
> Mark: Yeah, that would be it.
>
> Jake: It was so weird. Like, one minute I was this sport psychologist, and the next I was this horny bastard. Dr. Jekyll and Mr. Hyde.

Jake's literary reference holds a large component of negative evaluation. Robert Louis Stevenson's Mr. Hyde is a hedonistic id-like aspect of Dr. Jekyll who ends up committing some rather heinous acts. Jake's comparison of himself as someone who is essentially out of control and a kind of monster seems harsh, and Jake, who has a surfeit of charity for others, appears to be less than charitable to himself. The shock of finding Mr. Hyde within himself, especially in a professional relationship, is upsetting. I need to help Jake look at what he perceives to be his darker side and get an appreciation for the human qualities of his id impulses (e.g., seeking sensual gratification).

> Mark: So the horny bastard, Mr. Hyde, made an appearance. Sounds as if you recognized him. He's shown up before?
>
> Jake: Well, yeah, but that was with a girl I really had the hots for, and we were dating.
>
> Mark: And how was that?
>
> Jake: I was in love, and when we finally got together like that, I just got lost in the moment and . . .

Mark: And?

Jake: It was wonderful.

Mark: Of course it was! Those times when we're intimate with loved ones are a great chance to get lost in the moment and feel and enjoy. There's a lot about Mr. Hyde that is really human. But I sense there is a feeling of shame here about your response to Joanna.

Jake: But that sort of stuff shouldn't happen.

Mark: If you mean by "that sort of stuff" sexual intimacy with clients, then you have no argument from me. If you mean feeling erotic desires for a client, then we have an argument on our hands.

Jake: What do you mean?

Mark: There is a world of difference between feeling something sexual or romantic for a client and actually getting involved physically. I think you are equating a physical act with an internal state, and if one is prohibited, then so is the other. . . . OK, so what am I saying to you?

Jake: Sounds as if it's OK to get horny over an athlete.

Mark: No argument here, but what does it tell you if an athlete makes you hot and bothered?

Jake: I'd say I'd be way off track and in serious shit.

Mark: Why?

Jake: Because, I guess, it would be more about me and what I want and not about the athlete and what she needs. Seems kind of perfectly wrong. As you always said in class, "If the answer to 'Who is being served?' is not the athlete, then something is wrong."

Mark: Oh, crap! I knew that might come back to haunt me.

Jake: [Laughs.] You said it.

Mark: I know I did, and I probably didn't explain all the provisos well enough. I think I need to amend that maxim so it reads "Who is being served by my actions?" How you feel about your client and how you act with your client may be two different things at times. She kissed you; you didn't kiss back. You didn't cop a feel, and you brought the whole issue up immediately in supervision. I see a whole lot of right action here. I also see a whole lot of you beating yourself up for what is a really nice human reaction to someone who likes you a bunch and appreciates all you have done for her.

Jake: So it's OK?

Mark: Jake, it's more than OK. It's just about perfect for you at this point. You just had a walloping great experience. You just got to see yourself in the eyes of your client; and you just got to see your romantic, sexual response to her; and you got to talk about it. I couldn't have set up a better learning experience for a student if I tried. You are already way ahead of a lot of professionals who have never really confronted their own sexual responses to clients. [I stay quiet for a while.] So how are you doing?

Jake: I am trying to get my head around all this stuff.

OK, I am being a cheerleader here, but I think some cheerleading (essentially a subspecies of reframing) is what Jake can use now. I also think the cheerleading comes from my countertransferential responses to Jake. My questionable little fantasy earlier about hoping the goofy guy gets the girl has been transformed into the goofy guy getting a profound lesson in service delivery and emerging from the experience a more mature professional. Jake will need some time to "get his head around all this stuff," and we return to his erotic countertransference and his fears of disappointing me several times. His story triggers some of my own memories of how I struggled with erotic countertransference;

our conversation mirrors conversations I had with one of my supervisors. I feel an overwhelming sense of personal history, of passing on experience to the next generation. I am having one of those Eriksonian generativity moments (Erikson's psychosocial stage of midlife where the challenge is to begin to give back something to those coming after us or to lapse into midlife stagnation). Just as I still have my supervisors' voices in my head, I know Jake will hear this conversation again in his head as he progresses through his career. And some day he might have a similar talk with one of his supervisees. I believe Jake is thankful that I helped him understand himself, and in a true sense, I am thankful to Jake for giving me the opportunity to help him out. Supervisors have needs, too.

> Erotic transference and countertransference are truly heavy stuff, and supervisees may need lots of time to digest all the meanings and ramifications of these processes.

There is still another major issue, however, to be dealt with—how to handle Joanna's feelings for Jake. There are few things tougher to handle than when a client gets a crush on a psychologist. So what might be going on with Joanna? It is probably safe to assume that given the kiss on the lips (not a thank-you peck on the check), Joanna has developed some romantic feelings for Jake. Why has this situation occurred? A description of the professional relationship may help. Joanna is an extremely attractive young woman who, no doubt, has had her fair share of attention from males. She has probably been "hit on" many times in her life. But now she meets Jake, a fellow athlete who knows a lot about her world. He spends a good deal of time with her. His only interest appears to be her welfare. He cares for her. He's never hit on her. She feels safe with him, and he thinks she's awesome. How often do people get to experience such a caring, nonagendized relationship? It would be surprising if a romantic feeling did not occur occasionally under such conditions.

The situation with Jake and Joanna is a variation on what happens all the time with helping dyads. Students fall for their professors, patients want to marry their doctors, athletes develop romantic fantasies about their coaches, and supervisees get crushes on their supervisors. These transferential phenomena are the products of both the situation (i.e., the helping relationship) and the qualities of the characters involved. The comment at the beginning of the chapter—"I just wouldn't let it happen"—seems doubly naive in that the speaker (a) does not recognize that a caring, helping relationship is extremely fertile ground for the development of erotic transference and countertransference and (b) believes that one has the power to prevent it from happening.

So once it has happened, or it finally becomes recognized as happening (rather dramatically in Jake's case), what does one do? For several years, I have asked my psychology and physical therapy students (I also teach some classes in a physiotherapy program here in Australia) to role-play clients making veiled romantic overtures to their helpers. The results are always a combination of hilarity (lots of nervous laughter), awkwardness, confusion, bungled communication, hurt feelings, and a sense of being way out of their depths. How do you let the client down without damaging the relationship? All the fine talk about the professional relationship and boundaries, the respect one has for one's client, the ethics of helping, and so forth and so on cannot erase the fact that someone is going to get hurt; someone who has put himself or herself out on a romantic limb is going to feel more or less rejected. The whole situation is a major bummer. Not only will Joanna feel hurt, but Jake will feel awful as well in that he has done something to make his client feel bad. No one gets out unscathed.

> A major question in managing erotic transference and countertransference is how can we minimize the hurt for both parties and preserve the fine qualities of the relationship?

Mark:  So what happens when you go to practice tomorrow?

Jake:  I don't friggin' know. It's gonna be weird. What should I do?

Mark:  Hell, I don't friggin' know either. . . . Well, that's not totally right. I have a few ideas we can work on.

My identification with Jake and his "unknowing" state is intentional. I want him to know that this situation is extremely awkward for me, too, and that I am struggling along with him. I want to let Jake know that "we" are in a confused state, but we will be able to work something out together (collaborative empiricists in action).

Mark:   How about we do some role-playing of you and Joanna talking together tomorrow and see where that leads us? I'll be Joanna; talk to me as you might talk to her during warm-up and stretching.

Jake:   I don't even know where to start.

Mark:   OK, sorry. I am jumping ahead. Let's go back a step. What do you want to say to her? Let's get a little preparation going here.

Jake:   I'm not sure. I want to tell her . . . shit! I don't know what I want to tell her.

Mark:   OK, what comes first to mind?

Jake:   Well, first, I think I would want to tell her that we should run away to Tahiti together.

Mark:   Too expensive. Make it Mexico.

Jake is not denying his countertransferential feelings (a positive sign), but he is voicing them in a joking manner to lighten up a tense situation. I recognize his need to loosen up and push it along with another little joke. I think this small episode of humor helps both Jake and me because he then gets right back down to business.

Jake:   [Laughs and then is silent for a moment.] I guess I would want to say, "Wow, you kind of surprised me yesterday."

Mark:   All right, that's good. You're letting her know something about what happened to you.

Jake:   I have been playing this scene over and over. What if she says, "What do you mean?" and then I have to say, "That kiss and everything," and then she says, "Oh, that was just a thank-you—no worries, guy." And then I'll feel like a jerk for bringing it all up and for sort of putting her on the spot.

Mark:   Sounds as if the scenes in your head are minidisasters. Kind of rehearsing the unhappy outcomes over and over again? How about we build a couple of scripts? Maybe instead of "You surprised me" you could focus more specifically on your reaction rather than start with *her* making *you* react. Maybe when you have a moment that won't be interrupted by her having to do stuff, like at the end or beginning of practice, you could say, "Joanna, I felt kinda awkward after practice yesterday." You want to start there?

Jake:   OK, here goes. . . . Joanna, could I talk to you a moment? I felt awkward after practice yesterday, and I thought maybe we could talk about it.

Mark:   [As Joanna.] You mean the kiss?

Jake:   Mmm-hmm.

Mark:   Sorry, that was just a thank-you. You've been so great to me, and you've helped so much. I thought I needed to give you a big kiss. I really like you a lot.

Jake:   [Falling out of role.] Oh, crap! What do I say now, Mark?

Mark:   [Falling back to supervisor.] What do you want to say? I think you have good instincts when it comes to talking to people. Don't stifle what you are feeling by thinking too much right now. What is your gut instinct about what you want to say?

Jake:   I'd like to say I like her a lot too and that our work together has been really enjoyable, but we need to keep this professional.

Mark:   Perfect! See, you do know what to say.

Jake:   Won't telling her I like her a lot just take us down that path further?

Mark:   It probably would if you left it at that, but you have more to say, too.

Jake:   I don't want to hurt her feelings.

Mark:   I know you don't, but some feelings are going to get hurt. You can't avoid it. But now think of Joanna's situation. What if you were still wrestling, and you developed a crush on your female sport psychologist and had just kissed her? What message from her would let you down easy, hurt your feelings a bit, but also do the least damage to the relationship?

Jake:   I guess I would want to hear that everything was still cool, that she still cared for me, that she still wanted to work with me, and that she didn't think I was a fool.

Mark:   OK, think you got the tools now?

Jake:   Let's give it a shot.

Mark:   OK, I'll start where we left off. . . . [As Joanna.] I really like you a lot.

Jake:   And, Joanna, I really like you a lot, too. Working with you has been great. You're one of the most dedicated athletes I know. And working with you has helped me become a better professional. I am really happy about all I've learned from working with you, but that kiss kind of confused me. It was really nice of you to do, but it kinda crosses the professional boundaries that I am learning about as a psychologist. [Falling out of role.] I am just rambling on here.

Mark:   Keep going; you're doing fine.

Jake:   OK. [Back in role.] So I guess I'm saying that kiss seems like something different from what you and I usually do together as athlete and psychologist-in-training.

Mark:   [Also in role.] Oh, man, Jake. I'm sorry I made you uncomfortable. I just like you so much, and you have been so wonderful and helpful to me. I'm playing so much better now.

Jake:   What you just said, Joanna, is all the thanks I need. I am really pleased you think I've been helpful, and I would like to continue our working together just as it was. That's what I need to do as a psychologist . . . to be your sport psychologist . . . and that kiss sort of felt as if I wasn't exactly your psychologist anymore. I value what we do together, and I wouldn't want to hurt that for the world.

Mark:   [Falling out of role.] Damn, Jake. That was good! [Back in role, and becoming rather distant.] OK, Jake, no more kisses, I promise . . . won't happen again.

Jake:   [Falling out of role.] Now what? It's like she's doing a big-time retreat.

Mark:   [Falling back to supervisor.] Well, I am playing as if she's been rejected, and as much as she likes you, she feels embarrassed and uncomfortable. It's natural for her to become more distant. Knowing what I do of you and Joanna, I think something like this scenario will play out, but I don't believe she will stay distant for long . . . as long as you are willing to be as comfortable and helpful as you have been in the past. If you and Joanna were in therapy together, we would be treating this transference phenomenon entirely differently. You and Joanna would be examining what it says about you and her and what insights it provides into her other relationships in her life, but this ain't psychotherapy, and we want you two to get through this with a working relationship intact.

Jake:   So what do I do if she pulls away?

Mark:   What would you like to do?

Jake:   I guess just be there and let her know I'll be there. I'd probably want to tell her that I am her psychologist-in-training, and I am here for the duration and that I think we have a great working relationship going, and I want to continue it.

| | |
|---|---|
| Mark: | What you just said sounds good to me. Let her know that. I have no doubt that she will hear the message, and you'll be back working together, maybe not exactly as before but still in a solid helping relationship. |
| Jake: | I hope so. |
| Mark: | So, as you think of seeing her tomorrow, how are you doing? |
| Jake: | Well, I'm still a mess, but I think I'll do OK. |
| Mark: | You've got good instincts about what will be helpful and kind—just remember that, and follow them. |

Our role-playing has a distinctly parallel-process feel to it because in a cognitive–behavioral kind of mode, we are rehearsing an upcoming event to let Jake practice some behaviors he may need to call on in a delicate situation. This type of rehearsal, similar to mentally rehearsing facing a frightening opponent, helps Jake become a bit more comfortable with what may transpire. Jake and I had often moved into role-plays to help him feel more comfortable talking to athletes. For example, to help him with his introduction and delivery of relaxation (see Sherman & Poczwardowski, 2000), I would play an anxious athlete, and he would take me through the process. That he and I had done this type of rehearsal many times probably also helped him move into our most awkward role-play to date. I often use cognitive–behavioral techniques in supervision, and I hope they leave the message that what we do with athletes also works for us in a variety of situations.

Jake calls me the next day and tells me things were awkward but not bad. He talked to Joanna just before practice, and she avoided looking at him for a lot of the time, but during the end-of-practice sport psychology briefing, she participated in the group discussion, and on the way to the locker room she asked if their weekly appointment was still on for the following day. They continue working with each other for the rest of the season.

# Conclusion

Transference and countertransference crop up in all sorts of places, even in performance enhancement counseling. Jake experienced both phenomena in a rather dramatic fashion and felt shame, shock, confusion, and awkwardness, but he came away from the experience with an appreciation of psychologists' human reactions to clients. Once he got past the immediacy and the in-your-face quality of the experience, he began developing interests in examining the literature on erotic transference and countertransference and became fascinated with how such reactions occur and how they can be resolved, both in performance enhancement counseling and in psychotherapy.

My colleagues and I have written before about the state of fascination in supervisees (Andersen, Van Raalte, & Harris, 2000). When my supervisees become fascinated by their clients, by their reactions to athletes, and by their relationships with those they serve, I begin to see them move beyond the black and white thinking of "good and bad" feelings and thoughts about athletes. I see fascination; interest; and curiosity about self, others, and relationships to be signposts that a supervisee is moving beyond the concrete first stage of supervision to a more independently functioning professional who is developing a keen appreciation of his and others' all-too-human qualities.

# Commentary on Chapter 10

William B. Strean, PhD, and Herbert S. Strean, DSW

After reading and rereading Andersen's stimulating and informative chapter, we want to say (much to his chagrin) that we would describe his contribution as "awesome." We rarely see a comprehensive understanding of psychodynamic theory and its creative application to sport psychology in our professional literature. Furthermore, Andersen's authenticity, his courage to reveal himself, and his acknowledgment of his own vulnerabilities make him a delightful role model. His chapter does not give us any reason to have an ax to grind, and we have no major criticisms of it. We believe the substantive content and process learned by sharing case histories, coupled with revelations of one's own inner thoughts, have important roles in sport psychology. In our commentary, we expand on some of the concepts Andersen has presented to see if we can enlarge his focus on supervision. First, however, we locate this discussion in the field of sport psychology practice.

## Sex, Countertransference, and the Sport Psychologist

Let's talk about sex. Andersen takes on this unusual territory for sport psychology in several significant ways. First, he raises the issue of sex and sexual attraction that we experience as professionals toward our clients and students. The degree to which this phenomenon is rarely broached may be greater than he suggests. He describes a member of the audience who asked the conference panel about sexual attraction between graduate students and professors, but if memory serves correctly, it was Andersen himself who posed the question. Not that he is the only one drawing attention to the question, but the number of people who are asking us to think about these issues is small. This arena is very uncomfortable for most sport psychologists. But we want to underscore the importance of having open conversations about these all-too-human phenomena. If we are committed to promoting professionalism, helping graduate students develop, and providing optimal service for clients, we need to get comfortable enough with our own discomfort to talk about sexual attraction in sport psychology service delivery.

## What's on My Mind?

Another major path Andersen emphasizes is that of asking us, as practitioners, to take a more comprehensive look at ourselves. We see this approach as another, perhaps deeper, way of looking at what we "bring to the dance" (as the internationally regarded sport psychology practitioner and author, Ken Ravizza, likes to say). When we work with clients, we bring a whole range of thoughts, feelings, personal histories, wishes, desires, and fears. Acknowledging these subjectivities as the "human condition" of practicing sport psychology is important, but it may not relieve all the concerns we have about self-examination. Many of us enjoy being in the position of caregiver; we truly enjoy looking after others. Yet, we may dislike having the scrutiny turned on us. Understanding countertransference, as we describe later in this commentary, is an incredibly fruitful journey to take in becoming an increasingly effective practitioner.

We see exploring one's countertransference responses as an example of critical self-reflection. In openly sharing his own experiences with clients and graduate students, Andersen shows the tremendous value of this work on self. Professionals frequently advocate some form of evaluation as part of the appropriate sequence of sport psychology intervention (Andersen, 2002). We believe that a continuing analysis of one's own countertransference should be part of being in the dance.

## "Who You Talking About?"

One issue we would raise is that the scope and kind of sport psychology consultant–client relationships are quite diverse. Some of the points mentioned in chapter 10 about therapist–client relationships and APA guidelines may be less germane to some practitioners than to others. Some of the principles seem to warrant the "Talmudic quality" Andersen writes about when they are applied to professional psychologists. Yet when we are talking about graduate students giving group presentations about sport psychology skills, such strong dictums maybe could be relaxed.

# Exploring Concepts

Although we concur with Andersen's definition of transference as a phenomenon in which "past relationship patterns and the thoughts, feelings and behaviors that accompany them are getting transferred to the current therapeutic encounter," we suggested in a previous paper (Strean & Strean, 1998) that a simple one-to-one correspondence between the past and present does not always exist. We would like to emphasize that frequently a compensatory fantasy (Fine, 1982) counterbalances what was lacking in the client's childhood. In effect, the client fantasizes that the practitioner is someone whom a parent should have been. This dynamic may have been the way Jake experienced Andersen and the way Joanna experienced Jake—issues we shall discuss in more detail a little later.

Freud (1912, 1926) and other psychodynamic theorists discovered that transference reactions can take many forms. The client can proclaim loving feelings toward the helper, but dreams, fantasies, and resistances (e.g., forgetting an appointment, arriving habitually late for sessions, bouncing a check) may reveal the opposite. Similarly, statements of hatred can defend against warm feelings. Inasmuch as most people have mixed feelings toward parental figures, the sport psychologist should always be ready to be both idealized and chastised—sometimes in the same session.

One of the major advances in psychodynamic theory and practice since the mid-1980s has been the broadening of our understanding and use of the concept of countertransference. From Freud's (1910/1926) original dictum that "the countertransference arises [in the practitioner] as a result of the patient's influence on his unconscious feelings, and we are almost inclined to insist that he shall recognize the countertransference in himself and overcome it" (1910, pp. 144-145), current practitioners tend to view countertransference as including "all of the emotional reactions at work" (Abend, 1989, p. 374). Rather than an obstacle to be overcome, countertransference is now regarded by most clinicians as "all those reactions [of the therapist] to the patient that may help or hinder treatment" (Slakter, 1987, p. 3).

There is now a rather large literature on countertransference, and most authors acknowledge that it is as ever-present as transference and must be constantly examined by all helping professionals (Abend, 1982, 1989; Boesky, 1990; Brenner, 1985; Fine, 1982; Jacobs, 1986, 1991; Maroda, 1994; Renik, 1993; Strean, 1993, 1995, 1999, 2000). The increased examination and discussion of countertransference have helped most practitioners recognize that the therapeutic process is always an interactive one. Boesky (1990) stated the issue poignantly when he averred, "I consider the 'purity' of a theoretic [therapeutic] treatment, in which all of the resistances are created only by the patient, to be a fiction. If [the therapist] does not get emotionally involved sooner or later in a manner that he had not intended, [the therapy] will not proceed to a successful conclusion" (p. 573). Just as there can be no dynamically oriented counseling without constant transference reactions, most dynamically oriented clinicians would contend that no therapeutic process proceeds without constant countertransference reactions. The sport psychologist also becomes emotionally (or countertransferentially) involved with athletes, and that dynamic can be either beneficial or harmful depending on how the countertransference is understood and handled.

## Countertransference in Action

Jacobs (1986) has demonstrated that therapeutic technique is almost always "a countertransference enactment," even when the technical procedure is considered to be a valid and acceptable therapeutic intervention. In a sport setting, we might consider that the application of a specific mental skill, such as relaxation, is often a suitable intervention, but one that is also reflective of what the consultant brings to the situation. A corollary of Jacobs' position is that therapy and counseling are far more related to the personality of the therapist than they are to the therapist's technique. In effect, extensive countertransference participation and enactment are inevitable. Renik (1993), like many authors (Brenner, 1985; Fine, 1982; Jacobs, 1986, 1991; Strean, 1999, 2000), has demonstrated that the clinician "cannot eliminate or even diminish his or her subjectivity" (p. 562).

Since the mid-1990s, most practitioners have tended to view transference and countertransference as always in interaction. Consequently, if the client is in a state of sexual excitement toward the therapist, the therapist is probably, albeit subtly and unconsciously, inviting it. Furthermore, if the therapist is having sexual fantasies about the patient, the latter is probably in one way or another inducing it. We believe that similar processes took place between Jake and Joanna. As has been demonstrated repeatedly (Dahlberg, 1970; Fine, 1984; Strean, 1993), erotic transference and countertransference phenomena usually take place when the people involved have strong interpersonal needs and are yearning for a great deal of reassurance. Both Jake and Joanna may have frequently felt somewhat on the "outside" and probably unconsciously sensed this dynamic in each other. This narcissistic attraction was not consciously recognized by either of them, and hence it tended to be acted out rather than fully discussed and mastered by both parties. That is to say, both individuals were unaware that they were attracted to something of themselves that they saw in the other person. Without that awareness, they moved closer to each other rather than attend to the dynamics at work.

Inasmuch as both client and counselor are now being considered "more human than otherwise" (Sullivan, 1953), many clinicians advocate that at moments of impasse, resistance, or crisis, the therapist disclose his or her countertransference reactions to the client. Such revelations can help clarify the client's transference and improve the therapeutic alliance (Maroda, 1994; Renik, 1993; Strean, 1999, 2000), which in hindsight might have enhanced the working relationship between Jake and Joanna. For example, Jake might have discussed with Joanna how special she was to him and then reinforced the professional boundaries of their relationship. Unfortunately, Jake probably was not fully cognizant of his reactions to Joanna, and his supervisor was, at first, reluctant to lead Jake into a discussion of his countertransferential responses.

What is also being discussed more openly in the professional literature is that the supervisor's countertransference substantially influences treatment processes and outcomes (Lane, 1990; Rock, 1997; Strean, 2000). Such connections are best illustrated by Andersen's work with Jake. Andersen candidly shared with us his strong countertransference reactions toward his client, Jill. He unconsciously yearned for a symbiosis with Jill, whom in many ways he idealized and made the mother of his dreams (literally and figuratively). It would not be stretching the point too much to say that Andersen, as many parents do with their sons and daughters unconsciously, encouraged Jake to find a mother figure in the form of Joanna. If Andersen's countertransference issues, which involved a strong yearning for a mother, had been shared with Jake and discussed between them, we might have observed a more verbal interaction between Jake and Joanna that involved less acting on unconscious desires.

In working with clients and supervisees on the sexual dimension of the counseling situation, we believe timing is important. Just as enjoyable sex usually involves mutually pleasurable foreplay, we contend that our clients and supervisees need to know us for a while before we get into the subject of sexual attraction to clients. We believe Jake was possibly confronted about his "grin" prematurely and felt caught off guard when he was not ready to reveal too much of himself to Andersen or examine his suppressed feelings about his client. As a result, he felt humiliated, criticized, and uncomfortable in front of Andersen. Although Andersen offered a great deal of support and reassurance after he recognized that Jake was in distress, it might have been too late. We believe that Jake needed a lot of support, reassurance, and understanding *before* being confronted about his grin and all that it implied. With the kind of preparation and frank discussion of transference and countertransference mentioned previously, he might have been able to air more of his feelings toward Joanna and toward Andersen. Jake might also have been more enabled to help Joanna talk more with him about all that she was feeling toward him and what she fantasized that he felt toward her.

Just as psychotherapeutic interventions by the practitioner are always an expression of his or her countertransference, even when the technical procedure is considered to be valid and acceptable (Jacobs, 1986), so too can the supervisor's responses be colored by what Teitelbaum (1990) refers to as "supertransference." As we have suggested, more practitioners are shifting their conceptualization of countertransference away from the traditional classical model of a one-person psychology and nearer to a two-person psychology. It is now a virtual axiom that the therapist's countertransference and the patient's transference always influence both parties and, therefore, always affect the therapeutic outcome. Now, the same notion can be made about supervision—both parties affect each other, and both contribute to the supervisory and therapeutic outcome (Lane, 1990; Rock, 1997; Strean, 1991, 1999, 2000; Teitelbaum, 1990).

Searles (1955, 1962) was one of the first to discuss how supervisory interaction is influenced by transference and countertransference interactions in the treatment relationship. He suggested using supervision to clarify problems the practitioner experienced. This practice would not only diminish the resistances to learning but also foster change in the therapy. Ekstein and Wallerstein (1972) also discussed this "parallel process" in supervision (see also Van Raalte & Andersen, 2000) and delineated ways in which it could be used to understand the therapeutic atmosphere. They focused on the supervisee's inevitable "problems about learning" (interpersonal problems between supervisor and supervisee and the supervisee's resistance to supervision) in order to clarify the transference–countertransference problems between the supervisee and the client.

Doehrman (1976) substantiated empirically the Ekstein and Wallerstein (1972) concept of parallel process of supervision. She demonstrated that difficulties in the therapeutic relationship were unconsciously communicated to the supervisor by the way the practitioner interacted with his or her mentor. Unexpectedly, she found that the influence of the supervisor's emotional reactions to the supervisee and to the client was an outstanding feature of the processes observed. Similarly, we found that the overt and implied reactions of Andersen to Jake and Joanna were an outstanding feature of the processes we observed. For example, Andersen was clear about his investment in bringing Jake and Joanna emotionally close to each other. This emotional investment played a role in his supervision and was a factor contributing to Jake and Joanna's intense erotic transference–countertransference interaction.

Finally, we would like to offer our opinion on why erotic transference and erotic countertransference are so rarely confronted in the sport counseling situation and why discussion of the subject in our professional literature has been so limited for many years. If we endorse the notion that transference–countertransference for both parties tends to recapitulate a parent–child relationship, then we believe the mystery of the avoidance of the topic begins to unfold. The acceptance, understanding, and empathy that most counselors provide frequently induce responses in the client such as, "At last I have found the perfect parent I've always yearned for." This "honeymoon reaction" (Fine, 1982) of the client often stimulates a similar response in the therapist: "I too have found someone who loves me the way I've always wanted to be loved." The two parties feel like honeymooners, but they may begin to feel anxious when they encounter figures that they experience as parental. (For example, Andersen experienced Jill this way, and she probably felt the same toward him. It is also likely that Jake and Joanna experienced many childlike and parental emotions toward each other.) Because the interaction creates anxiety, it often activates "the first treatment crisis" (Fine, 1982), similar to the experience that the honeymoon is over; the idealized relationship is seen to be imperfect. Although recognition and discussion of sexual feelings are much less taboo today than they were in Freud's day, it is still truly difficult for most children and parents to allow themselves to experience erotic feelings toward each other. Repressing and suppressing them are par for the course in most homes in our society. Consequently, when these feelings emerge in the counseling situation, both parties tend to run away from them.

As Andersen suggests, if we want to provide future practitioners with the psychological and social equipment they need to help their clients, we must help them accept that sexual, romantic, parental, and childlike feelings and fantasies are universal phenomena that exist on some level between all sport psychologists and their clients, between all parents and their sons and daughters, between all supervisors and supervisees, and between all humans.

# Countertransference: Beyond the Erotic

Having commented on Andersen's exploration of erotic transference and countertransference, we would like to expand our consideration of the topic beyond the sexual realm. Awareness and self-management of countertransference can be valuable in a variety of other ways. To reiterate, countertransference can easily be misconstrued as the reaction that a sport psychology consultant should not be having; yet it is a rich source of information that can help with successful interventions in athletes' lives.

## "I Coulda Been a Contender"

With few exceptions, the sport psychologists we know are former athletes. Most of us have a great deal of experience with competition and performance; with a set of judgments and values about winning and losing; and with coaches, training, travel, and sundry other facets of the athletic milieu. How do our histories enter into our working relationships? If we have a positive countertransference and identify with a client, we may find that the client's struggles recapitulate some of our own (often unresolved) experiences. For example, we may work with an athlete who has had great success but now finds herself consistently getting results just below what is desired. She tells us about the one competitor who is frequently just above her in the standings. Her story may bring up in us recollections of similar situations we faced as athletes. If left unchecked, we may find ourselves relating to the situation through our own wish to "get it right this time" and beat that nasty opponent. On the other hand, we may, as athletes, have had little tolerance for teammates who showed such declines in their performances. We might begin to have some negative feelings about our client, who we believe should be tougher.

The specifics of such reactions are not important. What *is* crucial is that much of who we are as sport psychologists has roots in our being former athletes. There is great likelihood that we will experience many countertransference reactions as athletes share the vicissitudes of training and competition with us. Being aware of what is going on with us allows us to serve the client better. There are many particular ways in which the benefits of insight may occur. One example, similar to one Andersen used in another context, is sharing one's own countertransference experiences with the client to normalize what the client is feeling. Recently, when working with a developing athlete who was feeling pressure to perform from her parents and coaches, I (William) related what it was like for me to feel that kind of pressure when I was a child and how her current situation brought up those feelings for me. My sharing some of the resentment I felt as a child seemed to create an opening for the athlete to expose and explore some of her own feelings.

## Oh, Brother

Another way in which countertransference may frequently emerge is by experiencing the client as a family member. We believe that Andersen's indication of "big-brother feelings" for many of his clients is probably common. Especially among graduate students and young practitioners who may be close in age to clients, it is easy to have a big-brother or big-sister reaction to a patient. This response to athletes can be a positive experience that engenders wanting to lovingly support a client. It may also bring out competitive issues that could get in the way of working with a client (e.g., sibling rivalry). The range of associations is great and may include wanting a powerful and successful client to be like a younger sibling in whose glory one basks; an older sibling whom one admires and identifies with; or even a parent who will, by example, set everything right.

## Conclusion

We believe this chapter to be an unusually valuable contribution to the literature (as well as this volume and its companion [Andersen, 2000]), and we hope that the "family" of people embracing the concepts presented here will grow and prosper. As authors, we have a strong father–son transference relationship, and we would be happy to find a role for Mark in "our family."

# Expanding Repertoires and Understanding Self

*Diversity in Service Delivery*

# Raising the Bar

*Developing an Understanding of Athletes From Racially, Culturally, and Ethnically Diverse Backgrounds*

William D. Parham, PhD, ABPP

There is absolutely, positively no difference between consulting with or counseling athletes from culturally, ethnically, and racially diverse backgrounds and consulting with or counseling Anglo athletes. Both groups share the "love of the game"; are fueled by a seemingly insatiable desire to win; disdain losing; work long and arduous hours developing and maintaining their athletic skills; and comply willingly and steadfastly to nutritional, rehabilitation, and strength and conditioning regimens. Furthermore, both groups share long sports tenures that usually began with their involvement in youth sport. They have usually excelled and have basked in the limelight of their success. Just the thought of giving up sports through retirement or injury feels disarming emotionally, and actually terminating their involvement with the sport on which they have subsisted emotionally and psychologically for many years triggers a feeling of desperation, significant in magnitude to cause considerable distress.

Throughout their sport involvement, both culturally, ethnically, and racially diverse athletes and Anglo athletes trusted that their coaches always had their best interests in mind, and both groups respected the certified athletic trainers from whom they generously received expert and tailored sports medicine services. If fortune had its way, both groups accessed the services of a sport psychologist at some point in their athletic careers, and each learned performance enhancement skills that really made a difference. Finally, all these athletes have grown tremendously as human beings, are thankful for having had the opportunity to participate in sports, and almost without exception have learned life lessons that can be applied to their postsport personal and professional activities. Now that I have your attention, let's talk about reality.

Casual observation of a day in the life of culturally, ethnically, and racially diverse athletes (for the purposes of this chapter "diverse athletes" and "culturally, racially, and ethnically diverse athletes" will be used interchangeably) and their Anglo athlete peers, particularly as their lives are played out within the context of the athletic environment, generates the simplistic, naive, and caricature-like beliefs just illustrated. Somewhat surprising, at least to me, is the realization that many of my sport psychology consultant colleagues harbor long-held beliefs that are identical to the previous descriptions. For reasons I suspect have more to do with self-protection than ignorance, they view athletes from diverse backgrounds in ways that feel safe and that won't (apparently) jeopardize consultation relationships that might subsequently develop. Ironically, the "feel safe" approach clouds the lens through which they would see and appreciate individual and group differences and actually inhibits meaningfully tailored consultations.

Three premises guided the organization of my thoughts and the preparation of this chapter. First, I want to get across to the reader that context is everything when providing sport psychology consultation to culturally, ethnically, and racially diverse athletes—irrespective of age, talent, or performance level. Assessments of and interventions with these athletes must take into account the historical, social, political, economic, environmental, and familial context within which their athletic development and performance take place. Throughout this chapter, I use examples of African-descendant people, and athletes in particular, to make this point clearer.

Second, culture, ethnicity, and race as separate indices do little to inform us about either the client or the therapist who is providing the service. Culturally, ethnically, and racially diverse people do not represent homogeneous groups. Each group has distinct features, and there is considerable variability within each group. Likewise, therapists from different cultural, ethnic, or racial communities vary considerably in their levels of awareness about diversity and in their formal mental health–based education, training, and experience. Thus, "How does one work with culturally, ethnically, and racially diverse clients?" should never be the question that initiates one's desire to help therapeutically. Given the tremendous within-group variability of both clients and therapists, the question guiding the therapist's approach should be restated as "How do I work with this specific culturally, ethnically, or racially different client at this particular time and with this particular set of concerns?" For both the client and the therapist, the interplay between their respective levels of knowledge, understanding, and acceptance of self provides the most useful indices for measuring therapeutic effectiveness.

A third premise that frames the work I do in sport psychology underscores the importance of conceptualizing culturally, ethnically, and racially diverse athletes using paradigms that reflect diverse worldviews. The philosophical premises that frame diverse worldviews do a better job of capturing the essence and spirit of athletes from these backgrounds and are more in alignment with traditional ways in which their groups of origin were viewed. Cultural, ethnic, and racial worldviews are often in stark contrast to Euro-American psychology, which is anchored traditionally in oppressive ideologies often alleged to be universal.

# Psychology's Legacy With Respect to Culturally, Ethnically, and Racially Diverse People

Today's practitioners of the psychological sciences have been trained using theories and constructs emanating from Europe and alleged to describe universal human experiences.

Thus, the fact that most practitioners fail to appreciate individual differences from value-added versus deficient-laden perspectives makes some sense, at least conceptually. Close inspection of Euro-American theories, constructs, models, and paradigms reveals their limits in accurately depicting the lives and worldviews of non-Western populations. Especially noteworthy is the disfavor, enacted in appreciably significant ways, against culturally, ethnically, and racially diverse people throughout psychology's history.

African-descendant communities represent a case in point. In his classic book *Even the Rat Was White* (1976/1998), Robert V. Guthrie captures the zeitgeist of the different periods in the evolution of psychology in a way that brings to life psychology's past and exposes the roots that continue to feed modern-day psychological practice. He reminds us that the promotion and defense of relative affective, behavioral, and cognitive human capacities across racial lines filled the coffers of American anthropological and sociological "scholarship" for decades. The relativity of human capacities across racial lines actually found its seeds in 15th- through 18th-century European thought that supported the subjugation of the "degenerate," "savage," and "loathsome" dark-skinned people of Africa. The Romanus Pontifex and the Inter Caetera, papal documents that essentially legitimized the conquest, colonization, and exploitation of non-Christian nations, also fueled the subjugation of native inhabitants of Africa and other territories.

These past events and professional practices served as the backdrop for American psychology. A retrospective look reveals the practice of Euro-American psychologists using anthropomorphic measurements to categorize body characteristics (hair texture, lip size, skin color), from which they drew evidence to support racial superiority and inferiority. These race-based practices, along with the works of Charles Darwin, Francis Galton, and Gregor Mendel and the birth of structuralism (e.g., understanding the anatomy of conscious thought), were all grounded in pre-existing European and ecumenical beliefs. Collectively, these events ignited a mind-set within psychology that framed most, if not all, of the "important," "groundbreaking," and "cornerstone" research and theories of personality and human behavior that served as the foundation on which psychology now rests.

Essentially, social Darwinism emphasized that the strongest and most intelligent would dominate over the weaker, less intelligent individuals. This line of thinking led psychologists to revisit the studies of humans and of lower animals, and they often concluded that African-descendant people were just a notch above primates with respect to mental and other abilities. In *Hereditary Genius: Its Laws and Consequences,* Galton (1869) suggested that genius and greatness are a product of family lineage. His thinking about lineage-based intelligence gave birth to eugenics (the science of improving the qualities of the race by controlling inherited characteristics) and a belief in the value of selective mating and sterilization of the unfit. The rise of structuralism fed psychology's tendency to want to quantify and make concrete sense of everything, including the ways in which human beings process sensory information. Mendel's work on genetics stimulated discussion regarding the alleged usefulness of dominant and recessive traits in understanding aspects of human behavior.

Psychology's mind-set relative to racial differences can be seen in the work of Sir Cyril Burt, who fabricated his data on twins in an effort to support hypotheses of genetic superiority and inferiority. Other psychologists of distinction, some of whom were past presidents of the American Psychological Association, also embraced beliefs regarding the inferiority and subjugation of African-descendant people. Race-based formulations with psychological undertones were also evident in American political and judicial thought, thus adding to the ever-present feel and pervasiveness of oppressive ideologies. In the political arena, for example, I am reminded of then U.S. senator Daniel Patrick Moynihan's description of the negro family as a tangled web of pathology (1965). What also comes to mind in the legal and judicial arena are the laws that sanctioned sterilization of persons in mental institutions and prisons in America and Europe, many of whom were considered to be from inferior genetic stock.

In reviewing the stories of other cultural, ethnic, and racial groups such as Asian Americans, Latin Americans, and Native Americans, to name a few, a very similar picture surfaces in terms of their perceived value and worth within the historic and contemporary context of Anglo-America. Illuminating the social challenges of these groups within the American framework is beyond the scope of this particular chapter, but the literature on these groups is vast (e.g., Hu-DeHart, 1997; Dodd, Nelson, & Hofland, 1994; Kanellos, 1997; Mangan, Hong, Gersting, 2003; Padilla, 1995; Thomas, 1995).

Why is the foregoing important, and what do these facts have to do with developing performance or clinical profiles of diverse athletes? Collectively, all the previous information points to one undeniable reality. These groups were never, and are not now, inferior. They have been inferiorized. History actually reveals that many cultural, ethnic, and racial groups emerged from civilizations that flourished quite magnificently.

These situations of oppression and prejudice also invite us to consider that generations of therapists trained in Euro-American systems of psychology have inherited these past beliefs regarding the alleged inferiority of culturally, ethnically, and racially diverse people. Arguably, today's psychological practitioners are more sophisticated in their thinking about cultural and racial differences and are therefore less inclined to articulate ideologies and advocate positions based on cultural, ethnic, and racial hatred. Vestiges of themes throughout psychology's history that first promoted culturally, ethnically, and racially diverse people as genetically inferior and then shifted to believing that these groups were culturally deprived and deficient continue to be manifested in current practice. Socialized attitudes and behaviors patterned and reinforced in our educational, political, judicial, economic, and other life systems are difficult to break.

The fallacy in these views is apparent, yet aggressive promotion of fallacies frequently results in their believability. Conceptual schemes regarding the inferiority and deficiencies of people from diverse backgrounds were marketed so well by those in power that people in these groups began to internalize these beliefs and thus participated in their own subjugation. One challenge for sport psychology consultants when working with diverse clients is to realize that they are products of both social and political environments as well as a system of professional training that devalued—overtly and covertly—cultural, ethnic, and racial groups. It is simply not possible for consultants to have escaped the negative, pervasive, and nonaffirming influences relative to these oppressed people that permeated the dominant American and European consciousness. Sport psychology consultants might consider asking, "To what degree have I (and thus my professional practice) been influenced by the social, political, and other system forces that were, and continue to be, antagonistic to culturally, ethnically, and racially diverse people?"

It is equally important for sport psychology consultants to realize that people from diverse backgrounds are, and continue to be, survivors of a system of oppression. Their success, despite oppression, merits a conceptual shift in the consultant's thinking from believing deficiency or deprivation hypotheses to embracing views that capture their fervor and vitality.

What follows is an alternative way of viewing culturally, ethnically, and racially diverse people that capitalizes on their inherent strengths and resilience. A framework for therapists to think anew about the ways in which they conduct professional practice and research in light of this alternative and healing perspective will also be highlighted.

## History and "Other" Worldviews

Bringing the history of one particular culture, ethnic, or racial group to light runs the risk of downplaying the richness and vitality of all other groups equally worthy of such illumination. On the other hand, profiling the detailed histories and legacies of each diverse group is beyond the scope of this chapter. As a compromise, I will attempt to point out similarities in "other" worldviews of diverse groups as distinct from Euro-American ideological and philosophical thought, using African-descendant people as a specific example.

Historically, many non-Euro-American cultural, ethnic, and racial worldviews embraced the beauty and vitality that existed inherently in their groups and that was expressed by them in their thoughts, feelings, and behaviors. There existed tremendous within- and across-group variability among all cultural, ethnic, and racial groups in North America, yet despite their rich heterogeneity, their lives were usually guided by certain core principles. Spirit-driven energy was often considered the life force that fueled individuals yet lay dormant within each person until nurtured by family, community, and peers into its full expression. Culture, as experienced by these groups, consisted of a set of rules for living designed to facilitate the full expression of the spirit that lay within.

Many cultural, ethnic, and racial communities in North America believed (and still believe) in the power of a higher spirit or guiding force and practiced deference to this power, however identified, as a matter of course. They honored this spirit and divine force by aspiring to be better, and they saw challenging situations as opportunities to develop and maintain standards of personal excellence.

Culturally, ethnically, and racially diverse communities expected themselves to learn, wanted to learn, and appreciated and valued those from whom they learned. They felt empowered by their choices to respond to life's challenges and viewed the consequences of their actions as lessons on which they could base their continued growth and development. Most, if not all, of these groups recognized the interconnectedness of life forces, and they strove to be in alignment with the order and rhythm of the universe. Social relationships were as important and valued as executing morally and socially responsible behavior. People in diverse communities sought to discover their inherent capacity to self-heal, knowing that their not-yet-perfected being would succumb on occasion to temptations to stray from the correct path. By design, conflicts between competing life forces are inevitable, but conflict resolution is equally inevitable if one is inclined to persist in a quest to restore peace and balance.

## Eurocentric Orientations Versus "the Others"

This latter belief allows me to segue into an illumination of the difference between a mind-set rooted in principles emanating from many culturally, ethnically, and racially diverse populations and the Eurocentric mind-set (of which the American is a subset), which is rooted in principles borrowed from other traditional cultural, ethnic, and racial beliefs and reframed to justify domination-based ideologies.

With respect to beliefs about the universe, many cultural, ethnic, and racial communities (the others) believed in the interconnectedness of all things living and aspired to be one with nature. In contrast, Eurocentric orientations valued separateness, the hierarchical ordering of separated phenomena (often on the continuum of superior to inferior), and the control of nature versus harmonious coexistence with it. Eurocentric thought advocated mind–body dualism, assigning primacy to rational thought. Many cultural, ethnic, and racial communities saw no absolute mind–body distinction, choosing instead to see the interrelatedness of the mind and body in concert with ties to other life forms in the universe. Culturally, ethnically, and racially diverse populations looked to restore balance and harmony in their lives when they felt out of alignment with the rules for living that were inspired by their creator, spirit, or life force. Eurocentric ideology, values, and customs, however, dominated North America and represented the measure by which all things and people were judged; opposing thoughts, feelings, and behaviors were viewed as deviations that needed to be brought back into compliance with established "norms."

Many cultural, ethnic, and racial groups in North America embraced their communities and knew that survival was often dependent on the work of the collective whole. The individual, however, garnered the place of respect in Eurocentric ideology. Many cultural groups believed that people were seeded at birth with potential that would spring forth, develop, and mature into its full expression when nourished properly by family and community. In essence, life was a journey to discover the inner gift that was already present. On the other hand, Eurocentric thought fostered the belief that a person at birth was akin to an empty vessel or a tabula rasa (blank slate) and therefore was scripted to a lifelong quest "to strive to become whole," "to fill in the gaps," or "to come up to speed." In essence, life from a Eurocentric perspective was viewed as a process of adding continually to the inner vessel needing perpetually to be filled.

From the viewpoints of many cultural, ethnic, and racial groups, "existence" consisted of visible (e.g., people, animals, nature) and invisible (e.g., spirit, soul, energy) dimensions. Eurocentric thought primarily valued that which was visible, concrete, and verifiable and devalued that which was vague, intangible, or unseen. Regarding the concept of time, many cultural communities appreciated the fluidity of the past, present, and future and understood life's experiences within the context of all three time dimensions. The present, for example, was not viewed as a separate time and space dimension. The purpose-based enactment of present energies was always viewed within the context of its past manifestation and in anticipation of its future expression. By way of contrast, Eurocentric thinking viewed time metrically, as a commodity to be used and invested wisely because, after all, "time is money."

Why is the foregoing important? Residue of the conflicts that inevitably arose in times past from these competing ideologies is visible today. Many American ideologies promote the importance of the individual over the group as seen in the "cream will rise to the top" and "pyramid" concepts of success. Can anyone, however, ever really become divorced or "individuated" from his family, the unit from which he derived his core identity?

Hierarchical ordering based on status, coupled with aspirations to control one's environment, fuels current practices of double standards and discrepancies relative to cultural, ethnic, racial, and other disenfranchised groups. Vestiges of deficiency and deprivation ideologies can be seen in American psychology's propensity to emphasize pathology and weakness as opposed to qualities that bespeak creative resilience and resourcefulness. They can also be seen in the sport psychology consultant's tendency to teach athletes about performance "tools" with the frame of mind that the athletes do not already possess them. Short of dying, is it ever really possible for an athlete to "lose" the ability focus or concentrate? Do minds really wander? Are self-esteem, willpower, and motivation ever really low or high, or do these psychic realms alternate between levels? Could it be that these emotional energies are really present in abundance in every athlete even though he or she reports feeling emotionally depleted?

When responding to a consultation request, why is it that sport psychology consultants shy away from assessing personal problems or challenges that the athlete might be facing, choosing instead to focus only on the presence or absence of their mental performance tools? Don't the problems they experience, and the context within which the problems are expressed, feel "weighty"? Doesn't this additional weight merit identification of strategies that will relieve the burden and position them to perform optimally? Could the problems and life challenges that culturally, ethnically, and racially diverse groups face be accounted for at least in part by the lack of affirmation received in their environments regarding their humanness? Do responses from diverse people to a nonaffirming social, political, and economic system represent deviations from a normative standard or adaptations to abnormal conditions? How might an environment rooted in ideologies incongruent with a cultural, ethnic, and racial essence maim or kill the spirit of the people who are oppressed or marginalized? What inner forces propel culturally, ethnically, and racially diverse persons to persist and excel even under conditions of extreme adversity?

## Success Stories on the Hard Road to Glory

As an example of taking a historical perspective of "others" in sport, I will use African-descendant athletes and their past struggles. In a three-volume text, *A Hard Road to Glory: A History of the African American Athlete*, Arthur Ashe Jr. chronicled the story of African-descendant athletes from 1619 through the 1990s (see the 1946-1986 volume, Ashe, 1988).Wonderfully written, this project speaks eloquently about the struggles, pain, and suffering endured by these athletes and, more important, illuminates their resilience, creative resourcefulness, and perseverance to overcome imposed hardships. Included are the exploits of baseball heroes such as Leroy "Satchel" Paige, Jackie Robinson, and players in the Negro League. Basketball produced standout pioneers such as Nathaniel "Sweetwater" Clifton (one of the first three athletes of African descent in the NBA), William "Pop" Gates, and William "Dolly" King (also see *They Cleared the Lane: The NBA's Black Pioneers*, Thomas, 2002). Celebrities heralded in the sport of boxing include Joe Louis, Jersey Joe Walcott, and Muhammad Ali. Football's rich history bore giants such as Marion Motley (first African-descendant Hall of Famer), Dick "Night Train" Lane, and Eddie Robinson (legendary Grambling State University football coach who produced more players for the National Football League than any other coach). Track and field stars such as Jesse Owens, Alice Coachman (first African-descendant woman to win an Olympic gold medal), Wilma Rudolph (gold medalist, 1960 Summer Olympics), Lee Calhoun (first African-descendant athlete from a black college to win an Olympic gold medal), and Charles Dumas (first person to clear 7 feet in the high jump) all contributed memorably to the sports lore of African-descendant people. The successes of these African-descendant athletes, and their African-descendant athlete peers (of whom there were many more of prominence), were especially heroic given the often brutally antagonistic social and political climate of the times.

The "big five" sports (baseball, basketball, football, boxing, and track and field) were the few athletic venues that African-descendant athletes had access to. However, African-descendant athletes achieved success in all the sports in which they competed once they were given the chance to participate. Examples include notables such as Bill Spiller, Ted Rhodes, Madison Gunter, Charles Sifford, Ann Gregory, Lee Elder (first person of African descent to play in the Masters), and Tiger Woods (four-time Masters champion), who all achieved success in golf. *Forbidden Fairways: African Americans and the Game of Golf* (Sinnette, 1998) is unparalleled in its illumination of African-descendant golf history.

Althea Gibson and Arthur Ashe Jr. distinguished themselves in tennis. Nikki Frank and Peter Westbrook broke down barriers in fencing. Hazel Lyman, Ruth Coburn, Bob Robinson, and Ben Harding were noteworthy bowlers. Keturah "Kitty" Waterman Cox, Tina Sloan, and Gloria Jean Byard made names for themselves in field hockey. Willie O'Ree (first African-descendant player in the National Hockey League), Alton White, and Grant Fuhr were icebreakers in the sport of hockey. Mabel Fairbanks, Bobby Beauchamp, and Debi Thomas participated in figure skating. Other sports in which African-descendant athletes have not participated traditionally, including archery, judo, lacrosse, motor racing, powerboat racing, soccer, skiing, softball, swimming, table tennis, volleyball, weightlifting, wrestling, and even rodeo, produced African-descendant athletes with record-setting accomplishments.

The intrapersonal, social, and emotional struggles that African-descendant athletes experienced were tremendous. Imagine receiving death threats, as Henry "Hank" Aaron did when he approached the home run record of American icon Babe Ruth. What feelings might have emerged within African-descendant football players during the Great Depression upon hearing they could no longer participate in professional sports because whites were complaining about the scarcity of jobs? How might Jim Crow laws have influenced your mobility as a member of a traveling Negro League baseball team? To what heights might your frustrations, resentments, and anger soar knowing that around every corner were signs indicating "whites only" or attitudes reflected in statements such as "Blacks may not have some of the necessities to be a field or general manager"? How might you begin to feel about yourself hearing a constant barrage of racial epithets? Would drugs become problematic? What about gambling? Would your marriage result in divorce? Would you ever consider suicide?

What happens to the athlete client when the sport psychology consultant does not pay attention to the athlete's personal, historical, cultural, and ethnic experiences, believing that such issues have no link to the athlete's reported decrease in sport performance? Is it even possible to work with athletes qualitatively without considering their off-field personal struggles? What if the sport psychology consultant viewed an athlete's decreased sport performance as a symptom of a larger problem versus "a phase that all athletes go through at some point in their careers"?

# The Tre-Nine Grid Approach

The preceding narrative was offered in an attempt to frame the historical and multicultural mind-set with which I approach my work with athletes from culturally, ethnically, and racially diverse backgrounds. If you were the proverbial fly on the wall, you would see me using what I call the Tre-Nine grid (see the next page for a clearer layout of the process). The Tre-Nine grid identifies three phases of a counseling encounter during which general and specific self- and other-based questions are asked. The questions are designed to give me information about the client and to prompt me to be mindful of the ways in which my biases and assumptions influence the data I gather.

In the preconsultation phase, there are two component parts (self and other). The two major questions here are (1) do I possess the skills, knowledge, and abilities to respond to this request from the athlete? and (2) what do I know concretely about this athlete? The additional questions asked at this time involve issues of how my (and the athlete's) gender, race, ethnicity, and culture may influence the consultation process.

There are five component parts of the during-consultation phase. The questions, or processes, involve (a) an assessment and diagnostic impression or formulation, (b) the establishment of goals, (c) the discussion of intervention strategies, (d) an implementation of a strategic plan to accomplish the identified goals, and (e) an evaluative mechanism designed to measure and illuminate hoped-for change.

There are two component parts, or major questions I ask (self- and other-oriented), in the postconsultation phase. In this phase, probably the most self-reflective, I examine what I have learned about my client and myself. Other supplementary questions involve what mistakes I may have made, and if things went well, why they did so.

## Preconsultation Phase

Using this model within a culturally, ethnically, and racially sensitive framework, you would see me welcome the athletes with the belief that they are endowed from birth with tremendous gifts and talents. I also believe they have displayed and even showcased these talents many times in the sporting environment. Further, I believe they are now coming to me for sport psychology service having experienced some sort of impediment in the continued manifestation and execution of that talent. The impediment, often experi-

---

# Tre-Nine Consultation Grid

## Preconsultation Phase

Self

Do I possess the skills, knowledge, and abilities to respond appropriately and accurately to this request?

Subquestion: To what degree will my ethnicity, gender, age, and so on influence the work I do on behalf of my client?

Other

What do I know concretely about this client I am about to see?

Subquestion: How will his or her ethnicity, gender, age, and so on influence our consultation relationship?

## During-Consultation Phase

(a) Assessment: Why now? (e.g., events precipitating the problem, factors maintaining the problem)

(b) Establishment of goals: When all is said and done, how does the athlete want to be thinking, feeling, and behaving differently?

(c) Strategic interventions: What steps might be taken in order to accomplish the identified goals?

(d) Implementation: What can we do? (e.g., processes for putting suggested interventions into action)

(e) Evaluation: How effective were the interventions? Are there differences in thoughts, feelings, or behaviors now versus when the project began?

## Postconsultation Phase

Self

What have I learned about myself? How am I different as a result of having done this consultation?

Other

What have I learned about the person I just worked with? How has this individual changed and why?

---

enced by the athlete as a loss of essential psychological energy, is actually a self-imposed protective strategy designed to help him or her cope with possible failure. More on this point later.

I accept the consultation role shaped by my conviction that each athlete has the potential to succeed even though he or she has not always behaved or performed successfully. I also entertain a hypothesis that culturally, ethnically, and racially diverse athletes seeking my services for improved sport performance may be conflicted. I wonder, on the one hand, if their request to see me represents a desire to talk about the real intrapersonal struggles and concerns getting in the way of their flourishing athletically. I ask myself if their real concerns ever prompted them to consider abandoning the pressures associated with the athlete lifestyle. The pressures I speak of, and to which diverse athletes must respond daily, center not infrequently around the realities of prejudice, oppression, and race. There never has been a level playing field relative to culturally, ethnically, and racially diverse athletes participating in sports, and this reality is one that is almost always confronted as a matter of course. True, not all of these athletes confront these sorts of challenges with the same frequency or to the same degree of intensity. However, whether expressed overtly or covertly, by their coaches, teammates, the athletic systems they function within, or the communities where they live and from which their fan base is drawn, race is still the big news in America (and many other countries as well). Other realities that one might expect to be associated with an athlete's life, though important to consider in understanding the bigger picture, are not infrequently contextualized by race-based challenges. On the other hand, I find myself wondering if all they want to do is attend to their identified need to learn about tools for improved sport performance. Sometimes, this is all they are looking for.

I take on culturally, ethnically, and racially diverse clients because I believe I am fairly mindful in my self-examination regarding the degree to which my sense of success and personal accomplishments might influence the consultation relationship. I also believe I am mindful relative to my perceived success at navigating within the current social and political environment, especially with respect to racial politics. I believe that my education and training has positioned me to respond to their requests for assistance.

Finally, my agreement to work with culturally, ethnically, and racially diverse athletes comes with openness to the biases and assumptions I might have regarding my clients, their particular circumstances, and their abilities to navigate their life spaces. In essence, I want to provide my clients with an environment that is welcoming, that sets the stage for exploration of whatever they hope to address, and that prepares me to participate fully in the consultation experience. This desire requires me to look inward and to examine my own "stuff and baggage" with a mind toward anticipating possible convergence and divergence between the clients and me in ideas, values, and assumptions. Having done this self-examination, the doing of sport psychology with athletes from diverse backgrounds always provides me with a potential for wonderfully connecting experiences.

## During-Consultation Phase

During the various consultations, as the client–consultant relationship begins to take shape, I move into an assessment process, the necessary first step of any consultation in which I participate. In short, an assessment is an opportunity to gather relevant information that will enable me to construct the best possible picture of the problem the client appears to be struggling with. The assessment data are gathered using a template that stimulates responses to the following question: What is the present sport performance concern, and why are you seeking consultation now to address that concern? Questions designed to tease out the parameters of the problem include the following: What event(s) precipitated the concern that you experience currently? How long have you been experiencing the present concern? Under what circumstances does the present concern become evident? Is there a time or situation when the concern does not become manifest? What factors maintain the presence of the concern once it surfaces, and what factors are operative at the point where the concern ceases?

I am also interested in learning about other life experiences that elicit a concern and set off responses that are similar to those that prompted the client to seek my services. In this vein, I am particularly keen on learning about the internal and external resources the client called on when responding to the past challenges. These questions allow me to concretize and illuminate images in my own mind about what's going on in the client's life relative to his or her sport performance challenge(s). All the questions are asked within the context of the client's athletic developmental history, past and current family and community influences, gender, race, sexual orientation, physically challenged status, or other relevant life parameters.

Once I develop a snapshot of the sport performance challenge(s) that brought the culturally, ethnically, or racially diverse athlete to my office, I supplement my inquiry by asking about the challenges he or she experiences in other life domains (e.g., social, academic, leisure, spiritual). This allows me to develop a bigger-picture perspective of the athlete. It also provides other venues from which to draw evidence about how this particular athlete makes decisions, weighs pros and cons, implements action plans, and evaluates these plans. It is at this juncture that I begin to identify the athlete's thematic and patterned responses to life challenges. Snooping around in these other life venues provides the additional benefit of letting me assess the degree to which non-sport-related problems might be contributing to the client's stated concerns.

It is certainly not unusual for a performance enhancement request to represent a foot-in-the-door inquiry about the possibility of sharing and exploring personal concerns, issues, and struggles that have no initially apparent link to the reported sport performance problem. It feels legitimate to come to a sport psychology consultant for sport enhancement services. It feels more risky and threatening to display vulnerability that is triggered by intra- or interpersonal problems. In my experience, I have yet to receive a request for sport performance enhancement services that lacked a companion personal life challenge. The question at this point is not whether there is a coexisting personal problem but to what degree coexisting latent personal problems influence the manifest problem with sport performance.

Included in the assessment of sport performance problems and personal challenges and struggles is what might be considered a more traditional clinical interview. Issues such as depression, anxiety, family background, mental status, history of abuse (physical, sexual, emotional), substance use and abuse, medical history including use of medications, past and present suicidal ideation and behavior, and dangerousness to others are assessed as a matter of course during this early phase of the consultation.

In essence, early on in the consultation relationship I am interested in gathering data that allow me to develop a clear picture of the presenting problem, which more often than not is performance related. I am also interested in arriving at a bigger-picture perspective of the athlete's reported challenge(s), so my focus shifts from gathering data on the sport performance problem to seeking out information regarding the athlete's overall functioning within the other life domains that define his or her existence. This is all done within the larger context of past and current social, cultural, political, and economic dynamics relative to ethnic and racial groups.

This assessment section concludes with my providing the client with a formulation of what is going on. The construction of both a sport performance profile and a clinical profile that fits the data I gathered allows me to pay attention to the person versus the problem or concern. Realizing that I might have omitted or misunderstood certain data, I seek clarification of the athlete's concerns by asking him or her to provide a synopsis of our work together up to this point. I proceed in this manner because it is absolutely essential for the athlete and me to be on the same page with respect to the apparent problem(s) and our respective beliefs about the factors contributing to problem maintenance.

The process so far sets the stage for generating interventions that would bring about a satisfactory resolution to the athlete's presenting concern. I usually consider multiple interventions because, invariably, my assessment yields multiple concerns and multiple factors contributing to the multiple concerns. The suggested interventions are generated within personal and environmental contexts and are offered for client consideration. A decision is then made about what interventions to pursue.

The decision regarding which interventions to use is predicated, in part, on having developed outcome goals. In framing outcomes, there is a very clear attempt to articulate goals that are concrete, doable, and measurable. The operative question asked of the client at this juncture is "If you were 100% successful in achieving your goals, how would you be thinking, feeling, and behaving differently when compared with your customary way of self-managing?" Formulating outcome goals behaviorally, concretely, and measurably allows the client and me to develop a picture of where we are headed as we work collaboratively. It also provides a set of steps for us to follow as we embark on the athlete's quest.

Once the assessment is completed, behavioral goals are established, and interventions are suggested, we then begin sequentially implementing the interventions we hope will be effective. Frequently during this phase of our work, the client is assigned homework or is asked to consider doing or thinking about activities outside of our weekly meetings. Homework exercises bring the vision of change to life by allowing the client to participate in constructing the new reality he or she wants to achieve. The implementation phase is carried out within the context of the athlete's abilities, commitment to achieving articulated goals, and willingness to persist despite anticipated and unanticipated, actual or psychological roadblocks.

In working with culturally, ethnically, and racially diverse athletes to improve sport performance or increase satisfaction in non-sport-related personal domains, discussions regarding concentration, their ability to focus, self-esteem, willpower, and motivation inevitably arise. The clients usually introduce these subjects by reporting that they regularly experience deficits or depletions in these psychic realms. Further, they share their belief that the depletion or absence of the psychic realms prevents them from accomplishing their goals. The clients also express desire and commitment to follow through with the plan that will be devised for their improvement program.

## Specific Sport Psychology Considerations in the During-Consultation Phase

The great but often stifled potential I see in racially, ethnically, and culturally diverse athletes prompts me to consider some radically different propositions that fly in the face of the usual questions asked in classic sport psychology consultations. I would be a rich man if I were paid $1.00 every time I heard proclamations such as "I can't concentrate," "My mind wanders," "I lost my motivation," "I don't have the willpower I need," and the classic, "I have low self-esteem." In my examination of their willingness to improve sport performance or to function more satisfactorily in their personal domains, it becomes important that I address their beliefs about these psychic realms. Specifically, I invite them to consider that it is not humanly possible to lose motivation, to have minds wander, to have no willpower, or to have low self-esteem. I certainly acknowledge that they feel as if they are depleted in those psychic realms but push them to consider that they are not.

I offer an alternative viewpoint, one that encourages them to ask, "What if it were not humanly possible to lose motivation, willpower, or self-esteem?" "If I had endless amounts of each of these psychic energies, how would my life be different?" Fear is the emotional and instant reaction inevitably experienced by athletes when asking themselves questions such as these.

I have discovered that belief in high, low, absence, presence, or depletion of these psychic energies triggers success and failure fears that then feed their needs for self-protection. As a by-product of their successes in sports, these athletes have come to believe that their self-worth and self-esteem are tied to their performance. Thus, every evaluative situation (e.g., game-day competition, examinations) begins to feel like an indictment of their self-worth versus a barometer of their performance level at that particular time. Not surprising, temptations to avoid evaluative situations invariably emerge.

In essence, setting out, emotionally speaking, on a journey to locate and recover lost psychic energy delays pursuit of accomplishing the goals they established at the outset of their program. The benefits of pursuing their "yellow brick road" journey to find "lost" psychic energy (versus pursuing their stated success goals) translates to buying some time in hopes of avoiding perceived or real consequences for failing to achieve success, however defined. This self-protective strategy is examined with the goal of helping them resolve their problems. With culturally, ethnically, and racially diverse athletes who feel that their only life successes have resulted from their participation in sports, their struggle with self-esteem issues always seems more of a concern. Consequently, I take particular care in helping them disconnect their self-esteem issues from performance expectations, particularly those performance expectations based on race.

This viewpoint differs appreciably from what athletes have been socialized to believe about the aforementioned psychic energies. Professionals trained in the American system of psychology to provide sport psychology service have also been socialized to believe in variations in motivation, willpower, concentration, and self-esteem. Notions about high, low, or absent psychic energies, and the belief that certain levels of these energies are absolutely necessary for goal attainment, represent natural offshoots of Lockean tabula rasa formulations and of discussions about relative human capacities across race. Nonetheless, I invite my culturally, ethnically, and racially diverse clients to consider that what their ancestors said is true: They are seeded from the beginning with unlimited potential. When nurtured properly by family, community, and a professional consultant (me), that seed will bear fruit as success in athletics and in other life domains.

## Preparing to End the Relationship

Just before the client and I end our relationship, we go through some evaluation. Accountability is very important in my clinical work, so we spend a fair amount of time reviewing our work and determining the degree of success that has been achieved. Modifications of our original plan for change are implemented as needed, and the concrete, behavioral, and measurable goals that were established early in the consultation are realigned or committed to anew.

## Postconsultation Phase

The postconsultation phase is a continual process in my professional life. The overarching question is, what has been learned about myself, the athlete, and the whole consultation process? In many respects, the foregoing synopsis of how I respond to requests for sport psychology consultations from culturally, ethnically, and racially diverse athletes sounds identical to how I or another psychologist trained similarly might approach a typical consultation situation. Truthfully, there is considerable overlap. All consultations that I respond to, whether individual, group, or team and irrespective of gender, race, ethnicity, sexual orientation, or physically challenged status, include utilization of the Tre-Nine grid. Furthermore, how I proceed through each of the components (e.g., the questions I ask, the dynamic processes I attend to, and the within-component goals I hope to achieve) is identical across consultations.

There is, however, considerable difference in the mind-set I embrace when approaching my work with athletes from culturally, ethnically, and racially diverse backgrounds. I favor using a mind-set rooted in cultural, ethnic, and racial worldviews because they are more affirming and more consistent with the real essence of diverse athletes. As I look back and study my history as a person of African descent, what is particularly salient to me is how resilient, strong, and determined African-descendant people have been despite the horrific and vile atrocities they have had to endure for centuries. That African-descendant people (and most other marginalized groups) continue to struggle, survive, and succeed in the 21st century despite tremendously adverse circumstances speaks to their celebratory spirit, one that all of us could benefit from learning more about. At this juncture I make it a point to reaffirm a very clear reality. There is a lot in this world over which we have little to no control. But we have 100% control over how we respond to the challenges the world presents.

As I think about what it takes to have succeeded through generations despite the atrocities that have been perpetuated against African-descendant and other people of color, I feel a remarkably healing excitement and energy that serves as a source of strength and fuels continued persistence in my own growth and development. In every consultation with culturally, ethnically, and racially diverse athletes, I tap into this source of emotional nourishment as a prelude to my work.

In working with diverse athletes, I also pay attention to the multiple contexts within which they have developed and matured. The social, cultural, political, and environmental realities that frame their existence externally are manifest in the persons to whom I am providing service. The degree to which age, gender, sexual orientation, and physically challenged status influence their intrapersonal maturation is a critically important variable I consider in my work. It is simply not possible for me to understand culturally, ethnically, and racially diverse athletes without also understanding the multiple contexts that have influenced who they are and who they are striving to be.

I must also admit, however, that I rarely focus on statistical features of the adverse realities. Crime rates, disproportionate educational attainment, disparity in health care access and practices, underemployment, and unemployment tell me little about the person I am working with. I tend to direct my focus on learning as much as I can about the internal and external resources that culturally, ethnically, and racially diverse athletes have called on when negotiating their life spaces. For every marginalized person whose failure to negotiate the system has resulted in incarceration, dropping out of school, or poor health, many more people from these diverse backgrounds have been successful at managing their resources. As a result of these successes, they feel more in control of their careers, education, and health care options.

In working particularly with African-descendant athletes, I try to stay on top of my expression of overt or covert attitudinal and behavioral practices of bias and "isms" (e.g., sexism, ageism, ableism, xenophobia, homophobia, religious intolerance). I do recognize that being a professional of African descent does not excuse me from needing to keep myself in check with respect to my beliefs and values, particularly as they may conflict with those of the African-descendant athletes I work with.

In this vein, I am also mindful of the athletes' perceptions of me as a man, as an African-descendant male, as a mental health professional, or as whatever else I am believed to be or represent, and I invite them to share their perceptions. I have learned that who I think I am and how I think my clients perceive me is not always in concert with how they actually perceive me. I am reminded of a consultation with an African-descendant athlete who was feeling awkward until he disclosed his concern that I was looking down on him because his affluent family background was atypical of the African-descendant athletes he thought I was accustomed to seeing. His attempts to make himself "normal" in my eyes could be seen in his anglicized expression of language and demeanor in contrast to parlance between "brothers from the hood." Quite honestly, I was not even aware that he hailed from an affluent background, nor did his apparent economic fortunes factor into the concerns he was hoping to address by coming to see me. Nonetheless, it wasn't until we put this issue "on the table" that the process of our work seemed to smooth out.

# Conclusion

Conceptually limited, shallow, and race-based formulations of human behavior, often embraced as universal truths, have contaminated the thinking and practices of generations of mental health professionals. Evidence of present-day contamination is present in how we formulate client concerns and execute practice regimens. Given psychology's long history of pervasively misapplying theory and conceptual schemes relative to culturally, ethnically, and racially diverse athletes, transformation any time soon of these inappropriate race-based theories and practices into more appropriate, accurate, and affirming formulations seems unlikely.

Translating cultural traditions into innovative clinical practices when working with diverse athletes provides one means of getting beyond the constraints and shackles of race-hatred and envy-based ideologies. A practice long articulated by scholars of African descent is the transformation of negatively skewed formulations of human behavior relative to culturally, ethnically, and racially diverse people into beliefs that are more aligned with the rules for living as voiced by their foreparents. At least since 1968 (e.g., Cross, 1971; Grier & Cobbs, 1968; Nobles, 1976, 1991; Thomas & Sillen, 1972; White, 1991) and continuing through 2002 (e.g., Akbar, 1984; Azibo, 1996; Baldwin, 1990; Myers, 1985; Parham, 1989, 2002; Williams, 1981), scholars of African descent as well as other ethnic and nonethnic scholars (e.g., Atkinson, 1985; Axelson, 1993; Casas, 1985; Ivey, 1987; LaFromboise & Rowe, 1983; Lee, 1997; Paniagua, 2000; Sue & Sue, 1999) have provided ample suggestions for rethinking theory and practice of psychology relative to multicultural considerations. In doing so, they have extended an invitation to all of us to see through a different lens and thus capture a more complete vision of culturally, ethnically, and racially diverse clients.

Professional psychological associations (e.g., the Association of Multicultural Counseling and Development, a division of the American Counseling Association, American Psychological Association, Joint Task Force of Divisions 45 and 17) have responded to the calls for multicultural training and sensitivity in applied psychology service and in research. After a 20-plus-year effort among many psychologists of color, the American Psychological Association (APA) adopted the *Guidelines on Multicultural Education, Training, Research, Practice and Organizational Change for Psychologists* (2003) as an "official" document, thus raising the bar of professional practice expectations for all association members. In 2001, then Surgeon General of the United States, David Satcher, released a report titled *Mental Health: Culture, Race and Ethnicity*, wherein the adverse effect of racism on the mental health of cultural, ethnic, and racial communities is clearly articulated. This document represents the first time the U.S. government has come on board with an "official" recognition of racism as a significant mental health problem. The question now is, how will sport psychology organizations such as the Association for the Advancement of Applied Sport Psychology and the International Society of Sport Psychology respond to the challenges of multicultural service provision, and in what form will those responses appear?

# Commentary on Chapter 11

Heather Gridley, MA

"We are the same, we say the same things, we talk the same language. We act the same, and being Aboriginal, too, we have a very strong bond."

"If I didn't have Daniel and Shannon, it would have been a lot harder, and I might not have been so happy and probably would not have played as good footy as I have. That is how important it is."

Australian rules footballers
Daniel Motlop and Daniel Wells
*The Age*, July 17, 2004

Why would two Aboriginal athletes describe their friendship in this way? Was it their relocation to the urban east coast of Australia from the more sparsely populated far north and far west, respectively, of this vast country that cemented their bond? Do they sense the "safety in numbers" that partly explains the frequently observed collectivist mentality of many minority group members? Do they really possess the uncanny "sixth sense" often ascribed to Aboriginal players, in terms that serve to segregate even as they praise? Or are they just any pair of good teammates, period? The more I find myself writing "they," the less qualified I find myself to draw any conclusions at all—I am white, a woman, and most definitely not an elite athlete. And although I am a psychologist, I am not a sport psychology consultant. If I were, how might their comments help me understand the needs and resources of an Aboriginal client? How should I approach questions of diversity as they influence the lives of athletes who might seek my services?

After reading the thought-provoking chapter by William D. Parham, we can begin to appreciate some of the complexities inherent in the delivery of sport psychology service to athletes from diverse backgrounds. In asking questions such as "Who are these individuals called athletes?" Parham has laid down a challenge to sport psychologists to move beyond one-size-fits-all models of practice, to take account of the individual profile of each person who seeks their services, and moreover, to factor in the individual profiles of consultants themselves by raising the parallel question "Who is a sport psychologist?" Parham insists that on both sides of the consulting encounter, contextual variables such as race, ethnicity, age, gender, sexual orientation, and emotional and physical disability status provide ways to foster fortified working alliances.

What I really like about this chapter is the author's emphasis on the strengths inherent in each athlete's cultural profile. He writes with particular eloquence of the rich spiritual and philosophical heritage with which African-descendant Americans, himself included, are blessed. Although not glossing over or denying their shared transgenerational struggles with adversity and oppression, Parham prefers to focus on the value-added aspects of African-descendant people's history of survival. This approach is a welcome contrast to the deficit focus so common in psychology in general, and especially in Western psychology's treatment of cultural minorities, whom Parham notes have been inferiorized in subtle, as well as blatant, ways from the days when the scientific theorizing of Charles Darwin, his cousin Francis Galton, and others close to our discipline's roots lent support to the "civilizing mission" of colonization.

Parham uses a number of case examples to illustrate, simply, why attention to dimensions of diversity matters in so many practical applications of sport psychology service. He bases his work with African-descendant and other culturally diverse athletes on three premises:

1. An understanding of context (historical, social, political, economic, environmental, and familial) is essential for effective service provision.

2. Ethnically, racially, and culturally diverse athletes (and, indeed, therapists themselves) are not homogeneous groups and must not be treated as such.

3. Other cultural, ethnic, and racial worldviews are more helpful in conceptualizing the essence and spirit of diverse athletes than are the oppressive ideologies of traditional Euro-American psychology.

Taken together, all three of these premises are consistent with emergent theories of multi-cultural counseling (Essandoh, 1996; Sue & Sue, 2003) that argue for a balance between emic (within-group, culture-specific) and etic (across-group, universalist) approaches. Such theories tend to lean toward the emic perspective in order to decenter our professional practices from the mainstream assumptions in which they are likely to be embedded.

Sport is often described as the "great leveler," and much is made of the claim that sport and politics don't mix. Yet nowhere is politics, and the accompanying power differentials, more apparent than in the sporting arena. Global sporting domination, whether measured in Olympic medal tallies, golf or tennis Grand Slams, or team sport World Cups, closely parallels economic and political domination, especially in sports that cost money to play. In contrast, a glance at a list of boxing champions will indicate which groups in society at a given point in time have had to struggle hardest for survival—Joe Louis, Rocky Marciano, and Muhammad Ali in the United States; the names in Australia are disproportionately Aboriginal (Lionel Rose, Anthony Mundine) and immigrant (Rocky Gattellari, Jeff Fenech, Kostya Tzu). And the tennis achievements and atypical career patterns of the Williams sisters take on a substantially different aspect when the lens is widened to encompass the violent death of their half-sister in a Los Angeles ghetto. Context, as Parham says, is everything. Any sport psychologist who chooses to ignore it is dangerously naive and at risk of practicing unethically.

There is, however, a tension that arises from Parham's three core premises that occasionally threatens his own argument. His broad description of African-centered and other cultural beliefs and worldviews carries the very risk of overgeneralization that he cautions against. Assumptions about the enduring influence of such a cultural heritage on the particular African-descendant athlete seeking psychological services might be just as marginalizing (though probably not as destructive) as more overtly racist attitudes and practices. For example, fluctuations in an Aboriginal athlete's playing form, attendance at training, or concentration used to be attributed, in a derogatory manner, to the traditional nomadic cultural practice of "going walkabout." Aboriginal representation at elite levels is proportionally very high in the sports they have had access to (notably football, especially Australian rules; boxing; and track and field), in similar patterns to those Parham observes for African-descendant athletes. Most coaches and administrators have come to recognize, therefore, that it is simply good business to find ways to nurture these athletes and harness their talents. As well, a more sophisticated awareness of Aboriginal cultures is required, alongside concerted action to combat racism on and off the field.

To contribute positively to an Aboriginal player's welfare, a sport psychologist might need to understand that the life expectancy of Aboriginal Australian men is less than sixty years of age and falling; in some areas it is as low as mid-30s. That means a lot of funerals, especially in a culture that highly values extended family and community networks. In this light, is going walkabout a sign of racial inferiority, of being not up to the demands of elite performance, or a mark of solidarity, of deep loyalty to sometimes physically distant family in times of intolerable strain—or is it no different from any other athlete's form lapse, characterized differently on account of race? The sport psychologist might need to not only think through these contrasting constructions of the athlete's behavior but also act as an advocate with club officials and others involved. In so doing, he or she must also be aware that a quality that seems admirable to one person can still be twisted into a racist slur by another. "Another funeral! How many grandmothers does the black bastard have?" Above all, consultants need to be clear about their own assumptions and stereotypes to avoid overlooking or minimizing contextual cultural information on one hand and overgeneralizing from, or selectively attending to, such information on the other.

Although Parham is clear in his critique of psychology's past record on matters of race, he seems less critical of psychology's present—what I would describe as the discipline's insistence, almost exclusively, on a Western positivist paradigm of scientific inquiry and evidence-based practice. As a practitioner, he argues for a more clinical approach to sport psychology consultation, and his Tre-Nine grid model of assessment and intervention is highly individualistic and therapist driven. As a community psychologist, I am more inclined to look outward to a client's natural communities for resources and solutions. I start to feel uncomfortable when therapists begin to resemble protagonists of their own adventure stories. We are best seen as bit players with walk-on roles in clients' lives, even if a role is sometimes an important cameo part, a catalyst for positive change in a time of crisis or turmoil. This view of service is not just professional false modesty on my part. Duncan and Miller's (2000) review of four decades of outcome research confirmed that a massive 40% of positive change occurring in therapy can be attributed to client factors, whereas factors relating to the therapist's model and technique account for just 15%.

Let me expand on this question of what works in therapy—and why—because it has considerable relevance to issues of diversity in practice. Client factors are the kinds of things Parham describes when he talks about welcoming African-descendant and culturally diverse athletes "with the belief that they are endowed from birth with tremendous gifts and talents" and that "each athlete has the potential to succeed even though he or she has not always behaved or performed successfully." Beyond the individual athlete's ability and determination, there are also factors such as those illustrated in the quoted exchange that opens this commentary (e.g., a sense of belonging within a club or team, a best mate , strength drawn from a spiritual or religious community, or maybe a supportive grandmother). The sense of belonging might be enhanced by the presence of a critical mass of teammates from the same cultural background, the likelihood of which, in turn, might be influenced by an assertive club policy on minority recruitment and retention. Such policies are already in place, for example, in South African cricket (where the cultural majority is still the minority in terms of representation at elite levels). Australian rules football has also come a long way in a short time; it is barely 10 years since a national league club president announced that Aboriginal footballers would be welcome at his club as long as they conducted themselves "like white men" (McAlister, 1995). Unsurprisingly, there had been no Aboriginal players before that date in that particular club's history.

In areas such as business, the arts, tourism, and even politics, efforts have been made to appeal to "pink power" via strategies promoting inclusion of and safety for lesbian, gay, bisexual, and transgender (LGBT) persons. But homophobia is still the norm in most sporting contexts. It would be exciting to see sport psychologists involved in initiatives for attitude and behavior change at community, club, and individual levels of a similar kind to those that have tackled racism in sport over the past decade or more. Chapters 13 and 14 in this volume are fine contributions that describe these problems. Although Parham mentions sexual orientation and homophobia in his lists of diverse athletes and their concerns, gay and lesbian athletes form a substantial portion of the diversity that sport psychologists will encounter, and some more material on the gay and lesbian issues he sees in practice would have been nice additions. Parham does cite many examples in his section Success Stories on the Hard Road to Glory and notes that the pressures "to which African-descendant athletes must respond daily" center frequently around the realities of race, where "there never has been a level playing field." And in contrast, even when members of the dominant culture are in the minority, their resources are still substantial. For example, a white athlete on a predominantly black team might have a tough time but knows he or she has the support of the wider culture, including the media and public attitudes. So, too, the straight softball player in a dyke-ruled changing room.

A refreshing aspect of Parham's argument is his challenge of some long-treasured tenets of therapy, such as the notion that constructs such as self-esteem and motivation are measurable entities possessed in variable and fluctuating quantities by athletes (and by logical extension, all human beings). He names the dangers of uncritical acceptance of metaphors such as replacing lost energies, or topping up depleted "psychic" realms (e.g., motivation, concentration) and invites us to look instead at the barriers that might be impeding an athlete's fulfillment of his or her potential. Parham identifies diversity-related barriers as both internal (e.g., in the athlete's psychic structure and personal vulnerabilities) and external (e.g., professional ignorance, structural discrimination). Thus, he envisages the therapist's task as one of unlocking potential by tackling these barriers first via the therapeutic relationship and then via clinical as well as traditional performance enhancement strategies.

Parham expresses considerable frustration with approaches to sport psychology consultations that he describes as shallow, generic, and formula driven. How can they be otherwise, he asks, when little is known of the individual profiles of either the athletes or the service providers? Although I share this dissatisfaction, I would not be looking to clinical psychology for richer descriptions of an athlete's lived experience. Nor do I find manifest–latent and superficial–deep metaphors any more helpful than the "depleted psychic realm" analogies Parham rejects. He places a great deal of emphasis on what a client says or does not say, as indicators of surface reasons (pretexts) for consulting a sport psychologist, and the deeper or latent reasons that may emerge once a safe, congruent relationship is established. And he argues that such a relationship must be premised on recognition and incorporation of the dimensions of diversity inherent in both the athlete's and the consultant's personal profiles.

Certainly the establishment of a safe client-centered relationship is a sine qua non of successful counseling and therapy in a range of contexts. The client's perception of the relationship as one that is respectful and collaborative and that generates hope accounts for at least 30% of positive change (Duncan & Miller, 2000). And the client's experience of the relationship necessarily includes the degree to which the therapist demonstrates respect for diversity in all its manifestations. For example, a policy of never assuming the gender of someone's partner is a simple way of sending an initial message to LGBT clients that their relationships will not be undermined, insulted, or rendered invisible by the therapist. Carefully avoiding the use of gendered pronouns until such time as the client uses them might be dismissed as political correctness by the unaware practitioner, but as a strategy it costs nothing yet represents a micro-stand against an oppressive practice that marginalizes LGBT members of the wider community. Such marginalizing practices should never be replicated in a counseling environment.

The model of sport psychology consultation presented by Parham draws from publications and examples predominantly within the United States. Obviously, the theories and perspectives of many nations are missing. The present commentary is restricted to the context of Australian psychology, which is just as Eurocentric as the American psychology Parham describes. At the start of the 21st century, new paradigms are opening up spaces for minority voices to claim legitimacy in our discipline. In 2002, a group of postgraduate community psychology students at my university took an elective course on cross-cultural counseling that prompted a recognition on their part that their European–American-centered undergraduate psychology training had left them and their fellow students ill prepared to respond usefully to diversity issues (Darlaston-Jones et al., 2003). The four students set out to develop a semester-length project aimed at remedying this gap. They included approaches to the promotion of psychological well-being from a range of non-Western cultures: an Indigenous Australian approach to health and well-being, a Cuban community approach to wellness promotion, an approach based on the principles of an Indian ashram, and perspectives from Russian health professionals. There are many such resources available to the beginning (and experienced) practitioner that enable us to look beyond our own cultural and disciplinary blinkers. Where a gap exists between the cultural background of the psychologist and the client, it should not be the client who has to work hardest to bridge it—notwithstanding that the majority of us receive our most valuable lessons from clients themselves.

Parham invites sport psychology consultants to ask themselves questions such as the following: To what degree have I (and thus my professional practice) been influenced by social, professional, and other system forces that were and continue to be antagonistic to African-descendant people? He challenges consultants to acknowledge that African-descendant people are, and continue to be, survivors of a system of oppression. These are disturbing words for scientist-practitioners to hear. We have been trained from the outset to filter out contextual (read "extraneous") variables from our experimental designs and to stake our reputations on claims of value-free objectivity. Words such as *oppression*, *colonization*, and *patriarchy* can make us uncomfortable and defensive. But if we fail to deconstruct our own assumptions, especially those that sound just like common sense, we are more likely to be part of the problem than part of any solutions for clients whose life experiences and cultural heritages have been marginalized by those very assumptions.

Parham's own goal-oriented model of practice seems to me to reflect Western linear (exoteric) assumptions that stand in contrast to many Eastern esoteric philosophies and practices. A Victoria University sport psychology graduate student's thesis examined the differences between Western sport psychology's emphasis on the goal of winning and the traditions of Eastern martial arts that focus on personal discipline and mastery (Mathieson, 2001). Mathieson used an ancient story of a martial arts teacher (sensei) rebuking a student who believed that the more he trained with the master, the closer he would be to achieving his goals. The sensei's rebuke implied that an excessively goal-oriented approach would divert one's attention from the lessons to be learned from the journey itself.

As an outsider to sport psychology practice, I agree with Parham's observation that many standard sport psychology interventions appear generic and formula driven and hence shallow and limited in applicability to a diverse range of athlete client presentations, but I wonder if the answer is to magnify the person as a walking collection of latent disorders? Mainstream clinical psychology's individual change models and prescriptive treatments are not conducive to holistic service provision to a culturally diverse client population. Some feminist psychologists have long argued that all therapeutic models inevitably involve a view of the woman as patient and the therapist as healer and expert, with the problem itself being stripped of its social context (Kitzinger & Perkins, 1993).

Parham's emphasis on ethical practice as a fundamental component of service provision rather than as an afterthought is most welcome. It may be difficult, however, to rely on ethical codes if the consultants themselves do not promote critical reflection or acknowledge diversity issues and power dynamics (Brown, 1997). In the current climate of increasing awareness of racism, sexism, and homophobia in sport, as in all domains of society, sport psychologists' ethical responsibilities may include clarifying their own attitudes toward rape, their assumptions about whether dominant groups suffer from too little or too much self-esteem, or how far they have to stretch themselves to walk in the shoes of athletes from backgrounds far removed from their own. The Canadian Psychological Association's (1996) *Guidelines for Non-Discriminatory Practice* provides an encouraging example of an ethical framework for all practitioners seeking to incorporate diversity issues as more than a checklist of personal attributes within the therapist–client dyad. Similarly, Freedman and Combs (1996) pose a number of questions to guide a therapist's choice of models, theories, and practices. Questions such as "Does it [this practice] divide and isolate people or give them a sense of community and collaboration?" (p. 268) clearly resonate with the worldview of the Aboriginal footballer quoted at the start of this commentary. Such questions evaluate therapists not by how well they follow rules but by their actual effects on people's lives.

The chapter provides an excellent stimulus for reflecting on my experiences as a psychologist in my own social context and on my visions for a more culturally responsive and socially just discipline and practice. Essentially, the chapter inspired me to deconstruct and reconstruct my own model of community counseling. Constraints notwithstanding, Parham attends to how sport psychology consultants might incorporate a greater awareness of cultural diversity in its broadest sense into their everyday practice. Furthermore, his chapter provides useful reference points for our future work in whatever specialization we find ourselves practicing.

# Able Athletes
# With Disabilities

## *Issues and Group Work*

Stephanie Hanrahan, PhD

Writing a chapter on the application of sport psychology to athletes with disabilities is a challenge. First, there is danger that by doing so the differences between people with and without disabilities will be exaggerated. Within a sporting context, athletes are more alike than different, regardless of their intellectual, sensory, or physical capabilities. Something often missed in looking at different groups is that the variance within groups is almost always larger than the variance between groups. Second, what constitutes "a disability" is not always entirely clear. Third, the factors that may influence the development or use of mental skills, as well as the process of communication, vary depending on the disabilities involved. Nevertheless, I attempt to familiarize the reader with issues relevant to athletes with disabilities and then describe a group session for athletes with a variety of disabilities. In this group session, I hope to convey not only the considerations that may need to be made because of different disabilities but also some techniques that can be useful for group situations regardless of whether or not the participants have disabilities.

## What Is a Disability?

An impairment is "any loss of psychological, physiological or anatomical structure or function" (Bury, 1979, p. 36). A disability is "the impact of impairment upon the performance of activities commonly accepted as the basic elements of everyday living" (Thomas, 1982, p. 6). If individuals are hindered in their mobility, domestic routines, or occupational and communication skills, they are usually considered as having a disability. The phrase "everyday living" is important to keep in mind. In an elite sporting environment, a shortage of fast-twitch muscle fibers could be considered a disability because mobility in terms of sprinting would be impaired. Couched in terms of everyday living, however, the shortage of fast-twitch fibers is hardly a disability.

Using these definitions, the majority of athletes at some point in their careers have had a disability. Many sport injuries result in temporarily impaired mobility. Even a relatively minor injury, such as a dislocated finger, can hinder the successful completion of basic domestic chores. I will not attempt, in this chapter, to cover temporary disabilities but will instead focus on permanent disabilities.

Sticking to enduring impairments that affect everyday living does not completely overcome the difficulty of determining what is and what is not a disability. For example, people who are permanently deaf would fit the commonly accepted definition of disability. Many individuals in the deaf community, however, consider themselves to be members of a cultural group rather than people with disabilities. Within their culture, they are not hindered in the basic elements of everyday living. They may communicate using a different language from that of nearby communities, but within their cultural group they do not have a disability. This interpretation of deafness is supported in sporting circles in that deafness alone does not entitle one to be eligible to compete in the Paralympics. Deafness will not be included as a disability for the purposes of this chapter.

# Types of Disabilities and Accompanying Issues

Disabilities can be sensory, physical, or intellectual. All three types of disabilities can be congenital or acquired. People with congenital disabilities gradually grow to recognize that they are different from most other people in a way that tends to be negatively evaluated in the general community, and they slowly begin to understand that they have a disability (Vash, 1981). Other individuals acquire disabilities later in life. The disability may be acquired suddenly in an accident or slowly after weeks, months, or even years of illness (e.g., people with multiple sclerosis). Approximately 85% of athletes with physical or sensory disabilities have an acquired disability (Martin, 1999).

How people react to their own disabilities depends on the nature of the disability. A person's age at the onset of the disability will influence how others perceive and react to the person, as well as the learning experiences available to him or her. The type of onset can also affect how both the individual and other people react. Onset can be sudden or prolonged, and it can also be self-induced (e.g., spinal injury acquired by diving into a shallow lake) or other-induced (e.g., being hit by a drunk driver). Obviously, the specific functions impaired, the severity of the impairment, and the level and persistence of pain will influence how people react or adjust to a disability. Perhaps less obvious is the impact of how visible the disability is. Sometimes invisible disabilities are more difficult to deal with than are visibly obvious ones because people do not appear to be impaired and are assumed to be fully functioning (Vash, 1981).

Disabilities can be progressive or nonprogressive. Nonprogressive disabilities such as amputations, cerebral palsy, and spinal cord injuries are not going to change appreciably over time. Progressive disabilities, such as multiple sclerosis or neuromuscular diseases, require people to confront an active disease process as well as deal with the impairments that follow (Vash, 1981). When working with athletes with disabilities, it is not always obvious which disabilities are progressive. When I first worked in this area, I had the tendency to assume that people's disabilities were fixed variables. It was not until I worked with an athlete with Friedreich's ataxia who had a major decrease in functional ability over a four-month period that I began to recognize the instability of some disabilities.

Even athletes with apparently nonprogressive disabilities, such as amputations, can appear to be healthy when they are actually in remission or are having extended symptom-free periods. I naively had thought that amputations, particularly involving children or adolescents, were the result of accidents. When an amputee swimmer I had worked with for two years (and who had appeared to be healthy the entire time) died rather suddenly of cancer, I realized that many of the athletes who I thought had been in stable states were actually dealing with progressive diseases.

Another dimension of disabilities that is particularly relevant to sport is whether the disability is static or dynamic. With static disabilities (e.g., amputations, blindness, spinal cord injuries), generally no changes to physical conditions occur during sport and exercise activities. With dynamic disabilities (e.g., cerebral palsy, head injuries, neuromuscular diseases), the physical state or condition can be influenced or changed during physical activity (Lockette & Keyes, 1994).

There are a number of issues associated with disabilities that most able-bodied athletes never have to deal with. These issues are too numerous to cover in one chapter, but I will present a few examples to give readers an idea of the conditions and situations confronting many athletes with disabilities.

## Examples of Issues Confronting Athletes With Disabilities

I was working with a wheelchair basketball team, and they needed to find an alternative venue for training because the gym they normally used was being resurfaced. At the last minute, they found a gym that was available at the right time and at a reasonable price. The only problem was that the gym was on the second floor of a building without elevators. Accessibility can be an ongoing issue, not just of buildings but also of parking, transportation, and weight rooms. The design of some exercise and weight training facilities does not allow enough room between machines for wheelchairs. Similarly, the rearrangement of machines and weights can be problematic for athletes who are blind.

Discus throwers always have to deal with the tedium of retrieving the discuses after they have been thrown. That basic task would be difficult for a wheelchair athlete having to push a chair through thick grass or an athlete who is blind and cannot see where the discuses are. In many sports, basic aspects of training require exceptional effort, reliance on others, or both.

A paraplegic involved in recreational water skiing took a tumble from the ski chair. She didn't think much about it. Two weeks later it was discovered that she had broken bones in her foot. She had not been aware of the injury because of a lack of sensation in her lower limbs. Similarly, a junior wheelchair track athlete once teased me because I apologized for accidentally poking her shin while pinning her race number on her tracksuit. She had had no idea that my pinning was less than accurate. Athletes with spinal cord damage also have limited ability to regulate their temperatures. This thermoregulation impairment requires close monitoring of these athletes in extremely hot or cold weather to avoid hyperthermia or hypothermia (Lockette & Keyes, 1994).

Most disabilities require individuals to consider associated conditions. For example, amputees may need to deal with a decreased range of motion, orthopedic deformities of the spine (because of unilateral atrophy of some musculature), and impaired balance and coordination (Lockette & Keyes, 1994). Athletes with cerebral palsy are more likely than able-bodied athletes to have perceptual–motor disorders, visual difficulties, convulsive disorders, or speech and language difficulties (Lockette & Keyes, 1994). Athletes who are blind miss out on visual feedback. As a result, these athletes do not have access to a common source of information for improving physical skills. In addition, this lack of visual feedback may disrupt body orientation (Hanrahan, 1990). Athletes with intellectual disabilities may have problems thinking in abstract terms, poor short-term memory, limited literacy and numeracy skills, inconsistent concentration spans, and poor decision-making abilities (Hanrahan, 1990).

Regardless of the disabilities, however, the focus of the sport psychologist should be on the abilities of the athletes. As a sport psychologist, I work with these people because they are athletes, not because they have disabilities. In other words, I work with athletes within the context of disability. Awareness of the factors affecting how people cope with disabilities, as well as issues and conditions that may affect this population, serves as a background guide to my understanding. Only rarely do these considerations become the focus of a session.

> As a sport psychologist, you should focus on the abilities of your athletes.

## Equipment, Rules, and Classifications

Working with athletes with disabilities also may require the sport psychologist to become familiar with equipment and rules that may be specific to these competitors. Chairs and prostheses used in elite competition are extremely different technologically from those found in your average hospital. Also, an example of a basic rule difference is that in wheelchair tennis, two bounces are allowed instead of just one. Sport for people with disabilities also follows a unique classification system. Although the process of putting athletes into separate classes to ensure fair competition is not unique to sport for athletes with disabilities, the classification process for these athletes is much more complex than just the weight, age, or sex classifications used in able-bodied sports. The classification process is used to determine if athletes meet minimal disability criteria and to decide on the class in which they should compete. Those unfamiliar with the system may want to consider how unfair it would be for a person with an amputation below the elbow to compete against an individual with an amputation above the knee in a running event. Classification determines which athletes will compete against each other. The process can be stressful, particularly for athletes who come from areas without recognized classifiers or who have been poorly advised about their likely classifications (Tweedy, 1998).

Some sports (e.g., swimming) use a sport-specific functional classification system. The idea is to categorize people based on the functional ability they have in the sport, rather than by diagnostic groupings. This system can result in enhanced competition because it allows people from different diagnostic groupings to compete together in the same functional category. For example, swimmers who have cerebral palsy, spina bifida, or amputations can all compete together under the functional classification system. A potential problem with the system is that some individual athletes may be penalized for training. For example, athletes with cerebral palsy may, through training, increase their range of motion and strength. Although they still have the same disability, they have increased their functional ability. As a result, they may be given a new functional classification and forced to compete against those who have been less affected by disability.

## Prejudice

Prejudice comes in many different forms. Some members of the community believe that disability sports are not real sports. Sporting events that are restricted to people who fit particular descriptions are not real competitions. How can one be considered a world champion if the competition is restricted to those with limited eyesight, no use of lower limbs, or some other specific disability?

Rather than belittling the competitions of athletes with disabilities, some people display prejudice by having a condescending attitude toward the athletes themselves. Although rarely meaning any harm, comments such as "Oh, isn't it great they are having a go" convey the belief that people with disabilities cannot do much. When they do participate in sport, their abilities are not appreciated. There is no expectation of skill; rather the mere act of participating is seen as a major accomplishment, as if the athletes should spend their lives sitting at home. For example, wheelchair basketball players have commented on how frustrating it is when crowd members applaud an athlete getting up from a standard spill (a common occurrence). Applause for an offensive rebound, three-pointer, or great defensive play would be much more appreciated.

Potential barriers to participation or enhanced performance include overprotective parents, teachers, and even coaches. Some people with disabilities have spent a lot of time in hospitals and rehabilitation centers. It makes sense that the people close to them do not want to see them endure any additional discomfort due to sporting injuries. Being overprotective of athletes with disabilities—a well-meaning but counterproductive approach—limits their chances of meeting physical challenges and experiencing sporting achievements.

Able-bodied sporting organizations can also be the source of barriers to participation. Although some sports successfully have integrated athletes with disabilities at even the elite level (e.g., archery), many state and national governing bodies are hesitant to include athletes with disabilities at any level. Tenacious adherence to rules can make it impossible for some individuals to compete. For example, in a club swimming meet, a swimmer with an above-the-elbow amputation was disqualified in breaststroke for failing to touch the wall with both hands at the finish. Even more ludicrous, a bench press competitor with one leg was disqualified for not having both feet on the floor. When the participant put on his prosthesis so his artificial foot could be on the floor, he was disqualified because he had used unapproved extraneous equipment.

It is not just able-bodied sporting organizations, however, that can limit the opportunities of athletes with disabilities. Disability groups themselves can be prejudiced against other disability groups or have such narrow visions as to be ineffective. Rather than groups representing those with specific disabilities or conditions fighting against each other for limited government support, or for integration with able-bodied organizations at the expense of others, working together under an umbrella organization can be beneficial to all. These umbrella organizations do exist (e.g., Western Australia Disabled Sports Association, Sporting Wheelies and Disabled Sport and Recreation Association of Queensland) and have achieved a lot, but even within them, the perception sometimes exists that certain disability groups are second-class citizens.

## Personal Comfort or Discomfort

People may experience discomfort when working in unfamiliar environments or situations. Sport psychologists who have not spent time with people with disabilities may feel uncomfortable just because they don't know what to expect. Before becoming a psychologist, I coached ice skating for the Special Olympics and also helped out at the California Wheelchair Games. I attempted wheelchair basketball (with wheel burns and all on the insides of my upper arms) and worked at summer camps for kids with muscular dystrophy. I was by no means an expert in the area, but I felt fairly confident that I would be within my comfort zone when I was first asked to present some sport psychology workshops to a group of athletes with disabilities as part of a weekend camp.

I had no problems navigating around assorted limbs and wheelchairs left at the side of the pool. I could deal with some slightly unorthodox eating methods and quickly got used to having an athlete who was blind trailing me with a hand on my shoulder. I genuinely enjoyed the spontaneous demonstrations of affection by some of the athletes with intellectual disabilities. I was tricked into a debate with a double-leg amputee about which type of boots keeps one's feet warmest. I was less confident in my ability to understand the speech of some of those with cerebral palsy. My main personal issue was anxiety about saying the wrong thing. I felt embarrassed and guilty after asking athletes who were blind if they could "see what I mean." If I had not stumbled over my words trying to cover up what I thought was a major gaffe, the phrasing probably would not have been noticed. I was worried about my use of terminology. I eventually learned, though, that I was the only person concerned about it. Common phrases, such as "See what I mean?" are not suddenly given literal interpretations just because someone has a disability.

The other area I had to work at before becoming comfortable was using athletes as sources of information on themselves. At first, I almost pretended that the disabilities were not there and just continued on my way as I would with any group of athletes. After all, I was there because they were athletes, not because they had disabilities. Great in theory, but in practice the disabilities can influence the development of specific skills or techniques. I learned not to completely divorce the athletes from the context of disability. After some trials and errors, I finally realized that I needed to ask the athletes what would work best for them. If they did not know the answer, we would then explore some possibilities together. For example, when using imagery with athletes who are amputees, I need to know whether they image themselves performing with all limbs (based on previous experiences before amputation) or the limbs they currently have. I also need to know whether or not they should image their prostheses as part of themselves as athletes and if the wearing of artificial limbs affects their self-awareness in their imagery. The only way I can determine the answers to these questions is to speak directly with the athletes. Obviously, one cannot do that and at the same time ignore the disability.

> Don't be afraid that you will offend an athlete with a disability. Ask the athlete what works best for him or her in terms of language, visualization, and so on.

## Service Challenges

When running group sessions for athletes with disabilities, the sport psychologist usually must deal with a group of diverse athletes. In many cases the group is made up of individuals with different disabilities. When a group contains athletes with sensory, intellectual, and physical disabilities, the sport psychologist needs to be able to adapt to different needs at the same time. In addition to athletes with different disabilities being involved, the structure of services provided to athletes with disabilities often means that there will be participants from more than one sport. Sessions sometimes need to cater to team and individual sports, as well as open- and closed-skill sports, all at the same time. Of course these issues are not of concern when working with a specific team (e.g., a wheelchair basketball team or a goal ball team), but funding constraints often result in the merging of athletes from multiple sports to receive sport psychology services.

## Group Settings

Educational sessions about sport psychology commonly occur in group settings because of logistical concerns such as time, money, availability, and ease of organization. Although psychology clients who have been formally diagnosed tend to have better outcomes with individual rather than group therapy, clients with circumscribed issues or problems tend to achieve superior outcomes in group rather than individual settings (McRoberts, Burlingame, & Hoag, 1998). Interpersonal groups that encourage member-to-member communication allow for interactional learning to occur (MacKenzie, 1997). Some researchers predict that large-group treatments and advances in psychoeducational groups will play a significant role in the future of applied psychology (Barlow, Burlingame, & Fuhriman, 2000).

Group development, however, is not the focus of this chapter. A group that is "restricted to six or eight sessions is unlikely to move beyond engagement tasks" (MacKenzie, 1997,

p. 284), meaning that most of the stages discussed in linear and cyclical patterns of group development will not be reached. Groups structured for psychoeducational purposes also show limited developmental progress (MacKenzie, 1997). The example in the next section describes the first of five sessions and has a psychoeducational focus, so group development is not specifically explored. As promised in the first paragraph of this chapter, what follows is the description of a group session with athletes with a variety of disabilities. In addition to conveying some considerations made because of disabilities, this example provides some ideas that are useful for group sessions regardless of the specific population of participants.

# Introductory Group Session

A local umbrella organization for athletes with disabilities has asked me to run a series of five group sessions with the purpose of introducing the athletes to sport psychology. The athletes represent a range of sports, disabilities, ages, and experience. The sessions are being held in a large carpeted room at a sporting complex where some of the athletes train in swimming. Many of the athletes also go to the venue for weight training. I have been told that only a couple of the participants have had any previous formal experience with sport psychology. The athletes already know each other, so there is no need for me to use any icebreaking or get-to-know-you activities.

The first session I have with the group occurs as part of a weekend training camp. I meet with them on a Saturday afternoon from 3:00 to 4:30. They spent most of the morning training, had a break for lunch, and then had a session on nutrition. They had a 15-minute break before my session, but basically they look tired and in some instances bored, possibly because the nutrition session was a noninteractive lecture. Tables and chairs are placed in a roughly semicircular formation. Athletes are sitting at the tables in either their wheelchairs or in chairs available in the room. Because the athletes have just had a session in the same room, they have already established their territory. If the desks had been arranged in a classroom formation with rows and columns, I would have rearranged the furniture during the break before my session.

*Participants*

Jason (A1): single-leg amputee (A) below the knee; male; swimming; 35

Helen (A2): single-arm amputee (A) above the elbow; female; swimming; 16

Justin (A3): single-leg amputee (A) above the knee; male; sprinting; 19

Bruce (A4): double-leg amputee (A) above the knee; male; discus and shot put; 22

Scott (B1): completely blind (B); male; goal ball; 24

Rita (B2): visually impaired (B); female; cycling; 32

Sally (B3): completely blind (B); female; swimming; 15

Jeff (CP1): cerebral palsy (CP); ambulatory; male; soccer; 18

Kirsten (CP2): cerebral palsy (CP); electric wheelchair; female; bocce; 25

Ron (ID1): mild intellectual disability (ID); male; swimming; 17

Sarah (ID2): mild intellectual disability (ID); female; track and field; 21

Liz (FA1): Friedreich's ataxia (FA); wheelchair; female; water skiing; 27

Collin (W1): paraplegic; wheelchair (W); male; weightlifting; 28

Max (W2): incomplete quadriplegic; wheelchair (W); male; marathon; 43

Rachel (W3): paraplegic; wheelchair (W); female; wheelchair tennis; 20

Sharon (C): companion and aide (C) accompanying Kirsten (CP2)

In this group session, I am first introduced by the organizer, someone the athletes know. He uses the title "Dr." and my academic affiliation, and that may be a bit distancing, but he may have used it to add a note of credibility. I try to take care of the potential distancing right off the bat.

Organizer: Our next presenter is Dr. Stephanie Hanrahan from the University of Queensland. She is a sport psychologist. We have asked her to provide an introduction to sport psychology as well as run a relaxation session. After today, she will be making about four or five additional presentations to you over the next couple of months.

Stephanie Hanrahan (SH): Hi! Thanks for having me along today. I'd like to begin by saying that, yes, I do work at the University of Queensland, but I'm not just a stuffy academic locked up in my office reading journals and doing research. I do practice what I preach. In addition to working with athletes and coaches from a wide variety of sports, I also apply these mental skills to my own sporting performance. Please call me Stephanie.

I don't always say something along these lines, but I choose to take the emphasis off of the university side of things for two reasons. First, the group just sat through a lecture on nutrition; the participants are here because they are athletes, not because they want to be studying sport science. Second, more than one of the athletes seemed to roll their eyes or inaudibly groan when I was introduced as being from a university.

SH: Some of you might be dreading the fact that we have an hour and a half scheduled for this session. I promise I will do my best to keep you actively involved and to avoid turning the session into a two-hour lecture. [A few athletes smile at this, and a couple of athletes who were studiously avoiding eye contact look up.] To give me a quick idea of who's who, could we please just go around the room with brief introductions. Just your first name and your sport or main event would be great! Let's start here on my right.

I do this not only to learn who participates in which sport but also to get a glimpse of their basic communication skills. From these simple introductions, I can usually get a grasp of how well the group follows instructions, how much they listen to each other, and their ability to speak and enunciate. The process also briefly gives each participant the spotlight.

*[Because the person on my right has a seeing eye dog, I assume she is blind and gently tap her on the forearm to indicate to her that it is her turn to speak.]*

Sally (B3): Starting with me?

SH: Yes.

Sally (B3): Well, as most of you know, I'm Sally, and this [indicating her dog] is Baxter. My sport is swimming—everything except breaststroke.

Helen (A2): And I'm Helen. I also swim.

*[I nod to the next person.]*

Max (W2): I'm Max. I do road racing—marathons, half marathons, and 10Ks. [Pause.] Hey, Jason—your turn.

Jason (A1): Right. As he just said, I'm Jason. Swimming is my sport. I focus most on backstroke.

Bruce (A4): I do discus and shot put. The name's Bruce.

Collin (W1): I'm Collin, and my main sport is weightlifting.

Scott (B1): Is it my turn?

Max (W2): Yes.

This is the second time that Max has taken it upon himself to keep things on track. Because he is notably older than the others in the group, I may need to make a point of either individually challenging him to ensure he gets something out of the session or giving him greater responsibility. He seems impatient. He reminds me of an athlete I worked with a few years ago who always felt that being included with juniors or athletes with an intellectual disability was somehow demeaning. Now that I am aware of whom he reminds me of, I should be able to avoid assuming he is similar. He may think that a session on sport psychology is a waste of his time, or alternatively, he may be impatient to get to the parts of the session where he will learn specific skills that will help with his performance. Regardless of the underlying cause of his impatience, I am aware of it and will make a point to monitor whether or not he is getting anything out of the session.

Scott (B1):   OK, then, my name is Scott, and I play on the state goal ball team. I'm trying to make the national team.

Ron (ID1):   My name is Ron Clements. I compete in the 50 free, 100 free, 200 free, 100 back, 100 breast, and the 200 IM. Do you want to know my PBs?

When corresponding with the organizer of the training camp about what to include in my sessions, the organizer expressed concern that Ron might be disruptive because he has a short attention span and is easily distracted. During the sessions, I may need to check that Ron stays on task and make a point of keeping him occupied. At this point, however, Ron appears enthusiastic and ready to participate.

SH:   We don't have time at the moment, but maybe you can tell me your times at the end of the session. Next? [Nodding to the next person.]

Sarah (ID2):   [Very quietly.] Sarah. Athletics.

Sarah seems to be shy. I may actively need to encourage her to participate in the sessions. I will need to be sure she does not become just a spectator.

SH:   Athletics?

[Sarah nods.]

Liz (FA1):   I'm Liz, and I water ski. You know, sit skiing.

Rachel (W3):   I play tennis. I'm Rachel. And this [indicating the person next to her] is Kirsten. She plays bocce.

Kirsten is sitting in an electric wheelchair and obviously has very restricted motor ability. It may be useful for the future to remember that Rachel seems to be comfortable helping out Kirsten. That willingness can be helpful, but I will need to ensure that Rachel does not always speak for Kirsten.

SH:   Kirsten?

Kirsten (CP2):   [Difficult to understand because of severe motor impairment that affects her speech.] That's right.

It appears as though Kirsten will be unable to write. It is also evident that until I am able to spend some time with Kirsten, I will have difficulty comprehending her speech. I will need some help understanding her at first.

[I nod to the next person.]

Sharon (C):   I'm not really a participant. I'm just here with Kirsten.

I feel an immediate sense of relief. As a regular companion, Sharon should be able to understand Kirsten. I will still need to ensure that Kirsten is given a chance to participate and that others (whether it be Rachel or Sharon) do not help to the point of unintentional exclusion.

| SH: | That's fine. What's your name? |
|---|---|
| Sharon (C): | Sharon. |
| SH: | Thanks! And you? [Indicating the next person.] |
| Justin (A3): | I'm Justin. I do track—sprints. |
| Jeff (CP1): | And I'm Jeff. I play soccer with an able-bod club team as well as the national CP team. |
| *[Pause.]* | |
| Rita (B2): | I guess that must leave me. My name is Rita. I'm a cyclist. |
| SH: | OK. Thanks very much for that. [I mentally kick myself—I'm trying to get out of the habit of saying *OK*.] I may not remember everyone's name, but at least now I have an idea of who is here. What I'm going to do now is distribute this handout. On this handout is a list of factors that sometimes affect some people's performances. I'd like each of you to read each factor, then place a check mark next to it if it is something that sometimes affects your performance. If it really affects your performance, give it a double check mark. If it doesn't have a negative effect on you or your performance, go ahead and leave it blank. [See the next page for a copy of the handout.] I have pens and pencils here for anyone that needs them. Also, if anyone needs them, I have enlarged copies of the handout as well as a couple of braille copies. |

I previously believed that anyone who was blind could read braille. In fact, many people who have been blind from birth do not read braille. For those who do, it is relatively easy to print handouts in braille. Most large communities have a school for the blind or a community service organization that supports individuals who are blind. For a small fee (often no more than the cost of regular printing), you can print a text file on a braille printer. One word of advice—unless you can read braille, be sure to write on the printout what it is. I once dropped a stack of braille handouts. I didn't have a clue as to which was which.

| SH: | If you come to a question that doesn't make sense, feel free to give me a yell, and I'll try to help. |
|---|---|

*[There is a temporary flurry of activity while people collect pens and various forms of the handout. As they begin to read the handout, I circulate to ensure that everyone is on task.]*

| SH: | Kirsten, would you rather just read the handout and think to yourself what your answers are, or would you prefer that Sharon record your check marks? |
|---|---|
| Kirsten (CP2): | [Says about a dozen words, only one of which I pick up.] Sharon. |
| SH: | You'd rather have Sharon help out? |
| *[Kirsten nods.]* | |
| SH: | OK. Just be sure that Sharon writes down what you think, not what she thinks! |

I say this to emphasize that Kirsten is the one in control of what gets written, even though she is not doing the writing. Feelings of powerlessness are often an issue for individuals with severe disabilities (Martin, 1999). In addition, athletes completing questionnaires with the aid of another person sometimes modify their responses to reflect the opinions or unstated expectations of the person doing the writing (Hanrahan, Grove, & Lockwood, 1990).

*[I give a slightly questioning look to Sharon. She nods and smiles.]*

| SH: | [Quietly to Sharon.] Thanks. |
|---|---|

*[I wander around and see that Bruce and Collin are talking about one of the items on the handout.]*

| SH: | Anything I can help you with? |
|---|---|
| Bruce (A4): | No, we're just doing this together. |

# Factors That Affect Performance

Activity: For each of the situations in the following list, place a tick mark if you believe it is something that sometimes contributes to inconsistent performance, and place a double tick mark if you think it really affects performance.

___ Thinking about work or study

___ Being distracted by someone in the stands

___ Worrying about winning (thinking about the outcome)

___ Being uncertain about own abilities (self-doubt)

___ Worrying about the performance of teammates

___ Being indecisive (changing your mind halfway through an action)

___ Struggling with a new technique early on in a competition

___ Having no plan

___ Being too anxious

___ Feeling too much pressure from others

___ Thinking you have won

___ Thinking the competition is a lost cause

___ Thinking about the next round of competition (while still involved in the current round)

___ Worrying about what others might think

___ Being concerned about other people's performances

___ Thinking about what someone said or did to you before competition

___ Skipping the normal precompetition routine

___ Feeling like being somewhere else (mind wanders)

___ Feeling burned out

___ Having unrealistic expectations

___ Dwelling on mistakes

___ Having doubts about physical preparation or equipment

___ Falling in love

___ Trying too hard

___ Spacing out (visiting another planet)

___ Thinking about a previous injury

___ Being self-conscious performing in front of others

___ Disagreeing with officials

___ Losing your temper

___ Thinking about what it is you do not want to do

___ Being distracted by the opposition

___ Thinking about the weather, venue

___ Having no reason for being there

___ Realizing the competition is running late

___ Doing unexpectedly well

___ Doing unexpectedly poorly

___ Thinking about what impact the outcome of the competition might have

___ Swearing at yourself

___ Having ongoing arguments with others

___ (Add your own) _____

From *Sport Psychology in Practice*, edited by Mark B. Andersen, 2005, Champaign, IL: Human Kinetics. Reproduced with kind permission of Thomson Learning Australia, 2nd edition published by Dunmore Press Pty Ltd., 2004. Cite list reproduced as "The Coaching Process: A Practical Guide to Improving Your Effectiveness 2E", 2004.

SH:    I'd prefer it if you could each do it individually. Later you'll have time to share your answers.

Collin (W1):    OK.

*[Collin turns his chair so he is no longer facing Bruce.]*

*[I turn and see that Scott and Ron are involved in a lengthy discussion about work—the first item on the handout.]*

SH:    Hi, guys. How's it going?

Scott (B1):    Sorry, but I can't read braille. Ron's reading it to me.

SH:    That's fine. [To Ron.] Are you keeping your answers separate on two handouts? One for Scott and one for you?

Ron (ID1):    No, but I could.

SH:    Great. How about if we make this one yours [I write *Ron* at the top of the page] and this one Scott's? [I write *Scott* at the top of the other sheet.] You can just write on this one if the factor is something that affects you, and then on Scott's if it is something that he says affects him. Just try not to discuss right now why something does or doesn't affect you. It's OK to talk to make sure you both understand each question, but once you both understand the question, just write down whether it affects each of you. Since Ron is responsible for the reading and writing, how about if we make Scott responsible for both of you staying on task and making sure that you keep moving through the questions?

*[Ron eagerly nods, and Scott knowingly smiles.]*

Scott (B1):    Yep, that would be great. So does thinking about work or study affect my performance in goal ball? Yeah, sometimes. Ron—put a check mark there for me. What about for you?

*[I leave them to it and move on to Sarah, who is staring at the handout but hasn't written any check marks.]*

SH:    Hi, Sarah. Did I make it clear enough what I wanted you to do?

I am trying to take the blame for any lack of understanding. If she does not understand something, it is because I did not make it clear enough, not because she lacks ability.

Sarah (ID2):    [Mumbling.] Not really.

SH:    Sorry about that. What I want you to do is think about each sentence and whether or not it is something that keeps you from performing your best. Something that keeps you from running your fastest or throwing your farthest. So let's look at the first one, "thinking about work or study." Do you work or go to school?

*[Sarah nods.]*

SH:    Which one, work or school?

Sarah (ID2):    I work.

SH:    OK. Do you ever find yourself thinking about work when you are training or competing at the track?

Sarah (ID2):    No.

SH:    OK, let's go on to the next one. Have you ever been distracted by someone in the stands while you have been competing?

Sarah (ID2):    Yeah. My mom. I hate it when she comes to watch.

SH:    OK, then let's place a check mark next to that one.

*[Sarah places a check mark on the relevant line.]*

I've said OK three times in a row. I'm determined not to say it again.

SH:    Do you think you can keep going with the rest of them?

*[Sarah nods.]*

SH:    Great. I'll check back in case there are any questions that don't make any sense. If you come to one you don't understand, don't worry about it. Just skip it and move on to the next one.

*[Sally is raising her hand. I move to her and make a bit of noise as I approach.]*

SH:    Hi, Sally. What can I do for you?

Sally (B3):    Thanks for bringing the braille handouts—they're great. I can understand the statements and all, but even if I can manage to write a check mark next to it, I won't be able to tell which ones I have checked.

SH:    Good point. Will it work if you make a small tear in the side of the sheet next to any of the items that you think affect your performance?

Sally (B3):    Um, yeah, that should work. But could I get another copy of the handout that I don't tear just in case I tear too much or if it gets caught on something and tears across?

SH:    Sure. No problem.

Helen (A2):    Stephanie?

*[I move to Helen.]*

SH:    Yes?

Helen (A2):    What do you mean by "spacing out" or "visiting another planet"?

SH:    Do you ever have times when you mentally aren't at the pool even when you are physically there? You aren't thinking about anything in particular, but you aren't focused on your swimming either?

Helen (A2):    Do you mean when you're in la-la land?

SH:    Yes. Exactly.

Helen (A2):    OK. Thanks!

*[At this point I bring a second braille copy of the handout to Sally. I also check that the enlargement is adequate for Rita by observing that she is placing check marks in the correct places. I then eavesdrop on Scott and Ron to check that they are staying on task and that answers for both athletes are being recorded. I also observe Sharon and Kirsten to ensure that Kirsten is providing the answers to Sharon. I then stop by Sarah.]*

SH:    I see you're making good progress. Are there any words I used in the handout that don't make much sense?

Sarah (ID2):    Yeah . . . what's "inde . . . indecisive"?

SH:    Indecisive is when you can't make up your mind.

Sarah (ID2):    [Blank look.]

SH:    For example, being indecisive in middle distance running might mean that you end up getting boxed in because you can't decide when to make your move. Or in throwing and jumping events, have you ever noticed people waiting for the wind before throwing or jumping?

Sarah (ID2):    Yeah—you never want to go into a headwind.

SH:    Exactly, but sometimes athletes are indecisive about when to jump or throw, and as a result end up running out of time and having to perform in a terrible gust of wind or fouling because they are outside the time limit.

Sarah (ID2):    OK . . . yeah, I understand.

SH:    Was there anything else?

Sarah (ID2):    No, I think that's all.

SH:    OK. [Oops! I said "OK" again] I'll leave you alone so you can finish.

*[I then move to Max because he has finished his handout and is looking bored.]*

| | |
|---|---|
| SH: | Did you find any factors that sometimes affect your performance? |
| Max (W2): | Yes. None of them affect me all of the time, but most of them have affected me one time or another. When I think of the athletes that I sometimes coach, I think I could tick all of them. [Looking at the sheet, I notice that he has checked almost all of the factors.] |

My earlier concern that Max may think sport psychology is a waste of time is relieved. Although he continues to have an air of impatience, his finding almost all of the factors to be relevant to his sport indicates to me that he will get something out of this session.

| | |
|---|---|
| SH: | That makes sense. I actually created the list from athletes I have worked with, so all of the factors have affected somebody. Since you have finished sooner than some of the others, how about if you quickly go back through the factors you have checked and mark the four or five factors that you think have the greatest impact? |
| Max (W2): | Yep! |

*[At this point I float from person to person, checking that everyone understands the handout. To athletes who have finished, I recommend thinking about the factors that affect them in more than one event or that affect them frequently. I then make a general announcement.]*

| | |
|---|---|
| SH: | If I can just interrupt for a second. Most of you have probably noticed that there is room at the bottom of the list to add your own. I'm sure I haven't included everything, so if you can think of factors, other than illness or injury, that affect your performance, feel free to write them down. You can add more than one of your own if you want. If you can't think of any others though, don't worry about it. For a lot of athletes the list I have covers most things. |

While they are finishing the handout, I begin to sort out how I will put them into groups for the next part of the exercise. I have lots of choices. I could group the athletes by age, sex, disability, or sport. Alternatively I could use random groups. Because the discussion is going to be about the factors that affect performance, I think it may be useful for people from the same or similar sports to discuss their sporting experiences. Grouping athletes by disabilities would place the emphasis on something other than their abilities. Age groupings are not appropriate in this instance because some of the older athletes have less sporting experience than some of the younger athletes. While the athletes are completing the handout, I do my best to group people in my head according to sport. I end up with four swimmers and four track and field athletes. The remaining seven athletes are from closed-skill individual sports (cycling, water skiing, and weightlifting), open-skill individual sports (tennis and bocce), and team sports (goal ball and soccer). I do not see a lot of commonalities across the sports within these groupings (even the track and field athletes compete in vastly different events), so I decide to go with random groupings for the next exercise.

My inability to group people by sport in this situation is somewhat unusual. In a number of general principles of coaching courses that I teach, the diversity of sports represented in the class usually breaks into distinctly different groups more often than not. In this case, it does not work. Instead of my deciding who will go into which group or allowing the participants to group themselves (sometimes resulting in the exclusion of a person), I decide to have the athletes divide into groups on the basis of their birthdays. I find this technique to be useful for a number of reasons:

- It is truly random.
- It provides a short mental break.
- It almost always results in people working with individuals other than those who were already sitting next to them.

- It provides a little physical exercise, which can often energize people during a session.
- It allows participants to learn something about each other outside of sport.

I look around and see that everyone either has finished the handout or is working on the last item or two.

> SH: As you finish the handout, I'd like you to move to the front of the room. Please bring your handout and your pen or pencil with you. [There is no furniture at the front of the room that can get in the way. As the last two athletes begin to move to the front of the room, I continue.] What I'd like you to do now is to line up as quickly as possible by birthday. We'll only worry about month and day, not year. January is at the side of the room by the windows, and December is at the side of the room with the posters. The only hitch is that you cannot speak or write while lining up. You'll have to come up with other ways of communicating. So, as quickly as possible, get yourselves in the correct order, but remember, no talking!

*[The athletes begin to organize themselves into a line. Most of them communicate by holding up the number of fingers that correspond to the month in which they were born. When they find someone who was born in the same month, they then use the same process to indicate the day of the month. Sarah looks confused.]*

> SH: [Whispering.] Sarah, in what month is your birthday?
>
> Sarah (ID2): [Quietly.] August.
>
> SH: [Still whispering.] OK. August is the eighth month of the year. So if you hold up eight fingers, the others will know that you were born in August.

*[Sarah nods and holds up eight fingers.]*

I see that Sharon is helping Kirsten. I am a little concerned that this activity may be too challenging for the athletes who are blind. My concerns are put to rest when I see Sally feeling the hands of other athletes to learn how many fingers they are displaying. A different approach to overcome the challenge becomes obvious when I hear Scott clap three times. There is a pause and then he claps three times again. The people around him comprehend that his three claps indicate the month of March. The other person with a March birthday claps three times in reply. Scott finds the other March birthday. I then hear more clapping as they clap the day of the month on which they were born. When everyone seems to have found their place, I check that they were successful in forming the correct order.

> SH: Just a quick check to see if everyone is in the right place. . . . Starting at the January end, can you please call out your birthdays in order!
>
> Rachel (W3): January 17.
>
> Jason (A1): March 2.
>
> Scott (B1): The 5th of March.
>
> Collin (W1): April 3.
>
> Justin (A3): May 11.
>
> Jeff (CP1): May 18.
>
> Ron (ID1): June 22.
>
> Helen (A2): June 24.
>
> Liz (FA1): July 7.
>
> Rita (B2): August 6.
>
> Sarah (ID2): [With surprising conviction.] August 21.
>
> Kirsten (CP2): Sept 5.

| Max (W2): | October 20. |
| Bruce (A4): | December 14. |
| Sally (B3): | The same. December 14. |
| SH: | Excellent! Now I'm going to form you into groups of three, based on your birthdays. |

*[I move along the line indicating where the divisions in the line are to form the five groups of three.]*

| SH: | Each group needs to find a place where they can sit down as a group. |

*[The five groups quickly get settled.]*

| SH: | Just a warning to those who can't see. Some of the furniture has been moved, so please be careful when you next move around the room. [Slight pause.] Each of you has completed the handout. What I'd like each group to do now is decide on the two factors that affect performance the most. You don't have to stick to the exact words on the handout. If you think there are a couple of factors that are similar, you can lump them together under a heading that you think covers all of them. The idea is for the members of each group to agree on the two factors that they think most often lead to inconsistent performance. All members of the group must agree that the two factors are relevant to them. |

I engage in this process for a number of reasons. First, discussing the factors that can affect performance gives athletes the chance to explore in detail the specific items on the questionnaire that interest them. Discussing these issues with others often results in the realization that they are not the only people affected by these factors. Second, requiring each group of three to agree on two factors often results in participants looking at the big picture. They may have multiple factors checked on their lists that they consider to be important. Instead of excluding items, they merge them together by thinking about how they may be related. For example, a group may quickly decide that "being too anxious" is of importance to all of them, and this item will be one of their final two. They then may find that other items of importance to individuals actually have a common element. The athletes may have checked "being distracted by someone in the stands," "being distracted by the opposition," "thinking about the weather, venue," and "thinking about a previous injury." They may independently realize that these all have something to do with being distracted, or having an irrelevant focus of attention, and then create their own heading for this topic.

Third, the factors that the groups agree are of concern to them can guide me in determining the content of future sessions. Rather than using a pre-established plan for all sessions based on my perceptions of the needs of the particular group (or worse yet, a set protocol pulled out for any series of group sessions regardless of who the participants are), I prefer obtaining input from the participants themselves. I expect that most sport psychology practitioners have, at one time or another, been approached by coaches or managers to run sessions on topics that they believe to be of utmost concern to the athletes, only to learn that the athletes have entirely different opinions or perceptions about what the major issues are. I do not mean to suggest that the technique I am describing here is problem free, but it often provides a useful structure for future group sessions. (Note: I sometimes add sport-specific items or items based on the concerns of the coach.)

> Handouts and group discussions of those handouts can give you insight into what athletes want to discuss, thus forming future sessions.

A final purpose of this exercise is that it can result in people realizing the importance of mental factors without forcing the message down their throats. As an example, a few years ago I was invited to run an introductory session on sport psychology to approximately 150 rugby coaches as part of a five-day program for experienced coaches of this sport. All of the participants had already completed at least level one and level two rugby coaching courses, neither of which at the time contained any information about sport psychology. (Australia has a National Coaching Accreditation Scheme [NCAS], which has three levels of accreditation.) Saying that the coaches were less than impressed with the prospect of a two-hour session on sport psychology ("that psycho mumbo jumbo") with someone who was not only female (all of the coaches were male) but also American is an understatement. Anyway, having the coaches discuss the factors that affected their players' performance, in a manner similar to that described here, resulted in some of them informing me that all of the factors were important. When I later pointed out that all of these factors related to mental skills, they questioned why they had not received any of this important information in their previous coaching courses. But I digress. Back to the current session. . . .

While the groups are discussing the factors that affect performance and deciding on their final two, I float from group to group. I speak only if they ask me a question, if they seem lost or are completely off the topic, if I feel someone is dominating the discussion to the exclusion of others, or if I need to check on their progress. When I first began running group sessions, I had the tendency to speak too much. If activities are structured well, athletes can achieve a lot on their own without my giving my two cents' worth. Most of the groups in this situation are proceeding without any difficulties. The exception is the group that contains Rita, Kirsten, and Sarah. (These inconvenient groupings can happen when random methods of allocation are used.) Rita is quiet, Sarah is also quiet and can have some difficulties with new concepts, and Kirsten is difficult to understand. The potential advantage is that Sharon (the companion and aide accompanying Kirsten) is also sitting with the group. I need to be careful, though, that I don't take advantage of Sharon and just assume that she will facilitate the group process. Her role is to help Kirsten, not to become my assistant. When I approach the group, there is no evidence of any discussion.

> When groups are discussing among themselves, be careful that you don't talk too much.

SH: Have I made it clear enough to you what I am asking you to do?

*[Kirsten nods.]*

Rita (B2): Yes, you want us, as a group, to decide on the two factors that we think influence our sporting performances the most.

SH: Yes, exactly. [Sarah looks confused.] So, Sarah, see how you have checked about eight or nine of the situations on your handout? [Sarah nods.] Well, to start with we want to see which items you have ticked that maybe Rita and Kirsten have also marked. The first one that you have marked is "being distracted by someone in the stands." Rita and Kirsten, do either of you have that one marked?

Rita (B2): No, to me the spectators are a blur, so they don't really bother me.

I do not know whether the spectators are a blur because as a cyclist she is moving quickly past them or because her visual impairment does not allow her to focus. In the group situation, however, it is not the proper time to pursue the issue.

Kirsten (CP2): [Says something I can't make out, then laughs.]

SH: I'm sorry, I didn't understand what you said.

Sharon: Kirsten said that in bocce they hardly ever have any spectators, so there really isn't anyone there to distract her.

SH: So spectators are not a distraction for you.

Kirsten (CP2): No.

During this conversation, I make eye contact with Kirsten and speak directly to her even when Sharon is serving the role of interpreter. I am having the conversation with Kirsten, not with Sharon (Hanrahan, 1998).

SH: OK. So, Sarah, what is the next situation on the list that you thought might affect your performance?

Sarah (ID2): Being uncertain, self-doubt.

Rita (B2): Yep, I had that one, too.

Kirsten (CP2): Me too.

SH: Great! You have found one you all have in common. Rita, can you make a note of that? [She does so.] Now all you need to do is continue down the list to find the ones you have in common. If you have more than two in common when you finish, then you'll need to discuss which two most often have a negative effect on your performance. Just make sure that each person has a chance to say what she thinks. [There is a general indication of nonverbal agreement. As I leave the group, I can hear Sarah reading the next situation she has marked on her sheet. I sit back and observe the groups working.]

Max (W2): Stephanie?

*[I move over to the group containing Max, Bruce, and Sally.]*

SH: Yes?

Max (W2): Are you sure we can only have two? We all agree on about half of them.

SH: Yes, I want you to select the two that you think have the biggest impact. Remember though, if you want you can combine a few of them together under the same heading.

Bruce (A4): Right. "Being anxious," "thinking about what impact the outcome of the competition might have," and, let's see, "feeling too much pressure from others" all have something to do with being stressed.

*[I leave them to it as they debate how different items might be combined. I then quickly check how the other groups are progressing. Two groups have finished the activity, and the other three have found the items they have in common and are debating which are most important.]*

SH: May I have your attention please. [I wait a moment as voices die down.] As each group finishes, could you please select a member of the group to write the two factors you have decided on on the whiteboard. Try to pick someone who has legible writing. [A little bit of laughter.]

When doing group sessions, make sure you have a chalkboard or whiteboard. You can copy answers for use in future sessions.

In the past, I asked groups to read out their answers rather than write them on a board. I have since found that it is useful for me to have their responses in writing so I can copy them at the end of the session for use in future planning. I also find it easier to discuss their findings when I can see them in front of me. An added bonus is that writing the answers on the board gives the groups who finish first something to do. Participants begin to discuss the similarities and differences between groups while the final groups finish. See the responses that are written on the board in this session on the next page.

*[Selected individuals from the groups have written their responses on the board. The athletes who are blind or visually impaired have had someone else in their group read to them what has been written on the board.]*

SH: I understand that a number of you felt constrained by only being able to select two factors for your group. You can see on the board, though, that a number of different situations are seen to have a negative impact on performance. What you may have already figured out is that everything on that handout relates to mental skills. During the next sessions I have with you, I will cover techniques you can use to help you deal with these situations. For example, "mind on things it shouldn't be," "thinking about irrelevant things," and "thinking about what it is you don't want to do" all relate to the area of concentration and attention. Therefore, we will have a session on how to pay attention to what is important and ignore what's not. We

# Factors Perceived by Each Group to Negatively Affect Performance

Responses are written on the whiteboard.

### Group One

Feeling anxious or pressured

Mind on things it shouldn't be

### Group Two

Lacking confidence

Having no plan

### Group Three

Not feeling in control

Thinking about irrelevant things

### Group Four

Thinking about what it is you don't want to do

Losing your temper

### Group Five

Being uncertain about own abilities

Feeling burned out

---

will also spend some time covering techniques you can use to build your self-confidence. One group specifically mentioned "lacking confidence," and another listed "being uncertain about own abilities." The good news is that confidence is a skill you can develop; it's not just something you are born with a certain amount of. We will spend some time discussing what you expect to get out of your participation in sport, along with setting goals that will not only help you get there but also help you improve motivation as well as confidence. This should provide you with a plan as well as help with burnout. We'll also look at both precompetition plans and competition routines. These obviously help on the planning side of things but also can help you feel in control. We will finish today with a couple of relaxation-type exercises. Being able to relax when you want can help you counteract anxiety and even control your temper.

The list of factors developed by these athletes is similar to those I have seen from coaches and able-bodied athletes. Respondents usually include factors related to anxiety, confidence, motivation, and attention. The one possible difference is the mention of "not feeling in control." Although feeling in control is important for all athletes, it may be a bigger issue for athletes with disabilities because they are sometimes in situations where they are forced to rely on medication, equipment (e.g., wheelchairs), and other people (e.g., guide runners, transportation) (Martin, 1999).

As a result of this exercise, most (if not all) of the participants should be convinced of the importance of mental skills. Although somewhat time consuming, the exercise surreptitiously convinces the athletes of the relevance of sport psychology while at the same time provides them with a sense that future sessions will be tailored to them and their needs. As mentioned previously, it also gives me an indication as to what they consider to be important.

SH: To begin with, I'd like everyone to help move the furniture to the back of the room so we have a large open space. [As people are moving furniture, I move to Kirsten.] Kirsten, we are going to do some relaxation exercises. Would you be more comfortable in your chair or on the floor? I can easily help Sharon transfer you to the floor if that is what you would prefer.

| Kirsten (CP2): | [Speech that is difficult to understand, but I pick out two words—*stay* and *chair*. To be sure I have not incorrectly assumed that she indicated she would prefer to stay in her chair, I check my understanding of what she said.] |
| SH: | You'd prefer to stay where you are? |
| Kirsten (CP2): | Yes. |
| SH: | That's fine. |

*[Part of the room has been cleared of furniture, but one side of the room is experiencing a traffic jam.]*

| SH: | Not everybody is needed to move the remaining furniture. It would be most helpful if some of you moved to the front of the room to make room for the rest of the furniture at the back. |

*[While the rest of the furniture is being moved, I ask Liz the same question I asked Kirsten.]*

| SH: | Liz, we are going to do some relaxation exercises. Would you be more comfortable on the floor or in your chair? |
| Liz (FA1): | Probably the floor. |
| SH: | OK. Let me know how I can best help. |

*[Liz explains to me how to help transfer her to the floor. As I am doing so, I notice that the furniture is more or less at the back of the room.]*

| SH: | [To everyone.] Great! Now find yourself a place on the floor. I'd like you to lie down on your back. If you have any back trouble, feel free to place your feet on a chair to take the strain off your back. |

*[Looking around the room, the only two people (other than Kirsten) who are slow to make it to the floor are Max and Rachel.]*

| SH: | The exercise we are about to do is usually easiest if done lying down. Give me a yell if you would like a hand transferring. I also promise to help anyone that might need a hand transferring back to their chairs. |

For obvious biomechanical reasons, it is usually easier for people to move from a wheelchair to the floor than from the floor to a wheelchair. My offer of help tends to alleviate the fear that if they transfer to the floor they will be stuck there. In addition, I believe that by talking about transferring in an everyday voice, they realize that I may have some experience with the process. That I am tall and (hopefully obviously) strong probably boosts their confidence in my lifting ability. Not having ever been short or thin, I do not know for sure what effect my physical appearance has on athletes' with disabilities readily accepting physical help, but I feel it is probably an asset.

*[Everyone has found themselves a place on the floor. Ron is very close to Scott.]*

| SH: | Ron, could you please move over to your left? We have lots of space, so there is no reason to be too close to anyone else. Everyone should be able to move a little without worrying about touching someone else. |
| Ron (ID1): | [Moves to his left.] Is this far enough? |
| SH: | Yep! Thanks! [A couple of quiet conversations have sprung up around the room.] To begin, I'd like everyone to close their eyes and their mouths. [Instant quiet.] To the best of your ability, place your hands on your belly, just below your belly button. Now breathe in such a way that your belly and hands rise as you breathe in and fall as you breathe out. Tummy up as you breathe in, tummy down as you breathe out. Try to spend the same amount of time breathing in as you do breathing out. Try to make the transition between the two as natural and as smooth as possible, as if your breathing has a mind of its own. Tummy up as you breathe in, tummy down as you breathe out. If other thoughts come into your head, just let them float on past, and then refocus on your breathing—tummy up as you breathe in, and tummy down |

as you breathe out. [Pause.] Continue to breathe like that, but now add a picture in your head to go in time with your breathing. For example, you might imagine a wave as it rolls up onto the beach and as the water runs back into the ocean. The water is moving in time with your breathing, rolling up onto the beach as your belly moves up and rolling back down the beach as your belly moves down. Or, if you prefer, you might imagine a curtain blowing in an open window—blowing in and out in time with your breathing. If other thoughts come into your head, just refocus on the picture and your breathing. [Pause.] Now continue to focus on your breathing—tummy up as you breathe in, and tummy down as you breathe out. Stop the picture in your head, and just focus on your breathing. Continue breathing like that, but now, every time you breathe out, say the word *one* silently to yourself. Tummy up as you breathe in, and tummy down as you breathe out and say the word *one* silently to yourself. If other thoughts come into your head, just refocus on your breathing and saying the word *one*. [Pause.] Now slowly open your eyes and slowly sit up. [The athletes slowly begin to move and sit up. I move so I am near Liz so I can give her a hand to sit up. She is near the wall, so she can use the wall for support when sitting. I return to the front of the room and sit down.] What do you think the purposes of that exercise were?

| | |
|---|---|
| Max (W2): | To relax. |
| Ron (ID1): | Yes, to relax. |
| SH: | Yes, breathing like that physiologically relaxes you. It not only slows down your breathing but also lowers your heart rate. What other purpose do you think the exercise had? |
| Liz (FA1): | To focus. |
| SH: | Yes. Do any of you ever have trouble falling asleep because your brain won't shut up? You keep thinking about the same thing over and over and can't get to sleep? |
| Scott (B1): | Yes. |
| Collin (W1): | All the time. |
| SH: | Well, focusing on your breathing is a way of getting your mind off the treadmill. For example, suppose I tell you all right now *not* to think about pink elephants. Whatever you do, don't think about pink elephants. I don't want you thinking about pink elephants. [Pause.] How many of you had a pink elephant pop into your head? [Lots of hands go up.] |
| Ron (ID1): | I had a whole herd of them! |
| SH: | Right, so how do you not think of pink elephants? |
| Rachel (W3): | Think of blue crocodiles! |
| SH: | Yes, you have to give yourself something else to think about. That's the great thing about breathing. No matter what you are doing—with the possible exceptions of underwater hockey and synchronized swimming—you are always breathing. So if you find yourself thinking something you don't want to be thinking, you can refocus your attention on your breathing. Now for some people, just focusing on breathing isn't enough. They need something else for their brains to do as well. For visual people, adding a picture to go with the breathing is useful. Did any of you find it easier to focus on your breathing when you pictured the image of the beach or the curtain at the same time? |
| Jason (A1): | Yes, I love the ocean. I also heard the sound of the waves, which I think is really relaxing. |
| Ron (ID1): | I could see the curtain blowing. I once had a broken window in my room, and the curtain was always blowing. |
| SH: | Yes, we tend to base our images on past experiences. For some people, having the image to go along with the breathing makes it easier to block out unwanted |

thoughts because they are giving their brains something else to do. For other people, a word works better than a picture. Now, I just picked the word *one* to give you guys a word. You can use any word or phrase you want that will help you relax or focus. Some people like the word *relax*, others use the word *focus*. You can use any word or phrase that helps you focus on what is important or makes you feel the way you want to feel. You can remind yourself of specific aspects of technique or be your own cheerleader. The words you pick don't need to make sense to anyone but you. I had one Paralympian who used the word *rhubarb*. Rhubarb had nothing to do with her sport, but her family had a family joke about rhubarb. When she thought about it, it put her in a good mood and helped her relax, a state she found helpful for competition. I have here a list of cue words and phrases. In the next few days, I'd like each of you to go through the list and select a couple that you think might work for you. If you have your own words or phrases that you already use, feel free to add them to the list. I'll distribute the lists before you leave, but now I'd like to move on to one last quick exercise. The type of breathing you just did is called abdominal breathing because you breathe from your abdomen rather than shallowly from your chest. In addition to abdominal breathing, another method of relaxation is called progressive muscular relaxation, or PMR for short. What I would like each of you to do is make yourself comfortable. You can lie back down or remain sitting, whichever you prefer. [While the participants are making themselves comfortable, I approach Kirsten.]

SH: Kirsten, the exercise we are about to do involves tensing and then relaxing muscles. If you think that tensing your muscles might lead to muscle spasms, then just skip the tensing phase, and instead focus on the relaxation phase. Does that make sense?

Kirsten (CP2): Yes. Thanks.

> It is important to have a thorough knowledge of different conditions so that you know what activities may be unsuitable for athletes with certain disabilities.

The reason I speak to Kirsten separately is that approximately 70% of people with cerebral palsy have spasticity, an abnormal increase in muscle tone (Lockette & Keyes, 1994). For individuals with spastic cerebral palsy, trying to tense a muscle can result in uncontrolled movement of a group of muscles as well as an absence of isolated joint control (i.e., muscle spasms). I do not approach Jeff because he is a hemiplegic (i.e., only one side of his body is affected), and I will be doing a very short PMR exercise involving only one hand. Jeff writes with his unaffected hand, so I will ask everyone to use the hand they write with. Selecting the writing hand also overcomes any concerns about asking Helen, a single-arm amputee, to tense the hand she does not have.

SH: What I'd like you to do now is rest the hand that you write with on your lap or on the floor beside you. Now slowly begin to form that hand into a fist. Make it tighter, tighter still, as tight as you possibly can. Hold it. [Pause.] Now think to yourself, *stop* and *relax*. Let the tension drain out of your fingers. Notice the difference between the feeling of tension and the feeling of relaxation. [Pause.] Open your eyes and slowly sit up. [The athletes sit up and face me.] That was just a brief example of PMR. PMR works on the premise that we have a constant state of tension in our muscles. When we increase that tension and then relax, we automatically dip below that initial level of tension. [I visually draw a graph with my hands while explaining.] With practice, you can learn to go straight to relaxation without having to tense first. When doing PMR, you gradually work through the entire body—right hand, right arm, left hand, left arm, right foot, right calf, right thigh, left foot, left calf, left thigh, and so on—working all the way through the body. Now I realize that some of you either don't have all limbs or don't have muscular control over all limbs. I'd like to make an individual PMR tape for anyone who wants one, a cassette you can play to follow my voice through a relaxation session. In the past, I have seen some athletes get frustrated when they are asked to tense and relax a muscle group they do not have control over. On the other hand, I had an athlete with quadriplegia who liked mentally going through his whole body with the tape, even though there were only a few muscle groups he could actually contract. What I have here is a handout with a body drawn on it. If you don't have muscular control over all body parts, I'd like you to mark on this diagram the bits you either don't have or can't use. I'll then make you a PMR tape that mentions only the body parts you can use. I'll also give you a standard PMR tape, and then you can pick which one you prefer. [I distribute the diagram to the amputee athletes and the wheelchair athletes.] Be sure to write your name on the diagram so I know who is who. For everyone else, I'll have a standard PMR tape available for you at our next session. Ron, can you please do me a favor and give everyone a copy of this handout with the cue words and cue phrases on it. [Ron eagerly stands up, takes the handouts, and begins to distribute them. While he is doing this, I speak to Jeff.]

SH: Jeff, for the PMR tape, let me know if you want me to skip the tensing of the muscles on your left side and just have you focus on relaxing them. I understand that some people with cerebral palsy can have their muscles go into spasms.

Jeff (CP1): No, that's all right. I'm not spastic. . . . I don't mean that the way it might sound.

SH: Not a problem. I know what you mean. So I'll just make you a standard PMR tape?

Jeff (CP1): Yeah, that would be great.

*[Ron has finished distributing the handouts with the cue words and cue phrases. I check that Sally has a braille copy and that Rita has an enlarged copy.]*

SH: Thanks everybody for your participation. From today you should have an understanding of some of the mental factors that can affect performance. You should also be able to practice abdominal breathing and have a basic understanding of what PMR is. If nothing else, you may have learned when everyone's birthdays are. [Laughter.] As a reminder, in the next few days I would like each of you to select a couple of cue words or phrases that you think might be useful to you. I'd also like you to practice abdominal breathing every day, even if only for two minutes. While you're busy doing that, I'll make each of you a PMR tape to have ready for you when I see you in two weeks. If anyone has any questions, I'll stick around for a few minutes. Thanks again! [Some light applause and a few comments of thanks.]

I have learned that at the end of a group session it is better to stay back and answer questions than it is to require people to voice their questions in front of the group. First, some individuals may be more inclined to ask questions when they are not speaking in front of others. Second, they already sat through a session. Some people may want to leave. Their fidgeting can be distracting and could lead me to rush my responses. Because I will be having future sessions with the same group, if I get asked a question that I think is relevant to everyone, I will write down the issue and include that information in the next session.

> Don't hold up all people after a group session; do make yourself available for questions, however.

# So What?

This chapter has three main purposes:

- Familiarize the reader with issues relevant to athletes with disabilities
- Convey practical considerations for working with athletes with different disabilities
- Share some techniques that can be useful in introductory group sessions

The main points for each of these purposes are summarized as follows.

### Issues Relevant to Athletes With Disabilities

- How people react to their own disabilities depends on the nature of the disabilities, the age of onset, and the visibility of the disabilities.
- Disabilities can be progressive or nonprogressive.
- The physical state of some disabilities can be influenced or changed during physical activity.
- Accessibility can be an ongoing issue for training venues, parking, and transportation.
- Basic aspects of training may require exceptional effort, reliance on others, or both.
- Disabilities can affect thermoregulation and injury awareness.
- Most disabilities require individuals to consider associated conditions.
- Some sports for athletes with disabilities will have unique equipment and rules.
- Most athletes competing in disability sports must deal with the classification process.
- Athletes with disabilities experience different forms of prejudice.
- Although feeling in control is important for all athletes, it may be a bigger issue for athletes with disabilities.

### Practical Considerations

- Practitioners may need to deal with issues of personal discomfort.
- Practitioners should use the athletes as sources of information on themselves.
- Group sessions with this population often involve athletes with different disabilities from a variety of sports.
- Athletes who are blind obviously will not respond to nonverbal cues (unless tactile).
- Alternatives may need to be arranged for individuals who cannot write or have difficulty communicating verbally.
- Athletes who are blind or visually impaired may need enlargements, braille copies, or recorded versions of printed material.
- Visually impaired athletes need to be informed if furniture is rearranged.
- Carers or companions already have established roles. They are not employed to assist the sport psychologist.
- Practitioners should speak directly to athletes, even if someone else is serving the role of interpreter.
- Some athletes with physical disabilities may need help transferring to or from the floor.
- Athletes with cerebral palsy may get muscle spasms when tensing muscles.
- Progressive muscular relaxation tapes can be tailor-made to exclude body parts that athletes either cannot control or do not have, but some athletes will prefer the standard tape.

### Group Session Techniques

- Be aware of what the athletes have done or experienced before your session. When they arrive at your session, will they be bored, tired, or full of energy?

- Consider the arrangement of furniture. Change it if needed.
- Try to get everyone participating within the first few minutes of a session. It gets them involved and gives you an opportunity to get to know them.
- Be alert for athletes who may be feeling bored or excluded or who are easily distracted.
- Use a mixture of techniques (e.g., individual work, pair or small-group work, large-group activities).
- Allow athletes to help each other. You do not need to do everything or provide all the answers.
- Remember that if athletes do not understand something, it probably has more to do with how you presented the information than their ability to comprehend.
- If you are having individuals or small groups complete activities, have ideas ready concerning what the early finishers can do while waiting for the others.
- Instead of forcing the value of sport psychology down their throats, create an activity that allows athletes to realize the potential value of the field on their own.
- Consider different ways of breaking the larger group into smaller groups or pairs.
- Build energizers or breaks into your sessions.
- Base future sessions on the needs of the group. Do not automatically use the same format and content for every group.
- Realize that you do not need to talk the entire time.
- Use examples that are relevant to the people in the group.
- Provide a brief summary of the session at the end, and specify what, if anything, you want them to do before the next session.

# Conclusion

Many of the principles of good coaching (Kidman & Hanrahan, 2004) and competent sport psychology service apply when working with the athletes in this chapter, but being a sport psychologist for athletes with disabilities presents other challenges to the practitioner. One of the first places to start is with your own prejudices and stereotypes. Subtle, and not so subtle, prejudices can interfere with communication and the rapport-building process. Also, the sport psychologist is a learner, too, and allowing the athletes to be educators, admitting gaps in knowledge, and establishing a collaborative environment can go far to help ensure a good experience for all involved. I cannot emphasize enough the importance of doing your homework. As with any new sport, getting some background on the sport and the types of people involved will ease the transition into becoming a working member of the team. I hope this chapter serves as a place to begin to get some of that homework done.

## CHAPTER 13

# Straight Guys Working With Gay Guys

## *Homophobia and Sport Psychology Service Delivery*

Matthew P. Martens, PhD, and Michael Mobley, PhD

Imagine a life where a person cannot reveal who he is to many of his closest friends and respected mentors. Almost every day he has to lie to these people or at least hide information that he may not want them to know. He often hears jokes, phrases, and other remarks that, unbeknownst to the person making the statements, degrade him as a person. He is involved in activities that are often thought of as the ideal of masculinity, yet if his sexual preferences were discovered, he would be stereotyped as being among the most feminine of men. Unfortunately, these are some of the problems experienced by many gay male athletes.

The purpose of this chapter is to explore, from a sport psychology perspective, issues involved in working with gay male athletes. The chapter begins with a review of the literature regarding the experiences of gay male athletes. Next, current research and theory from clinical and counseling psychology are integrated, helping sport psychology professionals conceptualize the issues involved when working with this population. Finally, to address many of the issues we raise in this chapter, we conclude with a vignette of a sport psychology graduate trainee working with his supervisor.

# Gay Male Athletes in Sport

The experience of gay male athletes in sport has not been studied extensively by sport psychologists. Most of the published literature in this area involves anecdotal information or books published in the popular press (e.g., Barret, 1993; Bean & Bull, 2003; Kopay & Young, 2001; Pallone & Steinberg, 1990; Rotella & Murray, 1991). A review of this existing popular and professional literature does reveal several recurring themes regarding the experience of gay male athletes in sport:

- Contempt for gay males in general
- Sport as a definition of traditional masculinity
- Fear of being "outed"
- Issues related to HIV and AIDS

## Contempt for Gay Males

The most overt issue that gay male athletes often have to deal with is an open contempt for homosexuality among teammates, coaches, and opponents. Whereas most coaches and players today refrain from using overt racial or ethnic slurs, using terms such as *faggot* or *queer* (among others) to describe poor or "soft" performances is relatively common. Kopay and Young (2001) claim that coaches and players often feel an obligation to joke about homosexuality, playing into the myth of sport as a macho, heterosexual endeavor. Griffin (1994) expresses similar views, also interpreting the use of homophobic language as a way to maintain the traditional association between heterosexuality and athletics. Pronger (1990) states that athletes often use antigay humor as a shield against any hint of homosexuality, hypothesizing that this tactic may be a way male athletes deal with being nude around each other in locker rooms.

In an interview with David Kopay, a former National Football League running back who came out as a gay man at the end of his playing career in 1975, Barret (1993) discovered a more institutional reason for contempt of gay male athletes. Sport is big business in many societies, and in this interview, Kopay claims that it is important for professional sports to maintain a certain image for financial purposes. For whatever the reason, whether it be a shield against homosexuality, a desire to maintain a certain masculine image, or a business decision, contempt for gay men still seems to be a prevalent issue in the world of sport.

Unfortunately, some research indicates that contempt for lesbians and gay men may invade the practice of sport psychology. Rotella and Murray (1991) quote two sport psychologists regarding issues related to working with gay and lesbian athletes. One stated, "I cannot afford to be understanding and helpful to homosexual athletes. As a sport psychologist it would destroy my reputation and credibility with too many other athletes" (p. 355), whereas another is quoted as saying,

> As a sport psychologist I will work with homosexual athletes, but I must admit I do believe that there was a traumatic experience or a family or parent–child problem early in life causing the condition. I feel I must help them straighten out their sexual preferences. (p. 356)

One can imagine the experience a gay male athlete might have should he work with either of these individuals and reveal his sexual orientation. Although these views are probably not representative of most professionals involved in the practice of sport psychology, Rotella and Murray's work clearly indicates some have contempt for gay men and women, whether conscious and explicit or unconscious and implicit. Such attitudes may exist among many people who consider themselves sport psychologists.

For most gay and lesbian athletes, their sexual orientation is not the issue. The issue lies in the homophobia of the sporting world and the very real fears of reduced playing time, being kicked off the team, harassment, and physical violence if their sexual orientation were to be publicly known. Heterosexism and the cult of hypermasculinity pervade sport, and these worldviews can make the arena of sport an inimical place for people whose sexual preferences do not fit these rigid models of human love and interaction.

## Sport As a Definition of Traditional Masculinity

Related to the issue of contempt for gay men is the idea of sport as a definitive endeavor of traditional masculinity (Barret, 1993; Griffin, 1994; Kopay & Young, 2001). According to Griffin (1994, 1998), sport for men serves several functions in maintaining stereotypical gender roles, including the reinforcement of traditional conceptions of masculinity and the promotion of heterosexuality. Sport accomplishes these purposes by teaching boys and young men to suppress traditional feminine characteristics such as compassion or tenderness. Male athletes who do display these characteristics may be labeled with some of the derogatory names for gay men referred to earlier. More important, Griffin states that by embodying the traditional masculine image, male athletes promote an assumption of heterosexuality. This assumption allows male-to-male expression of emotions, such as intimacy and love, in a safe, nonsexual manner. For example, it is common to see male athletes physically embrace each other and affectionately slap backsides after successful athletic performances, behaviors that might be considered a sign of homosexuality outside of the sporting context.

Barret (1993) claims that it would be difficult for many people to accept the idea of a gay male athlete being engaged in the close physical contact commonplace in many sports without simultaneously experiencing sexual feelings. Thus, perhaps to maintain their own comfort level, many people simply assume that most male athletes (with the possible exception of "feminine" sports such as figure skating) are heterosexual. Pronger (1990) interprets this image in terms of health, stating that the image of athletes is quintessentially healthy, whereas gay men have been traditionally viewed as either physically or morally impure. This unhealthy image of gay men may be even more prevalent today, given the association of HIV and AIDS with the gay male community. In sum, according to the aforementioned authors, sport supports a traditional definition of masculinity—a definition that does not include gay males—in numerous ways.

## Fear of Being Outed

One of the biggest fears that gay male athletes may face on a day-to-day basis is that their teammates or coaches will discover their sexual orientation. Rotella and Murray (1991) note that athletes might fear physical retribution should their true identity be discovered. Regarding one of his interviews with gay male athletes, Pronger (1990) reports that one athlete believed coming out as a gay man would certainly end his career. Anecdotal evidence from gay men who played professional sports provides some support for this belief. David Kopay, a former National Football League running back, and Dave Pallone, a former Major League Baseball umpire, both stated that it was necessary for them to live double lives (as an umpire, Pallone would not technically be considered an athlete, but his experience may be representative of what it is like to be a gay male within organized sport). Had their sexual orientation been discovered, both men believed that their careers would have come to an end (Kopay & Young, 2001; Pallone & Steinberg, 1990). Kopay did not publicly announce that he was gay until after his playing career was over, but he was unable to obtain a job coaching or in any other professional capacity within the sport. Pallone stated that he acknowledged being gay to the commissioner of Major League

Baseball; as a result, his contract was not renewed. Pallone was also under investigation at the time for involvement in a sex scandal with underage boys (he was exonerated of all charges), which may have contributed to his dismissal. Nevertheless, both men believed that their sexuality was the factor that either caused them to be removed from professional sport or did not allow them to remain.

Given the contempt for gay men within organized sport, as well as the association between sport and "traditional" masculinity, it would not be surprising to discover that most gay male athletes have a strong fear of being discovered, or outed. On a positive note, attitudes within some sports may be changing. For example, in the hypermasculine world of Australian rugby, Ian Roberts, a star player by any standards, came out to his teammates and found a great deal of support and caring (Freeman, 1997). If such a reception can happen to a gay male rugby player in Australia, then there has to be hope for the rest of gay men in sport.

## Issues Related to HIV and AIDS

Another issue that gay male athletes may need to deal with is misconceptions related to HIV and AIDS. Despite continued improvements in educating the public about HIV and AIDS, the misconception of AIDS as a "gay disease" still exists. This misconception may be even more prevalent in the world of sport. For example, Dworkin and Wachs (1998) conducted a textual analysis of articles from the *Los Angeles Times*, *New York Times*, and *Washington Post* regarding the HIV-positive announcements of two heterosexual male athletes (Magic Johnson and Tommy Morrison) and one gay male athlete (Greg Louganis). Results indicate that the articles on the heterosexual athletes often conveyed a sense of shock and surprise at the announcement, tried to explain exactly how the athletes contracted HIV, and reaffirmed the athletes' heterosexuality. Such details were absent from articles about the gay athlete, insinuating that his life in and of itself explained his contraction of the virus. Although few published studies have examined athletes' views toward HIV and AIDS in the world of sport (Butki, Andersen, & Heyman, 1996), it is likely that many people in sport still consider AIDS a "gay disease," increasing the contempt for and fear of gay male athletes.

# What Kind of Issues Might Emerge?

Sport psychologists working with gay male athletes are asked to deal with virtually all of the same issues and problems (e.g., anxiety, team cohesion, performance failure) that face heterosexual male athletes. It is possible, however, that when working with gay athletes, sport psychologists will need to address several concerns that are specific to this population. These concerns include performance issues related to their sexual orientation and personal concerns related to the coming out process. In addition, sport psychologists may be forced to deal with their own prejudices and homophobic feelings when working with gay male athletes.

## Performance Issues Related to Sexual Orientation

It is certainly feasible to assume that, especially in team sports, gay male athletes may have to deal with performance issues that are in some way directly related to their sexual orientation. Given the issues that gay athletes must deal with in the world of sport (e.g., contempt for gays, fear of being outed), it is difficult to believe that these factors in some way do not affect athletic performance. For example, it may be difficult for a gay male athlete whose teammates often use antigay slurs, or who is often thinking about ways to make sure he is not outed, to focus on his athletic performance. Thus, sport psychologists may be called on to help gay male athletes cope with these issues and distractions in order to help them improve their athletic performance. In these situations, sport psychologists need to be careful about professional boundaries, especially in terms of competence issues. A gay male athlete trying to understand his sexuality, perhaps as part of the coming out process, is different from a gay male athlete trying to cope with external factors related to his sexuality that might be harming his athletic performance. In the latter situation, sport psychologists should use traditional sport psychology interventions (e.g., imagery and relaxation, teaching coping skills) to help the athlete improve his performance. The former situation of identity issues, however, involves a different set of psychological processes and thus may require a different set of professional competencies and suitable interventions.

> Performance in sport is often anxiety provoking enough without the constant added background fears associated with issues of outing and retribution.

## The Coming Out Process

For many gay males, coming to terms with their sexuality, and perhaps defining themselves publicly as gay men, is a difficult and complex process (Cass, 1996; Fukuyama & Ferguson, 2000; Newman & Muzzonigro, 1993; Reynolds & Hanjorgiris, 2000; Tremble, Schneider, & Appathurai, 1989; Troiden, 1989). It is possible that a gay male athlete working with a sport psychologist, an individual he has learned to trust and confide in, may seek to use that person to facilitate his own understanding of the coming out process. This use of services may raise professional issues for the sport psychologist, most notably in the areas of competence and ethical issues.

Sport psychologists who are either American Psychological Association (APA) or Association for the Advancement of Applied Sport Psychology (AAASP) members are ethically bound to practice within their areas of competence or to refer the client elsewhere (American Psychological Association, 1992, 1993; Association for the Advancement of Applied Sport Psychology, 1995). For sport psychologists trained only in performance enhancement issues, helping a client deal with sexual orientation issues and coming out processes may be outside their areas of competence. In such cases, the sport psychologist should either refer the athlete to a professional who is qualified to work with such issues or seek extensive consultation and supervision. The latter route is probably preferable because it may take a gay male athlete several months to confide in a sport psychologist about sexual orientation. Referring out at that point may be perceived (unconsciously) as a rejection, another message that being gay is not something "normal." If sport psychologists have the proper professional training, then they should work with athletes who are struggling with sexual orientation issues.

## Dealing With One's Own Homophobia

*Homophobia* has been traditionally defined as "the fear of homosexuals" (Herek, 1986a, 1986b; MacDonald, 1976), but the term may encompass a host of other reactions such as anger, pity, and disgust (Andersen, Butki, & Heyman, 1997). Although it is clear that homophobia is widespread within the general population (Herek, 1984, 1991; Weinberg, 1972), research also suggests that homophobia is common among both athletes and helping professionals. At least one study (Andersen et al., 1997) indicates that college athletes exhibit greater general homophobia, greater homophobia toward gay men, and more negative perceptions of gay men than do nonathletes. The most substantial finding in this study was clearly in the area of negative perceptions of gay men, indicating that perhaps this factor is the most salient in driving one's homophobia. Many people have no conscious contact or acute awareness of being in social, personal, or familiar relationships with men who self-identify as gay. Thus, within many individual circles of friends and family, nearly all men are assumed to be heterosexual, allowing gay men to be viewed in a negative manner. Research also indicates that mental health professionals often exhibit heterosexist biases in their work, which may result in dissatisfaction on the part of gay clients (Garnets, Hancock, Cochran, Goodchilds, & Peplau, 1991; Liddle, 1996; Rudolf, 1988, 1990). A sport psychologist working with a gay athlete may not only have to help the client deal with homophobia from his teammates but may also have to address his or her own homophobia and heterosexist attitudes to work effectively with the client.

When confronted with the presence of a gay male athlete, many teammates, coaches, and sport psychologists react with homophobic responses. Many of these straight men in a male-oriented sport feel fear, anxiety, uncertainty, and perhaps even hostile or aggressive emotions toward an openly identified gay athlete. Male teammates may fear that they have been or will become the object of affection of the gay athlete. It is not uncommon to hear men say, as has been voraciously stated in the policy debates about military gays, "I don't want any of them looking or staring at me in the locker room," "What if he decides to touch me or attack me one night?" or "It's not normal or moral for men to be with other men, so I don't want him around me, on my team." Indeed, such reactions may be more intense for those heterosexually identified male athletes who once considered themselves close friends of the newly identified gay male athlete. These men may become particularly self-conscious and suspicious of the possibility of being labeled "queer" themselves as a result of assumed guilt by association.

> Coaches often face substantial external and internal pressures and prejudices regarding having gay athletes on their teams.

In regard to male coaches, the recognition of having a gay athlete on the team potentially raises both internalized and externalized concerns. Internalized concerns may include self-doubt about the coach's ability to recruit and select "proper" athletes; a personal sense of failure as a man in serving as a role model for this gay male athlete; discomfort in being a father figure to this athlete; and perceived lack of control of the athlete's behavior, even though sexual orientation is a personal facet of one's identity expression.

Many coaches pride themselves on being able to scout out high-performance, high-intensity, and high-quality male athletes who will be strong team members and potential leaders among the group. After discovering an athlete is gay, a coach may assume that such a sexual orientation will jeopardize the athlete's ability to perform and to establish successful cohesive interactions with teammates. Sometimes coaches target and nurture future team members several years before the athletes join their teams, thereby establishing role-model relationships. Knowing that some male athletes highly regard their coaches, these men may feel as though they somehow "failed" gay athletes. The previously self-acknowledged father figure becomes distant, unaccepting, potentially demanding, and angry. Perhaps the coach will direct gay male athletes to seek help for their "problems" and forbid discussion of their personal lives within the context of the team. Such dialogues between coaches and gay male athletes may occur under the auspices of helping gay athletes survive and keep their positions on the team, an effort to strike the most amicable compromise of coexistence. Otherwise, the coach might seriously consider separating the athletes from the team. This directive, in essence, encourages gay athletes to return to the closet, perhaps even dictating such an action.

It is clear from such prejudicial reactions among male teammates and coaches that sport psychologists may be called on to help gay athletes deal with homophobic reactions. It is important, however, that sport psychologists examine any personal homophobic responses and issues. Most men within the sports organizational structure, including sport psychologists, have been socialized and raised in a culture that promotes homophobic tendencies. Thus, although many sport psychologists may not be overtly homophobic, some degree of internalized homophobia most likely exists. Such homophobic reactions will need to be addressed and overcome by male teammates, coaches, and sport psychologists. In the profession of sport psychology, there are many lesbian academics and practitioners who are "out." The same cannot be said for gay male sport psychologists. This difference between lesbian and gay sport psychologists indicates that homophobia is alive and well in the profession, at least when it comes to gay men. Gay sport psychologists are probably wary of coming out for many of the same reasons athletes are reluctant to let their sexual orientations be known.

Given the very few openly gay athletes in sport and its deeply rooted assumed masculinity and heterosexuality, gay male athletes have learned over the years that it is safest to remain "in the closet" about their true sexual orientation. People in most cultures implicitly make the assumption that people are heterosexual. Being gay, even among enlightened individuals, is often considered outside of the norm. This presumed sexual orientation status of heterosexuality among the general population and within many powerful institutions (such as education, the military, churches, politics, and sport) strongly suggests that many people are cloaked with vestiges of heterosexist notions and perspectives.

> Remaining in the closet may be perceived as the safest and most judicious choice given the often hostile atmosphere in the sporting world.

Homophobic or heterosexist views may be fostered as a result of highly biased cultural socialization processes, beginning with our initial unconscious experiences early in life. As babies, many of us were "tagged" based on our gender. Many new parents continue to dress newborn girls in pinks and yellows and newborn boys in blues and browns. One of the authors (Michael) remembers, and has numerous photos of, his 10-month-younger female sibling and himself—his blue suits and her frilly pink dresses and bonnets, particularly on Easter Sunday. These practices reflect behaviors rooted in perceived appropriate sex- and gender-role identification. Indeed, given the physical beauty and yet sometimes indistinguishable sex of newborn babies, parents seek to cloak babies in attire that will tell others this is little "Johnny" or little "LaShanda" to avoid any misidentification of the baby's biological sex. It is probably rare for parents to dress babies in nonstereotyped colors or even unisex clothing as a conscious act to avoid heterosexism and sexism.

From lessons about male and female children's clothing, we move to lessons about sex- and gender-appropriate verbal and nonverbal behaviors. Boys are expected to be little men: strong, aggressive, assertive, brave, tough, rough heroes. Girls are expected to be little women: dainty, submissive, fearful, tearful, gentle heroines in need of strong boys or men to rescue them (Bem, 1993; Eagly & Steffen, 1984; Hoffman & Hurst, 1990). When boys and girls display behavior outside these prescribed roles and expected norms, they may be perceived and labeled as being "sissies" or "tomboys," respectively. The intersection of sexual orientation roles and expected norms surfaces within the consciousness of parents, family members, and peers. In the context of sports, "tomboy" girls are acceptable depending on the sport and the degree of masculine gender-role identification perceived. On the other hand, "sissy" boys are generally unacceptable within many sports regardless of the degree of feminine gender-role identification perceived.

## Summary

A void certainly exists regarding the experiences of gay male athletes in the field of sport psychology. Much of the information we present was gleaned from anecdotal experiences reported in the popular press and some accounts in the sport sociology literature. Given this lack of information, much of our presentation is somewhat speculative in nature. Nonetheless, we believe that existing evidence does indicate problems with homophobia in the world of sport. Most athletes, coaches, and sport psychologists have in some way been exposed to—and to some degree have internalized—homophobic attitudes and beliefs. To effectively help gay male athletes, sport psychologists need to recognize the issues related to homophobia in sport, particularly how they affect the development and performance of gay male athletes. Just as important, sport psychologists need to become aware of their own homophobia and how homophobic reactions may emerge in work with gay male athletes. The following vignette highlights some of these issues and shows how effective supervision can help a sport psychology trainee conduct beneficial work with a gay male athlete.

# Coming Out, Backing Off, and Coming Back: The Story of Matt and Bryan

The following scenario involves a third-year graduate student in sport psychology beginning a session with his supervisor. The graduate student is a white male coming from a position of privilege in the dominant culture (Matt, first author), and the supervisor is an African American male, intimately familiar with racism and prejudice (Michael, second author).

> Matt:   Well, there is a certain issue I would like to begin with.
>
> Michael:   Sure, Matt. What's that?

At this point, I (Matt) am probably experiencing some degree of anxiety about even addressing an issue related to sexual orientation. I believe I have never personally known anyone who is gay, and I am uncomfortable with the topic. I do not view myself as homophobic, but when pressed would indicate that I am not particularly comfortable around gay men.

> Matt:   Remember I told you last week I started seeing a new client? Bryan, the baseball player.
>
> Michael:   Yeah, he's a new recruit. First baseman.
>
> Matt:   Well, something happened during our session this week that was pretty interesting. In the course of discussing team-related issues, Bryan mentioned to me that he is gay and that he has difficulty being with his teammates in social situations because they are not aware of his sexual orientation.
>
> Michael:   What was your reaction to Bryan's coming out to you?
>
> Matt:   I could not believe it! I mean, he just dropped it into the conversation as if it's no big deal.

Here I provide some initial indication that I may have problems dealing with gay men. I am clearly providing evidence that I assume homosexuality to be deviant in some way (e.g., the "no big deal" comment). To me, being gay is clearly a "big deal," which indicates that I, in some way, have a problem with the issue.

> Michael:   So you thought he "dropped" that information into your session? Before he told you this information, what were you talking about?

Here, Michael is trying to determine the context in which the athlete self-disclosed to me. Michael recognizes that this was an important step for the athlete to take, trusting me enough to come out to him. He also recognizes that I am unaware of the importance of this process and am instead too upset by my own fears and anxieties.

> Matt:   Well, we were talking about how he's been having trouble connecting with his teammates and that he really doesn't feel part of the team yet. In turn, he thinks this is hurting his performance. It was at this point that he said to me, "Well, I might as well tell you this. . . . Some of these problems I'm facing are

due to the fact I'm gay." When he said this I was completely floored, and it really threw me off for the rest of the session.

Such a revelation may be difficult initially for any sport psychology professional to deal with. It can be a challenge any time a client raises a personal issue that may be affecting his or her performance. This difficulty may be exacerbated when it involves sexual orientation because of factors such as internalized homophobia (as is the case in this scenario).

> Athlete revelations can initially be difficult to handle. Having steps in place is helpful.

> Michael: Sounds as if you were expecting to stay on the performance issue and adjusting to new teammates in your session with Bryan.
>
> Matt: Yeah! Anyway, this gay issue became our focus for the session, and I'm having some problems with it.
>
> Michael: What specific problems are you having, Matt?

What Michael is now doing is trying to get me to focus on my own feelings and concerns. In effect, he is trying to shift the focus of the supervision session from the client (Bryan) to the trainee (me). Earlier we mentioned the importance of dealing with one's own homophobia in effectively working with gay male athletes. Here Michael is trying to help me take that first step.

> Matt: Bryan says that he gets along well with his teammates, but he is getting nervous because they constantly tease him about not showing any interest in women. I think that this really gets to him, and it's affecting his performance. He's been really struggling at the plate this year, and his defense has been poor.

This deflection from my issues back to Bryan's performance issues might be a common response by a supervisee to such a query from the supervisor. I do not want to talk about my own gay issues; I want to focus on Bryan. Dealing with the client is much safer for me, so I avoid (perhaps unconsciously) Michael's direct question and try to guide the session back to a focus on Bryan. There is a bit of double avoidance in that I bring Bryan's issue back to a performance one. The message from me here is "I really don't want to talk in any depth about gay stuff."

> Michael: Matt, I hear you focusing on Bryan's performance and teammate concerns. Yet you stated that you had problems with it. Matt, what is it that you are having problems with?

> Sport psychologists need to address their own homophobic concerns before they can effectively work with gay athletes.

Michael gently confronts my avoidance. He in effect does not let me off the hook and again directly asks me to focus on myself. An alternative approach might have been to be a bit more gentle, asking permission to question me about my problems with this particular issue. In this situation, given that I already have a professional relationship with a gay client, Michael believes it is important to directly address the issue and get my feelings out in the open.

> Matt: Well, I feel for the guy and think he is having real problems, but I have no idea how to help him. First of all, as an ex–baseball player, I know that most of the people I played with would not have accepted a gay teammate, so I don't know if coming out to his teammates is an option. I suppose I would not even know how to help him come out if he wanted to. I mean, I can only imagine what this guy would have to go through in the locker room and on team trips.
>
> Michael: So, Matt, the difficulty for you at this time is whether or not you might be able to help Bryan come out, especially when you think about your own teammates during your playing days. As a baseball player, what messages did you hear about gay athletes while you were playing? And whom did those messages come from?

In this exchange, I display a hint of empathy for Bryan ("I can only imagine what this guy would have to go through"). This simpatico is important because it indicates that I am at least trying to relate to my client. I probably still have a lot of unconscious homophobia going on, however. My statement that "he is having real problems" may refer to teammate issues but also may indicate that being gay, for me, is seen as a problem. On the plus side, I have personal experience in the sport Bryan plays, which Michael then uses to further supervision. He continues to focus on me, asking me to relay personal experiences of my own playing days. By doing so, Michael is providing me the opportunity to feel, if only slightly, what it may be like for Bryan on his team.

> Matt: I don't know. . . . I suppose it was more the lingo. It was common to hear terms such as *faggot* or *queer* used among my teammates, especially when trying to put someone down. People would say things like, "Oh, that guy definitely is a fag," or "He likes to get it from behind," and other derogatory things like that. I can't imagine being gay and trying to sit through stuff like that, and I can't imagine people who talk like that ever accepting a gay teammate.
>
> Michael: That's a good issue to consider, Matt, how teammates might accept Bryan. But what about you? Are you able to accept Bryan's coming out? His being gay?

Michael first reinforces my concern about Bryan's teammates and then makes the transition from the teammates' feelings to my feelings. In this situation, in an attempt to enhance my empathy for Bryan, Michael might have considered asking me what I think Bryan is feeling if and when gay slurs are used. Again, though, Michael chooses to move directly into my personal feelings.

> Matt: I suppose I really don't know where I stand on the whole gay issue. I mean, I know that it is wrong to assault or discriminate against people because they're gay, but I've never really been around one of them.

My statement may be indicative of the feelings of many sport psychology trainees. One would hope that almost all sport psychology students (and professionals) would recognize that blatant discrimination and persecution of gays is wrong. Having such beliefs, however, does not preclude one from being homophobic. Because of societal and cultural factors, homophobia, to varying degrees, is probably internalized in most people. Thus, although I would not actively discriminate against a gay man, I might not feel comfortable interacting with him, which is clearly a problem given my current professional situation. My language is also indicative of my personal development and experiences—"I've never really been around one of them." Gay men are "them." They are not really real for me. In sport sociology parlance, they are the "other." As long as gay men and lesbians are "others" for sport psychologists, the potential threats of prejudice, stereotyping, and discrimination in the quality of service delivered are substantial. It would probably not be difficult for me to be on a team of straight men and to have a feeling of being part of "us." The interesting question is what prevents me from believing that Bryan is also one of us?

> Michael: Matt, this is real cool that you are being open and honest with me about your concerns in working with Bryan. In our society, despite the increased focus on gays and lesbians in the media, many people think they do not know how to deal with gay guys. Sounds as if you are aware of issues of hate crimes directed toward gay men. Is this true?
>
> Matt: Yeah, of course. That kid who was killed in Wyoming a few years ago received a ton of press, and I've seen a lot of other news reports and specials on various TV shows. I think that it's terrible, but I'm not sure how it directly relates to this situation.

When examining this issue, it is important for supervisors to reinforce the willingness of the supervisee to explore his or her personal feelings. Sexual orientation and preference are difficult for many people to talk about, so it is important that trainees be rewarded for taking such a risk.

> Michael:  Well, a minute ago you mentioned that you know it's wrong to assault or discriminate against gays. Are you concerned that someone might assault or discriminate against Bryan? Perhaps his teammates? The coach?
>
> Matt:  I don't know. It really would depend on his teammates. Hell, maybe they're completely fine with it. I doubt it, but you never know. But I guess that's not the real issue right now, although it seems to be there in the back of my mind.

Michael is trying to build on the fact that I think it is wrong to harm people because of their sexual preferences. This thinking may be a good starting point for me to begin changing my attitudes toward gay men, although I do not yet realize it. Michael wants to see if I am concerned about my client's safety, but that does not seem to be a particular concern of mine. Therefore, he decides to address another, more personal, issue.

> It is important that sport psychology trainees be reinforced for taking personal risks in exploring sexual orientation and getting in touch with their self-awareness and sensitivity about gay men, in general, and the potential relevant issues gay athletes may face.

> Michael:  Do you feel as though you yourself might act in a discriminatory manner in working with Bryan?
>
> Matt:  I don't know. I certainly wouldn't on purpose. But I'm afraid I might say something wrong or offend him in some way. I know I'm going to be uncomfortable with him, and I can't see how that would not affect my work.

What happens here is important because I allow myself to admit the possibility exists that I might harm or offend my client, which demonstrates some degree of insight. I am able to get to this point because my supervisor guided me in addressing my personal thoughts and feelings about the situation and did not allow me to deflect all of his queries toward the client. At this point, it would probably be beneficial for my supervisor to reinforce me for my willingness to admit I may not be qualified to work with this client.

> Michael:  I want to point something out to you, Matt. Since you began talking about Bryan's disclosure of his sexual orientation to you, are you aware that you have not used his name since that time? You have consistently referred to Bryan as "the guy," "him," "one of them," and "he," each of these being a rather nonpersonal, distancing reference to Bryan. As I listen to you, this seems unusual to me knowing that last week you consistently used Bryan's name. In fact, last week, I recall you stating that in many ways Bryan reminded you of yourself during your days as a baseball player. The two of you had similar stats and styles, and both of you are even lefties. Let's talk about how you are experiencing Bryan differently this week.

Michael again guides the session toward my personal feelings, this time by pointing out how I have distanced myself interpersonally from Bryan. He points out the way I have been describing Bryan in the session, then uses such evidence to get to the heart of the matter—how do I now view Bryan?

> Matt:  It's different because now I know that he's gay. It causes me to think and perceive him in a different way.
>
> Michael:  How is it different now? Matt, I understand that now you know Bryan is a gay man, but Bryan's personal self-disclosure about his sexual orientation suggests to me that he trusts you. What about that revelation makes him different?
>
> Matt:  Well, it's just that after Bryan came out to me, I spent the rest of the session thinking to myself, *"Man, this is weird—here I am having an important conversation with a gay guy."* I don't know if being gay is a choice or biological or what,

but I do know that I was not very comfortable in this situation with Bryan. So I don't know what I should do.

Michael: Well, you made an important first step—you chose to address the issue with me. To me, this indicates that you are willing to explore this issue and recognize that it is important. It is hard when we are confronted with situations that, for whatever reason, make us uncomfortable. I'm not angry with you or blaming you for being uncomfortable around gay men. Right now that is just part of who you are. To be an effective counselor or sport psychologist, though, I think it is important that you further explore your feelings toward homosexuality. Is this something you are willing to do?

Michael reinforces my decision to address my concerns in supervision, and he lets me know that he thinks I am capable of dealing with issues related to sexual orientation and homophobia. He makes it clear, however, that I must continue to work on my homophobia if I want to develop further as a sport psychologist. Should I choose not to do so, then Michael would be forced to take some type of action to ensure that I do not continue working with this particular client or any gay client.

Matt: Yes, I suppose so.

Michael: Good. I think it might be a good idea for you to even discuss with Bryan your reactions to his coming out to you. I know that in psychology we often talk about self-disclosure as a big no-no, but that opinion is being challenged by many in the field, and sometimes I think it can actually be therapeutic for the client. [Pause.] Actually, I have an idea. I imagine that your next session with Bryan might be somewhat anxiety provoking, given what we have talked about today. Why don't we role-play the next counseling session? I'll be Bryan, you be you, and we'll try to find the right words for you. How does that sound?

Matt: Well, I'm not real big on role-plays, but I'll give it a shot.

Michael: Okay, I'm Bryan. Let's say I just walked in, said hello, and sat down.

Matt: All right. . . . Ahhh, Bryan, I want to talk to you about something you said last week that made me uncomfortable.

Michael: [As himself.] Wait a second—stop right there. I don't think it would be a good idea to start things off with Bryan like that. Your tone is basically accusatory, as if Bryan did something to upset you, and you need to address it with him. Remember, Bryan didn't do anything wrong. Why don't you try first asking him if it would be okay to discuss something, and then phrase your statement in a more gentle way.

Matt: Okay. . . . Bryan, I was wondering if we could start this week by discussing something that came up last week.

Michael: [As Bryan.] Sure. What's up?

Matt: Well, I wanted to let you know that your coming out to me last week kind of shocked me—it was something I really wasn't ready for. I want to let you know that I've never worked with a gay athlete before and really have never known any gay men on a personal level. But, I'm still willing to work with you.

Michael: [As himself.] Now, that's much better. First, you asked for permission to discuss the issue, and you acknowledged some of your own limitations to your client, which I think is the ethical thing to do. The phrase "I'm still willing to work with you" bothers me, however, because it is still somewhat accusatory. It's almost as if you're saying, "I'll work with you even though something is wrong with you." I think that instead maybe you need to acknowledge your willingness to work with him, but you will have to do extra work to get up to speed on the needs of gay men, and gay athletes in particular. Does that make sense?

Matt: Yeah, I see where you're going. How about this: Umm, even though I've never worked with a gay athlete before, I've discussed the issue in supervision, and my supervisor is willing to work closely with me to help me better understand some of the issues that gay men have to face. At the same time, I might actually need you to educate me about the things you're going through from a gay athlete's perspective.

Michael: [As Bryan.] No problem. To be honest, I didn't really make a conscious decision to come out to you—it just sort of happened. But I appreciate your being honest with me. . . . [As himself.] Okay, how did that feel?

Matt: It's really hard to say, even though I know we're just role-playing. It's almost embarrassing to have to admit your weaknesses in terms of being uncomfortable working with someone.

Michael: Matt, one of the most important aspects of being a good counselor is being aware of and willing to address your own limitations, both professionally and personally. Your willingness to do so, I believe, is an important step in your professional development.

> As a sport psychologist, being willing to admit and address your limitations is all part of professional training and personal growth.

Fast forward one week, after my next session with Bryan.

Michael: How did the session with Bryan go?

Matt: Well, I was waiting in my office and had the plan of what I wanted to say. When Bryan arrived, however, I got very nervous, and we ended up small-talking for about 10 minutes or so. Finally, I just kind of blurted it out, but I did manage to phrase it in the way we talked about last week. I was really worried about how he would take it, but I was pleasantly surprised.

Michael: In what way?

Matt: He just kind of smiled and said that he wasn't surprised I was a little freaked out because, in retrospect, he realized he didn't really prepare me for his disclosure. But he said he trusted me and felt comfortable with me, and he wanted me to know the whole truth about him and his situation. He said he figured he owed it to me. Imagine that.

Michael: What do you mean, "imagine that"?

Matt: I mean, here I am totally freaked out about a gay man's self-disclosure and wishing that it never happened, but on his end he thought he almost had to do it. Kind of ironic.

Michael: Yes, I suppose so. So how did the rest of the session go?

Matt: Actually, it went pretty well. We didn't discuss anything related to his being gay specifically—mostly performance stuff. But I suppose that I was thinking a bit more broadly about his issues, now that I know a little more about him.

Michael: Matt, I think you really took an important step with Bryan. By being honest and by self-disclosing some of your feelings to him, I believe you've created a healthier environment for you two to work in. Could you imagine if you did not say anything to him or refused to address the sexual orientation issue? It would be like the proverbial elephant in the room that no one wants to talk about. Further, it also sounds as if you're thinking about Bryan's problems more holistically, which will only help your work together. I'm proud of you—I know how hard it must have been for you to bring this up, even after our role-play. [Pause.] Now, tell me a little more about what's going on with Bryan.

## Reaction to the Case Example

One aspect of this case that should be relatively clear is that the focus of supervision was not on client issues but on the supervisee's personal issues. Although such a style may not be the norm in sport psychology, it may be necessary when dealing with sensitive issues such as racism, sexism, and homophobia. For me to work effectively with Bryan, I needed to first understand my feelings toward gay men, then address those feelings as best as I possibly could. In our supervision session, Michael chose to help me work on this via a role-play. He reacted to me as my client might, thereby allowing me to see how the language I was choosing (perhaps unconsciously) was reflecting my feelings of discomfort. Michael helped me reframe my comments toward Bryan, which allowed Bryan and me to discuss the true issue—my own discomfort regarding his coming out.

It is important to note that my reactions to Bryan might be similar to those of many, if not most, sport psychology trainees placed in the same situation. In this case, Bryan's acknowledgment of being gay was the first time I had someone come out to me. This event was a shocker for me, and I appeared to lose my professional identity role as a sport psychologist trainee. Like many males, I operate under the assumption of heterosexuality. Thus, gay men are considered outside of the norm or deviant in some way. My personal identity as an individual surfaced as I struggled to understand how I might be able to assist Bryan. Such a reaction is not uncommon for graduate trainees who have no direct experience, knowledge, or contact with someone coming out to them. It is possible that I would find myself being concerned that Bryan was going to come on to me or was in some way romantically interested in me, which caused me to feel even more uncomfortable. All these factors resulted in my experiencing emotional and cognitive disruption. Michael was able to recognize this disruption in me, however, and he effectively addressed my difficulties in supervision.

Despite my initial responses, which indicated at least some degree of covert homophobia, a crucial aspect of the supervision session was that I chose to share Bryan's coming out. I could have easily chosen to ignore the issue by not addressing it with Michael.

> Supervisors need to create safe, trusting environments for their supervisees, just as sport psychologists need to create safe environments for their clients.

This willingness on my part to discuss an uncomfortable topic highlights the importance of fostering a supervisory environment where trainees are encouraged to share their concerns. In other words, just as counselors need to create safe environments for their clients, so do supervisors for their trainees. "Safe environment" does not mean that the supervisor does not challenge, confront, or direct the trainee but that such actions on the part of the supervisor occur in a supportive and empathetic atmosphere. In the case example, Michael demonstrated the safety of our supervisory environment by first trying to be supportive and considerate of my own interpersonal and personal concerns while also carefully helping me to begin developing a more human perspective on Bryan and how I might be able to work with him.

A second issue related to this example has to do with ethics. Although Michael and I were able to work through my difficulties, this may not be the case all of the time. If I was not willing to address my homophobia and take active steps to work on my feelings, then it would probably be unethical for me to work with this client (something that I verbalized). To continue working with Bryan under these conditions would probably fall under the principle of doing no harm, with me putting myself at risk for harming the client. Even if I closely worked with my supervisor on this issue, Michael might need to consider referring the client (perhaps to himself) until I had a better handle on my feelings toward gay men.

There are several ways in which I could further myself in becoming competent to work with gay clients. One way would be to work closely with Michael in supervision, devoting time to my own personal growth and development. A second would be to educate myself by reading on my own (the references cited earlier involving the anecdotal stories of various athletes might be a good starting point). A third option would be to engage in personal counseling to address my homophobic beliefs and attitudes. This last option would provide me the opportunity to explore my attitudes and feelings in a nonjudgmental, safe situation.

# Conclusion

It is fairly clear that, based on the little information that exists, it is often difficult for gay male athletes to exist in most sport environments. Societal homophobia and misperceptions regarding HIV and AIDS will probably cause many gay athletes to continue living double lives, choosing to not reveal who they truly are to teammates and coaches. Further, gay athletes will in all likelihood experience most of the same performance issues as their straight counterparts. When gay athletes turn to sport psychologists to help them deal with both performance concerns and personal issues related to their sexual orientation, sport psychologists must be able to handle such concerns in a professional, ethical manner. Some first steps in this area include educating oneself about the experiences of gay men in sport and recognizing how difficult it may be to live as a gay athlete in an environment that is heterosexist and homophobic.

One of the most important steps in working competently with gay athletes involves working through one's own internalized homophobia. The case example illustrates how a trainee might begin such a process, but professionals with little or no experience working with gay athletes may need to undergo such training themselves. As society becomes more accepting of sexual orientations that are considered alternative, the possibility exists that more gay athletes will be comfortable revealing their own sexual identities. Should this be the case, then it is possible that these individuals will be in need of support, both from personal and performance-related perspectives. Sport psychologists have the unique opportunity to be a part of this process within their professional roles and thus need to consider ways in which they can enhance their competencies in dealing with such issues.

# The Elephant in the Locker Room

## Opening the Dialogue About Sexual Orientation on Women's Sports Teams

Heather Barber, PhD, and Vikki Krane, PhD

Homophobia, and its cousin homonegativism, has been referred to as the "silence so loud, it screams" (Nelson, 1991). We call it the elephant in the locker room. Everyone knows it is there, but few in applied sport psychology are talking openly about it. So why open the dialogue? Why do we need to talk about sexual orientation in sport settings? For one, it is a performance issue. Issues surrounding sexual orientation influence, for example, team climate, individual focus, and coach credibility. Second, sport psychologists often focus on creating positive sport experiences and building character through sport. How can we encourage positive sporting behaviors and positive team climates if we are not creating dialogue about this pervasive issue? Griffin (1998) argues that sexual orientation affects all women in sport. If this statement is true, and we believe it is, an effort must be made by coaches, athletes, and sport psychologists to create environments where athletic achievement and positive social growth can occur.

In this chapter, we focus on sexual orientation, homonegativism, and heterosexism in women's sport. We approach nonheterosexuality broadly; some female athletes may self-identify as lesbian, bisexual, or transgendered (LBT). Thus, rather than consider lesbian, bisexual, and transgendered as a single identity, we either acknowledge all identities (i.e., use the term LBT) or use the term nonheterosexual to include all possible identities other than heterosexual. Using inclusive language when referring to nonheterosexual athletes and coaches opens the door for further dialogue and intervention. We also realize the importance of considering broader social and cultural forces when examining issues related to sexual orientation in women's sport. Thus, we include homonegativism and heterosexism when addressing issues related to nonheterosexuality.

Heterosexism is "an ideological system that denies, denigrates, and stigmatizes any nonheterosexual form of behavior, identity, relationship, or community" (Herek, 1992, p. 89). It is the belief that heterosexuality is the only acceptable mode of social interactions and sexuality. Through language, behaviors, values, and culture, heterosexist persons reinforce the belief that nonheterosexuality is wrong or unacceptable. "Homonegativism is negative stereotypes, prejudice, and discrimination against nonheterosexuals" (Krane, 1997, p. 145). Heterosexist environments fuel homonegativism. Heterosexism and homonegativism are an inherent part of women's sport (Barber & Krane, 1999; Lenskyj, 1992). They are endemic in men's sport as well, but this chapter focuses on women's teams. These issues may compromise team interactions, athlete and coach satisfaction, and athletic performances by creating distraction, increasing stress, and causing team conflict (Krane, 1995, 1997).

Sport psychologists have unique relationships with members of sport environments. Their positions may provide opportunities to challenge the heterosexist norms in women's sport. The culture of sport has interesting dynamics among the key players. A hierarchy exists in which administrators govern coaches, and coaches govern athletes. Generally, there are lines of communication between administrators and coaches and between athletes and coaches. Sport psychology consultants may be able to communicate and intervene with each group: administrators, coaches, and athletes. In the quest to create a climate of excellence, sport psychologists may also address social issues, such as heterosexism, that could otherwise increase stress and impede athletic success.

In the remainder of this chapter, we discuss specific strategies for working with LBT athletes and coaches. Our approach is consistent with our training as applied sport psychology consultants through exercise science programs. Performance and positive team interactions are our primary focus. We do not address clinical personal issues that may arise when considering sexual orientation in sport. As an aside, there is a false dichotomy in the sport psychology literature that divides issues into either performance concerns or personal concerns. How one performs in sport usually has deep personal significance tied to core issues of worth, identity, acceptance, and family dynamics (among other things). So how are performance issues different from personal issues? The truth of the matter is that they are not. And what could be more personal than sexual orientation?

We believe that applied interventions should be grounded in theory. Theory should provide a framework for understanding the issues at hand, as well as direct implications for sport psychology intervention. To this end, and consistent with our previous research (Krane & Barber, 2003), social identity (SI) perspective guides our discussion of the issues and interventions surrounding female nonheterosexual athletes and coaches.

SI perspective (Turner & Reynolds, 2001) is a broad social psychological framework that includes social identity and social categorization theories. This perspective covers a range of group processes, including the development of social identities, collective behaviors, and minority experiences, and their influences on self- and collective (e.g., team) esteem. SI perspective also explains the emergence of stereotypes and discrimination that often surround LBT athletes. Further, it proposes mechanisms for social change—by minimizing negative stereotypes and discrimination and by enhancing self- and collective esteem. SI perspective provides an ideal foundation for our discussion about creating a positive climate for both heterosexual and nonheterosexual female athletes. What follows includes an overview of the theory and three consultation scenarios dealing with sexual orientation and individual athletes, athletic teams, and coaches. Finally, we provide additional strategies, consistent with SI perspective, that sport psychology consultants may employ.

# Social Identity Perspective

Social identity (SI) perspective centers on the processes of self- and social categorization and social comparison. Social categorization provides the backdrop for alignment with a social identity. That is, people first make sense of their social worlds; they categorize groups of individuals into clusters based on similarities among people within the group and differences among people across groups (Deschamps & Devos, 1998). For example, we notice social groups based on athletes and nonathletes or on heterosexuals and nonheterosexuals. This process of social categorization allows people to organize and make sense of their social worlds.

People also notice the group(s) with which they have the most in common, and then they self-categorize as a member of that group. Upon self-categorization, persons learn the norms, values, and behaviors that are held in common among group members (Hogg & McGarty, 1990). Individual group members then adopt these values and behaviors, and socialization into the group results in their behaviors becoming more normative. This process explains how team norms, such as a strong emphasis on academic success, inside language or jokes, or involvement in community service, are perpetuated. New team members join a team because they share these values, or they are socialized to value these team characteristics.

Social comparison occurs as group members compare their social group with other social groups. This process is biased in favor of one's own group and against other groups. Therefore, individuals tend to perceive members within a group as similar and members across groups as different (Abrams & Hogg, 1990). Favorable comparison of one's social group enhances self- and collective esteem. Consequently, people are motivated to be biased in favor of their social group. Social comparison results in the development of stereotypes and may result in discrimination. Although stereotypes are not always negative, some stereotypes may perpetuate negative beliefs about some groups. As people support the status of their group, they may become prejudiced and discriminatory against other groups perceived as inferior (Abrams & Hogg, 1988). According to SI perspective, as long as group members are able to identify strengths of their group, self-esteem and collective esteem will be sustained. Collective esteem is the "feeling of self-worth derived from the collective aspects of the self, or group membership" (Krane, Barber, & McClung, 2002, p. 28). It is the pride people feel related to their group membership and social identity (Crocker & Luhtanen, 1990; Luhtanen & Crocker, 1992). Ideally, group membership results in positive social identity, self-esteem, collective esteem, and group status.

Social categorization and social comparison underlie heterosexism and homonegativism in sport. The process of social comparison helps us understand why negative stereotypes and discrimination against LBT females in sport emerge and are perpetuated. Theoretically, as people in the heterosexual social group, for example, compare themselves with members of the nonheterosexual social group in sport, they stress the differences between the groups. It becomes apparent to most females in sport that heterosexual females have higher status than females perceived as nonheterosexual (Kolnes, 1995; Krane, 2001; Pirinen, 1997). Further, differing sexual orientations become the primary focus rather than what female athletes have in common. As heterosexuals protect their privileged social status, some group members will denigrate lesbians and distance themselves from the LBT social group (Barber & Krane, 1999; Krane, 1997).

Through social categorization, women in sport are socialized to accept group norms and behaviors. In sport, these social norms and values often include heterosexist attitudes and behaviors that have become accepted and normalized (Barber & Krane, 1999;

Krane, 1997). Common heterosexist examples of group norm acceptance include sport administrators who do not punish coaches for enacting antilesbian or antigay policies, professional sports organizations that require athletes to adhere to a "morals clause" that is used to discriminate against lesbians, acceptance of antigay or antilesbian jokes in the athletic environment, and the labeling of "nonfeminine" athletes as lesbian.

As explained by SI perspective, social groups are in constant conflict for social status, power, and resources (Abrams & Hogg, 1990). Members of majority, or dominant, social groups attempt to sustain the social status quo to maintain their high power and the self- and collective esteem of group members. Members of lower-status social groups will engage in one of several possible strategies to enhance group status or self-esteem; these include social mobility and social change strategies. In social mobility strategy, a person attempts to become, or be perceived as, a member of a higher-status social group (Hinkle, Taylor, Fox-Cardamone, & Ely, 1998). Members of the LBT social group, realizing the higher social status afforded heterosexual women in sport, may pass as members of the dominant group (i.e., use social mobility) (Griffin, 1998; Krane, 1997; Krane & Barber, in press). For example, through "passing," LBT athletes reinforce the perception that they are heterosexual. This impression perpetuates the norm and promotes the value of concealing their lesbian identity (Barber & Krane, 1999). Ultimately, social mobility strategy perpetuates the status quo, or the perception that heterosexuals in sport deserve greater social status and power.

Social change strategies are attempts to gain status and power for the social group as a whole. SI perspective contains two social change strategies: social creativity and social competition. Social creativity involves attempting to change the status of a devalued social group by highlighting characteristics of the group that are valued by dominant social groups. Baird (2001) found that in social settings, female rugby players would dress and behave in a feminine manner to enhance how nonplayers perceived the athletes. The result of this action was greater social acceptability of the ruggers. Through social competition, members of a low-status social group attempt to increase their group's status and power, often through political means. For example, the U.S. women's national soccer team boycotted a major competition to protest that their salaries were substantially lower than those received by the men's team (Silver, 2001). This action led to more equitable compensation for the women. Krane and colleagues (2002) reveal that participation in the Gay Games encourages social creativity and social change strategies. For example, through social creativity, the athletes emphasize their athletic ability to increase acceptance by the dominant athletic social group. These athletes also apply social change strategies in their increased intentions to come out and to become more political after the Gay Games.

Attempts to change the status quo in women's sport and minimize heterosexism occur through social change strategies. Yet as Barber and Krane (1999) found through interviews with lesbian athletes and coaches in college sports, few lesbians feel empowered to employ overt strategies to confront discrimination. Their concerns about potential retribution (e.g., loss of job, loss of position on team) minimize the perception that they can safely challenge homonegativism. Examples of social change in sport do exist, however. In women's sport, social creativity occurs as nonheterosexual athletes demonstrate their skillfulness so that the dominant athletic social group accepts them. Athletes may become valued for their athletic prowess, regardless of their sexual orientation. Social competition occurs as coaches, administrators, sport psychologists, and athletes in traditional sport settings demand that discrimination be addressed and minimized. As these people expose and challenge homonegative incidents, changes in the environment may take place that create more equity among heterosexual and nonheterosexual women in sport. Throughout the remainder of this chapter, we describe a variety of strategies to minimize homonegativism and heterosexism. Social change strategies will be our primary focus toward creating positive climates for LBT athletes and coaches.

Before we can address more specific social change strategies in women's sport, it is important to consider the full complexity of this issue. SI perspective provides a framework for understanding social norms of female nonheterosexuals in sport; it also proposes that individuals have personal identities as well as multiple social identities. Sport psychologists should be aware that each individual athlete has a unique personality that will interact with social group characteristics. Further, athletes identify with multiple social groups. For example, it may be difficult for a Japanese American lesbian athlete to separate her experiences as a Japanese person from those as a female from those as a lesbian. As we address issues specific to female nonheterosexuals, we must remember that all people in sport face multiple social influences. Often athletes with multiple devalued identities have difficulty distinguishing marginal treatment due to their ethnicity, religion, race, or sexual orientation.

> There are many social influences on an athlete—ethnicity, religion, race, and sexual orientation, to name a few.

When creating positive environments for female nonheterosexuals in sport, social change strategies need to include administrators, coaches, athletes, and in some cases, parents and families of athletes. Additionally, we focus in this chapter on adolescent and college-age athletes. This is a critical developmental period during which many LBT females first self-categorize as nonheterosexuals. They may have been members of a team while self-categorized as heterosexual athletes, yet later they may shift social groups and learn new norms. Needless to say, this may be a confusing time for these people. To help these women develop and maintain high self-esteem, it is important to create positive and accepting environments. Coming out in a supportive environment greatly reduces the stress of this developmental period (Garnets & Kimmel, 1991). Sport environments with supportive climates for all members will assist athletes struggling with their new identities. Conversely, homonegative environments will make this adjustment more difficult and often create stressful situations for LBT athletes (Krane, 1997).

Homonegativism hurts heterosexual athletes as well. Kauer (2002) found that lesbian and heterosexual female college athletes identified common negative stereotypes about female athletes. All the women described negative implications of being labeled lesbian, regardless of whether it was true or not. Ultimately, decreasing discrimination toward LBT athletes will benefit all females in sport because a large source of social stress will be alleviated. This positive atmosphere will result in a stronger focus on being successful sportswomen.

SI perspective provides a framework for guiding practice in sport psychology settings involving sexual orientation. In this section, we use three case studies to illustrate the dialogue between individuals or teams and sport psychology consultants, as well as strategies that can facilitate self-esteem, collective esteem, and subsequent improvements in performance and team climate on women's sports teams. The strategies are introduced through three brief scenarios pertaining to sexual orientation, heterosexism, and homonegativism in women's sport. Each scenario includes the dialogue between the athlete or athletes, coach, and sport psychologist. This dialogue is typically emotionally charged and often characterized by false starts as individuals slowly gain confidence in the consultant and their own ability to express themselves. These examples illustrate common interactions we have had with athletes regarding sexual orientation issues on their teams.

## My Teammates Are So Negative: Jasmine's Story

Jasmine is a senior starting member of her college soccer team. Recently, she seems to lack focus and concentration during practices and appears to have withdrawn socially from her teammates. Her performances in practice and matches also are suffering. The coach suggests that Jasmine consult with a sport psychologist. In the first session with me (Vikki), she breaks down and laments that she just cannot put up with the team environment anymore.

Jasmine: My teammates are rude. They rarely speak to me, and when they do, they give me grief.

Vikki Krane
(VK): Do you know why they are acting that way?

Jasmine: They just are. I don't know why.

At this point, Jasmine does not reveal the details of the situation. Most likely, she is not ready, nor does she feel comfortable enough to discuss this sensitive issue. Knowing the team and some senior players, I have a hunch about what the issue may be. Still, I want to be careful not to push Jasmine to talk about it, or she is likely to pull away. Also, I may be wrong. Over time, however, as Jasmine becomes more comfortable, she does open up to me.

VK: How have things been going this week, Jasmine?

Jasmine: My teammates are being their usual selves.

VK: Have you tried to talk with them about why they are acting this way?

Jasmine: It won't matter. They think some of us are gay, and they've been acting really homophobic. They've always said bad stuff about gays, usually about people on other teams they assumed were gay. Now they are focusing their mean comments on us. [Pause.] It used to be only in the locker room or off the field. Now they are saying things on the field in practice. "Let's play dyke keep-away," or "We don't want any gays on the team."

It is important for me to let Jasmine talk without interruption. There may be long pauses as she explains her perceptions. My being understanding and not pushing Jasmine should allow her to feel more comfortable discussing the situation. Note that Jasmine has not actually come out to me; she has said only that her teammates perceive her as a lesbian. Because I cannot forget that initial discomfort and fear related to coming out to someone, I am very careful in choosing my language. I am careful that I do not label Jasmine or make her uncomfortable. I let her set the pace as to what details she is comfortable sharing. After Jasmine describes the problem, then I may offer suggestions.

VK: Have you thought about talking with your coach about this?

Jasmine: Like that would do much good; she's as homophobic as the rest of them.

VK: How do you know that?

Jasmine: I can just tell. She's never stopped players from making comments about people on other teams. I think she's even heard recent comments in practice but just won't deal with it. I'm so sick of this; I'm ready to just quit. [Pause.]

VK: What would you like to see happen?

Jasmine: I don't know.

VK: What would help you feel better?

Jasmine: If it all stopped.

VK: Let's think about this. How can we get it to stop?

Jasmine: [Sigh.] I just want to play soccer and not deal with all this.

VK: Unfortunately, Jasmine, one choice is to do nothing, in which case you'll continue to be miserable, or our second choice is to come up with some sort of plan.

Jasmine: I suppose I could try to ignore them.

VK: That's a start.

Although I want to offer suggestions, it is important to let Jasmine continue to take the lead in the discussion and explore her options. Consistent with my training in performance psychology, I focus our discussion on the sport environment. I also believe it is difficult to resolve team problems without the involvement of the coach or team leaders. If Jasmine felt comfortable talking with the team captains, we could develop a strategy beginning with Jasmine talking to them. As that is not the situation in this case, I suggest we approach her coach.

> Although it's tempting to offer your clients suggestions, be patient and let them come up with their own options.

> VK: How would you feel if I talked with your coach?
>
> Jasmine: No! She'll probably kick me off the team.
>
> VK: How about if I mention I've heard rumors that some team members believe someone on the team is a lesbian, and some players are being rude to her. I won't mention anyone's name, especially yours.

Here, I am trying to open lines of communication with the coach so that this issue can be addressed. By promising confidentiality, I attempt to reduce Jasmine's fears.

When people perceive their environments as intolerant, they are unlikely to willingly reveal a nonheterosexual identity. Jasmine says her teammates are not accepting of LBTs, and they treat athletes perceived as lesbian derogatorily. She further suggests that she does not trust the coach with this information. Because the coach determines playing status and her future role and involvement on the team, Jasmine is not willing to risk her current team standing. Sustaining the perception that she is heterosexual is an example of what Dworkin and Gutierrez (1989) consider survival tactics. Jasmine considers coming out to the coach, or even approaching the coach with this issue, as dangerous. A major focus of an intervention with this team is to create a more positive and accepting climate. The coach undoubtedly will be a key feature in sustaining climate changes and therefore must see the potential benefits to this environmental change to commit to this process. No doubt, obtaining this change in climate is not an easy task. There are, however, a variety of strategies that can be helpful.

Unfortunately, a strong social norm in women's sport is that female athletes present a feminine and heterosexual image (Hargreaves, 1993; Kolnes, 1995; Krane, 2001; Pirinen, 1997; Wright & Clarke, 1999). Athletes are socialized to believe that nonheterosexuals are bad for women's sport, that they will reduce the already marginalized status of female athletes. Consistent with SI perspective, some athletes and coaches are prejudiced against athletes perceived as nonheterosexual in order to maintain their privileged status as feminine females in sport. This process partially explains why heterosexism prevails, and is even nurtured, on some teams. One way to counter this norm is to create a new team norm—one accepting of diversity (not an easy task).

Ideally, creating a climate of acceptance should begin at the first team meeting of the season. A foundation for accepting individual differences, no matter what their basis, paves the way for accepting responses in light of future revelations. In other words, a social norm of acceptance and supportiveness needs to be nurtured. Including sexual orientation is a reasonable extension of many teams' acceptance policies. Many coaches already emphasize to their teams the importance of working with athletes who differ in race, ethnicity, or religion. In the current sport climate, few coaches will ignore the use of racial epithets by their players. Yet sexual vilification occurs when athletes call each other gay when referring to dumb actions or when athletes refer to their muscular competitors as amazons or dykes. One step in social change is creating an atmosphere where homonegative statements and actions are not accepted.

In my conversation with Jasmine's coach, Michelle, I first see if the coach will admit that she's noticed a problem.

> VK: I'd like to talk about something that several athletes have mentioned to me. It seems some of the athletes are not getting along. Have you noticed anything unusual?

Michelle: Not really—but now that you mention it, a couple of the players don't seem to mingle with the others as much as they used to. But working with young females, I see that often. What else have you heard?

Not knowing the coach well, I am not sure how she will react to "the lesbian issue." Being direct will let her know the problems on the team. In some cases, it also can close the door to further access to the team. Believing it is important for the coach to know what is going on with her team, I continue the conversation.

VK: It seems that some rumors are going around that one or more of the players are lesbian. Other players are reacting to that rumor by guessing who may be lesbian and treating those athletes poorly. Whether or not the rumor is true, we may want to address the cohesion or communication problems.

Here, I have taken a middle-of-the-road approach in which I state the problem (homonegativism) but also provide the coach the option to address it directly or to focus on team dynamics issues. Although I prefer to be much more direct with coaches, knowing the homonegative climate of women's sport compels me to let the coach focus the potential intervention. Even coaches who are open minded may be hesitant to discuss issues related to homonegativism with their teams. In this case, the coach wants to confront the homonegative climate.

Michelle: OK, I agree, we need to make some changes; what should I do?
VK: This doesn't have to be difficult. Some relatively simple changes will help. Let me give you an example. The other day I heard a player tell another, "I can't believe you did that . . . that is so gay!" You could respond by telling the athletes that you don't like that kind of talk, or that you'd rather they not use the word *gay* like that. You don't need to make a big deal about it, but simply state that their language is unacceptable.

Consistently reinforcing the unacceptability of heterosexism and homonegativism in a team environment serves multiple purposes. First, it creates a standard for all athletes. It also is the first step in creating a more positive climate for LBT athletes. When coaches regard homonegative comments as unacceptable, it sends a strong message, especially to the LBT athletes. LBT athletes are particularly tuned into coach reactions or nonreactions to homonegative or heterosexist statements. Simply knowing that the coach is supportive and aware of issues related to LBTs will reduce their stress and fear.

Unfortunately, in the case of this team, a negative climate already exists. Hence, new team standards (i.e., norms) need to be established. The sport psychology consultant and coaches can employ social creativity strategies to encourage acceptance of diverse teammates. First, the team needs to identify their salient identity (e.g., the Tigers varsity soccer team). Most likely, all players already identify as a team member. Now let them define the characteristics of their group. In a group discussion, athletes could brainstorm all the important qualities of team members.

VK: Okay, ladies, I want you to identify the strengths of the team and what makes our team work together to be successful. Let's start by brainstorming a list of our strengths.
Angela: We are committed to working hard.
Cathy: We work well together on the field.
Stephanie: And we communicate well in games.
Nia: We are mentally tough.
VK: Good. What other qualities make you a good team?

[Players continue to respond.]

This discussion could be taken a step further: Members can identify the strengths each individual brings to the team. For example, the team can sit in a circle and each player states the strengths of the person next to her.

Further discussion should address whether various social identities (e.g., race, religion, academic major) affect these characteristics.

> VK: Think about all the characteristics you have listed: committed, physically skilled, mentally tough. Also, think about the qualities each individual player brings to the team. Consider how the differences among players affect the team. In other words, does it matter what race, religion, ethnicity, or sexual orientation players are?

Ultimately, consultants want athletes to realize that the characteristics that make a strong and committed team cross social group boundaries. Notice that sexual orientation is overtly inserted into the discussion as another social category that does not detract from important group norms and goals.

> VK: Now, to be blunt, I've heard rumors that some players are lesbian. It really doesn't matter if this is true or not, but let's consider the possibility. Does it matter if anyone on the team is gay?
>
> Cathy: Well, yeah, it would mess up everything we just mentioned.
>
> VK: How?
>
> Cathy: I don't know. [Pause.] It would just get in the way of team cohesion.
>
> VK: How or why would it get in the way?
>
> Amy: It's just not right to be that way.
>
> Cathy: Gays are different. They just won't fit in.
>
> VK: If a teammate is a lesbian, does that have to get in the way?
>
> Shauna: Maybe not. If they don't bring it on the field, then it's not a problem.
>
> VK: What do you mean by bring it on the field?
>
> Shauna: You know, talk about it, act gay.
>
> Stephanie: We don't want to hear things about their girlfriends and stuff like that.
>
> VK: Do the rest of you talk about your boyfriends and whom you date?
>
> Cathy: Yeah, but that's different.
>
> VK: How?
>
> Amy: It's normal.
>
> VK: It may be normal for some people to be attracted to women. Do you like all of the guys your teammates date?
>
> Amy: No, but this isn't the same.
>
> VK: OK, in what ways isn't it the same?

Note how I keep the dialogue flowing yet gently challenge the players' opinions. Consultants also can ask players how their lives would be different if they were lesbian or how they would feel if they were asked not to talk about their social lives while in a team setting. Often athletes focus on their own feelings about nonheterosexuality but do not think about what it is like for someone to have to hide that she is LBT.

> You can challenge your athletes' opinions while also keeping the dialogue flowing.

Role-playing is another technique that could help team members consider how LBT athletes may feel. For example, a player could be asked to have a discussion with another player describing a date with her new boyfriend. Player 1 would describe him and her excitement about going out with him. Then ask that same player to reenact the same scene, only this time, do it from the perspective of a lesbian. Have the player consider what types of information she may or may not reveal to her teammate. Then role-play the situation. This exercise allows teammates to take the perspective of their lesbian teammates and may help them understand the situation from a different vantage point.

Another method for opening discussion related to sexual orientation is to ask the soccer players to identify factors that will detract from team success (Crace & Hardy, 1997).

| | |
|---|---|
| VK: | Okay, let's try something else. What are some factors that will interfere with team success? |
| Jasmine: | Not communicating on the field. |
| Nia: | Selfish playing—being ball hogs. |
| Hannah: | In general, not getting along. |
| VK: | Do any of these things occur on the team? And how can we overcome these problems? |

Putting athletes in pairs or small groups may facilitate their candid responses. Athletes also can be asked to develop strategies to overcome these potential problems. In essence, the athletes will suggest strategies that can be used to counter the team's homonegative atmosphere. Although the athletes most likely will not directly address sexual orientation in their strategies, the sport psychology consultant, after bringing the team together as a whole, should focus the discussion on acceptance of various social identities, including LBT athletes. Ultimately, the discussion should focus on applying the team-developed strategies (e.g., only say positive things to one another, leave personal problems off the field, focus on team goals) to create a positive climate for all athletes on the team. This intervention is very similar to the values-based team-building intervention Crace and Hardy (1997) describe.

| | |
|---|---|
| VK: | Think about our discussion about accepting all teammates, regardless of race, religion, ethnicity, or sexual orientation. How can the strategies you just described relate to that? |

In this case study, sexual orientation is an issue creating divisions within the team. This division created an environment that could not support positive team dynamics and good team performance when individual group members were being denigrated. The preceding interactions focus on encouraging discussion and enhancing understanding about LBT athletes. We also stress the development of strategies to encourage team cohesion, inclusive of LBT teammates. The ultimate goal is creating a sense of respect and appreciation in which all team members feel valued. This type of climate will foster personal growth, positive team communication, and possibly better team performance.

# I Know I'm the Only One: Susan's Story

Susan is a sophomore member of a Division I swimming team. The head coach heavily recruited her during her last two years of high school. During the current year, she has self-identified as a lesbian and has begun her first relationship with a woman. The woman she is seeing is a student at the university but not a member of her team. Susan has chosen to keep this relationship private. In fact, she has not told a soul. She believes that she is the only lesbian on the team and that she can successfully control (i.e., manage who knows) this information. She is unsure how her teammates and coach will accept her if they should find out about her sexual orientation.

Susan took an undergraduate sport psychology class from me (Heather). I also do some consulting in the university athletic program and have a private consulting practice. After a recent swim meet, Susan stops by my office and leans in the doorway.

Susan: Just wanted to pop in to say thanks for coming to the meet the other day. We don't draw big crowds, so we appreciate every body in the stands.

Heather Barber
(HB): I enjoyed it. I like being able to get out of the office and watch our students compete. It's definitely more fun than grading papers.

Susan: I can imagine.

HB: I know it's early, but how does the season look?

Susan: I think we're in an okay place. We've got a . . . unique . . . group this year. It'll be interesting to see if we can hold it together.

HB: What's different this year?

At this point, Susan begins to inch her way into my office, and I offer her a seat. This initial interaction can make or break the consultation. Athletes often sidle into my office without an agenda—which reflects the approach–avoidance nature of initially seeking consultation. Typically, athletes like Susan have not consciously decided to talk with anyone. When the opportunity presents itself, however, they may feel okay about taking the consultant up on it and may later acknowledge that they were hoping the conversation would occur. It also is important for the consultant to anticipate where the conversation is going. These encounters are not scheduled appointments, and if there really is no time to talk, do not shortchange the athlete. Say that you would like to sit down and talk, but you have a class or appointment coming up. Susan continues the conversation as she's getting situated.

Susan: I'm not sure if the team is different or if it's just me. [Long pause.] I still love swimming, I think. It's just that . . . that . . . I don't feel as close to the team as I did last year. They're [her teammates] nice . . . they're not jerks or anything. I know it's not them. In fact, they ask me to do things after practice, and I put them off. They probably think I'm whacked.

HB: It seems as if you are worried about your teammates and what they think of you. What's different? Can you tell me what you're worried about?

Susan: [Pauses, takes a deep breath, and blurts out.] I think I'm a lesbian. . . . At least I'm seeing a woman, so I guess that makes me one, and I know I'm the only one on the team.

This disclosure may come quickly in the conversation, as in this case, or may take a couple of conversations before enough comfort and trust is developed in the consultant. Susan has chosen not to share this information with anyone to date and carefully scrutinizes my response. Although we cannot anticipate this type of disclosure, consultants should be prepared for it and reinforce the athlete's willingness to share this information.

HB: I'm honored you felt comfortable sharing that information with me. It certainly came tumbling out. I hope that it feels good to talk.

Susan: I guess I've been holding it in, so it just flew out of my mouth. I haven't told anyone. I've been worried. . . . I just don't know how the team is going to deal with this. I don't even know how my coach will handle this. I spend half my day playing out the most awful scenarios in my head.

HB: We'll get to those in a minute, Susan, but first, how are you doing?

Initial conversations about sexual orientation can take many forms. In this scenario, I make sure that the focus is first and foremost on the well-being of the athlete and secondarily on performance and team dynamics issues.

Susan: I'm doing fine most of the time. When I'm with Ann, she's my girlfriend, I'm great. It all seems easy. Getting through the rest of life isn't quite as smooth.

I know my schoolwork and swimming are suffering. I'm working hard, but it isn't coming as easily as it used to.

HB: Why do you think that is? You say you're working hard.

Susan: I guess I'm just distracted, and I haven't been sleeping great. . . . I worry that some of my friends on the team know.

HB: What worries you about their knowing of your relationship with Ann?

Susan: Well, part of it's just that I don't know how they'll take it. It's not as if they say bad things, it's just that we don't talk about being gay. Maybe I'm just being paranoid. . . . Maybe they don't know anything, and I should just let it be. But what if they do? If I screw this up, things will never be the same. We have a great team, and I don't want to be the one who messes it up.

HB: Susan, you seem to be placing a lot of pressure on yourself to resolve this. What would feel most comfortable to you right now?

Susan: I'm thinking that maybe I should talk to Coach, but I'm not sure what to say. I have no idea how she'll handle this.

HB: Talking to Kate [the coach] might help relieve some of your uncertainty. What do you want to come out of a meeting with Kate?

Susan: I guess I want to know what she thinks I should do. Some part of me thinks she'll be okay, but it would be awful if she isn't.

HB: There is that risk, but I would trust your gut. If you're nervous about talking with Kate, we could do some role-playing, and you could practice what you want to say. Another possibility is for the three of us to sit down. I would mostly be there for moral support, and we would still practice ahead of time, but that's another option.

Susan: Would you do that for me?

HB: Not for you but with you.

Susan and I continue to talk about how we might approach the coach; we decide that I should call the coach and make an appointment to chat. When I call Kate, she is concerned that something is terribly wrong. I assure her that Susan just wants to talk over some personal issues. Kate says, "I'm glad Susan stopped in to talk with you. She hasn't been herself lately. I've tried to check in with her, but she assures me everything's fine."

The meeting with Kate is scheduled for the coach's office. It is a little uncomfortable at first. Having talked over the process beforehand with me, Susan begins the exchange and manages to carry the conversation. In this case, I am there primarily in a supportive role and to guide the discussion if need be. Allowing the athlete to initiate and steer the dialogue is critical. After all, it is her meeting.

Susan: Thanks for meeting with us. I know you've been worried about me, and I do appreciate your concern. There's been a lot going on lately, and I haven't done a great job handling it all. [Susan turns to me.] This is a lot harder than when we practiced it. [She sighs.] Okay, Coach, you can't help unless you know what's going on. I'm seeing someone, but it's not what you think . . . she's a woman.

Kate: Susan, first let me say, you're right, I have been worried about you, and I'm glad you talked with Heather, and I'm glad you wanted to talk with me. Obviously, this is your personal life, but parts of our lives spill into swimming all the time. Relationships are important, and they deserve our energy. We claim we're a family; that has to mean something. I will try to support you in your decisions. What do you want to do, and how can I help?

Susan: Thanks, Coach. I wasn't sure how this was going to go. Getting by you is a big step, but my big concern is that I don't want to hurt the team. At some point, they'll find out. I have to decide how that should happen. Heather and I have talked over some possible options if you are game. One would be to just keep on going, and if somebody asks, I'll deal with it. Second would be to begin to slowly let people in. I could start with Judy and Megan [teammates and friends] and go from there. The third option would be to have a team meeting to talk about it. I don't think I'm ready for that, and I'm not sure that it wouldn't make an issue of something that isn't there.

Kate: I want you to find a place where you're comfortable. At present, you're not having fun, and it shows in and out of the pool. I can't make decisions for you, but I can maybe help make life easier.

The meeting finishes with Susan saying she will think through the possibilities and talk with Kate and me in the coming days. After the meeting, Kate calls me to check in; she wants to know where I think things stand and see what she can do.

Kate: I learned a lot today, Heather. I never realized that my swimmers might be scared to come talk with me, but obviously Susan was worried about my reaction. I never say anything bad about gays or lesbians. I'm not sure why she was so worried.

HB: You know, often when people don't actually hear something positive come out of someone's mouth, then they assume that the person, like a lot of society, doesn't have a positive opinion of lesbians or gay men. Maybe it was because Susan had just never heard you say positive stuff that she figured you might have a negative reaction.

Kate: Hmm . . . possible. I've probably been so focused on what I say that I didn't even consider that what I don't say could create problems. Well, what can I do about it? I don't pretend to be very knowledgeable, but I certainly don't want my swimmers thinking I'm a homophobe or that it's okay for them to be.

In this case, the coach is trying to act in the best interests of the athlete and the team, and she should be reinforced for this behavior. She has recognized that she plays a role in the team climate, too, and is actively seeking strategies to change the status quo. At this point, I typically offer suggestions the coach can employ to increase the likelihood that Susan and future athletes will feel comfortable addressing issues about sexual orientation.

HB: Kate, you're doing great. . . . You're asking questions and seeking ways to create a more supportive environment. And there are several things you can do that don't take much effort. First, our university has a safe zone program. You can get a small sign for your office indicating it is free from heterosexism and homonegativism. This would send the message that your athletes can safely discuss any topic with you. The safe zone program also provides strategies for supporting nonheterosexual students. Here's the number to call to talk to the folks in the program. They are a good resource for you.

Kate: That seems doable. Anything else I can do?

HB: Another strategy is to add books to your shelves on gay and lesbian athletes. For example, Pat Griffin's *Strong Women, Deep Closets* or Eric Marcus' *Is It a Choice?* Biographies of famous lesbian and gay athletes such as Martina Navratilova, Billie Jean King, or Greg Louganis might be other possibilities. Placing books on a shelf may not seem to make a difference, but you'll be surprised. Athletes are very perceptive, and simply having such books in sight sends the message that they can safely address issues related to sexual orientation with you.

Kate: I can easily do that, too. I'll call the safe zone office tomorrow, and I'll get to a bookstore soon. If there's anything else you think of, let me know.

Although this coach is concerned about her approachability as a coach and about her athletes as individuals, she also expresses to me her concern about Susan's performance this year. Although her times have not been affected to date, Susan's been distracted in and out of practice. The coach is concerned that Susan's decreased training intensity at this point in the season will catch up with her and will negatively affect her ability to swim fast later in the season.

> Kate: I think today's conversation will help relieve some stress, but I am worried about Susan's ability to concentrate and focus on her training while all this is going on. She is already behind where she should be. Any suggestions for helping her stay focused? More to the point, any chance you'd be willing to work with her on keeping her head on the pool? She seems to trust you, and you may be able to bridge the personal and performance components.
>
> HB: I'll be glad to talk with Susan to see how she's doing. I'll broach the topic, but she has to be willing to take up the offer.

Addressing performance issues may provide Susan with opportunities to initiate conversations in an environment that she perceives to be less frightening. Having someone to talk to outside of the immediate athletic realm may be helpful at this juncture. Initiating conversations with Susan regarding her lack of focus and intensity during training will tie our previous conversations about her personal life to her current swimming experience. My primary role at this point is to help Susan talk about what is different in her training and her life that may be affecting her ability to focus. As always, listening is the key to asking the right questions. As the conversation unfolds, Susan will likely share information regarding how her concerns about the team's reaction to her sexual orientation may be influencing her performance. Strategies associated with attentional focus, getting quality sleep, and goal setting may be appropriate mechanisms to help Susan through what is, we hope, a transitional period.

> Listening is the key to asking the right questions.

Providing Susan with information that may assist her in creating positive support networks in and out of sport can also lessen the stress she is experiencing and may allow her to better focus her attention. Referring her to support systems such as a campus gay and lesbian alliance or a community support network might help her create a positive lesbian social identity and decrease isolation. It is important to realize, however, that LBT athletes often will not go to these support groups because they fear being publicly identified or labeled as LBT. Athletes rarely attend these groups even when they perceive they might be helpful.

The coach also has requested assistance in helping Susan and the team. Many of the strategies discussed in the previous case study could be modified to create a positive environment in this swimming program. Identifying new norms or characteristics of the group that enhance the team morale may increase Susan's self-esteem by placing a value on acceptance of diversity among team members. This does not necessitate Susan's coming out unless she chooses to, but it may make her feel that coming out is an option that would be supported.

In this case study, the issues differ greatly from those of the previous athlete. First, the coach is being proactive and looking for mechanisms to create a positive environment for her athletes. Although not all coaches are as supportive of lesbian athletes as this coach, in our experience coaches are far more supportive of lesbian athletes than expected. At times, we may mistakenly assume coaches are homonegative, when in actuality they merely lack knowledge, skills, or strategies to address these issues. All too often, coaches will do nothing when faced with uncertainty. Providing coaches and athletes with information and strategies for creating and sustaining a positive environment enhances both performance and satisfaction with the athletic experience.

# But It's My Personal Life: Ellen's Story

Ellen is the head coach of a mid-size Division I basketball program. She has been with the program for 15 years, first as an assistant and then as head coach. During her first

10 years, her teams finished in the top third of the conference and won the conference twice, ensuring NCAA tournament bids. In the past 5 years, however, her teams have not had successful seasons despite being very talented. Ellen has always taken pride in hearing people describe her as an intense coach whose focus is on performance. She has always distanced herself from her athletes, believing it is important to keep personal and professional issues separate. She has shared little with her team about her life outside of coaching.

Although Ellen believes that her athletes may have guessed she is a lesbian, she has not discussed her sexual orientation or personal life with them. She reinforces this sentiment with her players, telling them to leave differences and personal issues outside of the field house. Although she is approachable in times of crisis (e.g., death in the family, serious illness), when athletes approach her about sexual orientation issues, she is quick to refer them to the counseling center on campus.

As her teams have become less successful, she has become increasingly frustrated. Ellen believes she is recruiting athletes with the same skill levels and does not attribute this change in fortune to poor talent. In the past year, she has begun to hear bickering on the floor and in the locker room, and she has overheard some of the players talking about who is a dyke and who is straight. Ellen firmly believes that athletes should be able to separate the personal and professional, as she has always been able to do. Her "park it at the door" philosophy has created a problem for her. She calls me in hopes that I might provide some assistance to her and the team as they enter new territory.

Ellen's phone call, her first contact with me this year, is somewhat surprising. I have given a couple of one-shot sessions for her teams in the past on goal setting, but she has never been interested in pursuing anything more involved than that. After some opening chitchat, the initial conversation goes as follows.

> Ellen: In the past you've done some goal-setting stuff with the team, and it's been helpful. I was wondering if you might be willing to work with the team this year in a larger capacity. . . . I have to admit I'm not sure this is the right call, but I've got to do something different. We've got talent, but it doesn't seem to come together. Maybe you have some tricks up your sleeve that can help.
>
> HB: Coach, I'm glad to help in any way I can, but I don't want you to expect me to pull a rabbit out of the hat. Depending on what the issues are, I may be able to help. What do you think is the problem?
>
> Ellen: The players seem different from my players 10 years ago. This may be the most talented group I've ever had, but they bicker with each other . . . they bring their outside worries on the court. It's always something. They just don't seem to be together, and I don't seem to be able to bring them together.
>
> HB: First of all, kids are different today from how they were 10 years ago. Their experiences are different, and the pressures placed on them are different. Your expectations are probably different, too. How about I stop by a couple of practices and watch for a while? Then we can talk about where we might head.

Ellen and I talk a little while longer about her practice schedule. I also ask if I can talk with her assistant coaches, and she agrees. Finally, I outline some basic rules that I use when working with individuals and teams (e.g., basic philosophy of consulting, who has access to information).

During the next two weeks I attend four practices and observe the coaching staff as well as the players. My observations confirm that there seems to be some tension on the floor. Even though most teammates tease each other, the comments thrown out on the floor have an edge to them in many cases. I also note that a couple of the comments allude to issues around sexual orientation ("Are you sure you play on my team?" or "I think you like bumpin' under the boards with the big girls"). The assistant coaches also are concerned about the team dynamics. They are much more willing than the head coach to discuss what they perceive to be the issue—a major gay–straight split in the team. They even approached the coach about it, but she did not want to tackle the problem, saying the players have to learn to leave personal issues off the court.

I schedule a meeting with Ellen to talk about what I had seen and heard and where we might go. We start off talking about individuals and the team as a whole and ultimately get to the dynamics issue.

HB: You mentioned in our last conversation that players were at each other a bit and had trouble staying focused on basketball. What do you think is the trigger for this tension?

Ellen: You know kids, they just have trouble keeping their personal lives off the court.

HB: How do you deal with that when it happens?

Ellen: I don't. I tell them that their personal lives don't belong on the court. They're here to play basketball.

HB: Has that been very effective?

Ellen: Guess not . . . or you wouldn't be here.

HB: Although I understand your desire to keep their personal lives off the court, right now their personal lives are playing out on the court, and you will probably have to deal with it. So let's cut to the chase. It appears that you've got a mix of straight and lesbian women on your team. Most teams do. However, right now they see more differences between themselves than they do similarities, and they show little respect for each other. I don't think the admonishments to keep it off the court is going to make it go away. When they make snide remarks to each other pertaining to sexual orientation, what is your response? Do you ever stop them?

Ellen: No. I don't want to get into that. [Pause.] I've been thinking about this a lot, and I'll be honest with you, if I make their lives an issue, then my life becomes more of an issue, too. Do you know how hard it is to recruit these days? I can't afford for my life to be fair game.

Ellen's concerns about dealing with sexual orientation are not uncommon in the intercollegiate coaching ranks. Krane and Barber's (in press) recent research indicates that intercollegiate coaches are very concerned about controlling information regarding their programs and sexual orientation because they believe it will influence their ability to recruit top athletes. Many coaches believe that the mere perception that they or their athletes are anything other than heterosexual will be used against them in recruiting wars. In Division I, recruiting is critical for success, and success is essential for contract renewal. By not acknowledging this issue, Ellen has always been able to say that sexual orientation is not an issue on her teams.

Before Ellen will be willing to address this issue on her team, she has to feel less threatened about the potential impact on recruiting. Providing her with strategies to deal with her own anxieties is essential. Her concerns about recruiting are very real to her, and she is unwilling to initiate any strategies until she can envision the outcome. Identifying strategies for how she can address the makeup of her team with potential athletes and their parents provides a place to start.

HB: Let's talk about recruiting. It seems to be a real issue for you, and I can understand how important it is to attract top athletes to your program. When you talk with perspective athletes and their parents, you said that if they ask about lesbians on your team, you tell them it's not an issue on your team. That certainly is one strategy, but there may be another. What if you said, "Yes, I'm sure there are lesbians on my team. There have been in the past and will be in the future. If coaches from other Division I schools tell you that your daughter will be attending a school where there are no lesbians on the team, then the coaches are probably misrepresenting their programs, or they don't know their athletes very well. In either case, is that the kind of program you want to send your daughter to? All our athletes are respected and valued." How do you think that would play with parents?

Ellen: I'm not sure. It sounds easy when you say it, but there is a lot on the line.

HB: You don't have to do anything you're not comfortable with. This is just one possible way to begin to send the message that difference is important. I am certainly not advocating that you do anything that would hurt your recruiting. After you have a chance to think about it, why don't we try role-playing a recruiting visit with a mom or dad. I can be the parent, and you try it out. You said it sounds easy when I say it. This will give you a chance to try it with your own words. The offer is open anytime.

Ellen is beginning to realize that she needs to deal with this issue, and although she still has concerns about recruiting, she may be able to initiate a process that will help her current team.

Ellen: Okay, I'll think about what you've said. I'm still worried, but you make some good points about recruiting. [Pause.] I'll think about it . . . but what about my current team? I'm going to need your help. This is new territory. I hope you don't think I'm going to "come out" to my team, because that ain't happenin'.

HB: Whoa . . . no one said you had to come out to your team. Let's start slowly. How about we first meet with the rest of the coaching staff and talk about the climate you want to create on this team. What would it look like, and what would it feel like? Then we can talk as a group about how we can make it happen.

The meeting with the coaching staff goes well. We discuss the issues as a group and identify where and how we can make inroads. The assistant coaches are especially helpful in identifying examples where the actions of players have affected team and individual morale and subsequent performance. Ellen even enters the conversation when we begin to discuss what the climate on the team should feel like. After the meeting, Ellen is more confident about moving forward, although she still has concerns about how to do it.

Ellen: I can't just all of a sudden decide that now we're going to talk and now I'm a touchy feely coach. They won't buy it.

HB: I think you need to be yourself. You have always been about performance. This is an issue that's affecting the performance of your players. Begin the discussion about the concept of team and what it takes to create a team.

Ellen's focus has always been on performance, whereas I believe the strength of any team comes from the players and what they bring to the team. Constructing a team identity that welcomes individual difference can be a powerful tool for creating positive team dynamics. As a starting point, and consistent with Ellen's previous behavior, I initially keep the focus on performance. Intercollegiate athletic participation, however, is about more than just performance, and Ellen will need to start examining issues concerning the total development of athletes on her teams. This identity shift must result in changes on the team so that athletes actually do value individual differences, including sexual orientation. Creating this kind of dialogue will be a marked departure from previous behavior. Therefore, Ellen, her staff, and I need to open discussions that acknowledge differences on the team. To ensure that athletes do not mistrust this initial effort, Ellen needs to explain the reasoning behind the change. It is unlikely that she would decide to discuss sexual orientation if performance was not at issue, so it makes sense initially to address it as a performance issue. Issues surrounding sexual orientation are preventing the players from maximizing their potential.

One initiative that may be helpful in getting this group to come together is spending a morning at a challenge course. Challenge course activities provide a fresh environment to begin to recreate a sense of cohesion and team identity (Meyer & Wenger, 1998). These activities are a good starting point, but their success is limited unless there is continual follow-up. Creating a sense of team identity may allow this group to begin determining the strengths of their team and how individuals and individual differences contribute to the whole.

After returning from the challenge course, it is important to expand and reinforce the characteristics of the team and begin to recognize individual contributions. This also will be an important opportunity to regulate unacceptable and disrespectful behavior and show that the rules and values have changed. This is the part Ellen dreads most.

> Ellen: So what am I supposed to do when one of them makes one of their wisecracks, like the "under the boards" crack?
>
> HB: You don't have to make a big deal out of it. Just pull the player or players aside and let them know that their behavior is not okay. Interceding at this point may squelch it temporarily, but you may need to initiate a conversation after practice about respect. Another possibility is sitting down with your captains and helping them set the standard for respectful behavior. You can't dump this responsibility completely on them, however. It is a shared responsibility.

The second component of this intervention relates directly to the performance of the athletes. Ellen has always believed that her players should leave personal issues at home, and she has expressed this expectation clearly. Our conversations have helped her realize, however, that in addition to addressing issues on the team, the players need to learn strategies that will enhance their focus on the court. At this point, we can introduce strategies that will create new focus points for the group yet provide individual assistance to those who need it. A team meeting to create a program of specific, challenging team goals may be a good starting place. These goals encourage the group to recognize their reliance on each other. Following up with individual goals that directly tie into the team goals provides opportunities for recognition of individual contributions to the team's success. These individual goals can also be focus points for athletes on the floor every day during practice.

The goal-setting process also may focus on group dynamics. Changing communication patterns on the floor will prove critical for successful performance. Positive and productive talk on the floor is a central component in successful basketball teams and one that is disrupted by poor group dynamics. Creating goals around the amount of positive talk on the floor may be one example of how goal setting can transform behaviors that have reinforced interpersonal problems on the team. Negative talk will not change overnight, but providing specific strategies to change the talk can change the tenor on the court. Examples of these strategies include positively directing play by providing two upbeat comments to each player during each practice and enforcing specific rules regarding positive talk (e.g., if you don't have something positive to say, keep quiet).

This case study poses serious challenges for the consultant, coach, and team. Although this process can be unnerving to initiate, coaches and athletes have much to gain by a process that focuses on enhancing the quality of the experience for individuals and the group. Employing a combination of strategies can change the climate for individual players and the team as a whole, creating a focused and achievement-oriented team.

# Implications of the Cases

In each of these cases, social change is the ultimate goal. Consistent with SI perspective, the strategies used in these case studies may invoke lasting change in attitudes toward LBT females in sport and lead to more positive sport climates that will benefit all athletes. Although the employment of social creativity strategies may make some inroads toward reducing homonegativism on a team, the effect will be limited if broader social change also is not enacted.

An issue relevant to each of the previous cases is enhancing collective esteem, which is an important step toward social change. When social identity is salient and enhanced, collective esteem rises as well (Krane et al., 2002; Lalonde & Cameron, 1994). The suggestions to clarify a team's identity and to identify group values will positively influence players' collective esteem. Collective esteem also increases as the athletes identify the strengths and social status of their social group (i.e., team). Athletic teams may derive their social status through, for example, their athletic and academic success or their mental and physical toughness. Having coaches and athletes identify their team strengths should lead to increased collective esteem.

Many strategies employed to enhance team cohesion also may enhance collective esteem. For example, developing team goals should enhance both cohesion and collective esteem. Team discussions should result in consensus among the players as to what is important and what they want to accomplish. As players progress toward these goals, collective esteem will increase with each improvement in team play. In these cases, the players should discuss their primary long-term and short-term goals. Team norms and values are further reinforced as each athlete voices commitment to team goals. As their collective esteem increases, individuals in a social group are more likely to engage in social change strategies (Krane et al., 2002). In real life, things may not always progress so easily. Heterosexism and homonegativism are deeply woven into our social environments. Changing such a climate will take time. We can encourage athletes to change their behaviors toward team members, but it will likely take much longer for long-term changes in their attitudes. Once consultants address issues related to sexual orientation with a team, they should revisit the topic regularly. Sessions specifically devoted to homonegativism may not be necessary, but reminders of team values (e.g., respecting difference) and maintaining positive communication can be helpful.

Social change is the eventual goal of interventions to combat homonegativism and heterosexism on the athletic teams in the previous case studies. Ideally, team members will learn and accept that teammates will have diverse sexual orientations and that one orientation should not be privileged over others. In other words, athletes' behaviors should be supportive of their LBT teammates. Social change regarding LBT females in sport often begins with subtle changes that have a profound impact on the climate. For example, when athletes stop each other from using homonegative or heterosexist language, a tone is set. As athletes and coaches become more inclusive in their language (e.g., do not assume all team members date males, acknowledge same-gender partners), the atmosphere becomes more open. It may take time for some athletes to become used to this more open environment, and it is essential that coaches, administrators, sport psychology consultants, and team leaders act as role models for accepting behavior. When teams have high collective esteem, coupled with a strong desire to be successful, athletes will be concerned about the welfare of all team members, and teammates will be challenged to look out for one another

(Kauer, 2002). Team members speaking out against negative actions against their LBT teammates is social change in action. These behaviors will demonstrate that they are fully supportive of their teammates.

# Educating Ourselves

Whether or not acknowledged overtly, sport psychology consultants working with female athletes will most likely have nonheterosexual clients (Lenskyj, 1992, 1997). To implement successfully the strategies previously suggested, consultants must believe in them. Some sport psychology consultants may need to reflect on their own beliefs and confront potential biases and prejudices (House & Holloway, 1992; Reynolds, 1995; Sue, Arredondo, & McDavis, 1992).

The first step in confronting our biases is to identify them. Sport psychology consultants could list their perceptions and beliefs about LBTs. This list should be an honest assessment, acknowledging any potential biases and stereotypes as well as other perceptions about this social group. Next, each item on the list should be examined concerning why the consultant believes this and whether it is an accurate descriptor. Finally, any items on the list that may impede communication and successful consulting with LBTs should be challenged. Next to each negative item, a different interpretation or new belief could be listed. Possibly, consultants may need to engage in self-education to counter some stereotypic perceptions of LBT females.

Sport psychology consultants who want further education pertaining to LBTs have a variety of options available. Social identity theory is one framework that may facilitate a greater understanding of LBT experience. Reading scholarly literature on LBT athletes and coaches (e.g., Bredemeier, Carlton, Hills, & Oglesby, 1999; Greendorfer & Rubinson, 1997; Griffin, 1998; Krane, 1997; Lenskyj, 1997) or popular press writings on LBTs in sport (e.g., Nelson, 1991; Rogers, 1991; Young, 1995; Zipter, 1988) is also beneficial. Attending educational seminars at conferences and universities is another avenue for educating oneself about LBT issues. Not only will attendance enhance our understanding of LBT issues, but also our very presence signifies support of these sessions and LBT individuals (Krane & Pope, 1996).

Additionally, direct contact with culturally diverse groups enriches crosscultural sensitivity, knowledge, and understanding (Reynolds, 1995). Discussions with openly LBT athletes, coaches, administrators, and sport psychologists may enhance understanding about LBT issues. Interactions with these people will provide insights into their experiences with heterosexism in sport and as marginalized individuals in sport.

Through further understanding, new beliefs will emerge. Ultimately, personal biases will be set aside or eroded as consultants gain new insights. Still, consultants need to be aware of their limitations. Even sport psychology consultants who are supportive of nonheterosexuals may have limitations concerning the issues they are capable of addressing. For example, if an athlete is struggling with identity issues related to coming out, her sport psychology consultant might need to seek assistance from a counselor or psychologist with expertise in this area.

# Conclusion

This chapter describes a variety of strategies that may be employed by sport psychology consultants to decrease heterosexism and homonegativism in women's sport. Considering the general atmosphere around female athletes (e.g., concerns about femininity, innuendo about lesbians) (Krane, 2001), attention to these social issues is essential when creating a climate for athletic excellence and individual social development. Heterosexism, although often not an easy topic to tackle, can be addressed within sports teams. Doing so will provide many benefits for all athletes: reducing stress, removing a large distraction, enhancing team communication, increasing cohesion, and creating an environment for sporting excellence. The most positive benefit of confronting heterosexism is the consequent development of an atmosphere that supports the personal growth of all team members.

## CHAPTER 15

# Coming Full Circle
## From Practice to Research

Mark B. Andersen, PhD

At the start of the first book, *Doing Sport Psychology*, the goal the authors and I had set for ourselves was to take theory, models, and research and illustrate how they are translated into the real world of sport psychology service. I believe we were mostly successful at fulfilling those goals (more in some chapters, less in others). In this volume, we also keep that tradition going. That unidirectional model of theory and research to practice, however, is really only half the story. As academics and practitioners try to take what is known from research and translate that information into working with athletes, they come up against the phenomena of real people out in the messy and idiosyncratic world. Theory and research give us maps to navigate the territories of sport and exercise. But, as usual, we find that the map is not the territory, and the maps have areas on them labeled *terra incognita*. What we need are scouts, going out into those landscapes, to come back and help us fill in the missing bits on those cartographies. I think the authors here have scouted well, and their reconnoitering has brought back useful information. And that information is where practice can help inform research.

## Evidence-Based Practice

In counseling and clinical psychology, and in sport and exercise psychology, there is a constant call for evidence-based practice (Rowland & Goss, 2000). We need to present evidence that what we do is effective, helps people, and has a solid base in research. If we do not have that evidence, then the aroma of snake oil will begin to waft across the landscape of service delivery. What constitutes evidence, however, is a thorny question that challenges practitioners and researchers alike. The gold standard of evidence comes from controlled randomized clinical trials (RCTs) of intervention efficacy, a model intimately tied to biomedical research. RCTs can provide evidence that the interventions we use, when other variables are controlled for, actually help initiate and maintain change for the better.

Although I would not want to abandon the use of RCTs, we should recognize some of their limitations. One drawback is the problem of diagnosis. Now, we do not usually do clinical diagnosis in sport and exercise psychology, but we do diagnose, in at least some ways. For example, in studies of competition anxiety, the researcher may use a sport competition anxiety inventory to select those athletes who score high on the instrument. The researcher then divides these athletes into treatment and control groups, delivers an intervention to one group, and then tests for differences after the intervention to see if competition anxiety scores have gone down for the treatment group compared with the control group. Ostensibly, that would be fine evidence that those who have high competition anxiety would benefit from our interventions. One of the problems, however, stems from the designation of some participants as having high competition anxiety.

Athletes are anxious about competition for a wide variety of reasons. One athlete may be anxious because of a need to please a loving and caring coach; another may have anxiety about losing and the resultant withdrawal of parental affection. Still another may use winning to fill a void and a deep-seated feeling of worthlessness. Superficial diagnoses of high competition anxiety from inventories obfuscate the full picture of the athletes' worlds and homogenize them. In addition to this problem is the measurement issue of not really knowing what scores on paper-and-pencil tests really mean in terms of real-world behaviors. Anxiety tests are not usually calibrated against some metric that is meaningful, such as time to complete an 800-meter run, and so improvements in anxiety scores cannot reliably predict performance, at least at the individual level (see Sechrest, McKnight, & McKnight, 1996, for a discussion of this problem in psychotherapy outcome research).

Martin, Andersen, and Gates (2000) found that the Profile of Mood States (McNair, Lorr, & Droppleman, 1971), when used to monitor potential overtraining, has moderate predictive power to explain behavioral responses (performance times) to high-intensity training and taper at the group level. At the individual level, however, POMS profiles, when paired with performance, show the following patterns:

- POMS goes up (more mood disturbance), and performance after taper goes down.
- POMS goes up, and then performance improves.
- POMS goes down, and performance goes up.
- POMS goes down, and performance deteriorates.

At the group level, research tells us to use the Profile of Mood States to monitor overtraining; at the individual level, research tells us, at least, to be wary.

The strong internal validity of RCT research, although scientifically laudable, brings up questions of meaningfulness in the external world of sport and physical activity. Athletes are never randomly assigned to treatments. Any specific intervention is never given in isolation and is usually part of a larger treatment process. If a classic intervention is given, such as relaxation, it is often modified and remodified based on athlete feedback, so there is no uniformity of treatment delivery in real-word practice. In my practice, classic sport psychology interventions such as relaxation and imagery may occasionally be used, but rarely are they the focus of the work. As Murphy (2000) observes of his own practice in the afterword of *Doing Sport Psychology*, "Reading this book has caused me to reflect on my own work with elite athletes and to observe how infrequently I ever do straightforward interventions such as those we see studied so often in our journals" (p. 276). RCTs do provide evidence for effectiveness, but there are other sources, such as the realist and confessional tales Sparkes (2002) writes so eloquently about, along with the growing case study literature in our field.

# Confessing Prejudices on Research and the Field

I think confession truly is good for the soul. In keeping with that adage, I admit that I have a rather low opinion of the standard of both qualitative and quantitative research done in the sport and exercise sciences. I believe a large proportion of qualitative and quantitative studies in our field is questionable. And I must confess, I have written and published a bunch of that questionable research. In the quantitative realm of research in sport and exercise psychology, problems with interpretations of statistical results run from confusing numbers (crude maps) with behavior and meaningfulness (territories) to misunderstanding what statistical significance and effect sizes tell us in our quests for knowledge (see Andersen & Stoové, 1998; Speed & Andersen, 2000; Stoové & Andersen, 2003). In the qualitative research, there are limited models of what is seen as acceptable and worthy of publication (e.g., journals still do not publish in-depth case studies of individual athletes and their personal relationships with sport psychologists; see Krane, Andersen, & Strean, 1997, for more information).

Also, I am somewhat in the paradoxical position of being a sport psychologist who really doesn't like sport. I have spent a lot of my applied professional career trying to help people repair the damage that has been visited on them by being involved in sport and competition. Sport environments are often deeply pathogenic places where people learn really horrible lessons that twist their views of the world and of themselves. The focus of the major portion of research in sport psychology is on improving athletic performance, or more often than not, improving scores on inventories that we believe have something to do with performance. That focus is on behaviors and not really on individuals. Performance and scores on paper-and-pencil tests are clean. Individual lives are fairly messy. Rarely do we see research focusing on the happiness of the athletes, and happiness is not, generally, a group phenomenon.

Sport psychology service with athletes and coaches is also messy, and what we need to do is explore that messiness and bring it back to inform research so that research becomes more reflective of what really happens when we sit down with athletes. Some species of qualitative research are aimed at examining the lives of athletes, and that approach has huge potential to inform practice in a meaningful way, but a lot of qualitative research in sport psychology is executed on a rather limited level. Some of those limitations stem from the translation of the data of athletes' lives into "themes" and "verbal factor analyses" and the quantification of qualitative information (e.g., Scanlan, Russell, Beals, & Scanlan, 2003). Athletes' worlds become, once again, homogenized into higher- and lower-order themes, quantified by group, sanitized, and neatly boxed.

Another issue in sport psychology qualitative research is that the authors are usually noticeably absent. In many cases, the author or authors appear in a few sentences about background and research qualifications, and then they retreat and are never heard from again (e.g., Gould, Udry, Bridges, & Beck, 1997; also see Sparkes, 2002). From the study by Gould and colleagues on injuries comes the following statement: "These interviews were tape-recorded and conducted by the same individual (a 33-year-old female) who was trained in qualitative research methodology and who had experienced major knee injuries herself" (p. 382)—then the researcher disappears from the text completely. I do not want to imply that such "realist tales" as Gould and colleagues present are not valuable. I think they have immense value, but we need to recognize that they are also limited and still divorced from practice in significant ways. For example, in much qualitative research in sport psychology, little is reported about the relationship between the researcher and the interviewees, and what is reported is often perfunctory. A researcher may say, "The interviewer first established rapport with the athletes before delving into the main topics." Well, how did he do that? How was she sure rapport had been established? What depth of rapport was developed? Rapport is a mercurial phenomenon; it can wax and wane depending on the interviewee, the topics broached, the sensitivity of the interviewer, and a host of other factors. Rapport is messy, and that messiness cannot be dismissed in one sentence.

So, we have problems with the relevance of both qualitative and quantitative research to what we do with athletes in the real world. How do we solve this relevance problem? Not all the authors in *Doing Sport Psychology* and in *Sport Psychology in Practice* would call their contributions qualitative research, but they are precisely that. These authors take the stories of real-world experiences and bring that information back to practitioners and academics for perusal, criticism, and analysis. That is what good qualitative research does. The case studies in these two books bring practice back to inform research what needs to be explored if we are truly interested in the lives of athletes.

# Historical Roots

I would like to now make a diversion to some historical roots in psychotherapy that may help us get a grip on what relevant qualitative research and service delivery in applied sport psychology might be about. Back in the middle of the 20th century, one of America's great personality theorists and psychotherapists, George Kelly, wrote about the "client as scientist" (Hays, 2000, briefly discusses these issues). What he meant was that, like a scientist, the psychotherapy client is on a quest for knowledge, is an observer of his own life, formulates hypotheses about how his external and internal world operates, and conducts personal experiments to test his assumptions—often with repeated failures and frustrations stemming from self-fulfilling prophecies; rigid patterns of thinking; and intransigent modes of behaviors, leading to all sorts of unhappiness in the form of anxiety, depression, and a variety of other disturbances. In psychotherapy, the client learns to become a better scientist and, one hopes, ultimately a happier person.

Later, Aaron Beck, probably best known in quantitative circles for the Beck Depression Inventory (Beck, Ward, Mendelson, Mock, & Erbaugh1961), elaborated on Kelly's ideas and described the psychotherapeutic process as one of "collaborative empiricism." I love that term because it really gets to the heart of psychotherapy: the relationship between the psychotherapist and the client. Here we have two people engaged in collaboration, trying to figure out the experiential world of one of them, a world often filled with terrors, hopes, frustrations, joys, anxieties, and failures to change. It is amazing to me how many students come to us thinking that empirical evidence is the same as experimental evidence. In psychotherapy, the empirical data are the data of a life. And the two scientists are on a journey together to understand those data. Telling the tales of that collaborative empiricism, of that journey, is one of the best examples of qualitative research I know. This book does precisely that.

If we go back to an even earlier time in psychology's history, we find an example of qualitative inquiry that led to one of the most influential theories of the 20th century—a model of what it is to be human that has made a profound impact on the way we talk about ourselves, how we understand literature, and how we look at social movements. The language of this theory still pervades our communication. Phrases such as "anal retentive" still attest to Freud's legacy. Freud's psychoanalysis was not the product of randomized clinical trials but rather the result of intense case studies of individuals. One of the foundations of 20th-century thought, Freud's *The Interpretation of Dreams* (Freud, 1900/1965)—a type of autoethnography that no one has equaled since (cf. Sparkes, 2002)—was in large part a product of his own self-analysis. When one looks at so-called case studies in exercise and sport science, they pale in comparison with Freud's "Rat Man," but that is probably an unfair comparison. What journal editor would publish a case study on the "Aardvark

Decathlete"? And that is one problem, publishing qualitative studies, that I think really takes some time to figure out.

All people are in some ways like everyone else on the planet. We share the same evolutionary history and the same genetic code. In other ways, we are like members of our social and cultural groups, and finally, we are unique in some ways—like no one else. Good case studies illuminate the unique, and maybe the cultural aspects, of people. I hope many of the chapters have covered the first point well and have also delved into the second realm. The really wonderful case studies (e.g., Freud's) point us in the direction of the universal. Sport psychology case studies are a good start, but we have a long way to go.

# The Research Relationship

As discussed earlier, a great deal of research in sport psychology, especially in the quantitative realm, has focused on answering questions as to whether interventions, such as relaxation or imagery, help performance. On the surface, it would appear that a question such as "Does imagery work?" would be a good one to explore and try to answer. But that question, and the methods used to answer that question, is naive. The models used to explore the imagery question stem from that gold standard—the randomized clinical trials paradigm. The problem with this research is that the emphasis is on the treatment, with little or no attention paid to the deliverer of that treatment or the relationship between the sport psychologist and the athlete receiving imagery training. Imagery does not occur in a vacuum. It occurs within a relationship, and we know little about relationships in sport psychology. The few case studies available, and most all of the other qualitative studies, are about athletes; the researcher or sport psychologist is notably absent. In psychotherapy research, it was established several years ago that it really doesn't matter if you conduct cognitive–behavioral therapy, gestalt therapy, or psychodynamic therapy, or if you wave and slap codfish over people, for that matter (well, that is a bit of an exaggeration). The one variable that is always, and most strongly, connected to psychotherapy outcome, regardless of the therapy, is the quality of the relationship—the working alliance—between the client and the therapist. That point has been repeated ad infinitum in these texts, but it cannot be emphasized enough.

We might say, as a corollary of the findings in psychotherapy research, that the richness and meaningfulness of qualitative data gleaned from interpersonal interactions between researchers and participants depend on the quality of the relationships they establish. And that is why we need to think and act and interact with research participants like psychotherapists.

How do we train our qualitative research students to interact with participants? What skills do we try to impart? Can we help them think like psychotherapists? We are not in the business of turning out researchers who do therapy, but can we help students interact with the people they are interviewing in a therapeutic manner (a human, accepting, caring, insightful, and even loving manner)? I have found that many new graduate students want to do qualitative research, and this desire stems not from research questions that call for qualitative methods but rather from their dread fear of statistics. It becomes a problem of method driving research, not research questions driving method. The more sophisticated students argue that quantitative approaches are old hat, stem from positivistic models and thinking, and are not relevant to today's problems. I have heard that argument so often, I repeat it to myself just before I take a nap. They don't usually realize that about 80 years ago in physics—the queen of science—positivistic approaches, with the scientists as supposedly objective and detached observers, took a massive blow when the scientist observers became a central factor in the results of experiments.

Quantum mechanics gave us the Heisenberg Uncertainty Principle and the wonderful mythopoeic story of Schrödinger's cat. Students' arguments against quantitative methods are usually elaborate, pseudological defenses against their stats phobia. And then they proceed to ask questions that are really quantitative, such as, "Do people get better? Do people improve with this or that intervention?" I try to explain that quantitative questions and methods are just fine and that a lot of important research, such as drug efficacy trials, could not be done without them. In contrast, qualitative methods are enormously difficult, are much more convoluted than quantitative studies, take loads of training to get right, are often executed abysmally, and usually make the thesis or dissertation twice as long. Despite those warnings, they still want to do qualitative research. The defense against statistics anxiety is Samsonian in its strength. I say, "OK, you asked for it." Then we start training them how to interview and think like psychotherapists (and like a competent applied sport psychologist), how to examine closely their relationships with interviewees, and how to understand the main instrument of research (themselves)—and they come back and say, "I didn't think it would be this difficult." They had the impression, supported by a good deal of the qualitative sport psychology literature, that all you had to do was ask people some questions, report what they said, and maybe make some intelligent interpretations. It ain't that easy, and I won't let students loose on the public until they have had hours and hours of training in how to talk to people in a therapeutic manner.

# Examples of the Researcher's Own Stuff Making Things Messy

Let me tell a story about one of my doctoral students, Cadeyrn. I have his permission to use this tale. His narcissism is healthy and robust, and he loves to be talked about, so he will be delighted that I am mentioning him. His work examines the role of exercise and physical activity in the lives of people with cerebral palsy. He has cerebral palsy and is quite spastic, with a severe gait disorder and speech that at first is somewhat difficult to comprehend. He is also wonderfully sardonic and self-mocking. One day when discussing the often avoided issue of sexuality and people with disabilities, he said, "Chicks should really go for me. I'm a full-body vibrator." With comments such as that, you can see why I love him dearly. My countertransference to him is profound, but more on transference and countertransference in research later.

We were role-playing interviewing a person with cerebral palsy (CP), and I was the participant. I was playing a student going to university and starting to get involved in the student gym. He asked me what I was studying and how it was all going.

Cadeyrn: So when did you start studying at university?

Mark: [Role-playing the student with CP.] Just began my second semester.

Cadeyrn: What program are you in?

Mark: I'm doing information technology.

Cadeyrn: How did you choose that area?

Mark: Well, I think I would be good at it.

Cadeyrn: How is that going?

Mark: I'm doing OK.

Cadeyrn: Are you getting good grades?

Mark: [Falling out of the role-play.] OK, Cadeyrn. Let's take a time-out. Now where did that question come from?

Cadeyrn: [A long silence.] Probably me.

The value systems of the interviewer can help or hinder the interview process. Cadeyrn is a mammoth overachiever. Good grades are extremely important to him. Anything less than a high distinction (in U.S. terms, an A) in a class is cause for self-flagellation and existential crisis. His question to me about grades reflected his values and communicated those values. The participant may be just getting by gradewise, but for him that is a great accomplishment. Yet the question suggested that if he is not getting good grades, then he is not doing well. Cadeyrn had stepped in his own stuff and unwittingly foisted upon the interviewee the high demands he places on himself, possibly communicating that if the participant was not getting good grades, then he really was disabled. The question was not "Sounds as if things are going well at university. Can you tell me a bit more about what *OK* means for you in terms of school?" The question was more "Are you like me?" And that brings up the whole issue of the dynamics of the interview process and the problem of identification with the participant, and the participant's identification with the interviewer, and how those processes color the data. Cadeyrn had not examined his own prejudices, his own de-identification with people who have CP, and his own overachieving and overcompensation, along with how his issues could color the interactions with research participants. Just as we train sport psychologists to examine the instrument of service—themselves—we need to help qualitative researchers do the same, taking practice back to research.

Another example of not listening like a psychotherapist, and making sins of omission, comes from the training of another of my graduate students, David. I also have his permission to tell this story. Outside of his dissertation, David wanted to try his hand at taking a life history of a sport psychologist, his development, the crucial events in his life, how he got into sport psychology, his experiences working with athletes, and so forth. He chose me as the informant, and because it was going to be all about me, and I can talk about myself for hours, I naturally agreed. It was also an opportunity to train David in interview skills and to think like a psychotherapist. So the interviews were not only life history data gathering but also training sessions where we would go along and then take time-outs to discuss what was really happening, what he was getting right, where he was missing things, and how he might proceed. David is a good empathic reflector, a skill essential for good interviewing and for effective psychotherapy. He also has a gentle, caring, and receptive demeanor. We had gotten through my childhood and my involvement with sport (I was a mediocre swimmer who mainly liked to chat with the other guys working out in my lane), and then we came to my university days. There is a sadistic side to me that I sometimes use therapeutically (I hope) to shock and make students squirm and then to examine what all that squirming is about.

> David: OK, Mark, we have discussed your growing interest in psychology. Can you tell me some more about your university days?
>
> Mark: [In a matter-of-fact manner.] Well, the really big change in my early 20s at university was when I started sleeping with men.
>
> David: [Looking a bit stunned and lost.] I . . . uh . . . [Stumbling around, not knowing where to go or how to handle that information, so he lapsed into a weak type of reflection of what I had just said.] Oh, that must have been a big change.
>
> Mark: Yeah, I *said* it was a big change. [I was not going to help him out . . . yet.]
>
> David: Uh . . . I, uh . . . Oh, crap. [Falling out of the role of qualitative interviewer.] I don't know what to do.
>
> Mark: David, let's take a time-out. What's happening for you?
>
> David: Well . . . It's just that . . . you've told me something, and I simply don't know what to do with it.
>
> Mark: OK, but remember there is rarely anything that is just "just" or "simply." Your response to my outing myself in front of you is complex. And this gets to the heart of interviewing people. Your participants may give you stuff that tests you and your abilities to respond in an empathetic manner.

> David: I guess I failed then. You're my supervisor. . . . What am I to do when you say something like that?
>
> Mark: You have a good point. Our relationship really interfered with you in the role of interviewer. But I bet that is only a part of the story of your response. There's more stuff there, and it probably has to do with your own homophobia. We need to look at that.

I am not in the closet, nor do I wear my intimate life on my sleeve, so some students may know, others may not. David didn't. David comes from a strong Christian background and embodies the finest in Christian principles; he is also a straight male. His discomfort was apparent, and he did not know where to go with that information. We had discussed the importance of being able to handle sensitive material and explore any topic that comes up. I gave him that information as a kind of test. Interviewees will also test the researcher to see if they can trust him, to see if they will be comfortable, and to see how he handles really central stuff. If I were a regular participant and came out of the closet to my researcher and was met with befuddlement, awkwardness, and avoidance, then what happens to me? And what happens to the quality, honesty, and depth of the stories I tell from then on? *"Oh, this researcher is like all those other straight homophobes. Well . . . forget him."* What would happen if a participant told a story in her life history about having killed her sister in a car accident at 18, a defining and horrible event in her life, and then she was met with confusion and avoidance. I think "shutting down" would be likely.

David was embarrassed and apologetic and concerned that he had offended me. I felt so bad for him that I went overboard to explain that no offense was taken, that his awkwardness was really fascinating and a source of information that could be used to make him a better qualitative researcher. I probably didn't do a very good job of alleviating his anxiety. We ended the interview there for that day with a plan to begin discussing my PhD at our next session, but this story was not over. A few days later we started the next interview. I suggest to my qualitative research students that in consecutive interviews it is a good idea to try to make the process as seamless as possible by starting out with a quick review and summary of what went on in the previous encounter. This process lets the interviewee know that the researcher has studied what he said and has been thinking about him in the interim, and it helps to further rapport.

David did his summary of our session, but it was missing something. He then said, "So shall we start where we left off and talk some about your decision to go for the PhD?" Cadeyrn, whose work is also in the life history mode, was observing all these interviews as part of his training, and I could see him just chomping at the bit to say something. I said, "OK, but time-out. David, you did a fine job of summarizing, but I never heard the word *gay*. Why is that?" Well, David was crestfallen. In summarizing my life he had left out a defining feature, one that brought him anxiety. On a conscious level, David knew the importance of addressing sensitive material. We had gone through a lengthy discussion of how not addressing such issues forthrightly and with care was inimical to the interview process, yet his anxiety and discomfort and powerful unconscious motivation led him to "forget," a Freudian parapraxis, or "slip of the mind." We could not have asked for a more teachable moment if we had planned it. David's forgetting, his dynamic parapraxis, even in the face of working with a supervisor whom he wanted to impress (and certainly not offend), and even with an in-depth discussion a few days previously, illustrated perfectly just how powerful unconscious motivation is and how it trips us up again and again. If I were a regular participant listening to (or rather not hearing) David's underlying omission, I would probably have thought, *"OK, now I am really out of here."* End of all stories. I did my best to help David get past the "bad interviewer, insulting and disappointing his supervisor, beating himself up" mode he fell into, gain an appreciation of his own unconscious processes, and see how they can influence the stories he hears . . . and be fascinated.

Cadeyrn was helpful in lightening up the situation. He is truly polymorphously perverse and keenly interested in anything even vaguely sexual. He said, "Yeah, David, I was dying here, waiting for you to ask about all the sex and drugs and discos in the '70s." We had a good laugh, and today when we talk about it, we still laugh. David, like Cadeyrn, tripped over his own stuff. Sport psychologists in practice often trip over their own blind spots. We have seen that in the stories in these volumes. After almost 30 years of working in the realms of counseling, teaching, supervision, psychotherapy, and applied sport psychology, I still trip over my own issues. It is how we are built. The sport psychologist in practice can be a model for the qualitative researcher and bring back to research the valuable stories that can help and inform these modes of scientific inquiry, making them richer and more meaningful, and above all, useful.

## Missing the Point

Another good example of not listening like a psychotherapist comes from a presentation I heard by a respected qualitative researcher in sport psychology who has helped promote at least one species of qualitative research, or more accurately a qualitative–quantitative hybrid, in the field. In presenting her qualitative data on commitment to sport, she was using quotes from her interviews with an international soccer team (I have changed some details here, including the name of the team and the sport). As a prime example of emotional and cognitive commitment to sport, she quoted one player as saying something like, "This is the best and most important thing that has ever happened to me. It's been a lifelong dream. I am totally committed; I can't even think about not being a Demon." Sounds committed, dreams being fulfilled, and all that . . . wonderful! She let the quote stand, and that is where the story supports all the fantastic prejudices we have about involvement with sport. "Look at this guy; what a model of commitment," and by implication, a model for others to be committed to what they do. But something is amiss. What she did not listen to was the last bit: "I can't even think about not being a Demon." For me, those few words have as much, if not more, to say about the phenomenon of commitment in sport than most of the other data presented.

What do those words, "I can't even think about not being a Demon," mean for that player? Unfortunately, we will never know because that statement was never pursued, was taken at face value, and finally leaves us hanging. A psychotherapist, or any really therapeutically oriented qualitative interviewer, would have recognized in those few words that being a Demon has a dark side and said, "Ah ha! Now we are getting to something so important that just the thought of it brings about avoidance and anxiety." Here's one interpretation: Being a Demon is so precious, so wonderful, so completely tied to my sense of self and my worthiness as a human being that to lose it would mean something so terrible, so unspeakable, so devastating that I cannot allow myself to even entertain the thought—because if I were not a Demon then I would be nothing, empty, worthless. I have felt like that before, and I never want to feel like that again." The athlete puts on a brave face and a truly committed manner, plays hard, and trains hard, probably to the point of increasing his risk of injury. But the athlete also has this background anxiety about his position on the team and worries constantly about what the coaches and management are thinking. If something goes a bit wrong, then the threat of not being a Demon grows, and the background anxiety lurches into the foreground as insomnia, overly intense workouts, emotional lability, and possibly even more erratic performance.

It's funny; there are about five different themes in psychotherapy that keep coming up over and over again. One is "I am not worthy," with its sports correlate of good performance equals good person, probably the most damaging equation in sport and life. Another theme is that we behave in ways that ensure that the thing we fear most will happen, does happen. This player's anxiety about being dumped from the team may lead him down behavioral paths that will ensure he does get dumped. True, I made up this interpretation based on a few words, but it is too bad we did not get his whole story. There appeared to be so much more to tell, but taking what interviewees say at face value (and not listening like a psychotherapist) leaves our data not "rich," as many researchers claim theirs is, but superficial and impoverished, supporting in this case an underlying prejudice that commitment to sport is a good thing. I am sure being a Demon is a wonderful experience for many players. I am also sure that for others it is a personal horror.

# One Model
# for the Qualitative Researcher

When working with my graduate students, I take psychodynamic psychotherapy as a model when training them to interview participants in their qualitative studies. Psychodynamic psychotherapy comes from the work of Freud; he is such an easy target, and his work is so often poo-pooed (a term Freud would have loved), and fair enough—concepts such as castration anxiety or a female's penis envy strike us as somewhat quaint or odd. Oral, anal, phallic, and genital stages of psychosexual development aside, the core of psychodynamic psychotherapy lies in the relationship between the therapist and the client and the dynamic processes of transference and countertransference, key themes throughout these texts. In examining our transference and countertransference in psychotherapy, we begin to understand the patterns in the client's (and our own) lives. We hope in psychotherapy that the evolving relationship between the therapist and the client begins to replace past dysfunctional patterns with a model of a loving, caring involvement with others, a model that can be taken out into the real world and practiced.

Now that sounds a bit large and somewhat heavy, but I do not try to turn doctoral research students into psychotherapists. Rather, I encourage them to use the principles we are talking about to interact with and understand the people's stories they are trying to hear. Transference and countertransference do not occur, usually, without some substantial investment. So how do we get the research participant invested in the storytelling process? The best way I know is to embody all those qualities that Carl Rogers, in his client-centered therapy, talked about—being genuine, showing unconditional positive regard, being empathic, being honest and open, being accepting, being authentic, being truly interested, and communicating all that to participants (Rogers, 1961). In other words, being a model of what it is to be a loving, caring human being. Modeling such behavior helps the research participant in turn model honesty and openness and tell really fabulous stories.

# How Research and Practice
# Can Go Pear-Shaped

Readers can see the psychodynamic model in action in several of the chapters of both *Doing Sport Psychology* and *Sport Psychology in Practice*. There are, however, some dangers in the overapplication of a psychotherapeutic model of interaction and human behavior to the realm of qualitative research. In therapy, the client and the psychologist have an agreement that they are going to explore the client's life to try to help the person become less anxious, or happier, or more functional. Often when emotional buttons are pushed in psychotherapy, it is usually a good idea to keep the finger on that button and help the client stay with the emotional material to gain some insight into the roots of the unhappiness. That agreement to go to those emotionally valent places and stay there is not part of most qualitative research in sport psychology (athlete psychotherapy case studies, of course, being one exception). If students or qualitative researchers start to blur the goals of therapy and research, they may begin to push participants into realms where they did not agree to go. At that point, research would start to resemble emotional abuse and voyeuristic exploitation. Helping students make the distinction between helping people tell their stories in research and doing psychotherapy should be a central feature of good training in qualitative research methods.

One area of sport psychology service that has received scant attention is the impairment of the practitioner. Judy Van Raalte, Britt Brewer, and I have written about this issue (see Andersen, Van Raalte, & Brewer, 2000), but I have had trouble finding anything in sport psychology qualitative research reporting that even mentions the potential impairment of the researcher. Impairment comes in a variety of forms. Psychologists can be impaired because of personal situations (depression, pathological bereavement, family problems) that tax them, deplete their resources, and make their service substandard. Incompetence, or not knowing one's stuff, is another form of impairment where improper treatment and misunderstandings of the client's issues, and so forth, lead to possible further damaging of the athlete.

Other types of impairment concern characterological issues (e.g., the sport psychologist with the narcissistic personality disorder who uses clients for self-aggrandisement, exploiting their connections with sport stars to reflect their own glory). I am sure readers have heard not only sport psychologists but also other sport scientists name-drop who they are working with, a type of building up of one's own status. In light of some other narcissistic exploitation I have seen, name-dropping is just a moderate transgression (see Andersen, in press).

Now, what about qualitative researchers who are impaired and conducting research? If a researcher is exploring realms of deeply personal concerns and material emerges that is negatively valent (e.g., sexual abuse), and the informant becomes severely distressed, and then the researcher attempts to handle the crisis, does not have the gear to do so, but believes he does, then the evoking of past abuse becomes a retraumatization. For psychologists, "Do no harm" is a first principle. The same should be true of qualitative researchers. If one helps an informant open Pandora's box, then one better be able to handle the demons that emerge. To open the box and then run is a form of abuse. Researchers should also have a ready referral list (see Andersen & Van Raalte, chapter 9 in this volume) and be trained in how to make referrals with sensitivity and care.

And what about narcissistic or antisocial researchers who exploit informants for their own needs, such as admiration or sexual gratification? The damage they can cause to participants and to the reputation of the field is substantial. Also, impaired researchers who are incompetent and naive also set themselves at risk of exploitation by their informants. And as thesis advisers, if we send impaired students out to an environment and to people that they are not competent enough to deal with, such as a prison population, then we are responsible for putting them at risk.

I have been fortunate not to run across an impaired sport psychology researcher firsthand, but I am sure I will in time. In my work on university ethics and research committees, however, I have had to deal with qualitative researchers who were so blinded by their missions that they failed to see how they were putting their informants at risk. One researcher, who was doing life histories of German and Japanese people interned during World War II, believed there were no psychological risks in revisiting those painful memories because they were almost 60 years old. Insensitivity, ignorance, and thoughtless disregard of human frailty constitute impairment and lead to abuse of those people whose stories we should embrace with loving care.

# Conclusion

Coming full circle back to where we started with research, theory, and models helps me wrap these two books up in an Eriksonian way. Erikson's midlife challenge of generativity, of giving back something, seems to fit here on a couple of levels. The authors in these texts have been out there in the realm of sport psychology service delivery, and they have come back from that "brave new world" (Shakespeare's Miranda in *The Tempest*) with great stories and lessons for students just starting out and exploring those territories. They have "given back" to the next generation of sport psychologists. But those gifts don't stop there at the applied service level; they move beyond service and shed light on the potential research landscapes to explore. I can't thank them enough for their contributions.

The "play," however, is not quite over. In Shakespearean terms, we are not yet at the end of act V; there is one more scene to go. In echoing what Polonius said about the troupe of players in Hamlet, we have heard tales tragical, comical, historical, and even pastoral. But we are missing a denouement. To bring the curtain down on our play, Bob Eklund, in his afterword, will reflect on what we do when we do sport psychology.

# Afterword

Robert C. Eklund, PhD

A substantial part of my adolescence and early adulthood was organized around my athletic and coaching endeavors. My fascination with the psychological aspects of sport was an outgrowth of those adventures. I never imagined that my graduate study of sport psychology would do anything other than keep me closely involved with sport. By the time I read Mark Andersen's (2000) book, *Doing Sport Psychology*, however, I had almost completely removed myself from any involvement with applied sport psychology—be it with athletes, coaches, or even applied sport psychology aspirants. The demands of the academy and the pursuit of tenure and promotion left little time in my day for much beyond working on the responsibilities relevant to those ends—and applied involvement with coaches and athletes is applauded, but not rewarded, in academia. Even so, I found Andersen's book to be intriguing in many ways. The presentation of the "how" (instead of the "what") of real-life applied sport psychology actions, accompanied by relevant explanatory commentary and the attendant interpretations, reminded me of my initial interests in the area while also satisfying my more recent efforts to intellectualize the process.

I had mixed emotions earlier this year when Andersen asked me to write the afterword for this extension of that earlier work. Of course, it was not difficult for me to appreciate the privilege being extended, and so I was not confused on that account. To be among the very few people reading a new book before it goes to press and, moreover, to be invited to have the last word are an honor. The responsibility of fulfilling that honor, however, was more daunting. I wondered what I might say. The matter of my growing distance from involvement in the applied side of the field, which was primarily as an educator working in group settings, also made me wonder if I was the right person for the task. On top of my reservations about being able to say *the right things*, there is also the matter of finding *the right tone*. Sycophantic exuberance never really seems appropriate, and anyway, it's not my style. Fortunately, I am not often inclined toward being dogmatically bloody-minded either, although some of my colleagues may dispute that assertion. Even so, how does one find the right tone? Despite these reservations (and others), I decided I should accept the honor—and the arrival of the draft chapters quickly reminded me of the weight of the accompanying responsibility.

Since Andersen has taken a confessional stance in closing the circle of this book in chapter 15, I'll too start off with a couple of confessions. First, I enjoyed reading this book. It addresses matters meriting further consideration that had not been substantively touched on in its predecessor. Second, I think that, individually and collectively, the chapters represent a well-considered and significant contribution to scholarly dialogue on the application of psychology to sport. Certainly some contentious observations and stances are forwarded—I confess my contrarian urge was agitated at various points—but nonetheless, these specific matters serve well in inviting the reader to consider the larger set of ideas being advanced. I congratulate all of the authors of the chapters in this book, as well as Andersen for soliciting their contributions.

I have decided not to dwell on arguing the specifics inciting my contrarian urges. I believe that would be to miss the point of the compendium as a whole. Instead, I comment more broadly on the lacunae in *Doing Sport Psychology* that Andersen sought to tackle in this new book. These are areas that were not substantially addressed in the precursor to this book and ones that, nonetheless, merit thoughtful consideration.

# Part I

The first part of *Sport Psychology in Practice* focuses on the processes of presenting sport psychology to groups. This general notion appealed to me greatly because I've long thought of sport psychology group work as an important area that is often greatly underplayed in discussions of applied sport psychology service. It is likely that my interest and opinions on this account are biased by my training as an educator and sport scientist—and exacerbated by my experiences as an athlete and a coach. Indeed, my practical efforts in providing sport psychology service have been exclusively educational in nature. The overwhelming majority of these efforts have taken place in group settings—sometimes in a classroom, occasionally in locker rooms, and often in the settings where practices and games take place. I cannot claim that these encounters are representative of other service providers' experiences in the area. They do, however, make me dismissive of the idea that sport psychology, at least of the "real" sort, occurs only in dyads in remedial or therapeutic settings (and some chapters in this book have that unfortunate flavor, in my opinion). This is not to say that I'm dismissive of colleagues who deal with matters requiring dyadic interaction. Nothing could be further from the truth. I simply disagree with the idea that "real" sport psychology is only, or best, manifested in that manner.

Andersen's acknowledgment of group presentations as one of the most common types of service delivered by sport psychologists was a refreshing departure from the almost blinkered focus on (and exaltation of) therapeutic dyads that occurs in some quarters. Frankly, I think organizations such as the Association for the Advancement of Applied Sport Psychology could do more to advance sport psychology (and have a greater impact on sport) through broad-based educational intervention programs involving group presentations for sport providers and sport participants than their present focus affords. The chapters in the first part of the book do not take up that crusade per se, but they ably illustrate the importance and diverse possibilities of doing sport psychology in groups. Specifically, Speed, Andersen, and Simons' chapter illustrates that even getting to "do sport psychology" can require a type of crucially important group presentation, whereas the other chapters span from the primarily educational in nature (Sherman and Poczwardowski, chapter 2; Burke, chapter 3) through the frequent necessity of using group work as an entree for more serious intervention opportunities (Andersen and Peterson, chapter 4). Overall, there is plenty of scope for useful efforts in group settings in applied sport psychology that is worth acknowledging and promoting. Part I provides a helpful and reasonably rare acknowledgment of that utility and scope.

# Part II

The second part of *Sport Psychology in Practice* takes on the sensitive issues of presenting counseling and clinical concerns and the ethics of professional practice. I see the chapters in this section as covering fascinating, albeit sometimes tragic, territory. Some of the challenges and dilemmas facing sport psychology consultants seeking to behave ethically are amply illustrated in these contributions. Some areas have enjoyed a fair amount of open discussion in the past (e.g., Brewer and Petitpas' chapter on returning, or not, from injury), whereas others are too infrequently broached at sport psychology meetings (e.g., Stainback and Taylor's chapter on violence and alcohol abuse). And then, of course, there are issues that are almost never discussed in open debate among sport psychologists, and then only uncomfortably (e.g., discussions on transference and countertransference, erotic and otherwise, in chapter 10 and the associated commentary by Strean and Strean). These contributions are important and useful because they highlight the potential for pragmatic difficulties that a sport psychology consultant can face.

Even more important, fascinating ground is covered on the ethical bases and the management of difficulties in this second part of the book. "Doing the right thing" (or even figuring out what it is!) is not an easy task. It is often anything but clear-cut. The considerations and associated intricacies of service can verge on the overwhelming—especially for those not well familiarized with the ethical complexities attending the responsibilities of serving in the helping professions. The contributions in this part highlight these complexities and underscore the need for people providing sport psychology service to be ethically well grounded. It is a matter that I believe the relevant organizations in the field (e.g., AAASP, APA Division 47) could dwell on to a greater degree at their professional meetings.

There is a flip side to my overall feelings about part II of the book. I relay it not to undercut any of my previous comments. Specifically, it is undoubtedly true that clients can present for sport psychology intervention or assistance with interests (e.g., learning psychological skills to enhance performance) or difficulties (e.g., trouble maintaining competitive focus, lack of motivation) that are not the *core difficulties* (e.g., relationship problems, psychological traumas or pathologies, eating disorders). All professionals *must* consider these potential realities in working with clients. I find it unsettling, however, when this truth is employed as a bludgeon to belittle the merits and potential results of professionals whose training in sport and exercise science has *not* been primarily focused on detection and treatment of the underlying possibilities for these difficulties. The unspoken but implied agenda in raising this truism is that those whose training focused on the detection of underlying but unspecified difficulties are the ones with the best competencies for providing ethical service in the field. (I've witnessed occasions where it was asserted that they are the *only* professionals with suitable competencies for providing service in the field.)

As previously acknowledged, awareness that the manifest problem might not be the *real* problem is requisite. I suspect that very few professionals in the field would argue otherwise. Awareness of this potential, however, is only meaningful *to the extent that a professional has the ability to detect that the client's presenting concerns are, in fact, manifestations of an underlying difficulty.* I find it unsettling that the "to the extent" part of the formulation is never addressed when these observations are forwarded in these arguments. This is a crucial absence that, in my opinion, reduces the assertions about underlying problems to nothing more than clichés. Is comprehensive awareness of underlying potentialities and failsafe detection a possibility? (I'm sure the answer is no, but it is a good starting question anyway.) If not, then, what level of capability is necessary? What are the available options for developing that competency? How does this requisite level then translate into ethical practice across the variety of real-life settings that sport psychology professionals operate in? A meaningful discussion on this account could be fruitful—but it typically doesn't occur because too often that is not the purpose in advancing the manifest versus latent content truism.

In a related matter, I also note that practicing within one's competencies requires more than the ability to detect a client's underlying difficulties so that steps can be taken to ensure his or her needs are properly met (by referral if necessary). As discussed in chapter 9, becoming aware of the limits of one's competencies in the provision of service is a nontrivial accomplishment but one that is inherently requisite to guide ethical practice. A lack of awareness on the limits of one's knowledge is problematic. It provides a breeding ground for unwanted complications—both for the professional and for the client involved. I'm not sure that this self-awareness is as widely developed in the field as might be desired. Nonetheless, I have a strong sense that where this unfortunate lack of aware-ness exists, it is not the sole province of sport and exercise professionals. Of course, this lack of self-awareness is something the field needs to grapple with—with all practicing professionals.

More generally with regard to competencies, all professionals, including those whose training is in sport and exercise science, are ethically bound to seek assistance, or make referrals, when dealing with clients whose needs extend beyond their competencies. Prac-ticing beyond one's competencies, regardless of training and experience, is practicing unethically (Andersen and Van Raalte's chapter 9 comments on the expansion of one's capabilities under appropriate supervision). This issue is not a matter of debate—nor do I seek to create one—because no argument can justify practicing unethically. I simply point out that professionals trained in sport and exercise science have a set of competen-cies. These competencies arguably have utility. When these professionals practice legally within these competencies, they are practicing ethically.

Certainly, development of necessary competencies for ethical practice is inherently a difficult process. At some level I think it is often limited, ironically, by our institutional training experiences. As a necessary and pragmatic reality, institutional training pro-grams tend to be relatively narrowly focused. They are dependent on available expertise and limited, in large degree, by the mission of the host academic unit. Experiences in our various institutes (exercise science *and* psychology departments) do not tend to lend themselves to a broader awareness of other relevant avenues of expertise. This focused sort of training inherently restricts opportunities to evaluate personal com-petencies (and associated limitations) against a broader backdrop of possibilities. This state of affairs is unfortunate in my opinion—although I thoroughly appreciate the pragmatic difficulties associated with providing or requiring broader exposure after sitting through some of the passionate discussions that produced the AAASP certified consultant criteria.

Parenthetically, the rise and success of multidisciplinary support teams of relevant service professionals in settings such as the Australian Institute of Sport denote the limitations of any given training background. These teams can include psychologists, exercise physiolo-gists, biomechanists, dietitians, and others with relevant expertise and still afford external referrals when necessary. They demonstrate the breadth of competencies relevant in the provision of services to athletes, both for facilitating athletic performance and addressing other issues emerging in interactions with their athlete clients. In sum, these approaches highlight the competency limitations associated with any given training background and force professionals to consider where they might fit into a bigger picture in providing the best possible service to their clients.

There is a second aspect to the unease accompanying my enjoyment of the second part of this book that extends beyond my comments on competencies. Specifically, I think it is naive and presumptuous to observe that clients can present with problems that are *not the problem* when the argument is raised without mention of where the clients themselves fit into the intervention equation. This concern was deftly handled in several chapters in this book (e.g., Andersen and Fawkner's chapter 5, Stainback and Taylor's chapter 8), but I also offer my comments because I think it is a matter worth dwelling on.

Specifically, I become uncomfortable when the manifest versus latent issue is invoked in ways that ignore the fact that clients necessarily have a say in the treatments they are exposed to in working with their sport psychology professionals. Underlying difficulties, or even psychopathologies, when detected, do not prioritize and drive intervention efforts independent of the client's wishes (or even the consultant's professional judgment). The clients make the decisions and establish priorities—sometimes in conjunction with the consultant and consistent with his or her recommendations but sometimes despite that (hopefully) sage advice. Consideration of questions such as "What did the athlete come to see the consultant about?" and "What does he or she want from that exposure to sport psychology service?" cannot (and should not) be ignored just because psychopathology or adjustment difficulties are present. Detection of these problems does not mean they *have* to be treated at that moment—if at all.

For example, an athlete might present to acquire mental skills because he or she has recently developed an inability to maintain competitive focus that is affecting performance quality. Initial probing might uncover that the athlete is grieving the recent loss of a father. Although possibly aware that grief is causing at least part of the difficulty, the athlete may be interested only in learning how to compensate, for a short time, to compete in an upcoming event in which years of preparatory training have been invested. Would it be proper for a helping professional to push a different intervention agenda (e.g., working through the grief) at that point despite the athlete's wishes? I think not. The decision to attempt to postpone the grieving and sadness to this end is the athlete's to make. To do otherwise and lead athletes into territories where they do not wish to travel is, in Andersen's personal communication to me on this topic, "a form of professional abuse and hubris." I'll not delve into the ethical complexities involved in how sport psychology professionals pursue "doing the right thing" when a client's interests are in conflict with their professional judgments. Others have more expertise on this account, and commentaries in this book (e.g., chapters 5 and 10) address it better than I could anyway. I acknowledge that this is a nontrivial exercise, and I certainly do not seek to minimize its importance. Nonetheless, it is a matter that sits alongside the question of who (or what) makes the decisions on where the professional relationship will go. Comments by one of the wrestlers participating in the 1988 U.S. Olympic wrestling study that I was involved in as a doctoral student also illustrate the importance of this point nicely:

> There was this psychologist a few years back that came in. We did about two hours of written tests for him. Then he kind of made judgments and recommendations from there. . . . I don't think we need to know that I'm mentally or morally deficient. I think people wrestle for different reasons. For somebody to cut down 20 pounds to make weight is probably not real normal on the scale of normalcy—whatever normal is. So everybody—in their own little way—is off their rocker. Anybody 28 years old that is still running and spending 4-5 hours a day wrestling is probably not all there as far as all these tests. I don't think the mental tests are important—and those were sport psychology tests. That's not as important as getting somebody in there for us to work with as individuals. (Eklund, Gould, & Jackson, 1993, p. 36)

# Part III

The third part of *Sport Psychology in Practice* contains chapters about working with diverse athletes. These chapters differ in focus from more conventional treatments of these topics. The contributions on the challenges of working with diverse populations from the perspectives of involved professionals are refreshing, and the focus on processes of evolution in understanding personal prejudices, and how they might impede good service, is substantive. I particularly enjoyed the presentations in chapters 13 and 14. The various issues Martens and Mobley cover in their chapter on working with gay males are novel and make for fascinating reading. The related chapter by Barber and Krane is no less important. Their observations on intervening to create healthier environments on teams forming "in group" and "out group" splits between lesbian and straight athletes were insightful in my opinion. Overall, I have little doubt that these efforts contribute importantly to the extant literature on sport psychology consultation with diverse populations.

# Completing the Circle

The idea of closing out an applied sport psychology compendium by focusing attention on current research in the field is not something I had anticipated when I accepted Andersen's invitation. He reverses the frequently advocated relationship between research and practice by encouraging practice-to-research efforts to help inform the field. His comments are provocative—both on the extant literature and in his confessions—but I confess that his observations were not among the matters that incited my contrarian urge. Rather, I found his observations bracing and worthy of contemplation. Of course, speaking as a journal editor, I would not want to see all applied researchers jump fully on the practice-to-research bandwagon. I do, however, welcome his comments in whatever degree they stimulate a healthy interplay between the processes of both practice and research and the experiences of the professionals involved.

# And in Closing

I found *Sport Psychology in Practice* to be as satisfying to read as its predecessor. Like *Doing Sport Psychology*, this book has reminded me why I chose this field of study years ago. Of course, the scope and diversity of issues considered relevant, and worthy of study, have grown immensely during my time in sport psychology, but there is much to appreciate about that vitality. And things will change more in the coming years—so much so that, at some point in the future, state-of-the-art compendia, such as this book, will serve as important signposts of where the field has been and where involved professionals thought it should be headed. At this moment, however, the contributions in this book offer cutting-edge insight into sport psychology practice. Moreover, they provide the foundation for exciting future developments. The field is progressing quickly. Both contemplation and enthusiasm are required to keep pace with all the developments. I hope this book inspires both in all who read it.

*Robert C. Eklund*
*December, 2004*
*Tallahassee, Florida*

# References

## Preface

Andersen, M.B. (1993). Questionable sensitivity: A comment on Lee and Rotella. *The Sport Psychologist, 7*, 1-3.

Andersen, M.B. (Ed.). (2000). *Doing sport psychology.* Champaign, IL: Human Kinetics.

Lee, C.C., & Rotella, R.J. (1991). Special concerns and considerations for sport psychology consulting with black athletes. *The Sport Psychologist, 5*, 365-369.

Murphy, S.M. (2000). Afterword. In M.B. Andersen (Ed.), *Doing sport psychology* (pp. 275-279). Champaign, IL: Human Kinetics.

National Collegiate Athletics Association. (1989). *NCAA eating disorders project.* Overland Park, KS: Author.

## Chapter 1

Andersen, M.B. (2000). Beginnings: Intakes and the initiation of relationships. In M.B. Andersen (Ed.), *Doing sport psychology* (pp. 3-16). Champaign, IL: Human Kinetics.

Gardner, F. (1995). The coach and the team psychologist: An integrated organizational model. In S.M. Murphy (Ed.), *Sport psychology interventions* (pp. 147-175). Champaign, IL: Human Kinetics.

Ravizza, K. (1988). Gaining entry with athletic personnel for season-long consulting. *The Sport Psychologist, 2*, 243-254.

Simons, J.P., & Andersen, M.B. (1995). The development of consulting practice in applied sport psychology: Some personal perspectives. *The Sport Psychologist, 9*, 449-468.

## Chapter 2

American Psychological Association. (1992). Ethical principles of psychologists and code of conduct. *American Psychologist, 47*, 1597-1611.

Andersen, M.B. (Ed.). (2000). *Doing sport psychology.* Champaign, IL: Human Kinetics.

Andersen, M.B. (2001). When to refer athletes for counseling or psychotherapy. In J.M. Williams (Ed.), *Applied sport psychology: Personal growth to peak performance* (4th ed., pp. 401-415). Mountain View, CA: Mayfield.

Anderson, A. (1997). Learning strategies in physical education: Self-talk, imagery, and goal-setting. *Journal of Physical Education, Recreation and Dance, 68*(1), 30-35.

Bee, H. (1995). *The developing child* (7th ed.). New York: HarperCollins.

Bloom, B.S. (1981). *All our children learning: A primer for parents, teachers, and other educators.* New York: McGraw-Hill.

Botterill, C. (1990). Sport psychology and professional hockey. *The Sport Psychologist, 4*, 358-368.

Bredemeier, B.J.L., & Shields, D.L.L. (1995). *Character development and physical activity.* Champaign, IL: Human Kinetics.

Brewer, B.W. (2000). Doing sport psychology in the coaching role. In M.B. Andersen (Ed.), *Doing sport psychology* (pp. 237-247). Champaign, IL: Human Kinetics.

Brewer, B.W., & Shillinglaw, R. (1992). Evaluation of a psychological skills training workshop for male intercollegiate lacrosse players. *The Sport Psychologist, 6*, 139-147.

Bull, S.J. (1995). Reflections on a 5-year consultancy program with the England women's cricket team. *The Sport Psychologist, 9*, 148-163.

Burton, D. (1989). Winning isn't everything: Examining the impact of performance goals on collegiate swimmers' cognitions and performance. *The Sport Psychologist, 3*, 105-132.

Coakley, J.J. (1998). *Sport in society: Issues and controversies* (6th ed.). Boston: McGraw-Hill.

Corey, G. (1995). *Theory and practice of group counseling* (4th ed.). Pacific Grove, CA: Brooks/Cole.

Danish, S.J. (1996). Interventions for enhancing adolescents' life skills. *The Humanistic Psychologist, 24*, 365-381.

Danish, S.J., & Nellen, V.C. (1997). New roles for sport psychologists: Teaching life skills through sport to at-risk youth. *Quest, 49*, 100-113.

Danish, S.J., Petitpas, A., & Hale, B.D. (1995). Psychological interventions: A life development model. In

S.M. Murphy (Ed.), *Sport psychology interventions* (pp. 19-38). Champaign, IL: Human Kinetics.

Davis, K. (1991). Performance enhancement program for a college tennis player. *International Journal of Sport Psychology, 22,* 140-164.

Deci, E.L., & Ryan, R.M. (1985). *Intrinsic motivation and self-determination in human behavior.* New York: Plenum Press.

European Federation of Sport Psychology. (1996). Position statement of the European Federation of Sport Psychology (FEPSAC): II. Children in sport. *The Sport Psychologist, 10,* 224-226.

French, K.E., & Thomas, J.R. (1987). The relation of knowledge development to children's basketball performance. *Journal of Sport Psychology, 9,* 15-32.

Haywood, K.M., & Getchell, N. (2005). *Life span motor development* (4th ed.). Champaign, IL: Human Kinetics.

Hellison, D. (1996). Teaching personal and social responsibility in physical education. In S.J. Silverman & C.D. Ennis (Eds.), *Student learning in physical education: Applying research to enhance instruction* (pp. 269-286). Champaign, IL: Human Kinetics.

Kohlberg, L., & Ullian, D.Z. (1974). Stages in the development of psychosexual concepts and attitudes. In R.C. Friedman, R.L. Richart, & R.M. Vande Wiele (Eds.), *Sex differences in behavior* (pp. 209-222). New York: Wiley.

Lidor, R. (2000). On becoming a thinker–learner: Instructional applications of an integrated approach. *The Physical Educator, 57,* 14-21.

Lloyd, R.J., & Trudel, P. (1999). Verbal interactions between an eminent mental training consultant and elite level athletes: A case study. *The Sport Psychologist, 13,* 418-443.

Mercier, R., & Hutchinson, G. (1998). Social psychology. In B. Mohnsen (Ed.), *Concepts of physical education: What every student needs to know* (pp. 159-198). Reston, VA: National Association for Sport and Physical Education.

Mohnsen, B. (Ed.). (2003). *Concepts and principles of physical education: What every student needs to know* (2nd ed.). Reston, VA: National Association for Sport and Physical Education.

Mosston, M., & Ashworth, S. (1994). *Teaching physical education* (4th ed.). New York: Macmillan.

National Association for Sport and Physical Education. (2004). *Moving into the future: National standards for physical education* (3rd ed.). Reston, VA: Author.

National Education Goals Panel. (1999). *Data volume for the National Education Goals report.* Washington, DC: U.S. Government Printing Office.

Neff, F. (1990). Delivering sport psychology services to a professional sport organization. *The Sport Psychologist, 4,* 378-385.

Orlick, T. (1992). The psychology of personal excellence. *Contemporary Thought on Performance Enhancement, 1,* 109-122.

Orlick, T. (Ed.). (1998). *Journal of Excellence* [Online serial], *1.* Available: www.coach.ca/ismte/journal.htm

Orlick, T., & McCaffrey, N. (1991). Mental training with children for sport and life. *The Sport Psychologist, 5,* 322-334.

Page, S.J., Sime, W., & Nordell, K. (1999). The effects of imagery on female college swimmers' perceptions of anxiety. *The Sport Psychologist, 13,* 458-469.

Pangrazi, R.P., & Darst, P.W. (1997). *Dynamic physical education for secondary school students* (3rd ed.). Boston: Allyn & Bacon.

Partington, J., & Orlick, T. (1991). An analysis of Olympic sport psychology consultants' best-ever consulting experiences. *The Sport Psychologist, 5,* 183-193.

Payne, G.V., & Isaacs, L.D. (1999). *Human motor development: A lifespan approach* (4th ed.). Mountain View, CA: Mayfield.

Piaget, J., & Inhelder, B. (1969). *The psychology of the child.* New York: Basic Books.

Placek, J.H. (1996). Integration as a curriculum model in physical education: Possibilities and problems. In S.J. Silverman & C.D. Ennis (Eds.), *Student learning in physical education: Applying research to enhance instruction* (pp. 287-311). Champaign, IL: Human Kinetics.

Poczwardowski, A. (2001, May). Sport psychology service delivery model: A heuristic for systemizing and optimizing consulting practice. In A. Poczwardowski & K.P. Henschen, *Consultant variables, consultant–client relationships, immersion, and goodness of fit in successful sport psychology service delivery.* Symposium presented at the 10th World Congress of Sport Psychology, Skiathos, Greece.

Ravizza, K. (2001). Increasing awareness for sport performance. In J.M. Williams (Ed.), *Applied sport psychology: Personal growth to peak performance* (4th ed., pp. 179-189). Mountain View, CA: Mayfield.

Rink, J.E. (1998). *Teaching physical education for learning* (3rd ed.). Boston: McGraw-Hill.

Sage, G.H. (1990). *Power and ideology in American sport: A critical perspective.* Champaign, IL: Human Kinetics.

Sherman, C.P. (1999). Integrating mental management skills into the physical education curriculum. *Journal of Physical Education, Recreation and Dance, 70*(5), 25-30, 49.

Sherman, C.P. (2000). Teaching performance excellence through life skill instruction: An integrated curriculum (Part 1). *Strategies, 14*(2), 19-23.

Sherman, C.P. (2001). Teaching performance excellence through life skill instruction: An integrated curriculum (Part 2). *Strategies, 14*(3), 24-29.

Sherman, C.P., & Poczwardowski, A. (2000). Relax! It ain't easy (or is it?). In M.B. Andersen (Ed.), *Doing sport psychology* (pp. 47-60). Champaign, IL: Human Kinetics.

Simons, J.P., & Andersen, M.B. (1995). The development of consulting practice in applied sport psychology: Some personal perspectives. *The Sport Psychologist, 9,* 449-468.

Sinclair, G.D., & Sinclair, D.A. (1994). Developing reflective performers by integrating mental management skills with the learning process. *The Sport Psychologist, 8,* 13-27.

Singer, R.N. (1988). Strategies and metastrategies in learning and performing self-paced athletic skills. *The Sport Psychologist, 2,* 49-68.

Thompson, M.A., & Ravizza, K. (1998). The value of failure. In M.A. Thompson, R.A. Vernacchia, & W.E. Moore (Eds.), *Case studies in sport psychology: An educational approach* (pp. 247-256). Dubuque, IA: Kendall/Hunt.

Turatto, M., Benso, F., & Umilta, C. (1999). Focusing of attention in professional women skiers. *International Journal of Sport Psychology, 30,* 339-349.

Vanden Auweele, Y.V., Bakker, F., Biddle, S., Durand, M., & Seiler, R. (1999). *Psychology for physical educators.* Human Kinetics: Champaign, IL.

Vealey, R.S. (1988). Future directions in psychological skills training. *The Sport Psychologist, 2,* 318-336.

Vealey, R.S. (1994). Current status and prominent issues in sport psychology interventions. *Medicine and Science in Sports and Exercise, 26,* 495-502.

Weinberg, R.S., & Gould, D. (2003). *Foundations of sport and exercise psychology* (3rd ed.). Champaign, IL: Human Kinetics.

Weiss, M.R. (1991). Psychological skill development in children and adolescents. *The Sport Psychologist, 5,* 335-354.

Weiss, M.R. (1995). Children in sport: An educational model. In S.M. Murphy (Ed.), *Sport psychology interventions* (pp. 39-69). Champaign, IL: Human Kinetics.

Weiss, M.R., & Chaumeton, N. (1992). Motivational orientations in sport. In T.S. Horn (Ed.), *Advances in sport psychology* (pp. 61-99). Champaign, IL: Human Kinetics.

Wood, S.E., & Wood, E.G. (1999). *The world of psychology* (3rd ed.). Needham Heights, MA: Allyn & Bacon.

Wrisberg, C.A., & Anshel, M.H. (1989). The effect of cognitive strategies on the free throw shooting performance of young athletes. *The Sport Psychologist, 3,* 95-104.

Zhang, L., Ma, Q., Orlick, T., & Zitzelsberger, L. (1992). The effects of mental-imagery training on performance enhancement with 7–10-year-old children. *The Sport Psychologist, 6,* 230-241.

## Chapter 3

Anshel, M.H. (2002). *Sport psychology: From theory to practice* (4th ed.). San Francisco: Benjamin Cummings.

Beebe, S.A., Beebe, S.J., & Redmond, M.V. (1996). *Interpersonal communication: Relating to others.* Boston: Allyn & Bacon.

Berger, C.R. (1986). Uncertainty outcome values in predicted relationships: Uncertainty reduction theory then and now. *Human Communication Research, 13,* 34-38.

Bird, A.M. (1977). Development of a model for predicting team performance. *Research Quarterly, 48,* 24-32.

Bormann, E.G. (1986). Symbolic convergence theory and group decision making. In R.Y. Hirokawa & M.S. Poole (Eds.), *Communication and group decision making* (pp. 219-236). Beverly Hills, CA: Sage.

Burke, K.L. (1997). Communication in sports: Research and practice. *Journal of Interdisciplinary Research in Physical Education, 2,* 39-52.

Burke, K.L. (in press). Using sport psychology to improve basketball performance. In J. Dosil-Diaz (Ed.), *Sport Psychology: Improving performance in different sports.* West Sussex, England: Wiley.

Byrne, D.E.(1971). *The attraction paradigm.* New York: Academic Press.

Cahn, D.D. (1984). Teacher–student relationships: Perceived understanding. *Communication Research Reports, 1,* 65-67.

Carron, A.V., & Bennett, B.B. (1977). Compatibility in the coach–athlete dyad. *Research Quarterly, 48,* 671-679.

Carron, A.V., & Hausenblas, H.A. (1998). *Group dynamics in sport* (2nd ed.). Morgantown, WV: Fitness Information Technology.

Corey, G. (2001). *Theory and practice of counseling and psychotherapy* (6th ed.). Pacific Grove, CA: Brooks/Cole.

Delia, J. (1987). Communication research: A history. In C. Berger & S. Chaffee (Eds.), *Handbook of communication science* (pp. 20-98). Beverly Hills, CA: Sage.

Di Berardinis, J., Barwind, J., Flaningam, R.R., & Jenkins, V. (1983). Enhanced interpersonal relation as predictor of athletic performance. *International Journal of Sport Psychology, 14,* 243-251.

Fisher, B.A., & Hawes, L. (1971). An interact system model: Generating a grounded theory of small groups. *Quarterly Journal of Speech, 57,* 444-453.

Haney, W.V. (1979). *Communication and interpersonal relations.* Homewood, IL: Irwin.

Hanrahan, S., & Gallois, C. (1993). Social interactions. In R.N. Singer, M. Murphey, & L.K. Tennant (Eds.), *Handbook of research on sport psychology* (pp. 623-646). New York: Macmillan.

Hanson, G. (1986). *Determinants of firm performance: An integration of economic and organizational factors.* Unpublished doctoral dissertation, University of Michigan, Ann Arbor.

Hardy, C.J., Burke, K.L., & Crace, R.K. (2005). Coaching: An effective communication system. In S.M. Murphy (Ed.), *The sport psych handbook* (pp. 191-212). Champaign, IL: Human Kinetics.

Haselwood, D.M., Joyner, A.B., Burke, K.L., Geyerman, C.B., Czech, D.R., Munkasy, B.A., & Zwald, A.D. (in press). Female athletes' perceptions of head coaches' communication competence. *Journal of Sport Behavior.*

Infante, D.A., Rancer, A.S., & Womack, D.F. (1997). *Building communication theory* (3rd ed.). Prospect Heights, IL: Waveland Press.

Knapp, M.L. (1978). *Nonverbal communication in human interaction* (2nd ed.). Englewood Cliffs, NJ: Prentice Hall.

Lambrecht, K.W. (1987). An analysis of the competencies of sports and athletic club managers. *Journal of Sport Management, 1,* 116-128.

Martens, R. (2004). *Successful coaching* (3rd ed.). Champaign, IL: Human Kinetics.

Martens, R., & Peterson, J.A. (1971). Group cohesiveness as a determinant of success and member satisfaction in team performance. *International Review of Sport Sociology, 6,* 49-61.

McGough, E. (1974). *Understanding body talk.* New York: Scholastic.

Mehrabian, A. (1968, September). Communication without words. *Psychology Today, 1,* 52-55.

Nixon, H.L. (1976). Team orientations, interpersonal relations, and team success. *Research Quarterly, 47,* 429-435.

Ouchi, W. (1981). *Theory Z.* Reading, MA: Addison-Wesley.

Peters, T. (1988). *Thriving on chaos.* New York: Knopf.

Poole, M.S. (1983). Decision development in small groups, III: A multiple sequence of models of group decision development. *Communication Monographs, 50,* 321-341.

Smith, R.E., & Smoll, F.L. (1996). *Way to go coach: A scientifically-proven approach to coaching effectiveness.* Portola Valley, CA: Warde.

Smith, R.E., Smoll, F.L., & Curtis, B. (1979). Coach effectiveness training: A cognitive–behavioral approach to enhancing relationship skills in youth sport coaches. *Journal of Sport Psychology, 1,* 59-75.

Sullivan, P.A. (1993). Communication skills training for interactive sports. *The Sport Psychologist, 7,* 79-91.

Sunnafrank, M. (1986). Predicted outcome value during initial interactions: A reformulation of uncertainty reduction theory. *Human Communication Research, 13,* 3-33.

von Gunten, C.F., Ferris, F.D., & Emanuel, L.L. (2000). Ensuring the competency in end-of-life care: Communication and relational skills. *Journal of the American Medical Association, 284,* 3051-3057.

Watkins, B. (1991). Communications. In B.L. Parkhouse (Ed.), *The management of sport: Its foundation and application* (pp. 107-134). Chicago: Mosby.

Weinberg, R.S., & Gould, D. (2003). *Foundations of sport and exercise psychology* (3rd ed.). Champaign, IL: Human Kinetics.

Whetten, D.W., & Cameron, K.S. (1991). *Developing management skills* (2nd ed.). New York: HarperCollins.

Williams, J.M., & Widmeyer, W.N. (1991). The cohesion–performance outcome relationship in a coacting sport. *Journal of Sport & Exercise Psychology, 13,* 364-371.

Yukelson, D. (1997). Principles of effective team building interventions in sport: A direct service approach at Penn State University. *Journal of Applied Sport Psychology, 9,* 73-96.

Yukelson, D. (2001). Communicating effectively. In J.M. Williams (Ed.), *Applied sport psychology: Personal growth to peak performance* (4th ed., pp. 135-149). Mountain View, CA: Mayfield.

### Chapter 4

National Collegiate Athletics Association. (1989). *Nutrition and weight* [Videotape]. Overland Park, KS: Author.

Petrie, T.A., & Sherman, R.T. (2000). Counseling athletes with eating disorders: A case example. In M.B. Andersen (Ed.), *Doing sport psychology* (pp. 121-137). Champaign, IL: Human Kinetics.

### Chapter 5

Abell, S.C., & Richards, M.H. (1996). The relationship between body shape satisfaction and self-esteem: An investigation of gender and class differences. *Journal of Youth and Adolescence, 25,* 691-703.

Andersen, A.E., & Di Domenico, L. (1992). Diet vs. popular shape content of popular male and female magazines: A dose-response relationship to the incidence of eating disorders? *International Journal of Eating Disorders, 11,* 283-287.

Andersen, R.E., Barlett, S.J., Morgan, G.D., & Brownell, K.D. (1995). Weight loss, psychological, and nutritional patterns in competitive male body builders. *International Journal of Eating Disorders, 18,* 49-57.

Anderson, S.L., Zager, K., Hetzler, R.K., NahikianNelms, M., & Syler, G. (1996). Comparison of Eating Disorder Inventory (EDI-2) scores of male bodybuilders to the male college student subgroup. *International Journal of Sport Nutrition, 6*, 255-262.

Armstrong, J.E., Lange, E., & Mishra, S. (1992). Reported exercise practices and self-image of adult male and female recreational exercisers. *Family and Community Health, 14*, 20-28.

Beren, S.E., Hayden, H.A., Wifley, D.E., & Grillo, C.M. (1996). The influence of sexual orientation on body dissatisfaction in adult men and women. *International Journal of Eating Disorders, 20*, 135-141.

Berscheid, E., Walster, E., & Bohrnstedt, G. (1973). The happy American body: A survey report. *Psychology Today, 7*(6), 119-123, 126, 128-131.

Blouin, A.G., & Goldfield, G.S. (1995). Body image and steroid use in male bodybuilders. *International Journal of Eating Disorders, 18*, 159-165.

Brand, P.A., Rothblum, E.D., & Solomon, L.J. (1992). A comparison of lesbians, gay men, and heterosexuals on weight and restrained eating. *International Journal of Eating Disorders, 11*, 253-259.

Braun, D.L., Sunday, S.R., Huang, A., & Halmi, K. (1999). More males seek treatment for eating disorders. *International Journal of Eating Disorders, 26*, 413-424.

Brower, K.J. (1992). Addictive potential of anabolic steroids. *Psychiatric Annals, 22*, 30-34.

Buckley, W.E., Yesalis, C.E., Friedl, K.E., Anderson, W.A., Streit, A.L., & Wright, J.E. (1988). Estimated prevalence of anabolic steroid use among high school seniors. *Journal of the American Medical Association, 260*, 3441-3445.

Carlat, D.J., & Camargo, C.A. (1991). Review of bulimia nervosa in males. *American Journal of Psychiatry, 148*, 831-843.

Carlat, D., Camargo, C.A., & Herzog, D.B. (1997). Eating disorders in males: A report on 135 patients. *American Journal of Psychiatry, 154*, 1127-1132.

Cash, T.F. (1996). The treatment of body image disturbances. In J.K. Thompson (Ed.), *Body image, eating disorders, and obesity: An integrative guide for assessment and treatment* (pp. 83-107). Washington, DC: American Psychological Association.

Cash, T.F. (2002). Cognitive–behavioral perspectives on body image. In T.F. Cash & T. Pruzinsky (Eds.), *Body image: A handbook of theory, research, and clinical practice* (pp. 38-46). New York: Guilford Press.

Cash, T.F., & Brown, T.A. (1987). Body image in anorexia nervosa and bulimia nervosa. *Behavior Modification, 11*, 487-521.

Cash, T.F., & Grant, J.R. (1995). The cognitive–behavioral treatment of body-image disturbances. In V.V. Hasselt & M. Hersen (Eds.), *Sourcebook of psychological treatment manuals for adults* (pp. 567-614). New York: Plenum Press.

Cash, T.F., & Syzmanski, M.L. (1995). The development and validation of the Body-Ideals Questionnaire. *Journal of Personality Assessment, 64*, 466-477.

Cash, T.F., Winstead, B.A., & Janda, L.H. (1986). Body image survey report: The great American shape-up. *Psychology Today, 20*, 30-34, 36-37.

Catalano, A. (1996). Pecs appeal: Why men are the new cosmetic surgery junkies. *Marie Claire (Australia), 9*, 154-158.

Dally, P. (1969). *Anorexia nervosa.* London: Heinemann.

Davis, C. (1997). Body image, exercise, and eating behaviors. In K. Fox (Ed.), *The physical self: From motivation to well being* (pp. 143-174). Champaign, IL: Human Kinetics.

Davis, C., & Cowles, M. (1991). Body image and exercise: A study of relationships and comparisons between physically active men and women. *Sex Roles, 25*, 33-44.

Davis, C., Dionne, M., & Lazarus, L. (1996). Gender-role orientation and body image in women and men: The moderating influence of neuroticism. *Sex Roles, 34*, 493-505.

Davis, C., Durnin, J.V.G.A., Gurevich, M., LeMaire, A., & Dionne, M. (1994). The influence of body fat content and bone diameter measurements on body dissatisfaction in adult women. *International Journal of Eating Disorders, 15*, 257-263.

Davis, C., Fox, J., Cowles, M.P., Hastings, P., & Schwass, K. (1990). The functional role of exercise in the development of weight and diet concerns in women. *Journal of Psychosomatic Research, 34*, 563-574.

Deno, E. (1953). Self-identification among adolescent boys. *Child Development, 24*, 269-273.

Diabiase, W.J., & Hjelle, L.A. (1968). Body-image stereotypes and body-type preferences among male college students. *Perceptual and Motor Skills, 27*, 1143-1146.

Dion, K.K., Berscheid, E., & Walster, E. (1972). What is beautiful is good. *Journal of Personality and Social Psychology, 24*, 285-290.

Drewnowski, A., Hopkins, S.A., & Kessler, R.C. (1988). The prevalence of bulimia nervosa in the US college student population. *American Journal of Public Health, 78*, 1322-1325.

Drewnowski, A., & Yee, D.K. (1987). Men and body image: Are males satisfied with their body weight? *Psychosomatic Medicine, 49*, 626-634.

Durnin, J.V.G.A., & Passmore, R. (1967). *Energy, work and leisure.* London: Heinemann.

Fawkner, H.J. (2005). *Body image attitudes in men: An examination of the antecedents and consequent adjustive strategies and behaviours.* Unpublished doctoral dissertation, University of Melbourne, Australia.

Fawkner, H.J., & McMurray, N.E. (2002). Body image in men: Self-reported thoughts, feelings, and behaviors in response to media images. *International Journal of Men's Health, 1,* 137-161.

Feingold, A., & Mazzella, R. (1998). Gender differences in body image are increasing. *Psychological Science, 9,* 190-195.

Finch, C.B. (1991). *Sexual orientation, body image, and sexual functioning.* Unpublished master's thesis, Old Dominion University, Norfolk, Virginia.

Franco, K.S., Tamburrino, M.B., Carroll, B.T., & Bernal, G.A. (1988). Eating attitudes in college males. *International Journal of Eating Disorders, 7,* 285-288.

French, S.A., Story, M., Remafedi, G., Resnick, M.D., & Blum, R.W. (1996). Sexual orientation and prevalence of body dissatisfaction and eating disordered behaviors: A population-based study of adolescents. *International Journal of Eating Disorders, 19,* 119-126.

Fulkerson, J.A., Keel, P.K., Leon, G.R., & Door, T. (1999). Eating-disordered behaviors and personality characteristics of high school athletes and nonathletes. *International Journal of Eating Disorders, 26,* 73-79.

Gardner, R.M., Friedman, B.N., & Jackson, N.A. (1998). Methodological concerns when using silhouettes to measure body image. *Perceptual and Motor Skills, 86,* 387-395.

Garner, D.M., & Kearney-Cooke, A. (1997, January/February). The 1997 body image survey results. *Psychology Today, 30,* 30-36, 38-40, 42-44, 75-76, 78, 80, 84.

Gettelman, T.E., & Thompson, J.K. (1993). Actual differences and stereotypical perceptions in body image and eating disturbance: A comparison of male and female heterosexual and homosexual samples. *Sex Roles, 29,* 545-562.

Grogan, S., Williams, Z., & Conner, M. (1996). The effects of viewing same-gender photographic models on body-esteem. *Psychology of Women Quarterly, 20,* 569-575.

Halmi, K.A., Falk, J.R., & Swartz, E. (1981). Binge eating and vomiting: A survey of a college population. *Psychological Medicine, 11,* 697-706.

Herzog, D.B., Bradburn, I.S., & Newman, K. (1990). Sexuality in males with eating disorders. In A.E. Andersen (Ed.), *Males with eating disorders* (pp. 40-53). New York: Brunner/Mazel.

Herzog, D.B., Newman, K.L., & Warshaw, M. (1991). Body image dissatisfaction in homosexual and heterosexual males. *Journal of Nervous and Mental Disease, 179,* 356-359.

Herzog, D.B., Norman, D.K., Gordon, C., & Pepose, M. (1984). Sexual conflict and eating disorders in 27 males. *American Journal of Psychiatry, 141,* 989-990.

Hoek, H.W., & van Hoeken, D. (2003). Review and prevalence of eating disorders. *International Journal of Eating Disorders, 34,* 383-396.

Huddy, D.C., & Cash, T.F. (1997). Body-image attitudes among male marathon runners: A controlled comparative study. *International Journal of Sport Psychology, 28,* 227-236.

Huddy, D.C., Johnson, R.L., Stone, M.H., Proulx, C.M., & Pierce, K.A. (1997). Relationship between body image and percent body fat among male and female college students enrolled in an introductory 14-week weight-training course. *Perceptual and Motor Skills, 85,* 1075-1078.

Huddy, D.C., Nieman, D.C., & Johnson, R.L. (1993). Relationship between body image and percent body fat among college male varsity athletes and nonathletes. *Perceptual and Motor Skills, 77,* 851-857.

Jacobi, L., & Cash, T.F. (1994). In pursuit of the perfect appearance: Discrepancies among self-ideal percepts of multiple physical attributes. *Journal of Applied Social Psychology, 24,* 379-396.

Johnson, C., Powers, P.S., & Dick, R. (1999). Athletes and eating disorders: The National Collegiate Athletic Association study. *International Journal of Eating Disorders, 26,* 179-188.

Katz, J.L. (1986). Long distance running, anorexia nervosa, and bulimia: A report of two cases. *Comparative Psychiatry, 27,* 74-78.

Kearney-Cooke, A., & Steichen-Asch, P. (1990). Men, body image, and eating disorders. In A.E. Andersen (Ed.), *Males with eating disorders* (pp. 54-74). New York: Brunner/Mazel.

Keeton, W.P., Cash, T.F., & Brown, T.A. (1990). Body image or body images? Comparative, multidimensional assessment among college students. *Journal of Personality Assessment, 54,* 213-230.

Kiernan, M., Rodin, J., Brownell, K.D., Wilmore, J.H., & Crandall, C. (1992). Relation of level of exercise, age, and weight-cycling history to weight and eating concerns in male and female runners. *Health Psychology, 11,* 418-421.

Lerner, R.M., & Korn, S.J. (1972). The development of body-build stereotypes in males. *Child Development, 43,* 908-920.

Lindner, M.A., Ryckman, R.M., Gold, J.A., & Stone, W.F. (1995). Traditional vs. nontraditional women and men's perceptions of the personalities and physiques of ideal women and men. *Sex Roles, 32,* 675-690.

Loosemoore, D.J., Mable, H.M., Galgan, R.J., Balance, W.D.G., & Moriarty, R.J. (1989). Body image disturbances in selected groups of men. *Psychology: A Journal of Human Behavior, 26,* 56-59.

Lucas, A.R., Beard, C.M., O'Fallon, W.M., & Kurland, L.T. (1991). 50-year trends in the incidence of anorexia nervosa in Rochester, Minnesota: A population-based study. *American Journal of Psychiatry, 148,* 917-922.

Mangweth, B., Pope, H.G., Jr., Hudson, J.I., Olivardia, R., Kinzl, J., & Biebl, W. (1997). Eating disorders in Austrian men: An intracultural and crosscultural comparison study. *Psychotherapy and Psychosomatics, 66,* 214-221.

Marinos, S. (1997, April). You're so vain I bet you think this story is about you. *Elle Australia: Men,* 44-47.

McDonald, K., & Thompson, J.K. (1992). Eating disturbance, body image dissatisfaction, and reasons for exercising: Gender differences and correlational findings. *International Journal of Eating Disorders, 11,* 289-292.

McKay Parks, P.S., & Read, M.H. (1997). Adolescent male athletes: Body image, diet, and exercise. *Adolescence, 32,* 593-603.

McMurray, N.E., Bell, R., & Shircore, J. (1995, July). *Psychological factors influencing positive and negative health behaviours in a community sample of men and women.* Paper presented at the 9th European Congress of Psychology, Athens, Greece.

McMurray, N.E., & Gazis, J. (1995, November). *Factors associated with sexual risk taking in gay and bisexual men.* Paper presented at the 19th Annual Conference for the Advancement of Behavior Therapy, Houston, TX.

Mishkind, M.E., Rodin, J., Silberstein, L.R., & Striegel-Moore, R.H. (1986). The embodiment of masculinity: Cultural, psychological, and behavioral dimensions. *American Behavioral Scientist, 29,* 545-562.

Mort, F. (1988). Boys own? Masculinity, style and popular culture. In R. Chapman & J. Rutherfords (Eds.), *Male order: Unwrapping masculinity* (pp. 193-224). London: Lawrence & Wishart.

Ogden, J. (1992). *Fat chance: The myth of dieting explained.* London: Routledge.

Olivardia, R., Pope, H.G., Jr., Mangweth, B., & Hudson, J.J. (1995). Eating disorders in college men. *American Journal of Psychiatry, 152,* 1279-1285.

Oyebode, F., Boodhoo, J.A., & Schapira, K. (1988). Anorexia nervosa in males: Clinical features and outcome. *International Journal of Eating Disorders, 7,* 121-124.

Pasman, L., & Thompson, J.K. (1988). Body image and eating disturbance in obligatory runners, obligatory weightlifters, and sedentary individuals. *International Journal of Eating Disorders, 7,* 759-769.

Petrie, T.A., & Sherman, R.T. (2000). Counseling athletes with eating disorders: A case example. In M.B. Andersen (Ed.), *Doing sport psychology* (pp. 121-137). Champaign, IL: Human Kinetics.

Pope, H.G., Jr., Hudson, J.I., Yurgelun-Todd, D., & Hudson, M.S. (1984). Prevalence of anorexia nervosa and bulimia in three student populations. *International Journal of Eating Disorders, 3,* 45-51.

Pope, H.G., Jr., Olivardia, R., Gruber, A., & Borowiecki, J. (1999). Evolving ideals of male body image as seen through action toys. *International Journal of Eating Disorders, 26,* 65-72.

Pope, H.G., Jr., Phillips, K.A., & Olivardia, R. (2000). *The Adonis complex: The secret crisis of male body obsession.* New York: Free Press.

Raudenbush, B., & Zellner, D.A. (1997). Nobody's satisfied: Effects of abnormal eating behaviors and actual and perceived weight status on body image satisfaction in males and females. *Journal of Social and Clinical Psychology, 16,* 95-110.

Rosen, J.C. (1990). Body-image disturbance in eating disorders. In T.F. Cash & T. Pruzinsky (Eds.), *Body images: Development, deviance, and change* (pp. 190-214). New York: Guilford Press.

Ryan, J. (1995). *Little girls in pretty boxes: The making and breaking of elite gymnasts and figure skaters.* New York: Doubleday.

Salusso-Deonier, C.J., Markee, N.L., & Pedersen, E.L. (1993). Gender differences in the evaluation of physical attractiveness ideals for male and female body builds. *Perceptual and Motor Skills, 76,* 1155-1167.

Salusso-Deonier, C.J., & Schwarzkopf, R.J. (1991). Sex differences in body-cathexis associated with exercise involvement. *Perceptual and Motor Skills, 73,* 139-145.

Sarafino, E.P. (1998). *Health psychology: Biopsychosocial interactions* (3rd ed.). New York: Wiley.

Schneider, J.A., & Agras, W.S. (1987). Bulimia in males: A matched comparison with females. *International Journal of Eating Disorders, 6,* 235-242.

Schotte, D.E., & Stunkard, A.J. (1987). Bulimia vs. bulimic behaviors on a college campus. *Journal of the American Medical Association, 258,* 1213-1215.

Siever, M.D. (1994). Sexual orientation and gender as factors in socioculturally acquired vulnerability to body dissatisfaction and eating disorders. *Journal of Consulting and Clinical Psychology, 62,* 252-260.

Silberstein, L.R., Mishkind, M.E., Striegel-Moore, R.H., Timko, C., & Rodin, J. (1989). Men and their bodies: A comparison of homosexual and heterosexual men. *Psychosomatic Medicine, 51,* 337-346.

Silberstein, L.R., Striegel-Moore, R.H., Timko, C., & Rodin, J. (1988). Behavioral and psychological implications of body dissatisfaction: Do men and women differ? *Sex Roles, 19,* 219-232.

Singer, B.L., & Deschamps, D. (Eds.). (1994). *Gay and lesbian stats: A pocket guide of facts and figures.* New York: New Press.

St. Martin, M., & Garvey, N. (1996). Women's bodybuilding: Feminist resistance and/or femininity's recuperation. *Body and Society, 2,* 45-47.

Stoutjesdyk, D., & Jevne, R. (1992). Eating disorders among high performance athletes. *Journal of Youth and Adolescence, 22,* 271-282.

Striegel-Moore, R.H., Silberstein, L.R., Frensch, P., & Rodin, J. (1989). A prospective study of disordered eating among college students. *International Journal of Eating Disorders, 8,* 499-509.

Striegel-Moore, R.H., Silberstein, L.R., & Rodin, J. (1986). Toward an understanding of risk factors for bulimia. *American Psychologist, 41,* 246-263.

Thiel, A., Gottfried, H., & Hesse, F.W. (1993). Body experience in male athletes: A study on the mental health of wrestlers and rowers in the lower weight classes. *Psychotherapie Psychosomatik Medizinische Psychologie, 43,* 432-438.

Thompson, J.K., Heinberg, L.J., Altabe, M., & Tantleff Dunn, S. (1999). *Exacting beauty: Theory, assessment, and treatment of body image disturbance.* Washington, DC: American Psychological Association.

Thompson, R.A., & Sherman, R.T. (1993). *Helping athletes with eating disorders.* Champaign, IL: Human Kinetics.

Tucker, L.A. (1982). Effect of a weight-training program on the self-concepts of college males. *Perceptual and Motor Skills, 54,* 1055-1061.

Tucker, L.A. (1983). Weight training: A tool for the improvement of self and body concepts of males. *Journal of Human Movement Studies, 9,* 31-37.

Tucker, L.A. (1984). Physical attractiveness, somatotype, and the male personality: A dynamic interactional perspective. *Journal of Clinical Psychology, 40,* 1226-1234.

Wilkins, J.A., Boland, F.J., & Albinson, J. (1991). A comparison of male and female university athletes and nonathletes on eating disorder indices: Are athletes protected? *Journal of Sport Behavior, 14,* 129-143.

Williamson, I., & Hartley, P. (1998). British research into the increased vulnerability of young gay men to eating disturbance and body dissatisfaction. *European Eating Disorders Review, 6,* 160-170.

Yager, J., Kurtzman, F., Landsverk, J., & Wiesmeier, E. (1988). Behaviors and attitudes related to eating disorders in homosexual male college students. *American Journal of Psychology, 145,* 495-497.

Yates, A. (1991). *Compulsive exercise and the eating disorders: Toward an integrated theory of activity.* New York: Brunner/Mazel.

## Chapter 6

Alzate, R., Ramirez, A., & Lazaro, I. (1998, August). *Psychological aspect of athletic injury.* Paper presented at the 24th International Congress of Applied Psychology, San Francisco, CA.

Bramwell, S.T., Masuda, M., Wagner, N.N., & Holmes, T.H. (1975). Psychosocial factors in athletic injuries: Development and application of the Social and Athletic Readjustment Rating Scale (SARRS). *Journal of Human Stress, 1,* 6-20.

Brewer, B.W. (1993). Self-identity and specific vulnerability to depressed mood. *Journal of Personality, 61,* 343-364.

Brewer, B.W. (1994). Review and critique of models of psychological adjustment to athletic injury. *Journal of Applied Sport Psychology, 6,* 87-100.

Brewer, B.W. (1999a). Adherence to sport injury rehabilitation regimens. In S.J. Bull (Ed.), *Adherence issues in sport and exercise* (pp. 145-168). Chichester, England: Wiley.

Brewer, B.W. (1999b). Causal attribution dimensions and adjustment to sport injury. *Journal of Personal and Interpersonal Loss, 4,* 215-224.

Brewer, B.W. (2001). Psychology of sport injury rehabilitation. In R.N. Singer, H.A. Hausenblas, & C.M. Janelle (Eds.), *Handbook of sport psychology* (2nd ed., pp. 787-809). New York: Wiley.

Brewer, B.W., Andersen, M.B., & Van Raalte, J.L. (2002). Psychological aspects of sport injury rehabilitation: Toward a biopsychosocial approach. In D.L. Mostofsky & L.D. Zaichkowsky (Eds.), *Medical and psychological aspects of sport and exercise* (pp. 41-54). Morgantown, WV: Fitness Information Technology.

Brewer, B.W., Jeffers, K.E., Petitpas, A.J., & Van Raalte, J.L. (1994). Perceptions of psychological interventions in the context of sport injury rehabilitation. *The Sport Psychologist, 8,* 176-188.

Brewer, B.W., Linder, D.E., & Phelps, C.M. (1995). Situational correlates of emotional adjustment to athletic injury. *Clinical Journal of Sport Medicine, 5,* 241-245.

Brewer, B.W., Petitpas, A.J., & Van Raalte, J.L. (1999). Referral of injured athletes for counseling and psychotherapy. In R. Ray & D.M. Wiese-Bjornstal (Eds.), *Counseling in sports medicine* (pp. 127-141). Champaign, IL: Human Kinetics.

Brewer, B.W., Petitpas, A.J., Van Raalte, J.L., Sklar, J.H., & Ditmar, T.D. (1995). Prevalence of psychological distress among patients at a physical therapy clinic specializing in sports medicine. *Sports Medicine, Training and Rehabilitation, 6,* 138-145.

Brewer, B.W., & Petrie, T.A. (1995). A comparison between injured and uninjured football players on selected psychosocial variables. *Academic Athletic Journal, 10,* 11-18.

Brewer, B.W., Van Raalte, J.L., & Linder, D.E. (1991). Role of the sport psychologist in treating injured athletes: A survey of sports medicine providers. *Journal of Applied Sport Psychology, 3,* 183-190.

Brewer, B.W., Van Raalte, J.L., & Linder, D.E. (1993). Athletic identity: Hercules' muscles or Achilles heel? *International Journal of Sport Psychology, 24,* 237-254.

Brewer, B.W., Van Raalte, J.L., & Petitpas, A.J. (1999). Patient–practitioner interactions in sport injury rehabilitation. In D. Pargman (Ed.), *Psychological bases of sport injuries* (2nd ed., pp. 157-174). Morgantown, WV: Fitness Information Technology.

Caine, D.J., Caine, C.G., & Lindner, K.J. (Eds.). (1996). *Epidemiology of sports injuries.* Champaign, IL: Human Kinetics.

Cerny, F.J., Patton, D.C., Whieldon, T.J., & Roehrig, S. (1992). An organizational model of sports medicine facilities in the United States. *Journal of Orthopaedic and Sports Physical Therapy, 15,* 80-86.

Chan, C.S., & Grossman, H.Y. (1988). Psychological effects of running loss on consistent runners. *Perceptual and Motor Skills, 66,* 875-883.

Crossman, J., Gluck, L., & Jamieson, J. (1995). The emotional responses of injured athletes. *New Zealand Journal of Sports Medicine, 23,* 1-2.

Crossman, J., & Jamieson, J. (1985). Differences in perceptions of seriousness and disrupting effects of athletic injury as viewed by athletes and their trainer. *Perceptual and Motor Skills, 61,* 1131-1134.

Cupal, D.D. (1998). Psychological interventions in sport injury prevention and rehabilitation. *Journal of Applied Sport Psychology, 10,* 103-123.

Daly, J.M., Brewer, B.W., Van Raalte, J.L., Petitpas, A.J., & Sklar, J.H. (1995). Cognitive appraisal, emotional adjustment, and adherence to rehabilitation following knee surgery. *Journal of Sport Rehabilitation, 4,* 23-30.

Francis, S.R., Andersen, M.B., & Maley, P. (2000). Physiotherapists' and male professional athletes' views on psychological skills for rehabilitation. *Journal of Science and Medicine in Sport, 3,* 17-29.

Giges, B., & Petitpas, A. (2000). Brief contact interventions in sport psychology. *The Sport Psychologist, 14,* 176-187.

Gordon, S., Milios, D., & Grove, J.R. (1991). Psychological aspects of the recovery process from sport injury: The perspective of sport physiotherapists. *Australian Journal of Science and Medicine in Sport, 23,* 53-60.

Grove, J.R., Stewart, R.M.L., & Gordon, S. (1990, October). *Emotional reactions of athletes to knee rehabilitation.* Paper presented at the annual meeting of the Australian Sports Medicine Federation, Alice Springs, Australia.

Heil, J. (Ed.). (1993). *Psychology of sport injury.* Champaign, IL: Human Kinetics.

Johnson, U. (1997). Coping strategies among long-term injured competitive athletes: A study of 81 men and women in team and individual sports. *Scandinavian Journal of Medicine and Science in Sports, 7,* 367-372.

Johnson, U. (1998). Psychological risk factors during the rehabilitation of competitive male soccer players with serious knee injuries [Abstract]. *Journal of Sports Sciences, 16,* 391-392.

Johnston, L.H., & Carroll, D. (1998). The context of emotional responses to athletic injury: A qualitative analysis. *Journal of Sport Rehabilitation, 7,* 206-220.

Kleiber, D.A., & Brock, S.C. (1992). The effect of career-ending injuries on the subsequent well-being of elite college athletes. *Sociology of Sport Journal, 9,* 70-75.

Larson, G.A., Starkey, C.A., & Zaichkowsky, L.D. (1996). Psychological aspects of athletic injuries as perceived by athletic trainers. *The Sport Psychologist, 10,* 37-47.

Leddy, M.H., Lambert, M.J., & Ogles, B.M. (1994). Psychological consequences of athletic injury among high-level competitors. *Research Quarterly for Exercise and Sport, 65,* 347-354.

Little, J.C. (1969). The athlete's neurosis: A deprivation crisis. *Acta Psychiatrica Scandinavica, 45,* 187-197.

McDonald, S.A., & Hardy, C.J. (1990). Affective response patterns of the injured athlete: An exploratory analysis. *The Sport Psychologist, 4,* 261-274.

Meyers, M.C., Sterling, J.C., Calvo, R.D., Marley, R., & Duhon, T.K. (1991). Mood state of athletes undergoing orthopaedic surgery and rehabilitation: A preliminary report. *Medicine and Science in Sports and Exercise, 23*(Suppl.), S138.

Pargman, D. (Ed.). (1999). *Psychological bases of sport injuries* (2nd ed.). Morgantown, WV: Fitness Information Technology.

Pargman, D., & Lunt, S.D. (1989). The relationship of self-concept and locus of control to the severity of injury in freshmen collegiate football players. *Sports Training, Medicine and Rehabilitation, 1,* 203-208.

Pearson, L., & Jones, G. (1992). Emotional effects of sports injuries: Implications for physiotherapists. *Physiotherapy, 78,* 762-770.

Pearson, R., & Petitpas, A. (1990). Transitions of athletes: Pitfalls and prevention. *Journal of Counseling and Development, 69,* 7-10.

Petitpas, A.J. (2000). The Littlefoot approach to learned resourcefulness: Managing stress on and off the field. In M.B. Andersen (Ed.), *Doing sport psychology* (pp. 33-43). Champaign, IL: Human Kinetics.

Petitpas, A., & Danish, S.J. (1995). Caring for injured athletes. In S.M. Murphy (Ed.), *Sport psychology interventions* (pp. 255-281). Champaign, IL: Human Kinetics.

Petrie, T.A., Brewer, B., & Buntrock, C. (1997). A comparison between injured and uninjured NCAA Division I male and female athletes on selected psychosocial variables [Abstract]. *Journal of Applied Sport Psychology, 9*(Suppl.), S144.

Quinn, A.M. (1996). *The psychological factors involved in the recovery of elite athletes from long term injuries.* Unpublished doctoral dissertation, University of Melbourne, Australia.

Smith, A.M., Scott, S.G., O'Fallon, W.M., & Young, M.L. (1990). Emotional responses of athletes to injury. *Mayo Clinic Proceedings, 65,* 38-50.

Smith, A.M., Stuart, M.J., Wiese-Bjornstal, D.M., Milliner, E.K., O'Fallon, W.M., & Crowson, C.S. (1993). Competitive athletes: Preinjury and postinjury mood state and self-esteem. *Mayo Clinic Proceedings, 68,* 939-947.

Smith, A.M., Young, M.L., & Scott, S.G. (1988). The emotional responses of athletes to injury. *Canadian Journal of Sport Sciences, 13*(Suppl.), 84P-85P.

Sparkes, A.C. (1998). An Achilles heel to the survival of self. *Qualitative Health Research, 8,* 644-664.

Tedder, S., & Biddle, S.J.H. (1998). Psychological processes involved during sports injury rehabilitation: An attribution–emotion investigation [Abstract]. *Journal of Sports Sciences, 16,* 106-107.

Uemukai, K. (1993). Affective responses and the changes in athletes due to injury. In S. Serpa, J. Alves, V. Ferreira, & A. Paula-Brito (Eds.), *Proceedings of the 8th World Congress of Sport Psychology* (pp. 500-503). Lisbon, Portugal: International Society of Sport Psychology.

Wiese, D.M., Weiss, M.R., & Yukelson, D.P. (1991). Sport psychology in the training room: Implications for the treatment team. *The Sport Psychologist, 5,* 15-24.

Wiese-Bjornstal, D.M., Smith, A.M., Shaffer, S.M., & Morrey, M.A. (1998). An integrated model of response to sport injury: Psychological and sociological dimensions. *Journal of Applied Sport Psychology, 10,* 46-69.

Williams, J.M., & Andersen, M.B. (1998). Psychosocial antecedents of sport injury: Review and critique of the stress and injury model. *Journal of Applied Sport Psychology, 10,* 5-25.

## Chapter 7

Duda, J.L., & Hall, H. (2001). Achievement goal theory in sport: Recent extensions and future directions. In R.N. Singer, H.A. Hausenblas, & C.M. Janelle (Eds.), *Handbook of sport psychology* (2nd ed., pp. 417-443). New York: Wiley.

Egan, G. (1982). *The skilled helper* (2nd ed.). Monterey, CA: Brooks/Cole.

Hadfield, D. (1994). The query theory. *New Zealand Coach, 3*(4), 16-20.

Hamilton, L.H. (1997). *The person behind the mask: A guide to performing arts psychology.* Greenwich, CT: Ablex.

Hanrahan, C. (1995). In search of a "good" image: Use of imagery while performing dance movement. *Dissertation Abstracts International, 55*(8-A), 2189A.

Hanrahan, C., Tetreau, B., & Sarrazin, C. (1995). Use of imagery while performing dance movement. *International Journal of Sport Psychology, 26,* 413-430.

Hanrahan, S.J. (1996). Dancers' perceptions of psychological skills. *Revista de Psicologia del Deporte, 9/10,* 19-27.

Hardy, L., Jones, G., & Gould, D. (1996). *Understanding psychological preparation for sport: Theory and practice of elite performers.* Chichester, England: Wiley.

Macchi, R., & Crossman, J. (1996). After the fall: Reflections of injured classical ballet dancers. *Journal of Sport Behavior, 19,* 221-234.

Moore, W.E., & Stevenson, J.R. (1994). Training for trust in sport skills. *The Sport Psychologist, 8,* 1-12.

Ryan, R.M., & Deci, E.L. (2000). Self-determination theory and the facilitation of intrinsic motivation, social development, and well-being. *American Psychologist, 55,* 68-78.

Shaffer, S.M., & Wiese-Bjornstal, D.M. (1999). Psychosocial intervention strategies in sports medicine. In R. Ray & D.M. Wiese-Bjornstal (Eds.), *Counseling in sports medicine* (pp. 41-54). Champaign, IL: Human Kinetics.

Singer, R.N., Lidor, R., & Cauraugh, J.H. (1993). To be aware or not aware? What to think about while learning and performing a motor skill. *The Sport Psychologist, 7,* 19-30.

Taylor, J., & Taylor, C. (1995). *Psychology of dance.* Champaign, IL: Human Kinetics.

### *Commentary on Chapter 7*

Andersen, M.B. (2000). Introduction. In M.B. Andersen (Ed.), *Doing sport psychology* (pp. xiii-xvii). Champaign, IL: Human Kinetics.

Gould, D. (Ed.). (2002). Moving beyond the psychology of athletic excellence [Special issue]. *Journal of Applied Sport Psychology, 14.*

Hamilton, L.H. (1997). *The person behind the mask: A guide to performing arts psychology.* Greenwich, CT: Ablex.

Hamilton, L.H., & Hamilton, W.G. (1991). Classical ballet: Balancing the costs of artistry and athleticism. *Medical Problems of Performing Artists, 6,* 39-43.

Hamilton, L.H., & Hamilton, W.G. (1994). Occupational stress in classical ballet: The impact in different cultures. *Medical Problems of Performing Artists, 9,* 35-38.

Hays, K.F. (2000). Breaking out: Doing sport psychology with performing artists. In M.B. Andersen (Ed.), *Doing sport psychology* (pp. 261-274). Champaign, IL: Human Kinetics.

Hays, K.F. (2002). The enhancement of performance excellence among performing artists. *Journal of Applied Sport Psychology, 14,* 299-312.

Hays, K.F., & Brown, C.B., Jr. (2004). *You're on! Consulting for peak performance.* Washington, DC: American Psychological Association.

Kain, K. (1994). *Movement never lies: An autobiography.* Toronto: McClelland & Stewart.

Mainwaring, L.M., Krasnow, D., & Kerr, G. (2001). And the dance goes on: Psychological impact of injury. *Journal of Dance Medicine and Science, 5,* 105-115.

Starkes, J.L., Helsen, W., & Jack, R. (2001). Expert performance in sport and dance. In R.N. Singer, H.A. Hausenblas, & C.M. Janelle (Eds.), *Handbook of sport psychology* (2nd ed., pp. 174-201). New York: Wiley.

Taylor, J., & Taylor, C. (1995). *Psychology of dance.* Champaign, IL: Human Kinetics.

Wootten, C. (2001). Gender-based and relationship issues. In *Not just any body: Advancing health, well-being and excellence in dance and dancers* (pp. 58-62). Owen Sound, ON: Ginger Press.

**Chapter 8**

American Psychiatric Association. (1994). *Diagnostic and statistical manual of mental disorders* (4th ed.). Washington, DC: Author.

Chermack, S.T., & Giancola, P.R. (1997). The relation between alcohol and aggression: An integrated biopsychosocial conceptualization. *Clinical Psychology Review, 17,* 621-649.

DiClemente, C.C., & Prochaska, J.O. (1998). Toward a comprehensive, transtheoretical model of change. In A.S. Bellack & M. Hersen (Series Eds.) and W.R. Miller & N. Heather (Vol. Eds.), *Applied clinical psychology: Treating addictive behaviors* (2nd ed., pp. 3-24). New York: Plenum Press.

Dinh-Zarr, T., Diguiseppi, C., Heitman, E., & Roberts, I. (1999). Preventing injuries through interventions for problem drinking: A systematic review of randomized controlled trials. *Alcohol and Alcoholism, 34,* 609-621.

Institute of Medicine. (1990). *Broadening the base of treatment for alcohol problems.* Washington, DC: National Academy Press.

Johnston, L.D., O'Malley, P.M., & Bachman, J.G. (1998). *National survey results on drug use from the Monitoring the Future study, 1975-1997. Volume II: College students and young adults* (NIH Publication No. 98-4346). Rockville, MD: National Institute on Drug Abuse.

Lipsey, M.W., Wilson, D.B., Cohen, M.A., & Derzon, J.H. (1997). Is there a causal relationship between alcohol use and violence? A synthesis of evidence. *Recent Developments in Alcoholism, 13,* 245-282.

Miller, W.R. (1989). Matching individuals with interventions. In R.K. Hester & W.R. Miller (Eds.), *Handbook of alcoholism treatment approaches: Effective alternatives* (pp. 261-271). New York: Pergamon Press.

Miller, W.R., & Rollnick, S. (1991). *Motivational interviewing: Preparing people to change addictive behavior.* New York: Guilford Press.

Nattiv, A., Puffer, J.C., & Green, G.A. (1997). Lifestyles and health risks of collegiate athletes: A multi-center study. *Clinical Journal of Sport Medicine, 7,* 262-272.

Nephew, T.M., Williams, G.D., Stinson, F.S., Nguyen, K., & Dufour, M.C. (1999). *Apparent per capita alcohol consumption: National, state, and regional trends, 1977-1997* (NIAAA Surveillance Report #51). Bethesda, MD: National Institute on Alcohol Abuse and Alcoholism.

Prochaska, J.O., DiClemente, C.C., & Norcross, J.C. (1992). In search of how people change: Applications to addictive behaviors. *American Psychologist, 47,* 1102-1114.

Matching alcoholism treatments to client heterogeneity: Project MATCH three-year drinking outcomes. (1998). *Alcoholism: Clinical and Experimental Research, 22,* 1300-1311.

Rollnick, S., Mason, P., & Butler, C. (1999). *Health behavior change: A guide for practitioners.* Edinburgh, Scotland: Churchill Livingstone.

Stainback, R.D. (1997). *Alcohol and sport.* Champaign, IL: Human Kinetics.

Substance Abuse and Mental Health Services Administration. (1999). *Summary of findings from the 1998 national household survey on drug abuse* (DHHS Publication No. SMA 99-3328). Rockville, MD: Author.

U.S. Department of Health and Human Services. (1997). *Ninth special report to the U.S. Congress on alcohol and health* (NIH Publication No. 97-4017). Rockville, MD: National Institute on Alcohol Abuse and Alcoholism.

Wechsler, H., Dowdall, G.W., Maenner, G., Gledhill-Hoyt, J., & Lee, H. (1998). Changes in binge drinking and related problems among American college students between 1993 and 1997: Results of the Harvard School of Public Health College Alcohol Study. *Journal of American College Health, 47*(2), 57-68.

**Chapter 9**

American Psychiatric Association. (2001). *Diagnostic and statistical manual of mental disorders* (4th ed., text revision). Washington, DC: Author.

American Psychological Association. (1992). Ethical principles of psychologists and code of conduct. *American Psychologist, 47,* 1597-1611.

American Psychological Association Committee on Lesbian and Gay Concerns. (1990). *Bias in psychotherapy with lesbians and gay men.* Washington, DC: American Psychological Association.

Andersen, M.B. (1992). Sport psychology and procrustean categories: An appeal for synthesis and expansion of service. *Association for the Advancement of Applied Sport Psychology Newsletter, 7*(3), 8-9.

Andersen, M.B., Butki, B.D., & Heyman, S.R. (1997). Homophobia and sport experience: A survey of college students. *Academic Athletic Journal, 12*(1), 27-38.

Andersen, M.B., Denson, E.L., Brewer, B.W., & Van Raalte, J.L. (1994). Disorders of personality and mood in athletes: Recognition and referral. *Journal of Applied Sport Psychology, 6,* 168-184.

Andersen, M.B., & Tod, D. (in press). When to refer athletes for counseling or psychotherapy. In J.M. Williams (Ed.), *Applied sport psychology: Personal growth to peak performance* (5th ed.). Mountain View, CA: Mayfield.

Andersen, M.B., Van Raalte, J.L., & Brewer, B.W. (2000). When applied sport psychology consultants and graduate students are impaired: Ethical and legal issues in training and supervision. *Journal of Applied Sport Psychology, 12,* 134-150.

Andersen, M.B., Van Raalte, J.L., & Harris, G. (2000). Supervision II: A case study. In M.B. Andersen (Ed.), *Doing sport psychology* (pp. 167-180). Champaign, IL: Human Kinetics.

Baillie, P.H.F., & Danish, S.J. (1992). Understanding the career transitions of athletes. *The Sport Psychologist, 6,* 77-98.

Balague, G. (1999). Understanding identity, value, and meaning when working with elite athletes. *The Sport Psychologist, 13,* 89-98.

Barney, S.T., & Andersen, M.B. (2000). Looking for help, grieving love lost: The case of C. In M.B. Andersen (Ed.), *Doing sport psychology* (pp. 139-150). Champaign, IL: Human Kinetics.

Black, D. (Ed.). (1991). *Eating disorders among athletes: Theory, issues, and research.* Reston, VA: American Alliance for Health, Physical Education, Recreation and Dance.

Bobele, M., & Conran, T.J. (1988). Referrals for family therapy: Pitfalls and guidelines. *Elementary School Guidance, 22,* 192-198.

Brewer, B.W. (1994). Review and critique of models of psychological adjustment to athletic injury. *Journal of Applied Sport Psychology, 6,* 87-100.

Brewer, B.W., Petitpas, A.J., & Van Raalte, J.L. (1999). Referral of injured athletes for counselling and psychotherapy. In R. Ray & D.M. Wiese-Bjornstal (Eds.), *Counseling in sports medicine* (pp. 127-141). Champaign, IL: Human Kinetics.

Brewer, B.W., & Petrie, T.A. (2002). Psychopathology in sport and exercise. In J.L. Van Raalte & B.W. Brewer (Eds.), *Exploring sport and exercise psychology* (2nd ed., pp. 307-323). Washington, DC: American Psychological Association.

Brewer, B.W., Van Raalte, J.L., & Linder, D.E. (1991). Role of the sport psychologist in treating injured athletes: A survey of sports medicine providers. *Journal of Applied Sport Psychology, 3,* 183-190.

Burckes-Miller, M., & Black, D. (1988). Male and female college athletes: Prevalence of anorexia nervosa and bulimia nervosa. *Athletic Training, 23,* 137-140.

Butki, B.D., Andersen, M.B., & Heyman, S.R. (1996). Knowledge of AIDS and risky sexual behavior among athletes. *Academic Athletic Journal, 11*(1), 29-36.

Carr, C.M., & Murphy, S.M. (1995). Alcohol and drugs in sport. In S.M. Murphy (Ed.), *Sport psychology interventions* (pp. 283-306). Champaign, IL: Human Kinetics.

Cogan, K.D. (2000). The sadness in sport: Working with a depressed and suicidal athlete. In M.B. Andersen (Ed.), *Doing sport psychology* (pp. 107-119). Champaign, IL: Human Kinetics.

Cogan, K.D., & Petrie, T.A. (2002). Diversity in sport. In J.L. Van Raalte & B.W. Brewer (Eds.), *Exploring sport and exercise psychology* (2nd ed., pp. 417-436). Washington, DC: American Psychological Association.

Etzel, E.F., Ferrante, A.P., & Pinkney, J.W. (Eds.). (1996). *Counseling college student-athletes: Issues and interventions* (2nd ed.). Morgantown, WV: Fitness Information Technology.

Giges, B. (1998). Psychodynamic concepts in sport psychology: Comment on Strean and Strean (1998). *The Sport Psychologist, 12,* 223-227.

Gregg, E., & Rejeski, W.J. (1990). Social psychologic dysfunction associated with anabolic steroids: A review. *The Sport Psychologist, 4,* 275-284.

Griffin, P. (1992). Changing the game: Homophobia, sexism, and lesbians in sport. *Quest, 44,* 251-265.

Griffin, P. (1998). *Strong women, deep closets: Lesbians and homophobia in sport.* Champaign, IL: Human Kinetics.

Grove, J.R., Lavallee, D., Gordon, S., & Harvey, J.H. (1998). Account-making: A model for understanding and resolving distressful reactions to retirement from sport. *The Sport Psychologist, 12,* 52-67.

Heil, J. (1993). *Psychology of sport injury.* Champaign, IL: Human Kinetics.

Hellstedt, J.C. (1995). Invisible players: A family systems model. In S.M. Murphy (Ed.), *Sport psychology interventions* (pp. 117-146). Champaign, IL: Human Kinetics.

Kolt, G.S. (2000). Doing sport psychology with injured athletes. In M.B. Andersen (Ed.), *Doing sport psychology* (pp. 223-236). Champaign, IL: Human Kinetics.

Krane, V. (1995). Performance related outcomes experienced by lesbian athletes. *Journal of Applied Sport Psychology, 7*(Suppl.), S83.

Lavallee, D., & Andersen, M.B. (2000). Leaving sport: Easing career transitions. In M.B. Andersen (Ed.), *Doing sport psychology* (pp. 249-260). Champaign, IL: Human Kinetics.

Lenskyj, H. (1991). Combating homophobia in sport and physical education. *Sociology of Sport Journal, 8*, 61-69.

Lesyk, J.L. (1998). *Developing sport psychology within your clinical practice: A practical guide for mental health professionals.* San Francisco: Jossey-Bass.

Linder, D.E., Brewer, B.W., Van Raalte, J.L., & DeLange, N. (1991). A negative halo for athletes who consult sport psychologists: Replication and extension. *Journal of Sport & Exercise Psychology, 13*, 133-148.

Linder, D.E., Pillow, D.R., & Reno, R.R. (1989). Shrinking jocks: Derogation of athletes who consult a sport psychologist. *Journal of Sport & Exercise Psychology, 11*, 270-280.

Martin, K.A., & Hausenblas, H.A. (1998). Psychological commitment to exercise and eating disorder symptomatology among female aerobic instructors. *The Sport Psychologist, 12*, 180-190.

Miller, M.J., & Moore, K.K. (1993). Athletes' and nonathletes' expectations about counseling. *Journal of College Student Development, 34*, 267-270.

National Collegiate Athletic Association (Producer). (1989). *NCAA eating disorders project, Part 1, Afraid to eat: Eating disorders and student athletes* [Motion picture]. (Available from the National Collegiate Athletic Association, 700 W. Washington Street, Indianapolis, IN 46206-6222)

Petitpas, A., & Danish, S.J. (1995). Caring for injured athletes. In S.M. Murphy (Ed.), *Sport psychology interventions* (pp. 255-281). Champaign, IL: Human Kinetics.

Petitpas, A.J., Danish, S.J., & Giges, B. (1999). The sport psychologist–athlete relationship: Implications for training. *The Sport Psychologist, 13*, 344-357.

Petrie, T.A., & Sherman, R.T. (2000). Counseling athletes with eating disorders: A case example. In M.B. Andersen (Ed.), *Doing sport psychology* (pp. 121-137). Champaign, IL: Human Kinetics.

Poczwardowski, A., Sherman, C.P., & Henschen, K.P. (1998). A sport psychology service delivery heuristic: Building on theory and practice. *The Sport Psychologist, 12*, 345-356.

Putukian, M. (1994). The female triad: Eating disorders, amenorrhea, and osteoporosis. *Medical Clinics of North America, 78*, 345-356.

Rotella, R.J. (1992). Sport psychology: Staying focused on a common and shared mission for a bright future. *Association for the Advancement of Applied Sport Psychology Newsletter, 7*(3), 8-9.

Seime, R., & Damer, D. (1991). Identification and treatment of the athlete with an eating disorder. In E.F. Etzel, A.P. Ferrante, & J.W. Pinkney (Eds.), *Counseling college student-athletes: Issues and interventions* (pp. 175-198). Morgantown, WV: Fitness Information Technology.

Simons, J.P., & Andersen, M.B. (1995). The development of consulting practice in applied sport psychology: Some personal perspectives. *The Sport Psychologist, 9*, 449-468.

Sours, J.A. (1980). *Starving to death in a sea of objects: The anorexia nervosa syndrome.* New York: Jason Aronson.

Strean, W.B., & Strean, H.S. (1998). Applying psychodynamic concepts in sport psychology practice. *The Sport Psychologist, 12*, 208-222.

Strein, W., & Hershenson, D.B. (1991). Confidentiality in nondyadic counseling situations. *Journal of Counseling and Development, 69*, 312-316.

Sundgot-Borgen, J. (1994). Risk and trigger factors for the development of eating disorders in female elite athletes. *Medicine and Science in Sport and Exercise, 26*, 414-419.

Swoap, R.A., & Murphy, S.M. (1995). Eating disorders and weight management in athletes. In S.M. Murphy (Ed.), *Sport psychology interventions* (pp. 307-329). Champaign, IL: Human Kinetics.

Thompson, R.A., & Sherman, R.T. (1993). *Helping athletes with eating disorders.* Champaign, IL: Human Kinetics.

Van Raalte, J.L., & Andersen, M.B. (2000). Supervision I: From models to doing. In M.B. Andersen (Ed.), *Doing sport psychology* (pp. 153-165). Champaign, IL: Human Kinetics.

Van Raalte, J.L., & Andersen, M.B. (2002). Referral processes in sport psychology. In J.L. Van Raalte & B.W. Brewer (Eds.), *Exploring sport and exercise psychology* (2nd ed., pp. 275-284). Washington, DC: American Psychological Association.

Van Raalte, J.L., Brewer, B.W., Brewer, D.D., & Linder, D.E. (1992). NCAA Division II college football players' perceptions of an athlete who consults a sport psychologist. *Journal of Sport & Exercise Psychology, 14*, 273-282.

## Chapter 10

Abramowitz, S.I., Abramowitz, C.V., Roback, H.B., Corney, R.T., & McKee, W. (1976). Sex-role related countertransference in psychotherapy. *Archives of General Psychiatry, 33*, 71-73.

References

American Psychological Association. (1992). Ethical principles of psychologists and code of conduct. *American Psychologist, 47,* 1597-1611.

Andersen, M.B. (2000). Beginnings: Intakes and the initiation of relationships. In M.B. Andersen (Ed.), *Doing sport psychology* (pp. 3-16). Champaign, IL: Human Kinetics.

Andersen, M.B., Van Raalte, J.L., & Brewer, B.W. (2001). Sport psychology service delivery: Staying ethical while keeping loose. *Professional Psychology: Research and Practice, 32,* 12-18.

Andersen, M.B., Van Raalte, J.L., & Harris, G. (2000). Supervision II: A case study. In M.B. Andersen (Ed.), *Doing sport psychology* (pp. 167-179). Champaign, IL: Human Kinetics.

Avery, L.D., & Gressard, C.F. (2000). Counseling regulations regarding sexual misconduct: A comparison across states. *Counseling and Values, 45,* 67-78.

Barnhouse, R.T. (1978). Sex between therapist and patient. *Journal of the American Academy of Psychoanalysis, 6,* 533-546.

Bates, C.R., & Brodsky, A.M. (1989). *Sex in the therapy hour: A case of professional incest.* New York: Guilford Press.

Bouhoutsos, J.C. (1984). Sexual intimacy between psychotherapists and clients: Policy implications for the future. In L. Walker (Ed.), *Women and mental health policy* (pp. 207-227). Beverly Hills, CA: Sage.

Bouhoutsos, J.C., Holroyd, J., Lerman, H., Forer, B., & Greenberg, M. (1983). Sexual intimacy between psychotherapists and patients. *Professional Psychology: Research and Practice, 14,* 185-196.

Brodsky, A.M. (1989). Sex between patient and therapist: Psychology's data and response. In G.O. Gabbard (Ed.), *Sexual exploitation in professional relationships* (pp. 15-25). Washington, DC: American Psychological Association.

Brown, L.S. (1988). Harmful effects of posttermination sexual and romantic relationships with former clients. *Psychotherapy, 25,* 249-255.

Dahlberg, C.C. (1970). Sexual contact between client and therapist. *Contemporary Psychoanalysis, 5,* 107-124.

Davidson, V. (1977). Psychiatry's problem with no name. *American Journal of Psychoanalysis, 37,* 43-50.

Ethics Committee of the American Psychological Association. (1988). Trends in ethics cases, common pitfalls, and published resources. *American Psychologist, 43,* 564-572.

Feldman-Summers, S., & Jones, G. (1984). Psychological impacts of sexual contact between therapists or other health care practitioners and their clients. *Journal of Consulting and Clinical Psychology, 52,* 1054-1061.

Gabbard, G.O. (Ed.). (1989). *Sexual exploitation in professional relationships.* Washington, DC: American Psychiatric Press.

Gabbard, G.O., & Pope, K.S. (1989). Sexual intimacies after termination: Clinical, ethical, and legal aspects. In G.O. Gabbard (Ed.), *Sexual exploitation in professional relationships* (pp. 115-128). Washington, DC: American Psychiatric Press.

Gartell, N., Herman, J., Olarte, S., Feldstein, M., & Localio, R. (1986). Psychiatrist–patient sexual contact: Results of a national survey, I: Prevalence. *American Journal of Psychiatry, 143,* 1126-1131.

Guttman, H. (1984). Sexual issues in the transference and countertransference between female therapists and male patients. *Journal of the American Academy of Psychoanalysis, 12,* 187-197.

Hamilton, J.C., & Spruill, J. (1999). Identifying and reducing risk factors related to trainee–client sexual misconduct. *Professional Psychology: Research and Practice, 30,* 318-327.

Herman, J.L., Gartell, N., Olarte, S., Feldstein, M., & Localio, R. (1987). Psychiatrist–patient sexual contact: Results of a national survey, II: Psychiatrists' attitudes. *American Journal of Psychiatry, 144,* 164-169.

Holroyd, J.C., & Bouhoutsos, J.C. (1985). Biased reporting of therapist–client sexual intimacy. *Professional Psychology, 16,* 701-709.

Kavoussi, R.J., & Becker, J.V. (1987). Psychiatrist–patient sexual contact. *American Journal of Psychiatry, 144,* 1249-1250.

Koocher, G.P., & Keith-Spiegel, P. (1998). *Ethics in psychology: Professional standards and cases.* New York: Oxford University Press.

Ladany, N., O'Brien, K.M., & Petersen, D.A. (1997). Sexual attraction toward clients, use of supervision, and prior training: A qualitative study of predoctoral psychology interns. *Journal of Counseling Psychology, 44,* 413-424.

Nietzsche, F. (1966). *Beyond good and evil.* (W. Kaufmann, Trans.). New York: Vintage Books. (Original work published 1886)

Person, E. (1985). The erotic transference in women and in men: Differences in consequences. *Journal of the American Academy of Psychoanalysis, 13,* 169-180.

Petrie, T.A., & Buntrock, C. (1995). Sexual attraction and the profession of sport psychology. *Journal of Applied Sport Psychology, 7*(Suppl.), S98.

Pope, K.S. (1988). How clients are harmed by sexual contact with mental health professionals: The syndrome and its prevalence. *Journal of Counseling and Development, 67,* 222-226.

Pope, K.S. (1990a). Therapist–patient sex as sex abuse: Six scientific, professional, and practical dilemmas in addressing victimization and rehabilitation. *Professional Psychology: Research and Practice, 21,* 227-239.

Pope, K.S. (1990b). Therapist–patient sexual involvement: A review of the research. *Clinical Psychology Review, 10,* 477-490.

Pope, K.S., & Bouhoutsos, J.C. (1986). *Sexual intimacies between therapists and patients.* New York: Praeger.

Pope, K.S., Keith-Spiegel, P., & Tabachnick, B.G. (1986). Sexual attraction to patients: The human therapist and the (sometimes) inhuman training system. *American Psychologist, 34,* 147-158.

Pope, K.S., Levenson, H., & Schover, L.R. (1979). Sexual intimacy in psychology training: Results and implications of a national survey. *American Psychologist, 34,* 682-689.

Pope, K.S., Schover, L.R., & Levenson, H. (1980). Sexual behavior between clinical supervisors and trainees: Implications for professional standards. *Professional Psychology, 11,* 157-162.

Pope, K.S., Sonne, J.L., & Holroyd, J. (1993). *Sexual feelings in psychotherapy: Exploration for therapists and therapists in training.* Washington, DC: American Psychological Association.

Pope, K.S., Tabachnick, B.G., & Keith-Spiegel, P. (1987). Ethics of practice: The beliefs and behaviors of psychologists as therapists. *American Psychologist, 42,* 993-1006.

Pope, K.S., & Vasquez, M.J.T. (1998). *Ethics in psychotherapy and counseling: A practical guide.* San Francisco: Jossey-Bass.

Serban, G. (1981). Sexual activity in therapy: Legal and ethical issues. *American Journal of Psychotherapy, 35,* 76-85.

Sherman, C.P., & Poczwardowski, A. (2000). Relax! . . . It ain't easy (or is it?). In M.B. Andersen (Ed.), *Doing sport psychology* (pp. 47-60). Champaign, IL: Human Kinetics.

Somer, E., & Saadon, M. (1999). Therapist–client sex: Clients' retrospective reports. *Professional Psychology: Research and Practice, 30,* 504-509.

Sonne, J.L. (1989). Proscribed sex: Counseling the patient subjected to sexual intimacy by a therapist. *Medical Aspects of Human Sexuality, 16,* 18-23.

Sonne, J.L., Meyer, C.B., Borys, D., & Marshall, V. (1985). Clients' reactions to sexual intimacy in therapy. *American Journal of Orthopsychiatry, 55,* 183-189.

Sonne, J.L., & Pope, K.S. (1991). Treating victims of therapist–patient sexual involvement. *Psychotherapy, 28,* 174-187.

Stoltenberg, C. (1981). Approaching supervision from a developmental perspective: The counselor complexity model. *Journal of Counseling Psychology, 28,* 59-65.

Vinson, J.S. (1987). Use of complaint procedures in cases of therapist–patient sexual contact. *Professional Psychology: Research and Practice, 18,* 159-164.

Zicherman, G. (1984). Sociocultural considerations and the emergence of sexual feelings in male patients seeing female therapists. *Journal of the American Academy of Psychoanalysis, 12,* 545-551.

### Commentary on Chapter 10

Abend, S. (1982). Serious illness in the analyst: Countertransference considerations. *Journal of the American Psychoanalytic Association, 30,* 365-379.

Abend, S. (1989). Countertransference and psychoanalytic technique. *Psychoanalytic Quarterly, 58,* 374-396.

Andersen, M.B. (Ed.). (2000). *Doing sport psychology.* Champaign, IL: Human Kinetics.

Andersen, M.B. (2002). Developing comprehensive sport psychology interventions. In J.L. Van Raalte & B.W. Brewer (Eds.), *Exploring sport and exercise psychology* (2nd ed., pp. 13-24). Washington, DC: American Psychological Association.

Boesky, D. (1990). The psychoanalytic process and its components. *Psychoanalytic Quarterly, 59,* 550-584.

Brenner, C. (1985). Countertransference as a compromise formation. *Psychoanalytic Quarterly, 54,* 155-163.

Dahlberg, C. (1970). Sexual contact between patient and therapist. *Contemporary Psychoanalysis, 6,* 107-124.

Doehrman, M. (1976). Parallel processes in supervision and psychotherapy. *Bulletin of the Menninger Clinic, 40,* 9-84.

Ekstein, R., & Wallerstein, R. (1972). *The teaching and learning of psychotherapy.* New York: International Universities Press.

Fine, R. (1982). *The healing of the mind* (2nd ed.). New York: Free Press.

Fine, R. (1984). Countertransference reactions to the difficult patient. *Current Issues in Psychoanalytic Practice, 1,* 7-22.

Freud, S. (1926). The future prospects of psychoanalytic therapy. In J. Strachey (Ed. & Trans.), *The standard edition of the complete psychological works of Sigmund Freud* (Vol. 11, pp. 139-151). London: Hogarth Press.

Freud, S. (1912). The dynamics of transference. In J. Strachey (Ed. & Trans.), *The standard edition of the complete psychological works of Sigmund Freud* (Vol. 12, pp. 97-108). London: Hogarth Press.

Freud, S. (1926). Inhibitions, symptoms and anxiety. In J. Strachey (Ed. & Trans.), *The standard edition of the complete psychological works of Sigmund Freud* (Vol. 20, pp. 77-174). London: Hogarth Press.

Jacobs, T. (1986). On countertransference enactments. *Journal of the American Psychoanalytic Association, 43,* 289-307.

Jacobs, T. (1991). *The use of the self: Countertransference and communication in the analytic situation.* Madison, CT: International Universities Press.

Lane, R. (1990). *Psychoanalytic approaches to supervision.* New York: Brunner/Mazel.

Maroda, K. (1994). *The power of countertransference.* Northvale, NJ: Jason Aronson.

Renik, O. (1993). Analytic interaction: Conceptualizing technique in the light of the analyst's irreducible subjectivity. *Psychoanalytic Quarterly, 62,* 553-571.

Rock, M.H. (1997). *Psychodynamic supervision: Perspectives of the supervisor and the supervisee.* Northvale, NJ: Aronson.

Searles, H. (1955). The informational value of the supervisor's emotional experience. In H. Searles (Ed.), *Collected papers on schizophrenia* (pp. 157-176). New York: International Universities Press.

Searles, H. (1962). Problems of psychoanalytic supervision. In H. Searles (Ed.), *Collected papers on schizophrenia* (pp. 584-604). New York: International Universities Press.

Slakter, E. (1987). *Countertransference.* Northvale, NJ: Aronson.

Strean, H. (1991). Colluding illusions among analytic candidates, their supervisors, and their patients: A major factor in some treatment impasses. *Psychoanalytic Psychology, 8,* 403-414.

Strean, H. (1993). *Therapists who have sex with their patients: Treatment and recovery.* New York: Brunner/Mazel.

Strean, H. (1995). Countertransference and theoretical predilections as observed in some psychoanalytic candidates. *Canadian Journal of Psychoanalysis, 3,* 105-123.

Strean, H. (1999). Resolving some therapeutic impasses by disclosing countertransference. *Clinical Social Work Journal, 27,* 123-140.

Strean, H. (2000). Resolving therapeutic impasses by using the supervisor's countertransference. *Clinical Social Work Journal, 28,* 263-279.

Strean, W.B., & Strean, H.S. (1998). Applying psychodynamic concepts to sport psychology practice. *The Sport Psychologist, 12,* 208-222.

Sullivan, H. (1953). *Interpersonal theory of psychiatry.* New York: Norton.

Teitelbaum, S. (1990). Supertransference: The role of the supervisor's blind spots. *Psychoanalytic Psychology, 7,* 243-258.

Van Raalte, J.L., & Andersen, M.B. (2000). Supervision I: From models to doing. In M.B. Andersen (Ed), *Doing sport psychology* (pp. 153-166). Champaign, IL: Human Kinetics.

## Chapter 11

Akbar, N. (1984). Africentric social sciences for human liberation. *Journal of Black Studies, 14,* 395-414.

American Psychological Association. (2003). Guidelines on multicultural education, training, research, practice and organizational change for psychologists. *American Psychologist, 58,* 377-402.

Ashe, A.R., Jr. (1988). *A hard road to glory: A history of the African American athlete, 1946-1986.* New York: Warner Books.

Atkinson, D.R. (1985). A meta-review of research on cross-cultural counseling and psychotherapy. *Journal of Multicultural Counseling and Development, 13,* 138-153.

Axelson, J.A. (1993). *Counseling and development in a multicultural society* (2nd ed.). Pacific Grove, CA: Brooks/Cole.

Azibo, D.A. (1996). *African psychology in historical perspective and related commentary.* Trenton, NJ: African World Press.

Baldwin, J. (1990). *African personality from an Afrocentric framework.* Tallahassee, FL: A & M University Press.

Casas, J.M. (1985). A reflection on the status of racial/ethnic minority research. *The Counseling Psychologist, 13,* 581-598.

Cross, W.E. (1971). The negro to black conversion experience: Toward a psychology of black liberation. *Black World, 209,* 13-27.

Dodd, J.M., Nelson, J.R., & Hofland, B.H. (1994). Minority identity and self-concept: The American Indian experience. In T.M. Brinthaupt & R.P. Lipka (Eds.), *Changing the self: Philosophies, techniques and experiences* (pp. 307-336). Albany, NY: State University of New York Press.

Galton, F. (1869). *Hereditary Genius: Its Laws and Consequences.* London: Macmillan.

Grier, W.H., & Cobbs, P.M. (1968). *Black rage.* New York: Basic Books.

Guthrie, R.V. (1976/1998). *Even the rat was white: A historical view of psychology.* Needham Heights, MA: Allyn & Bacon.

Hu-DeHart, E. (Ed.). (1997). *Across the Pacific: Asian Americans and globalization.* Philadelphia: Temple University Press.

Ivey, A. (1987). The multicultural practice of therapy: Ethics, empathy and dialectics. *Journal of Social and Clinical Psychology, 5,* 195-204.

Kanellos, N. (1997). *Hispanic firsts: 500 years of extraordinary achievement.* Detroit: Visible Ink Press.

LaFromboise, T.D., & Rowe, W. (1983). Skills training for bicultural competence: Rationale and application. *Journal of Counseling Psychology, 30,* 589-595.

Lee, C.C. (1997). *Multicultural issues in counseling* (2nd ed.). Alexandria, VA: American Counseling Association.

Mangan, J.A., Fan, H., & Gersting, J.L. (Eds.). (2003). *Sports in Asian society: Past and present.* London: Frank Cass.

Moynihan, D.P. (1965). *The negro family: A case for national action.* Washington, DC: Office of Policy Planning & Research, U.S. Department of Labor.

Myers, L.J. (1985). Transpersonal psychology: The role of the Afro-centric paradigm. *Journal of Black Psychology 12*, 31-42.

Nobles, W. (1976). Black people in white insanity: An issue for community mental health. *Journal of Afro-American Issues, 4*(1), 21-27.

Nobles, W. (1991). African philosophy: Foundations for black psychology. In R.L. Jones (Ed.), *Black psychology* (3rd ed., pp. 47-65). New York: Harper & Row.

Padilla, A.M. (1995). *Hispanic psychology: Critical issues in theory and research.* Thousand Oaks, CA: Sage.

Paniagua, F.A. (2000). *Diagnosis in a multicultural context: A casebook for mental health professionals.* Thousand Oaks, CA: Sage.

Parham, T.A. (1989). Cycles of psychological nigrescence. *The Counseling Psychologist, 17*, 187-226.

Parham, T.A. (2002). *Counseling persons of African descent: Raising the bar of practitioner competence.* Multicultural Aspects of Counseling Series 18. Thousand Oaks, CA: Sage.

Satcher, D. (2001). *Mental health: Culture, race, and ethnicity.* Retrieved January 10, 2005, from http://www.surgeongeneral.gov/library/mentalhealth/cre

Sinnette, C. (1998). Forbidden fairways: African Americans and the game of golf. Chelsea, MI: Sleeping Bear Press.

Sue, D.W., & Sue, D. (1999). *Counseling the culturally different* (3rd ed.). New York: Wiley.

Thomas, A., & Sillen, S. (1972). *Racism and psychiatry.* Secaucus, NJ: Citadel Press.

Thomas, G.E. (Ed.). (1995). *Race and ethnicity in America: Meeting the challenges in the 21st century.* Washington, DC: Taylor & Francis.

Thomas, R. (2002). *They cleared the lane: The NBA's black pioneers.* Lincoln: University of Nebraska Press.

White, J.L. (1991). Toward a black psychology. In R.L. Jones (Ed.), *Black psychology* (3rd ed., pp. 5-15). New York: Harper & Row.

Williams, R.L. (1981). *Collective black mind: An Afrocentric theory of black personality.* St. Louis: Williams.

### Commentary on Chapter 11

Brown, L. (1997). Ethics in psychology: Cui Bono? In D. Fox & I. Prilleltensky (Eds.), *Critical psychology: An introduction* (pp. 51-67). London: Sage.

Canadian Psychological Association. (1996). *Guidelines for non-discriminatory practice.* Ottawa, ON: Author.

Darlaston-Jones, D., Sampson, E., Culbertson, H., Gridley, H., Gonzalez, R., & Kercheval, B. (2003, September). *Diversity and the scientist-practitioner model: Towards a more culturally responsive psychology.* Forum presentation at the 38th annual conference of the Australian Psychological Society, Perth, Western Australia.

Duncan, B., & Miller, S. (2000). *The heroic client: Doing client-directed, outcome-informed therapy.* San Francisco: Jossey-Bass.

Essandoh, P. (1996). Multicultural counseling as the "fourth force": A call to arms. *The Counseling Psychologist, 24*, 126-137.

Freedman, J., & Combs, G. (1996). *Narrative therapy.* New York: Norton.

Kitzinger, C., & Perkins, R. (1993). *Changing our minds: Lesbian feminism and psychology.* New York: Basic Books.

Mathieson, M. (2001, September). *The path and the goal: A comparative study of Zen concepts in Japanese martial arts and the tenets of Western sport psychology.* Paper presented at the 36th annual conference of the Australian Psychological Society, Adelaide, South Australia.

McAlister, A. (1995, May 8). Back to the Dark Ages. *Sydney Morning Herald.*

Sue, D., & Sue, D.W. (2003). *Counseling the culturally different: Theory and practice* (4th ed.). New York: Wiley.

### Chapter 12

Barlow, S.H., Burlingame, G.M., & Fuhriman, A. (2000). Therapeutic application to groups: From Pratt's "thought control classes" to modern group psychotherapy. *Group Dynamics: Theory, Research, and Practice, 4*, 115-134.

Bury, M.R. (1979). Disablement in society. *International Journal of Rehabilitation Research, 2*, 34-40.

Hanrahan, S.J. (1990). Coaching disabled individuals: Some practical considerations. *Commonwealth and International Conference on Physical Education, Sport, Health, Dance, Recreation and Leisure Conference Proceedings, 2*, 14-21.

Hanrahan, S.J. (1998). Practical considerations when working with athletes with disabilities. *The Sport Psychologist, 12*, 346-357.

Hanrahan, S.J., Grove, J.R., & Lockwood, R.J. (1990). Psychological skills training for the blind athlete: A pilot program. *Adapted Physical Activity Quarterly, 7*, 143-155.

Kidman, L., & Hanrahan, S. (2004). *The coaching process: A practical guide to improving your effectiveness* (2nd ed.). Palmerston North, New Zealand: Dunmore Press.

Lockette, K.F., & Keyes, A.M. (1994). *Conditioning with physical disabilities.* Champaign, IL: Human Kinetics.

MacKenzie, K.R. (1997). Clinical application of group development ideas. *Group Dynamics: Theory, Research, and Practice, 1,* 275-287.

Martin, J.J. (1999). A personal development model of sport psychology for athletes with disabilities. *Journal of Applied Sport Psychology, 11,* 181-193.

McRoberts, C., Burlingame, G.M., & Hoag, M.J. (1998). Comparative efficacy of individual and group psychotherapy: A meta-analytic perspective. *Group Dynamics: Theory, Research, and Practice, 2,* 101-117.

Thomas, D. (1982). *The experience of handicap.* London: Methuen.

Tweedy, S. (1998, August). B2 or not B2? A beginner's guide to classification and the Paralympics. *SportsMed News,* 10-11.

Vash, C.L. (1981). *The psychology of disability.* New York: Springer.

## Chapter 13

American Psychological Association. (1992). Ethical principles of psychologists and code of conduct. *American Psychologist, 47,* 1597-1611.

American Psychological Association. (1993). Guidelines for providers of psychological services to ethnic, linguistic, and culturally diverse populations. *American Psychologist, 48,* 45-48.

Andersen, M.B., Butki, B.D., & Heyman, S.R. (1997). Homophobia and sport experience: A survey of college students. *Academic Athletic Journal, 12,* 27-38.

Association for the Advancement of Applied Sport Psychology, Ethics Committee. (1995, Winter). Ethical principles and standards of the Association for the Advancement of Applied Sport Psychology. *AAASP Newsletter, 10,* 15-21.

Barret, R.L. (1993). The homosexual athlete. In L. Diamant (Ed.), *Homosexual issues in the workplace.* Series in clinical and community psychology (pp. 161-170). Washington, DC: Taylor & Francis.

Bean, B., & Bull, C. (2003). *Going the other way.* New York: Marlowe.

Bem, S.L. (1993). *The lenses of gender.* New Haven, CT: Yale University Press.

Butki, B.D., Andersen, M.B., & Heyman, S.R. (1996). Knowledge of AIDS and risky behavior among athletes. *Academic Athletic Journal, 11,* 29-36.

Cass, V. (1996). Sexual orientation identity formation: A Western phenomenon. In R. Cabaj & T. Stein (Eds.), *Textbook of homosexuality and mental health* (pp. 227-252). Washington, DC: American Psychiatric Press.

Dworkin, S.L., & Wachs, F.L. (1998). "Disciplining the body": HIV-positive male athletes, media surveillance, and the policing of sexuality. *Sociology of Sport Journal, 15,* 1-20.

Eagly, A.H., & Steffen, V.J. (1984). Gender stereotypes stem from the distribution of men and women into social roles. *Journal of Personality and Social Psychology, 46,* 735-754.

Freeman, P. (1997). *Ian Roberts: Finding out.* Sydney, Australia: Random House.

Fukuyama, M.A., & Ferguson, A.D. (2000). Lesbian, gay, and bisexual people of color: Understanding cultural complexity and managing multiple oppressions. In R.M. Perez, K.A. DeBord, & K.J. Bieschke (Eds.), *Handbook of counseling and psychotherapy with lesbian, gay, and bisexual clients* (pp. 81-105). Washington, DC: American Psychological Association.

Garnets, L., Hancock, K.A., Cochran, S.D., Goodchilds, J., & Peplau, L.A. (1991). Issues in psychotherapy with lesbians and gay men: A survey of psychologists. *American Psychologist, 46,* 964-974.

Griffin, P. (1994). Homophobia in sport: Addressing the needs of lesbian and gay high school athletes. *The High School Journal, 77*(2), 80-87.

Griffin, P. (1998). *Strong women, deep closets: Lesbians and homophobia in sport.* Champaign, IL: Human Kinetics.

Herek, G.M. (1984). Beyond "homophobia": A social psychological perspective on attitudes toward lesbians and gay men. *Journal of Homosexuality, 10*(1/2), 1-21.

Herek, G.M. (1986a). On heterosexual masculinity. *American Behavioral Scientist, 29,* 563-577.

Herek, G.M. (1986b). The social psychology of homophobia: Toward a practical theory. *Review of Law and Social Change, 14,* 923-934.

Herek, G.M. (1991). Stigma, prejudice, and violence against lesbians and gay men. In J.C. Gonsiorek & J.D. Weinrich (Eds.), *Homosexuality: Research implications for public policy* (pp. 60-80). Newbury Park, CA: Sage.

Hoffman, C., & Hurst, N. (1990). Gender stereotypes. *Journal of Personality and Social Psychology, 58,* 197-208.

Kopay, D., & Young, P.D. (2001). *The David Kopay story.* New York: Alyson.

Liddle, B.J. (1996). Therapist sexual orientation, gender, and counseling practices as they related to ratings of helpfulness by gay and lesbian clients. *Journal of Counseling Psychology, 43,* 394-401.

MacDonald, A.P., Jr. (1976). Homophobia: Its roots and meanings. *Homosexual Counseling Journal, 3*(1), 23-33.

Newman, G., & Muzzonigro, P. (1993). The effects of traditional family values on the coming out process of gay male adolescents. *Adolescence, 28,* 212-226.

Pallone, D., & Steinberg, A. (1990). *Behind the mask: My double life in baseball.* New York: Viking Penguin.

Pronger, B. (1990). Gay jocks: A phenomenology of gay men in athletics. In M.A. Messner & D.F. Sabo (Eds.), *Sport, men, and the gender order: Critical feminist per-spectives* (pp. 141-152). Champaign, IL: Human Kinetics.

Reynolds, A.L., & Hanjorgiris, W.F. (2000). Coming out: Lesbian, gay, and bisexual identity development. In R.M. Perez, K.A. DeBord, & K.J. Bieschke (Eds.), *Handbook of counseling and psychotherapy with lesbian, gay, and bisexual clients* (pp. 35-55). Washington, DC: American Psychological Association.

Rotella, R.J., & Murray, M.M. (1991). Homophobia, the world of sport, and sport psychology consulting. *The Sport Psychologist, 5,* 355-364.

Rudolf, J. (1988). Counselors' attitudes toward homosexuality: A selective review of the literature. *Journal of Counseling and Development, 67,* 165-168.

Rudolf, J. (1990). Counselors' attitudes toward homosexuality: Some tentative findings. *Psychological Reports, 66,* 1352-1354.

Tremble, B., Schneider, M., & Appathurai, C. (1989). Growing up gay or lesbian in a multicultural context. *Journal of Homosexuality, 17,* 253-267.

Troiden, R.R. (1989). The formation of homosexual identities. *Journal of Homosexuality, 17,* 43-73.

Weinberg, G. (1972). *Society and the healthy homosexual.* New York: St. Martin's Press.

**Chapter 14**

Abrams, D., & Hogg, M.A. (1988). *Social identifications: A social psychology of intergroup relations and group processes.* London: Routledge.

Abrams, D., & Hogg, M.A. (1990). An introduction to the social identity approach. In D. Abrams & M.A. Hogg (Eds.), *Social identity theory: Constructive and critical advances* (pp. 1-9). New York: Springer-Verlag.

Baird, S. (2001). *Femininity on the pitch: An ethnographic study of female rugby players.* Unpublished master's thesis, Bowling Green State University, Bowling Green, OH.

Barber, H., & Krane, V. (1999, September). *Closed lockers: A social identity theory interpretation of lesbian experience in sport.* Colloquium presented at the meeting of the Association for the Advancement of Applied Sport Psychology, Banff, Alberta, Canada.

Bredemeier, B.J.L., Carlton, E.B., Hills, L.A., & Oglesby, C.A. (1999). Changers and the changed: Moral aspects of coming out in physical education. *Quest, 51,* 418-431.

Crace, R.K., & Hardy, C.J. (1997). Individual value and the team building process. *Journal of Applied Sport Psychology, 9,* 41-60.

Crocker, J., & Luhtanen, R. (1990). Collective self-esteem and ingroup bias. *Journal of Personality and Social Psychology, 58,* 60-67.

Deschamps, J.C., & Devos, T. (1998). Regarding the relationship between social identity and personal identity. In S. Worshel, J.F. Morales, D. Paez, & J.C. Deschamps (Eds.), *Social identity: International perspectives* (pp. 53-74). Thousand Oaks, CA: Sage.

Dworkin, S.H., & Gutierrez, F. (1989). Counselors be aware: Clients come in every size, shape, color, and sexual orientation. *Journal of Counseling and Development, 68,* 6-8.

Garnets, L., & Kimmel, D. (1991). Lesbian and gay male dimensions in the psychological study of human diversity. In L. Garnets, J.M. Jones, D. Kimmel, S. Sue, & C. Tavris (Eds.), *Psychological perspectives on human diversity in America* (pp. 143-192). Washington, DC: American Psychological Association.

Greendorfer, S.L., & Rubinson, L. (1997). Homophobia and heterosexism in women's sport and physical education. *Women in Sport and Physical Activity Journal, 6,* 189-212.

Griffin, P. (1998). *Strong women, deep closets.* Champaign, IL: Human Kinetics.

Hargreaves, J.A. (1993). *Sporting females: Critical issues in the history and sociology of women's sports.* New York: Routledge.

Herek, G.M. (1992). The social context of hate crimes: Notes on cultural heterosexism. In G.M. Herek & K.T. Berrill (Eds.), *Hate crimes: Confronting violence against lesbians and gay men* (pp. 89-104). Newbury Park, CA: Sage.

Hinkle, S., Taylor, L.A., Fox-Cardomone, L., & Ely, P.G. (1998). Social identity and aspects of social creativity: Shifting to new dimensions of intergroup comparison. In S. Worshel, J.F. Morales, D. Paez, & J.C. Deschamps (Eds.), *Social identity: International perspectives* (pp. 53-74). Thousand Oaks, CA: Sage.

Hogg, M.A., & McGarty, C. (1990). Self-categorization and social identity. In D. Abrams & M. Hogg (Eds.), *Social identity theory: Constructive and critical advances* (pp. 10-27). New York: Springer-Verlag.

House, R.M., & Holloway, E.L. (1992). Empowering the counseling professional to work with gay and lesbian issues. In S.H. Dworkin & F.J. Gutierrez (Eds.), *Counseling gay men and lesbians: Journey to the end of the rainbow* (pp. 307-324). Alexandria, VA: American Association for Counseling and Development.

Kauer, K. (2002). *"Scary dykes and feminine queens": Stereotypes and female athletes.* Unpublished master's thesis, Bowling Green State University, Bowling Green, OH.

Kolnes, L.J. (1995). Heterosexuality as an organizing principle in women's sport. *International Review for Sociology of Sport, 30,* 61-77.

Krane, V. (1995, September). *Performance-related outcomes experienced by lesbian athletes*. Paper presented at the annual meeting of the Association for the Advancement of Applied Sport Psychology, New Orleans, LA.

Krane, V. (1997). Homonegativism experienced by lesbian collegiate athletes. *Women in Sport and Physical Activity Journal, 6*, 141-163.

Krane, V. (2001). We can be athletic and feminine, but do we want to? Challenging hegemonic femininity in women's sport. *Quest, 53*, 115-133.

Krane, V., & Barber, H. (2003). Lesbian experiences in sport: A social identity theory perspective. *Quest, 55*, 328-346.

Krane, V., & Barber, H. (in press). Identity tensions in lesbian college coaches. *Research Quarterly for Exercise and Sport*.

Krane, V., Barber, H., & McClung, L. (2002). The Gay Games as social change: A social identity theory explanation. *Journal of Applied Sport Psychology, 14*, 27-42.

Krane, V., & Pope, S. (1996, September). *Strategies to confront homonegativism in sport*. Paper presented at the annual meeting of the Association for the Advancement of Applied Sport Psychology, Williamsburg, VA.

Lalonde, R.N., & Cameron, J.E. (1994). Behavioral responses to discrimination: A focus on action. In M.P. Zanna & J.M. Olson (Eds.), *The psychology of prejudice: The Ontario Symposium* (Vol. 7, pp. 257-288). Hillsdale, NJ: Erlbaum.

Lenskyj, H.J. (1992). Unsafe at home base: Women's experiences with sexual harassment in university sport and physical education. *Women in Sport and Physical Activity Journal, 1*, 19-33.

Lenskyj, H.J. (1997). No fear? Lesbians in sport and physical education. *Women in Sport and Physical Activity Journal, 6*(2), 7-22.

Luhtanen, R., & Crocker, J. (1992). A collective self-esteem scale: Self-evaluation of one's social identity. *Personality and Social Psychology Bulletin, 18*, 302-318.

Marcus, E. (1993). *Is it a choice? Answers to 300 of the most frequently asked questions about gays and lesbians*. San Francisco: Harper.

Meyer, B.B., & Wenger, M. (1998). Athletes and adventure education: An empirical investigation. *International Journal of Sport Psychology, 29*, 243-266.

Nelson, M.B. (1991). *Are we winning yet? How women are changing sports and sports are changing women*. New York: Random House.

Pirinen, R.M. (1997). The construction of women's positions in sport: A textual analysis of articles on female athletes in Finnish women's magazines. *Sociology of Sport Journal, 14*, 290-301.

Reynolds, A.L. (1995). Challenges and strategies for teaching multicultural counseling courses. In J.G. Ponterotto, J.M. Casas, L.A. Suzuki, & C.M. Alexander (Eds.), *Handbook of multicultural counseling* (pp. 312-330). Thousand Oaks, CA: Sage.

Rogers, S.F. (1991). *Sportdykes: Stories from on and off the field*. New York: St. Martin's Press.

Silver, J. (2001, July/August). Playing for keeps. *Sports Illustrated for Women, 3*(4), 87-89.

Sue, D.W., Arredondo, P., & McDavis, R.J. (1992). Multicultural counseling competencies and standards: A call to the profession. *Journal of Counseling and Development, 79*, 477-486.

Turner, J.C., & Reynolds, K.J. (2001). The social identity perspective in intergroup relations: Theories, themes, and controversies. In R. Brown & S.L. Gaertner (Eds.), *Blackwell handbook of social psychology: Intergroup processes* (pp. 133-152), Malden, MA: Blackwell.

Wright, J., & Clarke, G. (1999). Sport, the media and the construction of compulsory heterosexuality. *International Review for the Sociology of Sport, 34*, 227-243.

Young, P.D. (1995). *Lesbians and gays in sport*. New York: Chelsea House.

Zipter, Y. (1988). *Diamonds are a dyke's best friend: Reflections, reminiscences, and reports from the field on the lesbian national pastime*. Ithaca, NY: Firebrand.

## Chapter 15

Andersen, M.B. (in press). "Yeah, I work with Beckham": Issues of confidentiality, privacy and privilege in sport psychology service delivery. *Sport and Exercise Psychology Review*.

Andersen, M.B., & Stoové, M.A. (1998). The sanctity of $p < .05$ obfuscates good stuff: A comment on Kerr and Goss. *Journal of Applied Sport Psychology, 10*, 168-173.

Andersen, M.B., Van Raalte, J.L., & Brewer, B.W. (2000). When applied sport psychology graduate students are impaired: Ethical and legal issues in supervision. *Journal of Applied Sport Psychology, 12*, 134-149.

Beck, A.T., Ward, C.H., Mendelson, M., Mock, J., & Erbaugh, J. (1961). An inventory for measuring depression. *Archives of General Psychiatry, 4*, 561-571.

Freud, S. (1965). *The interpretation of dreams*. (J. Strachey, Trans.). New York: Avon Books. (Original work published 1900)

Gould, D., Udry, E., Bridges, D., & Beck, L. (1997). Coping with season ending injuries. *The Sport Psychologist, 11*, 379-399.

Hays, K.F. (2000). Breaking out: Doing sport psychology with performing artists. In M.B. Andersen (Ed.), *Doing sport psychology* (pp. 261-274). Champaign, IL: Human Kinetics.

Krane, V., Andersen, M.B., & Strean, W. (1997). Issues in qualitative research methods and presentation. *Journal of Sport and Exercise Psychology, 19,* 213-218.

Martin, D.T., Andersen, M.B., & Gates, W. (2000). Using Profile of Mood States (POMS) to monitor high intensity training in cyclists: Group versus case studies. *The Sport Psychologist, 14,* 138-156.

McNair, D.M., Lorr, M., & Droppleman, L.F. (1971). *Profile of Mood States Manual.* San Diego, CA: Educational and Industrial Testing Service.

Murphy, S.M. (2000). Afterword. In M.B. Andersen (Ed.), *Doing sport psychology* (pp. 275-279). Champaign, IL: Human Kinetics.

Rogers, C. (1961). *On becoming a person.* Boston: Houghton Mifflin.

Rowland, N., & Goss, S. (Eds.). (2000). *Evidence-based counseling and psychological therapies: Research and applications.* New York: Routledge.

Scanlan, T.K., Russell, D.G., Beals, K.P., & Scanlan, L.A. (2003). Project on elite athlete commitment (PEAK): II. A direct test and expansion of the sport commitment model with elite amateur sportsmen. *Journal of Sport & Exercise Psychology, 25,* 377-401.

Sechrest, L., McKnight, P., & McKnight, K. (1996). Calibration of measures for psychotherapy outcome studies. *American Psychologist 51,* 1065-1071.

Sparkes, A.C. (2002). *Telling tales in sport and physical activity.* Champaign, IL: Human Kinetics.

Speed, H.D., & Andersen, M.B. (2000). What sport and exercise scientists don't understand. *Journal of Science and Medicine in Sport, 3,* 84-92.

Stoové, M.A., & Andersen, M.B. (2003). What are we looking at, and how big is it? *Physical Therapy in Sport, 4,* 93-97.

### *Afterword*

Andersen, M.B. (2000). *Doing sport psychology.* Champaign, IL: Human Kinetics.

Eklund, R., Gould, D., & Jackson, S.A. (1993). Psychological foundations of Olympic wrestling excellence: Reconciling individual differences and nomothetic characterization. *Journal of Applied Sport Psychology, 5,* 35-46.

# Index

Note: The italicized *f* following page numbers refers to figures.

## A

Aboriginal athletes, consulting example 217-222
abstract thinking, building in youth 20
academic model, of presentations 12-13
   disabled athletes case 229-245
acceptance
   of LBT female athletes 269, 271-272, 278, 283-284
   of services 3-16. *See also* selling
accidents, alcohol use and 137
accountability, in youth training 32
acknowledgment, in youth training 24
action stage, of addictive behavior change 138
activation levels
   awareness of. *See* awareness training
   control of. *See* arousal control
   positive transition of. *See* relaxation training
acute intervention stage, of alcohol treatment 140
adaptability
   of dancers 109-110, 130
   during presentations 12-13
addictive behavior, stage model of change for 138
aesthetic sports 127
   performing arts *vs.* 129-130
affirmations, positive, for dancers 125-126
African-descendant people
   historical portrayal of 203-204
   proven resiliency of 213-214, 218
   success stories as athletes 207-208, 218
aftercare, in alcohol treatment 140-141
"agony and ecstasy" game, for group presentations 65-66, 68
AIDS, misconception as "gay disease" 251-252, 263
alcohol use/abuse 135-158
   in dancers 133
   diagnostic terms for 137
   intervention/treatment for 135, 138-141
   problem drinking 137-139
      college football case 141-158
      professional issues 154-158
   referrals for 154, 156-157, 162
   risk taking and 136-137
   violence and 135, 137, 158
ambivalence, during injury rehabilitation 96-97
   downhill skier case 98-108
American Psychological Association (APA) 167
   ethical code of 172-173
   multicultural perspectives 203, 215
anger, substance abuse and 141-146, 151
anonymity, with weight/body image issues 63-65, 67
anorexia. *See* eating disorders
antidepressants, indications for 166-167
anxiety 163
   body image and
      athlete issues 62-63, 65-66
      coaches role 61-62, 67-74
      group work on 67-74
      practitioner issues 63-65
   competitive 114, 288
   control of 22, 34-36, 109, 116
   dancers and 113-116
   depression-related 165-166
   in disabled athletes 241
   with erotic attraction 174, 181, 183, 197
   gay athletes and 251-253, 257, 260
   during injury rehabilitation 96-97
      downhill skier case 98-108
   research on 288, 295-296
   with substance abuse intervention 141-144, 149
   with weigh-ins 70-73
anxiety disorders, referrals for 162
anxiolytic agents, indications for 166
APA. *See* American Psychological Association (APA)
approachability, sensitive topics and 64
argumentation, avoiding, with problem drinker 139, 143-144, 146, 156
arousal control, in youth sport teams 19, 21-22, 32-37, 40
artistic environment
   mental skills training for. *See* dance and dancers
   sports setting *vs.* 109-110, 127, 129-130, 132
Asian Americans 204, 269
assessment phase, in Tre-Nine grid 208-211
assistant coaches
   in sexual orientation dynamics 279-280
   team communication role 54-55
ass-kissing 13-14
Association for the Advancement of Applied Sport Psychology 167, 172, 215
assumptions, about diverse athletes 210, 214
   getting beyond 215, 218-219, 221-222
attention 20, 241
   performance value of 109, 116, 120

attention training
   for dancers 119-121, 132-133
   in youth sports 21-22, 25
attitudes
   as contagious 115-116
   learned in sport setting 17-19, 22
   respectful, importance of 8, 13-14
audience, spectators *vs.* 130
authority figures, substance abuse intervention and 141-142, 149
autogenic training, for young athletes 40-42
automaticity, in dancing 119
awareness training
   kinesthetic, for dancers 121-123, 131
   for young athletes 32, 35-40
away-from-practice arousal control 37

## B

"Band-Aid" orientation 7
banned substances 166
basketball, LBT female coach case 278-283
behavioral change, referrals for 162
behaviorism
   in body image disturbances 78, 81
   in communication theory 46, 50, 62
   in diverse population paradigms 203-206
   in group dynamics 62, 65
   in sports injury response 94-95, 94*f*
behaviors
   learned
      sex and gender 255
      in sport setting 17-19, 24
   risky, alcohol use and 136-137, 141, 147-148, 152
belonging, sense of 219
bias
   heterosexist 251, 254-255
      in women's sports 265-285
   toward diverse athletes 210, 214
big-brother/big-sister experience 198
bigorexia 79
biopsychosocial model, of injury rehabilitation 93, 94*f*
   downhill skier case 98-108
bisexual athletes 220-221, 265
BITR ("bull in the ring") session 55-56
body composition, nutrition referrals for 161-162
body dissatisfaction. *See* body image disturbance
body dysmorphia 77-79
   diver example 83-92
body image disturbance
   coaches role 61-62, 67-74
   cognitive-social learning framework 77-78
   current (maintaining) factors 77-78
   gender gap with 63, 65-67, 77, 79
   group presentations on 63-67
   group work on 67-74
   historical (causal) factors 77-78
   literature review 61, 77, 80-81
   male prevalence of 78-79
      reasons for 81-83
      at risk populations 80-81
   psychopathology related to 78, 80
   team issues with 61-63
   weight control and 63, 65-67, 79-80
      eating disorders related to 81-83
      male diver case 83-92
body shape image disturbance. *See* body dysmorphia
brainstorming
   team, for improved communication 55-56
   in youth training 33, 38, 40, 42
breathing techniques
   for dancers 115, 131-132
   for disabled athletes 242-244
bulimia. *See* eating disorders
"bull in the ring" (BITR) session 55-56
Byrne's theory, of interpersonal communication 47, 50, 52

## C

Cahn's theory, of interpersonal communication 46, 52
career transitions
   with career-ending injury 103, 106-108
   referrals for 162
   unwanted
      gay athletes' fear of 251-252
      LBT athletes' fear of 268
case studies, research value of 289-290
change model
   for addictive behavior 138, 140-141
      football case 141-158
      professional issues 139, 154-158
   for diverse athletes 221-222

character development, through sports 17-19
cheerleaders, eating disorders in 90-91
cheer leading 187
   by coaches 49, 51-52
chit chat
   as presentation opportunity 10-12
   for youth sport instruction 28-23
clarification, in youth training 24, 40
clinical issues. *See also* referrals
   as focus of service 8-10
   in youth sports 21-22
cliques, in team dynamics 55-56
coaches and coaching
   cheerleader type 49, 51-52
   communication skills importance 47-48
   competencies of 21-22, 161
   improprieties with touching 57, 171
   knowledge wealth of 4, 13-14
   LBT female case study 278-283
   quizzing, avoiding 6
   resistant 2, 15-16, 21
   respecting and involving 8, 13-14, 282
   role model for 14-15
   selling services to 3-16
   sexual orientation issues 254, 269, 277-279
   sharing stories with 5-7, 11, 15
   team eating disorders and 61-62
      group work involvement 67-74
co-ed teams, weight/body image issues 61, 63, 65
coercion, in substance abuse intervention 143-144
cognitive-behavioral model
   of sexual attraction processing 188-191
   of sport psychology 7-8, 18-20, 112, 117
   of sports injury reactions 94-95, 94*f*
      downhill skier case 98-108
   of substance abuse intervention 147-148, 150-151, 156
cognitive development. *See* mental skills
cognitive evaluation, of problem drinking 139-140
   intervention based on 147-148, 150-151, 156
cognitive restructuring 7, 21-23
cognitive-social learning framework, for body image disturbance 77-78
collaboration
   peer. *See* peer *entries*
   for skiing injury rehabilitation 99-108
   in sport psychology 8, 10, 222, 247
collaborative empiricism 290
   in sexual attraction 185-186, 189
collective esteem, of LBT female athletes 265-267, 283
collectivism, of diverse populations 206
college students
   alcohol use survey 136-137, 155
   substance abuse case 141-158
coming out process
   gay athletes 253
      graduate student dealing with 256-261
      supervision challenges 260-262
   LBT female athletes 271, 275
communication
   as central issue 6-7, 45-46
   disabled athletes and 230-232, 235, 237, 239, 242, 247
   disordered, in substance abuse intervention 142
   effective
      building in youth 18-19
      as performance predictor 47-48
   ineffective, as someone else's problem 46
   literature review 45-46
   misunderstandings and 48-55
   during presentations 10-12
   research on 47-48
   team enhancement of
      with LBT athletes 265-266, 269, 271-274, 278, 283-284
      volleyball example 48-59
   theories of 46-47
competence(ies)
   activity-specific, building in youth 20
   of coaches 21-22, 161
   of practitioners
      doubt about 159-161
      for team counseling 9, 14
      training background and 163, 202-204, 215
competition
   assignments on, in youth training 33, 37-40
   barriers to, for disabled athletes 226-227
   effective communication for 45
   "looking good for" 69-71, 74
   retirement from, due to injury 103, 106-108
   return to after injury 93-108
      downhill skier case 98-108
      psychological interventions for 95-98

psychological response factors 93-95, 94f
return to after referral 168
competitive anxiety 114, 288
competitiveness, of dancers 110, 127, 130
concentration skills 109, 116
for dancers 119-121
confidence. See self-confidence
confidentiality
eating disorders and 9-10, 87
in sexual orientation issues 271. See also coming out process
substance abuse intervention and 145, 151-152
confrontations 9-11
with substance abuse intervention 141-145
consciousness
of erotic attraction 178, 195-196
increased, of male body image 79
lack of, with countertransference 178, 195-196
social. See social consciousness
consciousness raising, for addictive behavior change 138, 144-145, 155
interviewing strategies for 139, 155-157
conscious thought, structuralism theory of 203
consent, in referral process 169
consultant-client alliance. See working alliance
consultations
for diverse athletes 206-208
Aboriginal example 217-222
generic vs. therapeutic 221-222
multidisciplinary network for 167-168
over lunch, as presentation 11-12
in performing arts 134
relationship-building for 11, 21-22, 38
for youth sports 21-23
contemplation stage, of addictive behavior change 138, 153, 155
coping skills/strategies
for clinical issues 9-10
during injury rehabilitation 95, 97-98
downhill skier case 98-108
integrating in youth sports 18-19, 21-23
for stress 17
counseling
for eating disorders, confidentiality and 9-10, 87
evidence-based 287-288
for male body image disturbances 83-92
multicultural, emergent theories of 218-222
research perspectives 287-298
as service model 8-10
Tre-Nine grid, for diverse athletes 208-214, 219
for youth sports 21-22
countertransference
awareness/self-management of 194-195, 197-198
in body image counseling 88, 91
erotic 171-174, 191, 193-194
swimmer example 176-178
track athlete case 174-176
volleyball case 179-191
therapeutic perspectives 195-197, 296
credibility
academic 230
building personal 63-64, 102
criminal acts, by athletes 145, 155, 214
criticism
communicating to coaches 50-51, 54
self-, by dancers 132-133
crossdisciplinary model, of physical education 18-19, 21
cue identification
for dancers 117, 119
for disabled athletes 245
in youth sports 19, 22, 24-26, 29
cultural context. See sociocultural context
culturally diverse athletes. See diverse athletes
cultural norms
of diverse athletes 205-207, 218-219, 224
on sexual orientation 254-255, 262, 269, 271, 283
curative model, of sport psychology 7-8

D

dance and dancers
attention training for 119-121
concentration training for 119-121
gender perspectives 130, 133
imagery training for 121-123, 125-126, 131
injury recovery strategies 112-113, 130
medical resources for 113, 134
mental skills training for 109-127
commentary on 131-132
milieu differences 127, 132-133
motivation perspectives 110-112
performance anxiety
others' 115-116
overcoming 113-115
performance plan for 131
self-confidence of 123-127
self-reflection by 117-119
self-talk by 116-117
sport setting vs. 109-110, 127, 129-130
dance diary, for self-reflection 117-119
Darwin, Charles 203, 218
data gathering 7
on diverse athletes 208-211

listening as 11-12
for referrals 167-168
for substance abuse intervention 141-143, 152
for youth sport consultations 22
decision making skills
building in youth 19-20, 26, 28-30
group 19-20, 47, 50
declarative knowledge 20
defensiveness, substance abuse and 141-145
depression 162, 164, 172
hammer thrower case 164-167
during injury rehabilitation 99-100
developmental model
of body image disturbance 77-78
of LBT female athletes 269
of sport psychology 7-8
of youth sport participation 17-20
diagnosis/diagnosing, in sport psychology 8, 69
directive approach, to youth training 39
disabled athletes 223-247
clinical dimensions 223-225, 246
comfort/discomfort issues 227-228
communication strategies 230-232, 235, 237, 239, 242, 247
doctoral student case 292-295
equipment issues 226
group sessions for
educational 228-229
introductory example 229-245
random selection strategies 236-237
techniques for 246-247
mental skills for 241-242
performance factors
having negative impact 240-241
questionnaire exercise 232-236
small-group selection of 237-240
prejudice toward 226-227
relaxation exercises for 242-245
service challenges with 224, 228, 246
sport classification issues 226
sport organizations for 227
sport rules and 226
training and sport setting issues 225-226, 246
discipline, need for consistent 55
discomfort
dancers' perception of 112-113, 130
emotional. See anxiety
personal, of disabled athletes 227-228
discrimination. See prejudice
discussions
group. See group discussions
open. See open discussion
sit-down, as presentation 10-12
divers, weight/body image issues 63, 65, 82
group work example 67-74
male example 77, 83-92
diverse athletes 201-215
Aboriginal footballer case 217-222
commentary on 219-222
cultural norms influence 205-207, 218-219, 224
Euro-American psychology mind-set for 202-204
innovative translations of 214-215
success stories with 207-208, 218
female nonheterosexual 269, 271
other historical worldviews of 204-205
Eurocentric orientation vs. 205-207
sports involvement similarities 201-202
Tre-Nine grid counseling approach 208-214, 219
doctor-patient dichotomy 8
"do no harm" edict, for group discussions 62
double lives, for gay athletes 251
double standards, for diverse athletes 206-207
dreams 290
erotic 177, 185-186
dual-role relationships 21
dysfunctional family
performance impact 163
substance abuse and 140-142, 151-152, 154
dysthymia, hammer thrower case 164-167

E

eating
social interaction opportunities 50, 52
team culture about 61-63, 65-66
diving team case 67-74
eating disorders 61-74
coaches role 61-62, 67-74
counseling confidentiality for 9-10, 87
in dancers 133
emotions resulting from 87-88
exercise motivations related to 81-83
gender comparisons 63, 65-67, 77, 79-80
group presentations on 63-67
effective presenter characteristics 63-64
outline for 65-67
tag-team 64-65
group work on 67-74
literature review 61, 80
in men 79-80
at-risk populations 80-81
body image disturbance and 81-83

male diver case 83-92
multidisciplinary team approach to 89-90
team issues with 61-63
ectomorphic physique 78
educational model
for disabled athletes 228-229
of sport psychology 7-8, 11
of youth sport participation 17-20
efficiency cues, in youth training 25-26
ego orientation, of dancers 112
emic approach, to multicultural counseling 218
emotional reactions
qualitative research and 296-297
to sport injury 94-95, 94f
downhill skier case 98-108
rapport-building considerations 96-97
with substance abuse intervention 142-144, 147
emotional states, negative, reframing in young athletes 22, 34-36, 39
emotions
about body image 61-63, 87
coaches, expression of 49
in dancers 119-120
with eating disorders 87-88
freedom to express 48-49, 55-56
gender differences 63
with weight control 81-82
empathy
for depressed athletes 165
gay athletes and 258, 262
for problem drinker 139, 143, 156
with weight/body image issues 71-72
empiricism, collaborative 290
in sexual attraction 185-186, 189
endomorphic physique 78
environmental adaptation, dancers' ability for 109-110, 127
eroticism. See also countertransference
as problematic 172, 174
psychodynamic theory of 171-174, 191, 193-194
swimmer example 176-178
track athlete case 174-176
volleyball case 179-191
ethics
for diverse athlete consultation 206-208, 218-219, 221-222
in homophobia challenges 257, 259-260, 262
scope of practice 21, 159-161
on sexual intimacy 172-173
ethnically diverse athletes. See diverse athletes
etic approach, to multicultural counseling 218
eugenics 203
Euro-American psychology
diverse populations and 205-207, 221
historical/worldview paradigms for 204-205
success stories of 207-208, 218
theory and practices 202-204
Eurocentric orientation, of diverse populations 205-207
evaluation
in dance auditions 113, 130
in Tre-Nine grid 208-209
in youth sport training 27-28
evidence-based practice 287-288
excellence model, of sport psychology 8
exercise science 163
expectations
during presentations 12-13
in referral process 168-169
experiences, sharing. See storytelling
expertise
activity-specific 20, 22
sharing wealth of 4, 13-14
extrinsic motivation, of dancers 112

F

facilitation approach, to problem drinking 139
football case 141-158
professional issues 154-158
failure, impact on self-confidence 123, 163
family relationships
core of diverse athlete identity 206-207
countertransference of 173-174, 177-178, 194, 196-198
dysfunctional 140-142, 151-152, 154, 163
fantasies
compensatory 194, 197
erotic 177, 185-186
fasting, health threats with 70
feedback
for coaches and assistants 50-51, 54
for dancers
during auditions 113, 130
during class/rehearsals 119-121
internal 121-123
for young athletes 40
female athletes
alcohol use survey 137
eating disorders and 63, 65-67
diving team case 67-73
general population vs. 77, 80
gymnasts example 74

Index

*female athletes (continued)*
sexual orientations of 265-267
case studies 269-284
educating ourselves about 284-285
social identity perspectives 265-269
team dimensions 265-267
flexibility
of dancers
athletes *vs.* 130
performance space demands 109-110
physical 110, 112
during presentations 12-13
focus training, for young athletes 21-22, 25
football, college, substance abuse case 141-158
Freud, Sigmund 171, 178, 194, 290
frustrations
of athletes
freedom to express 48-49, 55-56
with weight control 81-82
of dancers 115-116, 120-121

G
Galton, Francis 203, 218
gay men, as athletes 249-263
body image disturbance risks 80-81
eating disorders and 83, 90-91
coming out process 253
graduate student dealing with 256-261
supervision challenges 260-262
consultation considerations 220-221
contempt for 250-251. *See also* homophobia
discrimination of 251-252, 258
interpersonal reactions to 91, 220, 222
dealing with 253-256
performance issues 252-253, 268
sport experience of, recurring themes 250-252
sport psychologists as 255
gender issues
in alcohol use 136
in dance life 130, 133
integrated instruction and 21
with weight/body image 63, 65-67, 77, 79
diving team case 67-73
gymnasts example 74
gender-role identification 255
genetics, of human behavior 203
goal-oriented practice
diverse athletes deviation from 218-219
as Western-based 221
for youth sports 23-32
first step 23-26
second step 27-30
third step 30-32
goal setting
by problem drinkers 139, 141, 156
shared knowledge of 14
three-step, for youth sports 21, 23-32
in Tre-Nine grid 208-209
graduate students
dealing with homophobia 256-261
supervision challenges 260-262
sexual attraction and 174, 193-194
volleyball example 179-191
group communication
competitive advantage of 45
problem-solving 19-20, 47, 50
in sports. *See* team dynamics
theory and research on 46-48
group discussions
disabled athlete strategies 236-240, 247
on homonegativism 274
as presentation 10-12
on sensitive topics 62-63
for team communication enhancement 55-56
in youth training 33-34, 38
grouping, as learned process 20
group presentations
for disabled athletes
introductory session 229-245
psychoeducational focus 228-229
random selection strategies 236-237
techniques for 246-247
icebreakers for 65-67)
participant, during presentations 13
for performing arts consulting 134
for selling services 10-12, 15
on weight/body image 63-74
coaches role 61-62, 67-74
effective presenter characteristics 63-64
outline for 65-67
tag-team 64-65
growth and development, through youth sports 19-20
guided discovery. *See also* imagery
for dancer self-talk 117
in youth training 22, 25, 33
guilt, with sexual attraction issues 174, 181-183
gymnasts, weight/body image issues 74, 82

H
hammer thrower, mental health referral 164-167

health
alcohol use and 137, 139, 155
life-long, holistic skills for 18-21
male ideal for 78-79, 82
in weight/body image issues 70-73, 91, 133
heterosexism
in men's sports. *See* gay men
in women's sports 265-267
case studies 269-284
educating ourselves about 284-285
social identity perspective 265-269
heterosexuality
body image disturbance risks 80-81
female, social change impacts 265-269
male, traditional sport promotion 251, 254-255
hierarchical relationships
in dance company 130
in Eurocentric mind-set 205-206
of social groups, sexual orientation and 267-268, 283
high-level athletes
eating disorders in 81
gay men as 251-252, 254
sport psychology benefits for 8, 18
HIV, misconception as "gay disease" 251-252, 263
holistic skills
applicability to diverse athletes 221-222
coaches competencies in 21-22
for youth sport participants 18-20
homework, in youth training 33, 37
homoeroticism 174
homonegativism, in women's sport 265-267
case studies 269-284
educating ourselves about 284-285
social identity perspective 265-269
homophobia, in sports 91, 220, 222, 250-251
dealing with 253-255
doctoral student case 292-294
graduate student case 256-261
role playing for 260-262
supervision strategies 260-262
homosexuality. *See* gay men; lesbians
hostility, in coaches 2, 15-16
"human condition"
Eurocentric orientation for 202-204
of practicing sport psychology 194-196
worldview orientation for 204-208
humor
antigay 250, 252, 268
antilesbian 268
in body image disturbance 87-89
coaches sense of 49, 55, 58
in interactive youth training 36-37
during presentations 11, 64
hypermesomorphic physique 78

I
icebreakers, for group presentations 65-67
ignoring, in youth training 24
imagery
for dancers 121-123
from behind 131
self-confidence building 125-126
guided 40. *See also* guided discovery
for male body image disturbances 86
videotapes *vs.* 125
impairments
disability *vs.* 223-224
of practitioners 297
with problem drinking 137, 139
implementation phase, in Tre-Nine grid 208-209, 211-212
impotence, professional 160, 164
information-seeking behavior 50
information sharing, in referral process 168-169
injuries
alcohol use and 137
dancers' perception of 112-113, 130
sports. *See* sport injury
integration, in youth sport 18-19, 21-23
language and 21, 36, 41
interaction system (IS) model, of group communication 47
interactive learning, for disabled athletes 228-229
interactive presentations 10-13
interdisciplinary model, of physical education 18-19, 21
internalization, in body image counseling 89
interpersonal skills
building in youth 18-19
communication theory and research 45-48
misunderstandings and 48-55
with gay men 91, 220, 222, 253-256
practitioner competency and 159-161, 164
as research factor 290-292
substance abuse compromise of 140-141, 155, 158
for supervision 197
for working with diverse athletes 211
intervention
for addictive behavior 138-141
football case 141-158
professional issues 139, 154-158
in Tre-Nine grid 208-209, 211-212

intervention efficacy, randomized clinical trials of 287-288
interviews
psychodynamic psychotherapy model for 296
overapplication cautions 296-297
as research method 295-296
intimacy, sexual 57, 172-173
intrapersonal skills
diverse athletes and 207, 209-211, 214
integrated perspective of 19, 21-23
practitioner competency and 159-161, 164
intrinsic motivation
building in youth 17, 19, 22
in dancers 112, 125
introductory group sessions, for disabled athletes 229-245
techniques for 246-247
introductory talks, as presentation 10-12

J
judgment
avoiding
in injury rehabilitation 96
with weight/body image issues 69-70, 89
self-, by dancers 132-133

K
K-12 physical education, curriculum for 19
kinesthetic awareness, in dancers 121-123, 131
knowledge
building in youth 20
of performing arts, consultant's 109, 127, 133
research and quest for 290
sharing wealth of 4, 13-14

L
labeling 20, 69
language
inclusive, for nonheterosexual orientations 220-221, 265-266, 283
integrated youth instruction and 21, 36, 41
large-groups, educational, for disabled athletes 228-229
large-muscle movement sequences 129-130
Latin Americans 204
learning model, of youth sport participation 18-20
lecture model, of presentations 11-12
lesbian, bisexual, and transgender (LBT) females 265
coach example 278-283
collective esteem of 265-267, 283
coming out process 271, 275
discrimination *vs.* acceptance of 265-269, 271-272, 278, 283-284
social change strategies 266, 283-284
basketball example 278-283
complexity in sport 269, 283-284
educating ourselves about 284-285
soccer example 269-274
swim team case 274-278
social identity perspective 267-269
team communication enhancement 265-266, 273-274, 283-284
lesbian, gay, bisexual, and transgender (LGBT) persons 220-221
lesbians
contempt for 250
sport psychologists as 255
life skills 18-20, 162
"the lineup" exercise, for group presentations 66
listening 116
as data gathering 11-12
doctoral research example 292-295
log keeping, for eating disorders 91
"looking good"
for competition 69-71, 74
dancers emphasis on 133
male diver case 77, 83-92
loss, sense of, during injury rehabilitation 96-97, 99-100
loss of control, with eating disorders 88
lunch date, as presentation opportunity 11-12

M
maintenance stage
of addictive behavior change 138
of alcohol treatment 140-141, 158
maladaptive exercise, in body image disturbance 81-83
maladaptive thought patterns, reframing in young athletes 22, 34-36
male athletes
alcohol use survey 136-137
body image disturbances in 77-79
at-risk populations 80-81, 90-91
diving team case 67-73
weight control and 63, 65-67, 80
eating disorders in 80-83, 90-91
at-risk populations 80-81
general population *vs.* 79-80
team dynamics with gay athletes 252, 254-255, 258
marginalized athletes
racial/ethnic 207, 213-214, 218, 221. *See also* diverse athletes
sexual orientation and. *See* gay men; heterosexism
masculinity
male body image and 78-79
diver example 89-92

traditional, as sport definition 251, 254-255
maturation, youth sport participation and 19-20
mediator, sport psychologists as 50
medical history, in diverse athletes 211
medical model, of sport psychology 7-8
medical resources
    for athletes. See sports medicine practitioners
    for dancers 113, 134
medications
    abuse of. See substance abuse
    banned 166
    prescribed. See pharmacological treatment
meditation, for performance anxiety 115
megarexia 79
memory control, learned processes for 20
Mendel, Gregor 203
mental illness. See psychopathology
mental skills
    for alcohol treatment 157
    for dancers 109-127. See also dance and dancers
    for disabled athletes 241-242
    for injury rehabilitation 97-99
    maladaptive, reframing in young athletes 22, 34-36
    for performance enhancement 22-23
    for performing artists 109-127
    team building strategies 48-49, 53
    youth sports and 18-23
"menu approach," to confidence building 124-125
mesomorphic physique, as male ideal 78-79, 82
mind-body dualism 205-206
miscommunication, dealing with 6-7
mistakes, by dancers
    correction importance 132-133
    self-reflection for dealing with 117-119
modeling
    in body image counseling 89
    in group presentations 64-65
    in substance abuse intervention 143
mood, as contagious 115-116
motivational interviewing, of problem drinkers 139,
    151
    principles of 155-157
motivation theory
    dancers and 110-112, 125
    disabled athletes and 241
    of exercise related to eating disorders 81-83
    young athletes and 17, 19, 22
    youth sports and 17, 19, 22
motor skills. See physical skills
movement, in dancing
    concentration for fluidity 119-121
    internal imagery of 121-123, 125-126, 131
    as motivator 110-112
    in sports vs. 127, 129-130
movement sequences, large-muscle 129-130
multicultural counseling 215
    emergent theories of 218-222
multicultural training, for sport psychologists 204, 215,
    221
multidisciplinary consultants, network of 167-168
multidisciplinary team
    for eating disorders 89-90
    referrals vs. 89, 169
multiple sequence (MS) model, of group communication 47

N

National Education Goals, U.S. 19
Native Americans 204
natural community resources
    of deaf people 224
    of diverse athletes 206, 219
nature, interconnectedness with humans 205
negative emotions, reframing in young athletes 22, 34-36,
    9
negotiation process, in alcohol treatment 141
nicotine use, in dancers 133
Nietzsche, Friedrich 178
nonheterosexuality, in women's sports 265-267
    case studies 269-284
    educating ourselves about 284-285
    social identity perspective 265-269
non-Western populations
    athletes from. See diverse athletes
    worldview paradigms for 202
nutrition. See also eating
    in weight/body image issues 61-63, 65-66, 69, 79
nutritionists
    appropriate referrals to 161-162, 164
    for male eating disorders 89-91

O

open discussion
    on body image issues 62-63, 66-67, 69
        male diver case 62-63, 66-67, 69
    on sexual attraction
        avoidance of 173-174
        graduate student experience 179-191
        practitioner's experiences 174-178
operant conditioning, in communication theory 46
overachievers, pain associated with 113, 130

P

pain
    dancers' perception of 113, 130
    with disabilities 224, 227-228
parallel processes, in supervision and services 7, 169, 191, 196-197
parental emotions, countertransference of 177-178, 194, 196-197
patriarchy, in diverse populations 205-206, 221
peer collaboration
    empirical 185-186, 189
    in youth training 28, 31-32
peer evaluation, in youth sport training 28
peer pressure, integrated instruction and 21
perceived understanding theory, of interpersonal com-
    munication 46, 52
perceptions
    positive self-, building in youth 17, 19, 22
    of touching
        coach-athlete 57, 171-172
        by dancers 109-110
    of understanding, disabled athletes and 234-235
    in weight/body image issues 66, 70
        male discrepancies 77-79
perfectionism 7
    in dancers 132-133
performance
    building life-long skills for 18-20
    communication as predictor of 47-48, 54
    dancers' perception of 130
    disabled athlete factors
        having negative impact 240-241
        questionnaire exercise 232-236
        small-group selection of 237-240
    global domination of 218
    psychological state related to 8, 18, 33
    research perspectives 287-298
    sexual orientation factors 252-253, 266, 275, 282, 285
performance anxiety
    competitive anxiety vs. 114
    dancers and
        dealing with others' 115-116
        skills for overcoming 113-115
    relaxation training for 115, 163
performance enhancement
    barriers to, for disabled athletes 227
    communication as key 46-48
        volleyball team case 48-59
    as goal 8-9, 14
        counseling vs. 86
    mental methods for 22-23
    for performing arts 134
    personal factors related to 163-164
        countertransference of practitioner's 198
        in diverse athletes 206-208, 219
performance medicine 134
performance plan, for dancers 131
performance routines, facilitative, in youth sports 22
performance spaces, dancers' adaptation to 109-110
performing artists
    environment of, sports setting vs. 109-110, 127, 129-130, 132
    mental skills training for 109-127. See also dance and
    dancers
    personal sacrifice expectations of 112-113, 130, 133
performing arts medical center 113, 134
personal factors/issues
    credibility based on 63-64
    in diverse athletes 206-208, 210, 219
    of homonegativism awareness 266, 269, 278-280
    of homophobia awareness 256-262
    performance related to 163-164
        countertransference of practitioner's 198
        in diverse athletes 206-208, 219
    of sexuality awareness 178-179
    of weight/body image 63-65
personality attributes
    in body image disturbance 77-78
    in nonheterosexual females 269
    for self-confidence, in dancers 126-127
    in sports injury response 94-95, 94f
        downhill skier case 98-108
personality disorders, referrals for 162
personal relationships 7
    athlete-coach, value of 49-50, 52, 55-57
    therapeutic vs. 9-10
personal responsibility
    of problem drinker 139, 146-148, 156
    in youth training 26, 28-30
personal sacrifice, as dance ethic 112-113, 130, 132
personal space, dancers' perception of 109-110
pharmacological treatment
    for depression 166-167
    for problem drinkers 140
physical appearance. See also body image disturbance
    exercise perceptions related to 81
    self-appraisal disturbances of 74, 77-78
        in males 78-81
    weight control issues and 69-71, 74
physical education, for youth 17-18. See also youth sports
    developmental issues 19-20
    integrating instruction for 18-19, 21
physical fitness, male body image and 78-79, 82

physical flexibility, of dancers 110, 112
    athletes vs. 130
physical skills
    building in youth 18, 21
    referrals for 162
physical trauma. See sport injury
physicians. See sports medicine practitioners
polysubstance abuse, college football case 141-158
positive affirmations, for dancers 125-126
positive talk 282
postconsultation phase, of Tre-Nine grid counseling 209,
    213-214
power struggles, with substance abuse intervention 143-
    144
practice and evaluation phase, in injury rehabilitation 98
practice goals. See goal-oriented practice
preconsultation phase, of Tre-Nine grid counseling 208-
    210
precontemplation stage, of addictive behavior change
    138, 148-149, 155
predicted outcome value (POV) theory, of interpersonal
    communication 46, 54, 57
prejudice
    research perspectives 289-290
    toward disabled athletes 226-227
    toward diverse athletes 204, 210, 214
        getting beyond 210, 214-215, 218, 221-222
    toward gay men 251-252
        fearful 91, 220, 222, 253-256, 258
    toward LBT female athletes 265-269
preparation stage
    of addictive behavior change 138
    in referral process 168
pre-referral sources 167-168
presentations
    group. See group presentations
    interactive 10-13
    for selling services 10-12, 15
    tag-team, on weight/body image 64-65
presentation skills
    effective personal balance for 63-64
    training in 12-13
    for use with resistant coaches 15-16
privilege, importance of 9-10, 87
problem drinkers/drinking 137, 155
    college football case 141-154
    heavy drinkers vs. 137, 155, 157
    intervention/treatment for 138-141
    professional issues 139, 141, 154-158
problem-solving skills 19-20, 47, 50
procedural knowledge 20
procedural norms, decision making and 47
professional development, complex cases stimulation of 159-
    161
professional impotence 160, 164
Profile of Mood States (POMS), research validity of 288
progressive muscular relaxation (PMR), for disabled
    athletes 244-245
psychic energies, in diverse athletes 205-206, 213, 220
psychodynamic psychotherapy model, for research 296
    overapplication cautions 296-297
psychodynamic theory, of sexual attraction 171-174, 191,
    193-194
psychoeducational-developmental model
    for disabled athletes 228-229
    of sport psychology 7-8
    of youth sport participation 17-21
psychological development. See also mental skills
    through sports 17-20
psychological interventions
    for problem drinkers 140, 144-146, 150-151
    for sport injury 95-96
        downhill skier case 98-108
        phases of 96-98
psychological responses, to sport injury 93-95, 94f
    downhill skier case 98-108
    interventions for 95-98
psychological state, performance level related to 8, 18,
    33
psychologists and psychology
    ethics and 4, 21, 159
    Euro-American theory and practices 202-204
        diverse populations and 205-207, 221
        historical and other worldviews 204-205
        success stories of 207-208, 218
    learning and performance domains 21, 163
    romantic attractions and 171-172
    sexual ethics code for 172-173
    sharing stories about 5-7, 11, 15
psychopathology
    in diverse athletes 211
    during injury rehabilitation 96, 99-100
        downhill skier case 98-108
    in practitioners, research implications 297
    referrals for 162, 164, 168
        hammer thrower case 164-167
    related to body image disturbance 78, 80
psychotherapy, psychodynamic, in research 296
    overapplication cautions 296-297

**Index**

**Q**

qualitative research
  interview method 295-297
  methodology 291-292
  as questionable 289-290
quantitative research
  methodology 291-292
  as questionable 289-290
"query theory"
  for self-awareness, in dancers 116-117, 124
  in substance abuse intervention 142, 147
  in Tre-Nine grid 209-210
questionnaires, for disabled athletes 232-234

**R**

racially diverse athletes. *See* diverse athletes
racism
  getting beyond 210, 214-215, 218, 221-222
  in worldview paradigms 203-204, 218
randomized clinical trials (RCTs), of interventions 287-288
rapport building 7, 13
  with coaches 13-14
  with disabled athletes 228, 230, 234-235, 245
  research limitations 289-290
  in youth sports 21-22, 30
rapport-building phase, in injury rehabilitation 96-97
  downhill skier case 98-108
reasoning, building in youth 20, 22
recovery
  from dance injury 112-113, 130
  from problem drinking 139
    stage model of 138
  from sport injury. *See* sport injury rehabilitation
recruitment
  including practitioner in 50
  LBT female coaches and 280-281
  of minority athletes 219
recycling, in addictive behavior change 138
referrals 159-169
  appropriate disciplines for 161-162
  doubt as reason for 159-161
  follow-through concerns 159, 169
  multidisciplinary team *vs.* 89, 169
  networks for 167-168
  for performing arts consulting 134
  for personal issues 163-164
  process for 168-169
  for sport performance. *See* performance enhancement
  to sports medicine practitioners
    for clinical issues 21, 89, 167
    for eating disorders 89-91
    for injury rehabilitation 95-96, 98
  for substance abuse 141-145
  to treatment specialists 154, 157
"referring in" 169
rehabilitation, for injury. *See* sport injury rehabilitation
rehabilitation stage, of alcohol treatment 140
rehearsal 20
  for sexual attraction processing 188-191
reinforcement, positive *vs.* negative
  communicating 49-52, 54, 57-58
  in substance abuse intervention 142-143, 146
  in youth training 24, 36, 38, 40
reinforcement theory, of interpersonal communication 47, 50
  team example 50-52, 54, 57-58
relapsing, in addictive behavior change 138, 154, 158
  prevention of 140-141
relational track, in group communication 47
relationships
  adolescent, integrated instruction and 21
  consultative 11, 21-22, 38
  dual-role 21
  hierarchical. *See* hierarchical relationships
  personal *vs.* coaching 49-50, 52, 55
  personal *vs.* therapeutic 7, 9-10
  for referral sources 167-168
  research perspectives 290-292
  sexualization of professional 172, 176-177, 194
  working. *See* working alliance
relaxation training
  for disabled athletes 242-245
  for male body image disturbances 86
  for performance anxiety 115, 163
  for young athletes 22, 33-34, 40-43
research 287-298
  by disabled doctoral student 292-295
  historical roots of 290-291
  by impaired practitioners 297
  listening importance
    case study 292-295
    as psychotherapist 295-296
  prejudiced view of 289-290
  psychodynamic psychotherapy model 296
    overapplication cautions 296-297
  qualitative *vs.* quantitative
    methodology 291-292
    as questionable 289-290
  randomized clinical trials 287-288
  unidirectional model of 287

resiliency, of diverse populations 204, 213-214
resistance
  by coaches 2, 15-16, 21
  of problem drinker, to change 139, 141-144, 156
  to referrals 169
  to youth sport consultations 21-22
respect
  for coaches 8, 13-14, 282
  in referral process 168-169
responsibility. *See* personal responsibility
retirement
  from competition, due to injury 103, 106-108
  referrals for planning 162
retribution
  gay athletes' fear of 251-252
  LBT female athletes' fear of 268
return to sport
  after addiction intervention 141, 145-146, 150-154, 156-158
  after injury 93-108
    downhill skier case 98-108
    psychological interventions for 95-98
    psychological response factors 93-95, 94f
rhythm, in large-muscle movement sequences 130
risk taking
  alcohol use and 136-137
    football case 141-158
    professional issues 154-158
  as dance ethic 113, 130
role model, for coaches 14-15
role-play
  on homonegativism 273-274, 281
  for homophobia processing 260-262
  during presentations 13
  research applications 292-294
  for sexual attraction processing 188-191
romantic attraction, as problematic 171-172
rules of engagement, for group discussions 62-63

**S**

safety
  alcohol use and 136-137, 155
  for body image discussions 62-63, 66-67, 69
    male diver case 83-85
  for diverse athletes 218, 220
same-sex groups, for body image discussions 66-67
sandwich approach, to corrective communications 52
schema-driven attitudes, about physical appearance 77-78
scientists
  client as 290-291
  sport. *See* research; sport scientists
scope of practice, ethical guidelines for 21, 159-161
self-awareness training
  for arousal control 33-40
  for dancers 115-116
  for team communication 55-56
  on weight/body image 64, 88-89
self-confidence 109, 116
  building in youth 17, 19, 22, 25
  communication and 46-47
  for dancers 121, 123-127
  in disabled athletes 241
  maintaining, during injury rehabilitation 96-98
self-criticism, by dancers 132-133
self-definition. *See* self-identity
self-determination. *See* intrinsic motivation
self-disclosure
  for credibility 102
  by nonheterosexuals. *See* coming out process
  on sensitive topics 62-64, 69
  in youth training 30, 38, 41
self-efficacy. *See* self-worth
self-esteem 163
  building in youth 17, 19
  collective, of LBT female athletes 265-268, 283
  of diverse athletes 206, 212-213
  in weight/body image issues 72-73
self-evaluation skills, youth sports and 19
self-help groups, for problem drinkers 140, 156
self-identity
  integrated instruction and 21
  maintaining
    downhill skier case 98-108
    during injury rehabilitation 96-98
"self-medicate," dancers tendencies to 133
self-monitoring, for arousal control 33-40
self-motivation. *See* intrinsic motivation
self-perception, positive, building in youth 17, 19, 22
self-protection, in diverse athletes 212-213
self-reflection 109
  on countertransference 194
  by dancers 117-119
self-talk
  by dancers 116-117
  facilitative, in youth sports 22
  practitioners use of 50-51
self-worth
  maintaining, during injury rehabilitation 96-97
  qualitative research on 295-296
  reinforcing, during substance abuse intervention 139, 146-148, 156

selling, of services 3-16
  counseling model 8-10
  need for 3-5, 16
  parallel supervision processes 7
  presentations for 10-13
  psychology models for 7-8
  to resistant coaches 2, 15-16
  respecting and involving coaches 8, 13-14
  as role model for coaches 14-15
  sharing stories as 5-7, 11, 15
  shopping list model 5
  telling model 5-7
sex-role identification 255
sexual attraction
  commentary on 193-198
  exploration barriers 178-179
  incidence of 172
  as noncommonplace, in gay men 251
  psychodynamic theory of 171-174, 191, 193-194
  swimmer example 176-178
  track athlete case 174-176
  volleyball case 179-191
sexual behavior, as taboo 173, 297
sexual exploitation 171
sexual impropriety 57, 172
sexual intimacy 57, 172-173
sexuality
  barriers to exploration 178-179
  body image disturbance and 73, 80-81, 91
  integrated instruction and 21
sexual orientation
  mainstream. *See* heterosexuality
  male team dynamics and 252, 254-255, 258
  marginalized. *See* gay men; heterosexism
  as sport context 91, 174, 214, 220, 222
  women's teams and 265-285
    case studies 269-284
    educating ourselves about 284-285
    scope of 265-267
    social identity perspective 265-269
shame
  bulimia and 87-88
  with sexual attraction issues 174, 181-183, 185
sharing. *See* storytelling
shopping list model, of selling services 5
silence
  counseling value of 118
  criminal act reporting *vs.* 145
  in youth training 24
sit-down discussions, as presentation 10-12
situational characteristics, in sports injury response 94-95, 94f
  rapport-building considerations 96-97
situational opportunities, during presentations 12-13
skiing, sport injury case 98-108
skill development phase, in injury rehabilitation 97-98
small-group evaluation, in youth sport training 28
small-groups
  same-sex, for body image discussions 66-67
  selecting disabled athletes for 236
soccer, LBT female team case study 269-274
social categorization theory, of LBT female athletes 267-268
social change strategies, of LBT female athletes 266, 283-284
  basketball example 278-283
  complexity in sport 269, 283-284
  educating ourselves about 284-285
  identity perspectives of 268
  soccer example 269-274
  swim team case 274-278
social cohesion, group decision making and 46-48
social comparison theory, of LBT female athletes 267
social competition strategies, of LBT female athletes 268
social consciousness
  building in youth 17-19
  of homophobia 253-255, 258
social creativity strategies, of LBT female athletes 268
social identity (SI) perspective, of LBT female athletes 267-269
  categorization theory 267-268
  change strategies 268-269, 283
  comparison theory 267
  mobility strategies 268
  theoretical basis for 266-267
social interaction
  of athletes with coaches 49-50, 52, 55-57
  in sport experience 12-13
social learning framework, cognitive, for body image disturbance 77-78
social mobility strategies, of LBT female athletes 268
sociocultural context
  of body image disturbance 77-79
  counseling considerations 218-219, 222
  of dancers 109-110, 113, 130
  of diverse athletes 202, 211, 214, 222
  integrated instruction and 21
  of sexuality 178-179
Special Olympics 224, 227
spectators, audience *vs.* 130
speedskaters, young
  arousal control for 32-36, 40
  awareness training for 32, 35-40
  integrated instruction for 21-23

relaxation training for 33-34, 40-43
sport environment/setting
    attitudes and behaviors learned in 17-19
    dance environment *vs.* 109-110, 127, 129-130, 132
    disabled athletes and 225-226
    spending time in
        sexual attraction related to 173-174, 177
        of young athletes 22
sport injury 93-108
    career ending 98, 101, 107-108
    coping strategies for 95, 97-98
    downhill skier case 98-108
    literature review 93
sport injury rehabilitation
    biopsychosocial model of 93, 94f
    maintaining identity during 96-98
        downhill skier case 98-108
    outcomes of 94f, 107-108
    psychological interventions for 95-96
        education phase 97
        practice and evaluation phase 98
        rapport-building phase 96-97
        skill development phase 97-98
    psychological responses to 93-95, 94f
sport instruction, integrated
    consulting for 21-23
    language and 21, 36, 41
    for young athletes 18-19, 21
sport participation
    diversity of backgrounds 201-202, 217-218
    youth benefits from 17-19
sport psychologists
    competency limitations 159-161
    countertransference by
        awareness/self-management of 194-195, 197-198
        erotic 172-173, 193-194
        research implications 296
        therapeutic perspectives 195-197
    dance knowledge and skills 109, 127, 133
    desirable qualities of 11, 63-64
    impaired, research by 297
    mediator role 50
    as naive 13-14
    sexual involvement with clients 172-173
    sexual orientation of 255
    supervision of 7, 191, 196-197
    training background 163, 202-204
        multicultural 204, 215, 221
        research component 291-292
sport psychology. *See also* consultations
    evidence-based 287-288
    gaining acceptance of 3-5, 16
    for high-level athletes 18
    models of 7-8
    parallel processes in 7, 169, 191, 196-197
    research perspectives 287-298
    scope of practice 21, 159
        doubt levels within 159-161
    selling strategies for 5-16
    for youth sport participants 18, 21
sport scientists
    referrals to 162
    training background 163, 291-292
sports medicine practitioners
    injury rehabilitation role 95-96, 98
    referrals to 21, 89, 167
        for eating disorders 89-91
sport-specific activity
    building in youth 20, 22
    Tre-Nine grid counseling considerations 212-213
sport-specific functional classification, for disabled ath-
    letes 226, 228, 236, 238
sports teams. *See* team dynamics
stage fright 114, 130
stage model of change, for addictive behavior 138, 140-
    141
stereotyping
    of diverse athletes 210, 214, 218-219
    integrated instruction and 21
    of LBT female athletes 265, 267, 269
    of sport as masculine 251, 258
storytelling
    coaching cautions 54-55
    by research participants 296
    as selling strategy 5-7, 11, 15
    on weight/body image 62-64, 67
        by diving team 67-74, 88
    in youth training 30-32, 35, 37-38, 41-42
strategic knowledge 20
stress, coping abilities 17
structuralism theory, of conscious thought 203
student-athletes, alcohol use survey 136-137
study skills, referrals for 162
subjectivity
    of dance auditions 113, 130
    in sexual countertransference 194-195
substance abuse
    college football case 141-158
    in diverse athletes 211
    professional issues 154-158

referrals for 137, 154, 157, 162
suicidal ideation, in diverse athletes 211
suicide
    attempted, with sexual improprieties 171-172
    risk, in depressed athletes 165
supervision
    in dealing with homophobia 260-262
    interpersonal problems with 197
    involvement of, referring *vs.* 159-161, 169
    parallel processes of 7, 191, 196-197
support resources/systems
    for addiction recovery 140-142, 151-152, 154
    for clinical issues 9-10
    countertransference perspectives 173-174, 177-178, 194
    of diverse athletes 206-207, 219
    during injury rehabilitation 98-108
    for LBT female athletes 269, 271-272, 278, 283-284
    for referred clients 45, 168-169
survival tactics
    of LBT female athletes 271
    transgenerational, of African-descendant people 213-214,
        218
swimmers
    LBT female team case study 274-278
    sexual attraction case 176-178
    young
        goal-setting progression for 23-28
        integrated instruction for 21-23
symbolic convergence (SC) theory, of group communica-
    tion 46-47

**T**

tabula rasa, as diverse populations belief 206
tag-team presentations, on weight/body image 64-65
talent, identification *vs.* development of 8
target time, in youth training 26
task orientation, of dancers 112
task track, in group communication 47
team-building exercises, for group presentations 65-67
    weight/body image case 67-74
team culture, about eating 61-63, 65-66
team dynamics
    assistant coach role 54-55
    coaching misunderstanding case 48-54
    communication theory and research 45-48
    destructive, BITR session for 55-56
    as selling point 6, 8
    sexual orientation impact
        gay athletes and 252, 254-255, 258
        women case studies 269-283
        women's identities 265-266, 283-285
tension reduction strategies, building in youth 22
therapeutic model, of services 8-10
therapeutic relationships 9-10
    for diverse athletes 221-222
    personal *vs.* 7
    research perspectives 289-292
thinking skills. *See* cognitive restructuring; mental skills
time, cultural communities concept of 206
time management, referrals for 162
topical track, in group communication 47
touching
    coaches caution with 57, 171
    dancers' perception of 109-110
    inappropriate. *See* sexual impropriety; sexual intimacy
    nonsexual expressions of 251
    taboos for 171-191
track athlete, sexual attraction case 174-176
training programs, for sport psychologists 163, 202-
    204
    multicultural 204, 215, 221
    research component 291-292
training strategies. *See also* goal setting
    referrals for 162
    for team building 48-49, 53
    for young athletes 24-30, 36, 38, 40-41
transference
    erotic 171-174, 191
        swimmer example 176-178
        track athlete case 174-176
        volleyball case 179-191
    research and 296
transgendered athletes 220-221, 265
transgenerational survival, of African-descendant people
    213-214, 218
transpersonal psychologist 3-4
transtheoretical model of change, for addictive behavior
    138
trauma. *See* sport injury
travel, physiologic effects of 4
Tre-Nine grid counseling, for diverse athletes 208-209,
    219
    during-consultation phase 210-213
    postconsultation phase 213-214
    preconsultation phase 208-210
trust
    abuse of 171-172
    counseling strategies for 86
    personal characteristics for building 63-64
    substance abuse intervention and 145, 151-152

in youth sport consultations 22, 38
12-step programs, for problem drinkers 140, 156

**U**

uncertainty reduction (UR) theory, of interpersonal com-
    munication 46, 50, 291
    BITR session for 55-56
understanding, perceived
    disabled athletes and 234-235
    interpersonal communication and 46, 52

**V**

venting
    by athletes, freedom for 48-49, 55-56
    by dancers 115-116
videotapes
    for dancers 125
    track athlete case 174-176
    in weight/body image discussions 66-67
        male diver case 83-85
violence
    alcohol use and 135, 137, 158
        football case 141-158
    prevention strategies 135
    professional issues 154-158
vocational planning
    with career-ending injury 103, 106-108
    referrals for 162
volition, increasing 23
volleyball
    sexual attraction case 179-191
    team communication enhancement for 48-59

**W**

water polo players, young
    goal-setting progression for 28-32
    integrated instruction for 21-23
weigh-ins, anxiety with 70-73
weight and weight control 61-74
    body image disturbances and 63, 65-67, 79-80
        eating disorders related to 81-83
        male diver case 83-92
    coaches role 61-62, 67-74
    counseling confidentiality for 9-10
    in dancers 133
    gender comparisons 63, 65-67, 77, 79-80
    group presentations on 63-67
        effective presenter characteristics 63-64
        outline for 65-67
        tag-team 64-65
    group work on 67-74
    literature review 61
    nutrition referrals for 89-91, 161-162
    team issues with 61-63
weight training, body image disturbance and 78, 82
well-being
    life-long, holistic skills for 18-21
    for weight/body image issues 70-73
whistle-blower, in sexual taboos 179
working alliance 38
    countertransferential response 198. *See also* counter-
        transference
    with diverse athletes
        Aboriginal example 217-222
        client-centered 220-221
        personal factors component 206-208, 219, 222
        during injury rehabilitation 99-108
        for substance abuse recovery 141-144, 149, 154
        for Tre-Nine grid counseling 209-213
            preparing to end relationship 213
            specific sport considerations 212-213
workshops, educational, as selling strategy 11
worldview paradigms, for non-Western populations
    202
    American, as limited 203-204, 219, 221-222
    commentary on 217-222
    Eurocentric 205-207
    "other" and historical 204-205, 218
worthiness. *See* self-worth

**Y**

youth sports 17-43
    arousal control in 19, 21-22, 32-36, 40
    awareness training for 32, 35-40
    consulting in 18, 21-23, 43
    developmental aspects 17-19
    developmental issues 19-20
    goal-setting progression for 21, 23-32
    integrating mental skills for 18-19, 21
        language and 21, 36, 41
    introducing mental skills for 22-23
    relaxation training for 22, 33-34, 40-43

**Z**

zone of optimal functioning 8
    being in 37

# About the Editor

**Mark B. Andersen, PhD,** is a licensed psychologist in the USA and registered to practice psychology in Australia. Currently, he is an associate professor at Victoria University in Melbourne, Australia. He teaches in the School of Human Movement, Recreation, and Performance and coordinates the master and doctoral applied psychology degrees (sport and exercise psychology emphasis) in the School of Psychology. He received his bachelor degree in psychology from the University of California at Davis in 1973 and went on to complete a master of science in psychology at San Diego State University in 1978, where the two-year degree took four years to complete because he spent way too much time at the beach working on his tan. He completed his doctorate from the University of Arizona in 1988 and immigrated to Australia in 1994. He teaches graduate subjects in research design, psychology of rehabilitation, and the professional practice of psychology. His areas of research interest include the psychology of injury and rehabilitation, the role of exercise in mental health, well-being, and quality of life for those with chronic disorders (e.g., multiple sclerosis, arthritis, cerebral palsy), the training and supervision of applied psychology graduate students, and the professional practice of sport psychology service delivery. His first book, *Doing Sport Psychology* (2000, from Human Kinetics) is used worldwide in applied sport psychology graduate programs and has been translated into Japanese. He has deep familial and professional ties to Scandinavia, has published in Swedish, and recently completed and published work, in collaboration with colleagues at the University of Halmstad, on injury prevention in Swedish soccer players. He is also the former editor of the Professional Practice section of the international journal *The Sport Psychologist*. His most recent book, *Psychology in the Physical and Manual Therapies* (2004, edited with Gregory Kolt) was published by Elsevier Science. He has authored more than 100 refereed journal articles and book chapters and has made over 90 national and international conference presentations. Dr. Andersen has worked for many years counseling athletes and performing artists ranging from twelve-year old junior competitors to ballet dancers to American and Australian Olympians. He lives in the best eating city on the planet, Melbourne, and spends a great deal of time with his partner supporting the restaurants in their local district of St. Kilda.

# About the Contributors

**Heather Barber, PhD,** is an associate professor and chair of the department of kinesiology at the University of New Hampshire. Her research has focused on two areas: gender issues in sport and motivational influences in coaching. Specifically, her work has examined the influence of socialization processes and role-model selections on girls' and women's sport experiences, the influence of sexual orientation on girls' and women's sport experiences, and the role of perceived competence in coaches' motivation. Dr. Barber serves on the editorial board of *The Sport Psychologist* and on the executive board of the Association for the Advancement of Applied Sport Psychology (AAASP). She is an AAASP-certified consultant, and in her role as a psychological skills consultant she has worked with age-group through elite coaches and athletes in a variety of sports.

**Britton W. Brewer, PhD,** is a professor of psychology at Springfield College in Springfield, Massachusetts, where he teaches undergraduate and graduate psychology courses and conducts research on psychological aspects of sport injury. His research on anterior cruciate ligament rehabilitation has been funded by the National Institute of Arthritis and Musculoskeletal and Skin Diseases. Dr. Brewer is listed in the United States Olympic Committee Sport Psychology Registry, 2000-2004, and is an AAASP-certified consultant. He is a fellow of both the American Psychological Association and the Association for the Advancement of Applied Sport Psychology.

**Kevin L. Burke, PhD,** is professor and chair of the department of physical education, exercise, and sport sciences at East Tennessee State University in Johnson City, Tennessee. He is also a licensed professional counselor and fellow, certified consultant, charter member, and past secretary-treasurer of the Association for the Advancement of Applied Sport Psychology (AAASP). Dr. Burke served on AAASP's original executive board as the first student representative. He has presented and published through local, state, regional, national, and international channels. He has served on the editorial boards for the *Journal of Applied Sport Psychology* (associate editor), *Journal of Sport Behavior*, and *Strategies*. He is also past associate editor for the *Journal of Interdisciplinary Research in Physical Education*. He has served as a reviewer for *The Sport Psychologist, Journal of Sport & Exercise Psychology, Journal of Experimental Social Psychology,* and *Research Quarterly for Exercise and Sport*. Dr. Burke has coauthored two books: *Sport Psychology Library Series: Basketball* and *Tennis* and has served as coeditor of seven editions of the *Directory of Graduate Programs in Applied Sport Psychology.*

**Robert C. (Bob) Eklund, PhD,** works in the department of educational psychology and learning systems at Florida State University in Tallahassee. He has previously been employed at the University of Western Australia, the University of North Dakota, and Auburn University in Alabama after receiving his PhD in exercise and sport science from the University of North Carolina at Greensboro in 1991. His interest in sport psychology stems from his experiences as a freestyle wrestler while participating in collegiate and international competition and as a coach of athletes participating in youth sport, intercollegiate competition, and major international sporting events. He has authored or coauthored numerous refereed research publications, book chapters, and professional or applied practice articles on sport and exercise psychology and presented papers at regional, national, and international conferences. His reports have addressed issues on psychological experience associated with sport performance as well as self-presentational and self-relevant cognitions associated with sport and exercise participation. Dr. Eklund has been professionally active in providing peer review services to more than a dozen research journals. He is the editor of the *Journal of Sport & Exercise Psychology* and has served as an associate editor for the *Journal of Applied Sport Psychology* and a section editor for the *Research Quarterly for Exercise and Sport.*

**Helen J. Fawkner, PhD,** a former competitive diver, completed a master's of psychology at the University of Melbourne and has recently been awarded her PhD from that institute. Previously she taught sport and health psychology at the University of Ballarat in Victoria, Australia. She has published and presented internationally in the areas of sport and health psychology, principally on the relationship between psychosocial factors and athletic injury and on the antecedents and consequences of body image perceptions and disturbances in men. Dr. Fawkner has been invited to join the board of referees for the *Special Issue on Body Image and Health* in the *Journal of Health Psychology* that will be published in early 2006. In addition to research and teaching, Dr. Fawkner has conducted psychoeducational workshops with coaches from a wide range of sports.

**Heather Gridley, MA,** has held national positions in the Australian Psychology Society, primarily with the College of Community Psychologists and the Women and Psychology Interest Group, and more recently as director of social issues and membership. Her interest in both community psychology and narrative therapy stems from her work in community health, where she became aware of the limitations of interventions directed solely at individuals. Now as senior lecturer at Victoria University in Melbourne, Australia, she coordinates a postgraduate program in community and sport psychology. Heather's teaching and research are based on feminist and social justice principles, exemplified in her thesis on feminism and supervision and in her publications on women's health issues. Her sporting credentials are limited to an expired softball umpire's license and a longstanding tribal interest in Australian rules football that predates and runs counter to most of her feminist principles. She is about to reconcile this cultural conflict in a project addressing sexual assault within elite sporting contexts, titled *3Rs: Respect, Rights, and Responsibilities.*

**Stephanie Hanrahan, PhD,** is an associate professor and the director of the sport and exercise psychology program in the schools of human movement studies and psychology at the University of Queensland. Her research interests include attribution theory, achievement motivation, and psychological skills training for varied populations. As a registered psychologist, she works with athletes and coaches from a number of sports, as well as nonsport performers such as dancers, actors, and singers. Dr. Hanrahan is the coauthor of *Biophysical Foundations of Human Movement, Sociocultural Foundations of Human Movement, The Coaching Process: A Practical Guide to Improving your Effectiveness,* and *Game Skills: A Fun Approach to Learning Sport Skills.* She is also a fellow of the Australian Sports Medicine Federation.

**Kate F. Hays, PhD, CPsych,** established a practice in Toronto in 1998, The Performing Edge, emphasizing performance enhancement training for athletes and performing artists. Before that, she had practiced in New Hampshire for 25 years. Dr. Hays has authored four books on sport psychology, the mental benefits of physical activity, and performance psychology, as well as numerous articles and book chapters on these subjects. She has taught courses and workshops on these topics as well, to both the general public, graduate students, and colleagues.

**Vikki Krane, PhD,** is a professor in the school of human movement, sport, and leisure studies and the director of the women's studies program at Bowling Green State University in Ohio. Her research examines the experiences of athletes from a feminist perspective, specifically focusing on lesbians' experiences, body image, and heterosexism in sport. She is a former editor of *The Sport Psychologist* and is on the editorial board of the *Journal of Applied Sport Psychology.* Dr. Krane is also a fellow of the Association for the Advancement of Applied Sport Psychology (AAASP) and an AAASP-certified consultant. As a psychological skills consultant, she has worked with high school and college athletes as well as elite adolescent gymnasts and figure skaters. Her professional honors include the Mabel Lee Outstanding Young Professional Award from the American Alliance for Health, Physical Education, Recreation and Dance and the Dorothy V. Harris Young Scholar-Practitioner Award from AAASP.

**Matthew P. Martens, PhD,** is an assistant professor of counseling psychology at the State University of New York in Albany. He received his master's degree in sport psychology from the University of North Carolina and his doctoral degree in counseling psychology from the University of Missouri-Columbia. He has published and presented in the areas of sport psychology, substance abuse, and health psychology. His sport psychology publications have encompassed several domains, including diversity issues, alcohol use among college athletes, and career development considerations with athletes. Clinically, Dr. Martens has worked with a number of individual athletes and teams on issues such as performance enhancement, substance abuse, and general psychological health and well-being.

**Michael Mobley, PhD,** is an assistant professor in the department of educational, school, and counseling psychology at the University of Missouri-Columbia. He received his PhD in counseling psychology from Pennsylvania State University. He completed his doctoral internship at the University of Maryland Counseling Center in College Park, Maryland. Dr. Mobley's research areas of interest include perfectionism; multicultural counseling, training, and competencies; cultural identity development models (racial and ethnic, gay, lesbian, and bisexual); and self-empowerment theory of achievement as applied to African American adolescents. Since 1999 he has served as principal investigator and project director of a grant project titled GEAR UP MU REACH. This six-year, $2.7 million U.S. Department of Education program seeks to prepare low-income middle- and high-school-age youth for college. MU REACH has served African American students attending central middle and central high schools in the Kansas City, Missouri, public school district.

**William D. Parham, PhD, ABPP,** is the associate director of clinical services at the UCLA student psychological services and a psychologist for the department of intercollegiate athletics. A member of the USOC Sport Psychology Registry and a certified consultant with AAASP, he has consulted with the National Basketball Association (NBA), the National Football League (NFL), and Major League Baseball (MLB) and has worked with performing artists in music, theater, and drama. Dr. Parham is a fellow of APA Division 47 (sport psychology) and serves as their representative to the APA Council of Representatives. He also is a fellow in Divisions 17 and 45 and a two-time member of the APA Committee on Ethnic Minority Affairs. Dr. Parham is a member of the board of trustees of the American Board of Professional Psychology, and he chairs the Diversity Task Force. Finally, he was a member of the planning committee for the National Multicultural Conference and Summit in 2003 and 2005.

**Kirsten Peterson, PhD,** is a member of the United States Olympic Committee's sport psychology staff, providing counseling and performance enhancement services to athletes and coaches of numerous Olympic, Paralympic, and Pan American sports. She has traveled as part of the USOC sport psychology staff with three Olympic teams. Dr. Peterson is a licensed psychologist, a member of the American Psychological Association (APA), and a certified consultant through the Association for the Advancement of Applied Sport Psychology (AAASP).

**Albert J. Petitpas, PhD,** is a professor in the department of psychology and director of the National Football Foundation Center for Youth Development through Sport at Springfield College. He is a fellow and certified consultant of the Association for the Advancement of Applied Sport Psychology, and his research and applied work focus on the use of sport as a vehicle to enhance personal development across the life span. Dr. Petitpas has provided consulting services to a wide range of organizations including the National Collegiate Athletic Association's Youth Education through Sport program; the United States Olympic Committee's Career Assistance Program for Athletes; the National Football League and National Football Foundation's Coaching Academy, the First Tee; and the National Football Foundation's Play It Smart program.

**Artur Poczwardowski, PhD,** is an associate professor in the department of sport and exercise sciences at Barry University, Miami Shores, Florida. His teaching in Poland and the United States involved courses on motor learning and control, motor development, school psychology, applied sport psychology, and performance enhancement. He has consulted with children and youth athletic programs in a number of sports (e.g., judo, soccer, figure skating, speedskating, table tennis). At the elite level, he worked with the Polish national judo team (1992 Olympics) and the St. Lawrence University Division I women's hockey team. His research focuses on sport psychology service delivery, coach–athlete relationships, and coping strategies of elite performers. He has more than 20 publications and has given more than 40 professional presentations at the national and international levels. Dr. Poczwardowski received his PhD in exercise and sport science, with specialization in the psychosocial aspects of sport, from the University of Utah, Salt Lake City, and his two master's degrees from the University of Physical Education in Gdansk, Poland (physical education and coaching), and Gdansk University, Poland (psychology).

**Clay P. Sherman, PhD,** is an associate professor in the division of kinesiology and health science at California State University, Fullerton. He received his PhD in exercise and sport science from the University of Utah. His major research interests relate to the development and application of educational approaches for teaching children and youths preventative mental skills through the medium of sport and physical activity. Before beginning his graduate studies, Dr. Sherman was the head coach of an age-group swim team for six years and an alpine ski instructor, and he served three years as a caseworker and counselor for youths on probation. Dr. Sherman enjoys home brewing, water polo, mountain biking, and playing with his two sons, Luke and Jack (not necessarily in that order).

**Jeff Simons, PhD,** has more than 20 years' practical experience consulting to athletes, coaches, and organizations, including extensive work with competitors in four Olympics and numerous world championships, along with appointments to the 1996 and 2000 Australian Olympic teams. He is a faculty member in the department of kinesiology and physical education at California State University, Hayward. Dr. Simons previously had a private practice in Melbourne, Australia, from which he served as sport psychologist for the Victorian Institute of Sport (1995-2002), the professional Australian Rules Essendon Football Club (1999-2002), Athletics Australia (1995-2000), and Taekwondo Australia (1996-2002), as well as for many other sport organizations, programs, and individuals. He is on the board of directors for the Bluearth Institute, an Australian nonprofit organization promoting health and well-being through physical activity, and was instrumental in the creation and implementation of Discovery School Experience, a Bluearth Institute program designed to engage primary school children in physical activity and to facilitate lifelong attitudes for positive health choices. Dr. Simons received his PhD from the University of Illinois and has more than 16 years' experience as a lecturer and academic.

**Harriet D. Speed, PhD,** is a senior lecturer in the school of human movement, recreation, and performance at Victoria University in Melbourne, Australia, where she teaches graduate studies in sport and exercise psychology. Her current research interests include athlete transitions, eating behaviors and weight management in athletes, and the welfare of horse-racing jockeys. Dr. Speed was awarded a two-year (1995-1996) training scholarship in the psychology department at the Australian Institute of Sport. She serves as consultant to the Victorian Institute of Sport and several other state and national sporting bodies, working with athletes and coaches from a variety of sports including diving, golf, shooting, track and field, basketball, netball, taekwondo, and horse racing. Dr. Speed is a member of the Australian Psychological Society and the College of Sport Psychologists.

**Robert D. Stainback, PhD,** is a licensed clinical psychologist, a private practice consultant in sport psychology, and an AAASP-certified consultant. He has provided consultation to athletes in a variety of sports. In addition, he has 20 years of experience in the substance abuse treatment field. Dr. Stainback directed the substance abuse treatment program at the Birmingham Veterans Affairs Medical Center in Alabama and held faculty appointments in psychology and psychiatry at the University of Alabama at Birmingham. He has written articles and book chapters in sport psychology and addictions as well as a book titled *Alcohol and Sport,* published by Human Kinetics. He also has given numerous presentations to professional audiences in both areas. Dr. Stainback received his PhD and MBA from the University of Alabama.

**Herbert S. Strean, DSW,** was Distinguished Professor Emeritus at Rutgers University, having been a leader in social work education for nearly 50 years. Dr. Strean served as director for the New York Center for Psychoanalytic Training and contributed 35 books and more than 100 articles to social work, psychoanalysis, and professional practice. In *Sport Psychology in Practice,* Herb Strean addresses a favorite topic, that of countertransference; his final book, *Controversies on Countertransference,* published by Jason Aronson in 2001, includes an introduction, six of his papers—each reviewed by two discussants—and an epilogue. The chapter in this book, with his son Billy, marks a second foray into sport psychology, following an article in *The Sport Psychologist* that considered the contribution of psychodynamic principles in applied sport psychology practice. Herb Strean is remembered lovingly by his family, his friends, his colleagues, and the more than 4,000 professionals whom he enthusiastically taught.

**William B. Strean, PhD,** is an associate professor in the faculty of physical education and recreation at the University of Alberta, specializing in sport psychology. His primary research and applied interests are "play, fun, and games" and the role of laughter and humor in learning. Dr. Strean has also served as a sport psychology consultant with University of Alberta athletes, other elite athletes, and national teams. An NCCP Level III (C License) soccer coach, he coaches many youth sport teams. He is also a proud father and has done extensive work with children. Dr. Strean is a certified professional coactive coach who has helped many people to PLAY the game of life. He recently has become a certified laughter leader, and he speaks and conducts various workshops designed to teach people how to have more fun in their work and in their lives.

**Robert E. Taylor, PhD,** is a PhD graduate of the University of Tennessee, a diplomate of the American Board of Professional Psychology, a fellow of Divisions 12 and 31 of the American Psychological Association, and past president of the Georgia Psychological Association. He has provided psychotherapy services to myriad clients and professional consultation to independent practitioners for 40 years. Dr. Taylor has taught in undergraduate and graduate programs at Radford University, the University of Georgia, Mercer University, and the University of Alabama at Birmingham. He has published articles and book chapters ranging from *Science* to *The Psychotherapy Patient* and has given many presentations to national and international professional organizations. His special interests include biofeedback, clinical hypnosis, and stress management. Now in partial retirement, he continues to write and serve as a Red Cross disaster volunteer.

**Judy L. Van Raalte, PhD,** is a professor of psychology and director of the athletic counseling master's program at Springfield College in Springfield, Massachusetts. Dr. Van Raalte's research interests include self-talk and sport performance, the professional practice of sport psychology, body issues, and athletic injury. She served as coach for the Springfield College women's tennis team for five years, is coeditor of *Exploring Sport and Exercise Psychology* (now in its second edition), and is executive producer of 11 sport psychology videos. She is listed in the United States Olympic Committee Sport Psychology Registry and is an AAASP-certified consultant.